Frommer's®
Bahamas

Our Bahamas

by Darwin Porter & Danforth Prince

THE BAHAMAS ARCHIPELAGO STRETCHES FROM SOUTH FLORIDA almost to Haiti, comprising more than 700 islands. And the experiences that await you are as diverse as the islands themselves. On Paradise Island, you can order "surf and turf" from a tuxedo-clad waiter; buy Bulgari gems; partake of Las Vegas–style gambling; or sail on a James Bond–style yacht (many 007 films used Nassau and Paradise Island as backdrops). The waters off New Providence Island are dense with gardens of elkhorn coral and the sea floor is a graveyard of shipwrecks that draw boatloads of scuba divers.

Personally, we prefer the tranquil, less developed side of The Bahamas—from the underwater caverns of Lucayan National Park to Bimini's raffish End of the World Bar. If you move south from the megaresorts on Nassau and Paradise Island, you'll discover the Out Islands; here, virtually unchanged, is the kind of natural setting that Columbus and his crew first spotted in the 15th century. If you dream of lying under a sheltering palm tree on a deserted beach with talcum-fine sands, these are the islands to visit—some of them so underpopulated, electricity has yet to arrive.

The photos we've chosen reflect the best of these islands, whether you prefer action, relaxation, or a little of both.

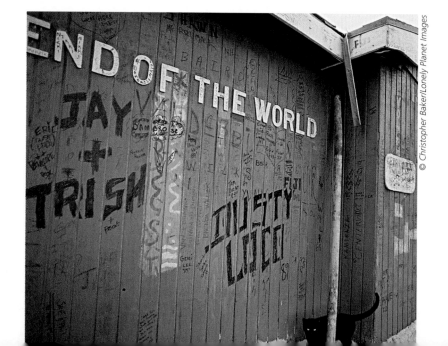

© Christopher Baker/Lonely Planet Images

© Kit Kittle/Corbis

Bimini's **END OF THE WORLD BAR (left),** with its sand floor and a back door that opens to the harbor, boasts a storied past; Adam Clayton Powell, the legendary congressman from Harlem, was a fixture here in the 1960s. These days, when the fishing is done, beer-bellied fishermen—each looking like a clone of another former patron, Ernest Hemingway—arrive with their suntanned dates to drink the night away.

Breathtaking **PINK SANDS BEACH (above)** is our favorite in The Bahamas. Its pristine beauty stretches for 5km (3 miles) along Harbour Island's eastern flank. In the wild pirate days, long past, "Calico Jack" Rackham—The Bahamas' most notorious freebooter—raced along this beach clad only in a red kerchief. These days you'll find tranquillity in the beach's northern bird sanctuary and pleasant swimming conditions.

First page: top, © Michael Lawrence/Lonely Planet Images; bottom, © Stephen Frink/Index Stock

Beginning at 3am on the day after Christmas, revelers in elaborate costumes celebrate **JUNKANOO.** The raucous street parade is an ancient ritual of African heritage that still lives on in The Bahamas and is a symbol of national pride. Some **JUNKANOO MASKS (above)** cover an entire face. This masked man joins stilt, street, and acrobatic dancers, along with clowns and monsters—perhaps a "fly" with red-and-chartreuse eyes and 2.7m (9ft.) wings. The **KING OF JUNKANOO (right)** wears an elaborate headdress, a caparison vest, and a giant hoop skirt made from cardboard and decorated with thin strips of crepe paper meticulously glued on. Part jive, part shuffle, and all dazzling gymnastics, parade participants dance to the syncopated beat of blowing bugles, tin whistles, clanking cowbells, conch shells, and Goombay drums (goat skins stretched over wooden frames).

Take a stroll through Nassau's vast bustling **STRAW MARKET (right)**, which dates from 1901, and you'll find all sorts of items made from the top of thatch palm—baskets with colorful embroidery, handbags, hats, tablemats, and even dolls.

The hub of market life from the Out Islands, Potter's Cay lies under the Paradise Island Bridge. **QUEENIE (below)** sells island staples such as papaya, bananas, coconuts, and pineapples. Fishing boats arrive at Potter's Cay, too, to unload their catch of the day, especially snapper and grouper—two mainstays of the Bahamian diet—and the "sexy conch," which Bahamian men view as an aphrodisiac.

© Jeff Greenberg/Alamy

© Bob Krist/Corbis

The 5.6ha (14-acre) sprawling "water city" at the Atlantis Paradise Island Resort & Casino justifies the resort's hype that "An ocean runs through it." The aquarium here is touted as the largest marine habitat in the world, with more than 100 species of tropical fish, some 14,000 in all. Take a stroll through this Plexiglas walkway at **MARINE PARK (left),** which provides a unique perspective to see marine life from down below as fish swim overhead.

Paying homage to the "lost continent" of Atlantis, the $850 million, 2,349-room **ATLANTIS PARADISE ISLAND RESORT & CASINO (above)** is a fantasy megaresort. It stands across from Nassau on Paradise Island, the poshest destination in The Bahamas. Atlantis, with a Disney-style replica of a Mayan temple, is not just a resort, but also a water park with marine life, underwater caves, waterfalls, blue lagoons, and a walk-through aquarium.

Built in 1838, this red-and-white banded **LIGHTHOUSE (left)** on Elbow Cay in the Abacos is one of the last hand-turned, kerosene-fueled beacons in The Bahamas. Climb 36m (120 ft.) to the top for a view of dazzling land- and seascapes. Local residents have repeatedly tried to destroy the lighthouse, hoping that ships near Hope Town would wreck on the reefs and they could salvage the profitable cargoes.

"THE CLOISTERS," (below) were once part of a 14th-century monastery near Lourdes, France. Newspaper baron William Randolph Hearst purchased the remains but when dismantled, they were not labeled. Paradise Island developer, Huntington Hartford, grandson of the founder of A&P, hired architects to reassemble the stones; the project took more than a year to complete.

The **HORSE-DRAWN SURREY (above)** is still the most romantic way to travel about Nassau. Drivers await passengers in the heart of Rawson Square and tell a colorful living history of Nassau—of all the blood, gore, lore, and legend. You'll pass the grounds of the 1859 Royal Victoria Hotel, once home to a man who inspired Margaret Mitchell to create the character of Rhett Butler in *Gone With the Wind*.

On October 12, 1492, Columbus landed on this frontier island, 122km (200 miles) southeast of Nassau. He named it San Salvador. In 1956, scholar Ruth Durlacher Wolper Malvin placed a lonely cross—known now as the **COLUMBUS MONUMENT (right)**—at what is believed, though disputed, to be the spot where Columbus made landfall.

PINK FLAMINGOS (left)—the graceful national birds of The Bahamas—strike elegant poses in the remote nature reserve of the Inagua National Park. The Romans killed these birds for their tongues—considered the greatest of all delicacies—but they are protected today and are no longer an endangered species. Every spring, flamingos flock to Great Inagua, the most southerly and the third-largest island of The Bahamas, to mate.

At the 16ha (40-acre) **LUCAYAN NATIONAL PARK (above)** on Grand Bahama Island, a wooden path winds through terrain that islanders call the "bush country." Along with rare birds, flora, and fauna, the park's environment ranges from dune-covered beaches to Golden Rock Creek, fed by what is touted as the world's largest underground freshwater cavern system. Bones, pottery, and other artifacts prove that this was a former stomping ground of the Lucayans, who came here to drink from the freshwater springs.

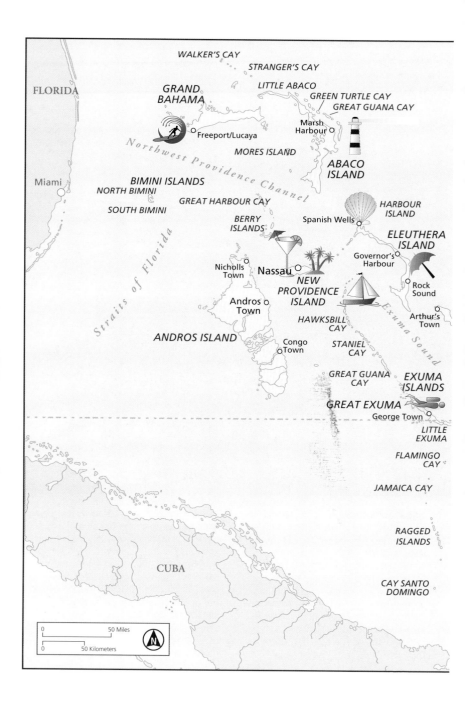

The Best Sun & Sand in the Bahamas

 Cable Beach

 Cabbage Beach

 Xanadu Beach

 Tahiti Beach

 Pink Sands Beach

 Ten Bay Beach

 Saddle Cay

 Stocking Island

 Cat Island's Beaches

CAT ISLAND

Cockburn Town   SAN SALVADOR

ATLANTIC
OCEAN

Stella Maris   RUM CAY

Tropic of Cancer

LONG ISLAND

Deadman's Cay

CROOKED ISLAND

ACKLINS ISLAND

MAYAGUANA ISLAND

NORTH CAICOS

MIDDLE CAICOS

PINE CAY

EAST CAICOS

PROVIDENCIALES   Grace Bay

CAICOS ISLANDS

SOUTH CAICOS

GRAND TURK ISLAND

LITTLE INAGUA

TURKS AND CAICOS ISLANDS

SALT CAY

TURKS ISLANDS

GREAT INAGUA

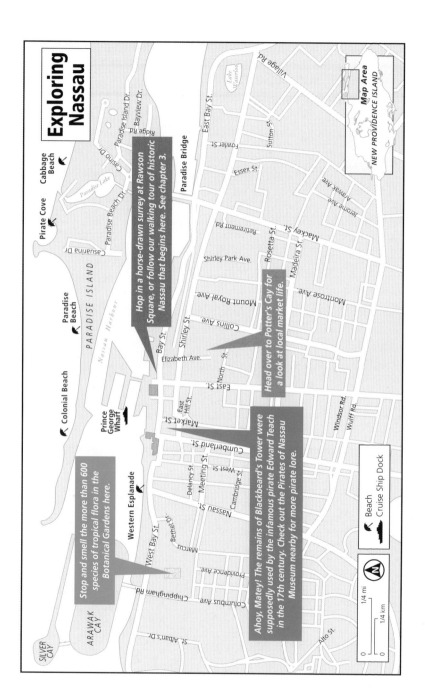

Exploring Nassau

Stop and smell the more than 600 species of tropical flora in the Botanical Gardens here.

Hop in a horse-drawn surrey at Rawson Square, or follow our walking tour of historic Nassau that begins here. See chapter 3.

Head over to Potter's Cay for a look at local market life.

Ahoy, Matey! The remains of Blackbeard's Tower were supposedly used by the infamous pirate Edward Teach in the 17th century. Check out the Pirates of Nassau Museum nearby for more pirate lore.

Map Area

NEW PROVIDENCE ISLAND

Pirate Cove
Cabbage Beach

Paradise Beach

Casuarina Dr.

Colonial Beach

PARADISE ISLAND

Paradise Lake

Casino Dr.

Paradise Island Dr.

Bayview Dr.

Ridge Rd.

Paradise Bridge

Paradise Beach Dr.

Nassau Harbour

Prince George Wharf

Western Esplanade

West Bay St.

Bethel Dr.

Marcus

Providence Ave.

Chippingham Rd.

Columbus Ave.

St. Alban's Dr.

ARAWAK CAY

SILVER CAY

Bay St.

Elizabeth Ave.

East St.

North St.

East Hill St.

Market St.

Cumberland St.

Delancy St.

Meeting St.

West St.

Cambridge St.

Nassau St.

Shirley St.

Collins Ave.

Mount Royal Ave.

Shirley Park Ave.

Retirement Rd.

Rosetta St.

Madeira St.

Montrose Ave.

Mackey St.

Arawak Ave.

Jerome Ave.

Windsor Rd.

Wulff Rd.

Alto St.

East Bay St.

Fowler St.

Essex St.

Sutton St.

Village Rd.

Lake Waterloo

Beach
Cruise Ship Dock

N

0   1/4 mi
0   1/4 km

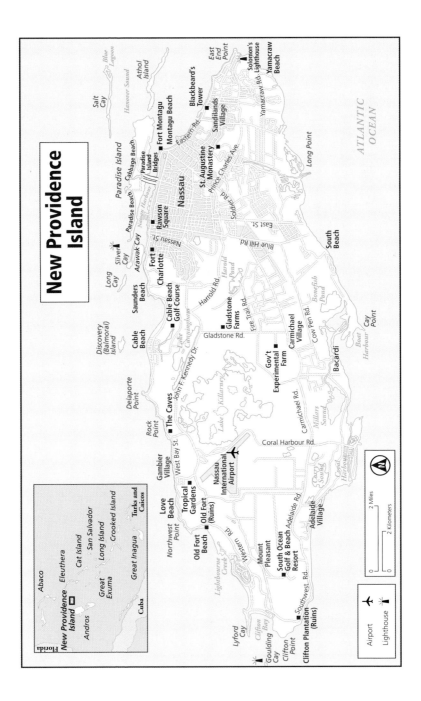

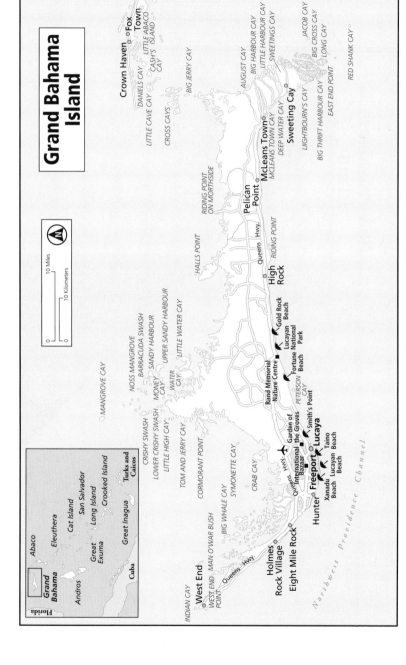

Grand Bahama Island

Florida

Abaco
Eleuthera
Cat Island
San Salvador
Andros
Great
Exuma
Long Island
Crooked Island
Great Inagua
Turks and
Caicos

Grand
Bahama

Cuba

10 Miles
10 Kilometers

Crown Haven
Fox Town
DANIELS CAY
LITTLE CAVE CAY
CASH'S CAY
LITTLE ABACO ISLAND

BIG JERRY CAY

AUGUST CAY
BIG HARBOUR CAY
LITTLE HARBOUR CAY
SWEETINGS CAY

MANGROVE CAY

CROSS CAYS

McLeans Town
McLEANS TOWN CAY
DEEP WATER CAY

Sweeting Cay
LIGHTBOURN'S CAY

JACOB CAY
BIG CROSS CAY
LONG CAY

BIG THRIFT HARBOUR CAY
EAST END POINT

RED SHANK CAY

NOSS MANGROVE
BARRACUDA SWASH
SANDY HARBOUR
MONEY CAY
UPPER SANDY HARBOUR
CRISHY SWASH
LOWER CRISHY SWASH
LITTLE HIGH CAY
WATER CAY
LITTLE WATER CAY

RIDING POINT
ON MORTHSIDE

Pelican
Point

HALLS POINT

Queens Hwy

RIDING POINT

High
Rock

TOM AND JERRY CAY

CORMORANT POINT

Gold Rock
Beach

Rand Memorial
Nature Centre
Lucayan
Beach
Fortune National
Park

Lucayan
National
Park

PETERSON
CAY

SYMONETTE CAY

Garden of
the Groves
Smith's Point

BIG WHALE CAY

CRAB CAY

International Bazaar
Freeport
Hunter
Lucaya
Queens Hwy
Xanadu
Beach
Lucayan
Beach
Taino
Beach

INDIAN CAY

WEST END MAN O'WAR
POINT BUSH

West End

Holmes
Rock Village

Eight Mile Rock

Queens Hwy.

Northwest Providence Channel

Frommer's®

Bahamas

2006

by Darwin Porter & Danforth Prince

Here's what the critics say about Frommer's:

"Amazingly easy to use. Very portable, very complete."

—*Booklist*

"Detailed, accurate, and easy-to-read information for all price ranges."
—*Glamour Magazine*

"Hotel information is close to encyclopedic."

—*Des Moines Sunday Register*

"Frommer's Guides have a way of giving you a real feel for a place."
—*Knight Ridder Newspapers*

WILEY
Wiley Publishing, Inc.

About the Authors

As a team of veteran travel writers, **Darwin Porter** and **Danforth Prince** have produced numerous titles for Frommer's, including best-selling guides to Italy, France, the Caribbean, England, and Germany. Porter, a former bureau chief of *The Miami Herald,* is also a Hollywood biographer, and his most recent release is *Howard Hughes: Hell's Angel.* Prince was formerly employed by the Paris bureau of the *New York Times,* and is today the president of Blood Moon Productions and other media-related firms.

Published by:

Wiley Publishing, Inc.

111 River St.
Hoboken, NJ 07030-5774

ISBN 13: 978-0-7645-8888-4
ISBN 10: 0-7645-8888-5

Editor: Jennifer Anmuth
Production Editor: M. Faunette Johnston
Cartographer: Elizabeth Puhl
Photo Editor: Richard Fox
Production by Wiley Indianapolis Composition Services

Front cover photo: Young man playing steel drum with band, on beach
Back cover photo: Beach chairs with umbrellas and sun bather

For information on our other products and services or to obtain technical support, please contact our Customer Care Department within the U.S. at 800/762-2974, outside the U.S. at 317/572-3993 or fax 317/572-4002.

Wiley also publishes its books in a variety of electronic formats. Some content that appears in print may not be available in electronic formats.

Manufactured in the United States of America

5   4   3   2   1

Contents

4 Paradise Island   121

5 Grand Bahama (Freeport/Lucaya)   139

6 Bimini, the Berry Islands & Andros   176

7 The Abacos   202

List of Maps

An Invitation to the Reader

In researching this book, we discovered many wonderful places—hotels, restaurants, shops, and more. We're sure you'll find others. Please tell us about them, so we can share the information with your fellow travelers in upcoming editions. If you were disappointed with a recommendation, we'd love to know that, too. Please write to:

Frommer's Bahamas 2006
Wiley Publishing, Inc. • 111 River St. • Hoboken, NJ 07030-5774

An Additional Note

Please be advised that travel information is subject to change at any time—and this is especially true of prices. We therefore suggest that you write or call ahead for confirmation when making your travel plans. The authors, editors, and publisher cannot be held responsible for the experiences of readers while traveling. Your safety is important to us, however, so we encourage you to stay alert and be aware of your surroundings. Keep a close eye on cameras, purses, and wallets, all favorite targets of thieves and pickpockets.

Other Great Guides for Your Trip:

Frommer's Portable Bahamas
Frommer's Caribbean
Frommer's Caribbean Cruises & Ports of Call
Frommer's Caribbean Ports of Call

Frommer's Star Ratings, Icons & Abbreviations

Every hotel, restaurant, and attraction listing in this guide has been ranked for quality, value, service, amenities, and special features using a **star-rating system.** In country, state, and regional guides, we also rate towns and regions to help you narrow down your choices and budget your time accordingly. Hotels and restaurants are rated on a scale of zero (recommended) to three stars (exceptional). Attractions, shopping, nightlife, towns, and regions are rated according to the following scale: zero stars (recommended), one star (highly recommended), two stars (very highly recommended), and three stars (must-see).

In addition to the star-rating system, we also use **seven feature icons** that point you to the great deals, in-the-know advice, and unique experiences that separate travelers from tourists. Throughout the book, look for:

Finds	Special finds—those places only insiders know about
Fun Fact	Fun facts—details that make travelers more informed and their trips more fun
Kids	Best bets for kids, and advice for the whole family
Moments	Special moments—those experiences that memories are made of
Overrated	Places or experiences not worth your time or money
Tips	Insider tips—great ways to save time and money
Value	Great values—where to get the best deals

The following **abbreviations** are used for credit cards:

AE	American Express	DISC	Discover	V	Visa
DC	Diners Club	MC	MasterCard		

Frommers.com

Now that you have the guidebook to a great trip, visit our website at **www.frommers.com** for travel information on more than 3,000 destinations. With features updated regularly, we give you instant access to the most current trip-planning information available. At Frommers.com, you'll also find the best prices on airfares, accommodations, and car rentals—and you can even book travel online through our travel booking partners. At Frommers.com, you'll also find the following:

- Online updates to our most popular guidebooks
- Vacation sweepstakes and contest giveaways
- Newsletter highlighting the hottest travel trends
- Online travel message boards with featured travel discussions

What's New in The Bahamas

Instead of opening new resorts and restaurants, many islands of The Bahamas spent a good part of 2005 recovering from massive hurricane damage in 2004. By the time of your visit, all the properties should be up and running again at peak capacity—that is, unless another fierce hurricane strikes, which is always a possibility in the autumn season. The biggest development this year puts one more thing in your suitcase: Your passport. Don't forget it. Under new Homeland Security regulations, Americans traveling to The Bahamas must show passports starting December 31, 2005, upon their return to the United States. Those returning to Canada will have to show passports starting December 31, 2006. A driver's license or a birth certificate will not be acceptable. See Chapter 2 for more details.

Here are the other changes that might affect your vacation decisions.

NEW PROVIDENCE ISLAND (NASSAU/CABLE BEACH) One of the most famous hotels on the island, **South Ocean Golf and Beach Resort,** has closed until further notice. The property had grown both tired and stale. Look for future developments to be announced.

On Cable Beach, bowing to pressure mainly from Britain and Canada, **Sandals Royal Bahamian Hotel** (© **800/SANDALS**) changed its former antigay discrimination policy and now admits "any couple in love," regardless of sexual preference.

Also on Cable Beach, the flashy megaresort of **Wyndham Nassau Resort & Crystal Palace Casino** (© **800/222-7466**) continues its decline, drawing fire from many guests, who find the bedrooms and general maintenance disappointing. Some clients continue to be faithful to it, whereas others are looking elsewhere for a place to spend their vacation dollars.

As for dining, many old-time favorites—long a mainstay of the culinary scene (including, for example, **Sun And . . .**)—have bit the dust, but others have emerged. The most recent opening that impressed us was **Provence** at Old Town Sandyport (© **242/327-0985**), bringing the Mediterranean cuisine of sunny Provence to Cable Beach. Dishes are prepared with superb simplicity, and first-rate ingredients are used.

PARADISE ISLAND Expect big things from **Atlantis Paradise Island Resort & Casino** (© **800/ATLANTIS**). Work continues throughout 2005 and 2006 for a massive expansion, including a 600-room all-suite luxury hotel and a 400-unit condo hotel. During the life of this edition, Atlantis is expected to open a branch of the world-renowned Nobu chain, funded in part by actor Robert DeNiro. And that's not all. Atlantis has purchased two former Paradise Island hotels—**Club Land'or** and **Club Med**—and has closed these properties for future development.

The big shakeup in the hotel scene for 2005 was when the Sheraton Grand closed in 2004 and blossomed again as the all-inclusive **Hotel Riu Paradise Island** (© 888/666-8816). It's basically the same beachfront hotel with minor improvements, but now it's a one-stop destination, offering all meals and entertainment.

GRAND BAHAMA ISLAND (FREEPORT)   After a major building boom, this island suffered massive damage in the storms of 2004 and spent most of 2005 restoring already existing properties instead of opening new ones. Hardest hit was the most famous hotel on the island, the **Crowne Plaza Golf Resort & Casino at the Royal Oasis** (© 800/545-1300). This mammoth resort limped through much of 2005, not operating at full capacity, but is expected to be fully operational by the time of your visit in 2006.

BERRY ISLANDS   In the remote and little visited Berry Islands, known only to the discerning few (often yachties), there is activity on sleepy Great Harbour Cay. The long-running **Great Harbour Cay Yacht Club & Marina** will be closed for most—or all—of 2006 as it's turned into a more luxurious and elegant resort. Check its status before heading here. But don't worry if you're planning to visit soon: Those wanting to experience the special charm of Great Harbour Cay can book into accommodations through **Tropical Diversions Resort** (© 800/342-7256), which isn't a real resort but a booking agency for a series of beach villas, town houses, and private homes. These often elegant living quarters can be rented when the owners have returned to their mainland homes.

THE ABACOS   At Marsh Harbour, a yachting center and chief port in the Abacos, the culinary news centers around the opening of the **Conch Crawl** (© 242/367-4444), at the ever-popular Conch Inn. Serving the resort's best Bahamian cuisine, this new restaurant was immediately adopted by the visiting yacht set as their favorite place to dine on local food such as fresh fish, especially grouper and conch.

HARBOUR ISLAND   If you want to visit Harbour Island, off the "mainland" of Eleuthera, it is now easier than ever, providing you are already in Nassau. From Potters Cay Dock in Nassau, **Bahamas Fast Ferries** (© 242/323-2166) takes you to remote Harbour Island in just 2 hours transit. The ferry company operates a speedy 177-seat catamaran.

THE EXUMAS   George Town, the capital of this mini-archipelago, is becoming the kayaking center of The Bahamas. You can rent kayaks at **Starfish Activity Center** (© 242/336-3033) and set out on your adventure, including taking time out for snorkeling on deserted beaches. Another good outfitter is **Ecosummer Expeditions** (© 800/465-8884), whose staff is skilled at guiding you through the government-protected nature reserve, Exumas Cays National Land and Sea Park.

LONG ISLAND   Just south of the Tropic of Cancer, **Chez Pierre** (© 242/338-8809) has been opened by two Canadian expats, Pierre and Anne Laurence. Set on 3.2 hectares (8 acres), their complex consists of comfortable bungalows. Pierre is a first-class chef, and his cuisine—a combination of French, Italian, and Caribbean—is the finest on this sleepy island.

1

The Best of The Bahamas

The Bahamas (that's with a capital "T") is one of the most geographically complicated nations of the Atlantic. A coral-based archipelago, it is composed of more than
700 islands, 2,000 cays (pronounced "keys," from the Spanish word for small islands),
and hundreds of rocky outcroppings that have damaged the hulls of countless ships
since colonial days.

The Commonwealth of The Bahamas came into being in 1973 after centuries of
colonial rule. After Great Britain granted The Bahamas internal self-rule in 1964, the
fledgling nation adopted its own constitution but chose not to sever its ties with its
motherland. It has remained in the Commonwealth, with the British monarch as its
head of state. In the British tradition, The Bahamas has a two-house Parliament, a
ministerial cabinet headed by a prime minister, and an independent judiciary. The
queen appoints a Bahamian governor-general to represent the Crown.

As The Bahamas moves deeper into the millennium, the government and various
investors continue to pump money into the tourism infrastructure, especially on Paradise Island, across from Nassau, as well as Freeport/Lucaya on Grand Bahama Island.
Cruise-ship tourism continues to increase, and a more upscale crowd is coming back
after abandoning The Bahamas for many years in favor of other Caribbean islands
such as St. Barts and Anguilla.

When Hubert Ingraham became prime minister in 1992, he launched the country
down the long road toward regaining its market share of tourism, which under Prime
Minister Lynden Pindling had seen a rapid decline. Exit polls revealed some first-time
visitors vowing never to return to The Bahamas under the administration of the notorious Pindling, whose government had taken over a number of hotels and failed to
maintain them properly.

When Ingraham took over as prime minister, however, he wisely recognized that
the government wasn't supposed to be in the hospitality business and turned many
properties back over to the professionals. After a painful slump, tourism in the post-
Pindling era is booming again in The Bahamas, and more than 1.6 million visitors
from all over the world now flock here annually. In the capital of Nassau, it's easy to
see where the government's money is being spent: on widened roads, repaved sidewalks, underground phone cables, massive landscaping, sweeping esplanades, a
cleanup campaign, and additional police officers walking the beat to cut down on
crime.

Perry Gladstone Christie—who was elected prime minister in the 2002 general
elections—continues to carry out those same policies to better Nassau. Christie is the
leader of the Progressive Liberal Party.

The Best Beaches of The Bahamas

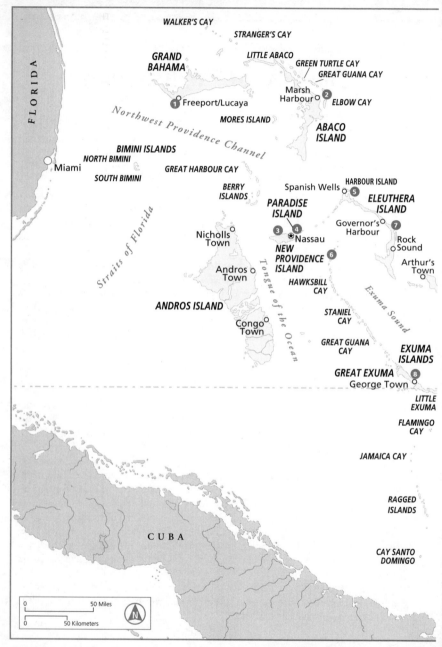

WALKER'S CAY

STRANGER'S CAY

LITTLE ABACO

GREEN TURTLE CAY

GREAT GUANA CAY

GRAND BAHAMA

FLORIDA

Northwest Providence Channel

1 Freeport/Lucaya

Marsh Harbour

2 ELBOW CAY

MORES ISLAND

ABACO ISLAND

BIMINI ISLANDS

NORTH BIMINI

Miami

SOUTH BIMINI

GREAT HARBOUR CAY

BERRY ISLANDS

Spanish Wells

HARBOUR ISLAND

5

ELEUTHERA ISLAND

Straits of Florida

PARADISE ISLAND

3 **4**

Nicholls Town

⚝ Nassau

NEW PROVIDENCE ISLAND

6

Governor's Harbour

7

Rock Sound

Arthur's Town

Andros Town

Tongue of the Ocean

HAWKSBILL CAY

ANDROS ISLAND

STANIEL CAY

Exuma Sound

Congo Town

GREAT GUANA CAY

EXUMA ISLANDS

GREAT EXUMA

8

George Town

LITTLE EXUMA

FLAMINGO CAY

JAMAICA CAY

RAGGED ISLANDS

CUBA

CAY SANTO DOMINGO

0   50 Miles
0   50 Kilometers

N

THE BEST BEACHES
Cabbage Beach **4**
Cable Beach **3**
Cat Island's Beaches **9**
Pink Sands Beach **5**
Saddle Cay **6**
Stocking Island **8**
Tahiti Beach **2**
Ten Bay Beach **7**
Xanadu Beach **1**

ATLANTIC
OCEAN

CAT ISLAND
⑨

Cockburn
Town   *SAN SALVADOR*

Stella
Maris   *RUM CAY*

Tropic of Cancer

*LONG
ISLAND*

Deadman's Cay

*CROOKED
ISLAND*

*ACKLINS
ISLAND*

*MAYAGUANA
ISLAND*

TURKS AND CAICOS
ISLANDS
(U.K.)

NORTH
CAICOS
PINE CAY   MIDDLE CAICOS
PROVIDENCIALES   EAST CAICOS
Grace
Bay   *CAICOS
ISLANDS*   SOUTH
CAICOS   *GRAND
TURK
ISLAND*

LITTLE INAGUA

SALT
CAY   TURKS
ISLANDS

GREAT INAGUA

Bahamas Beaches 101

In The Bahamas, the issue about public access to beaches is a hot and controversial subject. Recognizing this, the government has made efforts to intersperse public beaches near private ones, where access would otherwise be impeded. Although megaresorts discourage nonguests from easy access to their individual beaches, there are so many public beaches on New Providence Island and Paradise Island that all a beach lover has to do is stop his or her car (or walk) to many of the unmarked, unnamed beaches that flank the edge of these islands.

If you stay in one of the large beachfront resorts, all you need to do is leave the grounds of the hotel and head for the ocean via the sand in front the resort. But if your accommodation is not beachfront or you want to explore another beach, here are a few details:

Cabbage Beach ★★. On Paradise Island, this is the real showcase of the island. Its broad white sands stretch for at least 3km (2 miles). Casuarines, palms, and sea grapes border it. While it's likely to be crowded in winter, you can find a little more elbowroom by walking to the northwestern stretch of the beach. You can reach Paradise Island from downtown Nassau by walking over the bridge, taking a taxi, or boarding a ferryboat at Prince George Dock. Cabbage Beach does not have public facilities but you can patronize one of the handful of bars and restaurants nearby and use their facilities. Technically, you should be a customer even if that means buying only a drink, even a Coca-Cola.

Cable Beach ★★. No particular beach is actually called Cable Beach, yet this is the most popular beachfront on New Providence Island. Instead of an actual beach, Cable Beach is the name given to a string of resorts and beaches that lie in the center of New Providence's northern coast, attracting the most visitors. This beachfront offers 6.5km (4 miles) of soft white sand, and the types of food, restaurants, snack bars, and watersports offered at the hotels lining the waterfront vary. Calypso music floats to the sand from hotel pool patios where vacationers play musical chairs and see how low they can limbo. Vendors wind their way between sunblock-slathered bodies. Some sell armloads of shell jewelry, T-shirts, beach cover-ups, and fresh coconuts for sipping the sweet "water" straight from the shell. Others offer their hair-braiding services or sign up visitors for water-skiing, jet-skiing, and banana boat rides. Kiosks advertise parasailing, scuba diving, and snorkeling trips, as well as party cruises to offshore islands. Waters can be rough and

Unlike Haiti and Jamaica, The Bahamas has remained politically stable and made the transition from minority white rule to black majority rule with relatively little tension.

Economic conditions have slowly improved here as well. You do not see the wretched poverty in Nassau that you see in, say, Kingston, Jamaica, though many poor residents do still live on New Providence Island's "Over-the-Hill" section, an area where few tourists venture to visit (although the neighborhood is gritty and fascinating).

reefy, then calm and clear a little farther along the shore. There are no public toilets here, because guests of the resorts use their hotel facilities. If you're not a guest of the hotel, or not a customer, you are not supposed to use the facilities. The Cable Beach resorts begin 4.8km (3 miles) west of downtown Nassau. Even though resorts line much of this long swath of beach, there are various sections where public access is available without crossing through private hotel grounds.

Caves Beach. On the north shore, past the Cable Beach Properties, Caves Beach lies some 11km (7 miles) west of Nassau. It stands near Rock Point, right before the turnoff along Blake Road that leads to the airport. Since visitors often don't know of this beach, it's another good spot to escape the hordes. It's also a good beach with soft sands. There are no toilets or changing facilities.

Delaporte Beach. Just west of the busiest section of Cable Beach, Delaporte Beach is a public access beach where you can escape the crowds. It opens onto clear waters and boasts white sands, although it has no facilities. Nonetheless, it's an option.

Goodman's Bay. This public beach lies east of Cable Beach on the way toward the center of Nassau. Goodman's Bay and Saunders Beach (see below) often host local fundraising cookouts, where vendors sell fish, chicken, conch, peas 'n' rice, or macaroni and cheese. People swim and socialize to blaring reggae and calypso music. To find out when one of these beach parties is happening, ask the staff at your hotel or pick up a local newspaper. There is a playground here, plus toilet facilities.

Paradise Beach ☆☆. On Paradise Island, this is one of the best beaches in the entire area. The white sandy beach is dotted with *chikees* (thatched huts), which are perfect when you've had too much of the sun. Mainly used by guests of the Atlantis Resort (p. 123), it lies at the far western tip of the island. If you're not a resident, access is difficult. If you're staying at a hotel in Nassau and want to come to Paradise Island for a day at the beach, it's better to go to Cabbage Beach (see above).

Saunders Beach. East of Cable Beach, this is where many islanders go on the weekends. To reach it, take West Bay Street from Nassau in the direction of Coral Island. The beach lies across from Fort Charlotte, just west of Arawak Cay. Like Goodman's Bay (see above), it often hosts local fundraising cookouts open to the public. These can be a lot of fun. There are no public facilities.

Nassau really is the true The Bahamas. You'd think a city so close to the U.S. mainland would have been long since overpowered by American culture. Yet, except for some fast-food chain outlets, American pop music, and Hollywood films, Nassau retains a surprising amount of its traditionally British feel. (By contrast, Freeport/Lucaya on Grand Bahama Island has become almost completely Americanized, with little British aura or Bahamian tradition left.)

The biggest changes have occurred in the hotel sector. Sun International has vastly expanded its Atlantis property on Paradise Island, turning it into a virtual water world. Even more expansions have been announced, to be completed between now and late 2007. The Hilton interests have developed the decaying old British Colonial in Nassau, restoring it to life.

And Grand Bahama Island is in an interesting state of flux. Hotels along the entire Lucayan strip are being either built from scratch or upgraded; the fabled The Crowne Plaza Golf Resort & Casino at the Royal Oasis in Freeport is experiencing a renaissance under new owners.

If there's a downside to this boom, it's the emphasis on megahotels and casinos—and the corresponding lack of focus on the Out Islands, which include the Abacos, Andros, Bimini, Cat Island, Eleuthera, the Exumas, Long Island, and San Salvador. Large resort chains, with the exception of Four Seasons and Club Med, have ignored these islands; most continue to slumber away in relative seclusion and poverty. Other than the Four Seasons megaresort that recently opened in the Exumas—complete with an 18-hole golf course—development in the drowsy Out Islands has been minor. The very lack of progress here will continue to attract a certain breed of adventurous explorer, the one who shuns the resorts and casinos of Paradise Island, Cable Beach, and Freeport/Lucaya. Little change in this Out Islands-versus-the-rest situation is anticipated in the immediate future.

There's another interesting trend to note in The Bahamas: After a long slumber, the government and many concerned citizens here have awakened to eco-tourism. More than any government in the Caribbean except perhaps Bonaire, this nation is trying to protect its natural heritage. If nothing else, its residents realize doing this will be good for tourism, because many visitors come to The Bahamas precisely for a close encounter with nature.

Government, private companies, and environmental groups have drawn up a national framework of priorities to protect the islands. One of their first goals was to save the nearly extinct West Indian flamingo. Today, nearly 60,000 flamingos inhabit Great Inagua Island. Equally important programs aim to prevent the extinction of the green turtle, the white-crowned pigeon, the Bahamian parrot, and the New Providence iguana.

Although tourism and the environment are bouncing back, many problems still remain for this archipelago nation. While some Bahamians seem among the friendliest and most hospitable people in the world, others—particularly those in the tourist industry—can be downright hostile. To counter this, the government is working to train its citizens to be more helpful, courteous, and efficient. Sometimes this training has been taken to heart; at other times, however, it still clearly has not. Service with a smile is not assured in The Bahamas.

Drug smuggling remains a serious problem, and regrettably there seems to be no immediate solution. Because the country is so close to U.S. shores, it is often used as a temporary depot for drugs shipped from South America to Florida. The Bahamas previously developed a tradition of catering to the illicit habits of U.S. citizens, as well; during the heyday of Prohibition, long before cocaine, marijuana, and heroin were outlawed, many Bahamians grew rich smuggling rum into the United States. Things have improved, but you'll still see stories in the newspapers about floating bales of marijuana turning up in the sea just off The Bahamas' coastline and such.

Though this illicit trade rarely affects the casual tourist, it's important to know that it is a factor here—and so, armed with this knowledge, don't agree to carry any packages to or from the U.S. for a stranger while you're visiting. You could end up taking a much longer vacation on these islands than you had ever imagined.

Western Esplanade (also called Junkanoo Beach). If you're staying at a hotel in downtown Nassau, such as the British Colonial Hilton (p. 79), this is a good beach to patronize close to town. The narrow strip of sand is convenient to Nassau and has toilets, changing facilities, and a snack bar.

1 The Best Beaches

See also "Bahamas Beaches 101" box on p. 6.

- **Cable Beach** (New Providence Island): The glittering shoreline of Cable Beach has easy access to shops, casinos, restaurants, watersports, and bars. It's a sandy 6.5km-long (4-mile) long strip, with a great array of facilities and activities. See p. 97.

- **Cabbage Beach** (Paradise Island): Think Vegas in the Tropics. It seems as if most of the sunbathers dozing on the sands here are recovering from the previous evening's partying, and it's likely to be crowded near the megahotels, but you can find a bit more solitude on the beach's isolated northwestern extension (Paradise Beach), which is accessible only by boat or on foot. Lined with palms, sea grapes, and casuarinas, the sands are broad and stretch for at least 3km (2 miles). See p. 133.

- **Xanadu Beach** (Grand Bahama Island): Grand Bahama has 97km (60 miles) of sandy shoreline, but Xanadu Beach is most convenient to Freeport's resort hotels, several of which offer shuttle service to Xanadu. There's more than a kilometer of white sand and (usually) gentle surf. Don't expect to have Xanadu to yourself, but if you want more quiet and privacy, try any of the beaches that stretch from Xanadu for many miles in either direction. See p. 162.

- **Tahiti Beach** (Hope Town, the Abacos): Since the beach is so isolated at the far end of Elbow Cay Island, you can be sure that only a handful of people will ever visit these cool waters and white sands. The crowds stay away because you can't drive to Tahiti Beach: To get there, you'll have to walk or ride a rented bike along sand and gravel paths from Hope Town. You can also charter a boat to get there, which isn't too hard, since the Abacos are the sailing capital of The Bahamas. See p. 216.

- **Pink Sands Beach** (Harbour Island): Running the entire length of the island's eastern side, these pale pink sands stretch for 5km (3 miles) past a handful of low-rise hotels and private villas. A coral reef protects the shore from breakers, making for some of the safest swimming in The Bahamas. See p. 245.

- **Ten Bay Beach** (Eleuthera): Ten Bay Beach lies a short drive south of Palmetto Point, just north of Savannah Sound. Once upon a time, the exclusive Cotton Bay Club chose to build a hotel here because of the fabulous scenery. There may not be facilities here, but now that the hotel has closed, the white sands and turquoise waters here are more idyllic and private than ever. See p. 238.

- **Saddle Cay** (the Exumas): Most of the Exumas are oval-shaped islands strung end to end like links in a 209km (130-mile) chain. One notable exception is Saddle Cay, with its horseshoe-shaped curve near the Exumas' northern tip. It can be reached only by boat, but once achieved offers an unspoiled setting without a trace of the modern world—and plenty of other cays and islets where you can play Robinson Crusoe for a few hours if you like. See p. 256.
- **Stocking Island** (the Exumas): One of the finest white-sandy beaches in The Bahamas lies off Elizabeth Harbour, the main harbor of the archipelago, close to the little capital of George Town. You can reach Stocking Island easily by boat from Elizabeth Harbour, and the sands of this offshore island are rarely crowded; snorkelers and divers love to explore its gin-clear waters. In addition to its beach of powdery white sand, the island is also known for its "blue holes," coral gardens, and undersea caves. See p. 265.
- **Cat Island's Beaches:** The white sandy beaches ringing this island are pristine, opening onto crystal-clear waters and lined with coconut palms, palmettos, and casuarina trees—and best of all, you'll practically have the place to yourself. One of our favorite beaches here, near Old Bight, has a beautiful, lazy curve of white sand. Another fabulous beach lies 5km (3 miles) north of New Bight, site of the Fernandez Bay Village resort. This curvy, white-sandy beach is set against another backdrop of casuarinas, and is idyllic and unusually tranquil. Another good beach here is the long, sandy stretch that opens onto Hawk's Nest Resort and Marina on the southwestern side. None of the Cat Island beaches has any facilities (bring everything you need from your hotel), but they do offer peace, quiet, and seclusion. See "Cat Island," in chapter 10.

2 The Best Diving

- **New Providence Island:** Many ships have sunk near Nassau in the past 300 years, and all the dive outfitters here know the most scenic wreck sites. Other attractions are underwater gardens of elkhorn coral and dozens of reefs brimming with underwater life. The most spectacular dive site is the **Shark Wall**, 16km (10 miles) off the southwest coast of New Providence; it's blessed with incredible, colorful sea life and the healthiest coral offshore. You'll even get to swim with sharks (not as bait, of course). See p. 101.
- **Grand Bahama Island:** The island is ringed with reefs, and dive sites are plentiful, including the Wall, the Caves (site of a long-ago disaster known as Theo's Wreck), and Treasure Reef. Other popular dive sites include Spit City (yes, that's right), Ben Blue Hole, and the Rose Garden (no one knows how this one got its name). What makes Grand Bahama Island a cut above the others is the presence of a world-class dive operator, **UNEXSO** (the Underwater Explorer's Society; ✆ **800/992-DIVE** or 242/373-1244; www.unexso.com). See p. 167.
- **Andros:** Marine life abounds in the barrier reef off the coast of Andros, which is one of the largest in the world and a famous destination for divers. The reef plunges 1,800m (5,904 ft.) to a narrow drop-off known as the Tongue of the Ocean. You can also explore mysterious blue holes, formed when subterranean caves fill with seawater, causing their ceilings to collapse and exposing clear, deep pools. See p. 199.

- **Bimini:** Although Bimini is most famous for its game fishing, it boasts excellent diving, too. Five kilometers (3 miles) of offshore reefs attract millions of colorful fish. Even snorkelers can see black coral gardens, blue holes, and an odd configuration on the sea floor that is reportedly part of the lost continent of Atlantis (a fun legend, at any rate). Divers can check out the wreck of a motorized yacht, the *Sapona* (owned by Henry Ford), which sank in shallow waters off the coast in 1929. See p. 184.

- **Harbour Island** (Eleuthera): In addition to lovely coral and an array of colorful fish, divers can enjoy some unique experiences here, such as the Current Cut, an exciting underwater gully that carries you on a swiftly flowing underwater current for 10 minutes. Four wrecked ships also lie nearby, at depths of less than 12m (39 ft.), including a barge that was transporting the engine of a steam locomotive in 1865, reportedly after the American Confederacy sold it to raise cash for its war effort. See p. 252.

- **Long Island** (The Southern Bahamas): Snorkeling is spectacular on virtually all sides of the island. But experienced divers venturing into deeper waters offshore can visit underwater cages to feed swarms of mako, bull, and reef sharks. Dive sites abound, including the Arawak "green hole," a blue hole of incomprehensible depth. See p. 287.

- **Lucayan National Park:** This park on Grand Bahama Island is the site of a 9.5km-long (6-mile), underground, freshwater cave system, the longest of its type in the world. The largest cave contains spiral staircases that lead visitors into a freshwater world inhabited by shrimp, mosquito fish, fruit bats, freshwater eels, and a species of crustacean *(Spelionectes lucayensis)* that has never been documented elsewhere. On the 16 hectares (40-acre) preserve you'll find examples of the island's five ecosystems—pine forests, rocky coppice, mangrove swamps, whiteland coppice, and sand dunes. Pause to sunbathe on a lovely stretch of sandy beach, or hike along paths where you can spot orchids, hummingbirds, and barn owls. See p. 168.

- **Pelican Cays Land and Sea Park:** Known for its undersea caves, seemingly endless coral reefs, and abundant plant and marine life, this park, 13km (8 miles) north of Cherokee Sound at Great Abaco Island, is a highlight for scuba divers. See p. 210.

- **Exuma Cays National Land and Sea Park:** A major attraction of The Bahamas, this park is the first of its kind anywhere on the planet. The 35km-long (22-mile), 13km-wide (8-mile) natural preserve attracts scuba divers to its 453 sq. km (177 sq. miles) of sea gardens with spectacular reefs, flora, and fauna. Inaugurated in 1958, it lies some 35km (22 miles) northwest of Staniel Cay or 64km (40 miles) southeast of Nassau and is accessible only by boat. See p. 266.

3 The Best Snorkeling

- **New Providence Island/Paradise Island:** The waters that ring densely populated New Providence Island and nearby Paradise Island are easy to explore. Most people head for the Rose Island Reefs, the Gambier Deep Reef, Booby Rock Channel, the Goulding Reef Cays, and some easily seen, well-known underwater wrecks that lie in shallow water. Virtually every resort hotel on the island offers equipment and can book you onto a snorkel cruise to sites further off-shore. See p. 100 and 135.

- **Grand Bahama:** Resort hotels on island can hook you up with snorkeling excursions, such as the ones offered by **Ocean Motion Water Sports Ltd.** (© 242/374-2425; www.oceanmotionbahamas.com), which is the best outfitter for snorkeling. In addition, the outlet can connect you with any number of other watersports, from banana boating to water-skiing. The clear water around Grand Bahama is wonderful for snorkeling because it has a rich marine life. Snorkelers are fond of exploring Ben's Cave, a stunning cavern that's part of Lucayan Caves, as well as the coral beds at places like Silver Point Reef and Gold Rock. See p. 167.

- **Bimini:** Snorkelers are enthralled with the offshore black coral gardens, which are easily accessible from shore, and the colorful marine life around the island. Sometimes when conditions are right, snorkelers enjoy frolicking with a pod of spotted dolphins. Off North Bimini, snorkelers are attracted to a cluster of huge, flat rocks that jut from 6 to 9m (20–30 ft.) out of the water at Paradise Point. The most imaginative snorkelers claim these rocks, which seem hand-hewn, are part of a road system that once traversed the lost continent of Atlantis. See p. 184.

- **Long Island** (The Southern Bahamas): Shallow bays and sandy beaches offer many possibilities for snorkeling, and the staffs at both major resorts will direct you to the finest conditions near their stretches of beach. The southern end of the island is especially dramatic because of its unique sea cliffs. Many east-coast beach coves also offer fantastic snorkeling opportunities. See p. 284.

- **Elbow Cay:** With its 209km (130-mile) string of beautiful cays, and some of the best beaches in The Bahamas, the Abacos are ideal for snorkeling, especially in the waters off Elbow Cay. Visibility is often great because the cay lies close to the cleansing waters of the Gulf Stream. Mermaid Beach, a particularly colorful reef, is a favorite. **Froggie's Out Island Adventures** (© 242/366-0431; www.froggiesabaco.com) provides equipment and the best snorkeling advice. See p. 216.

- **Stocking Island:** George Town is the capital of the Exumas, which is celebrated for its crystal clear waters so beloved by yachties. From George Town, Stocking Island lies across Elizabeth Harbour, which is only 1.5 km (1 mile) away. Stocking Island is a long, thin, barrier island that attracts snorkelers who explore its blue holes (ocean pools of fresh water floating on heavier saltwater). The island is also ringed with undersea caves and coral gardens in stunning colors. You'll also find that Stocking Island has some of the most gorgeous white-sand beaches in the Southern Bahamas. See p. 267.

- **San Salvador:** Following in the footsteps of Columbus, snorkelers find a rich paradise on this relatively undiscovered island, with its unpolluted and unpopulated kilometers of beaches that are ideal for swimming, shelling, and close-in snorkeling. A week's stay is enough time to become acquainted only with the possibilities, including Bamboo Point, Fernandez Bay, and Long Bay, which are all within a few kilometers of Cockburn (the main settlement) on the western side of the island. At the southern tip of San Salvador is one of our favorite places for snorkeling, Sandy Point, and its satellite of Grotto Bay. See chapter 10.

4 The Best Fishing

- **New Providence:** The waters around New Providence are thick with game fish. In-the-know fishermen long ago learned the best months to pursue their catch: November to February for wahoo found in the reefs, June and July for blue marlin, and May to August for the oceanic bonito and blackfin tuna. Nassau is ideal for sportsfishing. Most boat charters allow their passengers to start fishing within 15 minutes after leaving the dock. The best outfitter is **Born Free Charters** (*C* **242/393-4144**) where anchoring and bottom-fishing are also options. See p. 99.

- **Grand Bahama:** Off the coast the clear waters are good hunting grounds for snapper, grouper, yellowtail, wahoo, barracuda, and kingfish. The tropical waters along Grand Bahama lure anglers in search of "the big one," because the island is home to some of the biggest game fish on earth. Many fishermen catch dolphins (not the Flipper kind, though). And Deep Water Cay is a fishing hot spot. The best outfitter is **Reef Tours, Ltd.** (*C* **242/373-5880**). See p. 164.

- **Green Turtle Cay:** The deep-sea fishing possibilities off the coast of this cay drew anglers from all over the world. An abundance of giant game fish as well as tropical fish live in these beautiful waters. Both dedicated fisherman and more casual sportsfishermen come to the little island, seeking yellowfin tuna, a few dolphinfish, and the big game wahoo, among other catches. Green Turtle Cay boasts some of the best fishing guides in The Bahamas, weather-beaten men who've spent a lifetime fishing the surrounding waters. The best place to hook up with one of these guides is **Green Turtle Club** (*C* **242/365-4070**). See p. 229.

- **Treasure Cay:** In the Abacos, some of the best fishing grounds are in the sea bordering this remote island. At the **Treasure Cay Marina** (*C* **242/365-8250**), fishermen from all over the world hire experienced skippers to take them out in their search for barracuda, grouper, yellowtail, snapper, tuna, marlin, dolphinfish, and wahoo. Deep-sea, bottom-, and drift fishing are yours for the asking. The cay's own bonefish flats are just a short boat cruise from the marina. See p. 223.

- **The Exumas:** Anglers from all over America descend on this beautiful archipelago for deep-sea or bottom-fishing. Fishermen hunt down kingfish, wahoo, dolphinfish, tuna, and bonito in the deepest waters off the coastline of the Exumas. Many visitors also fly here just to go bonefishing. Among other outfitters who can hook you up with fishing outings is **Club Peace & Plenty** (*C* **242/345-5555**), which rents the necessary equipment and can arrange experienced guides to accompany you. See p. 266.

5 The Best Sailing

- **Marsh Harbour and Hope Town** (the Abacos): Known among yachties for their many anchorages, sheltered coves, and plentiful marine facilities, the Abacos are considered one of the most perfect sailing areas in the world. You can charter boats of all shapes and sizes for a week or longer, with or without a crew. See "The Active Vacation Planner," in chapter 2, and p. 209 and 216 in chapter 7.

- The **Exumas:** Yachties flock to these beautiful sailing waters to see some of the most dramatic coastal scenery in The Bahamas. **The Family Island Regatta,** the most popular boating spectacle in The Bahamas, is held here annually. Most of the recreational boating is in the government-protected **Exumas Cays Land and Sea Park,** an area of splendid sea gardens and rainbow-hued coral reefs that stretches south from Wax Cay to Conch Cay. You can rent motorboats at **Minns Water Sports** (© 242/336-3483) in George Town. See p. 265.

- **New Providence Island:** Although sailing in the waters off New Providence Island isn't the equal of those yachting favorites, the Exumas and the Abacos, boaters can still find much to delight in. More organized boating excursions are offered in New Providence than anywhere else in The Bahamas, especially by outfitters such as **Barefoot Sailing Cruises** (© 242/393-0820; www.barefoot sailingcruises.com) and **Majestic Tours Ltd.** (© 242/322-2606). You can also choose from an array of sunset cruises, like the ones **Flying Cloud** (© 242/363-4430) offers, which feature its fleet of catamarans. The most popular—and the most scenic—trip is sailing to tranquil **Rose Island,** which is 13km (8 miles) east of the center of Nassau and is reached after sailing past several small, uninhabited cays. In addition, Blue Lagoon Island, 4.8 km (3 miles) northeast of Paradise Island, is a magnet for boaters in that it offers seven white sandy beaches along with seaside hammocks. The drawback to this island, however, is that cruise-ship passengers flock here and many beach buffs like to come over on day trips. See p. 72.

- **Grand Bahama Island:** On the beautiful waters off this large island, you can go sailing aboard *Ocean Wonder* (© 242/373-5880), which is supposedly the world's largest twin-diesel engine glass-bottom boat. This boat offers the best and most panoramic picture of underwater life off the coast of Grand Bahama Island—a view most often reserved for scuba divers. You can also go sailing aboard *Bahama Mama,* a two-deck 22m (72-ft.) catamaran on a Robinson Crusoe Beach Party. The catamaran also sails at sunset on a booze cruise. **Superior Watersports** (© 242/373-7863; www. superiorwatersports.com) operates this catamaran. See p. 164.

- **Marsh Harbour:** One of the finest anchorages in the Out Islands is found in Marsh Harbour, which is called "The Boating Capital of The Bahamas." **The Moorings** (© 800/535-7289 or 242/367-4000; www. moorings.com) is one of the leading charter sailboat outfitters in the world, and rents boats to sail the waters of the Abacos. Passengers discover white-sand beaches and snug anchorages on uninhabited cays. Sailing here is one of the great experiences of visiting The Bahamas. See p. 209.

6 The Best Golf Courses

- **Cable Beach:** The main course is the **Radisson Cable Beach Golf Course** (© 242/327-6000; www.radisson cablebeach.com) The oldest golf course in The Bahamas, this par-72 green was the private retreat of British expatriates in the 1930s. Today, it's managed by a corporate namesake of Arnold Palmer and owned by Cable Beach casino marketers. Small ponds and water traps heighten the challenge, amid more than 7,040 yards of well-maintained greens and fairways. See "The Active Vacation Planner," in chapter 2, and p. 100.

- **Paradise Island:** Tom Weiskopf designed **Ocean Club Golf Club** (*(C)* **242/363-6682;** www.oceanclub. com), an 18-hole, par-72 course, and it's a stunner. With its own pitfalls, including the world's largest sand trap and water hazards (mainly the Atlantic Ocean) on three sides, Jack Nicklaus and Gary Player have endorsed this course. For the best panoramic ocean view—good enough to take your mind off your game— play the par-3 14th hole. See "The Active Vacation Planner," in chapter 2, and p. 134.

- **Grand Lucaya, Grand Bahama Island:** Designed by Robert Trent Jones Jr., **The Reef Course** (*(C)* **242/ 373-1333**) opened in 2000. The Bahamian press called it a bit like a Scottish course, "but a lot warmer." The course boasts 6,920 yards of link-style greens. See p. 166.

- **Grand Bahama Island:** Megaresort **Crowne Plaza Golf Resort & Casino at the Royal Oasis** (*(C)* **242/350- 7000**) offers two golf courses, Emerald Golf Course and Ruby Golf Course. Both are par 72, with rolling, sandy terrain. See p. 165.

- **The Exumas:** At long last the Southern Bahamas has a world-class golf course: **Four Seasons Resort Emerald Bay Golf Club** opens onto the waters of Emerald Bay (*(C)* **242/ 366-6800**). The par-72, 18-hole course was designed by Greg Norman, the famous golf architect, who created six oceanfront holes. The course is challenging, yet not daunting, so that it appeals to golfers of various skills. See p. 266.

7 The Best Tennis Facilities

- **Paradise Island:** Well-heeled tennis buffs check into the **One&Only Ocean Club** (*(C)* **242/363-2501;** www.oneandonlyresorts.com). Many visitors go there just for tennis, which can be played day or night on their six Har-Tru courts. Guests booked into the cabanas and villas of the club can practically roll out of bed onto the courts. Although beginners and intermediate players are welcome, the courts are often filled with first-class competitors. Tennis is free for guests of the One&Only Ocean Club. The tennis complex at the **Atlantis** (*(C)* **242/363-3000;** www.atlantis. com) is more accessible to the general public, with ten courts (six regular asphalt and four hydro quartz), some lit for night games. See p. 135.

- **Freeport** (Grand Bahama Island): Freeport is another top choice for tennis buffs. **Crowne Plaza Golf Resort & Casino at the Royal Oasis** (*(C)* **242/350-7000**) has eleven state-of-the-art courts, three of them clay and eight lit for night games. You don't have to be a guest to play here, but you should call ahead for a reservation. See "The Active Vacation Planner," in chapter 2, and p. 167.

Eco-Tourism Highlights of The Bahamas

The Bahamas spreads over 258,998 sq. km (101,010 sq. miles) of the Atlantic Ocean—this is the largest oceanic archipelago nation in the tropical Atlantic Ocean, with miles of crystal-clear waters rich with fish and other marine resources—and thus is home to countless natural attractions, including a series of underwater reefs that stretch 1,224km (759 miles) from the Abacos in the northeast to Long Island in the southeast. It has the most extensive systems of blue holes and limestone caves in the world.

And, unlike Puerto Rico, Jamaica, Barbados, and other Caribbean island nations, The Bahamas also possesses large areas of undeveloped natural mainland.

It all adds up to plenty of opportunity for getting up close and personal with nature.

Start with the reefs. Lying off the coast of Andros, The Bahamas includes approximately 2,330 sq. km (909 sq. miles) of coral reef, comprising the third-largest barrier reef system in the world. Rich with diverse marine life, the reef attracts green moray eels, cinnamon clownfish, and Nassau grouper. When officials realized that long-line fishing threatened this fragile ecology, The Bahamas became one of the first Caribbean countries to outlaw the practice.

The nation's Parliament also passed the Wild Birds Protection Act to ensure the preservation of rare bird species. That law has made a significant difference: Great Inagua Island now shelters more than 60,000 pink flamingos, Bahamian parrots, and a large portion of the world's population of reddish egrets. These birds live in the government-protected, 743-sq.-km (290-sq.-mile) Inagua National Park.

And that's not all. The islands of The Bahamas are home to more than 1,370 species of plant life, plus 13 species of mammals; the majority of them, it must be said, are bats, but wild pigs, donkeys, raccoons, and the Abaco wild horse also roam the interiors of the nation's islands. You'll see whales and dolphins, including humpback and blue whales and the spotted dolphin, swimming in the sea.

To keep an eye on all this natural wealth, and share it with the public, the **Bahamas National Trust** administers 25 national parks and more than 283,279 hectares (699,699 acres) of protected land. Its headquarters, with one of the finest collections of wild palms in the western hemisphere, are located in Nassau at the **Retreat** on Village Road (© **242/393-1317**). Guided 30-minute tours are conducted Tuesday through Thursday. Volunteers at the Retreat can also help arrange visits to the national parks on the various islands. For more information, see p. 94.

8 The Best Honeymoon Resorts

- **Sandals Royal Bahamian Hotel** (Cable Beach, New Providence Island; © **800/SANDALS** or 242/327-6400; www.sandals.com): This Jamaican chain of couples-only, all-inclusive hotels is a honeymooners' favorite. The Bahamas's branch of the chain is more upscale than many of its Jamaican counterparts, and it offers 27 secluded honeymoon suites with semiprivate plunge pools. Staff members lend their experience and talent to on-site wedding celebrations; Sandals will provide everything from a preacher to flowers, as well as champagne and a cake. It's more expensive than most Sandals resorts, but you can usually get better rates through a travel agent or a package deal. See p. 86.

- **Compass Point** (New Providence Island; © 800/633-3284 or 242/327-4500; www.compasspointbahamas.com): This choice is a charming and personalized statement for those who shun megaresorts. The accommodations are found in floridly painted huts or cottages, some of which have kitchenettes and some of which are raised on stilts. Completely in harmony with the lovely natural setting, it's nevertheless state of the art. See p. 89.

- **One&Only Ocean Club** (Paradise Island; © 800/321-3000 in the U.S. only, or 242/363-2501; www.oneandonlyresorts.com): It's elegant, low-key, and low-rise, and it feels exclusive. The guests include many older couples celebrating honeymoons. With waterfalls, fountains, reflecting pools, and a stone gazebo, the Ocean Club's formal terraced gardens were inspired by the club's founder (an heir to the A&P fortune) and are the most impressive in The Bahamas. At the center is a French cloister, with carvings from the 12th century. See p. 124.

- **Old Bahama Bay** (Grand Bahama Island; © 800/572-5711 or 800/444-9469; www.oldbahamabay.com): Perfect for honeymooners seeking a quiet hideaway in a boutique-style hotel with cottages adjacent to a marina. The casinos, entertainment, shopping, and dining of Freeport/Lucaya are 40km (25 miles) away, but here you can sneak away to luxury, solitude, and romance. See p. 153.

- **Kamalame Cay** (Staniard Creek, Andros; © 242/368-6281; www.kamalame.com): You'll need deep pockets to afford one of the most exclusive resorts in the Out Islands, a perfect honeymoon retreat for the couple who want to escape casinos and resorts. With its 5km (3 miles) of white-sand beaches in both directions, this pocket of posh is a citadel of luxury and comfort. And don't worry if you've already taken your honeymoon; this is the perfect place to take a second one, or even a third. See p. 194.

- **Green Turtle Club** (Green Turtle Cay, the Abacos; © 800/963-5450, or 242/365-4271; www.greenturtleclub.com): Romantics appreciate this resort's winning combination of yachting atmosphere and well-manicured comfort. It's small (31 rooms) and civilized in an understated way; the charming, clapboard-covered village of New Plymouth is nearby, accessible by motor launch or, even better, a 45-minute walk across windswept scrublands. See p. 226.

- **The Bluff House Club Beach Hotel** (Green Turtle Cay, the Abacos; © 800/745-4911, or 242/365-4247; www.bluffhouse.com): This place was named because of its location high atop a 24m (80-ft.) cliff towering over a pink sand beach. Its 4.8 hectares (12 acres) front the Sea of Abaco on one side and the harbor of White Sound on the other. The accommodations are very private, with a rustic, seafaring decor that has its own kind of elegance. In addition to rooms, the hotel offers beach and hillside villas, and colonial suites with private balconies that overlook the water. See p. 225.

• **Pink Sands** (Harbour Island, Eleuthera; ✆ 800/OUTPOST or 242/333-2030; www.islandoutpost. com/PinkSands): You can have a spectacular getaway at this elite retreat on an 11-hectare (27-acre) beachfront estate owned by Chris Blackwell, the famous founder of Island Records. Its location on a 5km (3 mile) stretch of private pink sand, sheltered by a barrier reef, is just one of its assets. You can ask for a bedroom that evokes an upscale bordello in Shanghai to put you in a romantic mood, and you can also enjoy the best meals on the island. See p. 246.

• **Stella Maris Resort Club** (Long Island, the Southern Bahamas; ✆ **800/426-0466,** 242/338-2051, or 954/359-8238; www.stellamarisresort. com): Right on the Atlantic, built on the grounds of an old plantation, Stella Maris has become a social hub on Long Island. Sailing is important here, as are diving and getting away from it all. Many of the guests hail from Germany, and they lend the place a European flair. The sleepy island itself is one of the most beautiful in The Bahamas, and honeymooners fit into the grand scheme of things perfectly. See p. 286.

9 The Best Family Vacations

• **Radisson Cable Beach Hotel** (Cable Beach, New Providence Island; ✆ **800/333-3333** or 242/327-6000; www.radisson-cablebeach.com): A family could spend their entire vacation on the grounds of this vast resort. There's a pool area that features the most lavish artificial waterfall this side of Tahiti; a health club at the nearby Crystal Palace that welcomes both guests and their children; Camp Junkanoo, with supervised play for children 3 through 12; and a long list of in-house activities that includes dancing lessons. See p. 87.

• **Atlantis Paradise Island Resort & Casino** (Paradise Island; ✆ **800/ ATLANTIS** in the U.S., or 242/363-3957; www.atlantis.com): This is one of the largest hotel complexes in the world, with endless rows of shops and watersports galore. Both children and adults will enjoy the 5.6-hectare (14-acre) sea world with water slides, a lagoon for watersports, white sandy beaches, and underground grottoes plus an underwater viewing tunnel and 240m (787 ft.) of cascading waterfalls. Its children's menus and innovative,

creative children's programs are the best in The Bahamas and perhaps even in the Caribbean. See p. 123.

• **Crowne Plaza Golf Resort & Casino at the Royal Oasis** (Grand Bahama Island; ✆ **800/545-1300** or 242/350-7000): Many guests come here just to gamble and work on their tans, but others bring their kids. To divert them, the hotel maintains a pair of playgrounds and a swimming pool inspired by a tropical oasis, and offers children's platters in some of the restaurants. The architecture features lots of "Aladdin and His Lamp" accessories, such as minarets above a decidedly non-Islamic setting. See p. 145.

• **Best Western Castaways** (Grand Bahama Island; ✆ **800/780-7234** in the U.S., or 242/352-6682; www. bestwestern.com): Here's a good choice for families on a budget. The pagoda-capped lobby is set a very short walk from the ice-cream stands, souvenir shops, and fountains of the International Bazaar. Children under 12 stay free in their parent's room, and the in-house lounge presents limbo and fire-eating shows several evenings a month. The hotel offers a babysitting service and a free shuttle to Xanadu Beach. See p. 148.

- **Regatta Point** (George Town, Great Exuma; ℂ **800/688-0309** in the U.S.; www.regattapointbahamas.com): This resort offers efficiency apartments at moderate prices. On a palm-grove cay, it is family friendly, with its own little beach. Bikes are available, and Sunfish boats can be rented. There's also a grocery store nearby where you can pick up supplies. Many units are suitable for families of four or five. See p. 263.

10 The Best Places to Get Away from It All

- **Green Turtle Club** (Green Turtle Cay, the Abacos; ℂ **800/963-5450,** or 242/365-4271; www.greenturtle club.com): Secluded and private, this sailing retreat consists of tasteful one- to three-bedroom villas with full kitchens. It opens onto a small private beach with a 35-slip marina, which is the most complete yachting facility in the archipelago. Many rooms open onto poolside, and there's a dining room decorated in Queen Anne style. See p. 226.

- **Rock House Hotel** (Harbour Island, off the coast of Eleuthera; ℂ **242/ 333-2053;** www.rockhousebahamas. com): A glamorous and stylish inn—really, a glorified B&B—this posh little hideaway is drawing more and more of the glitterati to its shores. Set on a low buff above the harbor, it is tranquillity itself with whimsically decorated bedrooms. No one will find you if you decide to hide out here. See p. 248.

- **Club Med–Columbus Isle** (San Salvador, the Southern Bahamas; ℂ **800/** **CLUB-MED** or 242/331-2000; www. clubmed.com): This was the first large resort to be built on one of The Bahamas's most isolated islands, site of Columbus's first landfall in the New World. It's unusually luxurious, and unusually isolated, for a Club Med, and it occupies a gorgeous beach. The sheer difficulty of reaching it adds to the get-away-from-it-all mystique. See p. 280.

- **Fernandez Bay Village** (Cat Island, the Southern Bahamas; ℂ **800/ 940-1905** or 242/342-3043; www. fernandezbayvillage.com): The dozen stone and timber villas of Fernandez Bay Village are the closest thing to urban congestion Cat Island ever sees. There's a funky, thatch-roofed beach bar that'll make you feel like you're in the South Pacific, enjoying a cold beer each afternoon after you leave the stunning sands and turquoise waters behind for the day. There's only one phone at the entire resort, and your bathroom shower will probably open to a view of the sky. See p. 276.

11 The Best Restaurants

- **Chez Willie** (Nassau, New Providence Island; ℂ **242/322-5364**): This is one of the newest, but also the classiest, restaurants on New Providence Island, overshadowing its competitors on Cable Beach. It's a throwback to the grandeur of Old Nassau in its Duke and Duchess of Windsor cafe society heyday. Your host, Willie Armstrong, oversees a smoothly run operation serving some of the best French and Bahamian cuisine found on the island. See p. 91.

- **Buena Vista** (Nassau, New Providence Island; ⓒ **242/322-2811;** www.buenavista-restaurant.com): Overlooking Nassau Harbour, this restaurant retains the elegance that the city had when the Duke and Duchess of Windsor were in the governor's mansion. Its take on both a continental and Bahamian cuisine still attracts the serious foodie drawn both to the cuisine and the expert service by tuxedo-clad waiters. See p. 90.

- **Dune** (in the One&Only Ocean Club, Paradise Island; ⓒ **242/363-2501,** ext. 64739): The most cutting-edge restaurant in either Paradise Island or Nassau is this creation of French-born restaurant guru Jean-Georges Vongerichten, he of several of New York City's leading lights. Every dish served here is something special—from shrimp dusted with orange powder to chicken and coconut milk soup with shiitake cakes. See p. 130.

- **Bahamian Club** (Paradise Island; ⓒ **242/363-3000**): A notch down from the superb Dune, this establishment is one of the leading restaurants in The Bahamas and our favorite at the sprawling megaresort of Atlantis. Strictly upscale, it presents a superb French and international cuisine nightly against a backdrop that evokes the British Colonial era. The restaurant serves the island's finest cuts of meats. See p. 129.

- **Villa d'Este** (in the Atlantis Paradise Island Resort and Casino, Paradise Island; ⓒ **242/363-3000**): This is the finest Italian restaurant on Paradise Island, with nothing in Nassau to top it, either. The setting is gracious, tasteful, and Old World, but it's the food that keeps visitors and locals alike clamoring for reservations. All the old favorites are here, including veal parmigiana and fettuccine Alfredo as fine as any you'd find in Rome. Fresh herbs add zest to many dishes, and the pasta dishes are particularly good. See p. 132.

- **Mangoes Restaurant** (Marsh Harbour, the Abacos; ⓒ **242/367-2366**): For the best and most authentic Bahamian food in the Abaco chain, head for this welcoming spot, where both visiting yachties and locals flock for the fine cuisine. Order up a conch burger for lunch, then return in the evening for the catch of the day—straight from the sea and grilled to your specifications. The namesake mango sauce really dresses up a plate of grilled pork tenderloin. See p. 207.

- **The Landing** (Harbour Island, Eleuthera; ⓒ **242/333-2707;** www.harbourislandlanding.com): This attractive restaurant at the ferry dock has awakened the sleepy taste buds of Eleuthera. Brenda Barry and daughter Tracy feed you well from a choice of international cuisines, often prepared from recipes gathered during world travels. Under mature trees in their garden, you feast on delicious pasta dishes, freshly made gazpacho, pan-fried grouper, or a warm duck salad. See p. 250.

- **Rock House Restaurant** (Harbour Island; ⓒ **242/333-2053;** www.rockhousebahamas.com): On the increasingly chic Harbour Island, the restaurant in the Rock House Hotel serves a superb international cuisine. Its hip bodega aura evokes Miami, but it's thoroughly grounded on the island. At lunch you can get a rock lobster sandwich, but at night the chefs display their culinary prowess with an array of satisfying dishes. See p. 250.

12 The Best Nightlife

- **Cable Beach:** Cable Beach has a lot more splash and excitement than Nassau, its neighbor on New Providence Island, and wandering around Cable Beach is also much safer than exploring the back streets of Nassau at night. The main attraction is the **Wyndham Nassau Resort & Crystal Palace Casino** (© 242/327-6200; www.wyndhamnassauresort.com), with an 800-seat theater known for staging glitzy extravaganzas and a gaming room that will make you think you're smack dab in the middle of Vegas. One of the largest casinos on the islands, the Crystal Palace features 750 slot machines, 51 blackjack tables, nine roulette wheels, seven craps tables, and a baccarat table (we think the Paradise Island casino has more class, though). Despite all the glitter, you can still find cozy bars and nooks throughout the resort if you'd prefer a tranquil evening. See p. 119.

- **Atlantis Paradise Island Resort & Casino:** Paradise Island has the flashiest nightlife in all of The Bahamas, hands down. Not even nearby Nassau and Cable Beach can come close. Nearly all of the action takes place at the incredible **Atlantis Paradise Island Resort & Casino** (© 242/363-3000; www.atlantis.com), where you'll find high rollers from Vegas and Atlantic City alongside grandmothers from Iowa who play the slot machines when family isn't looking. It's all gloss, glitter, and showbiz, with good gambling (though savvy locals say your odds of beating the house are better in Vegas). For a quieter night out, you can also find intimate bars, discos, a comedy club, and lots more in this sprawling behemoth of a hotel. See p. 137.

- **Freeport:** Although the giant **Royal Oasis Casino** in the Crowne Plaza Golf Resort & Casino (© 242/350-7000; www.theroyaloasis.com) ranks third behind Paradise Island and Cable Beach, most of the nightlife in Freeport/Lucaya revolves around this glittering Moroccan-style palace, one of the largest casinos in either The Bahamas or the Caribbean. You get not only high- and low-stakes gambling, but also a splashy Vegas-like (well, maybe Reno-like) ambience. See p. 173.

2

Planning Your Trip to The Bahamas

You can be in The Bahamas after a quick 35-minute jet hop from Miami. And it's never been easier to take advantage of great package deals that can make these islands a terrific value.

1 The Islands in Brief

The Bahamian chain of islands, cays, and reefs stretches from Grand Bahama Island, 121km (75 miles) almost due east of Palm Beach, Florida, to Great Inagua, the southernmost island, which lies about 97km (60 miles) northeast of Cuba and fewer than 161km (100 miles) north of Haiti.

The most developed islands for tourism in The Bahamas are **New Providence Island,** site of Nassau (the capital) and Cable Beach; **Paradise Island;** and **Grand Bahama,** home of Freeport and Lucaya. If you're after glitz, gambling, bustling restaurants, nightclubs, and a beach-party scene, these big three islands are where you'll want to be. Package deals are easily found here.

Set sail (or hop on a short commuter flight) for one of the **Out Islands,** such as Andros, the Exumas, or the Abacos, and you'll find fewer crowds—and often lower prices, too. Though some of the Out Islands are accessible mainly (or only) by boat, it's still worth your while to make the trip if you like the idea of having an entire beach to yourself. This is really the place to get away from it all.

NEW PROVIDENCE ISLAND (NASSAU/CABLE BEACH) New Providence isn't the largest of the Bahamian Islands, but it's the historic heart of the nation, with a strong maritime tradition and the largest population in the country. Home to more than 125,000 residents, it offers groves of pines and casuarinas; sandy, flat soil; the closest thing in The Bahamas to urban sprawl; and superb anchorages sheltered from rough seas by the presence of nearby Paradise Island. New Providence has the country's busiest airport and is dotted with hundreds of villas owned by foreign investors. Its two major resort areas are Cable Beach and Nassau.

The resort area of **Cable Beach** is a glittering beachfront strip of hotels, restaurants, and casinos; only Paradise Island has been more developed. Its center is the Marriott Resort & Crystal Palace Casino. Often, deciding between Cable Beach and Paradise Island isn't so much a choice of which island you prefer as a choice of which hotel you prefer. But it's easy to sample both, since it takes only about 30 minutes to drive between the two.

Nassau, the Bahamian capital, isn't on a great stretch of shoreline and doesn't have as many first-rate hotels as either Paradise Island or Cable Beach—with the exception of the Bahama Hilton, which has a small private beach. The main advantages of Nassau are colonial charm and price. Its hotels may not be ideally located, but they are relatively inexpensive; some offer very low prices even during the winter high season. You can base yourself here and commute easily to the beaches at Paradise Island or Cable Beach. Some travelers even prefer Nassau because it's the seat of Bahamian culture and history—not to mention the shopping mecca of The Bahamas.

PARADISE ISLAND   If high-rise hotels and glittering casinos are what you want, along with some of the best beaches in The Bahamas, there is no better choice than Paradise Island, directly off the coast of Nassau. It has the best food, the best entertainment, terrific beaches, casinos, and the best hotels. Its major drawbacks are that it's expensive and often overcrowded. Boasting a colorful history, yet a host of unremarkable architecture, Paradise Island remains perhaps the most intensely marketed piece of real estate in the world. The sands and shoals of the elongated and narrow island protect the wharves and piers of Nassau, which rise across a narrow channel only 180m (590 ft.) away.

Owners of the 277-hectare (684-acre) island have included brokerage mogul Joseph Lynch (of Merrill Lynch) and Huntington Hartford, heir to the A&P supermarket fortune. More recent investors have included Merv Griffin. The island today is a carefully landscaped residential and commercial complex with good beaches, lots of glitter (some of it tasteful, some of it way too over-the-top), and many diversions.

GRAND BAHAMA ISLAND (FREE-PORT/LUCAYA)   The island's name derives from the Spanish term *gran bajamar* (great shallows), which refers to the shallow reefs and sandbars that, over the centuries, have destroyed everything from Spanish galleons to English clipper ships on Grand Bahama's shores. Thanks to the tourist development schemes of U.S. financiers such as Howard Hughes, Grand Bahama boasts a well-developed tourist infrastructure. Casinos, beaches, and restaurants are now plentiful here.

Grand Bahama's **Freeport/Lucaya** resort area is another popular destination for American tourists, though it has a lot more tacky development than Paradise Island or Cable Beach. The compensation for that is a lower price tag on just about everything. Freeport/Lucaya offers plenty of opportunities for fine dining, entertainment, and gambling. Grand Bahama also offers the best hiking in The Bahamas and has some of the finest sandy beaches. Its golf courses attract players from all over the globe, and the island hosts major tournaments several times a year. You'll find some of the world's best diving here, as well as UNEXSO, the internationally famous diving school. Grand Bahama Island is especially popular with families.

BIMINI   One of the smallest islands in The Bahamas and close enough to Miami (just 81km/50 miles away) to be distinctly separate from the other islands of the archipelago, Bimini is actually a pair of islands with a total area of 23 sq. km (9 sq. miles); smaller North Bimini is better developed than South Bimini. Luxurious yachts and fishing boats are always docked at the island's marinas. Throughout Bimini, there's a slightly run-down Florida-resort atmosphere mingled with some small-town charm (think old-time Key West, before the cruise-ship crowds ruined it).

Once the setting for Ernest Hemingway's *Islands in the Stream* (see below), Bimini attracts big-game fishers for big-league fishing tournaments. Sportfishing here is among the best in the world, and the scuba diving among the very best in The Bahamas. And if you'd like to follow in the footsteps of such famous anglers as Zane Grey and Howard Hughes, this is your island.

THE BERRY ISLANDS   Lying between Nassau and the coast of Florida, these 30-odd islands—which contain only about 77 sq. km (30 sq. miles) of dry land among them—attract devoted yachters and fishermen. This series of islets, cays, and rows of barely submerged rocks have extremely limited tourist facilities and are geared mostly toward well-heeled anglers, many of whom hail from Florida. Most of the full-time population (about 700 people) lives on Great Harbour. We find these islands a lot classier and charming than Bimini.

ANDROS   Andros is two islands, connected by a series of canals and cays called *bights*. The largest landmass in The Bahamas, it attracts divers, fishing enthusiasts, and sightseers.

Most of the island is uninhabited and unexplored. The main villages are Nicholl's Town, Andros Town, and Congo Town; all are accessible by frequent boat and plane connections from Miami and Nassau. Lodgings range from large resorts to small, plain guesthouses that cater mainly to fishermen.

Fun Fact   **Hemingway in Bimini**

One of the oddest pieces of real estate in the Atlantic—less than a few hundred feet wide in many places, with a surface area of only 23 sq. km (9 sq. miles)—Bimini has always floated like a magic lure, only 81km (50 miles) from some of the most crowded seashores in the United States. During the 1930s, it was famous as an alter ego to Key West. Soaked with liquor during U.S. Prohibition (Bimini served as a depot for outlawed contraband) and widely known today as a storage depot for illegal drugs, the place has always found itself bathed in controversy. Thanks to novelist Ernest Hemingway, its raunchy, no-holds-barred lifestyle became infamous throughout North America.

Hemingway's first boat (the *Pilar*) was a diesel-powered tub he skippered with fellow writer John Dos Passos for the express purpose of reaching Bimini. One of the bloodiest of his many self-destructive acts occurred off the coast of Bimini when, struggling to aim a revolver at the thrashing jaws of a captured mako shark, he accidentally shot himself in both legs. But don't let that fool you: Hemingway did some serious and successful fishing here. Among the most impressive catches of his life were a 356kg (785-lb.) mako and a 233 kg (514-lb.) tuna, both hauled in off the coast of Bimini.

Some of Hemingway's most famous fistfights happened on Bimini, too—one with wealthy publisher Joseph Knapp, others with a series of black contenders who stood to earn $250 if they could stay in the ring with him for three 3-minute rounds. (No one ever collected the money.)

Hemingway revised the manuscript of *To Have and Have Not* on Bimini in 1937. His evocative description of the seaport in *Islands in the Stream* was Alice Town, Bimini's still-seedy capital.

The world's third-largest barrier reef lies off the coast of Andros, and divers come from all over the world to explore it. The reef plunges 1,800m (5,904 ft.) to a narrow drop-off known as the Tongue of the Ocean. Bonefishing here is among the best on earth, and Andros is also known for its world-class marlin and bluefin tuna fishing.

Known as the "Big Yard," the central portion of Northern Andros is largely a dense forest of mahogany and pine where more than 50 varieties of orchids bloom. Southern Andros boasts a 103-sq.-km (40-sq.-mile) forest and mangrove swamp. Any hotel can arrange a local guide to give a tour.

THE ABACOS   Though this "island" is often called Abaco, it is actually a cluster of islands and islets. It is a mecca for yachters and other boaters who flock here year-round—particularly in July when the Regatta Time in Abaco race is held at the Green Turtle Yacht Club. For hundreds of years the residents of the Abacos have been boat builders, although tourism is now the main industry.

With the exception of Harbour Island in Eleuthera, you'll find more New England charm here than anywhere else in The Bahamas. Loyalists who left New England after the American Revolution settled here and built Cape Cod–style clapboard houses with white picket fences. The best places to experience this old-fashioned charm are Green Turtle Cay and Elbow Cay, which are accessible from Marsh Harbour. Marsh Harbour itself houses an international airport and a shopping center, although its hotels aren't as good as those on Green Turtle Cay and Elbow Cay (Hope Town).

Many of the Abaco islands are undeveloped and uninhabited. For the best of both worlds, visitors can stay at resorts on Walker's, Green Turtle, or Treasure cays, and then charter a boat to tour the more remote areas.

ELEUTHERA   Long and slender, this most historic of the Out Islands (the first English settlers arrived here in 1648) is actually a string of islands that includes Spanish Wells and Harbour Island, a chic destination. The length of the island (177km/110 miles) and the distances between Eleuthera's communities require access via three airports. The island lies about 97 km (60 miles) *east* of Nassau; frequent flights connect the two. Eleuthera is similar to Abaco, and visitors are drawn to the miles of barrier reef and fabulous, secluded beaches.

Gregory Town is the pineapple capital of the island chain. A bit farther south is Surfers Beach, one of the best surfing spots in The Bahamas. Several accommodations are available in this sleepy, slightly budget-oriented section of Eleuthera. The only major resort along the entire stretch of Eleuthera is the Club Med at Governor's Harbour. Other inns are more basic.

At the southern end of the island, **Rock Sound** is in a slump, waiting to see whether the fabled Cotton Bay Club will ever reopen.

Off the coast of Eleuthera, **Harbour Island** offers excellent hotels and food, picket fences, and pastel-colored houses that evoke Cape Cod. The beaches on Harbour Island are famed for their pink sand, tinted that color by crushed coral and shells. Another offshore island near Eleuthera, **Spanish Wells** has extremely limited accommodations, and the residents—descendants of long-ago Loyalists—aren't very welcoming to visitors.

THE EXUMAS   Just 56km (35 miles) southeast of Nassau, this 588km-long (365-mile) string of islands and cays—most of them uninhabited—is the great yachting hub of The Bahamas, rivaling (and some say surpassing) the Abacos. These waters, some of the prettiest in The Bahamas, are also ideal for fishing (bonefishing especially). Many secluded beaches open onto tranquil cays. Daily flights service the Exumas from both Nassau and Miami.

This island chain's commercial center is **George Town** on **Great Exuma,** while the Exuma National Land and Sea Park—protected by The Bahamas National Trust—encompasses much of the coastline. The park is accessible only by boat and is one of the major natural wonders and sightseeing destinations of The Bahamas, with an abundance of undersea life, reefs, blue holes, and shipwrecks. Portions of the James Bond thriller *Thunderball* were filmed at **Staniel Cay.** Each year in April, George Town hosts the interisland Family Island Regatta, a major event on the yachting calendar. A big new Four Seasons resort and golf course officially opened in the winter of 2004, at **Emerald Bay** in Great Exuma, bringing a new crowd here. The Four Seasons is also building a deep-water marina here, scheduled to open in August 2005 with 40 to 45 slips. Perhaps by 2006, 125 state-of-the-art slips will be available for ocean-going yachts, along with a dockmaster and eventually a restaurant. A few good inns are also on Great Exuma, centered mainly at George Town, and the locals are very hospitable. You'll feel like you practically have the archipelago to yourself.

THE SOUTHERN BAHAMAS This cluster of islands—with excellent beaches, good fishing, and dive sites—is known for its remoteness on the southern fringe of The Bahamas. Shaped like a skinny eel, **Cat Island** is only a few miles wide and 77km (48 miles) long. It's a lush, sleepy island in the southern Bahamian backwater, a great place to get away from it all.

Tradition holds that **San Salvador** was the first landmass that Christopher Columbus reached during his voyage to the New World in 1492. With its history and good beaches, the island is sure to undergo further development.

The appropriately named **Long Island** stretches for 93km (58 miles) and, despite a beautiful landscape—there are high cliffs in the north, wide shallow beaches, historic plantation ruins, and native caves—it has remained thoroughly off the beaten track. It's not always easy to get here; there are two minor airports with arrivals from Nassau, but flights do not occur daily. Both the Stella Maris Resort Club and the luxurious Cape Santa Maria Beach offer fishing and watersports.

Acklins Island and **Crooked Island** are hard to reach, have very limited tourist facilities, and appeal to people who want to escape civilization. The clear waters offshore offer good snorkeling and diving, and you'll have the sandy beaches to yourself. These islands are populated by only a mere 1,000 souls; lodging is available on Crooked Island only.

Moments Slow Boat to the Out Islands

Delivering goats, chickens, hardware, and food staples along with the mail, Bahamian mail boats greatly improve the quality of life for the scattered communities of the Out Islands. You can book passage on one to at least 17 different remote islands. All 30 boats leave from Nassau, and the round-trip takes a full day. For more information, consult an office of **The Bahamas Tourist Office** (see "Visitor Information," below) or the dockmaster at the Nassau piers at © **242/ 3326-9781** or 326-9772. See "Getting Around," later in this chapter, for additional details.

Set very close to the eastern tip of Cuba, **Great Inagua** is the most southerly island of The Bahamas and the third largest in the nation. Pink flamingos thrive here. For the serious bird-watcher, there is no place else like it in the Caribbean. A handful of no-frills inns provide accommodations.

2 Visitor Information

The "Planning Your Trip Online" section that begins on p. 47 is packed with invaluable advice about how to search for late-breaking information on the Web.

However, travel conditions are ever changing, and you'll want to marshal other resources as well. The two best sources to try before you leave home are your travel agent and **The Bahamas Tourist Office** nearest you. Visit the nation's official tourism office at www.bahamas.com, or call ℂ **800/BAHAMAS** or 242/302-2000. You can also walk in at the following branch offices:

> **Chicago:** 8600 W. Bryn Mawr Ave., Suite 580, North Chicago, IL 60631 (ℂ **773/693-1500**)
> **Los Angeles:** 11400 W. Olympic Blvd., Suite 204, Los Angeles, CA 90064 (ℂ **800/439-6993** or 310/312-9544)
> **Florida:** 1200 S. Pine Island Rd., Suite 750, Plantation, FL 33324 (ℂ **954/236-9292**)
> **New York:** 150 E. 52nd St., New York, NY 10022 (ℂ **212/758-2777**)
> **Toronto:** 121 Bloor St. E., Suite 1101, Toronto, ON M4W 3M5 (ℂ **416/968-2999**)
> **United Kingdom:** 10 Chesterfield St., London W1J 5JL (ℂ **020/7355-0800**)

You may also want to contact the U.S. State Department for background bulletins, which supply up-to-date information on crime, health concerns, import restrictions, and other travel matters. Call ℂ **202/512-1800** or visit www.travel.state.gov.

A travel agent can be a great source of information. Make sure your agent is a member of the American Society of Travel Agents (ASTA). If you get poor service from an ASTA agent, you can write to the ASTA Consumer Affairs Department, 1101 King St., Alexandria, VA 22314 (ℂ **800/440-ASTA** or 703/739-2782; www.astanet.com).

SEARCHING THE WEB

Bahamas websites include:

> **The Bahamas Ministry of Tourism** (www.bahamas.com or www.tourismbahamas.org): Official tourism site.
> **The Bahamas Out Islands Promotion Board** (www.boipb.com): Focuses on remote isles.
> **Bahamas Tourist Guide** (www.interknowledge.com/bahamas): Travelers' opinions.
> **Bahamas Vacation Guide** (www.bahamasvg.com): Service listings.
> **Nassau/Paradise Island Promotion Board** (www.nassauparadiseisland.com): Service listings.

3 Entry Requirements & Customs

ENTRY REQUIREMENTS
DOCUMENTS

To enter The Bahamas, **citizens of the United States, Britain,** and **Canada** coming in as visitors *must* bring a passport to demonstrate proof of citizenship. Under new Homeland Security regulations, starting December 31, 2005, Americans must show passports upon their return to the United States. A driver's license or a birth certificate will not be acceptable. Those returning to Canada will have to show passports starting December 31, 2006.

Tips Passport

Allow plenty of time before your trip to apply for a passport; the processing normally takes 3 weeks, and can take longer during busy periods (especially spring). Also keep in mind that if you need a passport in a hurry, you'll pay a higher processing fee. When traveling, safeguard your passport in an inconspicuous, inaccessible place like a money belt; keep a copy of the critical pages (including your passport number) in a separate place. If you lose your passport, visit the nearest consulate of your native country as soon as possible for a replacement.

Onward or return tickets must be shown to immigration officials in The Bahamas. Citizens of other countries, including Australia, Ireland, and New Zealand, should carry a valid passport.

For information on how to get a passport, go to the Fast Facts section of this chapter—the websites listed provide downloadable passport applications as well as the current fees for processing passport applications. For an up-to-date country-by-country listing of passport requirements around the world, go to the "Foreign Entry Requirement" Web page of the U.S. State Department at **www. travel.state.gov**.

The Commonwealth of The Bahamas does not require visas. On entry to The Bahamas, you'll be given an Immigration Card to complete and sign. The card has a carbon copy that you must keep until departure, at which time it must be turned in. You'll also have to pay a departure tax before you can exit the country (see "Taxes," under "Fast Facts: The Bahamas," later in this chapter).

CUSTOMS
What You Can Bring into The Bahamas

Bahamian Customs allow you to bring in 200 cigarettes, 50 cigars, or 1 pound of tobacco, plus 1 quart of spirits (hard liquor). You can also bring in items classified as "personal effects," and all the money you wish.

What You Can Take Home from The Bahamas

Visitors leaving Nassau or Freeport/ Lucaya for most U.S. destinations clear U.S. Customs and Immigration before departing The Bahamas. Charter companies can make special arrangements with the Nassau or Freeport flight services and U.S. Customs and Immigration for preclearance. No further formalities are required upon arrival in the United States once the preclearance has taken place in Nassau or Freeport.

Collect receipts for all the purchases you make in The Bahamas. *Note:* If a merchant suggests giving you a false receipt, misstating the value of the goods, beware— the merchant might be an informer to U.S. Customs. You must also declare all gifts received during your stay abroad.

If you purchased an item during an earlier trip abroad, carry proof that you have already paid customs duty on the item at the time of your previous reentry. To be extra careful, compile a list of expensive carry-on items and ask a U.S. Customs agent to stamp your list at the airport before your departure.

Returning U.S. citizens who have been away for 48 hours or more are allowed to bring back, once every 30 days, $800 worth of merchandise duty-free. You'll be charged a flat rate of 10% duty on the next $1,000 worth of purchases. Be sure to have your receipts handy. On gifts, the duty-free limit is $100. You cannot bring fresh foodstuffs into the United States; canned or packaged foods, however, are allowed, and you can bring back 1 liter of alcohol.

For specifics on what you can bring back, download the invaluable free pamphlet *Know Before You Go* online at **www. cbp.gov**. (Click on "Travel" then "Know Before You Go Online Brochure.") Or contact the **U.S. Customs & Border Protection (CBP),** 1300 Pennsylvania Ave. NW, Washington, DC 20229 (© **877/ 287-8667**) and request the pamphlet.

For a clear summary of **Canadian** rules, write for the booklet *I Declare,* issued by the **Canada Border Services** (© **800/ 461-9999** in Canada, or 204/983-3500; www.cbsa-asfc.gc.ca). Canada allows its citizens a C$750 exemption, and you're allowed to bring back duty-free 1 carton of cigarettes, 1 can of tobacco, 40 imperial ounces of liquor, and 50 cigars. In addition, you're allowed to mail gifts to Canada valued at less than C$60 a day, provided they're unsolicited and don't contain alcohol or tobacco (write on the package "Unsolicited gift, under $60 value"). All valuables should be declared on the Y-38 form before departure from Canada, including serial numbers of valuables you already own, such as expensive foreign cameras. *Note:* The C$750 exemption can only be used once a year and only after an absence of 7 days.

U.K. citizens returning from **a non-E.U. country** have a customs allowance of 200 cigarettes; 50 cigars; 250g of smoking tobacco; 2 liters of still table wine; 1 liter of spirits or strong liqueurs (over 22% volume); 2 liters of fortified wine, sparkling wine or other liqueurs; 60cc (ml) perfume; 250cc (ml) of toilet water; and

£145 worth of all other goods, including gifts and souvenirs. People under 17 cannot have the tobacco or alcohol allowance. For more information, contact **HM Customs & Excise** at © **0845/010-9000** or 020/8929-0152) or consult U.K.'s customs website at www.hmce.gov.uk.

The duty-free allowance in **Australia** is A$400 or, for those under 18, A$200. Citizens can bring in 250 cigarettes or 250 grams of loose tobacco, and 1,125 milliliters of alcohol. If you're returning with valuables you already own, such as foreign-made cameras, you should file Form B263. A helpful brochure available from Australian consulates or Customs offices is *Know Before You Go.* For more information, call the **Australian Customs Service** at © **1300/363-263,** or log on to www. customs.gov.au.

The duty-free allowance for **New Zealand** is NZ$700. Citizens over 17 can bring in 200 cigarettes, 50 cigars, or 250 grams of tobacco (or a mixture of all three if their combined weight doesn't exceed 250g); plus 4.5 liters of wine and beer, or 1.125 liters of liquor. New Zealand currency does not carry import or export restrictions. Fill out a certificate of export, listing the valuables you are taking out of the country; that way, you can bring them back without paying duty. Most questions are answered in a free pamphlet available at New Zealand consulates and Customs offices: *New Zealand Customs Guide for Travellers, Notice no. 4.* For more information, contact **New Zealand Customs Service,** the Customhouse, 17–21 Whitmore St., Box 2218, Wellington (© **04/473-6099** or 0800/ 428-786; www.customs.govt.nz).

4 Money

The currency is the **Bahamian dollar (B$1),** pegged to the U.S. dollar so that they're always equivalent. (In fact, U.S. dollars are accepted widely throughout The Bahamas.) There is no restriction on

bringing foreign currency into The Bahamas. Most large hotels and stores accept traveler's checks, but you may have trouble using a personal check. It's a good idea to exchange enough money to cover

What Things Cost in The Bahamas	US$/B$	UK£
Taxi from airport to Nassau's center	20.00	10.50
Local phone call	.25	.13
Double room at Graycliff (deluxe)	290.00	152.00
Double room at Holiday Inn Junkanoo Beach (moderate)	149.00	78.00
Dinner for one at Chez Willie (expensive)	60.00	32.00
Dinner at Bahamian Kitchen (inexpensive)	22.00	11.50
Bottle of beer in a bar/hotel	3.00–3.95	1.60–2.00
Rolls of ASA 100 color film (36 exposures)	6.50	3.40
Movie ticket	6.00	3.20

airport incidentals and transportation to your hotel before you leave home.

You can change currencies at a local American Express (© **800/807-6233;** www.americanexpress.com) or Thomas Cook (© **800/223-7373;** www.thomas cook.com) or at your bank.

Be sure to carry some small bills or loose change when traveling. Petty cash will come in handy for tipping and public transportation. Consider keeping the change separate from your larger bills, so that it's readily accessible and you'll be less of a target for theft.

ATMs

The easiest way to get cash away from home is from an ATM (automated teller machine). The **Cirrus** (© **800/424-7787;** www.mastercard.com) and **PLUS** (© **800/843-7587;** www.visa.com) networks span the globe; look at the back of your bank card to see which network you're on, then call or check online for ATM locations at your destination. Know your personal identification number (PIN) and your daily withdrawal limit. Ask your card carrier if your current PIN works in the Bahamas, particularly in the Out Islands. Every card is different, but some need a four-digit, rather than a six-digit, PIN to withdraw cash abroad.

Keep in mind that many banks impose a fee every time a card is used at a different bank's ATM, and that fee can be higher for international transactions (up to $5 or more) than for domestic ones (where they're rarely more than $1.50). On top of this, the bank from which you withdraw cash may charge its own fee.

You can also get cash advances on your credit card at an ATM. Credit card companies do try to protect themselves from theft by limiting the funds someone can withdraw outside their home country, so call your credit card company before you leave home. And keep in mind that you'll pay interest from the moment of your withdrawal, even if you pay your monthly bills on time.

On New Providence Island and Paradise Island, there are plenty of ATMs, including one at the Nassau International Airport. There are far fewer ATMs on Grand Bahama Island (Freeport/Lucaya), but those that are here are strategically located—including ones at the airport and the casino (of course).

Very few ATMs are in the Out Islands. If you must have cash on your Out Island trip, make arrangements before you leave Nassau or Freeport; outside of Freeport, we counted just seven ATMs in the entire remaining chain of Out Islands, including the one at the post office in Marsh Harbour. This situation is fluid, however, and more ATMs may be added in the future.

TRAVELER'S CHECKS

With 24-hour ATMs now available in most cities, traveler's checks are less necessary. However, keep in mind that you will likely be charged an ATM withdrawal fee if the bank is not your own, so if you're withdrawing money every day, you might be better off with traveler's checks—provided that you don't mind showing identification every time you want to cash one. You can get traveler's checks at almost any bank.

American Express (© 800/221-7282) offers denominations of $20, $50, $100, $500, and for cardholders only $1,000. You'll pay a service charge ranging from 1% to 4%; Amex gold and platinum cardholders are exempt from the 1% fee.

Visa (© 800/732-1322) offers traveler's checks at Citibank locations nationwide, as well as at several other banks. The service charge ranges between 1.5% and 2%; checks come in denominations of $20, $50, $100, $500, and $1,000. AAA members can obtain Visa checks for a $9.95 fee (for checks up to $1,500) at most AAA offices or by calling © 866/339-3378.

MasterCard (© 800/223-9920) also offers traveler's checks.

If you choose to carry traveler's checks, be sure to keep a record of their serial numbers separate from your checks in the event that they are stolen or lost. You'll get a refund faster if you know the numbers.

CREDIT CARDS

Credit cards generally offer relatively good exchange rates, are a safe way to carry money, and provide a convenient record of all your expenses. You can also withdraw cash advances from credit cards at banks or ATMs, provided you know your PIN. If you've forgotten yours, or didn't even know you had one, call the number on the back of your credit card and ask the bank to send it to you. It usually takes 5 to 7 business days, though some banks will provide the number over the phone if you tell them your mother's maiden name or some other personal information. Keep in mind that when you use your credit card abroad, most banks assess a 2% fee above the 1% fee charged by Visa or MasterCard or American Express for currency conversion on credit charges. But credit cards still may be the smart way to go when you factor in things like exorbitant ATM fees and higher traveler's check exchange rates (and service fees).

MONEYGRAMS

Sponsored by American Express, **Moneygram** (© 800/926-9400; www.moneygram.com) is the fastest-growing money-wiring service in the world. Funds can be transferred from one individual to another in less than 10 minutes between thousands of locations throughout the world. You don't even always have to go to an American Express office; some locations

---

Tips **Dear Visa: I'm Off to Marsh Harbour!**

Some credit card companies recommend that you notify them of any impending trip abroad so they don't become suspicious when the card is used in a foreign destination and your charges are blocked. If you don't call in advance, you can always call the card's toll-free emergency number (see "Fast Facts," later in this chapter) if a charge is refused—a good reason to carry the phone number with you. But the most important lesson: Carry more than one card with you on your trip; a card might not work for any number of reasons, so having a backup is smart.

are pharmacies and convenience stores in smaller communities. Acceptable forms of payment include cash, Visa, MasterCard, or Discover, and occasionally, a personal check. Service charges collected by American Express are $40 for the first $500 sent, with a sliding scale of commissions for larger sums. Included in the transfer is a 10-word telex-style message. The deal also includes a free 3-minute phone call to the recipient. Funds are transferred within 10 minutes, and can then be retrieved by the beneficiary at the most convenient location with a proper photo ID.

5 When to Go

THE WEATHER

The temperature in The Bahamas averages between 75°F and 85°F (24°C–29°C) in both winter and summer, although it can get chilly in the early morning and at night. The Bahamian winter is usually like a perpetual late spring—naturally the high season for North Americans rushing to escape snow and ice. Summer brings broiling hot sun and humidity. There's a much greater chance of rain during the summer and fall.

THE HURRICANE SEASON

The curse of Bahamian weather, the hurricane season, lasts (officially) from June 1 to November 30. But there is no cause for panic. More tropical cyclones pound the U.S. mainland than The Bahamas. Hurricanes are actually fairly infrequent here, and when one does come, satellite forecasts generally give adequate advance warning so that precautions can be taken.

If you're heading for The Bahamas during the hurricane season, you might want to visit the National Weather Service at www.nws.noaa.gov.

For an online 5-day forecast anytime, check the Weather Channel at www.weather.com (for free!) or call ℂ **900/WEATHER** (95¢ per min.).

Average Temperatures & Rainfall (in.) in The Bahamas

Note that these numbers are daily averages, so expect temperatures to climb significantly higher in the noonday sun and to cool off a good deal in the evening.

Month	Jan	Feb	Mar	Apr	May	June	July	Aug	Sept	Oct	Nov	Dec
Temp. °F	70	70	72	75	77	80	81	82	81	78	74	71
Temp. °C	21	21	22	24	25	27	27	28	27	26	23	22
Rainfall (in.)	1.9	1.6	1.4	1.9	4.8	9.2	6.1	6.3	7.5	8.3	2.3	1.5

THE "SEASON"

In The Bahamas, hotels charge their highest prices during the peak winter period from mid-December to mid-April, when visitors fleeing from cold north winds flock to the islands. Winter is the driest season.

If you plan to visit during the winter, try to make reservations at least 2 to 3 months in advance. And bear in mind that, at some hotels, it's impossible to book accommodations for Christmas and the month of February without even more lead time.

SAVING MONEY IN THE OFF SEASON

The Bahamas is a year-round destination. The islands' "off season" runs from late spring to late fall, when tolerable temperatures (see "The Weather," above) prevail throughout most of the region. Trade winds ensure comfortable days and nights, even in accommodations without air-conditioning. Although the noonday sun may raise temperatures to uncomfortable levels, cool breezes usually make the morning, late afternoon, and evening more pleasant here than in many parts of the U.S. mainland.

Dollar for dollar, you'll spend less money by renting a summer house or fully equipped unit in The Bahamas than you would on Cape Cod, Fire Island, Laguna Beach, or the coast of Maine.

The off season—roughly from mid-April to mid-December (rate schedules vary from hotel to hotel)—amounts to a summer sale. In most cases, hotel rates are slashed from 20% to a startling 60%. It's a bonanza for cost-conscious travelers, especially families who like to go on vacations together. In the chapters ahead, we'll spell out in dollars the specific amounts hotels charge during the off season.

OTHER OFF-SEASON ADVANTAGES

Although The Bahamas may appear inviting in the winter to those who live in northern climates, your trip may be more enjoyable if you go in the off season. Here's why:

- After the winter hordes have left, a less-hurried way of life prevails.
- Swimming pools and beaches are less crowded—perhaps not crowded at all.
- To survive, resort boutiques often feature summer sales.
- You can often appear without a reservation at a top restaurant and get a table for dinner.
- The endless waiting game is over: no waiting for a rented car, no long wait for a golf course tee time, and quicker access to tennis courts and watersports.

- The atmosphere is more cosmopolitan than it is in winter, mainly because of the influx of Europeans.
- Some package-tour fares are as much as 20% lower, and individual excursion fares may be reduced from 5% to 10%.
- Accommodations and flights are much easier to book.
- Summer is an excellent time for family travel, which is not always possible during the hectic winter season.
- Finally, the best Bahamian attractions—sea, sand, surf, and lots of sunshine—remain absolutely undiminished.

OFF-SEASON DISADVANTAGES

Let's not paint too rosy a picture. Although the advantages of off-season travel far outweigh the disadvantages, there are nevertheless some drawbacks to traveling here in summer:

- You might be staying at a construction site. Hoteliers save their serious repairs and their major renovations until the off season. You may wake up to the sound of hammers.
- Single tourists find the dating scene better in winter when there are more visitors, especially unattached ones.
- Services are often reduced. In the peak of winter, everything is fully operational. But in summer, many programs (such as watersports) might be curtailed in spite of fine weather.

Avoiding Spring Break

Throughout March and into mid-April, it's spring break season in the Caribbean for vacationing college and high school students. Expect beach parties, sports events, and musical entertainment; if the idea of hundreds of partying fraternity kids doesn't appeal to you, beware. When you make your reservations, ask if your hotel is planning to host any big groups of kids.

THE BAHAMAS CALENDAR OF EVENTS

For specific events, you can call your nearest branch of **The Bahamas Tourist Office** (see "Visitor Information," earlier in this chapter) at (℃ **800/BAHAMAS** or check their website at **www.bahamas.com**.

January

Junkanoo. This Mardi Gras–style festival begins 2 or 3 hours before dawn on New Year's Day. Throngs of cavorting, costumed figures prance through Nassau, Freeport/Lucaya, and the Out Islands. Jubilant men, women, and children wear elaborate headdresses and festive apparel as they celebrate their African heritage with music and dance. Mini-Junkanoos, in which visitors can participate, are regular events. Local tourist offices will advise the best locations to see the festivities. You can also call (℃ **242/324-1714** or visit www.junkanoo.com. January 1.

New Year's Day Sailing Regatta, Nassau and Paradise Island. Three dozen or more sailing sloops, ranging from 5 to 8.5m (16–28 ft.), converge off Montagu Bay in a battle for bragging rights organized by The Bahamas Boat Owners Association. For information, contact the **Regatta Desk at the Ministry of Youth, Sports & Culture** ((℃ **242/325-9370**). Early January.

Annual Bahamas Wahoo Championships, Berry Islands. Anglers from all over America take up the tough challenge to bait one of the fastest fish in the ocean, reaching speeds up to 70 mph. This fete takes place at Chub Cay Marina & Resort ((℃ **800/ 662-8555** or 242/367-2158; www. bahamaswahoo.com). Mid-January.

February

The Mid-Winter Wahoo, Bimini. The Bimini Big Game Resort & Marina draws Hemingway look-alikes and other anglers to this winter event that

is heavily attended by Floridians. For more information, call (℃ **800/737-1007** or contact the tournament director, Leonard Stuart, at the Bimini Tourist Office at (℃ **242/347-3539.** Early February.

Farmer's Cay Festival. This festival is a rendezvous for yachtsmen cruising the Exuma Islands and a homecoming for the people of Farmer's Cay, Exuma. Boat excursions will depart Nassau at Potter's Cay for the festival at 8pm on Friday, then return to Nassau at 8pm on Saturday from the Farmer's Cay Dock. For information contact Terry Bain in Little Farmer's Cay, Exuma, at (℃ **242/ 355-4006,** or the Exuma Tourist Office at (℃ **242/336-2430.** First Friday and Saturday in February.

March

Bacardi Billfish Tournament, Freeport. A prestigious weeklong tournament attracting the who's who of deep-sea fishing. Headquarters is the Port Lucaya Resort & Yacht Club. For more information, call (℃ **800/582-2921** or 242/373-9090. Mid-March.

April

Bahamas Family Island Regatta, George Town, the Exumas. Featuring Bahamian craft sloops, these celebrated boat races are held in Elizabeth Harbour. There's also a variety of onshore activities including basketball, a skipper's party, and a Junkanoo parade. Call (℃ **242/ 336-2430** or check www.georgetown cruisingregatta.org for exact dates and information. Usually third week of April.

Bahamas Billfish Championship. This annual event is divided into four competitions, taking place at four different venues and times, spanning April to June. Anglers can fish any and all of the tournaments taking place at Marsh Harbour (third week of Apr), Harbour Island (first week of May), Spanish Cay (mid-May), and Treasure

Cay (first week to second week of June). Since dates vary, contact the **Bahamas Billfish Championship** at Two Oakland Blvd., Suite 195, Hollywood, FL 33020 (℃ **888/303-2242** or 954/920-5577; www.bahamasbillfish.com). April to June.

Bahamas White Marlin Open, the Abacos. This is a rendezvous off Abaco drawing anglers seeking an action-packed billfish tournament. The headquarters is the Abaco Beach Resort & Marina. For more information, call ℃ **954/920-5577** or 242/367-2158. Dates vary.

May

Long Island Regatta, Salt Pond, Long Island. This even sees some 40 to 50 sailing sloops from throughout The Bahamas compete in three classes for trophies and cash prizes. Onshore, dancing to indigenous "rake 'n' scrape" music, sporting events, and local food specialties for sale make for a carnival-like atmosphere. For more information, call ℃ **242/394-1535.** Late May.

June

Eleuthera Pineapple Festival, Gregory Town, Eleuthera. This celebration devoted to the island's succulent pineapple features a Junkanoo parade, craft displays, dancing, a pineapple recipe contest, tours of pineapple farms, and a "pineathalon"—a .5km (¼-mile) swim, 5.5km (3½-mile) run, and 6.5km (4-mile) bike ride. For more information, call ℃ **242/332-2142.** First week of June.

July

Annual Racing Time in Abaco, Marsh Harbour. This weeklong regatta features a series of five sailboat races in the Sea of Abaco. Onshore festivities include nightly entertainment, cocktail parties, beach picnics, cultural activities, and a grand finale party. For registration forms and information, contact Abaco Tourist office at ℃ **242/367-3067.** Early July.

Independence Week. Independence celebrations are marked throughout the islands by festivities, parades, and fireworks. It all culminates on Independence Day. July 10.

Bahamas Summer Boating Fling/Flotilla. Boating enthusiasts and yachters make the 5-day crossing from Florida to The Bahamas (Port Lucaya's marina on Grand Bahama Island) in a flotilla of boats guided by a lead boat. All "flings" depart from the Radisson Bahia Mar Resort & Yacht Center in Fort Lauderdale. For more information, contact the **Bahamas Tourism Center** in Florida at ℃ **954/236-9292.** End of July to beginning of August.

August

Emancipation Day. The first Monday in August commemorates the emancipation of slaves in 1834. A highlight of this holiday is an early-morning "Junkanoo Rushout" starting at 4am in Fox Hill Village in Nassau, followed by an afternoon of "cook-outs," cultural events such as climbing a greased pole and the plaiting of the Maypole. First Monday in August.

Cat Island Regatta, Southern Bahamas. Sleepy Cat Island comes alive in the weekend of festive events, including sloop races, live "rake 'n' scrape" bands, quadrille dancing, old-fashioned contests and games, and local cuisine. Contact the **Regatta Desk** at ℃ **242/502-0600** in Nassau. Early August.

September

All Abaco Sailing Regatta. Local sailing sloops rendezvous at Treasure Cay Harbour for a series of championship races and onshore festivities. Contact the **Regatta Desk** in Nassau at ℃ **242/502-0600** or in Abaco at ℃ **242/367-3067.** Late September.

October

Discovery Day. The New World landing of Christopher Columbus, traditionally said to be the island of San Salvador, is celebrated throughout The Bahamas. Naturally, San Salvador has a parade every year on October 12.

North Eleuthera Sailing Regatta. Native sailing sloops take to the waters of North Eleuthera, Harbour Island, and Spanish Wells in a weekend of championship races. For information contact the **Eleuthera Tourist Office** at ℂ **242/332-2142.** Mid-October.

Great Bahamas Seafood and Heritage Festival, Heritage Village, Arawak Cay. This October festival is a combination of the Great Seafood Festival and Heritage festival. A cultural affair, it showcases authentic Bahamian cuisine, traditional music, and storytelling. For more information, exact time, and schedule of events, contact the **Ministry of Tourism** at ℂ **242/302-2072.**

November

Guy Fawkes Day. The best celebrations are in Nassau. Nighttime parades through the streets are held on many of the islands, culminating in the hanging and burning of Guy Fawkes, an effigy of the British malefactor who was involved in the Gunpowder Plot of 1605 in London. It usually takes place around November 5, but check with island tourist offices.

Bimini Big Game Fishing Club All Wahoo Tournament. Anglers take up the tough challenge of baiting one of the fastest fishes in the ocean. Headquarters is the Bimini Sands Resort & Marina. For information, contact ℂ **242/373-3500** or 242/347-3407; www.bahamas wahoo.com. Mid-November.

Annual One Bahamas Music & Heritage Festival. This 3-day celebration is staged at both Nassau and Paradise Island to celebrate national unity. Highlights include concerts featuring top Bahamian performing artists. Events include "fun walks" on the island and other activities. For more information, contact the **Nassau/Paradise Island Office** at the Ministry of Tourism, ℂ **242/356-5216,** ext. 4100. Last week of November.

December

Junkanoo Boxing Day. High-energy Junkanoo parades and celebrations are held throughout the islands on December 26. Many of these activities are repeated on New Year's Day (see "January," above). December 26.

6 The Active Vacation Planner

The more than 700 islands in the Bahamian archipelago (fewer than 30 of which are inhabited) are surrounded by warm, clear waters—ideal for fishing, sailing, and scuba diving. (Detailed recommendations and the costs of these activities are previewed under the individual destinations listings.) The country's perfect weather and its many cooperative local entrepreneurs allow easy access to more than 30 sports throughout the islands. For sports-related information about any of the activities listed below, call ℂ **800/32-SPORT.**

WATERSPORTS

FISHING   The shallow waters between the hundreds of cays and islands of The Bahamas are some of the most fertile fishing grounds in the world. Even waters where marine traffic is relatively congested have yielded impressive catches in the past, although overfishing has depleted schools of fish, especially big-game fish. Grouper, billfish, wahoo, tuna, and dozens of other species thrive in Bahamian waters, and dozens of charter boats are available for deep-sea fishing. Reef fishing, either from small boats or from shorelines, is popular everywhere, with grouper, snapper, and barracuda being the most commonly caught species. Specialists, however, or serious amateurs of the sport, often head for any of the following destinations.

The island of **Bimini** is known as the "Big-Game Fishing Capital of the World." Here anglers can hunt for the increasingly elusive swordfish, sailfish, and marlin. For tournament listings, see the "Calendar of Events," earlier in this chapter. Bimini maintains its own Hall of Fame, where many a proud angler has had his or her catch honored. World records for the size of catches don't seem to last long here; they are usually quickly surpassed.

Walker's Cay in the Abacos and **Chub Cay** in the Berry Islands are famous for both deep-sea and shore fishing. Some anglers return to these cays year after year. Grouper, jacks, and snapper are plentiful. Even spearfishing without scuba gear is common and popular.

Andros boasts the world's best bone-fishing. Bonefish (also known as "gray fox") are medium-size fish that feed in shallow, well-lit waters. Known as some of the most tenacious fish in the world, they struggle ferociously against anglers who pride themselves on using light lines from shallow-draft boats. **Andros Island Bone-fishing Club** in North Andros (© 242/368-5167; www.androsbonefishing.com) specializes in fishing adventures off some of the most remote and sparsely populated coastlines in the country.

SAILING   The Bahamas is one of the top yachting destinations in the Atlantic. Its more than 700 islands and well-developed marinas provide a spectacular and practical backdrop for sailing enthusiasts. For a listing of frequent regattas, see the "Calendar of Events," earlier in this chapter. The mini-archipelago of the **Abacos** is called "The Sailing Capital of the World." You might think it deserves the title until you've sailed the **Exumas,** which we think are even better.

Don't be dismayed if you don't own a yacht. All sizes and types of crafts, from dinghies to blue-water cruisers, are available for charter, and crew and captain are optional. If your dreams involve experiencing the seagoing life for an afternoon or less, many hotels offer sightseeing cruises aboard catamarans or glass-bottomed boats, often with the opportunity to snorkel or swim in the wide-open sea.

The Abacos have many marinas. The best arrangements for boating can be made at **Abaco Bahamas Charters** (© **800/626-5690** or 242/366-0151; www.abacocharters.com) and at the **Moorings** (© **800/535-7289** or 242/367-4000; www.moorings.com). In the Exumas it's difficult to rent boats, because most yachters arrive with their own. However, take a chance and contact **Happy People Marina** (© **242/355-2008**) on Staniel Cay.

SCUBA DIVING   The unusual marine topography of The Bahamas offers an astonishing variety of options for divers. Throughout the more than 700 islands are innumerable reefs, drop-offs, coral gardens, caves, and shipwrecks. In many locations, you may feel that you are the first human ever to explore the site. Since fewer than 30 of the Bahamian islands are

---

Tips **A Warning to Poachers**

It is illegal to take sponges or turtles from Bahamian waters. The Ministry of Agriculture, Fisheries, and Local Government also keeps a close eye on crayfish (spiny lobster) and prohibits the export of conch meat. Stone crab cannot be caught within 3km (2 miles) off Bimini or Grand Bahama.

inhabited, you can usually dive in pristine and uncrowded splendor.

Andros Island boasts the third-largest barrier reef in the world. Chub Cay in the Berry Islands, and Riding Rock, San Salvador, also offer premium spots to take a plunge in an underwater world teeming with aquatic life. The intricate layout of the Exumas includes virtually every type of underwater dive site, very few of which have ever been explored. The Abacos, famous for its yachting, and the extensive reefs off the coast of Freeport are also fabulous dive sites.

Freeport, incidentally, is home to the country's most famous and complete diving operation, **UNEXSO** (© **800/992-DIVE** or 242/373-1244; www.unexso.com). It offers a 5.2m-deep (17-ft.) swimming pool where divers can work toward certification, and the popular "Dolphin Experience," in which visitors are allowed to pet, swim, snorkel, and dive with these remarkable animals.

You can easily learn to dive for the first time in The Bahamas. Lots of Bahamian hotels offer resort courses for novices, usually enabling a beginner to dive with a guide after several hours of instruction. You'll probably start out in the swimming pool for your initial instruction, and then go out with a guide from the beach. A license proving the successful completion of a designated program of scuba study is legally required for solo divers. Many resort hotels and dive shops offer the necessary training as part of a 5-day training course. Participants who successfully complete the courses are awarded PADI- or NAUI-approved licenses.

For useful information, check out the website of the Professional Association of Diving Instructors (PADI) at www.padi.com. You'll find a description of the best dive sites and a list of PADI-certified dive operators. *Rodale's Scuba Diving Magazine* also has a helpful website at www.scubadiving.com. Both sites list dive-package specials and display gorgeous color photos of some of the most beautiful dive spots in the world.

SEA KAYAKING If you want to explore the pristine Exumas National Land and Sea Park, a spectacular natural area consisting of 365 mostly uninhabited cays that may be more impressive than anything in the Caribbean, **Ecosummer Expeditions** is your best bet. They'll take you on sea-kayaking itineraries that will allow you lots of time to enjoy the area's white-sand beaches and numerous reefs. You can also snorkel along the way. A 9-day trip leaving from Nassau costs $1,695. For more information, contact Ecosummer at P.O. Box 1765, Clearwater, BC, Canada V0E 1NO (© **800/465-8884** or 250/674-0102; www.ecosummer.com).

Another sea-kayaking outfit is **Ibis Tours** (© **800/525-9411** or 914/649-7526; www.ibistours.com).

OTHER ACTIVITIES

BIKE & SCOOTER RENTALS Most biking or scooter riding is done either on New Providence Island (Nassau) or on Grand Bahama Island; both have relatively flat terrain. Biking is best on Grand Bahama Island because it's bigger, with better roads and more places to go. Getting around New Providence Island is relatively easy once you're out of the congestion of Nassau and Cable Beach. In Nassau many hotels will rent you a bike or motor scooter.

On Grand Bahama Island, you can rent bikes at most big hotels (see chapter 5 for phone numbers and addresses of hotels). You can also rent motor scooters starting at about $35 per day. The tourist office at Freeport/Lucaya will outline on a map the best biking routes.

In the Out Islands, roads are usually too bumpy and potholed for much serious biking or scooter riding. Bike-rental places are almost nonexistent unless your hotel has some vehicles.

GOLF The richest pickings are on Grand Bahama Island, home to three courses that have been designated as potential PGA tour stops. The **Crowne Plaza Golf Resort & Casino** boasts two challenging and spectacular courses: the Ruby Golf Course and the Emerald Golf Course, site of The Bahamas National Open. The big news is the opening of the **Reef Course,** the first new golf course to open in The Bahamas since 1969. Designed by Robert Trent Jones, Jr., it features water along 13 of its 18 holes. The oldest course on Grand Bahama Island is the **Lucayan Park Golf & Country Club,** a heavily wooded course with elevated greens and numerous water hazards designed for precision golf. See chapter 5 for more information, and also refer to "The Best Golf Courses," in chapter 1.

Quality golf in The Bahamas, however, is not restricted to Grand Bahama Island. The **Cable Beach Golf Course,** part of the Radisson Cable Beach Hotel on New Providence, is the oldest golf course in the country, although not as good as the **South Ocean Golf Resort** in the secluded southern part of New Providence. The widely publicized **Ocean Club Golf Club** has unusual obstacles— a lion's den and a windmill—which have challenged the skill of both Gary Player and Jack Nicklaus. It also boasts the world's largest sand trap. After restoration, the course opened in 2000. See chapters 3 and 4 for more information, and also refer to "The Best Golf Courses," in chapter 1.

A spectacular Greg Norman-designed course opened in Great Exuma in 2003, part of the massive new **Four Seasons** resort. See chapter 9.

Golf is also available at a course in the Abacos at the **Treasure Cay Golf Club.** The design is challenging, with many panoramic water views and water obstacles. See chapter 7 for more information.

HIKING The Bahamas isn't the greatest destination for serious hikers. The best hiking is on Grand Bahama Island, especially in **Lucayan National Park,** which spreads across 16 hectares (40 acres) and is some 32km (20 miles) from Lucaya. A large map at the entrance to the park outlines the trails. The park is riddled with trails and elevated walkways. The highlight of the park is what may be the largest underground cave system in the world, some 11km (7 miles) long. Spiral steps let you descend into an eerie underground world.

Also on Grand Bahama Island, the **Rand Memorial Nature Centre** is the second-best place for hiking. It offers some 40 wooded hectares (99 acres) that you can explore on your own or with a tour guide. A .75km (½ mile) of winding trails acquaints you with the flora and fauna that call Grand Bahama home, everything from a native boa constrictor to the Cuban emerald hummingbird, whose favorite food is the nectar of the hibiscus.

HORSEBACK RIDING The best riding possibilities are at **Pinetree Stables** on Grand Bahama Island (© 242/373-3600 or 305/433-4809; www.pinetree-stables.com). Its escorted eco-tour trail rides are especially interesting. Rides are offered two times a day, Tuesday through Sunday; be sure to book rides a few days in advance. See chapter 5 for more information.

Virtually the only place on New Providence Island (Nassau) that offers horseback riding is **Happy Trails Stables,** Coral Harbour (© 242/362-1820; www.wind sorequestriancentre.com), which features both morning and afternoon trail rides and requires a reservation. These tours include transportation to and from your hotel. The trail rides are guided through the woods and along the beach. See chapter 3 for more information.

Horseback riding is hardly a passion on the other islands.

TENNIS   Most tennis courts are part of large resorts and are usually free for the use of registered guests during the day. Charges are imposed to light the courts at night. Nonguests are welcome but are charged a player's fee; they should call in advance to reserve. Larger resorts usually offer on-site pro shops and professional instructors. Court surfaces range from clay or asphalt to such technologically advanced substances as Flexipave and Har-Tru.

New Providence, with more than 80 tennis courts, wins points for offering the greatest number of choices. At least 21 of these lie on Paradise Island. Also noteworthy are the many well-lit courts at the Radisson Cable Beach Hotel. See chapters 3 and 4. After New Providence, Grand Bahama has the largest number of courts available for play—almost 40 in all. See chapter 5. Within the Out Islands, tennis courts are available on Eleuthera, the Abacos, the Berry Islands, and the Exumas. See chapters 6, 7, 8, and 9 for more information.

7 Travel Insurance

TRAVEL INSURANCE AT A GLANCE

Buying insurance might make sense because The Bahamas is not necessarily a "safe" destination. Although crimes against individual tourists are rare, your property, if left unprotected, could be stolen. Tour operators, airlines, and cruise ships can all go out of business suddenly, making default insurance a wise move on some Bahamian trips. Trip delay insurance might cover expenses that rise suddenly, as in the event of a hurricane.

Check your existing insurance policies and credit card coverage before you buy travel insurance. You may already be covered for lost luggage, canceled tickets, or medical expenses. The cost of travel insurance varies widely, depending on the cost and length of your trip, your age, health, and the type of trip you're taking, but expect to pay between 5% and 8% of the vacation itself.

TRIP-CANCELLATION INSURANCE

Trip-cancellation insurance helps you get your money back if you have to back out of a trip, if you have to go home early, or if your travel supplier goes bankrupt. Allowable reasons for cancellation can range from sickness to natural disasters to

the State Department declaring your destination unsafe for travel. (Insurers usually won't cover vague fears, though, as many travelers discovered in Oct 2001 after canceling trips because they were wary of flying.) In this unstable world, trip-cancellation insurance is a good buy if you're getting tickets well in advance—who knows what the state of the world, or of your airline, will be in 9 months? Insurance policy details vary, so read the fine print—and especially make sure that your airline or cruise line is on the list of carriers covered in case of bankruptcy. A good resource is **"Travel Guard Alerts,"** a list of companies considered high-risk by Travel Guard International (see website below). Protect yourself further by paying for the insurance with a credit card—by law, consumers can get their money back on goods and services not received if they report the loss within 60 days after the charge is listed on their credit card statement.

Note: Many tour operators include insurance in the cost of the trip or can arrange insurance policies through a partnering provider, a convenient and often cost-effective way for the traveler to obtain insurance. Make sure the tour company is a reputable one, however: Some experts suggest you avoid buying insurance from the tour or cruise company you're traveling with, saying it's better to buy from a "third-party" insurer than to put all your money in one place.

For more information, contact one of the following recommended insurers: **Access America** (© 866/807-3982; www.accessamerica.com); **Travel Guard International** (© 800/826-4919; www.travelguard.com); **Travel Insured International** (© 800/243-3174; www.travelinsured.com); and **Travelex Insurance Services** (© 888/457-4602; www.travelex-insurance.com).

MEDICAL INSURANCE Most health insurance policies cover you if you get sick away from home—but check, particularly if you're insured by an HMO. With the exception of certain HMOs and Medicare/Medicaid, your medical insurance should cover medical treatment— even hospital care—overseas. However, most out-of-country hospitals insist you pay your bills upfront, and then send you a refund after you've returned home and filed the necessary paperwork. In a worst-case scenario, that could include the high cost of an emergency evacuation. If you require additional medical insurance, try **MEDEX Assistance** (© 410/453-6300; www.medexassist.com) or **Travel Assistance International** (© 800/821-2828; www.travelassistance.com); for general information on services, call the company's Worldwide Assistance Services, Inc. at © **800/777-8710;** www.worldwideassistance.com).

LOST-LUGGAGE INSURANCE On domestic flights, checked baggage is covered up to $2,500 per ticketed passenger. On international flights (including U.S. portions of international trips), baggage coverage is limited to approximately $9.07 per pound, up to approximately $635 per checked bag. If you plan to check items more valuable than the standard liability, see if your valuables are covered by your homeowner's policy, get baggage insurance as part of your comprehensive travel-insurance package, or buy Travel Guard's "Bag Trak" product. Don't buy insurance at the airport, as it's usually overpriced. Be sure to take any valuables or irreplaceable items with you in your carry-on luggage, as many valuables (including books, money, and electronics) aren't covered by airline policies. If your luggage is lost, immediately file a lost-luggage claim at the airport, detailing the luggage contents. For most airlines, you must report delayed, damaged, or lost baggage within 4 hours of arrival. The airlines are required to deliver luggage, once found, directly to your house or destination free of charge.

8 Health & Safety

STAYING HEALTHY

Even on the remotest island, you'll find, if not a hospital, a local medicine man (or woman, in many cases). Many Bahamians are fond of herbal remedies. But you don't need to rely on these primitive treatments, as most resorts have either hospitals or clinics on-site.

The major health risk here is not tropical disease, as it is in some Caribbean islands, but rather the bad luck of ingesting a bad piece of shellfish, exotic fruit, or too many rum punches. If your body is not accustomed to some of these foods, or they haven't been cleaned properly, you may suffer diarrhea. If you tend to have digestive problems, then drink bottled water and avoid ice, unpasteurized milk, and uncooked food such as fresh salads. However, fresh food served in hotels is usually quite safe to eat.

The Bahamas has excellent medical facilities. Physicians and surgeons in private practice are readily available in Nassau, Cable Beach, and Freeport/Lucaya. A dozen or so health centers are in the Out Islands. Medical personnel hold satellite clinics periodically in small settlements, and there are about 35 other clinics, adding up to a total of approximately 50 health facilities throughout the outlying islands. (We've listed the names and telephone numbers of specific clinics in the individual island coverage that follows throughout this book.) If intensive or urgent care is required, patients are brought by the Emergency Flight Service to **Princess Margaret Hospital** (© 242/322-2861) in Nassau. Some of the big resort hotels have in-house physicians or can quickly secure one for you.

There is also a government-operated hospital, **Rand Memorial** (© 242/352-6735), in Freeport, and several government-operated clinics on Grand Bahama Island. Nassau and Freeport/Lucaya also have private hospitals.

Dentists are plentiful in Nassau, somewhat less so on Grand Bahama. You'll find dentists on Great Abaco Island, at Marsh Harbour, at Treasure Cay, and on Eleuthera. There aren't dentists on some of the remote islands, especially those in the Southern Bahamas, but hotel staff should know where to send you for dental emergencies.

Even if your interior plumbing is working fine, you face a danger of overexposure to the sun, which can be a real issue in The Bahamas. You must, of course, take the usual precautions you would anywhere against sunburn and sunstroke. Your time in the sun should be wisely limited for the first few days until you become accustomed to the more intense rays of the Bahamian sun. Also bring and use strong UVA/UVB sunblock products.

WHAT TO DO IF YOU GET SICK AWAY FROM HOME

In most cases, your existing health plan will provide the coverage you need. But double-check; you may want to buy **travel medical insurance** instead (see the section on insurance above). Bring your insurance ID card with you wherever you travel.

If you suffer from a chronic illness, consult your doctor before your departure. For conditions like epilepsy, diabetes, or heart problems, wear a **MedicAlert Identification Tag** (© 888/633-4298; www.medicalert.org), which will immediately alert doctors to your condition and give them access to your records through MedicAlert's 24-hour hot line.

Pack **prescription medications** in your carry-on luggage, and carry prescription medications in their original containers, with pharmacy labels—otherwise they won't make it through airport security. Also bring along copies of your prescriptions in case you lose your pills or run out. Don't forget an extra pair of contact lenses or prescription glasses. Carry the generic name of prescription medicines, in case a local pharmacist is unfamiliar with the brand name.

Contact the **International Association for Medical Assistance to Travelers** (IAMAT; © 716/754-4883, or in Canada 416/652-0137; www.iamat.org) for tips on travel and health concerns in The Bahamas. The United States **Centers for Disease Control and Prevention** (© 800/311-3435; www.cdc.gov) provides up-to-date information on necessary vaccines and health hazards. If you get sick, consider asking your hotel concierge to recommend a local doctor—even his or her own. You can also try the emergency room at a local hospital; many have walk-in clinics for emergency cases that are not life threatening. You may not get immediate attention, but you won't pay the high price of an emergency room visit.

STAYING SAFE

Crime is increasing, and visitors should exercise caution and good judgment when visiting The Bahamas. While most criminal incidents take place in a part of Nassau not usually frequented by tourists (the "Over-the-Hill" area south of downtown), crime and violence has moved into more upscale tourist and residential areas.

In the last year the U.S. Embassy has received several reports of sexual assaults, including against teenage girls. Most assaults have been perpetrated against intoxicated young women, some of whom were reportedly drugged. To minimize the potential for sexual assault, the embassy recommends that young women stay in groups, consume alcohol in moderation, and not accept rides or drinks from strangers.

Travelers should avoid walking alone after dark or in isolated areas, and avoid placing themselves in situations where they are alone with strangers. Be cautious on deserted areas of beaches at all hours. Hotel guests should always lock their doors and should never leave valuables unattended, especially on beaches. Visitors should store passport/identity documents, airline tickets, credit cards, and extra cash in hotel safes. Avoid wearing expensive jewelry, particularly Rolex watches, which criminals have specifically targeted. Use only clearly marked taxis and make a note of the license plate number for your records.

The loss or theft of a passport overseas should be reported to the local police and the nearest embassy or consulate. A lost or stolen birth certificate and/or driver's license generally cannot be replaced outside the United States. U.S. citizens may refer to the Department of State's pamphlets, *A Safe Trip Abroad* and *Tips for Travelers to the Caribbean,* for ways to promote a trouble-free journey. The pamphlets are available by mail from the Superintendent of Documents, U.S. Government Printing Office, Washington, DC 20402, via the Internet at www.gpoaccess.gov/index.html, or via the Bureau of Consular Affairs home page at www.travel.state.gov.

9 Specialized Travel Resources

TRAVELERS WITH DISABILITIES

A disability should not stop anyone from traveling to the Bahamian islands. Because these islands are relatively flat, it is fairly easy to get around, even for persons with disabilities.

You can obtain a free copy of *Air Transportation of Handicapped Persons,* published by the U.S. Department of Transportation. Write for Free Advisory Circular No. AC12032, Distribution Unit, U.S. Department of Transportation, Publications Division, 3341Q 75 Ave., Landover, MD 20785 (✆ **301/322-4961;** fax 301/386-5394; http://isddc.dot.gov). Only written requests are accepted.

Many travel agencies offer customized tours and itineraries for travelers with disabilities.

Flying Wheels Travel (✆ **507/451-5005;** fax 507/451-1685; www.flyingwheelstravel.com) offers escorted tours and cruises that emphasize sports and private tours in minivans with lifts. **Access-Able Travel Source** (✆ **303/232-2979;** www.access-able.com) offers extensive access information and advice for traveling around the world with disabilities. **Accessible Journeys** (✆ **800/846-4537** or 610/521-0339; www.disabilitytravel.com) caters specifically to slow walkers and wheelchair travelers, and their families and friends.

Tips Finding an Accessible Hotel

You can call the **Bahamas Association for the Physically Disabled** (© 242/ 322-2393) for information about accessible hotels in The Bahamas. This agency will also send a van to the airport to transport you to your hotel for a fee, and can provide ramps.

Organizations that offer assistance to travelers with disabilities include the **MossRehab Hospital** (www.mossresource net.org), which provides a library of accessible travel resources online. The **SATH (Society for Accessible Travel and Hospitality;** © 212/447-7284; fax 212/725-8253; www.sath.org) offers a wealth of travel resources for all types of disabilities and informed recommendations on destinations, access guides, travel agents, tour operators, vehicle rentals, and companion services. Annual membership costs $45 for adults, $30 for seniors and students. The **American Foundation for the Blind (AFB;** © 800/232-5463; www.afb.org) provides information on traveling with Seeing Eye dogs.

For more information specifically targeted to travelers with disabilities, the community website **iCan** (www.ican online.net/channels/travel/index.cfm) has destination guides and several regular columns on accessible travel. Also check out the quarterly magazine *Emerging Horizons* (www.emerginghorizons.com), which costs $15 annually, $20 outside the U.S; and *Open World Magazine,* published by the Society for Accessible Travel and Hospitality (see above; subscription: $13 annually, $21 outside the U.S.).

TIPS FOR BRITISH TRAVELERS WITH DISABILITIES Contact the Royal Association for Disability and Rehabilitation (RADAR), Unit 12, City Forum, 250 City Rd., London, EC1V 8AF (© 020/7250-3222; fax 020/7250-0212; www.radar.org.uk).

GAY & LESBIAN TRAVEL

Think twice before choosing The Bahamas. Although many gay people visit or live here, the country has very strict antihomosexual laws. Relations between homosexuals, even when between consenting adults, are subject to criminal sanctions carrying prison terms. If you would like to make visiting gay beaches, bars, or clubs part of your vacation, consider South Miami Beach, Key West, or Puerto Rico instead.

Of course, the big resorts welcome one and all, even if forced to do so. For many years, the all-inclusive Sandals Royal Bahamian on Cable Beach refused to accept same-sex couples and booked only heterosexual guests. However, rights groups in Canada and Great Britain lobbied successfully, and the Sandals people found they could no longer advertise their resorts, and their discriminatory policies, in those countries. As a result, Sandals capitulated and ended its previous ban. However, gay and lesbian couples looking for a carefree holiday should seriously consider if they want to spend their hard-earned dollars in a resort like Sandals that did not voluntarily end its ban against homosexuals until forced to do so by more liberal and far-sighted governments.

Generally speaking, The Bahamas isn't a gay-friendly destination. Single gays or gay couples should travel here with great discretion. If you're intent on visiting, check out the **International Gay & Lesbian Travel Association (IGLTA;** © 800/ 448-8550 or 954/776-2626; fax 954/

776-3303; www.iglta.com), which links travelers up with gay-friendly hoteliers, tour operators, and airline and cruise-line representatives. It offers monthly newsletters, marketing mailings, and a membership directory that's updated once a year.

Many agencies offer tours and travel itineraries specifically for gay and lesbian travelers. **Above and Beyond Tours** (© 800/397-2681; www.abovebeyond tours.com) is the exclusive gay and lesbian tour operator for United Airlines. **Now, Voyager** (© 800/255-6951; www.now voyager.com) is a well-known, gay-owned and -operated travel service. **Olivia Cruises & Resorts** (© 800/631-6277 or 415/962-5700; www.olivia.com) charters entire resorts and ships for exclusive lesbian vacations and offers smaller group experiences for both gay and lesbian travelers.

The following travel guides are available at most travel bookstores and gay and lesbian bookstores, or you can order them from the bookstore Giovanni's Room, 1145 Pine St., Philadelphia, PA 19107 (© 215/923-2960; www.giovannisroom. com): *Out and About* (© 800/929-2268; www.outandabout.com), which offers guidebooks and a newsletter ($20 a year for 10 issues) packed with solid information on the global gay and lesbian scene; *Spartacus International Gay Guide* (Bruno Gmünder Verlag; www.spartacus world.com/gayguide) and *Odysseus: The International Gay Travel Planner* (Odysseus Enterprises Ltd.), both good, annual English-language guidebooks focused on gay men; the *Damron* guides (www.damron.com), with separate, annual books for gay men and lesbians; and *Gay Travel A to Z: The World of Gay & Lesbian Travel Options at Your Fingertips* by Marianne Ferrari (Ferrari International; Box 35575, Phoenix, AZ 85069), a very good gay and lesbian guidebook series.

SENIOR TRAVEL

In The Bahamas, the standard adult rate usually applies to all ages more than 21 years of age. The careful, frugal travel shopper, however, might find some deals if arrangements are made before you go.

Members of **AARP** (formerly the American Association of Retired Persons), 601 E St. NW, Washington, DC 20049 (© 888/687-2277 or 202/434-2277; www.aarp.org), get discounts on hotels, airfares, and car rentals. AARP offers members a wide range of benefits, including *AARP The Magazine* and a monthly newsletter. Anyone over the age of 50 can join.

Many reliable agencies and organizations target the 50-plus market. **Elderhostel** (© 877/426-8056; www.elderhostel. org) arranges study programs for those aged 55 and over (and a spouse or companion of any age) in the U.S. and in more than 80 countries around the world. Most courses last 5 to 7 days in the U.S. (2–4 weeks abroad), and many include airfare, accommodations in university dormitories or modest inns, meals, and tuition. **ElderTreks** (© 800/741-7956; www.eldertreks.com) offers small-group tours to off-the-beaten-path or adventure-travel locations, restricted to travelers age 50 and older.

Recommended publications offering travel resources and discounts for seniors include: the quarterly magazine *Travel 50 & Beyond* (www.travel50andbeyond. com); *Travel Unlimited: Uncommon Adventures for the Mature Traveler* (Avalon); *101 Tips for Mature Travelers,* available from Grand Circle Travel (© 800/221-2610 or 617/350-7500; www.gct.com); *The 50+ Traveler's Guidebook* (from St. Martin's Press); and *Unbelievably Good Deals and Great Adventures That You Absolutely Can't Get Unless You're Over 50* (from McGraw Hill), by Joann Rattner Heilman.

FAMILY TRAVEL

The Bahamas is one of the top family-vacation destinations in North America. The smallest toddlers can spend blissful hours on sandy beaches and in the shallow seawater or in swimming pools constructed with them in mind. There's no end to the fascinating pursuits offered for older children, ranging from boat rides to shell collecting to horseback riding, hiking, or even dancing. Some children are old enough to learn to snorkel and to explore an underwater wonderland. Some resorts will even teach kids to swim or windsurf.

Most families with kids head for New Providence (Nassau), Paradise Island, or Grand Bahama Island (Freeport). Look for our "Kids" icon, indicating attractions, restaurants, or hotels and resorts that are especially family friendly. See also "The Best Family Vacations," in chapter 1, for additional recommendations.

Familyhostel (℄ 800/733-9753; www.learn.unh.edu/familyhostel) takes the whole family, including kids ages 8 to 15, on moderately priced domestic and international learning vacations. Lectures, field trips, and sightseeing are guided by a team of academics.

Recommended family travel Internet sites include **Family Travel Forum** (www.familytravelforum.com), a comprehensive site that offers customized trip planning; **Family Travel Network** (www.familytravelnetwork.com), an award-winning site that offers travel features, deals, and tips; **Traveling Internationally with Your Kids** (www.travelwithyourkids.com), a comprehensive site offering sound advice for long-distance and international travel with children; and **Family Travel Files** (www.thefamilytravelfiles.com), which offers an online magazine and a directory of off-the-beaten-path tours and tour operators for families.

AFRICAN-AMERICAN TRAVEL

Agencies and organizations that provide resources for black travelers include: **Rodgers Travel, Inc.** (℄ 800/825-1775 or 215/473-1775; www.rodgerstravel.com), a Philadelphia-based travel agency with an extensive menu of tours in

---

Traveling with Minors

It's always wise to have plenty of documentation when traveling in today's world with children. For details on entry requirements for children traveling abroad, keep up to date by going to the U.S. Department of State website: www.travel.state.gov.

To prevent international child abduction, E.U. governments have initiated procedures at entry and exit points. These often (but not always) include requiring documentary evidence of relationship and permission for the child's travel from the parent or legal guardian not present. Having such documentation on hand, even if not required, facilitates entries and exits. All children must have their own passport. To obtain a passport, the child **must** be present—that is, in person—at the center issuing the passport. Both parents must be present as well. If not, then a notarized statement from the parents is required.

Any questions parents or guardians might have can be answered by calling the **National Passport Information Center** at ℄ 877/487-2778 Monday to Friday 8am to 8pm Eastern Standard Time. For more information—especially regarding residents of countries other than the United States—see the section on passports in "Fast Facts," later in this chapter.

Women Traveling Alone in The Bahamas

Should a woman travel alone to The Bahamas? Opinions and reports vary. A woman traveling alone in such countries as Jamaica face certain dangers, and safety is often an issue. Women traveling alone in The Bahamas rarely encounter aggressive, potentially dangerous behavior from males, and are usually treated with respect. However, some Bahamian men may assume that a woman traveling alone is doing so in order to find a male partner. To avoid such unwanted attention, dress a bit conservatively and don't go wandering the streets of Nassau unescorted at night. It's always advisable to wear a cover-up to your swimsuit when leaving the beach and heading into town.

Women Welcome Women World Wide (5W; ✆ 01494/465441; www. womenwelcomewomen.org.uk) works to foster international friendships by enabling women of different countries to visit one another (men can come along on the trips; they just can't join the club). It's a big, active organization, with more than 3,500 members from all walks of life in some 70 countries. Check out the award-winning website **Journeywoman** (www.journeywoman. com), a "real-life" women's travel information network where you can sign up for a free e-mail newsletter and get advice on everything from etiquette and dress to safety.

Also check out the travel guide *Safety and Security for Women Who Travel,* by Sheila Swan Laufer and Peter Laufer (Travelers' Tales, Inc.), offering advice and tips on safe travel.

destinations worldwide, including heritage and private group tours; and the **African-American Association of Innkeepers International** (✆ 877/422-5777; www. africanamericaninns.com), which provides information on member B&Bs in the U.S., Canada, and the Caribbean.

The Internet offers a number of helpful travel sites for the black traveler. **Black Travel Online** (www.blacktravelonline. com) posts news on upcoming events and includes links to articles and travel-booking sites. **Soul of America** (www.soulof america.com) is a more comprehensive website, with travel tips, event and family reunion postings, and sections on historically black beach resorts and active vacations.

10 Planning Your Trip Online

SURFING FOR AIRFARES

The "big three" online travel agencies, **Expedia.com, Travelocity,** and **Orbitz,** sell most of the air tickets bought on the Internet. (Canadian travelers should try expedia.ca and Travelocity.ca; U.K. residents can go for expedia.co.uk and opodo. co.uk.) Each has different business deals with the airlines and may offer different fares on the same flights, so it's wise to shop around. Expedia and Travelocity will also send you **e-mail notification** when a cheap fare becomes available to your favorite destination. Of the smaller travel agency websites, **SideStep** (www. sidestep.com) has gotten the best reviews from Frommer's authors. It's a browser add-on that purports to "search 140 sites at once," though in reality only beats competitors' fares as often as other sites do.

Also remember to check **airline websites,** especially those of low-fare carriers, whose fares are often misreported or simply missing from travel agency websites. Even with major airlines, you can often shave a few bucks from a fare by booking directly through the airline and avoiding a travel agency's transaction fee. But you'll get most of these discounts only by booking online; even their phone agents know nothing about the cheapest fares. For the websites of airlines that fly to and from your destination, go to "Getting There: Flying to The Bahamas," below.

Great **last-minute deals** are available through free weekly e-mail services provided directly by the airlines. Most of these are announced on Tuesday or Wednesday and must be purchased online. Most are only valid for travel that weekend, but some can be booked weeks or months in advance. Sign up for weekly e-mail alerts at airline websites or check megasites that compile comprehensive lists of last-minute specials, such as **SmarterTravel.com**. For last-minute trips, **site59.com** in the U.S. and **lastminutetravel.com** in the U.S. and **lastminute.com** in Europe often have better air and hotel package deals than the major label sites. A website listing numerous bargain sites and airlines around the world is **www.itravelnet. com**.

If you're willing to give up some control over your flight details, use what is called an "**opaque**" **fare service** like **Priceline** (www.priceline.com; www.priceline.co.uk for Europeans) or its smaller competitor **Hotwire** (www.hotwire.com). Both offer rock-bottom prices in exchange for travel on a "mystery airline" at a mysterious time of day, often with a mysterious change of planes en route. The mystery airlines are all major, well-known carriers—and the possibility of being sent from Philadelphia to Chicago via Tampa is remote; the airlines' routing computers have gotten a lot better than they used to be. But your chances of getting a 6am or 11pm flight are pretty high. Hotwire tells you flight prices before you buy; Priceline usually has better deals than Hotwire, but you have to play their "name our price" game. If you're new at this, the helpful folks at **BiddingForTravel** (www.biddingfortravel. com) do a good job of demystifying Priceline's prices and strategies. Priceline and Hotwire are great for flights within North America and between the U.S. and Europe. But for flights to other parts of the world, consolidators will almost always beat their fares. *Note:* In 2004 Priceline added nonopaque service to its roster. You now have the option to pick exact flights, times, and airlines from a list of offers—or opt to bid on opaque fares as before.

For much more about airfares and savvy air-travel tips and advice, pick up a copy of *Frommer's Fly Safe, Fly Smart* (Wiley Publishing, Inc.).

SURFING FOR HOTELS

Shopping online for hotels is a possibility in The Bahamas, although many small hotels and B&Bs don't show up on websites at all. Of the "big three" sites, **Expedia.com** may be the best choice, thanks to its long list of special deals. **Travelocity** (www.travelocity.com) runs a close second. Hotel specialist sites **hotels. com** and **quikbook.com** are also reliable. An excellent free program, **TravelAxe** (www.travelaxe.net), can help you search multiple hotel sites at once, even ones you may never have heard of.

Priceline and Hotwire are even better for hotels than for airfares; with both, you're allowed to pick the neighborhood and quality level of your hotel before offering your money. *Note*—Hotwire overrates its hotels by one star—what Hotwire calls a four-star is a three-star anywhere else.

Frommers.com: The Complete Travel Resource

For an excellent travel-planning resource, we highly recommend Frommers.com (www.frommers.com), voted best travel site by *PC Magazine*. We're a little biased, of course, but we guarantee that you'll find the travel tips, reviews, monthly vacation giveaways, and online-booking capabilities thoroughly indispensable. Among the special features are our popular **Message Boards,** where Frommer's readers post queries and share advice (sometimes even our authors show up to answer questions); the **Frommers.com newsletter,** for the latest travel bargains and insider travel secrets; and **Frommer's Destinations Section,** where you'll get expert travel tips, hotel and dining recommendations, and advice on the sights to see for more than 3,000 destinations around the globe. When your research is done, the **Online Reservations System** (www.frommers.com/book_a_trip) takes you to Frommer's preferred online partners for booking your vacation at affordable prices.

SURFING FOR RENTAL CARS

For booking rental cars online, the best deals are usually found at rental-car company websites, although all the major online travel agencies also offer rental-car reservations services. Priceline and Hotwire work well for rental cars, too; the only "mystery" is which major rental company you get, and for most travelers the difference between Hertz, Avis, and Budget is negligible.

11 The 21st-Century Traveler

INTERNET ACCESS AWAY FROM HOME

Travelers have any numbers of ways to check their e-mail and access the Internet on the road. Of course, using your own laptop—or even a PDA (personal digital assistant) or electronic organizer with a modem—gives you the most flexibility. But even if you don't have a computer, you can still access your e-mail. In lieu of the cybercafe that exists in most cities today, in The Bahamas you may have to rely on the good graces of your hotel to get your mail.

WITHOUT YOUR OWN COMPUTER

To retrieve your e-mail, ask your **Internet Service Provider (ISP)** if it has a Web-based interface tied to your existing e-mail account. If your ISP doesn't have such an interface, you can use the free **mail2web** service (www.mail2web.com) to view (but not reply to) your home e-mail. For more flexibility, you may want to open a free, Web-based e-mail account with **Yahoo! Mail** (www.yahoo.com). Microsoft's Hotmail (www.hotmail.com) is another popular option, though it has encountered some spam problems. Your home ISP may be able to forward your e-mail to the Web-based account automatically.

If you need to access files on your office computer, look into a service called **GoToMyPC** (www.gotomypc.com). The service provides a Web-based interface for you to access and manipulate a distant PC from anywhere—even a cybercafe—provided your "target" PC is on and has an always-on connection to the Internet (such as with RoadRunner cable access). The service offers top-quality security, but if you're worried about hackers, use your own laptop to access the GoToMyPC system.

WITH YOUR OWN COMPUTER

Wi-Fi (wireless fidelity) is the buzzword in computer access, and more and more hotels, cafes, and retailers are signing on as wireless "hotspots" from where you can get high-speed connection without cable wires, networking hardware, or a phone line (see below). You can get Wi-Fi connection one of several ways. Many laptops sold in the last year have built-in Wi-Fi capability (an 802.11b wireless Ethernet connection). Mac owners have their own networking technology, Apple AirPort. For those with older computers, an 802.11b/**Wi-Fi card** (around $50) can be plugged into your laptop. You sign up for wireless access service much as you do cellphone service, through a plan offered by one of several commercial companies that have made wireless service available in airports, hotel lobbies, and coffee shops, primarily in the U.S. (followed by the U.K. and Japan). **T-Mobile Hotspot** (www.t-mobile.com/hotspot) serves up wireless connections at more than 1,000 Starbucks coffee shops nationwide. **Boingo** (www.boingo.com) and **Wayport** (www.wayport.com) have set up networks in airports and high-class hotel lobbies. IPass providers (see below) also give you access to a few hundred wireless hotel lobby setups. Best of all, you don't need to be staying at the Four Seasons to use the hotel's network; just set yourself up on a nice couch in the lobby. The companies' pricing policies can be byzantine, with a variety of monthly, per-connection, and per-minute plans, but in general you pay around $30 a month for unlimited access—and as more and more companies jump on the wireless bandwagon, prices are likely to get even more competitive.

You can also find places that provide **free wireless networks** in cities around the world. To locate these free hotspots, go to www.personaltelco.net/index.cgi/WirelessCommunities.

If Wi-Fi is not available at your destination, most business-class hotels throughout the world offer dataports for laptop modems, and a few thousand hotels in the U.S. and Europe now offer free high-speed Internet access using an Ethernet network cable. You can bring your own cables, but most hotels rent them for around $10. **Call your hotel in advance** to see what your options are.

In addition, major Internet Service Providers (ISP) have **local access numbers** around the world, allowing you to go online by simply placing a local call. Check your ISP's website or call its toll-free number and ask how you can use your current account away from home, and how much it will cost.

If you're traveling outside the reach of your ISP, the **iPass** network has dial-up numbers in most of the world's countries. You'll have to sign up with an iPass provider, who will then tell you how to set up your computer for your destination(s). For a list of iPass providers, go to www.ipass.com and click on "Individual Purchase." One solid provider is **i2roam** (www.i2roam.com; ✆ **866/811-6209** or 920/235-0475).

Wherever you go, bring a **connection kit** of the right power and phone adapters, a spare phone cord, and a spare Ethernet network cable—or find out whether your hotel supplies them to guests.

USING A CELLPHONE OUTSIDE THE U.S.

The three letters that define much of the world's **wireless capabilities** are GSM (Global System for Mobiles), a big seamless network that makes for easy cross-border cellphone use. In the U.S., T-Mobile, AT&T Wireless, and Cingular use this quasiuniversal system; in Canada, Microcell and some Rogers customers are GSM, and all Europeans and most Australians use GSM. If your cellphone is on a GSM system, and you have a world-capable multiband phone such as many (but not all) Sony Ericsson, Motorola, or Samsung models, you can make and receive calls across civilized areas on much of the globe. Just call your wireless operator and ask for "international roaming" to be activated on your account. Unfortunately, per-minute charges can be high. World-phone owners can bring down their per-minute charges with a bit of trickery. Call up your cellular operator and say you'll be going abroad and want to "unlock" your phone to use it with a local provider. Usually, they'll oblige. Then, in your destination country, pick up a cheap, prepaid phone chip at a mobile phone store and slip it into your phone. (Show your phone to the salesperson, as not all phones work on all networks.) You'll get a local phone number in your destination country—and much, much lower calling rates.

Otherwise, **renting** a phone is a good idea. While you can rent a phone from any number of overseas sites, including kiosks at airports and at car-rental agencies, we suggest renting the phone before you leave home. That way you can give loved ones your new number, make sure the phone works, and take the phone wherever you go—especially helpful when you rent overseas, where phone-rental agencies bill in local currency and may not let you take the phone to another country.

Phone rental isn't cheap. You'll usually pay $40 to $50 per week, plus airtime fees of at least a dollar a minute.

Two good wireless rental companies are **InTouch USA** (✆ 800/872-7626; www.intouchglobal.com) and **RoadPost** (www.roadpost.com; ✆ 888/290-1606 or 905/272-5665). Give them your itinerary, and they'll tell you what wireless products you need. InTouch will also, for free, advise you on whether your existing phone will work in The Bahamas; simply call ✆ 703/222-7161 between 9am and 4pm Eastern Time, or go to http://intouch global.com/travel.htm.

12 Getting There: Flying to The Bahamas

Lying right off the east coast of Florida, the archipelago of The Bahamas is the easiest and most convenient foreign destination you can fly to unless you live close to the Canadian or Mexican borders.

Nassau is the busiest and most popular point of entry (this is where you'll fly if you're staying on Paradise Island). From here, you can make connections to many of the more remote Out Islands. If you're headed for one of the Out Islands, refer to the "Getting There" section that appears at the beginning of each island's coverage later in this book for details. Freeport, on Grand Bahama, also has its own airport, which is served by flights from the U.S. mainland, too.

Flight time to Nassau from Miami is about 35 minutes; from New York, 2½ hours; from Atlanta, 2 hours and 5 minutes; from Philadelphia, 2 hours and 45 minutes; from Charlotte, 2 hours and 10 minutes; from central Florida, 1 hour and 10 minutes; and, from Toronto, 3 hours.

THE MAJOR AIRLINES

From the U.S. mainland, about a half-dozen carriers fly nonstop to the country's major point of entry and busiest airline hub, **Nassau International Airport** (✆ 242/377-7281). Some also fly to the archipelago's second-most-populous city of Freeport. Only a handful (see below) fly directly to any of the Out Islands.

American Airlines (✆ 800/433-7300; www.aa.com), has several flights per day from Miami to Nassau as well as four daily flights from Fort Lauderdale to Nassau. In addition, the carrier flies three times daily from Miami to Freeport. It also offers three flights daily from Miami to Georgetown and one flight daily from Miami to Marsh Harbour.

The Gulf of Mexico & the Caribbean

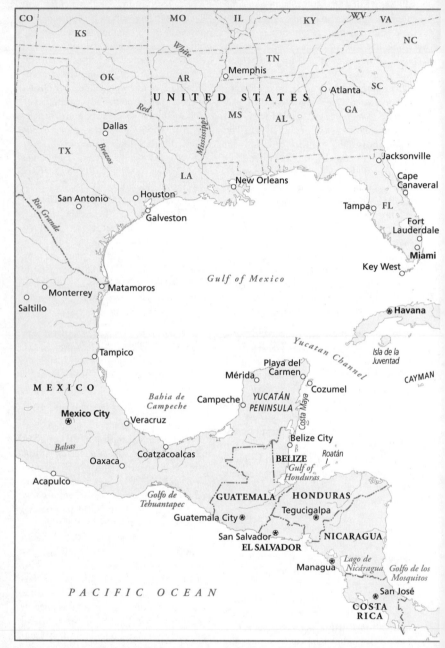

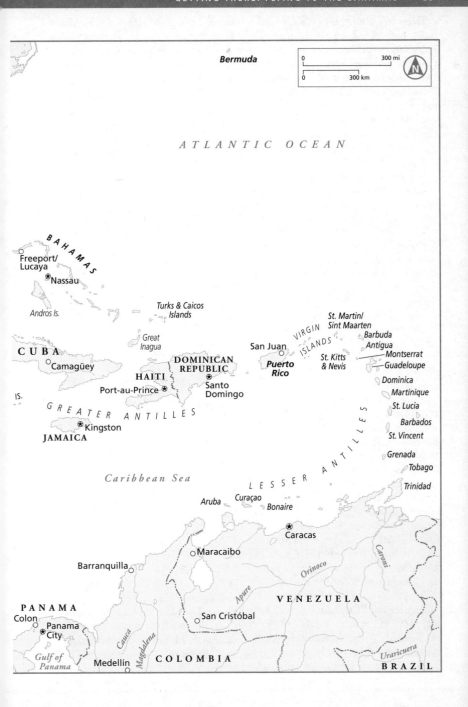

Bermuda

0   300 mi

0   300 km

N

ATLANTIC OCEAN

BAHAMAS

Freeport/
Lucaya

Nassau

Andros Is.

Turks & Caicos
Islands

St. Martin/
Sint Maarten

*VIRGIN
ISLANDS*

Barbuda

Antigua

Montserrat

Guadeloupe

*Great
Inagua*

San Juan

CUBA

Camagüey

**DOMINICAN
REPUBLIC**

HAITI

Port-au-Prince

*Puerto
Rico*

St. Kitts
& Nevis

Santo
Domingo

Dominica

Martinique

St. Lucia

IS.

GREATER ANTILLES

Barbados

St. Vincent

Kingston

JAMAICA

Grenada

Tobago

Trinidad

Caribbean Sea

LESSER ANTILLES

Curaçao

Aruba

Bonaire

Caracas

Maracaibo

Barranquilla

Orinoco

Caroní

Apure

VENEZUELA

PANAMA

Colon

Panama
City

San Cristóbal

Cauca

Magdalena

*Gulf of
Panama*

Medellín

COLOMBIA

Uraricuera

BRAZIL

Delta (℡ 800/221-1212; www.delta.com) has several connections to The Bahamas, with service from Atlanta, Orlando, and New York's LaGuardia.

The national airline of The Bahamas, **Bahamasair** (℡ 800/222-4262; www.bahamasair.com), flies to The Bahamas from Miami and Fort Lauderdale, landing at either Nassau (with seven nonstop flights daily) or Freeport (with two nonstop flights daily).

US Airways (℡ 800/428-4322; www.usairways.com) offers daily direct flights to Nassau from Philadelphia and Charlotte, North Carolina.

Other carriers include **Continental Airlines** (℡ 800/525-0280; www.continental.com), through its regional affiliate, Gulfstream International, has greatly expanded its link to The Bahamas through South Florida. Continental operates flights between Fort Lauderdale and Andros Town on Andros, with four round-trip flights each week. The airline also offers daily service from Fort Lauderdale to both Georgetown and Governors Harbour. In addition, it maintains frequent links between Fort Lauderdale and Marsh Harbour, North Eleuthera, and Treasure Cay. **Twin Air** (℡ 954/359-8266; www.flytwinair.com) flies from Fort Lauderdale three times a week to Rock Sound and Governor's Harbour and four times a week to North Eleuthera.

Air Canada (℡ 888/247-2262; www.aircanada.com) is the only carrier offering scheduled service to Nassau from Canada. Direct flights from Toronto and Montreal leave daily; flights from Toronto and Montréal, as well as other Canadian cities, make connections in the U.S.

British travelers opt for transatlantic passage aboard **British Airways** (℡ 800/247-9297 in the U.S. or 0870/850-9850 in the U.K.; www.britishairways.com), which offers four weekly direct flights from London to Nassau. The airline also

has at least one flight daily to Miami. From here, a staggering number of connections are available to Nassau and many other points within the archipelago on several carriers.

FLYING TO THE OUT ISLANDS

Many frequent visitors to The Bahamas do everything they can to avoid the congestion, inconvenience, and uncertain connections of the Nassau International Airport. A couple of U.S.-based airlines offer service directly to some of the Out Islands. **American Eagle** (℡ 800/433-7300; www.aa.com) offers frequent service from Miami's International Airport to the Abacos, Eleuthera, and the Exumas. **US Airways** (℡ 800/428-4322; www.usairways.com) flies nonstop every day from Fort Lauderdale to Eleuthera, usually making stops at both Governor's Harbour and North Eleuthera. US Airways also flies every day from West Palm Beach to the Abacos, stopping in both Treasure Cay and Marsh Harbour.

Chalk's Ocean Airways (℡ 800/424-2557; www.chalksoceanairways.com) operates 17-passenger amphibious aircraft that take off and land in waters near the company's portside terminals. From the Florida mainland, a nonstop flight departs for Bimini from Fort Lauderdale International Airport. The flight then continues on to Paradise Island. There's also a one-stop flight from Fort Lauderdale's International Airport to Bimini. (The airline also offers charter flights to virtually anywhere in The Bahamas.)

GETTING THROUGH THE AIRPORT

With the federalization of airport security, security procedures at U.S. airports are more stable and consistent than ever. Generally, you'll be fine if you arrive at the airport **1 hour** before a domestic flight and **2 hours** before an international flight.

Bring a **current, government-issued photo ID** such as a driver's license or passport. Keep your ID at the ready to show at check-in, the security checkpoint, and sometimes even the gate. (Children under 18 do not need government-issued photo IDs for domestic flights, but they do for international flights to most countries.)

E-tickets have made paper tickets nearly obsolete. Passengers with e-tickets can beat the ticket-counter lines by using airport **electronic kiosks** or even **online check-in** from your home computer. Online check-in involves logging on to your airlines' website, accessing your reservation, and printing out your boarding pass—and the airline may even offer you bonus miles to do so. If you're using a kiosk at the airport, bring the credit card you used to book the ticket or your frequent-flier card. Print out your boarding pass from the kiosk and simply proceed to the security checkpoint with your pass and a photo ID. If you're checking bags or looking to snag an exit-row seat, you will be able to do so using most airline kiosks. Even the smaller airlines are employing the kiosk system, but always call your airline to make sure these alternatives are available. **Curbside check-in** is also a good way to avoid lines, although a few airlines still ban curbside check-in; call before you go.

Security lines are getting shorter than they were during 2001 and 2002, but long ones still remain. If you have trouble standing for long periods of time, tell an airline employee; the airline will provide a wheelchair. Speed up security by **not wearing metal objects** such as big belt buckles or clanky earrings. If you've got metallic body parts, a note from your doctor can prevent a long chat with the security screeners. Keep in mind that only **ticketed passengers** are allowed past security, except for folks escorting passengers with disabilities or children.

Federalization has also stabilized **what you can carry on** and **what you can't.** The general rule is that sharp things are out, nail clippers are okay, and food and beverages must be passed through the X-ray machine—but that security screeners can't make you drink from your coffee cup. Bring food in your carry-on rather than checking it, as explosive-detection machines used on checked luggage have been known to mistake food (especially chocolate, for some reason) for bombs. Travelers in the U.S. are allowed one carry-on bag, plus a "personal item" such as a purse, briefcase, or laptop bag. Carry-on hoarders can stuff all sorts of things into a laptop bag; as long as it has a laptop in it, it's still considered a personal item. The Transportation Security Administration (TSA) has issued a list of restricted items; check its website (www.tsa.gov/public/index.jsp) for details.

At press time, the TSA is also recommending that you **not lock your checked luggage** so screeners can search it by hand if necessary. The agency says to use plastic "zip ties" instead, which can be bought at hardware stores and can be easily cut off.

FLYING FOR LESS: TIPS FOR GETTING THE BEST AIRFARE

Passengers sharing the same airplane cabin rarely pay the same fare. Travelers who need to purchase tickets at the last minute, change their itinerary at a moment's notice, or fly one-way often get stuck paying the premium rate. Here are some ways to keep your airfare costs down.

- Passengers who can book **long in advance, stay over Saturday night,** or **fly midweek** or **at less-trafficked hours** can often pay a fraction of the full fare. If your schedule is flexible, say so, and ask if you can secure a cheaper fare by changing your flight plans.

- You can also save by keeping an eye out in local newspapers for **promotional specials** or **fare wars,** when airlines lower prices on their most popular routes. You rarely see fare wars offered for peak travel times, but if you can travel in the off-months, you may snag a bargain.
- Search **the Internet** for cheap fares (see "Planning Your Trip Online").
- **Consolidators,** also known as bucket shops, are sources for international tickets, although they usually can't beat the Internet on fares within North America. Start by looking in Sunday newspaper travel sections; U.S. travelers should focus on the *New York Times, Los Angeles Times,* and *Miami Herald. Beware:* Bucket shop tickets are usually nonrefundable or rigged with stiff cancellation penalties, often as high as 50% to 75% of the ticket price, and some put you on charter airlines with questionable safety records. **FlyCheap** (© **800/**

FLY-CHEAP; www.1800flycheap. com) is owned by package-holiday megalith MyTravel and so has especially good access to fares for sunny destinations. **Air Tickets Direct** (© **800/778-3447;** www.airtickets direct.com) is based in Montreal and leverages the currently weak Canadian dollar for low fares; it'll also book trips to places that U.S. travel agents won't touch, such as Cuba.

- Join frequent-flier clubs. Accrue enough miles, and you'll be rewarded with free flights and elite status. It's free, and you'll get the best choice of seats, faster response to phone inquiries, and prompter service if your luggage is stolen, your flight is canceled or delayed, or if you want to change your seat. You don't need to fly to build frequent-flier miles—frequent-flier credit cards can provide thousands of miles for doing your everyday shopping.

13 Packages for the Independent Traveler

Before you search for the lowest airfare on your own (see earlier in this chapter), you may want to consider booking your flight as part of a package deal—a way to travel independently but pay group rates.

A package tour is not an escorted tour, in which you're led around by a guide. Except by cruise ships visiting certain islands, the option of being escorted around six or so Bahamian islands on an escorted tour does not exist.

Often—and especially when booking popular destinations like The Bahamas—a package that includes airfare, hotel, and transportation to and from the airport will cost you less than just the hotel alone would have, had you booked plane tickets, hotels, and car rentals independently. Packages are sold in bulk to tour operators who resell them to the public at a cost that drastically undercuts standard rates.

It's important to spend a little time shopping around; just be sure to compare apples to apples, since the package offerings can vary. You can use the reviews and rack rates given in this book to evaluate whether a package is really a good deal.

Here are a few tips to help you tell one package from another, and figure out which one is right for you:

- **Read the fine print.** Make sure you know *exactly* what's included in the price you're being quoted, and what's not. Hotel taxes? Airport transfers? Don't pay for a rental car you don't need. Before you commit to a package, make sure you know how much flexibility you have, say, if your child gets sick or your boss suddenly asks you to adjust your vacation schedule. Some packagers require ironclad commitments, whereas others charge only minimal fees for changes or cancellations.

- **Use your best judgment.** If a deal appears to be too good to be true, it probably is. Go with a reputable firm with a proven track record. When in doubt, ask your travel agent.

The best place to start your search is the travel section of your local Sunday newspaper. Also check the ads in the back of national travel magazines like *Travel & Leisure, National Geographic Traveler, Travel Holiday,* and *Condé Nast Traveler. Arthur Frommer's Budget Travel* always has lots of ads and frequent articles about good-value packages.

Vacation Together (© 877/444-4547; www.vacationtogether.com) allows you to search for and book packages offered by a number of tour operators and airlines. The **United States Tour Operators Association**'s website (© 212/599-6599; www.ustoa.com) has a search engine that allows you to look for operators that offer packages to a specific destination.

RECOMMENDED PACKAGE-TOUR OPERATORS

Liberty Travel (© 888/271-1584; www.libertytravel.com) is one of the biggest packagers in the Northeast, and it usually boasts a full-page ad in Sunday papers.

One good source of package deals is the airlines themselves. Most major airlines offer air/land packages, including **American Airlines Vacations** (© 800/321-2121; www.aavacations.com), **Delta Vacations** (© 800/221-6666; www.deltavacations.com), **US Airways Vacations** (© 800/455-0123; www.usairwaysvacations.com), and **Continental Airlines Vacations** (© 800/301-3800; www.covacations.com).

The biggest hotel chains and resorts also offer package deals. If you already know where you want to stay, call the resort itself and ask if it can offer land/air packages.

There's also **TourScan, Inc.,** 1051 Boston Post Rd., Darien, CT 06820 (© 800/962-2080 in the U.S.; www.tourscan.com), which researches the best value vacation at each hotel and condo.

For one-stop shopping on the Web, go to **www.vacationpackager.com**, a search engine that will link you to many different package-tour operators offering Bahamas vacations, often with a company profile summarizing the company's basic booking and cancellation terms.

ALL-INCLUSIVE TOURS

Just-A-Vacation, Inc., 2910 Hamilton St., Hyattville, MD 20782 (© 800/683-6313; www.justavacation.com) specializes in all-inclusive resorts on the islands of The Bahamas, plus other destinations in the Caribbean including Barbados, Jamaica, Aruba, St. Lucia, and Antigua.

Club Med (© 888/WEB-CLUB; www.clubmed.com) has various all-inclusive options throughout the Caribbean and The Bahamas.

SPECIAL TOURS FOR FISHERMEN

Frontiers International (© 800/245-1950 or 724/935-1577; www.frontierstrvl.com) features fly- and spin-fishing tours of The Bahamas and is a specialist in saltwater-fishing destinations.

FOR BRITISH TRAVELERS

Package tours to The Bahamas can be booked through **Harlequin Worldwide Connoisseurs Collection,** 2 North Rd., South Ockendon, Essex RM15 6AZ (© 01708/850-300; www.harlequinholidays.com). This agency offers both air and hotel packages not only to Nassau, but to most of the Out Islands as well. The company also specializes in scuba-diving and golf holidays.

Another specialist is **Kuoni Travel,** Kuoni House, Dorking, Surrey RH5 4AZ (© 01306/744-442; www.kuoni.co.uk), which offers both land and air packages to

The Bahamas, including such destinations as Nassau and Freeport, and to some places in the Out Islands. They also offer packages for self-catering villas on Paradise Island.

14 For the Cruise-Ship Traveler

Cruises to The Bahamas are usually either 3- or 4-day weekend getaways or week-long itineraries in which the ship may stop at Nassau, Freeport, and/or one of several privately owned Bahamian islands for a day at the beach.

Regardless of the ship you choose, your cruise will probably depart from the cruise capital of the world, Miami. A handful of vessels also depart for Bahamian waters from Port Everglades (adjacent to Fort Lauderdale), Port Canaveral, and, in very rare instances, from New York. Many cruise-ship passengers combine a cruise with visits to Orlando's theme parks, Miami's South Beach, the Florida Everglades, or the Florida Keys and Key West.

Nearly all cabins aboard ships today have two twin beds that can be pushed together, plus storage space (of varying size), a shower and a toilet (ditto), and sometimes a TV showing a rotating stock of programs. If you want to keep costs to a minimum when booking, ask for one of the smaller, inside cabins (one without windows). If you like to be active all day and stay out late enjoying the ship's bars and nightclubs, you won't miss the sunshine anyway. On the other hand, ships offer suites today that have an amazing array of pampering options (including hot tubs on their own private verandas!).

Because they buy in such bulk, cruise lines typically offer some of the best deals on airfare to your port of embarkation, and also typically offer extension packages that allow pre- or post-cruise stays at a hotel or resort.

Getting around Freeport/Lucaya or Nassau is relatively easy, and the official shore excursions offered by most ships are dull and sometimes restrictive, so it's best to decide what you want to do (shopping, swimming, snorkeling, or gambling) and head off on your own during your stop at each port of call. You'll certainly have time to relax at the beach if you choose, or to enjoy watersports (the chapters that follow will give you details on what companies or outfitters to contact for equipment, so you needn't feel dependent on the cruise line for everything).

In Nassau, cruise ships anchor at piers along Prince George Wharf. Taxi drivers meet all arrivals and will transport you into the heart of Nassau, center of most shopping and sightseeing activities. Duty-free shops also lie just outside the dock area, but for that, you'd do better to go inside the city's commercial and historic core.

As you disembark, you'll find a tourist information office in a tall pink tower, where you can pick up maps of New Providence Island or of Nassau itself. One-hour walking tours are conducted from here if you'd like an overview of the city, with a guide pointing out historic monuments. Outside this office, an ATM will supply you with U.S. dollars if your cash is running low.

THE MAJOR CRUISE LINES

For detailed information, and reviews of each of the ships spending significant time in either the Caribbean or The Bahamas, consider picking up a copy of *Frommer's Cruises & Ports of Call 2006.* Most of the major cruise lines we list here focus on Nassau (see chapter 3) and/or Freeport (see chapter 5):

- **Carnival Cruise Line** (© 888/ CARNIVAL; www.carnival.com): The cruise line everyone's heard of offers a big, loud, flashy cruise party with lots of gambling, glitz, and crowds, so if you're looking for some quiet, reflective time, this might not be your cup of rum.

Carnival's best bet for The Bahamas is aboard the *Fantasy.* Three-night loops go to Nassau; 4-night excursions visit Freeport and Nassau. The *Fantasy* departs from Port Canaveral rather than from the more southerly port of Miami. Refurbished in 2003, this vessel has an entertainment complex that attempts to evoke the heyday of Pompeii. If you like theme decor, such as a piano bar where Cleopatra would feel at home, sail on the *Fantasy.*

Similar in appeal, the *Fascination* visits Nassau from a base in Miami. These cruises especially appeal to passengers seeking a "long weekend" at sea and in port. Movie buffs like the *Fascination* because of its backdrop featuring legends from Hollywood or Broadway (Marilyn Monroe, among others). The average on-board age of most passengers on these Bahamian jaunts is a relatively youthful mid-40s, although ages range from 3 to 95 and usually include lots of children.

Celebration, refurbished in 1999, sails on 4- to 5-night trips to The Bahamas from Jacksonville, Florida. Outdated and a bit frumpy compared to newer Carnival vessels, *Celebration* is nonetheless seaworthy, evoking cruising in the mid-1980s.

- **Disney Cruise Line** (© **800/951-3532;** www.disneycruise.com): Launched in 1999, the *Disney Wonder* mingles state-of-the-art technology and audio-visuals with lots of Disney razzle-dazzle. Disney's ships also offer the best-designed family cabins of any cruise ship, the biggest children's facilities, and a number of adults-only areas, including one swimming pool, a piano bar, a comedy club, and various social venues.

Disney Wonder itineraries begin and end in Port Canaveral, last between 3 and 4 days, and include daylong visits to Nassau and Castaway Cay, the latter a privately owned Bahamian island featuring extensive children's facilities, an adults-only beach area, a family beach area, and all the sports and recreation choices you could want.

Most Disney cruises are sold as 7-night packages that include either 3 days at Disney World and 4 days at sea, or vice versa. The 4-night cruise offers a full day at sea as well as visits to the ports.

A day at Walt Disney World and you'll see the kind of people Disney attracts to its ships—families, honeymooners, adults without children, and seniors. Just about everybody, actually. Although Disney is certainly family-oriented, it's estimated that 30% of the passengers are child-free married couples or singles. Also, 10% to 15% of Disney's passengers are Europeans eager to experience that patented Disney magic.

- **Norwegian Cruise Line** (© **800/327-7030;** www.ncl.com): NCL offers 7-night Florida-Bahamas transits aboard the *Norwegian Dawn,* visiting Nassau and either Great Stirrup Key (NCL's private island). Generally inexpensive and emphasizing sports, NCL's ships attract a lot of active travelers in the 24-to-45 age bracket. Activities and cuisine are routine but adequate enough for short cruises.

Passengers who book on NCL want to travel to a hot weather destination in winter, but don't want to spend lavish sums for the experience. The line offers a wide variety of cabins at a range of prices to cater to a fairly diverse clientele than those usually found aboard HAL or Celebrity ships.

- **Royal Caribbean International** (© 800/398-9819; www.royal caribbean.com): This cruise line vies with Carnival in offering The Bahamas as a specific destination instead of including the archipelago as a 1-night stopover with most of the cruise devoted to other destinations south toward the Caribbean. Things run smoothly on this middle-of-the-road cruise line, which has a less frenetic atmosphere than that aboard Carnival's megaships. The company is well run, and there are enough on-board activities to suit virtually any taste and age level. Though accommodations and facilities are more than adequate, they're not upscale, and cabins aboard some of the line's older vessels tend to be a bit more cramped than the industry norm.

Your best bet if you want The Bahamas only (not the Caribbean) is to sail aboard the *Majesty of the Seas* or the *Sovereign of the Seas. Majesty* sails on 3-night Bahamian jaunts going round-trip from Miami year-round, visiting Nassau with a stopover at Coco Cay. The latter is a private Bahamian island that RCCL has filled with such facilities as beach barbecues and watersports. This vessel also features year-round 4-night trips from Miami that include Nassau and Coco Cay, but with a day in Key West as well.

For those who'd like the same itinerary but find departures from Port Canaveral more convenient, *Sovereign of the Seas* offers 3- to 4-night sails year-round that call on Nassau and Coco Cay. Another RCCL vessel, *Explorer of the Seas,* includes Nassau as part of 7-night itineraries going through either the western or eastern Caribbean.

Defining the typical passenger aboard a line that is noted for its broad-based, mass-market appeal is about as treacherous as sailing a megaship over a shallow Bahamian reef. Forced to generalize, though, we'd define Royal Caribbean's typical passengers as couples (and, to a lesser extent, singles) aged 30 to 60. A good number of families, sometimes with children, are thrown into the mix as well.

HOW TO GET THE BEST DEAL ON YOUR CRUISE

If you have a travel agent you trust, leave the details to him or her. If not, try contacting a travel agent who specializes in booking cruises. Some of the most likely contenders include the following:

Cruises, Inc., 1415 NW 62 St., Fort Lauderdale, FL 33009 (© **866/280-8198;** www.cruisesinc.com); **Cruises Only,** 1011 E. Colonial Dr., Orlando, FL 32803 (© **800/278-4737;** www.cruisesonly. com); **The Cruise Company,** 10760 Q St., Omaha, NE 68127 (© **800/289-5505;** www.thecruisecompany.com); **Kelly Cruises,** 1315 W. 22nd St., Ste. 105, Oak Brook, IL 60523 (© **800/837-7447;** www.kellycruises.com); **Hartford Holidays Travel,** 129 Hillside Ave., Williston Park, NY 11596 (© **800/828-4813;** www. hartfordholidays.com); and **Mann Travel** and **Cruises,** 4400 Park Rd., Charlotte, NC 28209 (© **866/591-8129;** www. manntravelandcruises.com).

A FEW MONEY-SAVING TIPS

- **Book early**
- **Book an inside cabin**
- **Take advantage of senior discounts**
- **Don't sail alone;** cruise lines base their rates on double occupancy, so solo passengers usually pay between 150% and 200% of the per-person rate. If you're traveling alone, most lines have a program that allows two solo passengers to share a cabin.

15 Getting Around

If your final destination is Paradise Island, Freeport, or Nassau (Cable Beach) and you plan to fly, you'll have little trouble in reaching your destination. However, if you're heading for one of the Out Islands, you face more exotic choices, not only of airplanes but also of other means of transport, including a mail boat, the traditional connecting link in days of yore.

As mentioned, each section on one of the Out Island chains has specific transportation information, but in the meantime, we'll give you a general overview.

BY PLANE

The national airline of The Bahamas, **Bahamasair** (© **800/222-4262;** www. bahamasair.com), serves 19 airports on 12 Bahamian islands, including Abaco, Andros, Cat Island, Eleuthera, Long Island, and San Salvador. Many of the Out Islands have either airports or airstrips, or are within a short ferry ride's distance of one. You can usually make connections to these smaller islands from Nassau.

BY RENTAL CAR

Many travelers don't really need to rent a car in The Bahamas, especially those who are coming for a few days of soaking in the sun at their resort's own beach. In Nassau and Freeport, you can easily rely on public transportation or taxis. In some of the Out Islands, there are a few car-rental companies, but most rental cars are unusually expensive and in poor condition (the roads are often in the same bad state as the rental cars).

Most visitors need transportation only from the airport to their hotel; perhaps you can arrange an island tour later, and an expensive private car won't be necessary. Your hotel can always arrange a taxi for you if you want to venture out.

You may decide that you want a car to explore beyond the tourist areas of New Providence Island, and you're very likely to want one on Grand Bahama Island.

Just remember: Road rules are much the same as those in the U.S., but you *drive on the left.*

For the Out Islands, turn to the relevant "Getting Around" sections of the chapters that follow to determine if you'll want a car (you may want one on Eleuthera, or to explore on Great Abaco Island); perhaps you'll stay put at your resort but rent a car for only 1 day of exploring.

The major U.S. car-rental companies operate in The Bahamas, but not on all the remote islands. We always prefer to do business with one of the major firms if they're present because you can call ahead and reserve from home via a toll-free number; they tend to offer better-maintained vehicles; and it's easier to resolve any disputes after the fact. Call **Budget** (© **800/ 472-3325;** www.budget.com), **Hertz** (© **800/654-3131;** www.hertz.com), **Dollar** (© **800/800-3665;** www.dollar car.com), or **Avis** (© **800/331-1212;** www.avis.com). Budget rents in Nassau and Paradise Island. Liability insurance is compulsory.

"Petrol" is easily available in Nassau and Freeport, though quite expensive. In the Out Islands, where the cost of gasoline is likely to vary from island to island, you should plan your itinerary based on where you'll be able to get fuel. The major towns of the islands have service stations. You should have no problems on New Providence or Grand Bahama Island unless you start out with a nearly empty tank.

Visitors may drive with their home driver's license for up to 3 months. For longer stays, you'll need to secure a Bahamian driver's license.

As you emerge at one of the major airports, including those of Nassau (New Providence) and Freeport (Grand Bahama Island), you can pick up island maps that are pretty good for routine touring around those islands. However, if you plan to do extensive touring in the Out Islands, you should go first to a bookstore in either Nassau or Freeport and ask for a copy of *Atlas of The Bahamas.* It provides touring routes (outlined in red) through all the major Out Islands. Once you arrive on these remote islands, it may be hard to obtain maps.

BY TAXI

Once you've reached your destination, you'll find that taxis are plentiful in the Nassau–Cable Beach–Paradise Island area and in the Freeport/Lucaya area on Grand Bahama Island. These cabs, for the most part, are metered—but they take cash only, no credit cards. See "Getting Around," in the chapters on each island that follow for further details.

In the Out Islands, however, it's not so easy. In general, taxi service is available at all air terminals, at least if those air terminals have "port of entry" status. They can also be hailed at most marinas.

Taxis are usually shared, often with the local residents. Out Island taxis aren't metered, so you must negotiate the fare before you get in. (Expect to pay a rate of around $20 per hour.) Cars are often old and badly maintained, so be prepared for a bumpy ride over some rough roads if you've selected a particularly remote hotel.

BY MAIL BOAT

Before the advent of better airline connections, the traditional way of exploring the Out Islands—in fact, about the only way unless you had your own craft—was by mail boat. This service is still available, but it's recommended only for those who have lots of time and a sense of adventure. You may ride with cases of rum, oil drums, crawfish pots, live chickens, or even an occasional piano.

The boats—19 of them composing the "Post Office Navy" under the direction of the Bahamian Chief of Transportation—are often fancifully colored, high-sided, and somewhat clumsy in appearance, but

the little motor vessels chug along, serving the 30 inhabited islands of The Bahamas. Schedules can be thrown off by weather and other causes, but most morning mail boats depart from Potter's Cay (under the Paradise Island Bridge in Nassau) or from Prince George Wharf. The voyages last from 4½ hours to most of a day, sometimes even overnight. Check the schedule of the particular boat you wish to travel on with the skipper at the dock in Nassau.

This is a cheap way to go: The typical fare from Nassau to Marsh Harbour is $45 per person, one-way. Many of the boats offer two classes of passenger accommodations, first and second. In first class you get a bunk bed; in second, you may be entitled only to deck space. (Actually, the bunk beds are usually reserved for the seasick, but first-class passengers on larger boats sit in a reasonably comfortable enclosed cabin.)

For information about mail boats to the Out Islands, contact the **Dockmasters Office** in Nassau, under the Paradise Island Bridge on Potter's Cay (© **242/ 393-1064**).

BY CHARTERED BOAT

For those who can afford it, this is the most luxurious way to see The Bahamas. On your private boat, you can island-hop at your convenience. Well-equipped marinas are on every major island and many cays. There are designated ports of entry at Great Abaco (Marsh Harbor), Andros, the Berry Islands, Bimini, Cat Cay, Eleuthera, Great Exuma, Grand Bahama Island (Freeport/Lucaya), Great Inagua, New Providence (Nassau), Ragged Island, and San Salvador.

Vessels must check with Customs at the first port of entry and receive a cruising clearance permit to The Bahamas. Carry it with you and return it at the official port of departure.

The Yachtsman's Guide to The Bahamas (Tropical Island Publishers) covers the entire Bahamas. Copies are available at major marine outlets and bookstores, and by mail direct from the publisher for $40, U.S. post-paid: Tropical Island Publishers, P.O. Box 12, Adelphia, NJ 07710 (© **877/923-9653;** www. yachtsmansguide.com).

Experienced sailors with a sea-wise crew can charter **"bareboat"** (a fully equipped boat with no crew). You're on your own, and you'll have to prove you can handle it before you're allowed to take out such a craft. You may want to take along an experienced yachter familiar with local waters, which may be tricky in some places.

Most yachts are rented on a weekly basis. Contact **Abaco Bahamas Charters** (© **800/626-5690** or 242/366-0151; www.abacocharters.com), or the **Moorings** (© **800/535-7289** or 242/367-4000; www.moorings.com).

16 Tips on Accommodations

The Bahamas offers a wide selection of accommodations, ranging from small private guesthouses to large luxury resorts. Hotels vary in size and facilities, from deluxe (offering room service, sports, swimming pools, entertainment, and so on) to fairly simple inns.

There are package deals galore, and they are always cheaper than "rack rates." (A rack rate is what an individual pays if he or she literally walks in from the street. These are the rates we've listed in the chapters that follow, though you can almost always do better—especially at the big resorts.) It's sometimes good to go to a reliable travel agent to find out what, if anything, is available in the way of a land-and-air package before booking a particular accommodation. See section 13, "Packages for the Independent Traveler," earlier in this chapter, for details on a number of companies that usually offer good-value packages to The Bahamas.

There is no rigid classification of hotel properties in the islands. The word "deluxe" is often used (or misused) when "first class" might have been a more appropriate term. "First class" itself often isn't. For that and other reasons, we've presented fairly detailed descriptions of the properties so that you'll get an idea of what to expect. However, even in the deluxe and first-class resorts and hotels, don't expect top-rate service and efficiency. When you go to turn on the shower, sometimes you get water and sometimes you don't. You may even experience power failures.

What the Hotel Symbols Mean

As you're shopping around for your hotel, you may see the following terms used:

- **AP (American Plan):** Includes three meals a day (sometimes called full board or full pension).
- **EP (European Plan):** Includes only the room—no meals.
- **CP (Continental Plan):** Includes continental breakfast of juice, coffee, bread, and jam.
- **MAP (Modified American Plan):** Sometimes called half board or half pension, this room rate includes breakfast and dinner (or lunch instead of dinner if you prefer).

The winter season in The Bahamas runs roughly from the middle of December to the middle of April, and hotels charge their highest prices during this peak period. Winter is generally the dry season in the islands, but there can be heavy rainfall regardless of the time of year. During the winter months, make reservations 2 months in advance if you can. You can't book early enough if you want to travel over Christmas or in February.

The off season in The Bahamas—roughly from mid-April to mid-December (although this varies from hotel to hotel)—amounts to a sale. In most cases, hotel rates are slashed a startling 20% to 60%. It's a bonanza for cost-conscious travelers, especially for families who can travel in the summer. Be prepared for very strong sun, though, plus a higher chance of rain. Also note that hurricane season runs through summer and fall.

MAP VS. AP, OR DO YOU WANT TO GO EP?

All Bahamian resorts offer a **European Plan (EP)** rate, which means that you pay for the price of a room. That leaves you free to dine around at night at various other resorts or restaurants without restriction. Another plan preferred by many is the **Continental Plan (CP),** which means you get a continental breakfast of juice, coffee, bread, and jam included in a set price. This plan is preferred by those who don't like to look around for a place to eat around breakfast time.

Another major option is the **Modified American Plan (MAP),** which includes breakfast and one main meal of the day, either lunch or dinner. The final choice is the **American Plan (AP),** which includes breakfast, lunch, and dinner. At certain resorts you will save money by booking in on either MAP or AP, because discounts are granted. If you dine a la carte often for lunch and dinner, your dining costs will be much higher than if you stay on the MAP or AP.

Dining at your hotel at night cuts down on transportation costs. Taxis especially are expensive. Nonetheless, if dining out and having many different culinary experiences is your idea of a vacation, and you're willing to pay the higher price, avoid AP plans or at least make sure the hotel where you're staying has more than one dining room (see above).

One option is to ask if your hotel has a dine-around plan. You might still keep costs in check, but you can avoid a culinary rut by taking your meals in some other restaurants if your hotel has such a plan. Such plans are rare in The Bahamas, which does not specialize in all-inclusive resorts the way that Jamaica or some other islands do.

Before booking a room, check with a good travel agent or investigate on your own what you are likely to save by booking on a dining plan. Under certain circumstances in winter you might not have a choice if MAP is dictated as a requirement for staying there. It pays to investigate, of course.

THE RIGHT ROOM AT THE RIGHT PRICE

Ask detailed questions when booking a room. Specify your likes and dislikes. There are several logistics of getting the right room in a hotel. In general, back rooms cost less than oceanfront rooms, and lower rooms cost less than upper-floor units. Therefore, if budget is a major consideration with you, opt for the cheaper rooms. You won't have a great view, but you'll pay less and save your money for something else. Just make sure that it isn't next to the all-night drummers.

Of course, all first-class or deluxe resorts feature air-conditioning, but many Bahamian inns do not, especially in the Out Islands. Cooling might be by ceiling fans or, in more modest places, the breeze from an open window, which also brings the mosquitoes. If sleeping in a climate-controlled environment is important to your vacation, ascertain this in advance.

If you're being your own travel agent, it pays to shop around by calling the local number given for a hotel and its toll-free number if it has one. You can check online and call a travel agent to see where you can obtain the best price.

Another tip: Ask if you can get an upgrade or a free night's stay if you stay an extra few days. If you're traveling during the marginal periods between low and high season, you can sometimes delay your travel plans by a week or 10 days and get a substantial reduction. For example, a $300 room booked on April 12 might have been lowered to $180 by April 17, as mid-April marks the beginning of the low season in The Bahamas.

Tip for seniors: Ask if an AARP card will get you a discount.

Transfers from the airports or the cruise dock are included in some hotel bookings, most often in a package plan but usually not in ordinary bookings. This is true of first-class and deluxe resorts but rarely of medium-priced or budget accommodations. Always ascertain whether transfers (which can be expensive) are included.

When using the facilities at a resort, make sure that you know exactly what is free and what costs money. For example, swimming in the pool is nearly always free, but you might be charged for use of a tennis court. Nearly all watersports cost extra, unless you're booked on some special plan such as scuba package. Some resorts seem to charge every time you breathe and might end up costing more than a deluxe hotel that includes most everything in the price.

Some hotels are right on the beach. Others involve transfers to the beach by taxi or bus, so factor in transportation costs, which can mount quickly if you stay 5 days to a week.

THE ALL-INCLUSIVES

A hugely popular option in Jamaica, the all-inclusive resort hotel concept finally has a foothold in The Bahamas. At most resorts, everything is included—sometimes even drinks. You get your room and all meals, plus entertainment and many watersports (although some cost extra). Some people find the cost of this all-inclusive holiday cheaper than if they'd paid individually for each item, and some simply appreciate knowing in advance what their final bill will be.

The first all-inclusive resort hotel in The Bahamas was **Club Med** (© 800/258-2633; www.clubmed.com) on Paradise Island. This is not a swinging-singles kind of place; it's popular with everybody, from honeymooners to families with kids along. There's another mammoth Club Med at Governor's Harbour on Eleuthera. Families with kids like it a lot here, and the resort also attracts scuba divers. There's a third branch in San Salvador, in the Southern Bahamas, which has more of a luxurious hideaway atmosphere.

The biggest all-inclusive of them all, **Sandals** (© 800/SANDALS; www.sandals.com), came to The Bahamas in 1995 on Cable Beach. This Jamaican company is now walking its sandals across the Caribbean, having established firm beachheads in Ocho Rios, Montego Bay, and Negril. The most famous of the all-inclusives (but not necessarily the best), it recently ended its ban against same-sex couples. See Chapter 3 for details.

RENTAL VILLAS & VACATION HOMES

You might rent a big villa, a good-size apartment in someone's condo, or even a small beach cottage (more accurately called a cabana).

Private apartments come with or without maid service (ask upfront exactly what to expect). This is more of a no-frills option than the villas and condos. The apartments may not be in buildings with swimming pools, and they may not have a front desk to help you.

Many cottages or cabanas ideally open onto a beach, although others may be clustered around a communal swimming pool. Most of them are fairly simple, containing no more than a plain bedroom plus a small kitchen and bathroom. In the peak winter season, reservations should be made at least 5 or 6 months in advance.

Hideaways International (© **888/ 843-4433** in the U.S. or 603/430-4433; www.hideaways.com) publishes *Hideaways Guide,* a 148-page pictorial directory of home rentals throughout the world, with full descriptions so you know what you're renting. Rentals range from cottages to staffed villas to whole islands! On most rentals you deal directly with owners. At condos and small resorts, Hideaways offers member discounts. Other services include specialty cruises, yacht charters, airline ticketing, car rentals, and hotel reservations. Annual membership costs $185.

Sometimes local tourist offices will also advise you on vacation-home rentals if you write or call them directly.

THE BAHAMIAN GUESTHOUSE

Many Bahamians stay at a guesthouse when traveling in their own islands. In The Bahamas, however, the term "guesthouse" can mean anything. Sometimes so-called guesthouses are really like simple motels built around swimming pools. Others are small individual cottages, with their own kitchenettes, constructed around a main building in which you'll often find a bar and restaurant serving local food.

FAST FACTS: The Bahamas

American Express Representing American Express in The Bahamas is **Destinatinos,** on Shirley Street (between Charlotte and Parliament sts.), Nassau (© **242/ 322-2931**). Hours are 9am to 5pm Monday through Friday. The travel department is also open Saturday 9am to 1pm. If you present a personal check and an Amex card, you can buy traveler's checks here.

Area Code The area code for The Bahamas is **242.**

ATMs See "Money," earlier in this chapter.

Business Hours In Nassau, Cable Beach, and Freeport/Lucaya, commercial banking hours are 9:30am to 3pm Monday through Thursday, 9:30am to 5pm on Friday. Hours are likely to vary widely in the Out Islands. Ask at your hotel. Most government offices are open Monday through Friday from 9am to 5pm, and most shops are open Monday through Saturday from 9am to 5pm.

Camera & Film Purchasing film in Nassau/Paradise Island or Freeport/Lucaya is relatively easy, if a little expensive. But stock up if you're going to the Out Islands and need a special kind.

Car Rentals See "Getting Around," earlier in this chapter. We do not recommend renting a car in The Bahamas.

Climate See "When to Go," earlier in this chapter.

Crime See "Safety," below.

Currency See "Money," earlier in this chapter.

Drug Laws Importing, possessing, or dealing unlawful drugs, including marijuana, is a serious offense in The Bahamas, with heavy penalties. Customs officers may at their discretion conduct body searches for drugs or other contraband goods.

Drugstores Nassau and Freeport are amply supplied with pharmacies (see individual listings). However, if you're traveling in the Out Islands, it is always best to carry your prescribed medication with you, since pharmacies are harder to find.

Electricity Electricity is normally 120 volts, 60 cycles, AC. American appliances are fully compatible; British or European appliances will need both converters and adapters.

Embassies & Consulates The U.S. Embassy is on 42 Queen St., P.O. Box N-8197, Nassau (② **242/322-1181**), and the Canadian consulate is on Shirley Street Shopping Plaza, Nassau (② **242/393-2123**). The British High Commission is at Ansbacher House (3rd floor), East Street, Nassau (② **242/325-7471**).

Emergencies Throughout most of The Bahamas, the number to call for a medical, dental, or hospital emergency is ② **911**. In the Out Islands, the number is ② **919**. To report a fire, however, call ② **411**.

Etiquette & Customs When encountering a person, even if a stranger in the Out Islands, it is customary to exchange greetings. A "good morning" or "afternoon" will suffice. But that custom doesn't prevail in bustling Freeport and Nassau. It is impolite anywhere to rush up to someone and demand that they supply you with directions to a place; Bahamians gently lead into conversations with a greeting and friendly comments before getting down to business.

Business in offices is conducted rather formally with exchange of business cards, elaborate handshakes, and the like. If you're doing business in The Bahamas, wear business clothes as you would to any office in America. Don't show up in resort wear or shorts for any formal meetings or functions.

When leaving the beach, it's recommended that men put on a shirt and pants, even a pair of jeans, before heading into a town. Women should wear a cover-up for their bathing suit, or else slip into a tropical dress or pants.

If you're planning to attend religious services, wear the best clothes you brought along. Bahamians believe in dressing up for their "Sunday-go-to meeting."

Regardless of how much you want to take a snapshot of an islander, it is extremely rude to photograph anyone without his or her permission.

Holidays Public holidays observed in The Bahamas are New Year's Day, Good Friday, Easter Sunday, Easter Monday, Whitmonday (7 weeks after Easter), Labour Day (the first Fri in June), Independence Day (July 10), Emancipation Day (the first Mon in Aug), Discovery Day (Oct 12), Christmas, and Boxing Day (the day after Christmas). When a holiday falls on Saturday or Sunday, stores and offices are usually closed on the following Monday.

Information See "Visitor Information," earlier in this chapter.

Internet Access Access is limited on the islands, but it can be obtained. **Cyber-cafe,** in the Mall at Marathon in Nassau (*©* **242/394-6254**), is open daily from 8:30am to 8pm, charging 15¢ per minute; there are four computers available. Web access is increasingly common at hotels in The Bahamas—even in the Out Islands, you can usually access the Web. But if this issue is especially important to you, check with specific accommodations before booking.

Language In The Bahamas, locals speak English, but sometimes with a marked accent that provides the clue to their ancestry—African, Irish, or Scottish, for example.

Liquor Laws Liquor is sold in liquor stores and various convenience stores; it's readily available at all hours though not sold on Sundays. The legal drinking age is 18.

Lost & Found Be sure to tell all of your credit card companies the minute you discover your wallet has been lost or stolen and file a report at the nearest police precinct. Your credit card company or insurer may require a police report number or record of the loss. Most credit card companies have an emergency toll-free number to call if your card is lost or stolen; they may be able to wire you a cash advance immediately or deliver an emergency credit card in a day or two. **Visa's** U.S. emergency number is *©* **800/847-2911. American Express** cardholders and traveler's check holders should call *©* **800/221-7282. MasterCard** holders should call *©* **800/307-7309.** For other credit cards, call the toll-free number directory at *©* **800/555-1212.**

If you need emergency cash over the weekend when all banks and American Express offices are closed, you can have money wired to you via **Western Union** (*©* **800/325-6000;** www.westernunion.com).

Identity theft or fraud are potential complications of losing your wallet, especially if you've lost your driver's license along with your cash and credit cards. Notify the major credit-reporting bureaus immediately; placing a fraud alert on your records may protect you against liability for criminal activity. The three major U.S. credit-reporting agencies are **Equifax** (*©* **888/766-0008;** www.equifax.com), **Experian** (*©* **888/397-3742;** www.experian.com), and **TransUnion** (*©* **800/680-7289;** www.transunion.com). Finally, if you've lost all forms of photo ID, call your airline and explain the situation; they might allow you to board the plane if you have a copy of your passport or birth certificate and a copy of the police report you've filed.

Mail & Postage Rates You'll need Bahamian (not U.S.) postage stamps to send postcards and letters. Most of the kiosks selling postcards also sell the stamps you'll need to mail them, so you probably won't need to visit the post office. Sending a postcard or an airmail letter (up to ½-oz. in weight) from The Bahamas to anywhere outside its borders (including the U.S., Canada, and the U.K.) costs 65¢, with another charge for each additional half ounce of weight.

Mail to and from the Out Islands is sometimes slow. Airmail may go by air to Nassau and by boat to its final destination. If a resort has a U.S. or Nassau address, it is preferable to use it.

Newspapers & Magazines Three newspapers are circulated in Nassau and Freeport: the *Nassau Guardian* (www.thenassauguardian.com), the *Tribune,* and the *Freeport News.* Circulation in the Out Islands is limited and likely to be slow. You can find such papers as the *New York Times, Wall Street Journal, USA Today, The Miami Herald, Times of London,* and *Daily Telegraph* at newsstands in your hotel and elsewhere in Nassau.

Passports Passport requirements vary according to your country of origin.

For Residents of the United States: Whether you're applying in person or by mail, you can download passport applications from the U.S. State Department website at **www.travel.state.gov**. For general information, call the **National Passport Agency** (© **202/647-0518**). To find your regional passport office, either check the U.S. State Department website or call the **National Passport Information Center** (© **877/487-2778**).

For Residents of Canada: Passport applications are available at travel agencies throughout Canada or from the central **Passport Office,** Department of Foreign Affairs and International Trade, Ottawa, ON K1A 0G3 (© **800/567-6868;** www.ppt.gc.ca).

For Residents of the United Kingdom: To pick up an application for a standard 10-year passport (5-year passport for children under 16), visit your nearest passport office, major post office, or travel agency or contact the **United Kingdom Passport Service** at © **0870/521-0410** or search its website at **www.ukpa.gov.uk**.

For Residents of Ireland: You can apply for a 10-year passport at the **Passport Office,** Setanta Centre, Molesworth Street, Dublin 2 (© **01/671-1633;** www.irlgov.ie/iveagh). Those under age 18 and over 65 must apply for a €12 3-year passport. You can also apply at 1A South Mall, Cork (© **021/272-525**) or at most main post offices.

For Residents of Australia: You can pick up an application from your local post office or any branch of Passports Australia, but you must schedule an interview at the passport office to present your application materials. Call the **Australian Passport Information Service** at © **131-232,** or visit the government website at **www.passports.gov.au**.

For Residents of New Zealand: You can pick up a passport application at any New Zealand Passports Office or download it from their website. Contact the **Passports Office** at © **0800/225-050** in New Zealand or 04/474-8100, or log on to **www.passports.govt.nz**.

Pets You'll have to get a valid import permit to bring any animal into The Bahamas. Application for such a permit must be made in writing, accompanied by a $10 processing fee and a $5 fax fee, to the **Director of Agriculture,** Department of Agriculture, P.O. Box N-3028, Nassau, The Bahamas (© **242/325-7413**), at least 4 weeks in advance.

Police Dial © **911**. In the Out Islands, the number is © **919**.

Safety When going to Nassau (New Providence), Cable Beach, Paradise Island, or Freeport/Lucaya, exercise the same caution you would if visiting Miami. Whatever you do, if people peddling drugs approach you, steer clear of them.

Women, especially, should take caution if walking alone on the streets of Nassau after dark, particularly if those streets appear to be deserted. Pickpockets (often foreigners) work the crowded casino floors of both Paradise Beach and Cable Beach. See that your wallet, money, and valuables are well secured.

If you're driving a rental car, always make sure your car door is locked, and never leave possessions in view in an automobile. Don't leave valuables such as cameras and purses lying unattended on the beach while you go for a swim. If you are traveling with valuables, especially jewelry, don't leave them unguarded in hotel rooms. Many of the larger hotels will provide safes. Keep your hotel room doors locked at all times.

You're less likely to be mugged or robbed in the Out Islands, where life is generally more peaceful. There are some hotels there that, even today, don't have locks on the doors.

Taxes Departure tax is $15 ($18 from Grand Bahama Island) for visitors ages 7 and up. An 8% tax is imposed on hotel bills; otherwise there is no sales tax in The Bahamas.

Telephone Although some of the Out Islands are still difficult to reach, direct long-distance dialing between North America and Nassau, Grand Bahama, the Abacos, Andros, the Berry Islands, Bimini, Eleuthera, Harbour Island, Spanish Wells, the Exumas, and Stella Maris on Long Island is available.

To call The Bahamas from the U.S. or Canada, dial 1-242 plus the seven-digit local number. From the U.K., dial 001-242 plus the local seven-digit number.

To make a direct international call from The Bahamas to the U.S. or Canada, dial 1 plus the area code and local number. To call other countries, dial 011 plus the country code (the U.K. is 44, for example), the area code (usually without its initial zero), and the local number.

For local calls within The Bahamas, simply dial the seven-digit number. To call from one island to another within The Bahamas, dial 1-242 and then the seven-digit local number.

Note that the old coin-operated phones are still prevalent and still swallow coins. Each local call costs 25¢; you can use either Bahamian or U.S. quarters. Those old phones, however, are gradually being replaced by phones that use calling cards (debit cards), similar in appearance to a credit card, that come in denominations of $5, $10, $20, and $50. They can be bought from any office of BATELCO (Bahamas Telephone Co.).

BATELCO's main branch is on Kennedy Drive, Nassau (© **242/302-7008**), although a popular local branch lies in the commercial heart of Nassau, on East Street off Bay Street.

To get **directory assistance** within The Bahamas, dial © **916.** To reach an international or a domestic operator within The Bahamas, dial **0.** There is no distinction made in The Bahamas between the two types of operators.

To reach the major international services of **AT&T,** dial © **800/CALLATT,** or head for any phone with AT&T or USA DIRECT marked on the side of the booth. Picking up the handset will connect you with an AT&T operator. These phones are often positioned beside cruise-ship docks to help passengers disembarking on shore leave for the day. **MCI** can be reached at © **800/888-8000.**

Time Eastern Standard Time is used throughout The Bahamas, and daylight saving time is observed in the summer.

Tipping Many establishments add a service charge, but it's customary to leave something extra if service has been especially fine. If you're not sure whether service has been included in your bill, don't be shy—ask.

Bellboys and porters, at least in the expensive hotels, expect a tip of $1 per bag. It's also customary to tip your maid at least $2 per day—more if she or he has performed special services such as getting a shirt or blouse laundered. Most service personnel, including taxi drivers, waiters, and the like, expect 15% (20% in deluxe restaurants).

Tourist Offices See "Visitor Information," earlier in this chapter, and also specific island chapters.

Water Technically, tap water is drinkable throughout The Bahamas. But we almost always opt for bottled. Resorts tend to filter and chlorinate tap water more aggressively than other establishments; elsewhere, bottled water is available at stores and supermarkets, and tastes better than that from a tap. On many of the Out Islands, rainfall is the main source of water. Definitely drink bottled water there.

Weddings The bride and groom must both be in The Bahamas at the moment they apply for the $40 wedding license here. If both are single and U.S. citizens, they must obtain an affidavit to that effect from the U.S. Embassy in Nassau. The fee is $55 per person; you'll need to appear in person with ID such as a passport (and, if applicable, proof of divorce). If all of these requirements are met, you can then get married after staying for 24 hours in The Bahamas. No blood test is necessary. Contact the **Ministry of Tourism** at P.O. Box N-3701, Nassau, The Bahamas (© **888-NUPTIAL** or **242-356-0435**) for more details.

3

New Providence
(Nassau/Cable Beach)

One million visitors a year have cast their vote: They want to visit Nassau, adjoining Cable Beach, or Paradise Island (which is covered separately in chapter 4). This is the center of all the action: the best shopping, the best entertainment, the most historic attractions—plus some of the best beaches in The Bahamas.

The capital of The Bahamas, the historic city of Nassau is a 35-minute flight from Miami. Despite the development and the modern hotels, a laid-back tropical atmosphere still hangs over the city, and it still offers a good dose of colonial charm. The commercial and banking hub of The Bahamas, as well as a mecca for shoppers, Nassau lies on the north side of New Providence, which is 34km (21 miles) long and 11km (7 miles) wide at its greatest point.

Cable Beach, a stretch of sand just west of the city, is lined with luxury resorts—in fact, the Nassau/Cable Beach area has the largest tourist infrastructure in The Bahamas, though there's another concentration of luxury hotels on Paradise Island. (If you want to stay right on the sands, don't choose a hotel in downtown Nassau itself. Head for Cable Beach or Paradise Island. You can easily reach the beach from a base in Nassau, but it won't be right outside your window.)

When you're based in Nassau/Cable Beach, you have an array of watersports, golf, tennis, and plenty of duty-free shopping nearby—not to mention those fine, powdery beaches. In addition, the resorts,

restaurants, and beaches of Paradise Island, discussed in the next chapter, are just a short distance away. (Paradise Island, which lies just opposite Nassau, is connected to New Providence Island by a toll bridge that costs $1 for cars, $2 for taxis, and is free for pedestrians; there's also frequent ferry and water-taxi service between Nassau and Paradise Island.)

As the sun goes down, Cable Beach and Paradise Island heat up, offering fine dining, glitzy casinos, cabaret shows, moonlight cruises, dance clubs, and romantic evening strolls. (We'd confine the evening stroll to Cable Beach or Paradise Island, and not the streets of downtown Nassau, which can be dangerous at night.)

The shops might draw a lot more business than the museums, but no city in The Bahamas is as rich in history as Nassau. You can take a "royal climb" up the Queen's Staircase to Fort Fincastle. These 66 steps lead to a fort said to have been cut in the sandstone cliffs by slaves in the 1790s. Other Nassau attractions include Ardastra Gardens, which feature 2 hectares (5 acres) of landscaping and more than 300 exotic birds, mammals, and reptiles. (Most popular are the trained pink flamingos that march for audiences daily to their trainer's commands.)

It's surprising that Nassau has retained its overlay of British colonial charm despite its proximity to Florida. It truly hasn't become Americanized; despite new development, traffic, and cruise-ship

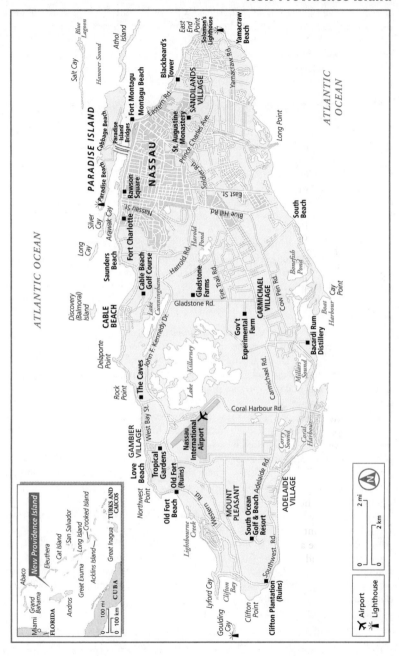

New Providence Island

73

crowds, Nassau's a long way from becoming another Miami. Stately old homes and public buildings still stand proudly among the modern high-rises and bland government buildings. Tropical foliage lines streets where horse-drawn surreys still trot by, carrying visitors on leisurely tours. Police officers in white starched jackets and colorful pith helmets still direct traffic on the main streets as they have long done. It could almost be England—but for the weather, that is.

1 Orientation

ARRIVING

BY PLANE   Planes land at **Nassau International Airport** (© 242/377-1759), which lies 13km (8 miles) west of Nassau by Lake Killarney.

No bus service goes from the airport to Cable Beach, Nassau, or Paradise Island. Your hotel may provide airport transfers if you've made arrangements in advance; these are often included in package deals. There are also any number of car-rental offices here if you plan to have a car while on New Providence Island (see "Getting Around," below), though we don't really think you need one.

If you don't have a lift arranged, take a taxi to your hotel. From the airport to the center of Nassau, expect to pay around $20; from the airport to Cable Beach, $15; from the airport to Paradise Island, $28 plus toll. Drivers expect to be tipped 15%, and some will remind you should you "forget." You don't need to stop at a currency exchange office before departing the airport: U.S. currency is fine for these (and any other) transactions.

BY CRUISE SHIP   Nassau has spent millions of dollars expanding its port so that a number of cruise ships can come into port at once. Sounds great in theory. Practically speaking, however, facilities in Nassau, Cable Beach, and Paradise Island become extremely overcrowded as soon as the big boats dock. You'll have to stake out your space on the beach, and you will find shops and attractions overrun with visitors every day you're in port.

Cruise ships dock near Rawson Square, the heart of the city and the shopping area—and the best place to begin a tour of Nassau. Unless you want to go to one of the beach strips along Cable Beach or Paradise Island, you won't need a taxi. You can go on a shopping expedition near where you dock: The site of the Straw Market is nearby, at Market Plaza; Bay Street—the main shopping artery—is also close; and the Nassau International Bazaar is at the intersection of Woodes Rogers Walk and Charlotte Street.

The government has added **"Festival Place"** (© 242/322-7680) to the Prince George dock (where the cruise ships arrive). Festival Place is a multicolored structure worth visiting. This facility is open daily 8am to 5pm. It provides booths where you can find Reception Services (© 242/323-3182), tourist information, and merchants selling arts, crafts, and Bahamian candy. You can lounge and have a daiquiri while you listen to the live calypso entertainment, or even get your hair braided. You can ride a horse and surrey, or catch a water taxi.

VISITOR INFORMATION

The Bahamas Ministry of Tourism maintains a **tourist information booth** at the Nassau International Airport in the arrivals terminal (© 242/377-6806; www.bahamas.com). Hours are from 8:30am to 11pm daily.

Information can also be obtained from the Information Desk at the **Ministry of Tourism's Office,** Rawson Square (℗ **242/328-7810**), which is open Monday to Friday 9am to 5pm.

THE LAY OF THE LAND

Most of the hotels in Nassau are city hotels and are not on the water. If you want to stay right on the sands, choose a hotel in Cable Beach (later in this chapter) or on Paradise Island (see chapter 4).

Rawson Square is the heart of Nassau, lying just a short walk from **Prince George Wharf,** where the big cruise ships, usually from Florida, berth. Here you'll see the Churchill Building, which contains the offices of the Bahamian prime minister along with other government ministries.

Busy **Bay Street,** the main shopping artery, begins on the south side of Rawson Square. This was the street of the infamous "Bay Street Boys," a group of rich, white Bahamians who once controlled all political and economic activity on New Providence.

On the opposite side of Rawson Square is **Parliament Square,** with a statue of a youthful Queen Victoria. Here are more government houses and the House of Assembly. These are Georgian and neo-Georgian buildings, some dating from the late 1700s.

The courthouse is separated by a little square from the **Nassau Public Library and Museum,** which opens onto Bank Lane. It was the former Nassau Gaol (jail). South of the library, across Shirley Street, are the remains of the **Royal Victoria Hotel,** which opened the year the American Civil War was launched (1861) and once hosted blockade runners and Confederate spies.

A walk down Parliament Street leads to the post office, and philatelists may want to stop in, since some Bahamian stamps are collector's items.

Favorite New Providence Experiences

Listening to the Sounds of Goombay. At some local joint, you can enjoy an intoxicating beat and such island favorites as "Goin' Down Burma Road," "Get Involved," and "John B. Sail."

A Ride in a Horse-Drawn Surrey. If you'd like to see Nassau as the Duke of Windsor did when he was governor, consider this unique form of transportation. It's elegant, romantic, and nostalgic. Surreys await passengers at Rawson Square, in the exact center of Nassau.

A Glass-Bottomed Boat Ride. Right in the middle of Nassau's harbor, numerous boats wait to take you through the colorful sea gardens off New Providence Island. In the teeming reefs offshore, you'll meet all sorts of sea creatures that inhabit this underwater wonderland.

An Idyllic Day on Blue Lagoon Island. It's like an old Hollywood fantasy of a tropical island. Located off the eastern end of Paradise Island, Blue Lagoon Island has seven sandy beaches. Boats from Nassau Harbour take you there and back.

Going south, moving farther away from the water, Elizabeth Avenue takes you to the **Queen's Staircase,** one of the major landmarks of Nassau, leading to Bennet's Hill and Fort Fincastle.

If you return to Bay Street, you'll discover the tent of the **Straw Market,** a handcrafts emporium where you could buy all sorts of souvenirs. At the intersection of Charlotte Street is another major shopping emporium, the **Nassau International Bazaar.**

In Nassau, and especially in the rest of The Bahamas, you will seldom, if ever, find street numbers on hotels or other businesses. Sometimes in the more remote places, you won't even find street names. Get directions before heading somewhere in particular. Of course, you can always ask along the way, as most Bahamians tend to be very helpful.

2 Getting Around

BY TAXI

You can easily rely on taxis and skip renting a car. The rates for New Providence, including Nassau, are set by the government. Working meters are required in all taxis, although you will also find gypsy cabs without meters. When you get in, the fixed rate is $3, plus 35¢ for each additional .5km (⅓-mile). Each passenger over two pays an extra $3. Taxis can also be hired at the hourly rate of $45 for a five-passenger cab. Luggage is carried at a cost of 75¢ per piece, although the first two pieces are transported free. The radio-taxi call number is © **242/323-4555.** It's also easy to get a taxi at the airport or at one of the big hotels.

BY CAR

You really don't need to rent a car. It's a lot easier to rely on taxis when you're ready to leave the beach and do a little exploring.

However, if you choose to drive (perhaps for a day of touring the whole island), some of the biggest U.S. car-rental companies maintain branches at the airport, downtown, and on Paradise Island. **Avis** (© **800/331-1212** or 242/377-7121; www.avis.com) operates at the airport, and also has branches at the cruise-ship docks at Bay Street and Cumberland Street, across from the British Colonial Hilton (© 242/326-6380). **Budget Rent-a-Car** (© **800/527-0700** or 242/377-9000; www.budgetrentacar.com) has a branch at the airport. **Dollar Rent-a-Car** (© **800/800-4000** or 242/377-7231; www.dollar.com) rents at the airport. **Hertz** (© **800/654-3131** or 242/377-8684; www.hertz.com) has an airport location.

Remember: Drive on the left!

⌢Moments **A Surrey with a Fringe on Top**

The elegant, traditional way to see Nassau is in a horse-drawn surrey—the kind with the fringe on top and a wilted hibiscus stuck in the straw hat shielding the horse from the sun. Before you get in, you should negotiate with the driver and agree on the price. The average charge is $10 per person for a 25-minute ride. The maximum load is three adults plus one or two children under the age of 12. The surreys are available daily from 9am to 4:30pm, except when the horses are resting (that's 1–3pm May–Oct, and 1–2pm Nov–Apr). You'll find the surreys at Rawson Square, off Bay Street.

Tips **On Your Own Sturdy Feet**

This is the only way to see Old Nassau, unless you rent a horse and carriage. All the major attractions and the principal stores are close enough to walk to. You can even walk to Cable Beach or Paradise Island, although it's a hike in the hot sun. Confine your walking to the daytime, and beware of pickpockets and purse snatchers. In the evening, avoid walking the streets of downtown Nassau, where muggings occur.

BY JITNEY

The least-expensive means of transport is by jitney—medium-size buses that leave from the downtown Nassau area to outposts on New Providence. The fare is $1, and exact change, in coins or with a dollar bill, is required. The jitneys operate daily from 6:30am to 7pm. Some hotels on Paradise Island and Cable Beach run their own free jitney service. Buses to the Cable Beach area leave from the Navy Lion Road depot. Buses to the eastern area depart from the Frederick Street North depot, and buses to the malls leave from Fredrick Street North Depot.

BY BOAT

Water taxis operate daily from 9am to 6pm at 20-minute intervals between Paradise Island and Prince George Wharf at a round-trip cost of $6 per person. Ferry service runs from the end of Casuarina Drive on Paradise Island across the harbor to Rawson Square for a round-trip fare of $6 per person. The ferry operates daily from 9:30am to 4:15pm, with departures every half-hour from both sides of the harbor.

BY MOPED

Lots of visitors like to rent mopeds to explore the island. Unless you're an experienced moped rider, stay on quiet roads until you feel at ease. (Don't start out in all the congestion on Bay St.!) Many hotels have rentals on the premises. If yours doesn't, try **Knowles** (© 242/356-0741), at Festival Place, which rents mopeds for $45 per day. Included in the rental price are insurance and mandatory helmets for both drivers and passengers.

FAST FACTS: **New Providence**

American Express The local representative is **Destinations,** 303 Shirley St., between Charlotte and Parliament streets, Nassau (© **242/322-2931**). Hours are Monday to Friday 9am to 5pm.

ATMs Major banks with ATMs in Nassau include the **Royal Bank of Canada** (© **242/322-2420**), **Bank of Nova Scotia** (© **242/356-1517**), and **Barclays** (© **242/356-8000**). However, some accept cards only in the **Cirrus** network (© **800/424-7787**), while others take only **PLUS** (© **800/843-7587**). ATMs at both the Paradise Island and Cable Beach casinos dispense quick cash. You can also find ATMs at the airports.

Babysitting Hotel staff can help you hire an experienced sitter. Expect to pay around $10 to $15 an hour, plus $3 an hour for each additional child.

Climate See "When to Go," in chapter 2.

Complaints The government of The Bahamas is becoming more user friendly. If you have a complaint about any establishment, call the **Ministry of Tourist Complaint Unit** at ✆ **242/356-0435.**

Dentist Try the dental department of the **Princess Margaret Hospital** on Sands Road (✆ **242/322-2861**).

Doctor For the best service, use a staff member of the **Princess Margaret Hospital** on Sands Road (✆ **242/322-2861**).

Drugstores Try **Lowes Pharmacy,** Palm Dale (✆ **242/322-8594**), open Monday through Saturday from 8am to 6:30pm. They also have two branches: **Harbour Bay Shopping Center** (✆ **242/393-4813**), open Monday to Saturday 8am to 8:30pm and Sunday from 9am to 5pm; and **Town Center Mall** (✆ **242/325-6482**), open Monday to Saturday 10am to 9pm. Nassau has no late-night pharmacies.

Embassies & Consulates See "Fast Facts: The Bahamas," in chapter 2.

Emergencies For any major emergency, call ✆ **919.**

Eyeglass Repair The **Optique Shoppe,** 22 Parliament St. at the corner of Shirley Street (✆ **242/322-3910**), is convenient to the center of Nassau. Hours are Monday to Friday 9am to 5pm and on Saturday 9am to noon.

Hospitals The government-operated **Princess Margaret Hospital** on Sands Road (✆ **242/322-2861**) is one of the major hospitals in The Bahamas. The privately owned **Doctors Hospital,** 1 Collins Ave. (✆ **242/322-8411**), is the most modern private health care facility in the region.

Hot Lines For help or assistance of any kind, call ✆ **242/326-HELP.**

Information See "Visitor Information," above.

Internet Access Check out Cybercafe at the **Mall at Marathon** (✆ **242/394-6254**). Here you can get online from your own laptop or log on to one of the computers. The cost is 15 cents per minute. Some of the larger hotels also offer guests Internet access for a small fee.

Laundry & Dry Cleaning The **Laundromat Superwash** (✆ **242/323-4018**), at the corner of Nassau Street and Boyd Road, offers coin-operated machines; it's open 24 hours a day, 7 days a week. In the same building is the **New Oriental Dry Cleaner** (✆ **242/323-7249**). Another dry cleaner a short drive north of the center of town is the **Jiffy Quality Cleaner** (✆ **242/323-6771**) at the corner of Blue Hill Road and Cordeaux Avenue.

Newspapers & Magazines *The Tribune Daily* and *The Nassau Guardian,* both published in the morning, are the country's two competing daily newspapers. At your hotel and visitor information stations, you can find various helpful magazines, brochures, and booklets.

Photographic Needs The largest camera store in Nassau is John Bull (✆ **242/322-3328**), on Bay Street 3 blocks west of Rawson Square.

Police Dial ✆ **911** or ✆ **919.**

Post Office The **Nassau General Post Office,** at the top of Parliament Street on East Hill Street (✆ **242/322-3344**), is open Monday through Friday from 9am to

5pm and on Saturday from 9am to 1pm at the Festival Place. Note that you can buy stamps from most postcard kiosks.

Safety Avoid walking in downtown Nassau at night, where there are sometimes robberies and muggings. (Most tourists are never affected, but better safe than sorry.) Cable Beach and Paradise Island are safer places to be in the evening.

Taxes There is no sales tax, though there is a 12% hotel tax. Each visitor leaving The Bahamas pays a $20 departure tax.

3 Where to Stay

In the hotel descriptions that follow, we've listed regular room prices or "rack rates," but these are simply for ease of comparison. They are likely to be accurate for smaller properties, but you can almost always do better at the larger hotels and resorts. ***Note:*** Read the section "Packages for the Independent Traveler" in chapter 2 before you book a hotel separately from your airfare, and if you do book yourself, always inquire about honeymoon specials, golf packages, summer weeks, and other discounts. In many cases, too, a travel agent can get you a package deal that would be cheaper than these official rates.

Hotels add a 12% "resort levy" tax to your rate. Sometimes this is quoted as part of the price; at other times, it's added to your final bill. When you are quoted a rate, always ask if the tax is included. Many hotels also add a 15% service charge to your bill. Ask about these charges in advance so you won't be shocked when you receive the final tab.

Taxes and service are not included in the rates listed below. We'll lead off with a selection of hotels within the heart of Nassau, followed by accommodations in Cable Beach. Most visitors prefer to stay at Cable Beach since the resorts here are right on the sand. But you can stay in Nassau and commute to the beaches at Cable Beach or Paradise Island; it's cheaper but less convenient. Those who prefer the ambience of Old Nassau's historic district and being near the best shops may decide to stay in town.

NASSAU
EXPENSIVE

British Colonial Hilton ☆☆   In the restored British Colonial Hilton, there's a palpable air of the long-ago days when The Bahamas was firmly within the political and social orbit of Britain. This landmark seven-story hotel has seen its share of ups and downs over the years. Plush and glamorous when it was built in 1900, it burned to the ground in 1920, and was rebuilt 3 years later before deteriorating into a flophouse. Between 1996 and 1999, a Canadian entrepreneur poured $68 million into its restoration.

Don't expect the glitz and glitter of Cable Beach or Paradise Island here—the Hilton is after business travelers rather than the casino crowd. It also lacks the aristocratic credentials of Graycliff (see below). Nonetheless, it's a dignified and friendly, but rather sedate, hotel with a discreetly upscale decor (no Disney-style themes or gimmicks). Bedrooms are a bit on the small side, but capped with rich crown moldings

Where to Stay & Dine in Nassau

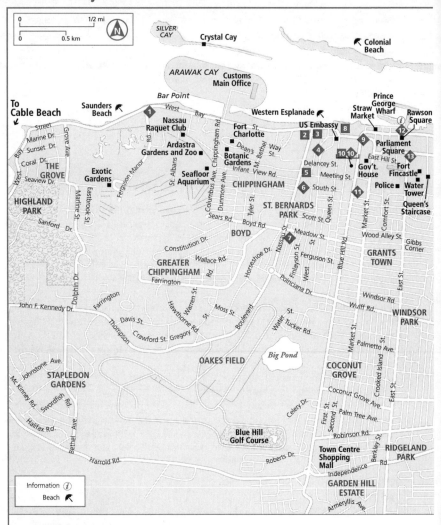

ACCOMMODATIONS ■

British Colonial Hilton **8**
Buena Vista Hotel **5**
El Greco Hotel **3**
Graycliff **10**
Holiday Inn
  Junkanoo Beach **2**
Nassau Harbour Club **17**

DINING ◆

Bahamian Kitchen **12**
Buena Vista **6**
Café Matisse **13**
Café Skans **1**
Chez Willie **4**
Conch Fritters
  Bar & Grill **9**

Crocodiles Waterfront
  Bar & Grill **14**
Double Dragon **16**
East Villa Restaurant
  and Lounge **18**
Gaylord's **15**
Graycliff **10**

Palm Tree **11**
Poop Deck **19**
Shoal Restaurant
  and Lounge **7**

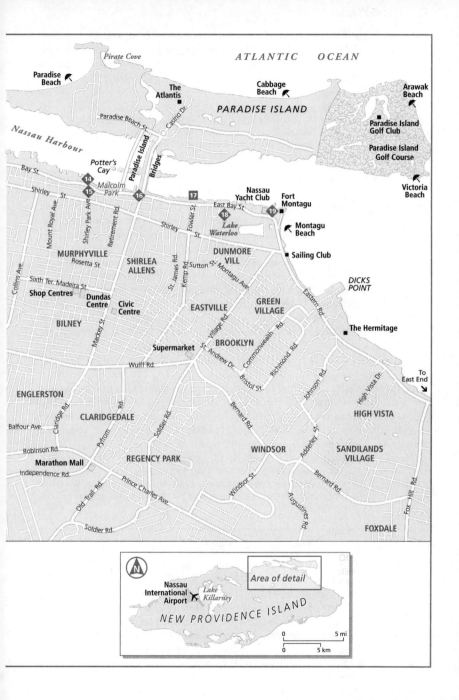

ATLANTIC OCEAN

Pirate Cove

Paradise Beach

The Atlantis

Cabbage Beach

PARADISE ISLAND

Arawak Beach

Paradise Beach St.

Casino Dr.

Paradise Island Golf Club

Paradise Island Golf Course

Nassau Harbour

Bay St.

Potter's Cay

Paradise Island Bridges

Victoria Beach

Shirley St.

Malcolm Park

14

15

16

17

18

Nassau Yacht Club

Fort Montagu

19

Montagu Beach

Mount Royal Ave.

Shirley Park Ave.

Retirement Rd.

Shirley

East Bay St.

Fowler St.

Lake Waterloo

Sailing Club

DICKS POINT

Collins Ave.

MURPHYVILLE

Rosetta St.

SHIRLEA ALLENS

St. James Rd.

Kemp Rd.

Sutton St.

Montagu Ave.

DUNMORE VILL

Sixth Ter. Madeira St.

Shop Centres

Dundas Centre

Civic Centre

EASTVILLE

GREEN VILLAGE

Eastern Rd.

The Hermitage

BILNEY

Mackey St.

Supermarket

BROOKLYN

Village Rd.

St. Andrew Dr.

Commonwealth Rd.

Richmond Rd.

Johnson Rd.

Wulff Rd.

Bristol St.

ENGLERSTON

Claridge Rd.

Rd.

CLARIDGEDALE

Soldier Rd.

Bernard Rd.

WINDSOR

High Vista Dr.

To East End

HIGH VISTA

Balfour Ave.

Pyfrom

Adderley St.

SANDILANDS VILLAGE

Robinson Rd.

Marathon Mall

Independence Rd.

REGENCY PARK

Old Trail Rd.

Prince Charles Ave.

Windsor St.

Bernard Rd.

Fox Hill Rd.

Soldier Rd.

Augustines Rd.

FOXDALE

N

Nassau International Airport

Lake Killarney

Area of detail

NEW PROVIDENCE ISLAND

0   5 mi

0   5 km

and accessorized with tile or stone-sheathed bathrooms with shower/tub combinations. The staff, incidentally, is superbly trained and motivated; we've found them upbeat and hardworking. There's a small beach a few steps away, but it's not very appealing (it's on the channel separating New Providence from Paradise Island, with no "cleansing" wave action at all).

1 Bay St. (P.O. Box N-7148), Nassau, The Bahamas. ℂ **800/HILTONS** in the U.S. and Canada, or 242/322-3301. Fax 242/302-9009. www.hilton.com. 291 units. Winter $205–$325 double, $435–$2,000 suite; off season $190–$210 double, $440–$900 suite. AE, DC, DISC, MC, V. Bus: 10. **Amenities:** 2 restaurants; 2 bars; outdoor pool; health club; full-service spa; Jacuzzi; tour desk; business center; secretarial service; limited room service; babysitting; laundry service; dry cleaning. *In room:* A/C, TV, dataport, minibar, coffeemaker, hair dryer, iron, safe, trouser press.

Graycliff ✿   Now in a kind of nostalgic decay, Graycliff remains the grande dame of downtown Nassau hotels even though her tiara is a bit tarnished and her age showing. In spite of its drawbacks, this place still has its devotees, especially among older readers. Originally an 18th-century private home and an example of Georgian colonial architecture, it's now an intimate inn, with an old-fashioned atmosphere. Even though the inn isn't on the beach, people who can afford to stay anywhere often choose Graycliff because it epitomizes the old-world style and grace that evokes Nassau back in the days when the Duke and Duchess of Windsor were in residence. Churchill, of course, can no longer be seen paddling around in the swimming pool with a cigar in his mouth, and the Beatles are long gone, but the three-story Graycliff continues without the visiting celebs, who today head for Paradise Island. Beach lovers usually go by taxi to either nearby Goodman's Bay or to the Western Esplanade Beach, nearly adjacent to Arawak Cay. The bigger British Colonial Hilton is Graycliff's main competitor; they both have a rather staid, deliberately unflashy ambience.

The historic garden rooms in the main house, are large and individually decorated with antiques, though the better units are the more modern garden rooms. The Yellow Bird, Hibiscus, and Pool cottages are ideal choices, but the most luxurious accommodation of all is the Mandarino Suite, with Asian decor, a king-size bed, an oversize bathroom, and a private balcony overlooking the swimming pool. Bathrooms are spacious, with shower/tub combinations, deluxe toiletries, and robes.

8–12 W. Hill St. (P.O. Box N-10246), Nassau, The Bahamas. ℂ **800/688-0076** in the U.S., or 242/322-2796. Fax 242/326-6110. www.graycliff.com. 18 units. Winter $290–$400 double, $400 cottage; off season $200 double, $310 cottage. AE, MC, V. Bus: 10 or 21A. **Amenities:** 2 restaurants; 2 bars; 3 outdoor pools; spa; Jacuzzi; sauna; limited room service; massage; babysitting; laundry service; dry cleaning. *In room:* A/C, TV, dataport, minibar, hair dryer, iron, safe.

⟮*Fun Fact* **In Suite Double O, a "License to Kill"**

In both *Thunderball* and *Never Say Never Again,* James Bond, or secret agent 007, was served shaken martinis at the British Colonial. To commemorate that historic event, the Hilton-owned property now has a "Double-O" suite filled with Bond memorabilia, including posters, books, CDs, movie stills, and all the best Bond flicks, including *Goldfinger* and *Live and Let Die.* Guests can take a Bond book from the suite, perhaps *Tomorrow Never Dies,* and curl up on a chaise longue at the beach. The suite is a one-bedroom unit with living room and ocean views. When you get tired of the movie Bond, you might be able to stroll over to the next chair and meet the real Bond—Sean Connery is often at his island home on nearby Lyford Cay.

MODERATE

Holiday Inn Junkanoo Beach *(Value)*   West of downtown Nassau, this hotel over-looks Junkanoo Beach. Although not as fine as Cable Beach, Junkanoo is also a safe beach with tranquil waters, white sands, and a lot of shells; the hotel offers lounge chairs on the beach but no waiter service for drinks. This place is a good value for those who don't want to pay the higher prices charged by the more deluxe hotels along Cable Beach. All the motel-style bedrooms have a view of either the beach or Nassau Harbour, and they come with extras you don't always find in a moderately priced choice, such as alarm clocks, two-line phones, and a working desk. All come with well-maintained bathrooms containing shower/tub combinations.

The on-site Bay Street Grille is not reason enough to stay here, although you can dine outside in a tropical courtyard overlooking the pool. The West Coast Bar and Grill is another dining option.

W. Bay St. (P.O. Box SS-19055), Nassau, The Bahamas. (*C*) **800/465-4329** or 242/356-0000. Fax 242/323-1408. www.holiday-inn.com. 183 units. Winter $149 double, $179 suite; off season $95–$150 double, $149 suite. AE, DISC, MC, V. Bus: 10 or 17. **Amenities:** Restaurants; bar; 2 outdoor pools; health club; spa; salon; tour desk; 24-hr. room service; laundry service; dry cleaning; nonsmoking rooms; Internet cafe; rooms for those w/limited mobility. *In room:* A/C, TV, dataport, fridge, coffeemaker, hair dryer, iron, safe.

INEXPENSIVE

Buena Vista Hotel   Although this place really revolves around its restaurant (p. 90), it rents a few spacious bedrooms upstairs. It's a good bargain if you don't mind the lack of resort-style facilities. The building, with a pale pink facade, started out a century ago as a private home, and stands about 1km (⅔-mile) west of downtown Nassau. Expect a pastel decor, with a tasteful mix of antiques and reproductions. Each room comes with a small bathroom containing a shower/tub combination; staff might be a bit distracted because of the demands of the busy restaurant downstairs.

Delancy and Augusta sts. (P.O. Box N-564), Nassau, The Bahamas. (*C*) **242/322-2811.** Fax 242/322-5881. www.buenavista-restaurant.com. 5 units. Mid-Apr to mid-Dec $70 double; mid-Dec to mid-Apr $100 double. AE, MC, V. Bus: 16. **Amenities:** Restaurant; limited room service. *In room:* A/C, TV, fridge, coffeemaker, iron.

El Greco Hotel   Across the street from Lighthouse Beach, and a short walk from the shops and restaurants of Bay Street, El Greco is a well-managed bargain choice that attracts many European travelers. The Greek owners and staff genuinely seem to care about their guests—in fact, the two-story hotel seems more like a small European B&B than your typical Bahamian hotel.

The midsize rooms aren't that exciting, but they're clean and comfortable, with decent beds and small tile bathrooms, containing shower/tub combinations. Bed-rooms have a bright decor—a sort of Mediterranean motif, each with two ceiling fans and carpeted floors. Accommodations are built around a courtyard that contains stat-ues crafted in the Italian baroque style, draped with lots of bougainvillea. A restaurant isn't on-site, but you can walk to many places nearby for meals.

W. Bay St. (P.O. Box N-4187), Nassau, The Bahamas. (*C*) **242/325-1121.** Fax 242/325-1124. www.bahamasnet.com. 27 units. Winter $109 double, $150 suite; off season $79 double, $125 suite. AE, MC, V. Free parking. Bus: 10. **Ameni-ties:** Restaurant (dinner only); bar; pool; limited room service; babysitting. *In room:* A/C, TV.

Nassau Harbour Club Hotel & Marina   Don't expect lush and sprawling gardens, or much peace and privacy here—this hotel is in the heart of Nassau's action and is usually overrun in March and early April with college kids on spring break. A com-pound of two-story pink buildings from the early 1960s arranged like a horseshoe around a concrete terrace, it occupies a bustling strip of land between busy Bay Street and the edge of the channel that separates New Providence from Paradise Island. From your room, you'll have views of yachts and boats moored at a nearby marina, and easy access to the shops, bars, and restaurants of downtown Nassau and within the Harbour Bay Shopping Centre. Throughout, it's down-to-earth and just a bit funky. Bedrooms are simple and small but comfortable and equipped with bathrooms containing shower/tub combinations. However, they are a little worn and located near the animated hubbub of the busy bar.

E. Bay St. (P.O. Box SS-5755), Nassau, The Bahamas. © **242/393-0771.** Fax 242/393-5393. 50 units. Winter $90–$130 double, $140 suite; off season $80–$110 double, $110 suite. Extra person $25 per day. AE, MC, V. Free parking. Bus: 11 or 19. **Amenities:** Restaurant; bar; outdoor pool. *In room:* A/C, TV, fridge.

CABLE BEACH

The glittering shoreline of Cable Beach, located west of Nassau, is topped only by Paradise Island (see chapter 4). It has loyal fans, many of whom think Paradise Island is too snobbish. Cable Beach has for years attracted visitors with its broad stretches of beachfront, a wide array of sports facilities, and great nightlife, including casino action. Deluxe or first-class resorts, two of which are all-inclusive, line the shoreline.

VERY EXPENSIVE

Breezes Bahamas ⚶ SuperClubs, which competes successfully with Sandals (see below), spent $125 million transforming a tired old relic, the Ambassador Beach Hotel, into this all-inclusive resort. The nearby Sandals is more imposing, elegant, stylish, and upscale, with better amenities and views. Rowdier and more raucous, and located on a prime 450m (1,476-ft.) beachfront along Cable Beach, Breezes attracts a more middle-of-the-road crowd; it's unpretentious and more affordable (though it ain't exactly cheap, and we think it's rather overpriced for what it is). This U-shaped beachfront resort has two wings of rooms plus a main clubhouse facing a large pool area. Except between March and May, when no one under 21 is admitted, both couples and single travelers over 16 are accepted here. Everything is included—the room, meals, snacks, unlimited wine (not the finest) with lunch and dinner, even premium brand liquor at the bars, plus activities and airport transfers.

The refurbished hotel rooms contain pastel-painted wooden furniture with Formica tops, and a working air-conditioning system. Rooms, however, are not as luxurious as those at Sandals. Tiled bathrooms are medium-size but well equipped with a shower and bathtub.

Diners can sample unremarkable international fare at the food court, although the Italian restaurant serves a better dinner. A beachside grill and snacks are available throughout the day. Entertainment includes a high-energy disco, a piano bar, and a nightclub. Karaoke is inevitable, but the professional Junkanoo live shows, which are presented every Saturday night, are better, and local bands often perform. The social centerpiece is a sometimes-overcrowded terrace with a swimming pool.

P.O. Box CB-13049, Cable Beach, Nassau, The Bahamas. © **800/GO-SUPER** or 242/327-5356. Fax 242/327-5155. www.superclubs.com. 400 units. Winter $297–$540 double, $775 suite; off season $292–$513 double, $680 suite. Rates include all meals, drinks, tips, airport transfers, and most activities. AE, DISC, MC, V. Free parking. Bus: 10. No children under 14 year-round; no one under 18 Mar–May. **Amenities:** 4 restaurants; 4 bars; 2 outdoor pools; 2 tennis courts; health club; watersports equipment; laundry service; nonsmoking rooms; rooms for those w/limited mobility. *In room:* A/C, TV, coffeemaker, hair dryer, iron, safe.

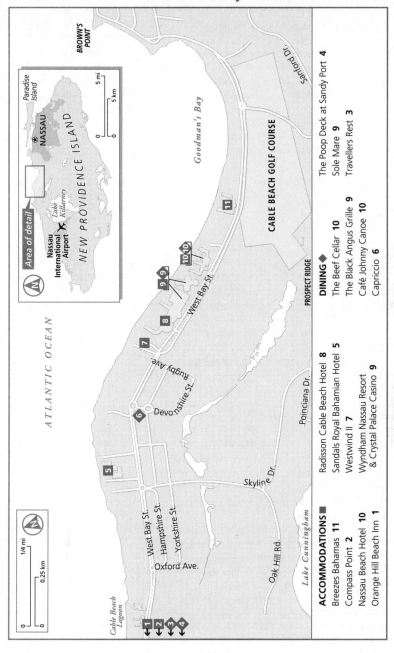

ACCOMMODATIONS ■
Breezes Bahamas **11**
Compass Point **2**
Nassau Beach Hotel **10**
Orange Hill Beach Inn **1**

Radisson Cable Beach Hotel **8**
Sandals Royal Bahamian Hotel **5**
Westwind II **7**
Wyndham Nassau Resort
& Crystal Palace Casino **9**

DINING ◆
The Beef Cellar **10**
The Black Angus Grille **9**
Café Johnny Canoe **10**
Capriccio **6**

The Poop Deck at Sandy Port **4**
Sole Mare **9**
Travellers Rest **3**

85

Moments Junkanoo Festivals

No Bahamian celebration is as raucous as the Junkanoo (which is also the name of the music associated with this festival). The special rituals originated during the colonial days of slavery, when African-born newcomers could legally drink and enjoy themselves only on certain strictly predetermined days of the year. In its celebration, Junkanoo closely resembles Carnaval in Rio and Mardi Gras in New Orleans. Its major difference lies in the costumes and the timing (the major Junkanoo celebrations occur the day after Christmas, a reminder of the medieval English celebration of Boxing Day on Dec 26, and New Year's Day).

In the old days, Junkanoo costumes were crafted from crepe paper, often in primary colors, stretched over wire frames. (One sinister offshoot of the celebrations was that the Junkanoo costumes and masks were used to conceal the identity of anyone seeking vengeance on a white or on another slave.) Locals have more money to spend on costumes and Junkanoo festivals today than they did in decades past. Today, the finest costumes can cost up to $10,000 and are sometimes sponsored by local bazaars, lotteries, and charity auctions, though everyday folks from all walks of Bahamian life join in, too, usually with their own homemade costumes, many of which are sensual or humorous. The best time and place to observe Junkanoo is New Year's Day in Nassau, when throngs of cavorting, music-making, and costumed figures prance through the streets. Find yourself a good viewing position on Bay Street. Less elaborate celebrations take place in major towns on the other islands, including Freeport.

Sandals Royal Bahamian Hotel ★★★   This is the most upscale Sandals resort in the world. It's shockingly expensive, though you can often get special promotional rates that make it more reasonable. It originated as a very posh hotel, the Balmoral Beach, in the 1940s. In 1996, the Jamaica-based Sandals chain poured $20 million into renovating and expanding this property on a sandy beach a short walk west of the more glittery megahotels of Cable Beach. Everywhere, you'll find manicured gardens, rich cove moldings, hidden courtyards tastefully accentuated with sculptures, and many of the trappings of Edwardian England in the tropics.

A favorite for honeymoon getaways, Sandals offers well-furnished and often elegant rooms, all classified as suites. Some are in the Manor House, while others are in outlying villas. The villas are preferred because they have romantic, secluded settings and easy access to nearby plunge pools. Some units have Jacuzzis and private pools, and some of the bathrooms are enormous. The bedrooms have thick cove moldings, formal English furniture, and shower/tub combination bathrooms loaded with perfumed soaps and cosmetics. The rooms that face the ocean offer small, curved terraces with ornate iron railings and views of an offshore sand spit, Sandals Key.

For a long time, only heterosexual guests were allowed at this resort. Recently, the British and Canadian governments said they wouldn't allow Sandals to advertise its resorts if it continued discriminatory policies against same-sex couples. In 2004, Sandals capitulated and ended the ban. Today gay couples are allowed in as guests.

Bahamian and international fare is offered in generous portions in the property's restaurants. In addition to spectacular buffets, the options include white-glove service and continental dishes in the Baccarat Dining Room. The two latest additions include Kimono's, offering Japanese cuisine, and Casanova, specializing in Italian fare. Other choices are the Royal Café for southwestern grilled specialties, and Spices, for upscale buffets at breakfast, lunch, and dinner. The pool here is one of the most appealing on Nassau, with touches of both Vegas and ancient Rome (outdoor murals and replicas of ancient Roman columns jutting skyward above the water). Complimentary shuttle bus service goes to the casino and nightlife options at the nearby Crystal Palace complex, plus concierge service is offered in suites and upper-tier doubles.

W. Bay St. (P.O. Box CB-13005), Cable Beach, Nassau, The Bahamas. ⓒ 800/SANDALS or 242/327-6400. Fax 242/327-6961. www.sandals.com. 405 units. Winter $4,760–$8,820 per couple for 7 days ($1,620–$3,000 per couple for 2 days); off season $4,470–$8,590 per couple for 7 days ($1,520–$2,920 per couple for 2 days). Rates include all meals, drinks, and activities. AE, DISC, MC, V. Free parking. Bus: 10. Couples only; no children or singles allowed. **Amenities:** 8 restaurants; 9 bars; 6 outdoor pools; 2 tennis courts; health club; full-service spa; watersports equipment; nonsmoking rooms; rooms for those w/limited mobility. *In room:* A/C, TV, coffeemaker, hair dryer, iron, safe.

EXPENSIVE

Radisson Cable Beach Hotel 🅠 *Kids*   Right in the middle of Cable Beach (its best asset) this high-rise is connected by a shopping arcade to the Crystal Palace Casino. The nearby Wyndham Nassau Marriott Resort is glitzier and has better facilities, but the Radisson is still one of the most desirable choices for families, as it has the best children's programs in the area, and because many of its bedrooms contain two double beds, suitable for a family of four. The nine-story property has an Aztec-inspired facade of sharp angles and strong horizontal lines, built in a horseshoe-shaped curve around a landscaped beachfront garden. You'll think of Vegas when you see the rows of fountains in front, the acres of marble sheathing inside, and the four-story lobby with towering windows. Big enough to get lost in, but with plenty of intimate nooks, the hotel offers an almost endless array of things to do. Note, however, that readers frequently complain of staff attitude and slow service at this sprawling resort.

Bedrooms are modern and comfortable if rather standard, with big windows that open onto views of the garden or the beach. Units are equipped with one king-size bed or two doubles, along with phones with voice mail, plus tiled combination bathrooms (tub and shower).

The hotel contains six restaurants, the most glamorous of which is the Amici, serving a traditional Italian cuisine in a two-story garden setting. You can also spice up your evening at Islands, which sometimes has karaoke and other entertainment. We try to avoid the overpriced Avocado's or Bimini's, both of which have poor service and an uninspired cuisine. The Mini-Market Grill serves Caribbean/continental breakfast and lunch buffets, and the Forge is a steak-and-seafood restaurant where guests are

---

The Art of the Massage
The Ultra Spa at Sandals Royal Bahamian Resort & Spa in Nassau has repeatedly made the top 10 list of spa resorts in the *Condé Nast Traveler* reader's choice survey. The decor features walls and floors of Italian Satumia stone, rich mahogany doors and a collection of pre-Raphaelite prints in gilded frames. One service offered, Massage Duet, allows couples to learn the art of massage from a professional so they can practice on each other in the comfort of one's hotel room.

---

seated around a tabletop grill to prepare their own steaks, seafood, or chicken. Beach parties and revues are often staged.

W. Bay St. (P.O. Box N-4914), Cable Beach, Nassau, The Bahamas. ✆ **800/333-3333** or 242/327-6000. Fax 242/327-6987. www.radisson-cablebeach.com. 685 units. Winter $175–$250 double; off season $150–$250 double; year-round $550–$950 suite. AE, DISC, MC, V. Free parking. Bus: 10. **Amenities:** 6 restaurants; 3 bars; 3 outdoor pools; 5 tennis courts; gym; kid's camp (ages 4–12); shopping arcade; salon; limited room service; babysitting; laundry service; dry cleaning; rooms for those w/limited mobility. *In room:* A/C, TV, dataport, coffeemaker, hair dryer, iron, safe.

Wyndham Nassau Resort & Crystal Palace Casino (Overrated (Kids) This big, flashy megaresort on the lovely sands of Cable Beach is so vast and all-encompassing that some of its guests never venture into Nassau during their stay on the island. The complex incorporates five high-rise towers, a futuristic central core, and a cluster of gardens and beachfront gazebos—all linked by arcades, underground passages, and minipavilions. Guest rooms come in several different price brackets ranging from standard island view to ocean vista, each with private balconies. If you're a big spender, corner suites with lots of space are the way to go, complete with wraparound balconies and king-sized beds looking out onto the water through floor-to-ceiling glass. Combination bathrooms (shower/tub) most often come with dressing areas and dual basins. We continue to get complaints from readers who found their bedrooms disappointing. Yet other readers have praised the accommodations. If at all possible, it's better to look at your room before checking in. The hotel seems to be in some sort of chaotic flux, so proceed carefully before making it your choice for a vacation.

Aside from a massive casino, the largest in The Bahamas, the complex contains a wide array of dining and drinking facilities. Two of its restaurants, Black Angus Grille for succulent steaks and other American fare, and Sole Mare with a gourmet Italian cuisine, are among the finest in New Providence. Even if you're not a guest of the hotel, you might want to avail yourself of the drinking and dining options or the casino action here.

W. Bay St. (P.O. Box N-8306), Cable Beach, Nassau, The Bahamas. ✆ **800/222-7466** in the U.S., or 242/327-6200. Fax 242/327-5227. www.wyndhamnassauresort.com. 850 units. Winter $179–$250 double, $250–$500 suite; off season $149–$169 double, $220–$230 suite. AE, DC, DISC, MC, V. Free self-parking, valet parking $5. Bus: 10. **Amenities:** 8 restaurants; 3 bars; outdoor pool; nearby golf course; 10 tennis courts; health club; Jacuzzi; sauna; children's programs (4–12); business center; 24-hr. room service; babysitting; laundry service; dry cleaning; nonsmoking rooms; rooms for those w/limited mobility. *In room:* A/C, TV, dataport (in some), minibar, coffeemaker, hair dryer, iron, safe.

MODERATE

Nassau Beach Hotel (Kids) This place has been somewhat overshadowed by the glitzy properties a short walk away, but a crowd of loyal fans—often families—comes every year, enjoying a 900m (2,952-ft.) white-sand beach. Guests here avoid the carnival at such neighboring megaresorts as the Wyndham Nassau Resort. A good value, the Nassau Beach is a conservative, moderately priced choice with a lively but restrained atmosphere.

The hotel was built in the 1940s, with three separate wings in a beige-and-white twin-towered design, and it features modified Georgian detailing and tile- and marble-covered floors. Today, the place has been enhanced by fresh landscaping and touches that include ceiling fans and mahogany, English-inspired furniture. Each of the midsize accommodations contains summery rattan pieces, comfortable beds, and a marble bathroom with a tub/shower combination.

On-site are five restaurants (including the Beef Cellar, which is reviewed under "Where to Dine"), plus entertainment in the evening (including live bands and dancing). It's also near the Crystal Palace Casino.

Family-Friendly Hotels

Camp Junkanoo at the Radisson Cable Beach (p. 87) provides a supervised program for children 4 to 11 at no additional cost. Activities include swimming, treasure hunts, and nature walks. Kids Klub at the Wyndham Nassau Resort offers supervised activities in the hotels own beachfront clubhouse, the Kids Klub Pavilion, for children aged 4 to 12. Activities range from scavenger hunts to nature exploration to beach games to Sega and Nintendo.

W. Bay St., P.O. Box N-7756, Cable Beach, Nassau, The Bahamas. © **888/627-7282** in the U.S., or 242/327-7711. Fax 242/327-8829. www.nassaubeachhotel.com. 400 units. $95–$150 double; $250–$300 1-bedroom suite; $350–$400 2-bedroom suite. AE, DISC, MC, V. Free parking. Bus: 10. **Amenities:** 5 restaurants; 3 bars; 2 pools; 6 tennis courts; health club; watersports equipment/rentals; babysitting; laundry service; nonsmoking rooms; Internet cafe; rooms for those w/limited mobility. *In room:* A/C, TV, hair dryer, iron, safe.

Westwind II *(Kids)*   Set on the western edge of Cable Beach's hotel strip, 9.5km (6 miles) from the center of Nassau, the Westwind II is a cluster of two-story buildings that contain two-bedroom, two-bathroom timeshare units, each with a full kitchen (there's a grocery store nearby). The size and facilities of these units make them ideal for traveling families. These units are available to the public whenever they're not otherwise occupied by investors. All the diversions of the megahotels are close by and easily reached, but in the complex itself, you can enjoy a low-key, quiet atmosphere and privacy. (A masonry wall separates the compound from the traffic of W. Bay St. and the hotels and vacant lots that flank it.) Each unit has a pleasant decor that includes white tiled floors, rattan furniture, bathrooms with shower/tub combinations, and either a balcony or a terrace. Since units are identical, price differences depend on whether the units face the beach, the pool, or the garden. The manicured grounds feature palms, flowering hibiscus shrubs, and seasonal flower beds. Don't stay here if you expect any of the luxuries or facilities of the nearby Nassau Beach Hotel (see above). Westwind II is more for do-it-yourself types.

W. Bay St. (P.O. Box CB-11006), Cable Beach, Nassau, The Bahamas. © **866/369-5921** or 242/327-7019. Fax 242/327-7529. www.westwindii.com. 54 units. Nov–Apr $1,579–$1,825 per week for up to 4 people; May–Oct $1,282–$1,400 per week for up to 4 people. MC, V. Bus: 10. **Amenities:** Bar; 2 pools; 2 tennis courts; babysitting; coin-operated laundry; rooms for those w/limited mobility. *In room:* A/C, TV, kitchen, fridge, coffeemaker, iron.

WEST OF CABLE BEACH

Compass Point *★★ (Finds)*   Charming, personalized, and casually upscale, this is an alternative to the megahotels of Cable Beach, which lie about 9.5km (6 miles) to the east. Think British colonial hip, with guests straight out of Soho (either London or New York) and a smattering of music-industry types. The place isn't as snobby as Graycliff, but for those who want an intimate inn and like the vibrant Bahamian colors, there is no other place like it on the island. Scattered over .8 hectares (2 acres) of some of the most expensive terrain in The Bahamas, the property lies beside one of the few sandy coves along the island's northwest coast, about 20 minutes from downtown Nassau and near a great snorkeling beach. The beach is very small, a sandy crescent that virtually disappears at high tide.

Each unit is a private, fully detached "hut" or cottage painted in pulsating, vivid colors. Everything larger than a studio has a kitchenette. Designed for privacy, all the units have exposed rafters, high ceilings with fans, and windows facing ocean breezes, and they have all been renovated, the furnishings replaced, the bathrooms and kitchens redone, and an air-conditioning system installed. Some of the huts are raised on stilts.

W. Bay St., (P.O. Box CB13842), Gambier, Love Beach, New Providence, The Bahamas. ℂ 800/633-3284 in the U.S., or 242/327-4500. Fax 242/327-2407. www.compasspointbahamas.com. 18 units. Winter $245 cabana, $305–$390 1-bedroom cottage, $470 2-bedroom cottage; off-season rates 20% lower. AE, MC, V. Free parking. Bus: Western Bus. **Amenities:** Bar; outdoor pool; limited room service; laundry service; dry cleaning; babysitting. *In room:* A/C, TV, mini-bar, coffeemaker, hair dryer, iron, safe.

Orange Hill Beach Inn ✹ *Finds*   This hotel, set on 1.4 landscaped hillside hectares (3½ acres), lies about 13km (8 miles) west of Nassau and 1.5km (1 mile) east of Love Beach, which has great snorkeling. It's perfect for those who want to escape the crowds and stay in a quieter part of New Providence Island; it's easy to catch a cab or jitney to Cable Beach or downtown Nassau. The welcoming owners, Judy and Danny Lowe, an Irish-Bahamian partnership, jokingly refer to their operation as "Fawlty Towers Nassau."

This place was built as a private home in the 1920s and became a hotel in 1979 after the Lowes added more rooms and a swimming pool. Rooms and apartments come in a variety of sizes, although most are small. The bathrooms, likewise, are small but well maintained. Each has a balcony or patio, and a few apartments are equipped with kitchenettes. Many of the guests are European, especially in summer. It has been renovated with updated furniture in the rooms, as well as upgrading the bathroom units.

On-site is a bar serving sandwiches and salads throughout the day, and a restaurant that offers simple but good dinners. Diving excursions to the rich marine fauna of New Providence's southwestern coast are among the most popular activities here.

W. Bay St., just west of Blake Rd. (P.O. Box N-8583), Nassau, The Bahamas. ℂ 888/399-3698 or 242/327-7157. Fax 242/327-5186. www.orangehill.com. 32 units. Winter $119–$130 double, $164 apt; off season $102–$117 double, $117–$140 apt. MC, V. Free parking. Bus: Western Bus. **Amenities:** Restaurant; bar; outdoor pool; laundry service and coin-operated laundry; rooms for those w/limited mobility. *In room:* A/C, TV, kitchenette (in some).

4 Where to Dine

NASSAU

Nassau restaurants open and close often. Even if reservations aren't required, it's a good idea to call first just to see that a place is still functioning. European and American cuisine are relatively easy to find in Nassau. Surprisingly, it used to be difficult to find Bahamian cuisine, but in recent years, more places have begun to offer authentic island fare.

VERY EXPENSIVE

Buena Vista ✹ CONTINENTAL/BAHAMIAN/SEAFOOD   Although not quite up there with Graycliff, this restaurant is definitely a runner-up in Nassau's culinary sweepstakes. It's a block west of Government House (Delancy St. is opposite the cathedral close off St. Francis Xavier, and only a short distance from Bay St.). It opened back in the 1940s in a colonial mansion set on 2 hectares (5 acres) of tropical foliage. Traditional elegance and fine preparations have always characterized this place.

You're likely to be shown to the main dining room, unless you request the cozy and intimate Victoria Room or, even better, the Garden Patio, which has a greenhouse setting and a ceiling skylight. The chef scours Nassau's markets to collect the freshest and finest ingredients, which he puts together in menus bursting with flavor and full of originality. Look for impromptu daily specials such as breaded veal chop or Long

Island duckling. Besides the nouvelle cuisine here, you'll also find respect for tradition. The rack of lamb Provençale is a classic, but you might want to try instead some of the lighter veal dishes. The cream of garlic soup has plenty of flavor but never overpowers. Instead of wildly fanciful desserts, Buena Vista sticks to the classics—say, cherries jubilee or baked Alaska flambé au cognac. Service is deft, efficient, and polite. Calypso coffee finishes the meal off nicely as you listen to soft piano music.

Delancy and Meeting sts. (✆) 242/322-2811. www.buenavista-restaurant.com. Reservations recommended. Main courses $28–$40; fixed-price dinner $38–$48. AE, MC, V. Mon–Sat 7–9:30pm.

Chez Willie ☆☆ FRENCH/BAHAMIAN   Elegant and romantic in aura, Chez Willie is a hot dinner reservation along Bay Street, luring visitors to Nassau in the evening. (*Note:* Most people arrive at the restaurant by taxi in lieu of wandering the deserted streets, which can be a bit dangerous at night.)

Jackets are preferred for men, and you can dine alfresco, listening to live piano music. Somehow this place recaptures some of the grandeur of Nassau in its cafe society days. In this relaxing atmosphere, you are likely to meet the host Willie Armstrong himself. You'll recognize him by his bow tie with jeweled clip, kissing the hand of female guests. In the courtyard is a fountain and regal statuary.

The food is exquisite. Launch into your repast by trying the stone crab claws with a Dijon mustard sauce or perhaps a fresh Bahamian tuna and crab mousse in a light sauce. Much of the fare here is familiar but beautifully prepared with first-rate ingredients. Main courses range from lobster thermidor to sautéed Dover sole in a tarragon-and-tomato-laced sauce. We often opt for the broiled seafood platter in a sauce made with fresh herbs. The chef's special is grouper in puff pastry with crabmeat, served with a coconut cream sauce. Special dinners for two, taking an hour, feature beef Wellington, a delicate chateaubriand, or roast rack of lamb.

W. Bay St. (✆) 242/322-5364. Reservations required. Jacket preferred for men. Main courses $30–$52; fixed-price menu for 2 $60–$100 per person. AE, DISC, MC, V. Daily 6:30–10pm.

Graycliff ☆ CONTINENTAL   Part of the Graycliff hotel, an antiques-filled colonial mansion located opposite Government House, this restaurant is the domain of connoisseur and bon vivant Enrico Garzaroli. The chefs use local Bahamian products whenever available and turn them into an old-fashioned, heavy cuisine that still has a lot of appeal for tradition-minded visitors, many of whom return here year after year. Young diners with more contemporary palates might head elsewhere, though, as the food has fallen off a bit of late. The chefs, neither completely traditional nor regional, produce such dishes as grouper soup in puff pastry, and plump, juicy pheasant cooked with pineapples grown on Eleuthera. Lobster is another specialty, half in beurre blanc and the other sided with a sauce prepared with the head of the lobster. Other standard dishes include escargots, foie gras, and *tournedos d'agneau* (lamb). The pricey wine list is the finest in the country, with more than 180,000 bottles. The collection of Cuban cigars here—almost 90 types—is said to be the most varied in the world.

W. Hill St. (✆) 242/322-2796. Reservations required. Jacket advised for men. Main courses lunch $20–$30, dinner $38–$52. AE, DISC, MC, V. Mon–Fri noon–3pm; daily 6:30–10pm. Bus: 10.

MODERATE

Café Matisse ☆ INTERNATIONAL/ITALIAN   Set directly behind Parliament House, in a peach building that was built a century ago as a private home, this restaurant is on everybody's short list of downtown Nassau favorites. It serves well-prepared

Italian and international cuisine to businesspeople, workers from nearby government offices, and all kinds of deal makers. There are dining areas within an enclosed courtyard, as well as on two floors of the interior, which is decorated with colorful Matisse prints. It's run by the sophisticated Bahamian-Italian team of Greg and Gabriella Curry, who prepare menu items that include an enticing cannelloni with lobster sauce; mixed grill of seafood; grilled rack of lamb with grilled tomatoes; a perfect filet mignon in a green-pepper sauce; and a zesty curried shrimp with rice. There are also meal-size pizzas.

Bank Lane at Bay St., just north of Parliament Sq. ✆ **242/356-7012.** Reservations recommended. Main courses lunch $14–$20, dinner $16–$35. AE, MC, V. Tues–Sat noon–3pm and 6–10pm. Bus: 17 and 21.

East Villa Restaurant and Lounge CHINESE/CONTINENTAL
You might imagine yourself in Hong Kong during the 1980s in this well-designed modern house across the road from the headquarters of the Nassau Yacht Club. It's somewhat upscale, sometimes attracting rich Florida yachters to its dimly lit precincts, where aquariums bubble in a simple but tasteful contemporary setting. Zesty Szechwan flavors appear on the menu, but there are less spicy Cantonese alternatives, including sweet-and-sour chicken and steamed vegetables with cashews and water chestnuts. Lobster tail in the spicy Chinese style is one of our favorites. Dishes can be ordered mild, medium, or zesty hot.

E. Bay St. ✆ **242/393-3377.** Reservations required. Lunch $8–$16; main courses $10–$38. AE, MC, V. Sun–Fri noon–3pm; daily 6–10pm. Bus: 11 or 19.

Gaylord's NORTHERN INDIAN
The Indian owners of this restaurant arrived in The Bahamas via Kenya and then England, and they are wryly amused at their success in "bringing India to The Bahamas." Within a room lined with Indian art and artifacts, you'll dine on a wide range of savory and zesty Punjabi, tandoori, and curried dishes. Some of the best choices are the lamb selections, although such concessions to local culture as curried or tandoori-style conch have also begun cropping up on the menu. If you don't know what to order, consider a tandoori mixed platter, which might satisfy two of you with a side dish or two. Any of the *korma* dishes, which combine lamb, chicken, beef, or vegetables in a creamy curry sauce, are very successful. Takeout meals are also available.

Dowdeswell St. at Bay St. ✆ **242/356-3004.** Reservations recommended. Main courses $15–$50; vegetarian dinner $25. AE, MC, V. Mon–Fri noon–3pm; daily 6:30–11pm. Bus: 10 or 17.

Poop Deck BAHAMIAN/SEAFOOD
This is a favorite with yachters and others who find a perch on the second-floor, open-air terrace, which overlooks the harbor and Paradise Island. If you like dining with a view, you won't find a better place than this in the heart of Nassau. At lunch, you can order conch chowder (perfectly seasoned) or a juicy beef burger. The waiters are friendly, the crowd is convivial, and the festivities continue into the evening with lots of drinking and good cheer. Native grouper fingers served with peas 'n' rice is the Bahamian soul food dish on the menu. Two of the best seafood selections are the fresh lobster and the stuffed mushrooms with crabmeat. The creamy homemade lasagna with crisp garlic bread is another fine choice.

Nassau Yacht Haven Marina, E. Bay St. ✆ **242/393-8175.** Reservations recommended. Lunch $15–$30; main courses $25–$52. AE, MC, V. Daily noon–4:30pm and 5–10:30pm. Bus: 10, 19, or 23.

Shoal Restaurant and Lounge BAHAMIAN
Many of our good friends in Nassau swear that this is the best joint for authentic local food. We're not entirely convinced

this is true, but we rank it near the top. The place is a beehive of activity on Saturday mornings, when seemingly half of Nassau shows up for the chef's specialty, boiled fish and johnnycake. This may or may not be your fantasy, but to a Bahamian it's like pot liquor and turnip greens with cornbread to a Southerner. Far removed from the well-trodden tourist path, this restaurant is a real favorite of residents. After all, where else can you get a good bowl of okra soup these days? Naturally, conch chowder is the preferred opener. Many diners follow the chowder with more conch, "cracked" this time. But you can also order some unusual dishes such as Bahamian-style mutton using native spices and herbs. The seafood platter—with lobster, shrimp, and fried grouper— is more international in appeal. Peas 'n' rice accompanies everything. The restaurant even offers to transport you to and from the restaurant from your hotel free of charge.

Nassau St. ⓒ **242/323-4400.** Main courses $9–$38. AE, DISC, MC, V. Daily 7:30am–10:30pm.

INEXPENSIVE

Bahamian Kitchen *Value* *Kids* BAHAMIAN   Next to Trinity Church, this is one of the best places for good Bahamian food at modest prices. Down-home dishes, full of local flavor, include lobster Bahamian style, fried red snapper, conch salad, stewed fish, curried chicken, okra soup, and pea soup and dumplings. Most dishes are served with peas 'n' rice. You can order such old-fashioned Bahamian fare as stewed fish and corned beef and grits, all served with johnnycake. If you'd like to introduce your kids to Bahamian cuisine, this is an ideal choice. There's takeout service if you're planning a picnic.

Trinity Place, off Market St. ⓒ **242/325-0702.** Lunch $6–$13; main courses $9–$23. AE, MC, V. Mon–Sat 11am–10pm. Bus: 10.

Café Skans *Value* INTERNATIONAL   This is a straightforward, Formica-clad diner with an open kitchen, offering flavorful food that's served without fanfare in generous portions. It's next door to the Straw Market site, attracting local residents and office workers from the government buildings nearby. Menu items include Bahamian fried or barbecued chicken; bean soup with dumplings; souvlakia or gyros in pita bread; and burgers, steaks, and various kinds of seafood platters. This is where workaday Nassau comes for breakfast.

Bay St., adjacent to the Straw Market. ⓒ **242/322-2486.** Reservations required. Breakfast $4–$9; sandwiches $6–$19; main-course platters $6–$25. MC, V. Mon–Fri 8am–5pm; Sat–Sun 8am–6pm.

Conch Fritters Bar & Grill BAHAMIAN/INTERNATIONAL   A true local hang-out with real island atmosphere, this light-hearted restaurant changes its focus several times throughout the day. Lunches and dinners are high-volume, high-turnover affairs mitigated only by attentive staff who seem genuinely concerned about the well-being of their guests. Live music is presented every day except Monday from 7pm until closing, when the place transforms again into something of a singles bar. Food choices are rather standard but still quite good, including cracked conch, fried shrimp, grilled salmon, six different versions of chicken, blackened rib-eye steak, burgers, and sandwiches. Specialty drinks from the active bar include a Goombay Smash.

Marlborough St. (across from the British Colonial Hilton). ⓒ **242/323-8801.** Burgers, sandwiches, and platters $10–$40. AE, MC, V. Daily 10am–11:30pm.

Crocodiles Waterfront Bar & Grill INTERNATIONAL/BAHAMIAN   One of the most appealing, funky bar/restaurants in Nassau lies about a 2-minute walk from the Nassau side of the Paradise Island Bridge, with a view over the water. Set on a deck that's partially protected with thatched parasols but mostly open to the sky and a view of the channel, it's completely casual. (You'll recognize the place by the hundreds of stenciled crocodiles happily cavorting on the wall that separates the place from the dense traffic of E. Bay St.) After one of the rum concoctions from the bar, you might get into the swing of things. If you're hungry, order up cracked or grilled conch, a grilled 10-ounce sirloin steak, teriyaki-marinated tuna, grilled lobster tail, Bahamian-style fried chicken, crab cakes, or the standard but creamy lasagna. A particularly good sandwich choice is blackened mahimahi. There's a lounge on the premises with frequent live entertainment.

E. Bay St. ℂ 242/323-3341. Main courses $11–$33. AE, DISC, MC, V. Daily 11am–midnight. Bus: 10 or 17.

Double Dragon CANTONESE/SZECHWAN   The chefs hail from the province of Canton in mainland China, and that's the inspiration for most of the food here. If you've ever really wondered about the differences between Cantonese and Szechwan cuisine, a quick look at the menu here will highlight them. Lobster, chicken, or beef, for example, can be prepared Cantonese style, with a mild black-bean or ginger sauce; or in spicier Szechwan formats of red peppers, chiles, and garlic. Honey-garlic chicken and orange-flavored shrimp are always popular and succulent. Overall, this place is a fine choice if you're eager for a change from grouper and burgers.

Bridge Plaza Commons, Mackey St. ℂ 242/393-5718. Main courses $8–$22. AE, DISC, MC, V. Mon–Thurs noon–10pm; Fri noon–11pm; Sat 4–11pm; Sun 5–10pm. Bus: 10.

Palm Tree ⊛ (Value) BAHAMIAN/AMERICAN   This restaurant occupies the homestead of a Bahamian matriarch, Lydia Russell, who died in the 1980s. This place is set within a white-and-green-colored stucco house in the heart of Nassau. Inside, you'll find lots of exposed wood, a color scheme of white and black, and lots of local paintings inspired by Junkanoo. Menu items are as down-home as you can get (cracked conch, baked pork chops, fried or steamed grouper, minced or broiled lobster, and baked chicken) and are served with two of at least seven side dishes like potato salad, creamed corn, beets, coleslaw, macaroni and cheese, peas 'n' rice, or fried plantains.

Corner of Market and Cockburn sts. ℂ 242/322-4201. Main courses $6–$10. No credit cards. Mon–Sat 8am–10pm. Bus: 8.

CABLE BEACH
VERY EXPENSIVE
The Black Angus Grille ⊛ INTERNATIONAL/STEAKS/SEAFOOD   This is your best bet for dining if you're testing your luck at the Crystal Palace Casino nearby (and you may need to win to pay the hefty bill here). The Rotisserie in the Sheraton

---

(Finds) The Secret Garden

The Retreat, Village Road (ℂ 242/393-1317), consists of 4.4 hectares (11 acres) of the most unspoiled gardens on New Providence, even more intriguing than the Botanical Gardens. They're home to about 200 species of exotic palm trees. You'll think you've wandered into *1001 Arabian Nights* in this true oasis in the heart of Nassau. Tours are self-guided. This is the home of The Bahamas National Trust, and the grounds (without the tours) can be visited Monday through Friday from 9am to 5pm for a $2 admission for adults and $1 for children/students.

Grand Resort Paradise Island has the edge and is also more reasonably priced, but this is a close runner-up. Serving some of the best beef and steaks along Cable Beach, it's the favorite of hundreds of casino goers. Set one floor above the gambling tables, it has a boldly geometric decor of brightly colored tile work and comfortable banquettes.

Although steaks are frozen and flown in from the mainland, they are well prepared—succulent, juicy, and cooked to your specifications. The filet mignon is especially delectable, although the T-bone always seems to have more flavor. Prime rib is a nightly feature. The kitchen also prepares a number of sumptuous seafood platters, and Bahamian lobster tails here are fresh and flavorful.

In the Wyndham Nassau Resort & Crystal Palace Casino, W. Bay St. (*) 242/327-6200. Reservations recommended. Main courses $35–$60. AE, DC, DISC, MC, V. Daily 6–11pm. Bus: 10.

Sole Mare 🏆🏆 NORTHERN ITALIAN   This is our top choice for elegant dining along Cable Beach, and it also serves the best Northern Italian cuisine along the beach strip. The chefs are well trained and inventive. A filet of whatever fresh fish is available that day appears on the menu and is the keynote of many a delectable meal here. Many of the other ingredients have to be imported from the mainland, but the chefs still work their magic with them. Our lobster tail stuffed with crabmeat was a splendid choice, as was our dining partner's veal scaloppine sautéed with fresh mushrooms. Veal also appears rather delectably sautéed with endive, a dish you might enjoy in an upmarket tavern in northern Italy. The dessert soufflés are excellent, especially when served with the vanilla sauce.

In the Wyndham Nassau Resort & Crystal Palace Casino, W. Bay St. (*) 242/327-6200. Reservations required. Main courses $35–$70. AE, DC, DISC, MC, V. Thurs–Sat 3–11pm (hours may vary, call ahead). Bus: 10.

EXPENSIVE

The Beef Cellar 🏆 STEAKS/SEAFOOD   If you like steak, look no farther than Cable Beach and its Nassau Beach Hotel. The steaks here are juicy, succulent, and tender—and cooked just as you like. Located downstairs from the hotel's lobby, within a short walk of the casino at the neighboring Wyndham Nassau Resort, the Beef Cellar features a warmly masculine decor of exposed stone and leather, two-fisted drinks, and tables that have individual charcoal grills for diners who prefer to grill their own steaks. The seafood platters are also superb, including shrimp kabob and grilled salmon in a dill sauce. The prices here are more reasonable than those at the Black Angus Grille in the Wyndham Resort.

In the Nassau Beach Hotel. (*) 242/327-7711. Main courses $20–$40. AE, DC, MC, V. Daily 6:30–10pm.

Provence 🏆 MEDITERRANEAN   The best dishes in Nassau that feature the sunny cuisine of Provence in France are showcased here with the chef's self-styled *cuisine du soleil.* Lying near the end of West Bay Street, Provence prepares many dishes with superb simplicity—Atlantic salmon with citrus butter, for example—so as not to mar the natural flavor. Other dishes are heavily spiced such as the rib-eye steak in a fire-breathing pepper sauce. Although lacking certain key ingredients (such as hogfish), the chefs also turn out a delightful bouillabaisse evocative of the type served in Marseille. Daily seafood specials are featured—our favorite being the pan-seared sea bass, or else you might order the filet of black grouper.

Old Town Sandyport. (*) 242/327-0985. Reservations required. Main courses $27–$40. AE, DISC, MC, V. Mon–Sat 11:30am–3pm and 6–10:30pm.

MODERATE

Capriccio ITALIAN/INTERNATIONAL   Set beside a prominent roundabout, about .5km (⅓-mile) west of the megahotels of Cable Beach, this restaurant lies within a grandly Italian building with Corinthian columns and an outdoor terrace. Inside, it's a lot less formal, outfitted like a luncheonette, but with lots of exposed granite, busy espresso machines, and kindly Bahamian staff who have been trained in their understanding of Italian culinary nuance. At lunch you get pretty ordinary fare such as fresh salads, sandwiches, and a few hot platters like cracked conch. But the cooks shine at night, offering dishes such as chicken breast with sage and wine sauce, spaghetti with pesto and pine nuts, and seafood platters.

W. Bay St. *©* 242/327-8547. Reservations recommended. Lunch items $6–$17; dinner main courses $15–$28. MC, V. Mon–Sat 11am–10pm; Sun 5–10pm.

The Poop Deck at Sandy Port INTERNATIONAL/SEAFOOD   This is the largest and most imposing restaurant west of Cable Beach, convenient for the owners of the many upscale villas and condos that surround it. It's set within a pink concrete building that's highly visible from West Bay Street—but despite its impressive exterior, it's a bit sterile-looking on the inside. This simple island restaurant evolved from a roughneck bar that occupied this site during the early 1970s. Lunch is usually devoted to well-prepared burgers, pastas, sandwiches, and salads. Dinners are more substantial, featuring filet mignon, surf and turf (seafood and steak combo), cracked conch, and fried shrimp caught off the Bahamian Long Island. The house drink is a Bacardi splish-splash, containing Bacardi Select, Nassau Royal Liqueur, pineapple juice, cream, and sugar-cane syrup.

Poop Deck Dr., off W. Bay St. *©* 242/327-DECK. Reservations recommended. Main courses lunch $10–$30, dinner $19–$60. AE, DISC, MC, V. Tues–Sun noon–10:30pm.

INEXPENSIVE

Café Johnny Canoe *(Kids* INTERNATIONAL/BAHAMIAN   There's absolutely nothing stylish about this place (it was originally a Howard Johnson's), but because of its good value and cheerful staff, it's almost always filled with satisfied families. Within a yellow-painted interior that's accented with Junkanoo memorabilia, you can order filling portions of diner-style food with a Bahamian twist: cracked conch and lobster, grilled mahimahi, grouper fingers with tartar sauce, homemade soups, and fried fish. Sandwiches always come with one side order; platters always come with two. The place is named after the legend of a Bahamian slave who escaped in the canoe of a Junkanoo band. There's live Junkanoo music, accented with goatskin drums and synchronized cowbells, on Friday nights.

In the Nassau Beach Hotel, W. Bay St. *©* 242/327-3373. Breakfast $6–$14; salads, sandwiches, and lunch and dinner platters $12–$30. AE, DISC, MC, V. Daily 7:30am–11pm.

WEST OF CABLE BEACH

Travellers Rest *(★ (Value* BAHAMIAN/SEAFOOD   Set in an isolated spot about 2.5km (1½ miles) west of the megahotels of Cable Beach, this restaurant feels far away from it all. Its owners will make you feel like you're dining on a remote Out Island. Travellers Rest is set in a cozy cement-sided house that stands in a grove of sea-grape and palm trees facing the ocean. It was established by Winnipeg-born Joan Hannah in 1972, and since then has fed ordinary as well as famous folks like Stevie Wonder, Gladys Knight, spy novelist Robert Ludlum, Julio Iglesias, Eric Clapton, and Rosa Parks. You can dine outside, but if it's rainy (highly unlikely), you can go inside the tavern with its small bar decorated with local paintings. Many diners use the white-sand beach across from the restaurant to get here; others pull up in their own boats. In this laid-back atmosphere, you can feast on well-prepared grouper fingers, barbecue ribs, curried chicken, steamed or cracked conch, or minced crawfish, and finish perhaps with guava cake, the best on the island. The conch salad served on the weekends is said to increase virility in men.

W. Bay St., near Gambier (14km/8¾ miles west of the center of Nassau). ℭ 242/327-7633. Main courses lunch $7.50–$25, dinner $14–$28. AE, MC, V. Daily noon–11pm. Bus: Western Bus.

5 Beaches, Watersports & Other Outdoor Pursuits

One of the great sports centers of the world, Nassau and the islands that surround it are marvelous places for swimming, sunning, snorkeling, scuba diving, boating, water-skiing, and deep-sea fishing, as well as tennis and golf.

You can learn more about most of the available activities by calling **The Bahamas Sports Tourist Office** (ℭ **800/32-SPORT** or 954/236-9292) from anywhere in the continental United States. Call Monday through Friday from 9am to 5pm, EST. Or, write the center at 1200 South Pine Island Rd., Suite 750, Plantation, FL 33324.

HITTING THE BEACH

In the Bahamas, as in Puerto Rico, the issue about public access to beaches is a hot and controversial subject. Recognizing this, the government has made efforts to intersperse public beaches with easy access between more private beaches where access may be impeded. Although megaresorts discourage nonresidents from easy access to their individual beaches, there are so many public beaches on New Providence Island and Paradise Island that all a beach lover has to do is stop his or her car (or else walk) to many of the unmarked, unnamed beaches that flank the edge of these islands.

The average visitor will not have a problem with beaches because most people stay in one of the large beachfront resorts where the ocean meets the sand right outside of the hotel.

For those hoping to explore more of the coast, here are the "no problem, man" beaches—the ones that are absolutely accessible to the public:

Cable Beach ✮✮   No particular beach is actually called Cable Beach, yet this is the most popular beachfront on New Providence Island. Instead of an actual beach, Cable Beach is the name given to a string of resorts and beaches that lie in the center of New Providence's northern coast, attracting the most visitors. This beachfront offers 6.5km (4 miles) of soft white sand, with many different types of food, restaurants, snack bars, and watersports offered by the hotels lining the waterfront. Calypso music floats to the sand from hotel pool patios where vacationers play musical chairs and see how low they can limbo. Vendors wend their way between sunblock-slathered bodies. Some sell armloads of shell jewelry, T-shirts, beach cover-ups, and fresh coconuts for sipping the sweet "water" straight from the shell. Others offer their hair-braiding services or sign up visitors for water-skiing, jet skiing, and banana boat rides. Kiosks advertise parasailing, scuba-diving, and snorkeling trips, as well as party cruises to offshore islands. Waters can be rough and reefy, then calm and clear a little farther along the shore. There are no public toilets here, because guests of the resorts use their hotel facilities. If you're not a guest of the hotel, or not a customer, you are not supposed to use the facilities. Cable Beach resorts begin 4.8km (3 miles) west of downtown Nassau. Even though resorts line much of this long swath of beach, there are various sections where public access is available without crossing through private hotel grounds.

Caves Beach   On the north shore, past the Cable Beach Hotel properties, Caves Beach is 11km (7 miles) southwest of Nassau. It stands near Rock Point, right before the turnoff along Blake Road that leads to the airport. Since visitors often don't know of this place, it's a good spot to escape the hordes. It's also a good beach with soft sands. There are no toilets or changing facilities.

Delaporte Beach   Just west of the busiest section of Cable Beach, Delaporte Beach is a public access beach where you can also escape the crowds. It opens onto clear waters and boasts white sands, although it has no facilities, including toilets. Nonetheless, it's an option.

Goodman's Bay   This public beach lies east of Cable Beach on the way toward the center of Nassau. Goodman's Bay and Saunders Beach (see below) often host local fund-raising cookouts, where vendors sell fish, chicken, conch, peas 'n' rice, or macaroni and cheese. People swim and socialize to blaring reggae and calypso music. To find out when one of these beach parties is happening, ask the staff at your hotel or pick up a local newspaper. A playground is here, along with toilet facilities.

Old Fort Beach ★   We often head here to escape the crowds on weekdays, a 15-minute drive west of the Nassau International Airport (take W. Bay St. toward Lyford Cay). This lovely sandy beach opens onto the turquoise waters of Old Fort Bay near the western part of New Providence. The least developed of the island's beaches, it attracts many homeowners from swanky Lyford Cay nearby. In winter, the beach can be quite windy, but in summer it's as calm as the Caribbean Sea.

Saunders Beach   East of Cable Beach, this is where many islanders go on the weekends. To reach it, take West Bay Street from Nassau in the direction of Coral Island. This beach lies across from Fort Charlotte, just west of Arawak Cay. Like Goodman's Bay (see above) it often hosts local fund-raising cookouts open to the public. These can be a lot of fun. There are no public facilities.

Western Esplanade   If you're staying at a hotel in downtown Nassau, such as the British Colonial, this one (also known as Junkanoo Beach) is a good beach to patronize close to town. On this narrow strip of sand convenient to Nassau, you'll find toilets, changing facilities, and a snack bar.

BIKING

A half-day bicycle tour with **Bahamas Outdoors Ltd.** (© **242/362-2772;** about $60) can take you on a 5km (3-mile) bike ride along some scenic forest and shoreline trails in the Coral Harbour area on the southwestern coast of New Providence. You pass along a trail that has mangrove creeks and pine forests as a scenic backdrop and can take time off for a kayak trip to a shallow for snorkeling. Some of the major hotels on Paradise Beach and Cable Beach rent bikes to their guests. You can bike along Cable Beach or the beachfront at Paradise Island, but Nassau traffic is too congested.

BOAT CRUISES

Cruises from the harbors around New Providence Island are offered by a number of operators, with trips ranging from daytime voyages for snorkeling, picnicking, sunning, and swimming, to sunset and moonlight cruises.

Finds **A Beach for Lovers**

Continuing west along West Bay Street, you reach **Love Beach,** across from Sea Gardens, a good stretch of sand lying east of Northwest Point. Love Beach, although not big, is a special favorite with lovers. The snorkeling is superb, too. It's technically private, though no one bothers visitors who come, and locals fervently hope it won't ever become overrun like Cable Beach.

Barefoot Sailing Cruises, Bay Shore Marina (✆ **242/393-0820;** www.barefoot sailingcruises.com) runs the *Wind Dance,* which leaves for all-day cruises from this dock, offering many sailing and snorkeling possibilities. This is your best bet if you're seeking a more romantic cruise and don't want 100 people aboard. The cruises usually stop at Rose Island, which is a charming, picture-perfect spot, with an uncrowded white sandy beach and palm trees. You can also sail on a ketch, the 16m (52-ft.) *Riding High,* which is bigger than the 12m (39-ft.) *Wind Dance.* Cruise options are plentiful, ranging from a half-day of sailing, snorkeling, and exploring ($55), to a full day ($89), to private dinner cruises of 3 moonlit hours ($650 for two people). If the cruise becomes a party, $500 is charged for the first two guests, then $65 for each additional person.

Flying Cloud, Paradise Island West Dock (✆ **242/363-4430**), features catamaran cruises carrying 50 people on day and sunset trips. It's a good bet for people who want a more intimate cruise and shy away from the heavy volume carried aboard Majestic Tours catamarans (see below). Snorkeling equipment is provided free. Monday to Saturday half-day charters cost $50 per person; a 2½-hour sunset cruise goes for $50. Evening bookings are on Monday, Wednesday, and Friday. A 5-hour cruise leaves on Sunday at 10am that costs $65 per person.

Majestic Tours Ltd., Hillside Manor (✆ **242/322-2606**), will book 3-hour cruises on two of the biggest catamarans in the Atlantic, offering views of the water, sun, sand, and outlying reefs. This is the biggest and most professionally run of the cruise boats, and it's an affordable option; but we find that there are just too many other passengers aboard. The *Yellow Bird* is suitable for up to 250 passengers. It departs from Prince George's Dock; ask for the exact departure point when you make your reservation. The cost is $18 per adult, $9 for children under 10, and snorkeling equipment is $10 extra. The outfitter has also added another boat, the *Robinson Crusoe,* holding 350 passengers. On Wednesday, Friday, and Sunday, there are cruises from 10am to 4:30pm, costing $45 for adults and half price for children 11 and under. Sunset dinner cruises from 7 to 10pm on Tuesday and Friday cost $50 per adult, again half price for children.

FISHING

May to August are the best months for the oceanic bonito and the blackfin tuna; June and July for blue marlin; and November through February for the wahoo found in reefy areas.

Arrangements can be made at any of the big hotels, but unfortunately, there's a hefty price tag. Prices are usually $350 for a half-day boat rental for parties of two to six, or $700 for a full day's fishing.

One of the most reliable companies, **Born Free Charters** (✆ **242/393-4144**), offers a fleet of three vessels that can seat six comfortably; they can be rented for a half-day

($450–$600) or a full day ($900–$1,200). Each additional person is charged $50 depending on boat size. Fishing choices are plentiful: You can troll for wahoo, tuna, and marlin in the deep sea, or cast in the shallows for snapper, grouper, and yellowtail. Anchoring and bottom-fishing are calmer options. We recommend this charter because Born Free offers so many types of fishing and gives you a lot of leeway regarding where you want to fish and how much time you want to spend.

Occasionally, a boat owner will configure him- or herself and their boat as a venue for deep-sea fishing, and unless you're dealing with a genuinely experienced guide, your fishing trip may or may not be a success. Two of the most consistently reliable deep-sea fishermen are the father-son team of John and Teddy Pratt, who maintain 11m (36-ft.) and 13m (43-ft.) boats, either of which is available for full- or half-day deep-sea fishing excursions. Both boats dock every night at the island's largest marina, the 150-slip **Nassau Yacht Haven,** on East Bay Street (② **242/393-8173**), where a member of the staff will direct you toward either of the two boats. Alternatively, you can call ② **242/422-0364** to speak to one of the men directly. It takes about 20 minutes of boat travel to reach an offshore point where dolphin and wahoo may or may not be biting, depending on a raft of complicated seasonable factors. These trips need to be booked weeks in advance.

GOLF

Some of the best golfing in The Bahamas is found in Nassau. The following courses are open to the public, not just to guests of the hotels that operate the properties.

Radisson Cable Beach Golf Course ★★ on West Bay Road, Cable Beach (② **242/ 327-6000**), is a spectacular 18-hole, 7,040-yard, par-72 championship golf course that's better than ever. The redesign of the course features a reshaping of the course's fairways, repositioning of greens, and the creation of new hazards and water-lined holes through two-thirds of the course. Better year-round playing conditions have been assured by the addition of a salt-tolerant grass known as paspalum that is greener, firmer and more upright, withstanding the salty breezes and tropical climate while offering a premium putting surface. The development was overseen by veteran designer and consultant Fred M. Settle, Jr., of International Golf Design, Inc. The Cable Beach course is under the management of the Radisson Cable Beach Hotel, but it's often used by guests of the other hotels nearby. Greens fees are $105 for residents of The Bahamas and for people staying at the Radisson, $135 to $150 for all other players. Carts are included.

HORSEBACK RIDING

Happy Trails Stables, Coral Harbour, on the southwest shore (② **242/362-1820;** www.windsorequestriancentre.com), offers a 90-minute horseback trail ride for $95, including free transportation to and from your hotel. Riders must weigh less than 200 pounds. The stables are signposted from the Nassau International Airport, which is 3km (2 miles) away. Children must be 12 or older, and reservations are required, especially during the holiday season.

SNORKELING, SCUBA DIVING & UNDERWATER WALKS

There's great snorkeling off most of the beaches on New Providence, especially **Love Beach.** Most any of the hotels and resorts will rent or loan you snorkeling equipment. Several of the companies mentioned above under "Boat Cruises" also offer snorkel trips, as does Bahamas Divers, below. See also "Easy Side Trips to Nearby Islands," later, for additional snorkeling excursions.

Our favorite sight for snorkeling is **Goulding Cay,** lying off the western tip of New Providence. Underwater you'll find a virtual field of hard corals, especially the elegant elkhorn. The clear waters here and the shallow coral heads make it ideal for filmmakers. In fact, it's been featured in many films, ranging from a number of 007 movies to *20,000 Leagues Under the Sea.* More elkhorn coral awaits you to the south at **Southwest Reef,** which also has some stunning star coral found in water less than 2.4m (8 ft.) deep in many places. To the north is the curiously named **Fish Hotel,** which is not much on coral but is graced with large schools of fish, especially red snapper, jacks, and grunts.

There are more dive sites around New Providence than you can see in one visit, so we've included a few of our favorites. **Shark Wall** ✿✿ is the most intriguing, which is a diving excursion 16km (10 miles) off the coast; others include the **Rose Island Reefs,** the **Southwest Reef,** the **Razorback,** and **Booby Rock Reef.** Dive outfitters can also lead you to many old shipwrecks off the coast, along with caves and cliffs. Wrecks include *Mahoney* and *Alcora,* plus the wreck used in the James Bond film, *Never Say Never Again.* Divers also explore the airplane propeller used in another Bond film, *Thunderball.* All dive outfitters feature one or more of these sites.

Bahamas Divers, East Bay Street (✆ **242/393-5644**), has packages that range from a half-day of snorkeling at offshore reefs for $30 per person, to a half-day scuba trip with preliminary pool instruction for beginners for $89 for two tanks or $55 for one tank; other equipment is an additional cost. Half-day excursions for certified divers to deeper outlying reefs, drop-offs, and blue holes can be arranged.

Participants receive free transportation from their hotel to the boats. Children must be 10 or older, and reservations are required, especially during the holiday season.

Hartley's Undersea Walk ✿, East Bay Street (✆ **242/393-8234**), offers an exciting and educational experience. They take you out from Nassau Harbour aboard the yacht *Pied Piper.* During the 3½-hour cruise, you take a boat ride out to a reef. After donning a lead and glass helmet, you descend a ladder into 4 to 5m (12–15 ft.) of water. Air is pumped into the helmet through a long tube. You can keep your glasses on or your contact lenses in, because your face and hair stay completely dry. For about 25 minutes, you walk through a garden of tropical fish, sponges, and other undersea life.

Entire families can go on this safe adventure, which costs $125 (no reduced child's fare). You don't even have to be able to swim. Two trips run per day, at 9:30am and 1:30pm, Tuesday through Saturday. Arrive 30 minutes before departures, and make reservations 5 to 10 days in advance. Free transportation is available to and from your hotel.

Stuart Cove's Dive Bahamas, Southwest Bay Street, South Ocean (P.O. Box CB13137, Nassau; ✆ **800/879-9832** in the U.S. or 242/362-4171), is about 10 minutes from top dive sites, including the coral reefs, wrecks, and an underwater airplane structure used in filming James Bond thrillers. Divers on expeditions here are taken to the island's most thrilling underwater site, the wreck of the *Caribe Breeze,* depicted in the film, *Open Water.* The staff here feeds reef sharks some 15m (49 ft.) below the surface, and, from a position of safety, snorkelers above can see the show down below. The Porpoise Pen Reefs, named for Flipper, and steep sea walls are also on the diving agenda. A two-tank dive in the morning costs $88, or an all-day program goes for $135. All prices for boat dives include tanks, weights, and belts. An open-water certification course starts at $695. Bring along two friends, and the price drops to $495 per person. Escorted boat snorkeling trips cost $48; children under 12 are $24. A special feature is a series of shark-dive experiences priced from $135. In one outing, Caribbean reef sharks swim among the guests. In one dive, called Shark Arena, divers kneel down while a dive master feeds the sharks off a long pole. Another experience, the Shark Buoy in 1,800m (5,904 ft.) of ocean, involves a dive among silky-skinned sharks at about 9m (30 ft.). They swim among the divers while the dive master feeds them.

The outfitter has generated much excitement with its introduction of yellow "submarines," actually jet bikes called Scenic Underwater Bubbles. An air-fed bubble covers your head as these self-contained and battery-powered jet bikes propel you through an underwater wonderland. The subs are popular with nondivers, and they're viewed as safe for kids as well (that is, those older than 12). An underwater armada is escorted along to view the reefs, all for a cost of $99. The whole experience, from pickup at your hotel or cruise ship to return, takes about 3 hours.

TENNIS

Courts are available at some hotels. Guests usually play free or for a nominal fee, whereas visitors are charged.

Most of the courts at Cable Beach are under the auspices of the **Radisson Cable Beach Hotel,** West Bay Street (© 242/327-6000). Residents of Radisson play free until sunset. Non-Radisson guests pay $10 per person per hour.

Another hotel offering tennis courts is the **Nassau Beach Hotel,** West Bay Street and Cable Beach (© 242/327-7711), with six Flexipave night-lit courts. Guests play for free between 9am to 5pm (after 5pm $7 per hr.) and nonguests play for $7 per hour.

6 Seeing the Sights

Most of Nassau can be explored on foot, beginning at Rawson Square in the center. Here is where Bahamian fishers unload a variety of produce and fish—crates of mangoes, oranges, tomatoes, and limes, plus lots of crimson-lipped conch. To experience this slice of Bahamian life, go any morning Monday through Saturday before noon.

The best way to see some of the major public buildings of Nassau is to take our walking tour (see below), which will give you not only an overview of the historic sights, but also a feel for the city as a whole. Then you can concentrate on specific sights you'd like to take in, notably Ardastra Gardens and Coral Island Bahamas.

THE TOP ATTRACTIONS

Ardastra Gardens ★   The main attraction of the Ardastra Gardens, almost 2 hectares (5 acres) of lush tropical planting about 1.5km (1 mile) west of downtown Nassau near Fort Charlotte, is the parading flock of **pink flamingos.** The Caribbean flamingo, national bird of The Bahamas, had almost disappeared by the early 1940s but was brought back to significant numbers through the efforts of the National Trust. They now flourish in the rookery on Great Inagua. A flock of these exotic feathered creatures has been trained to march in drill formation, responding to the drillmaster's commands with long-legged precision and discipline. A flock of marching flamingos perform daily at 10:30am, 2:10pm, and 4:10pm.

Other exotic wildlife at the gardens include boa constrictors (very tame), kinkajous (honey bears) from Central and South America, green-winged macaws, peacocks and peahens, blue-and-yellow macaws, capuchin monkeys, iguanas, ring-tailed lemurs, red-ruff lemurs, margays, brown-headed tamarins (monkeys), and a crocodile. There are also numerous waterfowl to be seen in Swan Lake, including black swans from Australia and several species of wild ducks. Parrot feedings are at 11am, 1:30pm, and 3:30pm.

You can get a good look at Ardastra's flora by walking along the signposted paths. Many of the more interesting and exotic trees bear plaques with their names.

What to See & Do in Nassau

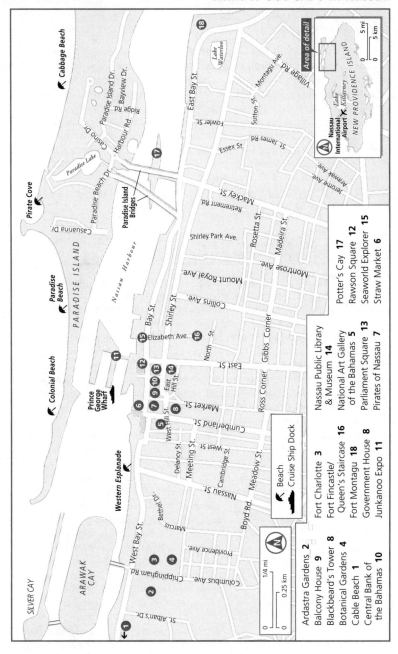

Ardastra Gardens **2**
Balcony House **9**
Blackbeard's Tower **8**
Botanical Gardens **4**
Cable Beach **1**
Central Bank of
the Bahamas **10**

Fort Charlotte **3**
Fort Fincastle/
Queen's Staircase **16**
Fort Montagu **18**
Government House **8**
Junkanoo Expo **11**

Nassau Public Library
& Museum **14**
National Art Gallery
of the Bahamas **5**
Parliament Square **13**
Pirates of Nassau **7**

Potter's Cay **17**
Rawson Square **12**
Seaworld Explorer **15**
Straw Market **6**

Chippingham Rd. © 242/323-5806. www.ardastra.com. Admission $12 adults, $6 children 4–12 years old, under 4 free. Daily 9am–4:30pm. Bus: 10.

National Art Gallery of The Bahamas ⭐ At long last this archipelago nation has a national showcase to display its talented artists. In a restored historic building in the center of Nassau, the gallery showcases Bahamian art, past and present. Bahamian art as an entity has existed for only 50 years. Museum curators claim that the present collection is only the nucleus of a long-range strategy to beef up the present number of works. Most of the paintings on exhibit are divided into a historical and a contemporary collection. Pioneering Bahamian artists are honored, as are younger and more modern painters. Perhaps in the realm of primitive or even native art, many of the paintings are quite sophisticated, especially Amos Ferguson's *Snowbirds*. He used house paint on cardboard to create a remarkable portrait.

Villa Doyle, West Hill St. © 242/328-5800. www.nagb.org.bs. Admission $3 adults, $2 seniors and students, $1 children 14 and under. Tues–Sat 11am–4pm.

Finds   **Hanging Out at Potter's Cay**

The liveliest place in Nassau during the day is Potter's Cay, a native market that thrives beneath the Paradise Island Bridge. From the Out Islands, fishing boats and heavily laden sloops arrive early in the morning to unload the day's catch. These boats carry the most expensive catch, the spiny lobster, but grouper is king along with fresh crab, jack, mackerel, and other fish,

If grouper is king, then "sweet, sexy conch," as the locals say, is queen. Conch is arguably the Bahamian's favorite dish. At dozens of stands you can watch the conch being extracted from its shell. These shells are later dried out (they're really smelly for days) and sold as highly polished souvenirs. Vendors make the freshest conch salad right on the spot here; if you haven't eaten the delicacy before, this is the place to try it.

You'll see chefs eagerly buying the best of the day's catch to inspire their menus for the day. Fish is sold dead or alive and in some cases dried or filleted. What we don't like to see are fishmongers chopping up sea turtles, an endangered species. The vendors are not of the politically correct sort, and they're more likely interested in catering to the Bahamian life-long love of turtle flesh than they are in preserving the species for future generations.

Not just fish is sold here. Sloops from the Out Islands also bring in cartons of freshly harvested vegetables, including the fiery hot peppers so beloved by locals, along with paw-paws (papaya), stalks of bananas, fresh herbs, various root vegetables, tomatoes, and squash along with an array of luscious exotic fruits. *Here's a tip:* Many of these vendors have a wicked sense of humor and will offer you a taste of the tamarind fruit, claiming it's the "sweetest taste on God's earth." Invariably tricked visitors spit it out. The taste is horrendously offensive.

You can also see mail boats leaving and coming to this quay. Watching the hysterical departure or arrival of a mail boat is one of the more amusing scenes to be viewed on Paradise Island.

Seaworld Explorer 🔍 If you are curious about life below the waves but aren't a strong swimmer, hop aboard this submarine, which holds about 45 passengers. Tours last 90 minutes and include 55 minutes of actual underwater travel at depths of about 3.5m (11 ft.) below the waves. Big windows allow big views of a protected ecology zone offshore from the Paradise Island Airport. About 20 minutes are devoted to an above-water tour of landmarks on either side of the channel that separates Nassau from Paradise Island.

Deveaux St. Docks. 📞 **242/356-2548**. Reservations required. Tours $37 adults, $19 children ages 2–12. Tours Thurs–Sun 11:30am year-round; additional departure at 1:30pm Dec–June.

MORE ATTRACTIONS

Balcony House The original design of this landmark house is a transplant of late-18th-century southeast American architecture. The pink, two-story structure is named for its overhanging and much photographed balcony. Restored in the 1990s, the House has been returned to its original design, recapturing a historic period. The mahogany staircase inside was thought to have been salvaged from a wrecked ship in the 1800s. You visit the house on a guided tour.

Trinity Place and Market St. 📞 **242/302-2621**. Free admission, but donation advised. Mon–Wed and Fri 10am–4:30pm; Thurs 10am–1pm.

Blackbeard's Tower These crumbling remains of a watchtower are said to have been used by the infamous pirate Edward Teach in the 17th century. The ruins are only mildly interesting—there isn't much trace of buccaneering. What's interesting is the view: With a little imagination, you can see Blackbeard peering out from here at unsuspecting ships. Blackbeard also purportedly lived here, but this is hardly well documented.

Yamacraw Hill Rd. (8km/5 miles east of Fort Montagu). No phone. Free admission. Daily 24 hr. Reachable by jitney.

Botanical Gardens More than 600 species of tropical flora are found in this 7.2 hectare (18-acre) park, located within a former rock quarry near Fort Charlotte. The garden features vine-draped arbors, two freshwater ponds with lilies, water plants, tropical fish, and a small cactus garden. After viewing them, you can take a leisurely walk along one of the trails.

Chippingham Rd. No phone. Admission $3 adults, $1.50 children under 12. Mon–Fri 8am–4pm; Sat–Sun 9am–4pm. Bus: 10 or 17.

Central Bank of The Bahamas The nerve center that governs the archipelago's financial transactions is also the venue for a year-round exhibition of paintings that represent some of the emerging new artistic talent of the island. The cornerstone of the building itself was laid by Prince Charles on July 9, 1973, when the country became independent from Britain. His mother, in February of 1975, officially inaugurated the bank.

Trinity Place and Frederick St. 📞 **242/322-2193**. Free admission. Mon–Fri 9:30am–4:30pm.

Fort Charlotte Begun in 1787, Fort Charlotte is the largest of Nassau's three major defenses, built with plenty of dungeons. It used to command the western harbor. Named after King George III's consort, it was built by Gov. Lord Dunmore, who was also the last royal governor of New York and Virginia. Its 42 cannons never fired a shot, at least not at an invader (only seven cannons remain on-site). Within the complex are underground passages, which can be viewed on free tours. Tour guides at the fort are free but are very happy to accept a tip.

Off W. Bay St. on Chippingham Rd. 📞 **242/325-9186**. Free admission. Daily 8am–4pm. Bus: 10.

Fort Fincastle   Reached by climbing the Queen's Staircase, this fort was constructed in 1793 by Lord Dunmore, the royal governor. You can take an elevator ride to the top and walk on the observation floor (a 38m-/125-ft.-high water tower and lighthouse) for a panoramic view of the harbor. The tower is the highest point on New Providence. The so-called bow of this fort is patterned like a paddle-wheel steamer, the kind used on the Mississippi; it was built to defend Nassau against a possible invasion, though no shot was ever fired.

Although the ruins of the fort hardly compete with the view, you can walk around on your own. Be wary, however, of the very persistent young men who will try to show you the way here. They'll try to hustle you, but you really don't need a guide to see some old cannons on your own.

Elizabeth Ave. No phone. Free admission to fort; tickets to water tower $1. Mon–Sat 8am–5pm. Bus: 10 or 17.

Fort Montagu   Built in 1741, this fort—the oldest one on the island—stands guard at the eastern entrance to the harbor of Nassau. The Americans captured it in 1776 during the War of Independence. Less interesting than Fort Charlotte and Fort Fincastle, the ruins of this place are mainly for fort buffs. Many visitors find the nearby park, with well-maintained lawns and plenty of shade, more interesting than the fort itself. Vendors often peddle local handcrafts in this park, so you can combine a look at a ruined fort with a shopping expedition if you're so inclined.

Eastern Rd. Free admission. No regular hours. Bus: 10 or 17.

Junkanoo Expo   This museum is dedicated to Junkanoo—the colorful, musical, and surreal festival that takes place on December 26 when Nassau explodes into a riot of sounds, festivities, celebrations, and masks. It is the Bahamian equivalent of the famous Mardi Gras in New Orleans. If you can't visit Nassau for Junkanoo, this exhibition is the next best thing. You can see the lavish costumes and floats, which the revelers use during this annual celebration. The bright colors and costume designs are impressive if for no other reason than the sheer size of the costumes themselves. Some of the costumes are nearly as big as one of the small parade floats, but they are worn and carried by one person. The Expo has been installed in an old customs warehouse at the entrance to the Nassau wharf. The Expo also includes a souvenir boutique with Junkanoo paintings and a variety of Junkanoo handcrafts.

Prince George Wharf, Festival Place. ℂ 242/323-3182. Free admission. Daily 9am–5pm.

Pirates of Nassau *Kids*   This museum, which opened in 2003, celebrates the dubious "golden age of piracy" (1690–1720). Nassau was once a bustling and robust town where pirates grew rich from plundered gold and other goods robbed at sea. Known as a paradise for pirates, it attracted various rogues and the wild women who flooded into the port to entertain them—for a price, of course. The museum recreates those bawdy, lusty days in a series of exhibits illustrating pirate lore. You can walk through the belly of a pirate ship (the *Revenge*) as you hear "pirates" plan their next attack. You can smell the dampness of a dungeon, and you'll even hear the final prayer of an ill-fated victim before he walks the gangplank. It's fairly cheesy, but fun for kids. Exhibits also tell the saga of Captain Woodes Rogers, who was sent by the English crown to suppress pirates in The Bahamas and the Caribbean.

Marlborough and George sts. ℂ 242/356-3759. Admission $12 adults, $6 children 3–18, free for children 2 and under. Mon–Sat 9am–6pm; Sun 9am–12:30pm. Bus: 10.

Finds   Going Over-the-Hill

Few visitors take this trip any more, but it used to be a tradition to go "Over-the-Hill" to Nassau's most colorful area. "Over-the-Hill" is the actual name of this poor residential district, where the descendants of former slaves built compact, rainbow-hued houses, leaving the most desirable lands around the harbor to the rich folks. This, not the historic core of Nassau around Rawson Square, is truly the heart of Bahamian-African culture.

The thump of the Junkanoo-Goombay drum can be heard here almost any time of the day or night. The area never sleeps, or so it is said. Certainly not on Sunday morning, when you can drive by the churches and hear hell and damnation promised to all sinners and backsliders.

This fascinating part of Nassau begins .5km (⅓-mile) south of Blue Hill Road, which starts at the exclusive Graycliff hotel. But once you're "Over-the-Hill," you're a long way from the vintage wine and expensive Cuban cigars of Graycliff. Some people—usually savvy store owners from abroad—come here to buy local handcrafts from individual vendors. The area can be explored on foot (during the day *only*), but many visitors prefer to drive. *Note:* This area is well worth a visit, but keep your eyes open; most criminal incidents in Nassau take place in this part of town.

WALKING TOUR   HISTORIC NASSAU

Start:	Rawson Square.
Finish:	Prince George Wharf.
Time:	2 hours.
Best Times:	Monday through Saturday between 10am and 4pm.
Worst Times:	Sunday when many places are closed and a day when lots of cruise ships are in port.

Begin your tour at:

❶ Rawson Square

The center of Nassau, Rawson Square lies directly inland from Prince George Wharf, where many of the big cruise ships dock. Everyone seems to pass through this crossroads, from the prime minister to bankers and local attorneys, to cruise-ship passengers, to shoppers from Paradise Island, to Junkanoo bands. On the square is the Churchill Building, where the controversial Prime Minister Lynden Pindling conducted his affairs for 25 years before his ouster in 1992. The

current prime minister and some other government ministries use the building today. Look for the statue of Sir Milo Butler, a former shopkeeper who became the first governor of The Bahamas after Britain granted independence in 1973.

Across Rawson Square is:

❷ Parliament Square

A statue of a youthful Queen Victoria dominates the square. To the right of the statue stand more Bahamian government office buildings, and to the left is the House of Assembly, the oldest governing body in continuous session in the New

World. In the building behind the statue, the Senate meets; this is a less influential body than the House of Assembly. Some of these Georgian-style buildings date from the late 1700s and early 1800s. Immediately south of Parliament Square in a Georgian-inspired building, between Parliament Street and Bank Lane, is the Supreme Court. The bewigged and begowned judges here, looking very British, interpret Bahamian law and dispense justice at the highest authority.

TAKE A BREAK
If you'd like to relax, try **Café Matisse**, Bank Lane and Bay Street, behind Parliament Square (© **242/356-7012**). The house specialty is pizza topped with *frutti di mare,* or fresh local seafood. Lunch is served from noon to 3pm.

The Supreme Court building stands next to the:

❸ Nassau Public Library and Museum

This 1797 building was once the Nassau Gaol (jail). If you want to pop in here for a look, you can do so Monday through Thursday from 10am to 8pm, Friday from 10am to 5pm, and Saturday from 10am to 4pm. Chances are you will have seen greater libraries. But what's amusing here is that the small prison cells are now lined with books. Another item of interest is the library's collection of historic prints and old documents dating from colonial days. It became the public library in 1873.

Across from the library on Shirley Street is the former site of the:

❹ Royal Victoria Hotel

In its day, the hotel was the haunt of Confederate spies, royalty, smugglers of all sorts, and ladies and gentlemen. Horace Greeley pronounced it "the largest and most commodious hotel ever built in the Tropics," and many agreed with this American journalist. The hotel experienced its

heyday during the American Civil War. At the Blockade Runners' Ball, some 300 guests reportedly consumed 350 magnums of champagne. Former guests have included two British prime ministers, Neville Chamberlain and his replacement, Winston Churchill. Prince Albert, consort of Queen Victoria, also stayed here once. The hotel closed in 1971. After it was destroyed by fire, it was demolished and razed to the ground. Today, on its former site sits one of Nassau's showcase parking lots. Ironically, the parking lot seems to be such a source of pride to the city that it is unlikely the Royal Victoria will ever be rebuilt, at least in that spot.

After imagining the former splendor of the Royal Victoria, head south along Parliament Street. At the end of Parliament Street stands:

❺ Nassau General Post Office

If you're a collector, you may want to purchase Bahamian stamps, which might be valuable. You can also mail letters and packages here.

Armed with your colorful purchases, walk east (right) on East Hill Street and turn left onto East Street, then right onto Shirley Street, and head straight on Elizabeth Avenue. This will take you to the landmark:

❻ Queen's Staircase

The stairway leads to Bennet's Hill. In 1793, slaves cut these 66 steps out of sandstone cliffs.

These stairs provided (and still provide) access from the center of Old Nassau to:

❼ Fort Fincastle

Lord Dunmore built this fort in 1793. Designed in the shape of a paddle-wheel steamer, the fort was a place to look out for marauders who never came. It was eventually converted into a lighthouse, because it occupied the highest point on the island. The tower is more than 60m (197 ft.) above the sea, providing a panoramic view of Nassau and its harbor.

A small footpath leads down from the fort to Sands Road. Once you reach it, head west (left) until you approach East

Walking Tour: Historic Nassau

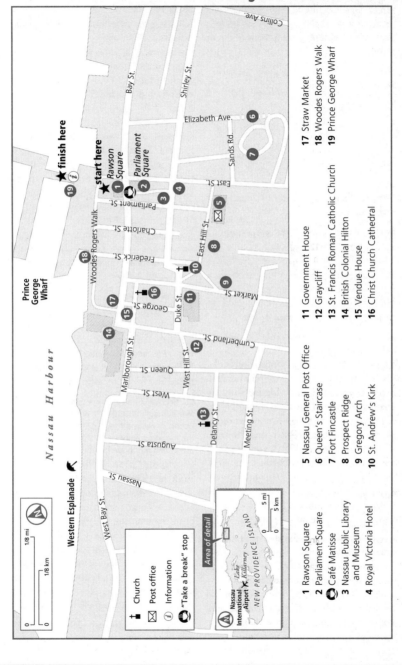

1 Rawson Square
2 Parliament Square
3 Café Matisse
4 Nassau Public Library and Museum
4 Royal Victoria Hotel

5 Nassau General Post Office
6 Queen's Staircase
7 Fort Fincastle
8 Prospect Ridge
9 Gregory Arch
10 St. Andrew's Kirk

11 Government House
12 Graycliff
13 St. Francis Roman Catholic Church
14 British Colonial Hilton
15 Vendue House
16 Christ Church Cathedral

17 Straw Market
18 Woodes Rogers Walk
19 Prince George Wharf

Prince George Wharf

Nassau Harbour

Western Esplanade

start here
Rawson Square
Parliament Square

finish here

Church
Post office
Information
"Take a break" stop

Area of detail

Nassau International Airport
Lake Killarney
NEW PROVIDENCE ISLAND

0 — 5 mi
0 — 5 km

0 — 1/8 mi
0 — 1/8 km

Bay St.
Shirley St.
Elizabeth Ave.
Sands Rd.
East St.
Parliament St.
Charlotte St.
East Hill St.
Frederick St.
Woodes Rogers Walk
George St.
Duke St.
Market St.
Cumberland St.
Marlborough St.
Queen St.
West Hill St.
West St.
Augusta St.
Delancy St.
Meeting St.
Nassau St.
West Bay St.
Collins Ave.

Street again, then bear right. When you come to East Hill Street (again), go left, because you will have returned to the post office.

Continue your westward trek along East Hill Street, which is the foothill of:

❽ Prospect Ridge

This was the old dividing line between Nassau's rich and poor. The rich people lived along the waterfront, often in beautiful mansions. Black Bahamians went "Over-the-Hill" to work in these rich homes during the day but returned to Prospect Ridge to their own homes (most often shanties) at night.

Near the end of East Hill Street, you come to:

❾ Gregory Arch

This tunnel was cut through the hill in 1850; after it opened, working-class black Bahamians didn't have to go "Over-the-Hill"—and steep it was—but could go through the arch to return home.

At the intersection with Market Street, turn right. On your right rises:

❿ St. Andrew's Kirk (Presbyterian)

Called simply "the Kirk," the church dates from 1810 but has seen many changes over the years. In 1864, it was enlarged, and a bell tower was added along with other architectural features. This church had the first non-Anglican parishioners in The Bahamas.

On a steep hill, rising to the west of Market Street, you see on your left:

⓫ Government House

This house is the official residence of the governor-general of the archipelago, the queen's representative to The Bahamas. (The post today is largely ceremonial, as an elected prime minister does the actual governing.) This pink-and-white neoclassical mansion dates from the early 19th century. Poised on its front steps is a rather jaunty statue of Christopher Columbus.

Opposite the road from Government House on West Hill Street rises:

⓬ Graycliff

A Georgian-style hotel and restaurant from the 1720s, this stamping ground of the rich and famous was constructed by Capt. John Howard Graysmith in the 1720s. In the 1920s, it achieved notoriety when it was run by Polly Leach, a pal of gangster Al Capone. Later, under royal ownership, it attracted such famous guests as the Duke and Duchess of Windsor and Winston Churchill.

Upon leaving Graycliff, you will see a plaque embedded in a hill. The plaque claims that this site is the spot where the oldest church in Nassau once stood.

On the corner of West Hill Street and West Street is Villa Doyle, former home of William Henry Doyle, chief justice of the Bahamian Supreme Court in the 1860s and 1870s.

Opposite it stands:

⓭ St. Francis Roman Catholic Church

Constructed between 1885 and 1886, it was the first Catholic church in The Bahamas. The Archdiocese of New York raised the funds to construct it.

Continue along West Street until you reach Marlborough. Walk the short block that leads to Queen Street and turn right, passing the front of the American embassy. At the corner of Queen Street and Marlborough rises:

⓮ British Colonial Hilton

Built in 1923, the most famous hotel in The Bahamas was once run by Sir Harry Oakes, who was at the time the most powerful man on the islands and a friend of the Duke of Windsor. Oakes's murder in 1943, still unsolved, was called "the crime of the century." A set for several James Bond thrillers, this historic location was also the site of Fort Nassau. In the summer of 1999, it became a Hilton hotel.

One part of the hotel fronts George Street, where you'll find:

⓯ Vendue House

One of the oldest buildings in Nassau, Vendue House was once called the

Bourse (Stock Exchange) and was the site of many slave auctions. It is now a museum.

Not far from Vendue House on George Street is:

16 Christ Church Cathedral

Dating from 1837, this Gothic Episcopal cathedral is the venue of many important state ceremonies, including the opening of the Supreme Court: a procession of bewigged, robed judges followed by barristers, accompanied by music from the police band.

Continue north on George Street to the intersection with Bay Street.

17 Straw Market

The market—largely destroyed by a fire in the fall of 2001, and still not rebuilt by the Bahamian government—opens onto Bay Street at George Street. It has long been a favorite of cruise-ship passengers. You'll find not only straw products but all sorts of souvenirs and gifts, as well. Bahamian women at the market have traditionally woven baskets and braided visiting women's hair with beads. Due to the fire's destruction of its infrastructure, the market is temporarily housed in a tent, about 2 blocks from its original premises. Hours of the Straw Market are daily from 7am to around 8pm, although each individual vendor (there are around 200 of them) sets his or her own hours.

Continue north toward the water until you reach:

18 Woodes Rogers Walk

The walk was named for a former governor of the colony who was thrown into debtors' prison in London before coming back to Nassau as royal governor. Head east along this walk for a panoramic view of the harbor, with its colorful mail and sponge boats. Markets here sell vegetables, fish, and lots of conch.

The walk leads to:

19 Prince George Wharf

The wharf was constructed in the 1920s, the heyday of American Prohibition, to provide harbor space for hundreds of bootlegging craft defying the American blockade against liquor. The yacht of Queen Elizabeth II, the HMS *Britannia,* has been a frequent visitor over the years. Cruise ships also dock here.

ORGANIZED TOURS

There's a lot to see in Nassau, and many tour options to suit your taste and take you through the colorful historic city and outlying sights of interest.

Walking tours, arranged by the Ministry of Tourism, leave from the Tourist Information Booth on Rawson Square at 10am to 2pm daily. Tours last for 1 hour and include descriptions of some of the city's most venerable buildings, with commentaries on Nassau's history, customs, and traditions. The cost is $10 for all ages. Call © 242/323-3102 to confirm that tours are on schedule.

Majestic Tours, Hillside Manor, Cumberland Street, Nassau (© 242/322-2606), offers a number of trips, both night and day. A 2-hour city-and-country tour leaves Monday to Saturday at 2pm and goes to major points of interest in Nassau, including the forts, the Queen's Staircase, the water tower, and the former site of the Straw Market (passing but not entering it). The tour costs $30 per person. An extended city-and-country tour also leaves daily at 2pm and includes the Ardastra Gardens. The charge is $38 per person, half price for children 12 and under. Combination tours depart Tuesday, Wednesday, and Thursday at 10am and combine all the sights you see on the first tour listed above, plus the Retreat Gardens and lunch. It costs $48 per person, half price for children. Many hotels have a Majestic Tours Hospitality Desk in

Moments   Journeys into the Wilds

You can take a day off from the beach and join one of the wildlife tours offered by **Bahamas Outdoors,** P.O. Box CB12564 (© **242/362-1574;** www.bahamasoutdoors.com). We highly recommend Carolyn Wardle, president of Bahamas Outdoors, for hands-on insight into the best of the island's remaining wildlife habitats. Born in England, and a resident of New Providence for at least 40 years, Ms. Wardle, a passionate conservationist, is a well-known figure to residents of New Providence's more isolated regions. Armed with sturdy shoes, a Bahamas Outdoors T-shirt, sunglasses, a hat, and binoculars, she knows the island's wildlife habitats (forest, seashore, and freshwater ponds) better than anyone on the island. Consider signing on for a half-day tour, priced at $59 per person, or a full-day tour, at $99 per person. Tours rarely include more than a half-dozen participants, and can be conducted either within a vehicle (with frequent stops along the way for closer observation) or on an all-terrain bike. Depending on what you communicate in advance, the focus of your island tour could include birds, native flora and fauna, butterflies, national parks, historic sites, or—best of all—a combination of all of them. Access to binoculars and a battered collection of field guides are included as part of the price of any tour. The full-day tours also include a picnic lunch.

Advance reservations at least a day in advance are advised. Most tours begin in front of the tour participants' hotel at whatever time was pre-arranged. Bird-watching tours tend to begin earlier, around 7am, than biking and/or historic and nature tours, which begin just a bit later. Ms. Wardle, incidentally, is a director of the Society for the Conservation and Study of Caribbean Birds (SCSCB).

the lobby, for information about these tours, as well as for reservations and tickets. Other hotels can supply brochures and tell you where to sign up.

EASY SIDE TRIPS TO NEARBY ISLANDS

A short boat trip will take you to several small islands lying off the north coast of New Providence. One of these, **Blue Lagoon Island** ⚓, has become so popular that several cruise ships offer their passengers day trips here. Just 5km (3 miles) north of the Narrows at the eastern end of Paradise Island, Blue Lagoon has seven beaches. Although the name recalls images of Brooke Shields, barely clad, cavorting on a desert isle, the reality is quite different. Visitors can dance to a live band, dive with sea creatures at Stingray City, parasail, snorkel, kayak, shop, and lunch at a buffet, among many other things. They also have hammocks and a children's play area with toys.

Blue Lagoon Island has had several owners, including the British Navy, cartoonist John McCutcheon, and the author of *Sophie's Choice,* William Styron. McCutcheon built a watchtower in the 1940s to replace one that was destroyed by an earlier hurricane, and added his own special touch to the structure. He covered the walls of the first floor with his collection of rocks from famous places around the world, including a brick from the Great Wall of China.

Now Ludwig Meister owns the island, and **Nassau Cruises Ltd.** ★★★, Paradise Island Bridge (© **242/363-3333**), leases it and provides the transportation. Nassau Cruises maintains three motorized yachts, the *Calypso I, the Calypso II,* and the *Calypso IV.* These are the most luxurious cruises you can book. Their trip to uninhabited Blue Lagoon Island is reason enough just to sail with them. Equipped with bars, their yachts depart from a point just west of the tollbooth on the Paradise Island Bridge. Daytime trips depart every day for the scheduled beaches of Blue Lagoon Island, a 6.5km (4-mile) sail east of Paradise Island. The day sails leave at 10 and come back from the island at 2 and 4pm. A day pass is $25 for adults and $15 for children and covers the boat ride only. The all-inclusive day pass is $65 for adults and $35 for children (ages 3–12) and covers transportation, the boat ride, lunch, one daiquiri for adults, and all nonmotorized watersports, including snorkeling.

Remote **Rose Island** is a sliver of land poking up out of the sea northeast of the Prince George waterfront docks of Nassau. Shelling is one of the lures of this little islet. If you want to escape the crowds of Nassau, you can take a boat, the *Robinson Crusoe,* which leaves Wednesday, Friday, and Sunday at 10am from Nassau and returns at 4:30pm. The cost is $50, $25 for children ages 5 through 11, and free for kids under 5. You can relax in a hammock, snorkel among the coral reefs, and enjoy the white-sand beach before and after your sizzling barbecue lunch with unlimited white wine (included in the price). Bookings for this island retreat trip are available through **Majestic Tours** (© **242/322-2606;** www.majesticholidays.com).

If you want to see the Exuma island chain on a daylong excursion, try the **Fantastic Exuma Powerboat Adventure.** The name may sound silly, but the trip provides an excellent overview of the area. The boat departs Nassau Harbour at 9am and arrives in the Exuma Cays about an hour later. There are several stops, with snorkeling at a private cay (Ship Channel), a visit with the iguanas on Allan's Cay, feeding stingrays along the shore, and a barbecue lunch. A full bar is available all day, and the drinks are free. The cost is $175 per adult or $99 for children 2 through 12. For more information and prices, contact **Powerboat Adventures** (© **242/393-7116;** www.powerboat adventures.com).

7 Shopping

Nassau shopping is now more upscale than in decades past. Swanky jewelers and a burgeoning fashion scene have appeared. There are still plenty of T-shirts claiming that "It's Better in The Bahamas," but in contrast you can also find platinum watches and diamond jewelry.

The range of goods is staggering; in the midst of all the junk souvenirs, you'll find an increasing array of china, crystal, or watches from such names as Bally, Herend, Lalique, Baccarat, and Ferragamo.

But can you really save money on prices stateside? The answer is "yes" on some items, "no" on others. To figure on what's a bargain and what's not, you've got to know the price of everything back in your hometown, turning yourself into a sort of human calculator about prices.

Don't try to bargain with the salespeople in Nassau stores as you would do with merchants at the local market. The price asked in the shops is the price you must pay, but you won't be pressed to make a purchase. The salespeople here are courteous and helpful in most cases.

There are no import duties on 11 categories of luxury goods, including china, crystal, fine linens, jewelry, leather goods, photographic equipment, watches, fragrances, and other merchandise. Antiques, of course, are exempt from import duty worldwide. But even though prices are "duty-free," you can still end up spending more on an item in The Bahamas than you would back in your hometown. It's a tricky situation.

If you're contemplating a major purchase, such as a good Swiss watch or some expensive perfume, it's best to do some research in your hometown discount outlets before making a serious purchase in The Bahamas. While the alleged 30% to 50% discount off stateside prices might apply in some cases, it's not true in most cases. Certain cameras and electronic equipment, we have discovered, are listed in The Bahamas at, say, 20% or more below the manufacturer's "suggested retail price." That sounds good, except the manufacturer's suggested price might be a lot higher than what you'd pay in your hometown. You aren't getting the discount you think you are. Some shoppers even take along department-store catalogs from the States to determine if they are indeed getting a bargain.

A lot of price-fixing seems to be going on in Nassau. For example, a bottle of Chanel is likely to sell for pretty much the same price regardless of the store.

How much you can take back home depends on your country of origin. For more details, plus Customs requirements for some other countries, refer to "Entry Requirements & Customs," in chapter 2.

The principal shopping areas are **Bay Street** and its side streets downtown, as well as the shops in the arcades of hotels. Not many street numbers are used along Bay Street; just look for store signs.

ANTIQUES

Marlborough Antiques   This store carries the type of antiques you'd expect to find in a shop in London: antique books, antique maps and engravings, English silver (both sterling and plate), and unusual table settings (fish knives and so on). Among the most appealing objects is the store's collection of antique photographs of the islands. Also displayed are works by Bahamian artists Brent Malone, Davide White, and Maxwell Taylor. Corner of Queen and Marlborough sts. © 242/328-0502.

ART

Kennedy Gallery   Although many locals come here for custom framing, the gallery also sells original artwork by well-known Bahamian artists, including limited-edition prints, handcrafts, pottery, and sculpture. Parliament St. © 242/325-7662.

(Fun Fact   **The "Pirate" of The Bahamas**

Chances are you'll be seeing expat actor Johnny Depp, star of *Pirates of the Caribbean,* shopping and walking around the streets of Nassau. He hasn't moved here, but he's purchased Little Halls Pond Cay, 96km (60 miles) south of Nassau, for $3.6 million. Nassau will be his refueling stop. The private island for this reclusive star is hardly open for tours and is accessible only by helicopter, seaplane, or private boat, plus an invitation. When not in The Bahamas, and when not on location, Depp spends most of his time in Paris with singer/actress Vanessa Paradis.

⸜Finds⸝ Going up in Smoke

What do Pierce Brosnan, Ben Kingsley, Michael Jordan, and Salma Hayek (yes, Salma herself) have in common? They are aficionados of a Graycliff Cigar. The owner of Nassau's fabled old antique, the **Graycliff** hotel (p. 82), Enrico Garzaroli, operates the **Graycliff Cigar Company** on the grounds of his hotel at 12 West Hill St. (✆ **242/302-9150**). This is the only cigar factory in The Bahamas. If you call for an appointment, you can see the old-fashioned way that Cuban cigars were created—from breeding to planting and leaf selection, right up to the final hand-rolling and shaping in the factory itself. Avelino Lara, hailed as Cuba's most famous cigar maker, is in charge of the operation.

BRASS & COPPER

Brass and Leather Shop   With two branches on Charlotte Street, this shop offers English brass, handbags, luggage, briefcases, attachés, and personal accessories. Shop no. 2 has handbags, belts, scarves, ties, and small leather goods from such famous designers as Furla, Tumi, HCL, and others. If you look and select carefully, you can find some good buys here. 12 Charlotte St., between Bay and Shirley sts. ✆ **242/322-3806**.

CIGARS

Remember, U.S. citizens are prohibited from bringing Cuban cigars back home because of the trade embargo. If you buy them, you're supposed to enjoy them in The Bahamas.

Tropique International Smoke Shop   Many cigar aficionados come here to indulge their passion for Cubans, which are handpicked and imported by Bahamian merchants. The staff at this outlet trained in Havana, so they know their cigars. In Wyndham Nassau Resort & Crystal Palace Casino, W. Bay St. ✆ **242/327-7292**.

COINS & STAMPS

Bahamas Post Office Philatelic Bureau   Here you'll find beautiful Bahamian stamps slated to become collector's items. One of the most sought-after stamps has a seashell motif. *Insider's tip:* If you don't want to take the trouble to go to the main office, try the smaller philatelic bureau at the Welcome Center, Festival Place, Prince George Dock, open Monday to Saturday 9am to 1pm. In the General Post Office, at the top of Parliament St. on E. Hill St. ✆ **242/322-1112**.

Coin of the Realm   This family-run shop is in a lovely building that was hewn out of solid limestone more than 200 years ago. The shop offers not only fine jewelry, but also Bahamian and British postage stamps, mint and used, and rare (and not-so-rare) Bahamian silver and gold coins. It also sells old and modern paper Bahamian currency. Bahama pennies that were minted in 1806 and 1807 are now rare and expensive items. Charlotte St., just off Bay St. ✆ **242/322-4497**.

CRYSTAL, CHINA & GEMS

Solomon's Mines   Evoking the title of a 1950s MGM flick, this is one grand shopping adventure. This flagship store, with many branches, is one of the largest duty-free retailers in either The Bahamas or the Caribbean, a tradition since 1908. Entering the store is like a shopping trip to London or Paris; the amount of merchandise is staggering, from a $50,000 Patek Philippe watch to one of the largest collections of Herend china in the West. Most retail price tags on watches, china, jewelry, crystal,

Herend, Baccarat, Ferragamo, Bally, Lalique, and other names are discounted 15% to 30%—and some of the merchandise and oddities here are not available in the States, such as their stunning collection of African diamonds. The selection of Italian, French, and American fragrances and skin-care products are the best in the archipelago. Bay St. ⓒ **242/356-6920.** Charlotte and Bay sts. ⓒ **242/325-7554.**

FASHION

Barry's Limited   One of Nassau's more formal and elegant clothing stores, this shop sells garments made from lamb's wool and English cashmere. Elegant sportswear (including Korean-made guayabera shirts) and blazers are sold here. Most of the clothes are for men, but women often stop in for the stylish cuff links, studs, and other accessories. Bay and George sts. ⓒ **242/322-3118.**

Bonneville Bones   The name alone will intrigue, but it hardly describes what's inside. This is the best men's store we've found in Nassau. You can find everything here, from standard T-shirts and designer jeans to elegant casual clothing, including suits. Bay St. ⓒ **242/328-0804.**

Cole's of Nassau   This boutique offers the most extensive selection of designer fashions in Nassau. Women can be outfitted in everything from swimwear to formal gowns, from sportswear to hosiery. Cole's also sells gift items, sterling-silver designer and costume jewelry, hats, shoes, bags, scarves, and belts. Parliament St. ⓒ **242/322-8393.**

Fendi   This is Nassau's only outlet for the well-crafted Italian-inspired accessories endorsed by this famous leather-goods company. With handbags, luggage, shoes, watches, wallets, and portfolios to choose from, the selection may well solve some of your gift-giving quandaries. Charlotte St. at Bay St. ⓒ **242/322-6300.**

HANDICRAFTS

Sea Grape Boutique   This is the finest gift shop on New Providence, with an inventory of exotic decorative items that you'll probably find fascinating. It includes jewelry crafted from fossilized coral, sometimes with sharks' teeth embedded inside, and clothing that's well suited to the sometimes-steamy climate of The Bahamas.

Finds Goin' Local—Coconut Gin & a Fish Fry

Locals call the small artificial island of **Arawak Cay** "Fish Fry." It lies right in the heart of Nassau, across West Bay Street (from the Botanical Gardens, walk back along Chippingham Rd.). Early in the day, you'll be able to buy ultrafresh conch; vendors will crack the mollusk before your eyes (this isn't everybody's favorite attraction). They'll give you some hot sauce and tell you to chow down. Beginning around noon, you'll find at least a half-dozen simple bars and kiosks dispensing cracked conch, fried fish, and grits garnished with either spicy corned beef or tuna salad. With it, you can sample a favorite drink of the islands, coconut milk laced with gin (an acquired taste, to say the least, but you'll feel like a real Bahamian). It's at its most crowded and popular every Sunday night, beginning around 5pm until around midnight, when hundreds of Bahamians gather together next to bonfires to gossip, flirt, raise hell, and hang out.

There's a second branch of this outfit, Sea Grape Too, in the Radisson Hotel's Mall, on Cable Beach (℃ 242/327-5113). W. Bay St. (next to Travelers Restaurant). ℃ **242/327-1308.**

JEWELRY

Colombian Emeralds Famous around the Caribbean, this international outlet is not limited to emeralds, although its selection of that stone is the best in The Bahamas. You'll find an impressive display of diamonds, as well as other precious gems. The gold jewelry here sells for about half the price it does Stateside, and many of the gems are discounted 20% to 30%. Ask about their "cyber-shopping" program. Bay St. ℃ **242/326-1661.**

John Bull The jewelry department here offers classic selections from Tiffany & Co.; cultured pearls from Mikimoto; the creations of David Yurman, Carrera y Carrera, Greek and Roman coin jewelry; and Spanish gold and silver pieces. It's the best name in the business. The store also features a wide selection of watches, cameras, perfumes, cosmetics, leather goods, and accessories. It is one of the best places in The Bahamas to buy a Gucci or Cartier watch. Bay St. ℃ **242/322-4253.**

LEATHER

In addition to the stores mentioned below, another good store for leather goods is the **Brass and Leather Shop,** described under "Brass & Copper," above.

Gucci This shop, opposite Rawson Square, is the best place to buy leather goods in Nassau. The wide selection includes handbags, wallets, luggage, briefcases, gift items, scarves, ties, for men and women, umbrellas, shoes, sandals, watches, and perfume, all by Gucci of Italy. Saffrey Sq., Bay St., corner of Bank Lane. ℃ **242/325-0561.**

Leather Masters This well-known retail outlet carries an internationally known collection of leather bags, luggage, and accessories by Ted Lapidus, Lanvin, and Lancel of Paris; Etienne Aigner of Germany; and "i Santi" of Italy. Leather Masters also carries luggage by Piel and Travel Pro; leather wallets by Bosca; and pens, cigarette lighters, and watches by Colibri. Silk scarves, neckties, and cigar accessories are also featured. 8 Parliament St. ℃ **242/322-7597.**

LINENS

The Linen Shop This is the best outlet for linens in Nassau. It sells beautifully embroidered bed linens, Irish handkerchiefs, and tablecloths. Look also for the most exquisite children's clothing and christening gowns in town. In the Ironmongery Building, Bay St., near Charlotte St. ℃ **242/322-4266.**

MAPS

Balmain Antiques This place offers a wide and varied assortment of 19th-century etchings, engravings, and maps, many of them antique and all reasonably priced. Other outlets have minor displays of these collectibles, but this outlet has the finest. Some items are 400 years old. It's usually best to discuss your interests with Mr. Ramsey, the owner, so he can direct you to the proper drawers. His specialties include The Bahamas, America during the Civil War, and black history. He also has a collection of military historical items. The shop now features Haitian primitive art. You'll find the shop on the second floor, three doors east of Charlotte Street. In the Mason's Building, Bay St., near Charlotte St. ℃ **242/323-7421.**

MARKETS

The **Nassau International Bazaar** consists of some 30 shops selling international goods in a new arcade. A pleasant place for browsing, the $1.8-million complex sells

What Happened to the Straw Market?

A tremendous fire on September 4, 2001 destroyed virtually all of the merchandise and most of the infrastructure of the permanent home of **Nassau's Straw Market,** a concrete shell a few steps from the administration of the Bahamian Tourist Board, at the corner of Bay and Market streets. Since then, the Straw Market has occupied a tent on Bay Street, opposite the intersection of Bay Street with George Street, about 2 blocks from its original premises. Hours of the Straw Market are daily from 7am to around 8pm, although each individual vendor (there are around 200 of them) sets his or her own hours. Merchandise is what it's always been: Hats, weavings, baskets, valises, all woven from reeds, straw, and grasses.

goods from around the globe. The bazaar runs from Bay Street down to the waterfront (near the Prince George Wharf). With cobbled alleyways and garreted storefronts, the area looks like a European village.

Prince George Plaza, Bay Street, is popular with cruise-ship passengers. Many fine shops (Gucci, for example) are found here. When you get tired of shopping, you can dine at the open-air rooftop restaurant that overlooks Bay Street.

PERFUMES & COSMETICS

Nassau has several good perfume outlets, notably **John Bull** and **Little Switzerland,** which also stock a lot of nonperfume merchandise.

The Beauty Spot   The largest cosmetic shop in The Bahamas, this outlet sells duty-free cosmetics by Lancôme, Chanel, YSL, Elizabeth Arden, Estée Lauder, Clinique, Christian Dior, and Biotherm, among others. It also operates facial salons. Bay and Frederick sts. ⓒ 242/322-5930.

The Perfume Bar   This little gem has exclusive rights to market Boucheron, and it also stocks the Clarins line (though not exclusively). Bay St. ⓒ 242/322-7216.

The Perfume Shop   In the heart of Nassau, within walking distance of the cruise ships, the Perfume Shop offers duty-free savings on world-famous perfumes. Treat yourself to a flacon of Eternity, Giorgio, Poison, Lalique, Shalimar, or Chanel. Those are just a few of the scents for women. For men, the selection includes Drakkar Noir, Polo, and Obsession. Corner of Bay and Frederick sts. ⓒ 242/322-2375.

STEEL DRUMS

Pyfroms   If you've fallen under the Junkanoo spell and want to take home some steel drums, you've come to the right place. They'll always be useful if island fever overtakes you after you return home. This shop also carries many souvenirs and T-shirts. Bay St. ⓒ 242/322-2603.

8 New Providence After Dark

Gone are the days when tuxedo-clad gentlemen and elegantly gowned ladies drank and danced the night away at such famous nightclubs as the Yellow Bird and the Big

Bamboo. You can still find dancing, along with limbo and calypso, but for most visitors, the major attraction is gambling.

Cultural entertainment in Nassau is limited, however. The chief center for this is the **Dundas Center for the Performing Arts,** which sometimes stages ballets, plays, or musicals. Call ℂ **242/393-3728** to see if a production is planned at the time of your visit.

ROLLING THE DICE

As another option, you can easily head over to Paradise Island and drop into the massive, spectacular casino in the Atlantis resort. See chapter 4.

Wyndham Nassau Resort & Crystal Palace Casino   This dazzling casino—the only one on New Providence Island—is now run by Wyndham Nassau Resort. Although some experienced gamblers claim you get better odds in Vegas, the Crystal Palace stacks up well against the major casinos of the Caribbean. The 3,252-sq.-m (35,000-sq.-ft.) casino is filled with flashing lights, and the gaming room features hundreds of slot machines, blackjack tables, roulette wheels, craps tables, a baccarat table, and a big six. W. Bay St., Cable Beach. ℂ **242/327-6200.**

THE CLUB & MUSIC SCENE

Club Waterloo   They've seen it all over the years at the Club Waterloo, located in an old colonial mansion set beside a narrow saltwater estuary known as Lake Waterloo. To qualify for the $5 cover charge, you can purchase a visitors' pass from most taxi drivers, which will get you inside the door. If you're not registered at a hotel, the cover charge is $20 Wednesday to Sunday, going up to $30 on Friday and Saturday. But despite these high prices, you'll get the feeling that very few people actually pay full price: It's management's way of screening out the bad drunks. The main bar is open nightly from 4pm to 4am, and the Shooters Sports bar is open from midnight to 4am. You'll also find an open-air pool bar, and a Bacardi Bar, which specializes in its namesake. The crowd tends to be an eclectic mix of locals, Europeans, and American vacationers, both singles and couples. E. Bay St. ℂ **242/393-7324.** Cover $5–$30, including 1 or 2 drinks.

King & Knights Native Calypso Show   This is the only folkloric Bahamian show on New Providence. Its linchpin is Eric Gibson ("King Eric"), a talented musician and calypso artist from Acklins Island. He has functioned as the semiofficial ambassador of Bahamian goodwill, conducting concert tours throughout North America, Europe, and Australia. A musical staple here since the late 1950s, his act includes a half-dozen musicians, four or five dancers, a "calypsonian" who might double as a comedian, and a limbo contortionist. The shows are a little short (only 90 min.), but end with a sequence that emulates the Junkanoo festival. If you opt for a dinner here, you can schedule it for whenever you want, before, during, or after the show. Shows are Monday to Saturday at 8:30pm. In the Nassau Beach Hotel, Cable Beach. ℂ **242/327-7711.** Reservations recommended. Cover charge $25, dinner and show $45.

The Zoo   Set midway between Cable Beach and the western periphery of Nassau, this is the largest and best-known nightspot of its kind on New Providence. It's housed on two floors of what was once a warehouse, with five bars, an indoor/outdoor restaurant (Zoo Cafe), and a sometimes-crowded dance floor that attracts mainly an under-30 crowd. Each of the five bars has a different theme, including an underwater theme, a jungle theme, and a *Gilligan's Island* theme. The sports bar is complete with pool tables and wide-screen broadcasts. The most raucous area of the complex is on the street level, where a young crowd congregates to drink and dance. If you're looking for a respite from the brouhaha below, climb a flight of stairs to the "VIP Lounge," which offers stiff drinks and the chance for conversation. Most of the complex is open Tuesday to Sunday 8am to 3am. W. Bay St. at Saunders Beach. ✆ 242/322-7195. Cover $10–$25.

VEGAS-STYLE SHOWS

Rain Forest Theater   This 800-seat theater (previously known as the Palace Theater) is a major nightlife attraction. Fake palm trees on each side and lots of glitz set the scene for the Las Vegas–style extravaganzas and Caribbean revues that are presented on its stage. Shows are presented every Monday, Wednesday, and Friday, at 8:30pm. The show is complimentary, however there is a 1-drink minimum. In the Crystal Palace Casino, W. Bay St., Cable Beach. ✆ 242/327-6200.

THE BAR SCENE

Charlie's on the Beach/Cocktails 7 Dreams   The focus within this sparsely decorated club is local gossip, calypso and reggae music, and stiff drinks, all of which can combine into a high-energy night out in Nassau. The setting is a simple warehouse-like structure a few blocks west of the British Colonial Hilton, though management warns that during some particularly active weekends (including spring break), the entire venue might move, short-term, to a larger, and as yet undetermined, location. Open only Wednesday and Friday to Sunday 9pm to 4am. W. Bay St. near Long Wharf Beach. ✆ 242/328-3745. Cover $10–$30.

Crocodiles Waterfront Bar & Grill   Look for the hundreds of crocodiles stenciled into the wall that shields this watering hole from busy East Bay Street, and venture into the funky bar for a rum drink. There's a relaxed vibe on the deck, which offers a bit of shade under thatched parasols. You can order moderately priced steak, seafood, or sandwiches (see the full review under "Where to Dine," earlier in this chapter). Both the restaurant and bar are open daily 11am to midnight. E. Bay St. (a 2-min. walk from the Nassau side of the Paradise Island Bridge). ✆ 242/323-3341.

The Drop Off   Every harbor town has a rowdy, raucous, and sudsy dive with whiffs of spilled beer and ample doses of iodine from the nearby sea, and in Nassau, this is it. Most of its clients are either local residents, or workers aboard one of the fishing and cargo boats that bob at anchor in nearby Nassau Harbor. The setting is a cavernous room lined with murals of underwater life, all within a cellar that's usually several degrees cooler than the baking sidewalks outside. There's disco music some evenings after 11pm, and a short list of two-fisted platters that includes grilled or fried snapper or grouper, steaks, burgers, and sandwiches. Call for hours. E. Bay St. at East St. ✆ 242/322-3444.

Out Island Bar/The Beach Bar   These bars, both within the same hotel, are used primarily by its guests, but are open to all, attracting everybody from newlyweds to those who married when Eisenhower was in office. The more central of the two is the Out Island Bar, set adjacent to the lobby and outfitted in a breezy wicker and rattan theme that goes well with the party-colored drinks that are its specialty. If you want a view, head for the Beach Bar, which is thatch-covered and set directly on the sands of one of the best beaches in the area. Call for hours. In the Nassau Beach Hotel, Cable Beach. ✆ 242/327-7711.

My, what an inefficient way to fish.

Ring toss, good. Horseshoes, bad.

Faster! Faster! Faster!

We take care of the fiddly bits, from providing over 43,000 customer reviews of hotels, to helping you find our best fares, to giving you 24/7 customer service. So you can focus on the only thing that matters. Goofing off.

travelocity
You'll never roam alone.™

travelocity.com   **1**-888-TRAVELOCITY   AOL Keyword: Travel

4

Paradise Island

Located just 180m (590 ft.) off the north shore of Nassau, Paradise Island is a favorite vacation spot for East Coast Americans, who flee their icy winters for the stunning white sands of Paradise Beach. In addition to its gorgeous beaches, the island boasts beautiful foliage, including brilliant red hibiscus and a grove of casuarina trees sweeping down to form a tropical arcade.

Now the priciest piece of real estate in The Bahamas, this island once served as a farm for Nassau and was known as Hog Island. Purchased for $294 by William Sayle in the 17th century, it cost A&P grocery chain heir Huntington Hartford $11 million in 1960. He decided to rename the 6.5km-long (4-mile) sliver of land Paradise before selling out his interests. Long a retreat for millionaires, the island experienced a massive building boom in the 1980s. Its old Bahamian charm is now gone forever, lost to the high-rises, condos, second homes of the wintering wealthy, and gambling casino that have taken over. The centerpiece of Paradise Island is the mammoth Atlantis Paradise Island Resort & Casino, which has become a nightlife mecca and a sightseeing attraction in its own right.

For those who want top hotels, casino action, Vegas-type revues, fabulous beaches, and a posh address, Paradise Island is the place. It's now sleeker and more upscale than Cable Beach, its closest rival, and Freeport/Lucaya. True, Paradise Island is overbuilt and overly commercialized, but its natural beauty still makes it a choice vacation spot, perfect for a quick 3- or 4-day getaway.

Paradise Island is treated as a separate entity in this guide, but it is actually part of New Providence, connected by a bridge. You can travel between the two on foot, by boat, or by car. So you can stay in Nassau or Cable Beach and come over to enjoy the beaches, restaurants, attractions, and casino on Paradise Island. You can also stay on Paradise Island and easily go into Nassau for a day of sightseeing and shopping. So view this section as a companion to chapter 3. Refer to "Fast Facts: New Providence" on p. 77 for transportation details, nearby sights, and a wider array of sports and recreation choices.

1 Orientation

ARRIVING

Most visitors to Paradise Island arrive in Nassau and commute to Paradise Island by ground transport. However, **Chalks International Airways** (© **800/424-2557,** or 242/363-3114; www.chalksoceanairways.com) flies daily from Fort Lauderdale International Airport directly into Paradise. There are about five flights on weekdays, rising to around eight flights on Saturday and Sunday. The airplanes are Grumman G-73T; each aircraft carries up to 17 passengers. The airline's headquarters are at 704 SW 34th St., Fort Lauderdale, FL 33315.

When you arrive at the **Nassau International Airport** (see chapter 3 for information on flying into Nassau), you won't find bus service to take you to Paradise Island. Many package deals will provide hotel transfers from the airport. Otherwise, if you're not renting a car, you'll need to take a taxi. Taxis in Nassau are metered and take cash only, no credit cards. It will usually cost you $30 to go by cab from the airport to your hotel. The driver will also ask you to pay the one-way $1 bridge toll (this charge will be added onto your metered fare at the end).

VISITOR INFORMATION

Paradise Island does not have a tourist office, so refer to the tourist facilities in downtown Nassau (see "Orientation," at the beginning of chapter 3). The concierge or the guest services staff at your hotel can also give you information about the local attractions.

ISLAND LAYOUT

Paradise Island's finest beaches lie on the Atlantic (northern) coastline; the docks, wharves, and marinas are located on the southern side. Most of the island's largest and glossiest hotels and restaurants, as well as the famous casino and a lagoon with carefully landscaped borders, lie west and north of the roundabout. The area east of the roundabout is less congested, with only a handful of smaller hotels, a golf course, the Versailles Gardens, the Cloister, the airport, and many of the island's privately owned villas.

2 Getting Around

You don't need to rent a car. Most visitors walk around Paradise Island's most densely developed sections and hire a taxi for the occasional longer haul. For information on renting a car, refer to "By Rental Car," on p. 61 in chapter 2.

The most popular way to reach nearby Nassau is to **walk across the toll bridge.** There is no charge for pedestrians.

If you want to tour Paradise Island or New Providence by **taxi,** you can make arrangements with either the taxi driver or the hotel reception desk. Taxis wait at the entrances to all the major hotels. The going hourly rate is about $60 in cars or small vans.

If you are without a car and don't want to take a taxi or walk, you can take a **ferry to Nassau.** The ferry to Nassau leaves from the dock on Casino Drive every half-hour, and the 10-minute ride costs $3 one-way. Quicker and easier than a taxi, the ferry deposits you right at Bay Street. Daily service is from 9:30am to 4:15pm.

Water taxis also operate between Paradise Island and Prince George Wharf in Nassau. They depart daily from 8:30am to 6pm at 20-minute intervals. Round-trip fare is $6 per person.

If you are a guest at one of the properties of Atlantis Paradise Island Resort & Casino, you can take a complimentary tour of the island, leaving daily at noon.

Unlike New Providence, no public buses are allowed on Paradise Island.

3 Where to Stay

In the off season (mid-Apr to mid-Dec), prices are slashed by at least 20%—and perhaps a lot more, though the weather isn't as ideal. But because Paradise Island's summer business has increased dramatically, you'll never see some of the 60% reductions that you might find at a cheaper property in the Greater Nassau area. Paradise Island

Tips **Make a Deal Before You Go**

The rates given below are rack rates, and you should be able to avoid paying them. Always ask if special promotional rates are available, or see if a travel agent can help you do better. Package deals often greatly reduce the prices of these resorts, too. Be sure to read the section "Packages for the Independent Traveler" in chapter 2, before you book a hotel yourself.

doesn't have to lower its rates to attract summer business. For inexpensive accommodations, refer to the recommendations on New Providence Island (see chapter 3). Paradise Island ain't cheap!

VERY EXPENSIVE

Atlantis Paradise Island Resort & Casino ★★★ *Kids*   This megaresort of The Bahamas is *massive,* opening onto a long stretch of white-sand beach with a sheltered marina. Think Vegas in the Tropics, with a fairly interesting ancient mythology theme thrown in, and you'll get the picture. The advantage is that you'll never be bored; the downside is that it's sprawling, and the service just can't keep up with the number of guests here. The Atlantis is a self-contained "water world," with the Lost Continent of Atlantis as its theme. It's a great choice for a family vacation, since kids love all the facilities and gimmicks, and the children's program is outstanding. Singles and young couples who want a lot of action like it, too, though some people find it too over-the-top and impersonal. The Atlantis proudly offers so many sports, dining, and entertainment options that many guests never set foot off the property during their entire vacation.

A soaring "Royal Tower"—one of the tallest buildings in The Bahamas—is replete with decorative sea horses, winged dragons, and megasize conch shells sprouting from cornices and rooflines. The casino and entertainment complex lie in an area over the watery depths of a lagoon. The best and most plush accommodations are in the Royal Tower. (Rooms in the Royal Tower's Imperial Club have a personal concierge and upgraded amenities.) But even in the older, less expensive sections, rooms have a comfortable tropical decor. Every unit sports a balcony or terrace with water views, individually controlled air-conditioning, in-room movies, and voice mail and modem access, plus roomy bathrooms with tubs and showers. The most deluxe accommodation is the Bridge Suite, renting for $25,000 a day and sometimes occupied by Michael Jordan while hosting his celebrity invitational at the on-site golf course.

Any old hotel might sport tropical gardens, but the Atlantis goes one better by featuring the world's largest collection of outdoor open-air marine habitats, each of them aesthetically stunning. A few of these were conceived for snorkelers and swimmers, but most were designed so guests could observe the marine life from catwalks above and from glassed-in underwater viewing tunnels. Even folks who don't stay here—including thousands of cruise-ship passengers—come to check out these 11 distinctly different exhibition lagoons containing millions of gallons of water and at least 200 species of tropical fish. They include a shark tank, a stingray lagoon, and separate holding tanks for lobsters, piranhas, and underwater exotica. Swimmers can meander along an underwater snorkeling trail (Paradise Lagoon) and explore a five-story, Disney-style replica of a Mayan temple complete with 18m (59-ft.) water slides.

Where to Stay & Dine in Paradise Island

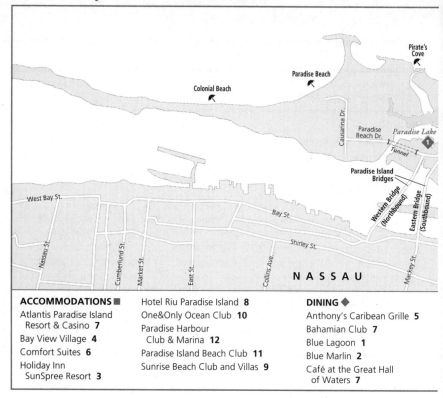

ACCOMMODATIONS ■
Atlantis Paradise Island
  Resort & Casino **7**
Bay View Village **4**
Comfort Suites **6**
Holiday Inn
  SunSpree Resort **3**

Hotel Riu Paradise Island **8**
One&Only Ocean Club **10**
Paradise Harbour
  Club & Marina **12**
Paradise Island Beach Club **11**
Sunrise Beach Club and Villas **9**

DINING ◆
Anthony's Caribean Grille **5**
Bahamian Club **7**
Blue Lagoon **1**
Blue Marlin **2**
Café at the Great Hall
  of Waters **7**

   The focal point of this extravagance is the massive **Paradise Island Casino,** the best-designed casino in The Bahamas. There are 13 bars, nightclubs, and lounges, including a cigar bar (see "Paradise Island After Dark," later in this chapter). There are also 17 restaurants, some reviewed under "Where to Dine," below; expect to pay a lot to dine in most of them.

Casino Dr. (P.O. Box N-4777), Paradise Island, The Bahamas. ⓒ 800/ATLANTIS in the U.S., or 242/363-3957. Fax 242/363-6300. www.atlantis.com. 2,349 units. Winter $360–$720 double, from $810 suite; off season $285–$565 double, from $685 suite. Package deals available. AE, DC, DISC, MC, V. Free self-parking, valet parking $5 day. **Amenities:** 17 restaurants; 18 lounges and clubs; 11 pools; golf course; 10 tennis courts; health club; spa; sauna; watersports equipment/rentals; children's programs (5–12); salon; 24-hr. room service; massage; babysitting; laundry service; dry cleaning; nonsmoking rooms; rooms for those w/limited mobility. *In room:* A/C, TV, dataport, minibar, fridge, hair dryer, iron, safe.

One&Only Ocean Club 🌟🌟🌟   This resort is the most exclusive address on Paradise Island, with sky-high prices that match the pampering service (the best in The Bahamas) and refined ambience. The white-sand beach that lies adjacent to the hotel is the finest in the Nassau/Paradise Island area. This is also one of the best-developed tennis resorts in The Bahamas. In 1999, the property began a major expansion and renovation. A favorite honeymoon spot, it's more upscale than the megahotel Atlantis,

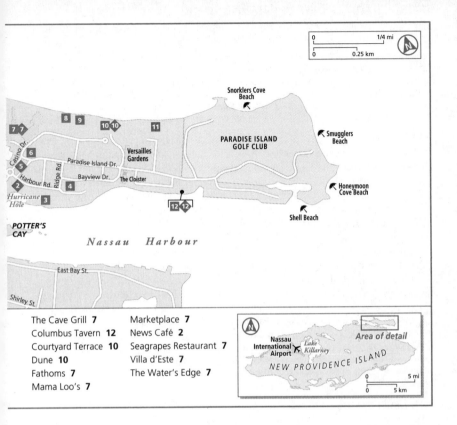

The Cave Grill **7**	Marketplace **7**
Columbus Tavern **12**	News Café **2**
Courtyard Terrace **10**	Seagrapes Restaurant **7**
Dune **10**	Villa d'Este **7**
Fathoms **7**	The Water's Edge **7**
Mama Loo's **7**	

which is really a fun family resort. Guests can revel in the casino and nightlife activities of Atlantis nearby, and then retire to this more tranquil, secluded, and intimate retreat.

The tasteful and spacious rooms are plushly comfortable with king-size beds, gilt-framed mirrors, and dark-wood armoires. The marble bathrooms in the suites are massive, and each contains a bidet, twin basins, and both a tub and shower.

The real heart and soul of the resort lies in the surrounding gardens, which were designed by the island's former owner, Huntington Hartford. This resort, in fact, was once his private home. Formal gardens surround a French cloister set on 14 hectares (35 acres) of manicured lawns. The 12th-century carvings of the Cloister are visible at the crest of a hill, across a stretch of terraced waterfalls, fountains, a stone gazebo, and rose gardens. Larger-than-life statues dot the vine-covered niches on either side of the gardens. Begin your tour of the gardens at the large swimming pool, which feeds a series of reflecting pools that stretch out toward the cloister. A new addition is the child-friendly family pool, replete with aqua toys and a waterfall.

Arguably the best dining on Paradise Island can be found at the resort's Dune restaurant, creation of culinary legend Jean-Georges Vongerichten. In addition, a pair of fountains illuminates the Courtyard Terrace at night. See "Where to Dine," later in this chapter for a review of both restaurants. Another option is a beachfront restaurant and bar, where you can dine under cover but still in the open air.

Ocean Club Dr. (P.O. Box N-4777), Paradise Island, The Bahamas. **℃ 800/321-3000** in the U.S., or 242/363-2501. Fax 242/363-2424. www.oneandonlyresorts.com. 106 units, 3 private villas. Winter $725–$1,025 double, $1,280–$2,000 suite, $5,000–$6,000 villa; off season $475–$760 double, $775–$1,400 suite, $4,500–5,500 villa. AE, MC, V. Free parking. **Amenities:** 3 restaurants; 4 bars; 2 pools; golf course; 6 tennis courts; health club; spa; steam room; shuttle to Atlantis casino; 24-hr. room service; babysitting; laundry service; dry cleaning; nonsmoking rooms. *In room:* A/C, TV, dataport, kitchenette (in some), minibar, hair dryer, iron, safe, butler service.

EXPENSIVE

Holiday Inn SunSpree Resort ⚓ *Kids*   This older, 12-floor property adjacent to the waters of Nassau Harbour opens onto a marina with very little beach, but a good-sized swimming pool. It was rescued from oblivion in the late 1990s when a Florida-based investment group, Driftwood Ventures, renovated it. This group turned it into an all-inclusive resort, which lies just a short stroll away from the popular Atlantis and all its attractions. Bedrooms are midsize with twin or king-size beds, plus well-maintained private bathrooms with tub and shower combinations. The decor is comfortable, airy and sunny, and outfitted with tropically inspired colors and upholstery. All third-floor rooms and select units on the fourth floor are designated for nonsmokers only. The food served at the restaurants is palatable but needs much improvement, and service is very slow, so be duly warned. However, there are nightly live shows to spice up the lackluster gourmet, including fire dancing and Bahamian bands.

Harbour Dr. (P.O. Box SS-6249), Paradise Island, The Bahamas. **℃ 800/HOLIDAY** in the U.S., or 242/363-2561. Fax 242/363-3803. www.paradiseislandbahama.com. 246 units. Winter $320–$437 double, $537 suite; off season $269–$374 double, $474 suite. Rates are all-inclusive. AE, DC, DISC, MC, V. **Amenities:** 3 restaurants; 2 bars; pool; 2 tennis courts; health club; Jacuzzi; watersports equipment/rental; children's programs; car rental; massage; non-smoking rooms; rooms for those w/limited mobility. *In room:* A/C, TV, dataport, fridge, beverage maker, hair dryer, iron, safe.

Hotel Riu Paradise Island ⚓ *Kids*   Opening onto a 5km (3-mile) stretch of sandy beach, this is the newest addition to the beachfront. In December 2004, the Riu Hotels chain refurbished the old Sheraton Grand here into an all-inclusive megaresort. Among the renovations was the enlargement of the pool, the addition of a restaurant, and general room enhancement. This 14-story ecru high-rise offers some of the most comfortably appointed bedrooms on Paradise Island. It's more understated than the Atlantis, a lot cheaper, and more user friendly and manageable in terms of size and layout. Your kids would be happier with all the spectacular events at the Atlantis, but the Riu is a viable runner-up for the family trade. Guests can leave the shelter of the poolside terrace

---

Tips Coming Attractions

Atlantis's next phase of development includes a 600-room all-suite luxury hotel, to be situated west of the Royal Towers; a 400-unit condo hotel; additional water-themed attractions, including a dolphin encounter; and 9,290 sq. m (100,000 sq. ft.) of additional group and meeting facilities. Nobu, a world-renowned Japanese restaurant headed by namesake chef Nobu Matsuhisa and funded by partner Robert DeNiro, will replace the Five Twins restaurant in the Atlantis casino. This is expected to take place by Christmas 2006.

and settle almost immediately onto one of the waterside chaise longues at the beach. The hotel is within walking distance of the casino, restaurants, and nightlife facilities of the Atlantis Paradise Island Resort & Casino properties.

Welcoming drinks are served while you relax on comfortable chairs in the lobby bar amid palm trees and tropical foliage. All the spacious accommodations here are deluxe and tastefully decorated, and equipped with medium-size bathrooms containing tub/shower combos. Many have spacious balconies that afford sweeping water views or luxurious terraces.

For an extra charge, you can skip the all-inclusive dinner fare and dine at Tengoku, a Japanese-themed restaurant. Other choices available to jaded buffet-goers include Atlantic Restaurant—serving some of Paradise Island's finest steaks and featuring a nonsmoking section, plus a terrace—and Sir Alexander, which is Riu's gourmet a la carte restaurant featuring highly refined, mainly continental gourmet cuisine with first-rate ingredients. Live entertainment is available 6 nights a week.

6307 Casino Dr. (P.O. Box SS-6307), Paradise Island, The Bahamas. (C) **888/666-8816** in the U.S., or 242/363-3500. Fax 242/363-3900. www.riu.com. 379 units. Winter $424–$454 double, $514–$576 jr. suite; off season $394–$424 double, $484–$546 jr. suite. Rates are all-inclusive. AE, DISC, MC, V. **Amenities:** 3 restaurants; 2 bars; pool; 4 tennis courts; gym; spa; Jacuzzi; sauna; kids' club; watersports equipment; salon; limited room service; massage; babysitting; laundry service; dry cleaning; nonsmoking rooms; rooms for those w/limited mobility. *In room:* A/C, ceiling fan, TV, dataport, minibar, hair dryer, safe.

Paradise Island Beach Club ⭐   Set near the eastern tip of Paradise Island, adjacent to a relatively isolated strip of spectacular beachfront, this two- and three-story timeshare complex was built in 1985. Managed by Marriott, it's more of a self-catering condo complex than a full-fledged resort. Many guests cook at least some meals in their own kitchens and head elsewhere, often to bigger hotels, for restaurants, watersports, gambling, and entertainment. Views from the bedrooms are usually ocean panoramas; overall, the setting is comfortable and, at its best, even cozy. You'll feel like you have your own Florida apartment, with easy access to the beach. Apartments have either one or two bedrooms, with wicker and rattan furnishings, and luxuries that include double basins in each bathroom, plus a tub and shower.

On the premises are both a round and a triangular-shaped swimming pool, one with a simple snack bar that's open only at lunchtime, except on Monday and Wednesday when there's a Bahamian buffet. The entertainment and casino facilities of the more densely developed sections of Paradise Island are just a short walk away. The major drawback here is the service, which is very laissez-faire.

Ocean Ridge Dr. (P.O. Box N-10600), Paradise Island, The Bahamas. (C) **242/363-2814** or 242/363-2992. Fax 242/363-2130. www.pibc-bahamas.com. 44 units. Winter $275 1-bedroom apt, $479 2-bedroom apt; off season $250 1-bedroom apt, $350 2-bedroom apt. AE, MC, V. **Amenities:** Pool bar; 2 pools; exercise room; salon; massage; coin-operated laundry service; rooms for those w/limited mobility. *In room:* A/C, TV, kitchen, hair dryer, iron, safe.

Sunrise Beach Club and Villas ⭐ *Kids*   This cluster of Spanish-inspired low-rise town houses occupies one of the most desirable stretches of beachfront on Paradise Island. Midway between the Hotel Riu and the One&Only Ocean Club, it's a short walk from the casino and a variety of sports and dining options. Accommodations are clustered within five separate groupings of red-roofed town houses, each with access to the resort's two swimming pools (one of which has a waterfall) and a simple snack bar. The hotel is usually full of lots of Germans, Swiss, and Austrians, many of whom stay for several weeks, preparing most of their own meals, since units have kitchens.

Expect pastel colors, summery-looking furniture, and a private patio or veranda, plus king-size beds and floor-to-ceiling mirrored headboards, as well as average-size bathrooms with tub and shower. The best units are the three-bedroom apartments, situated directly on the beach. This is a good bet for "quieter" families who want a more subdued and relaxed vacation, and who want to avoid the "circus" going on 24 hours at the Atlantis.

P.O. Box SS-6519, Paradise Island, The Bahamas. ✆ 800/451-6078 or 242/363-2250. Fax 242/363-2308. www.sunrise beachclub.com. 100 units. Winter $315 1-bedroom apt, $551 2-bedroom apt, $695–$987 3-bedroom apt; off season $243 1-bedroom apt, $441 2-bedroom apt, $719–$987 3-bedroom apt. AE, MC, V. **Amenities:** Restaurant; bar; 2 pools; babysitting; coin-operated laundry; nonsmoking rooms; rooms for those w/limited mobility. *In room:* A/C, TV, kitchen, beverage maker, hair dryer, iron, safe.

MODERATE

Bay View Village ✿ More than 20 kinds of hibiscus and many varieties of bougainvillea beautify this 1.6-hectare (4-acre) condo complex. The condos here are near the geographic center of Paradise Island, and also only a 10-minute walk to either the harbor or the white sands of Cabbage Beach (the complex has no beach of its own). The restaurants, nightlife, and casino of Atlantis are only a few minutes away, although the modest Terrace restaurant here is nothing to be ashamed of.

We particularly recommend rooms near the center of the resort, because they are closest to the three swimming pools and laundry facilities. Each accommodation has its own kitchen with dishwasher, plus a patio or balcony and daily maid service. A shopping center is only 3 minutes away. Some units open onto views of the harbor. A full-time personal cook can be arranged on request. The units come in a wide variety of sizes; the largest can hold up to six. Rates are slightly less for weekly rentals. Penthouse suites contain roof gardens that open onto views of the harbor. Bedrooms come with king-, queen-, or twin-size beds. Bathrooms are medium in size, well maintained, and equipped with tub/shower combos.

Bayview Dr. (P.O. Box SS-6308), Paradise Island, The Bahamas. ✆ 242/363-2555. Fax 242/363-2370. 75 units. www. bayviewvillage.com. Winter $215 1-bedroom suite, $365 town house, $385 villa; off season $170 1-bedroom suite, $290 town house, $320 villa. AE, DC, DISC, MC, V. **Amenities:** Restaurant; bar; 3 pools; tennis court; babysitting; coin-operated laundry; nonsmoking rooms; rooms for those w/limited mobility. *In room:* A/C, TV, kitchen, coffeemaker, hair dryer, iron, safe.

Comfort Suites ⓥ*alue* A favorite with honeymooners and a good value, this three-story, all-suite hotel is across the street from the Atlantis. If the mammoth Atlantis seems too overpowering, Comfort Suites is a nice alternative. You get the splash and wonder of the Atlantis, but you don't have to stay there all night or when the cruise-ship crowds descend. Although there are both a pool bar and a restaurant on the premises, guests are granted signing privileges at each of the drinking-and-dining spots, as well as the pool, beach, and sports facilities of the nearby Atlantis. Accommodations are priced by their views, over the island, the pool, or the garden. The medium-size bathrooms have beach towels, and ample vanities. Bedrooms are standard motel size with two double beds or one king.

Paradise Island Dr. (P.O. Box SS-6202), Paradise Island, The Bahamas. ✆ 877/424-6423 in the U.S. or Canada, or 242/363-3680. Fax 242/363-2588. www.comfortsuites.com. 227 units. Winter $205–$255 double; off season $190–$230 double. Rates include continental breakfast. AE, DISC, MC, V. **Amenities:** Restaurant; bar; pool; tennis court; health club; babysitting; laundry service and coin-operated laundry; nonsmoking rooms; rooms for those w/limited mobility. *In room:* A/C, TV, dataport, fridge, beverage maker, hair dryer, iron, safe (in some).

INEXPENSIVE

Paradise Harbour Club & Marina   The noteworthy thing about this place is its sense of isolation, despite heavily developed Paradise Island. Built in 1991 near the island's extreme eastern tip, it's just a few steps from the also-recommended Columbus Tavern (see review below). It's pale pink, with rambling upper hallways, terra-cotta tile floors, and clean, well-organized bedrooms with tub/shower combos in the bathrooms. If available, opt for one of the top-floor accommodations so you can enjoy the view. Some of its quaint amenities, all free, include a water taxi to downtown Nassau, a beach shuttle (albeit in a golf cart), snorkeling gear, and bikes.

In room: A/C, TV, kitchen (in some), minibar, coffeemaker, hair dryer, iron, safe (in some).

Paradise Island Dr. (P.O. Box SS-5804), Paradise Island, The Bahamas. (✆) **242/363-2992.** Fax 242/363-2840. www. phc-bahamas.com. 23 units. Winter $150 double, $210 jr. suite, $275 1-bedroom apt, $410 2-bedroom apt; off season $120 double, $180 jr. suite, $250 1-bedroom apt, $350 2-bedroom apt. MC, V. **Amenities:** Restaurant; bar; pool; exercise room; Jacuzzi; watersports equipment/rental; golf cart shuttle to the beach; limited room service; babysitting; coin-operated laundry; rooms for those w/limited mobility. In room: A/C, TV, kitchen (in some), minibar, coffeemaker, hair dryer, iron, safe (in some).

4 Where to Dine

Paradise Island offers an array of the most dazzling, and the most expensive, restaurants in The Bahamas. If you're on a strict budget, cross over the bridge into downtown Nassau, which has far more reasonably priced places to eat. Meals on Paradise Island are often expensive but unimaginative. (Surf and turf appears on many a menu.) Unfortunately, you may not get what you pay for.

The greatest concentration of restaurants, all near the casino, is owned by Sun International. There are other good places outside this complex, however, including Dune at the Ocean Club, which is that hotel's showcase restaurant.

EXPENSIVE

Bahamian Club (★★ FRENCH/INTERNATIONAL   Overall, this is our favorite restaurant at the Atlantis. With an upscale British colonial–era feel, it's a big but civilized and clubby spot, with spacious vistas, mirrors, gleaming mahogany, and forest-green walls. The excellent food is served in two-fisted portions. Meat is king here, all those old favorites from roasted prime rib to Cornish hen, plus the island's best T-bone, along with a selection of veal and lamb chops. The retro menu also features the inevitable Dover sole, lobster, and salmon steak. All of these dishes are prepared only with top-quality ingredients imported from the mainland. Appetizers also harken back to the good old days, with fresh jumbo shrimp cocktail, baby spinach salad with a bleu-cheese dressing, and onion soup. Try the Bahamian conch chowder for some local flavor. Side dishes are excellent here, especially the penne with fresh tomato sauce and the roasted shiitake mushrooms. Proper attire required—no jeans or sneakers.

In the Atlantis, Casino Dr. (✆) **242/363-3000.** Reservations required. Main courses $41–$45. AE, DC, DISC, MC, V. Wed–Mon 6–11pm.

Blue Lagoon (★ SEAFOOD   Across the lagoon from Atlantis, this restaurant is located two floors above the former reception area of the now closed Club Land'or, which was purchased by the Atlantis group and closed down for a major restoration and configuration. Call ahead to check on construction status.

Views of the harbor and Paradise Lake, along with music from an island combo, complements your candlelight meal here—a nice escape from the casino's glitter and glitz. Many of the fish dishes, including stone crab claws or the Nassau conch chowder, are excellent. The chef even whips up a good Caesar salad for two. The ubiquitous broiled grouper almondine is on the menu, or try some of the other dishes such as steak au poivre with a brandy sauce, or duck a l'orange. Yes, you've probably had better versions of these dishes elsewhere, but they are competently prepared and served here, even though the meats are shipped in frozen.

In the former Club Land'or, Paradise Dr. ✆ 242/363-2400. Reservations required. Main courses $29–$75. AE, DISC, MC, V. Daily 5–10pm.

Café at the Great Hall of Waters ★ Kids INTERNATIONAL   This restaurant
gives you a splashy look at the megaresort and water wonderland of Atlantis, even if you're not a guest of the hotel. Paradise Island has better restaurants, but none is this dramatic. You feel like a scuba diver as you peer through gigantic picture windows displaying the illuminated "ruins" of Atlantis. Everywhere you look, rainbow-hued fish swim past stone archaeological remains, and rows of lobsters parade through the sand. With a ceiling that seems miles away, the Café's multilevel dining areas are located on the lower floor of the Royal Towers. There's a kids' menu, and little ones love taking walks along the aquarium walls between courses. In such a setting, the food becomes almost secondary, although it's quite good. The chef imports top-quality ingredients for such dishes as rack of lamb with an arugula pesto. Lobster is a specialty, and you can also order well-prepared versions of smoked salmon with lemon grass and jumbo lump Andros crab cakes. Desserts are uniformly delicious.

Royal Towers, Atlantis Resort, Casino Dr. ✆ 242/363-3000. Reservations required. Main courses $35–$50. AE, DC, MC, V. Thurs–Mon 7–11am, 11:30am–2:30pm, and 6–10pm.

Courtyard Terrace ★ CONTINENTAL/BAHAMIAN   Okay, so the food isn't the
island's finest, which it ought to be for these prices. The on-site Dune is better. But when the moon is right, an evening meal here can be heavenly for people who don't have to watch their wallets. You dine amid palms, flowering shrubs, and a fountain in a flagstone courtyard surrounded by colonial verandas. Live music wafts from one of the upper verandas to the patio below. This isn't the most glittering dining room, but it's the most sophisticated. Women should bring some kind of evening wrap in case it becomes chilly.

The menu includes a strong showing of the classics: beefsteak tartare, steak Diane, prime sirloin, lobster quiche, and chateaubriand. Such a menu also calls for rack of lamb; though the shrimp Provençale or the calf's liver lyonnaise, if featured, may have more zest. With candles flickering in the breeze, music floating down, and tables set with Wedgwood china and crisp linen, you might not even mind the slow service.

In the Ocean Club, Ocean Club Dr. ✆ 242/363-2501. Reservations required. Jacket and tie recommended for men. Main courses $40–$52. AE, DC, DISC, MC, V. Daily 6:30–9pm.

Dune ★★★ INTERNATIONAL   The most sophisticated and cutting-edge restau-
rant on Paradise Island is in the west wing of the lobby level of the Ocean Club. Created and still owned by French-born restaurant guru Jean-Georges Vongerichten—who's already a big star in New York—it has a charcoal-gray and black decor that looks like it was plucked directly from a chic enclave in Milan; a sweeping view of the ocean; a teakwood floor that evokes a yacht's; and very attentive service. If you approach the place from the grounds, rather than from the interior of the hotel, you'll pass by the herb garden from which many of the culinary flavorings are derived. The chefs here invariably select the very finest ingredients, which are then handled with a razor-sharp technique.

Every dish has a special something, especially shrimp dusted with orange powder and served with artichokes and arugula. A splendid choice is tuna spring rolls with soybean salsa. Also charming to the palate is a chicken-and-coconut milk soup served with shiitake cakes. The goat cheese–and–watermelon salad is an unexpected delight. Filet of grouper—that standard throughout The Bahamas—is at its savory best here when served with a zesty tomato sauce.

In the Ocean Club, Ocean Club Dr. ℭ 242/363-2501, ext. 64739. Reservations required. Main courses lunch $12–$25, dinner $22–$50. AE, DC, DISC, MC, V. Daily 7–11am, noon–3pm, and 6–10:30pm.

Fathoms ⋇ SEAFOOD   You'll feel as if you're dining under the sea in this very dark seafood palace, with menus printed on stainless-steel sheets and an almost-mystical decor. Illuminating its glossy, metallic interior and four enormous plate-glass windows, sunlight filters through the watery aquariums that surround the Dig, Atlantis's recreation of an archaeological excavation of the underwater ruins of the Lost Continent.

At first you'll think the best appetizer is a selection of raw seafood in season. But then you're tempted by the blackened sashimi flavored with red ginger as it passes by. The lobster gazpacho is the best on the island, and you can also dig into a bowl of steamy black mussels flavored with chardonnay, garlic, and tomato. The wood-grilled yellowtail appears perfectly cooked with a wasabi potato mash and caviar, and the grilled Atlantic salmon is made extra inviting with its side dish of Parmesan garlic fries, a first for many diners. The meat devotee will find a wide selection here. Save room for dessert, and make it a light, feathery soufflé—a different one is served every night.

In the Atlantis Aquarium, Casino Dr. ℭ **242/363-3897**. Reservations recommended. Main courses $27–$50. AE, DC, MC, V. Daily 5:30–10pm.

Mama Loo's ⋇ ASIAN   Many people come here just to hang out in the bar, but if you're in the mood for a good Chinese meal, you'll be ushered to a table in a dining room with spinning ceiling fans, flaming torches from an overhead chandelier, and lots of potted palms. It evokes Shanghai during the British colonial age. The menu includes dishes from the Szechwan, Cantonese, Polynesian, and Caribbean repertoire. The best dish on the menu is Mama Loo's stir-fried lobster, beef, and broccoli with ginger. Two specialties we also like are shrimp in spicy chile sauce with a peanut sauce on the side, and deep-fried chicken filets with honey-flavored garlic sauce.

In the Coral Tower, Atlantis, Casino Dr. ℭ **242/363-3000**. Reservations recommended. Main courses $26–$40. AE, DC, DISC, MC, V. Tues–Sat 6–10pm.

Marketplace ⋇ *Value* INTERNATIONAL   Decorated with old vases and terra-cotta tiles, this large buffet-style restaurant is reminiscent of a sprawling market. It serves the best buffet on Paradise Island. You come here to fill up with an amazingly varied choice of food. Before you start loading onto your plate, browse past the various cooking stations and do some strategic planning. From fresh fruit to omelets, you can make breakfast as light or as heavy as you want. At lunch and dinner, you'll find everything from fresh seafood and made-to-order pastas to freshly carved roast beef and lamb. No intimate affair, this place seats some 400 diners. Sit inside or on the patio overlooking a lagoon.

Royal Towers, Atlantis Resort, Casino Dr. ℭ **242/363-3000**. Reservations not needed. Full buffets $34–$60. AE, DC, MC, V. Daily 7–11am, 11:30am–2:30pm, and 5:30–10pm.

The Water's Edge ⋇ SEAFOOD BUFFET   Three 4.5m (15-ft.) waterfalls splash into an artificial lagoon just outside the dining room's windows. Huge chandeliers illuminate the room, which has views of an open kitchen, where a battalion of chefs work to create a nightly seafood buffet. Many guests come here just to sample the pizza and pasta specialties. The pizzas are standard, but some of the pastas have a bit of zest, including penne *a l'arrabbiata* (with a spicy tomato sauce). The chef pays special attention to the antipasti, which evokes the tangy flavors of the Mediterranean, especially the *soup au pistou* (vegetables with basil and roasted garlic). Depending on the night, some of these dishes are better than others. The main problem here is that the food has a hard time competing with the ambience.

At the Atlantis, Casino Dr. © **242/363-3000.** Reservations recommended. Seafood buffet $45. AE, DC, DISC, MC, V. Daily 6–10pm.

Villa d'Este ✦ ITALIAN   Paradise Island's most elegant Italian restaurant offers classic dishes prepared with skill and served with flair. It's become less oriented to Tuscan dishes and is more Americanized Italian now. Italian murals decorate the walls.

Main dishes have flair, including pan-fried chicken breast with artichokes and mushrooms in a lemon-laced white-wine sauce, or a whole roasted rack of lamb coated with red-wine sauce and rosemary potatoes. The freshly made fettuccine tomato sauce and basil is almost perfect. The sea bass is quite delectable here, served with a perfect seafood broth.

In the Atlantis, Coral Tower, Casino Dr. © **242/363-3000.** Reservations required. Main courses $30–$50. AE, DC, MC, V. Fri–Tues 6–10pm.

MODERATE

Blue Marlin ✦ *Finds* BAHAMIAN/SEAFOOD   This could be both your nightclub and dining choice for the evening. With a name like Blue Marlin, you expect and get fish and seafood dishes, although there are other choices as well. The catch always tastes fresh, and it's well prepared. If you've never had that famous Bahamian dish, cracked conch, here is a good place to introduce yourself to it. (Think breaded veal cutlet.) That favorite of the 1950s, lobster thermidor, is still a popular choice here, and the chef always fashions a linguine studded with morsels of fresh seafood. For the meat or poultry fancier, there are tender spare ribs basted with guava and Eleuthera coconut chicken. Every night at 7:30, a steel-pan band and limbo show is presented along with a slightly gruesome live glass-eating act. You have a choice of dining inside or out.

Hurricane Hole Plaza. © **242/363-2660.** Reservations recommended. Main courses $10–$24. DISC, MC, V. Daily 5pm to "last customer."

Columbus Tavern ✦ *Finds* CONTINENTAL/BAHAMIAN   Far removed from the glitz and glamour of the casinos, the tavern seems relatively little known, even though Freddie Lightbourne of the Poop Deck restaurant has been running it for years now. It deserves to be discovered, because it serves good food at reasonable (for Paradise Island) prices. The tavern has the typical nautical decor (don't come here for the setting), with tables placed both inside and outside overlooking the harbor. The bar is worth a visit in itself, with its long list of tropical drinks. You can go local by starting off with the conch chowder, or opt for cheese-stuffed mushrooms with foie gras. Even though it's imported frozen, the rack of lamb are flawless. You can also order a decent veal cutlet and a quite good filet of grouper with a tantalizing lobster sauce.

Paradise Island Dr. © **242/363-2534.** Reservations required for dinner. Main courses lunch $11–$26, dinner $20–$48. AE, MC, V. Mon–Fri 11:30am–10:30pm; Sat–Sun 8:30–10:30pm.

INEXPENSIVE

Anthony's Caribbean Grill AMERICAN/CARIBBEAN   Its owners think of this place as an upscale version of Bennigan's or TGI Fridays. But the decor is thoroughly Caribbean, thanks to psychedelic tropical colors, underwater sea themes, and jaunty maritime decorative touches. A bar dispenses everything from conventional mai tais to embarrassingly oversized, 48-ounce "sparklers"—with a combination of rum, amaretto, vodka, and fruit punch that is about all most serious drinkers can handle. Menu items include burgers, pizzas capped with everything from lobster to jerk chicken, barbecued or fried chicken, ribs with Caribbean barbecue sauce, and several meal-size salads.

Paradise Island Shopping Center, at the junction of Paradise and Casino drives. ℂ 242/363-3152. Lunch $7–$15; dinner $11–$39. AE, DISC, MC, V. Daily 7:30am–11pm.

The Cave Grill *Kids* BURGERS/SALADS/SANDWICHES   This burger-and-salad joint is near the Atlantis's beach, catering to the bathing suit–and–flip-flops crowd, most often families. To reach the restaurant, you pass beneath a simulated rock-sided tunnel illuminated with flaming torches. The selection of ice cream will cool you off in the midafternoon sun.

At the Atlantis, Casino Dr. ℂ 242/363-3000. Lunch platters $10–$24. AE, DISC, MC, V. Daily 10am–6pm.

News Café DELI   Low-key and untouristy, this is where you'll find most of the island's construction workers, groundskeepers, and hotel staff having breakfast and lunch. They maintain a stack of the day's newspapers, so you can have something to read as you sip your morning cappuccino or latte. You can also stock up here on sandwiches for your beach picnic.

In the Hurricane Hole Plaza, Paradise Island. ℂ 242/363-4684. Reservations not accepted. Breakfast, lunch sandwiches, and platters $5–$11. Assorted coffees $2–$3.50. AE, DC, DISC, MC, V. Daily 7am–11pm.

Seagrapes Restaurant *Kids* INTERNATIONAL   Buffet lunches and dinners are the specialty of this pleasantly decorated tropical restaurant. This is the most affordable and family-oriented choice in the Atlantis, offering Cuban, Caribbean, and Cajun dishes. It's pretty straightforward fare, but you get a lot of food for not a lot of money—a rarity on pricey Paradise Island. The restaurant, which can seat 200 to 300 diners at a time, overlooks the lagoon and has a marketplace look, with buffet offerings displayed in little stalls and stations.

In the Atlantis, Casino Dr. ℂ 242/363-3000. Breakfast and lunch buffet $19; dinner buffet $40. AE, DC, DISC, MC, V. Daily 7–11am, noon–3pm, and 5:30–10pm.

5 Beaches, Watersports & Other Outdoor Pursuits

Visitors interested in something more than lazing on the beaches have only to ask hotel personnel to make the necessary arrangements. Guests at the **Atlantis** (ℂ 242/363-3000), for example, can have access to a surprising number of diversions without so much as leaving the hotel property. They can splash in private pools; play tennis, Ping-Pong, and shuffleboard; ride the waves; snorkel; or rent Sunfish, Sailfish, jet skis, banana boats, and catamarans from contractors located in kiosks.

HITTING THE BEACH

On Paradise Island, **Cabbage Beach** ⭐⭐ is the real showcase. Its broad white sands stretch for at least 3km (2 miles). Casuarines, palms, and sea grapes border it. It's likely to be crowded in winter, but you can find a little more elbowroom by walking to the northwestern stretch of the beach. You can reach Paradise Island from downtown Nassau by walking over the bridge, taking a taxi, or boarding a ferryboat at Prince George Dock. Cabbage Beach does not have public facilities but you can patronize one of the handful of bars and restaurants nearby and use their facilities. Technically, to use the facilities, you should be a customer—even if that means buying only a drink.

Our other favorite beach in this area is the white-sand **Paradise Beach** 🌸🌸, dotted with *chikees* (thatched huts), which are perfect when you've had too much of the sun. The beach is used mainly by guests of the Atlantis (p. 123), as it lies at the far western tip of the island. If you're not a resident, access is difficult. If you're staying at a hotel in Nassau and want to come to Paradise Island for a day at the beach, it's better to go to Cabbage Beach (see above).

FISHING

Anglers can fish close to shore for grouper, dolphin fish, red snapper, crabs, even lobster. Farther out, in first-class fishing boats fitted with outriggers and fighting chairs, they troll for billfish or giant marlin.

The best way to hook up with this pastime is to go to the activities desk of your hotel. All hotels have contacts with local charter operators who take their passengers out for a half or full day of fishing. For other possibilities, refer to "Beaches, Watersports & Other Outdoor Pursuits," in chapter 3.

GOLF

Ocean Club Golf Club 🌸🌸 on Paradise Island Drive (📞 **242/363-6682;** www.one andonlyresorts.com), at the east end of the island, is an 18-hole championship golf course designed by Tom Weiskopf that overlooks both the Atlantic Ocean and Nassau

---

Favorite Paradise Island Experiences

A Dazzling Stage Show. In the Las Vegas tradition, you can catch one of the show-biz extravaganzas that are staged at the Atlantis showroom of the Atlantis Paradise Island Casino.

The Sunset at the Cloister. Here, amid the reassembled remains of a 12th-century French stone monastery once owned by William Randolph Hearst, you can enjoy one of the most beautiful pink and mauve sunsets in all The Bahamas.

A Day at Paradise Beach. It's one of the best beaches in the entire Caribbean. When you've had too much of the sun, relax in one of the *chikees* (thatched huts) that dot the beach.

A Night at the Casino. The Paradise Island Casino is one giant pleasure palace. Many visitors arrive on the island just to test their luck in this 2,787-sq.-m (30,000-sq.-ft.) casino. The echoing interior passageway that interconnects the various parts of this far-flung resort is home to a medley of shops and restaurants, some of them among the finest in The Bahamas.

Finds Spa Serenity

The 2,323-sq.-m (25,000-sq.-ft.) **Mandara Spa** at the **Atlantis** (p. 123) is designed to make guests feel like gods and goddesses. Services include exotic body scrubs and wrap treatments with names like Caribbean Coffee Scrub, Tropical Coconut Scrub, and Sunburn Cooler. Spa guests also get to take a dip in Poseidon's Thalassotherapy Pool, a beautiful, open-air natural seawater pool.

Harbour. Attracting every caliber of golfer, the par-72 course is known for its hole 17, which plays entirely along the scenic Snorkelers Cove. Greens fees, including cart, are $245 per player, and rental clubs and shoes are available.

Golfers who want more variety will find one other course on New Providence Island (see "Beaches, Watersports & Other Outdoor Pursuits," in chapter 3).

SNORKELING & SCUBA DIVING

For more scuba sites in the area, see "Snorkeling, Scuba Diving & Underwater Walks," in chapter 3.

Bahamas Divers, East Bay Street, Yachthaven Marina Drive (© **242/393-5644;** www.bahamadivers.com), is the best all-around center for watersports on the island, specializing in scuba diving and snorkeling. They're located in Nassau near the Paradise Island Bridge. A one-tank dive, all equipment included, costs $55; a two-tank dive goes for $89. Snorkeling reef trips depart daily at 8:30am and 1:30pm, costing $39 with all equipment included.

TENNIS

Well-heeled tennis buffs check into **Ocean Club,** Ocean Club Drive (© **242/363-2501**). Many visitors go there just for tennis, which can be played day or night on their six Har-Tru courts. Guests booked into the cabanas and villas of the club can practically roll out of bed onto the courts. Although beginners and intermediate players are welcome, the courts are often filled with first-class competitors. Tennis is free for guests of the Ocean Club.

Other hotels with courts include the **Atlantis** (© **242/363-3000**), with 10 hard-surface courts. At least two major tennis championships a year are held at the Atlantis courts, drawing players from the world's top 20.

6 Seeing the Sights

Most of the big hotels here have activity-packed calendars, especially for that occasional windy, rainy day that comes in winter. Hordes of Americans can be seen taking group lessons in such activities as backgammon, whist, tennis, and cooking and dancing Bahamian style. They're even taught how to mix tropical drinks, such as a Goombay Smash (spicy rum, coconut rum, apricot brandy, and orange juice served in a high-ball glass with ice) or a Yellow Bird (dark rum, white rum, Galliano herbal liqueur, and both orange and lime juice strained into a Collins glass half filled with crushed ice). To an increasing degree, hotels such as the Atlantis have configured themselves as destinations in their own right.

Atlantis Paradise Island Resort & Casino ⋆⋆   Regardless of where you're staying—even if it's at the most remote hotel on New Providence—you'll want to visit this lavish theme park, hotel, restaurant complex, casino, and entertainment center. It's Paradise Island's big attraction. You could spend all day here—and all night, too—wandering through the glitzy shopping malls; sampling the international cuisine of the varied restaurants; gambling at the roulette wheels, slot machines, and blackjack tables; or seeing Vegas-style revues. And once you're here, don't even think about leaving without a tour of the Dig, a Disney-style attraction that celebrates the eerie and tragic legend of the lost continent of Atlantis. During the day you can dress casually, but at night you should dress up a bit, especially if you want to try one of the better restaurants.

The most crowded time to visit Atlantis is between 9am and 5pm on days when cruise ships are berthed in the nearby harbor. (That's usually every Tues and Sat 9am–5pm.) The most crowded time to visit the casino is between 8 and 11pm any night of the week. There is no cover to enter: You pay just for what you gamble away (and that could be considerable), eat, and drink. The big shows have hefty cover charges, although some entertainment in the bars is free, except for the price of the liquor.

Casino Dr. ✆ **242/363-3000**. Free admission. Daily 24 hr.

The Cloister ⋆   Located in the Versailles Gardens of the One&Only Ocean Club, this 12th-century cloister, originally built by Augustinian monks in southwestern France, was reassembled here stone by stone. Huntington Hartford, the A&P heir, purchased the cloister from the estate of William Randolph Hearst at San Simeon in California. Regrettably, after the newspaper czar originally bought the cloister, it was hastily dismantled in France for shipment to America, but the parts had not been numbered—they all arrived unlabeled on Paradise Island. The reassembly of the complicated monument baffled most conventional methods of construction, until artist and sculptor Jean Castre-Manne set about to reassemble it piece by piece. It took him 2 years, and what you see today, presumably, bears some similarity to the original. The gardens, which extend over the rise to Nassau Harbour, are filled with tropical flowers and classic statues. Unfortunately, although the monument retains a timeless beauty, recent buildings have encroached on either side, marring Huntington Hartford's original vision.

One&Only Ocean Club, Ocean Club Dr. ✆ **242/363-2501**. Free admission. Daily 24 hr.

Moments   **A Special Place of Beauty**

If you head up Paradise Island Drive, you'll reach Ocean Club Drive and a garden of tranquillity known as the **Versailles Gardens at the Ocean Club.** This is the loveliest spot on Paradise Island, far removed from the glitz and faux-glamour of the casinos. Its seven terraces frequently host weddings. Statues of some of A&P heir Huntington Hartford's favorite people are found in the gardens, including Mephistopheles, Franklin D. Roosevelt, and even Napoleon. The gardens are open any time, day or night—and admission is free.

---

7 Shopping

For serious shopping, you'll want to cross over the Paradise Island Bridge into Nassau (see chapter 3). However, many of Nassau's major stores also have shopping outlets on Paradise Island.

The Shops at the Atlantis, in the Atlantis (© 242/363-3000), is the largest concentration of shops and boutiques on Paradise Island, rivaling anything else in The Bahamas in terms of size, selection, and style. The boutiques are part of the recently rebuilt Crystal Court Arcade within the sprawling Atlantis. Most of them are set adjacent to the resort's casino, in a well-appointed arcade that meanders between the Royal Tower and the Coral Tower, although a handful, as noted below, are scattered strategically throughout the resort. It's all about conspicuous consumption, so if you want to do more than browse, bring your platinum card and make sure it's Amex.

There are two separate branches of **Colombian Emeralds** (one in the Crystal Court arcade, another closer to the beach within the Atlantis's Beach Tower), where the colored gemstones far outnumber the relatively limited selection of diamonds. Other choices include **Mademoiselle,** with branches in both the Beach Tower and the Coral Tower, where chic but simple clothing for women focuses on festive beach and resort wear.

The richest pickings lie within the **Crystal Court Arcade.** Here, 3,252 sq. m (35,000 sq. ft.) of merchandising space features **Lalique,** France-based purveyor of fine crystal and fashion accessories for men and women; **Cartier; Versace,** the late designer to the stars (this boutique also has a particularly charming housewares division); **Armani,** whose clothes make almost any woman look like Michelle Pfeiffer and any man at least a bit thinner; **Façonnable,** a youthful, sporty designer for young and beautiful club-hoppers; **Bulgari,** purveyor of the most enviable jewels in the world, as well as watches, giftware, and perfumes; and **Gucci** and **Ferragamo,** in case you forgot your dancing shoes. And if you want a bathing suit, **Coles of Nassau** sells swimwear by Gottex, Pucci, and Fernando Sanchez. Finally, **John Bull,** known for its Bay Street store in Nassau and as a pioneer seller of watches throughout The Bahamas, also has an interesting assortment of watches, jewelry, and designer accessories at this outlet.

8 Paradise Island After Dark

Paradise Island has the best nightlife in The Bahamas, and most of it centers on the Atlantis.

The Atlantis Resort's Casino and Discothèque

There's no other spot in The Bahamas, with the possible exception of the Crystal Palace complex on Cable Beach, with such a wide variety of after-dark attractions, and absolutely nothing that approaches its inspired brand of razzle-dazzle. Even if you stay in Nassau or Cable Beach, you'll want to drop into this artfully decorated, self-contained temple to decadence, even if gambling isn't really your passion. Love it or hate it, this place is simply a jaw-dropper.

The casino is the most lavishly planned, most artfully "themed" casino this side of Vegas. The only casino in the world built above a body of water, it was designed as an homage to the lost continent of Atlantis, and it appears to have risen directly from the waters of the lagoon. The gaming area is centered on buildings representing a Temple of the Sun and a Temple of the Moon with a painted replica of the zodiac overhead.

Rising from key locations in and around the casino are five of the most elaborate sculptures in the world. Massive and complex, they were crafted by teams of artisans spearheaded by Dale Chihuly, the American-born resident of Venice whose glass-blowing skills are the most celebrated in the world. Other than the decor, the casino's gaming tables, open daily from 10am to 4am, are the main attraction in this enormous place, and about a thousand whirring and clanging slot machines operate 24 hours a day.

One side of the casino contains **Dragons,** a disco that manages to attract a few local hipsters as well as guests of the Atlantis. Come here anytime during casino hours for a drink. A sweaty, flirty crowd parties all night on the dance floor. Often, you can catch some of the best live music in The Bahamas, as bands take to the stage that's cantilevered above the dance floor. The disco gets going around 9pm nightly, with a cover charge of $30 required from all nonguests of the Atlantis. Ringing the casino are some 3,252 sq. m (35,000 sq. ft.) of retail shopping space (see "Shopping," above) and an impressive cluster of hideaway bars and restaurants.

Also in the same Atlantis complex, **Joker's Wild** (© 242/363-3000) is the only real comedy club in The Bahamas, with a talented company of funny people who work hard to make their guests laugh. Show times are Tuesday through Sunday at 9:30pm. At least two comedians will appear on any given night, most of them hailing from The Bahamas, with occasional appearances of performers from London and New York. Midway between the Royal Tower and the Coral Tower, Casino Dr. © 242/363-3000. No cover charge for casino, but a cover charge of $25 applies to clubs and shows.

THE BAR SCENE

Dune Bar   Recommended as the top restaurant on Paradise Island, this deluxe dining room is also the setting for the island's most elegant and sophisticated lounge; it's becoming increasingly popular as a plush, appealing (and permissive) meeting spot for singles. The bar is centered around a translucent white marble bar skillfully illuminated from behind. At the Ocean Club, Ocean Club Dr. © 242/363-2501, ext. 64739. Call for open hours.

Plato's Lounge   This is the Atlantis resort's most romantic bar, a sensual spot where you can escape the din of the slot machines. There's a glow from dozens of flickering candles set within lavish candelabras, and ocean views through the oversize windows. A pianist sets the mood during cocktail hour and early evening. In the morning, the site doubles as a cafe, serving pastries and snacks from 6am until 4pm. It's open around the clock daily. On the lobby level of the Royal Towers, Atlantis Resort, Casino Dr. © 242/363-3000.

5

Grand Bahama
(Freeport/Lucaya)

Big, bold, and *brassy* describe Grand Bahama Island, home to the resort area of Freeport/Lucaya. Though there's a ton of tourist development, it doesn't have the upscale chic of Paradise Island, but it does have fabulous white-sand beaches and a more reasonable price tag.

It may never return to its high-roller days with the gloss and glitz of the '60s, when everybody from Howard Hughes to Frank Sinatra and Rat Packers showed up, but recent improvements and massive redevelopment have brought a smile back to its face, which had grown wrinkled and tired over the latter part of the 20th century.

The second-most-popular tourist destination in The Bahamas (Nassau/Cable Beach/Paradise Island is first), Grand Bahama lies just 81km (50 miles) and less than 30 minutes by air off the Florida coast. That puts it just 122km (76 miles) east of Palm Beach, Florida. The island is the northernmost and fourth-largest landmass in The Bahamas (118km/73 miles long and 6.5–13km/4–8 miles wide).

Freeport/Lucaya was once just a dream. Wallace Groves, a Virginia-born financier, saw the prospect of developing the island into a miniature Miami Beach, and in the 1950s, almost overnight, the low-lying pine forest turned into one of the world's major resorts. Today, with the casino, the International Bazaar, high-rise hotels, golf courses, marinas, and a bevy of continental restaurants, Groves's dream is fully realized.

The Lucaya district was developed 8 years after Freeport, as a resort center along the coast. It has evolved into a blend of residential and tourist facilities. As the two communities grew, their identities became almost indistinguishable. But elements of their original purposes still exist today. Freeport is the downtown area and attracts visitors with its commerce, industry, and own resorts, whereas Lucaya is called the "Garden City" and pleases residents and vacationers alike with its fine sandy beaches.

Grand Bahama is more than an Atlantic City clone, however. If you don't care for gambling at one of the island's two casinos, or if you're not interested in Vegas-style cabaret revues, try one of the alternatives. Because the island is so big, most of it remains relatively unspoiled. You can get close to nature at plenty of quiet places, including the Rand Nature Centre and the Garden of the Groves. Lucayan National Park—with its underwater caves, forest trails, and secluded beach—is another major attraction. Just kilometers from Freeport/Lucaya are serene places where you can wander in a world of casuarina, palmetto, and pine trees. During the day, you can enjoy long stretches of open beach, broken by inlets and little fishing villages.

The reviews of Grand Bahama Island are definitely mixed. Some discerning travelers who could live anywhere have built homes here; others vow never to set foot on the island again, finding it "tacky" or "uninspired." Judge for yourself.

1 Orientation

For a general discussion on traveling to The Bahamas, refer to chapter 2.

ARRIVING

A number of airlines fly to Grand Bahama International Airport from the continental United States, including **American Airlines** (© 800/433-7300; www.aa.com) and **Bahamasair** (© 800/222-4262; www.bahamasair.com), both with daily flights from Miami. **GulfStream Continental Connection** (© 800/231-0856; www.gulfstream air.com) flies to Freeport from Miami and West Palm Beach once daily, and from Fort Lauderdale five times daily. **US Airways** (© 800/428-4322; www.usairways.com) flies once daily from Charlotte, North Carolina.

Other competing airlines include **AirTran** (© 800/247-8726), flying daily non-stop from Atlanta as well as Baltimore Thursday to Monday. **Delta Connection** (© 800/221-1212) flies daily from Atlanta.

Many visitors arrive in Nassau, then hop on one of the five daily Bahamasair flights to Freeport. These 35-minute hops run $162 round-trip.

No buses run from the airport to the major hotel zones. But many hotels will provide airport transfers, especially if you've bought a package deal. If yours does not, no problem; taxis meet arriving flights and will take you from the airport to one of the hotels in Freeport or Lucaya for about $11 to $20. The ride shouldn't take more than about 10 minutes.

A great way to get from the eastern coast of The Bahamas to Freeport is aboard a modern ferryboat, the sleek *Cloud X,* which will transport you there in 3 hours. Launched in 2004, this 367-passenger ferry embarks from the port of Palm Beach Wednesday to Monday, offering one daily departure and one daily return. The round-trip fare is $99 for adults, $49 for children 6 to 12, and free for kids 5 and under. A $34 port charge is levied on passengers of all ages. On board are a trio of comfortable lounges, two bars, and a casino. For more information call © 866/Go-Ferry (fax 561/841-0472; www. cloudx.com). MasterCard and Visa are accepted. The main office for booking is at 301 Broadway, Suite 142, Riviera Beach, FL, 33404, open Monday to Friday 9am to 5pm.

Discovery Cruise Lines (© 888/213-8253; www.discoverycruiseline.com) offers daily passage between the Fort Lauderdale Seaport and Grand Bahama Island. Frankly, the Discovery vessels making this 89km (55-mile) jaunt haven't been the newest or glitziest cruise ships sailing in the past 3 or 4 decades, but they are shipshape and fit the bill. The trip over from Florida takes about 5 hours, and they have the required pool deck and bar, along with a casino, bar show lounge, and dining facilities. They feed passengers very well. A round-trip fare runs $157 per person, and you can make reservations online.

VISITOR INFORMATION

Assistance and information are available at the **Grand Bahama Tourism Board,** International Bazaar in Freeport (© 242/352-6909; www.grand-bahama.com). Two other information booths are located at the **Freeport International Airport** (© 242/352-2052) and at the Port Lucaya Marketplace (© 242/373-8988). There's also a branch at the cruise-ship docks. Hours are 9am to 5pm Monday to Saturday.

Grand Bahama Island

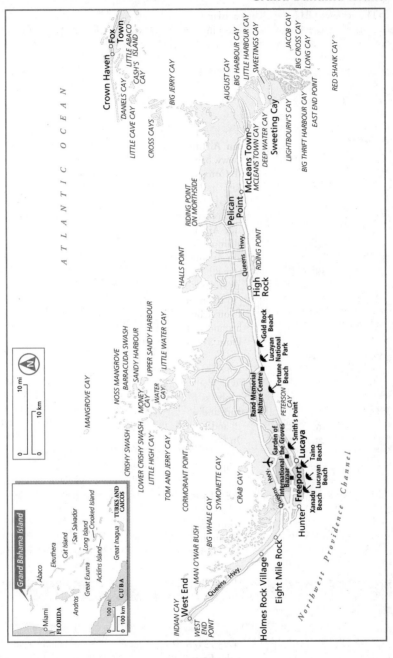

ISLAND LAYOUT

Getting around Freeport/Lucaya is fairly easy because of its flat terrain. Although Freeport and Lucaya are frequently mentioned in the same breath, newcomers should note that Freeport is a landlocked collection of hotels and shops rising from the island's center, while Lucaya, about 4km (2½ miles) away, is a waterfront section of hotels, shops, and restaurants clustered next to a saltwater pond on the island's southern shoreline.

Freeport lies midway between the northern and southern shores of Grand Bahama Island. Bisected by some of the island's largest roads, it contains the biggest hotels, as well as two of the most-visited attractions in the country: the Crowne Plaza Golf Resort & Casino at the Royal Oasis and the International Bazaar shopping complex. The local straw market, where you can buy inexpensive souvenirs, lies just to the right of the entrance to the International Bazaar.

To reach **Port Lucaya** from Freeport, head east from the International Bazaar along East Sunrise Highway, then turn south at the intersection with Seahorse Road. Within about 4km (2½ miles), it will lead to the heart of the Lucaya complex, Port Lucaya.

Set between the beach and a saltwater pond, Port Lucaya's architectural centerpiece is **Count Basie Square,** named for the great entertainer who used to have a home on the island. Within a short walk east or west, along the narrow strip of sand between the sea and the saltwater pond, rise most of the hotels of Lucaya Beach.

Heading west of Freeport and Lucaya, the West Sunrise Highway passes industrial complexes such as The Bahamas Oil Refining Company. At the junction with Queen's Highway, you can take the road northwest all the way to **West End,** a distance of some 45km (28 miles) from the center of Freeport. Along the way you pass Freeport Harbour, where cruise ships dock. Just to the east lies Hawksbill Creek, a village known for its fish market.

Much less explored is the **East End** of Grand Bahama. It's located some 72km (45 miles) from the center of Freeport and is reached via the Grand Bahama Highway, which, despite its name, is rather rough in parts. Allow about 2 hours of driving time. First you pass the **Rand Nature Centre,** about 5km (3 miles) east of Freeport. About 11km (7 miles) on is **Lucaya National Park,** and 8km (5 miles) farther lies the hamlet of **Free Town;** east of Free Town is **High Rock,** known for its Emmanuel Baptist Church. From here, the road becomes considerably rougher until it ends in **MacLean's Town,** which celebrates Columbus Day with an annual conch-cracking contest. From here, it's possible to take a water taxi across Runners Creek to the exclusive Deep Water Cay club, catering to serious anglers.

In Freeport/Lucaya, but especially on the rest of Grand Bahama Island, you will almost never find a street number on a hotel or a store. Sometimes in the more remote places, you won't even find a street name. In lieu of numbers, locate places by prominent landmarks or hotels.

2 Getting Around

BY TAXI

The government sets the taxi rates, and the cabs are metered (or should be). Metered rates are $3 for the first quarter mile (⅕km) and 40 cents each additional mile (1.6km). Additional passengers over the age of 2 are $3 each. If there's no meter, agree on the price with the driver in advance. You can call for a taxi, although most taxis wait at the major hotels or the cruise-ship dock to pick up passengers. One major taxi company is

Freeport Taxi Company, Logwood Road (© **242/352-6666**), open 24 hours. Another is **Grand Bahama Taxi Union** at the Freeport International Airport, Old Airport Road (© **242/352-7101**), also open 24 hours. *Note:* Typical taxi rates are as follows: From the Harbour to: Royal Oasis Golf Resort & Casino, $16; Xanadu Beach Hotel, $17; Port Lucaya Marketplace, $24; Taíno Beach Resort/The Ritz, $24; Viva Fortuna Beach, $29. From the airport to: Lucaya, $19; Viva Fortuna, $15; Royal Oasis, $11; Xanadu/Woodbourne/Running Mon Marina, $14. By Bus

Public bus service runs from the International Bazaar to downtown Freeport and from the Pub on the Mall to the Lucaya area. The typical fare is $1 for adults, 50¢ for children. Check with the tourist office (see "Visitor Information," above) for bus schedules. There is no number to call for information.

BY CAR

If you plan to confine your exploration to the center of Freeport with its International Bazaar and Lucaya with its beaches, you can rely on public transportation. However, if you'd like to branch out and explore the rest of the island (perhaps finding a more secluded beach), a rental car is the way to go. Try **Avis** (© **800/331-2112** or 242/352-7666; www.avis.com) or **Hertz** (© **800/654-3001** or 242/352-9250; www.hertz.com). Both of these companies maintain offices in small bungalows outside the exit of the Freeport International Airport.

One of the best local companies is **Dollar Rent-a-Car,** Old Airport Road (© **242/352-9325;** www.dollar.com), which rents everything from a new-style Kia Sportage to a Toyota Corolla. Rates range from $49 per day manual or $55 automatic, with unlimited mileage, plus another $15 per day for a CDW (Collision Damage Waiver; $500 deductible). Gas is usually $3 per gallon, and remember to drive on the left as British rules apply.

BY SCOOTER

A scooter is a fun way to get around as most of Grand Bahamas is flat with well-paved roads. Scooters can be rented at most hotels, or, for cruise-ship passengers, in the Freeport Harbour area. Helmets are required and provided by the outfitter. You can find dozens of stands along the road in Freeport and Lucaya and also in the major parking lots, charging rates ranging from $40 to $55 a day.

ON FOOT

You can explore the center of Freeport or Lucaya on foot, but if you want to venture into the East End or West End, you'll need to rent a car, hire a taxi, or try Grand Bahama's erratic public transportation.

Tips Island Hopping

If you'd like to visit some other islands while on Grand Bahama, you can do so aboard a small commuter-type airline, **Major's Airlines,** Freeport International Airport (© **242/352-5778** or 242/352-5781; www.thebahamasguide.com/major air), which offers regular round-trip flights to Bimini for $130, to the Abacos for $150, to Andros for $205, or to Eleuthera for $215. Most of its carriers transport 9 to 15 passengers. Flights are not available every day, so call for schedules, reservations, and more information.

FAST FACTS: **Grand Bahama**

Banks In Freeport/Lucaya, banks are open from 9:30am to 3pm, Monday to Thursday, and 9:30am to 5pm on Friday. Most banks here have ATMs that accept VISA, MasterCard, American Express, and any other bank or credit card on the Cirrus, Honor, Novus, and PLUS networks.

Climate See "When to Go," in chapter 2.

Currency Exchange Americans need not bother to exchange their dollars into Bahamian dollars, because the currencies are on par. However, Canadians and Brits will need to convert their money, which can be done at local banks or sometimes at a hotel, though hotels tend to offer less favorable rates.

Doctors For the fastest and best service, just head to Rand Memorial Hospital (see "Hospitals," below).

Drugstores For prescriptions and other pharmaceutical needs, go to Mini Mall, 1 West Mall, Explorer's Way, where you'll find **L.M.R. Drugs** (© **242/352-7327**), next door to Burger King. Hours are Monday to Saturday 8am to 8pm and Sunday 8am to 3pm.

Embassies & Consulates See "Fast Facts: The Bahamas," in chapter 2.

Emergencies For all emergencies, call © **911,** or dial 0 for the operator.

Eyeglass Repair The biggest specialist in eyeglasses and contact lenses is the **Optique Shoppe,** 7 Regent Centre, downtown Freeport (© **242/352-9073**).

Hospitals If you have a medical emergency, contact the government-operated, 90-bed **Rand Memorial Hospital,** East Atlantic Drive (© **242/352-6735** or 242/352-2689 for ambulance emergency).

Internet Access Visit the **Cyberclub** at Seventeen Center (© **242/351-4560;** cyberclub@grandbahama.net), open Monday to Saturday 9am to 8pm.

Information See "Visitor Information," earlier in this chapter.

Laundry & Dry Cleaning Try **Jiffy Cleaners and Laundry,** West Mall at Pioneer's Way (© **242/352-7079**), open Monday to Saturday 8am to 6pm.

Newspapers & Magazines The Freeport News is a morning newspaper published Monday through Saturday except holidays. The two dailies published in Nassau, the *Tribune* and the *Nassau Guardian,* are also available here, as are some New York and Miami papers, especially the *Miami Herald,* usually on the date of publication. American news magazines, such as *Time* and *Newsweek,* are flown in on the day of publication.

Police In an emergency, dial © **911.**

Post Office The main post office is on Explorer's Way in Freeport (© **242/352-9371**).

Safety Avoid walking or jogging along lonely roads. There are no particular danger zones, but stay alert: Grand Bahama is no stranger to drugs and crime.

Taxes All visitors leaving The Bahamas from Freeport must pay a $5 departure tax—in cash. (Both U.S. and Bahamian dollars are accepted.) You're also outrageously hit with another $20 departure tax, which is factored into your ticket. No sales tax is charged, but you will have to pay a 12% hotel tax.

Taxis See "Getting Around," earlier in this chapter.

Weather Grand Bahama, in the north of The Bahamas, has temperatures in winter that vary from about 60°F to 75°F (16°C–24°C) daily. Summer variations range from 78°F to the high 80s (26°C to the low 30s Celsius). In Freeport/Lucaya, phone *📞* **915** for weather information.

3 Where to Stay

Your choices are the Freeport area, near the Bahamia Casino and the International Bazaar, or Lucaya, closer to the beach.

Remember: In most cases, a resort levy of 8% and a 15% service charge will be added to your final bill. Be prepared, and ask if it's already included in the initial price you're quoted.

FREEPORT
EXPENSIVE
Island Seas Resort A timeshare property open to nonmembers, this resort opens onto a secluded beach, although it also offers its own water fun in the form of a pool, hot tub, and waterfall. Also on-site is a Tiki-hut restaurant and bar. The location is convenient for the Port Lucaya Market and the Lucaya Golf and Country Club. Depending on their individual owners, each condo is different, ranging from one-bedroom units to large two-bedroom suites. Each contains a full bathroom with tub/shower, plus a full kitchen and balcony. Although not part of the hotel facilities, many watersports outfitters are right on the beach.

William's Town (P.O. Box F-44735), Freeport, Grand Bahamas, The Bahamas. *📞* **242/373-1271.** Fax 242/373-1275. www.islandseas.com. 149 units. Winter $399 double, $499 2-bedroom suite; off season $219 double, $319 2-bedroom suite. AE, DISC, MC, V. **Amenities:** Restaurant; bar; pool; tennis court; bike rentals; limited room service (9am–4pm). *In room:* A/C, TV, fridge, coffeemaker, iron/ironing board, safe.

MODERATE
Crowne Plaza Golf Resort & Casino at the Royal Oasis *⭐* *Kids* Badly hit during the 2004 hurricane, this hotel—the most famous one on the island—spent most of 2005 under restoration. It should be up and running for your visit, but ask about rates: There's a chance the prices will increase. This mammoth complex actually consists of two differently styled resorts combined under one umbrella: the 10-story Crowne Plaza tower and the less glamorous, three-story Crowne Plaza Country Club. Reinventing itself to stay competitive, the resort spent some $42 million on its once-tired, built-in-the-1960s properties, hoping to revive some of their old glitz and glamour.

Flanked by a pair of fine golf courses, the Ruby and the Emerald, and thus catering to the convention crowd, the resorts are set on 1,000 hectares (2,470 acres) of tropical grounds. As it lies inland from the sea, the complex doesn't have its own natural beach. One of the grandest additions is a marine park and a man-made, landlocked beach; otherwise, you can take frequent shuttle buses to good natural beaches nearby, where watersports are available. The two sections, also jointly share one of the largest casinos in the entire country, a serviceable site that's functional—though nowhere near as flashy or cutting edge as, say, the Atlantis Casino on Paradise Island.

Where to Stay & Dine in Freeport/Lucaya

ACCOMMODATIONS ■

Best Western Castaways **7**
Coral Beach **11**
Crowne Plaza Golf Resort & Casino at the Royal Oasis **3**
Flamingo Bay Yacht Club & Marina Hotel **19**
Island Palm Resort **8**
Island Seas Resort **10**
Lakeview Manor Club **2**

Old Bahama Bay **1**
Paradise Cove **1**
Pelican Bay at Lucaya **13**
Port Lucaya Resort & Yacht Club **12**
Ritz Beach Resort **17**
Royal Islander **7**
Taino Beach Vacation Club **18**
The Westin & Sheraton at Our Lucaya **15**
Wyndham Viva Fortuna **24**

DINING ◆

Barracuda's **15**
Becky's Restaurant **4**
Bishop's Restaurant **21**
Café Michel **4**
China Beach **15**
China Temple **4**
Churchill's **15**
Club Caribe **23**
Fatman's Nephew **14**

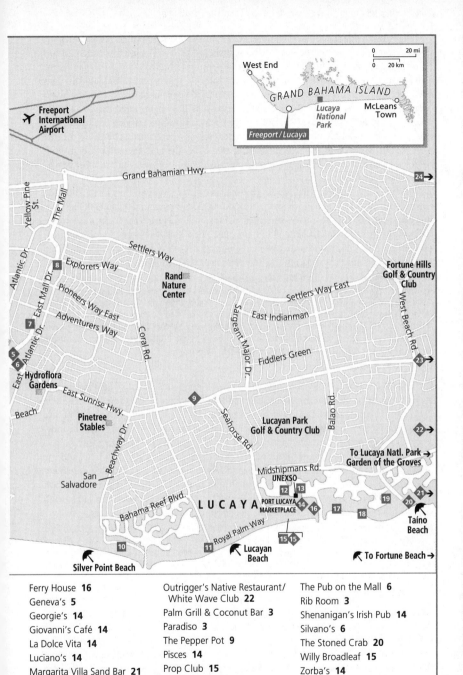

Ferry House **16**	Outrigger's Native Restaurant/	The Pub on the Mall **6**
Geneva's **5**	White Wave Club **22**	Rib Room **3**
Georgie's **14**	Palm Grill & Coconut Bar **3**	Shenanigan's Irish Pub **14**
Giovanni's Café **14**	Paradiso **3**	Silvano's **6**
La Dolce Vita **14**	The Pepper Pot **9**	The Stoned Crab **20**
Luciano's **14**	Pisces **14**	Willy Broadleaf **15**
Margarita Villa Sand Bar **21**	Prop Club **15**	Zorba's **14**
Oasis Café **3**	Pub at Lucaya **14**	

The Crowne Plaza Country Club attracts families, honeymooners, frugal couples, golfers, and others who don't need or want luxury. The hotel's design is rather like an enormous low-rise wagon wheel, with a Disney-inspired minimountain surrounded by a swimming pool at its core. The hotel is so spread out, guests often complain that they need ground transport just to reach their bedrooms. (Nine wings radiate from the pool.) Some of the rooms have kitchenettes and are sold as timeshare units. Regular accommodations come in several classifications; even standard rooms are well equipped, with two comfortable double beds, dressing areas, and full-size bathrooms. Rooms in the 900 wing are the largest and best furnished—and are usually the ones that sell out first. Both resorts also rent out a number of suites, each furnished in summery fabrics plus beachy but durable furniture.

Crowne Plaza Tower, lying across the mall from its larger sibling, is smaller and more tranquil, and a bit more posh, containing 32 suites and 362 luxuriously furnished large units. The tower structure adjoins the Casino and the International Bazaar. A light, California-style decor prevails, with a skylit lobby and rooms that most often contain cherry hardwood furnishings. Lots of conventioneers and folks on quick getaways from Florida tend to stay here, as do high rollers.

The Mall at W. Sunrise Hwy. (P.O. Box F-207), Freeport, Grand Bahama, The Bahamas. ✆ **800/545-1300** in the U.S. and Canada, or 242/350-7000. Fax 242/350-7002. www.theroyaloasis.com. 876 units. Crowne Plaza Country Club: Winter $145–$155 double, $240 suite; off season $115–$125 double, $180 suite. Crowne Plaza Tower: Winter $175–$205 double, $350 suite; off season $145–$155 double, $250 suite. Up to 2 children under 12 stay free in parent's room. AE, MC, V. **Amenities:** 6 restaurants; 6 bars; nightclub; casino; 3 pools; golf; 11 tennis courts; fitness center; spa; kids' activity center; limited room service (6:30am–11pm); massage; babysitting. *In room:* A/C, TV, dataport (in some), minifridge, beverage maker, hair dryer, iron/ironing board, safe.

INEXPENSIVE

Best Western Castaways (Kids)   Castaways is a modest and unassuming hotel despite its platinum location adjacent to the International Bazaar and the casino. You stay here because of its location and the low price. It's not on the beach, but a free shuttle will take you to nearby Williams Town Beach or Xanadu Beach. Surrounded by gardens, the four-story hotel has a pagoda roof and an indoor/outdoor garden lobby with a gift shop, a clothing shop, a game room, and tour desks. Rooms are your basic motel style, and the best units are on the ground. The Flamingo Restaurant features remarkable Bahamian and American dishes daily from 7:30am to 10pm; it also serves one of the island's best breakfasts. There's also a swimming pool area with a wide terrace and a pool bar serving sandwiches and cool drinks. A children's playground adjoins the pool.

42629 E. Mall Dr., Freeport, Grand Bahama, The Bahamas. ✆ **800/780-7234** or 242/352-6682. Fax 242/352-5087. www.bestwestern.com. 118 units. Winter $125–$155 double, $205 suite; off season $95–$125 double, $145 suite. Children under 12 stay free in parent's room. AE, DISC, MC, V. **Amenities:** Restaurant; 2 bars; pool; bike rentals; babysitting; self-service laundry; nonsmoking rooms; rooms for those w/limited mobility. *In room:* A/C, TV, dataport, hair dryer, iron/ironing board, safe.

Island Palm Resort (Value)   Set within the commercial heart of Freeport, this simple three-story motel consists of four buildings separated by parking lots and greenery. Within an easy walk from virtually everything in town, and 2km (1¼ miles) from the International Bazaar, it offers good value in no-frills, eminently serviceable rooms with well-kept bathrooms equipped with shower/tub combinations. Complimentary shuttle-bus service ferries anybody who's interested to nearby Williamstown Beach (also called Island Seas Beach), where you can use the beachfront facilities (including jet skis and snorkeling equipment) of its sibling resort, a timeshare unit known as Island Sea.

E. Mall Dr. (P.O. Box F-44881), Freeport, Grand Bahama, The Bahamas. Ⓒ **242/352-6648.** Fax 242/352-6640. http://islandpalm.tripod.com. 143 units. Winter $85 double; off season $75 double. Extra person $5. AE, DISC, MC, V. **Amenities:** Restaurant; bar; nightclub; pool; nonsmoking rooms; rooms for those w/limited mobility. *In room:* A/C, TV, iron/ironing board, safe.

Lakeview Manor Club   Today this 1970s-era resort is a timeshare, but it was originally built as private apartments. It's a good bargain for those who want peace and privacy, but the staff seems a bit lax. Catering to self-sufficient types, it offers midsize one-bedroom and studio apartments, each with tropical furniture, a private balcony, plus small bathrooms with shower/tub combinations. The club overlooks the 5th hole of the PGA-approved Princess Ruby Golf Course. It's 8km (5 miles) from the beach, but it's ideal for golfers or for anyone to whom a sea view isn't important. A complimentary shuttle bus travels to the International Bazaar, the supermarket, Port Lucaya, and beach areas.

Cadwallader Jones Dr. (P.O. Box F-42699), Freeport, Grand Bahama, The Bahamas. Ⓒ **242/352-9789.** Fax 242/352-2283. www.bahamasvg.com/lakeview. 52 units. Year-round $75 double, $100 1-bedroom apt; weekly $450 double; $600 1-bedroom apt. DC, DISC, MC, V. Closed last week of Oct. **Amenities:** Pool; 2 tennis courts; activities' desk; self-service laundry; babysitting. *In room:* A/C, ceiling fan, TV, full kitchen, beverage maker.

Royal Islander   Don't be fooled by the corny-looking, storm-battered exterior of this place. It was built during an unfortunate Disney-style period in Freeport's expansion, during the early 1980s, with an improbable-looking pyramidal roof inspired by a cluster of Mayan pyramids. Inside, it's a lot more appealing than you might think, with rooms arranged around a verdant courtyard that seems far, far removed from the busy traffic and sterile-looking landscape outside. Rooms have white-tile floors and bathrooms that are on the small side, with tiny sinks and shower stalls. Otherwise, the motif is Florida/tropical, with some pizzazz.

There's a coffee-shop-style snack bar and a small restaurant on the premises, but other than that, you'll have to wander a short distance, perhaps to the International Bazaar just across the street, to find diversions and dining. Free transport to the beach is available, but you'll have to take a bus or taxi anywhere else.

E. Mall Dr. (P.O. Box F-42549), Freeport, Grand Bahama, The Bahamas. Ⓒ **242/351-6000.** Fax 242/351-3546. www.bahamasvacationguide.com/royalislander.html. 100 units. Winter $97 double; off season $87 double. Children under 14 stay free in parent's room. AE, MC, V. **Amenities:** Restaurant; snack bar; bar; pool; Jacuzzi; self-service laundry; nonsmoking rooms. *In room:* A/C, TV, safe.

LUCAYA
EXPENSIVE
The Westin & Sheraton at Our Lucaya ★★ *Kids*   This massive $400-million resort, one of the largest in The Bahamas, is firmly anchored at the center of two of the best white sandy beaches in The Bahamas—Lucayan Beach and Taíno Beach. Expect nearly 3.2 hectares (8 acres) of soft white sand. Freeport/Lucaya, which had been losing tourist business to Paradise Island, got a big boost in 1999 when this sprawling metropolis opened its doors.

The first of the three sections was completed late in 1998 under the name **Sheraton at Our Lucaya.** It's the only one of the three branches of Our Lucaya to focus exclusively on all-inclusive holidays, whereby all meals, drinks, and most activities are included in one set price. With a vague South Beach Art Deco design, it's a massive, open-sided hexagon, with rooms facing the beach and the swimming pool. The 528-room resort is contemporary but relaxed; the developers have created a young vibe that draws a high number of families. Bedrooms are whimsical and fun, thanks to fabrics you'd expect on a loud Hawaiian shirt from the Elvis era and maple-veneered furniture, all put together with the kind of artful simplicity you'd expect in a California beach house.

In 2000, two newer subdivisions of Our Lucaya were opened, neither of which is marketed as an all-inclusive property. The smaller and somewhat more private of the two is **Westin Lighthouse Pointe,** a 322-unit, low-rise complex that focuses specifically on an adult clientele. Its larger counterpart is the 528-unit **Westin-Breakers Cay,** a grand, 10-story, white-sided tower. The three sections stretch in a glittering profile along a narrow strip of beachfront, allowing residents to drop into any of the bars, restaurants, and gardens. A complex this big contains a staggering diversity of restaurants, each designed with a different theme and ambience. The best of the resort's cuisine selections will be reviewed under "Where to Dine," later in this chapter. And consistent with the broad themes, each of the subdivisions has a dramatic and/or unconventional swimming pool. For example, the Sheraton at Our Lucaya's pool is designed around a replica of a 19th-century sugar mill, complete with an aqueduct that might be worthy of the ancient Romans.

A spa and fitness center, a quintet of tennis courts, a convention center, a state-of-the-art casino, and a shopping mall have all also been added in recent years, and there's an increasing emphasis on golf, thanks to the opening of the spectacular Reef Course (p. 166). An innovative feature for tennis players is the Fast Grand Slam of Tennis, which features replicas of the world's best known court surfaces—red clay at the French Open, manicured grass at Wimbledon, Rebound Ace at the Australian Open, and DecoTurf at the U.S. Open.

Children aged 2 to 12 can be amused and entertained throughout daylight hours every day at Camp Lucaya.

Royal Palm Way (P.O. Box F-42500), Lucaya, Grand Bahama, The Bahamas. © **877-OUR-LUCAYA** in the U.S., or 242/373-1333. Sheraton fax 242/373-8804; Westin fax 242/350-5060. www.ourlucaya.com. 1,260 units. Sheraton (all-inclusive) year-round $169–$249 double; from $469 suite; $30 extra per day for 3rd and 4th occupant. Westin Lighthouse Pointe or Breakers Cay year-round $199–$259 double; from $749 suite; $30 extra per day for 3rd and 4th occupant. AE, DISC, MC, V. **Amenities:** 10 restaurants; 10 bars; 44 pools; 2 golf courses; 5 tennis courts; health club; spa; watersports equipment/rentals; kids' camp and children's programs; business center; salon; 24-hr. room service; babysitting; laundry service; dry cleaning; nonsmoking rooms; rooms for those w/limited mobility. *In room:* A/C, TV, dataport (Westin only), kitchenette (in some units), minibar, iron/ironing board, safe.

MODERATE

Pelican Bay at Lucaya ★★ Here's a good choice for travelers with champagne tastes and beer budgets, a hotel with more architectural charm than any other small property on Grand Bahama. It's built on a peninsula jutting into a labyrinth of inland waterways, with moored yachts on virtually every side. Pelican Bay evokes a Danish

---

Tips **Never Pay Top Price**

Before you try to book your hotel on your own, be sure to read the section in chapter 2 on "Packages for the Independent Traveler" and the tips on how to lower hotel costs. Never pay the rack rate. Use the rates given in this section as a point of comparison only.

seaside village, with rows of "town houses," each painted a different color and sporting whimsical trim, and each overlooking the harbor. The hotel opened in the fall of 1996 and later expanded with another wing in 1999. Its location couldn't be better, right next to Port Lucaya Marketplace, where restaurants and entertainment spots abound. Lucayan Beach, one of the best stretches of white sand on the island, is just across the street, and Taíno Beach, with equally good sands, lies immediately to the east of the hotel. UNEXSO, providing some of the best dive facilities in The Bahamas, is next door. If that's not enough, the extensive amenities of Our Lucaya (see previous listing) are available for use.

The spacious accommodations have Italian tile floors and whitewashed furniture, with either a king-size bed or twin beds. The end rooms have cross ventilation and are the ideal choices for those who don't want to rely entirely on air-conditioning. Each unit comes with satellite TV, as well as a balcony with a view of the nearby waterway and marina. Bathrooms, although of standard size, contain oversize cotton robes and tub/shower combos.

The hotel has one main restaurant, the Ferry House, which specializes in American and Bahamian food and serves breakfast, lunch, and dinner daily. The Yellow Tail Pool Bar offers drinks and snacks all day.

Seahorse Rd. (P.O. Box F-42654), Lucaya, Grand Bahama, The Bahamas. © **800/600-9192** in the U.S., or 242/373-9550. Fax 242/373-9551. www.pelicanbayhotel.com. 186 units. Winter $165–$215 double, $275 suite; off season $135–$190 double, $250 suite. Rates include breakfast. AE, MC, V. **Amenities:** Restaurant; bar; 3 pools; Jacuzzi; business center; babysitting; nonsmoking rooms. *In room:* A/C, TV, dataport (in suites); minibar (in suites), minifridge, coffeemaker, hair dryer, iron/ironing board, safe.

Port Lucaya Resort & Yacht Club ⭐   With its own 100-slip marina lying next to the Port Lucaya Marketplace, this club opened in 1993 in the heart of the Port Lucaya restaurant, hotel, and nightlife complex. The resort consists of a series of pastel-colored two-story structures that guests reach via golf cart after checking in. The wings of guest rooms separate the piers—site of some very expensive marine hardware—from a verdant central green space with a gazebo-style bar and a swimming pool. Although set back inland on a waterway, Lucayan Harbour, this resort lies within a few minutes' walk of Lucayan Beach, one of the island's finest, and is also close to Taíno Beach. Even though it's not right on the beach, it's such an easy walk that no one seems to complain. Many guests are drawn to the nautical atmosphere of the resort and its nearness to Port Lucaya Marketplace.

The medium-size rooms have tile floors and are attractively and comfortably furnished with rattan pieces and big wall mirrors. The rooms are divided into various categories, ranging from standard to deluxe, and open onto the marina (preferred by yachting guests), the Olympic-size swimming pool, or the well-landscaped garden. (If you don't want to hear the sounds coming from the lively marketplace, request units 1–6, which are more tranquil and away from the noise.) Bathrooms with newer shower/tub combinations are tidy and well maintained, with adequate shelf space.

The hotel's restaurant, Tradewinds Cafe, offers standard Bahamian, American, and international dishes but only to groups of 50 or more. Finding a restaurant, however, shouldn't be difficult in the Port Lucaya Marketplace.

Bell Channel Rd. (P.O. Box F-42452), Lucaya, Grand Bahama, The Bahamas. © **800/LUCAYA-1** or 242/373-6618. Fax 242/373-6652. www.portlucayaresort.com. 160 units. Winter $100–$145 double, $175–$250 suite; off season $80–$120 double, $125–$200 suite. Extra person $25 per day. Children 12 and under free in parent's room. AE, DISC, MC, V. **Amenities:** Restaurant; 2 bars; pool; Jacuzzi; babysitting; nonsmoking rooms. *In room:* A/C, TV, hair dryer, iron/ironing board.

INEXPENSIVE

Coral Beach   Built in 1965 as privately owned condominiums, this peacefully isolated property near a sandy beach sits amid gardens and groves of casuarinas in a residential neighborhood. Some of the apartments and rooms have verandas, and four contain kitchenettes. More suitable for older travelers, the complex rents large but rather sparsely furnished units, with shower/tub combinations in the bathroom. A poolside bar provides finger food at reasonable prices and is open daily from 10am to 4pm. A beauty salon is on the premises. You're also within walking distance of the Port Lucaya Marketplace.

Coral Rd. at Royal Palm Way (P.O. Box F-42468), Lucaya, Grand Bahama, The Bahamas. ⓒ **242/373-2468.** Fax 242/373-5140. www.bahamasvg.com/coralbeach. 10 units. Winter $95–$115 double, $550–$650 weekly double; off season $80–$95 double, $490–$550 weekly double. MC, V. **Amenities:** Pool bar; pool; salon. *In room:* A/C, TV, kitchenette (in some), minifridge, coffeemaker.

TAINO BEACH

MODERATE

Ritz Beach Resort ⚡ (Kids)   Rated five stars by the government, this hotel lies adjacent to the Taíno Beach Vacation Club, sharing all the fun and amenities of its elaborate water park. Enveloped by semitropical gardens, the Ritz (not related to other fabled world hotels of the same name) also is adjacent to the Pirates of The Bahamas Beach Theme Park.

Actually, the origins of this resort date back to 1995. Over the years it was constructed in three different phases. Made up of two buildings, it also comprises a 50-room complex called Coral Suites. All the bedrooms are in concrete coral buildings, and units range from both efficiency and studio units to one-bedroom suites to elaborate villa and penthouse accommodations. The bedrooms are spacious and well furnished and handsomely maintained, with a tub-and-shower combo in the efficiency rooms and a walk-in shower in the studios.

Everything depends on how much you want to pay. Penthouses are on the fourth levels, and include such accommodations as a studio penthouse, which is multilevel with its own sun deck and private pool. The hotel's eating facilities are actually at the Taíno Beach Vacation Club where guests can patronize two international restaurants and five bars. The Ritz also has its own pool bar.

Jolly Roger Dr., Taíno Beach, Lucaya (P.O. Box F-43819), Grand Bahama Island, The Bahamas. ⓒ **888/311-7945** or 242/373-9354. Fax 242/373-4421. www.timetravelcorp.com. 110 units. Year-round $199 efficiency, $299 studio, $499 penthouse. Children 12 and under stay free in parent's room. **Amenities:** Restaurant; pool bar; pool; tennis court; babysitting; laundry service; nonsmoking rooms (all); rooms for those w/limited mobility. *In room:* A/C, TV, beverage maker, hair dryer, iron/ironing board.

Taíno Beach Vacation Club   This fun resort on the southern shore offers attractively furnished and breezy one-, two-, and three-bedroom condos furnished in a semitropical motif. The setting of the beach club is near an excellent 457m (1,500-ft.) strip of white sands. Although no beach here is actually private, this one comes the closest; you won't be subject to harassment from beach vendors pestering you to sell unwanted souvenirs. Yet, when you want to remove yourself from this relatively tranquil beach, you can walk over to the adjacent water park and the Pirates of the Caribbean Theme Park, where you'll find plenty of visitors and touristy attractions. These oceanfront accommodations are highly desirable, each well equipped with several extras. The location here is only a 6-minute ride from Port Lucaya and a 15-minute drive from the International Bazaar. Accommodations are divided into a series

---

Kids **Especially Fun Places for Kids**

Crowne Plaza Golf Resort & Casino at the Royal Oasis (p. 145)   Campo Seashell is a fully supervised program for children 5 to 11. Activities include volleyball on the beach, lizard-watching, and limbo contests. Day and evening activities are available.

The Westin & Sheraton at Our Lucaya (p. 149)   Camp Lucaya is the only interactive children's camp in The Bahamas, a full-service, free-standing center available for infants to 12-year-olds. With a menu of enriching experiences, children can participate in a variety of activities, from learning native dances and creating island-inspired arts and crafts to coconut bowling, a just-for-kids garden and tykes-only gecko pool. The Marine Explorer's Club, co-sponsored with UNEXSO, teaches ocean and marine experiences to youngsters, including an opportunity to go nose-to-nose with dolphins.

Wyndham Viva Fortuna (p. 154)   Kids Club is designed for children aged 2 to 11 and provides sports, games, and lessons under the supervision of trained staff members.

---

of two buildings rising three floors in this concrete structure with ocean views. Set among tropical gardens, the emphasis here is on sports, such as volleyball and basketball.

Jolly Roger Dr., Taíno Beach, Lucaya (P.O. Box F-43819), Grand Bahama Island, The Bahamas. ℭ **242/373-4682.** Fax 242/373-4421. www.tainobeach.com. 37 units. Year-round $150 efficiency; $375 1-bedroom unit; $475 2-bedroom unit; $650 3-bedroom unit. AE, DISC, MC, V. **Amenities:** Restaurant; pool bar; pool; laundry service; nonsmoking rooms (all); rooms for those w/limited mobility. *In room:* A/C, TV, kitchenette, beverage maker, iron/ironing board.

INEXPENSIVE
Flamingo Bay Yacht Club & Marina Hotel   Unlike the Ritz Beach Resort and the Taíno Vacation Club (its sibling properties), this hotel is set back but lies only about a 5-minute walk from a strip of 457m (1,500 ft.) of white sand. A three-story concrete building, offers midsize bedrooms that are comfortable and attractively furnished in a Caribbean motif, with a sleek new bathroom with tub/shower combination. You have a choice of renting a room with a king-size bed or two double beds, and each unit comes with such extras as a microwave and toaster. Across the street is the Pirates of The Bahamas (p. 169). At a 20-slip marina, a water taxi runs every hour to the center of the Lucaya area. Although amenities are sparse, customers are permitted to use of the Ritz Beach Resort's, which are plentiful.

Jolly Roger Dr., Taíno Beach, Lucaya, Grand Bahama Island, The Bahamas. ℭ **800/824-6623** or 242/373-4677. Fax 954/484-4757. www.timetravelcorp.com. 58 units. Year-round $70 double. Children 12 and under stay free in parent's room. AE, DISC, MC, V. **Amenities:** Coin-operated laundry; nonsmoking rooms. *In room:* A/C, TV, kitchenette, beverage maker.

OUTSIDE FREEPORT/LUCAYA
EXPENSIVE
Old Bahama Bay ★★   A cottage-style resort, this complex is the centerpiece of an 11-hectare (28-acre) site with home sites and a marina. In an oceanfront setting, the

boutique hotel has cottages adjacent to the 72-slip marina complex; a private beach is steps away. The colonial-style architecture graces a setting 40km (25 miles) west of Freeport, consisting of suites set in six two-story beach houses and three spacious buildings overlooking the marina. The living space is the most generous on the island, with custom-designed furnishings along with private beachfront terraces. The elegant marble bathrooms are luxurious with deluxe toiletries, and a whirlpool tub. The most recent addition added 12 "beachcomber" junior suites and four two-bedroom Grand Bay suites, each designed in a British colonial style. Dockside Grille serves quite good Bahamian and international dishes for three meals a day. The gourmet restaurant on-site is Aqua, featuring Caribbean, Asian, and Bahamian-inspired dishes.

West End (P.O. Box F-42546), Grand Bahama Island, The Bahamas. © **800/572-5711** in the U.S. or 800/444-9469. Fax 242/346-6546. www.oldbahamabay.com. 49 units. Winter $259–$509 suite, from $649 2-bedroom suite; off season $199–$399 suite, from $569 2-bedroom suite. $50 per extra person. Breakfast and dinner $80 per person extra per day. AE, MC, V. **Amenities:** 3 restaurants; 2 bars; pool; 2 tennis courts; fitness center; watersports equipment/rentals; car rental; limited room service (7am–10pm); massage; babysitting; laundry service; nonsmoking rooms (all). *In room:* A/C, TV, dataport, kitchenette, minifridge, beverage maker, hair dryer, iron/ironing board, safe.

MODERATE

Paradise Cove ★ *(Finds)*   Paradise Cove teems with rainbow-hued tropical marine life and a vast array of coral to delight the snorkeler in you. If you want to escape the glitz and glam of Freeport or Lucaya, this secluded hideaway on a beach is the perfect place. You'll find an informal series of one-bedroom apartments and two-bedroom cottages for rent here. Away from the crowds, Paradise Cove is like Grand Bahama used to be before the tourist hordes invaded. Yet you are only a 20-minute drive east of West End. Snorkeling, swimming, kayaking, and sunbathing fill the day here. At twilight, attend the breathtaking sunset bonfire. All units are good size and have full kitchens for those who want to cook their own grub.

Paradise Cove (P.O. Box F-42771), Freeport, Grand Bahama Island. © **242/349-2677.** www.deadmansreef.com. Fax 242/352-5471. 12 units. Year-round $100 1-bedroom apt, $575 weekly; $195 2-bedroom villa, $1,225 weekly. Extra person $15 per day. **Amenities:** Bar; watersports equipment/rentals. *In room:* A/C, TV, kitchen.

Wyndham Viva Fortuna ★ *(Kids)*   Think of this as an Italian Club Med. It caters to a mostly European, relatively young crowd, who appreciate the 14 secluded hectares (35 acres) of beachfront and the nonstop sports activities that are included in the price. Established in 1993, Viva Fortuna lies 9.5km (6 miles) east of the International Bazaar in the southeastern part of the island, amid an isolated landscape of casuarinas and scrubland. Midsize bedrooms lie in a colorful group of two-story outbuildings. About three-quarters have ocean views; the others overlook the garden. Each has a private balcony, and two queen-size beds, with a small bathroom with shower stalls. Singles can book one of these rooms, but they are charged 40% more than the per-person double-occupancy rate.

All meals, which are included in the rates, are served buffet-style in a pavilion near the beach, and the Italian cuisine is actually some of the best on Grand Bahama Island. In addition to the buffet, you'll find a casual Italian restaurant, La Trattoria, where you can order sit-down dinners within a candlelit setting.

1 Dubloon Rd. (P.O. Box F-42398), Freeport, Grand Bahama, The Bahamas. © **800/898-9968** or 242/373-4000. Fax 242/373-5594. www.wyndham.com. 276 units. Winter $124 double, $74 per extra person; off season $98 double, $59 per extra person. Rates are all-inclusive. AE, DC, MC, V. **Amenities:** 2 restaurants; 3 bars; disco; pool; 2 tennis courts; gym; sauna; watersports equipment/rentals; kids' club; babysitting; nonsmoking rooms; rooms for those w/limited mobility. *In room:* A/C, TV, hair dryer, iron/ironing board, safe.

4 Where to Dine

Foodies will find that the cuisine on Grand Bahama Island doesn't match the more refined fare served at dozens of places on New Providence (Nassau/Paradise Island). However, a few places in Grand Bahama specialize in fine dining; others get by with rather standard fare. The good news is that the dining scene is much more affordable here.

FREEPORT

EXPENSIVE

Rib Room ⟨ SEAFOOD/STEAKS   The Rib Room serves the island's best steaks, in huge portions. Everything is served in the atmosphere of a British hunting lodge. If you don't want one of the steaks, opt instead for the blue-ribbon prime rib of beef with a passable Yorkshire pudding. Special praise goes to the broiled Bahamian lobster, but steer clear of the grouper. Shrimp can be succulent when it's not overcooked, and steak Diane, although rather fully flavored, is meltingly textured. The wine list is reasonably priced.

Crowne Plaza Golf Resort & Casino at the Royal Oasis, the Mall at W. Sunrise Hwy. ✆ **242/352-6721.** Reservations recommended. Jackets required for men. Main courses $22–$36. AE, DC, MC, V. Fri–Wed 5:30–10:30pm.

MODERATE

Silvano's ⟨ ITALIAN   The only authentic Italian dining spot in Freeport, this 80-seat restaurant with its Mediterranean decor serves a worthy but not exceptional cuisine. The standard repertoire from Mama Mia's kitchen is presented here with quality ingredients, most often shipped in from the United States. Service is polite and helpful. The grilled veal steak is our favorite, although the home pastas are equally alluring. They're served with a wide variety of freshly made sauces. The chef also works his magic with fresh shrimp. Other traditional Italian dishes round out the menu.

Ranfurley Circle. ✆ **242/352-5111.** Reservations recommended. Lunch specials $5.50–$11; main courses $13–$36. AE, DISC, MC, V. Daily noon–3pm and 5–11pm.

INEXPENSIVE

Becky's Restaurant BAHAMIAN/AMERICAN   This pink-and-white restaurant offers authentic Bahamian cuisine prepared in the time-tested style of the Out Islands. Go here to rev up before a day of serious shopping at the International Bazaar, which is right at hand. Owned by Becky and Berkeley Smith, the place offers a welcome dose of down-to-earth noncasino reality. Breakfasts are either all-American or Bahamian and are available all day. Also popular are minced lobster, curried mutton, fish platters, baked or curried chicken, and conch salads. Stick to the local specialties instead of the lackluster American dishes.

E. Sunrise Hwy. and E. Beach Dr. ✆ **242/352-5247.** Breakfast $5–$11; main courses $7–$22. AE, MC, V. Daily 7am–10pm.

Geneva's BAHAMIAN/SEAFOOD   If you want to eat where the locals eat, head for Geneva's, where the food is made the old-fashioned way. This restaurant is one of the best places to sample conch, which has fed and nourished Bahamians for centuries. The Monroe family will prepare it for you stewed, cracked, or fried, or in a savory conch chowder that makes an excellent starter. Grouper also appears, prepared in every imaginable way. The bartender will get you into the mood with a rum-laced Bahama Mama.

Kipling Lane and E. Mall, at W. Sunrise Hwy. ✆ **242/352-5085.** Lunch sandwiches and platters $6–$12; dinner main courses $9–$25. DISC, MC, V. Daily 7am–11pm.

The Pepper Pot BAHAMIAN   This might be the only place on Grand Bahama that specializes in Bahamian takeout food. You'll find it after about a 5-minute drive east of the International Bazaar, in a tiny shopping mall. You can order takeout portions of the island's best guava duff (a dessert specialty of The Bahamas that resembles a jelly roll), as well as a savory conch chowder, the standard fish and pork chops, chicken souse (an acquired taste), cracked conch, sandwiches and hamburgers, and an array of daily specials. The owner is Ethiopian-born Wolansa Fountain.

E. Sunrise Hwy. (at Coral Rd.). © **242/373-7655.** Breakfast $3–$5; main courses $7–$9; vegetarian plates $3–$5. No credit cards. Daily 24 hr.

The Pub on the Mall INTERNATIONAL   Located on the same floor of the same building and under the same management, three distinctive eating areas lie across the boulevard from the International Bazaar and attract many locals. The **Prince of Wales** serves such Olde English staples as shepherd's pie, fish and chips, platters of roast beef or fish, and real English ale. One end of the room is devoted to the **Red Dog Sports Bar,** with a boisterous atmosphere and at least four TV screens blasting away for dedicated sports fans. **Silvano's** (see above) is an Italian restaurant serving lots of pasta, usually with verve, as well as veal, chicken, beefsteaks, seafood, and such desserts as tiramisu. The Bahamian-themed **Islander's Roost** has a tropical decor of bright island color and a balcony overlooking the Bazaar. The food is good if not great; the main platters are a good value, usually very filling and satisfying. Menu items include sandwiches, salads, grilled fish, beefsteaks, and prime rib.

Ranfurley Circle, Sunrise Hwy. © **242/352-5110.** Reservations recommended. Main courses $6–$36. AE, MC, V, DISC. Prince of Wales and Red Dog daily noon–midnight; Silvano's daily noon–3pm and 5–11pm; Islander's Roost Mon–Sat 5–11pm.

IN THE INTERNATIONAL BAZAAR
INEXPENSIVE

Café Michel BAHAMIAN/AMERICAN   The name implies that you've found a real French bistro set amid the bustle of the International Bazaar, but alas, it turns out to be a mere coffee shop. Nevertheless, it's a good place for refueling when you're shopping the bazaar. About 20 tables are outside under red and white umbrellas and bistro-style tablecloths. Inside are about a dozen more. Local shoppers know to come here not only for coffee, but also for platters, salads, and sandwiches throughout the day. Both American and Bahamian dishes are served, including seafood platters, steaks, and, of course, grouper. The house specialty is a Bahamian lobster platter with all the fixings.

International Bazaar. © **242/352-2191.** Reservations recommended for dinner. Main courses $5–$36. AE, MC, V. Mon–Sat noon–11pm. Closes at 6pm in off season.

China Temple CHINESE   This Chinese joint—and don't expect more than just that—also does takeout. Over the years it's proved to be the dining bargain of the bazaar. The menu is familiar and standard: chop suey, chow mein, and sweet-and-sour chicken. It's certainly not gourmet Asian fare, but it's cheap, and it might hit the spot when you're craving something different.

International Bazaar. © **242/352-5610.** Lunch $7–$9; main courses $10–$14. AE, MC, V. Mon–Sat 11am–10pm.

LUCAYA
EXPENSIVE

Churchill's ⭐ AMERICAN   One of the island's most elegant restaurants, Churchill's lures discerning palates to the Westin & Sheraton at Our Lucaya—even guests staying in Freeport. We like to arrive early for drinks in the colonial-style bar with its dark-wood floors, potted plants, and ceiling fans, even a grand piano. (All the setting needs to feel complete is a new Bogie-and-Ingrid-Bergman combo willing to remake *Casablanca* on-site.) This is the island's best chophouse, featuring both succulent steaks flown over from the mainland and locally caught seafood. The manor house setting is a perfect foil for the finely honed service and top-quality ingredients, deftly prepared.

At the Westin & Sheraton at Our Lucaya, Royal Palm Way. ✆ 242/373-1333. Reservations required. Main courses $25–$65. AE, DC, DISC, MC, V. Mon–Sat 6–11pm.

The Stoned Crab ✿ SEAFOOD   Tired of frozen seafood shipped in from the mainland? Come here for the sweet stone crab claws and the lobster, both caught in Bahamian waters. There's none better on the island. You can't miss this place—a triple pyramid (ca. 1968) whose four-story wood-and-steel framework is strong enough to withstand any hurricane. Swiss-born Livio Peronino is the manager and chef, preparing a seafood platter with everything on it, including grouper, conch fritters, and all kinds of shellfish. The best pasta on the menu is linguine al pesto with lobster and shrimp. For starters, try the zesty conch chowder. Have a lobster salad with your meal and finish with Irish coffee.

At Taíno Beach, Lucaya. ✆ 242/373-1442. Reservations recommended. Main courses $22–$45. AE, MC, V. Daily 5–10pm.

Willy Broadleaf ✿ INTERNATIONAL   At the first-class Westin & Sheraton at Our Lucaya, you're treated to one of the most lavish buffet dinners in the entire Bahamian chain. The chefs conceive of their lavish offering as a giant spread of exotic dishes based on recipes from around the globe. The decor fits the cuisine, evoking a courtyard patio in Mexico, a marketplace in old Cairo, the dining hall of an Indian maharajah, even an African village; from India comes tandoori chicken, from Greece moussaka. Another tasty treat is a sausage made from wild boar. Expect freshly made salads, both hot and cold dishes, and luscious, often fruit-based desserts.

The Westin & Sheraton at Our Lucaya, Royal Palm Way. ✆ 242/373-1333. Breakfast buffet $20, Tues–Fri $34 buffet, Sat–Sun $50 seafood buffet. AE, DC, DISC, MC, V. Daily 6:30–11am and 6–10pm.

MODERATE

Barracuda's ✿ AMERICAN   With high ceilings and big windows, this space is the size of an airplane hanger, and it's done up with playful art and a whimsical, hip decor that would be at home in Miami's South Beach. The kitchen turns out hearty breakfast dishes that are loaded with flavor. The best examples are omelets and French toast. The weekend buffet is a table-groaning event of freshly made American and Bahamian dishes—it's one of the best food values on island.

At the Westin & Sheraton at Our Lucaya, Royal Palm Way, Lucaya. ✆ 242/373-1333. Breakfast $14 or under; buffet $16. DC, MC, V. Daily 7–10:30am; Sat–Sun 6:30pm–midnight.

China Beach ✿ ASIAN FUSION   At the Westin & Sheraton at Our Lucaya, you can cruise the Pacific Rim, feasting on exotic delights, including the spicy hot cuisines of Vietnam and Thailand, with calls at Korea, Indonesia, and Malaysia. The menu changes every month but some dishes appear with regularity. Our favorites among these are a savory Hong Kong roast duckling and a zesty Thai chicken. The beef marinated in soy sauce is served with fresh spring onion, and the grouper filet appears with fresh ginger and scallions. Other Far East specialties include a seafood teppanyaki and stir-fry conch.

At the Westin & Sheraton at Our Lucaya, Royal Palm Way. ✆ 242/373-1333. Reservations recommended. Main courses $19–$33. AE, DC, DISC MC, V. Tues–Sat 6–11pm.

Oasis Café BAHAMIAN/AMERICAN This restaurant on the lobby of the Royal Oasis resort adjoins the casino. As you eat, you can view the gamblers winning and losing (mostly the latter). If you order a la carte, the menu consists mainly of snacks and sandwiches. But many diners come here for the hot and cold dishes on the buffet. The chefs do a good job with their roasting at night, especially with the prime rib, which can be carved for you. Homemade soups are featured daily, along with fresh salads and tasty desserts. The best time to come for island flair and fun is on Bahamian night each Friday. During most of 2005, the Royal Oasis resort—including this restaurant— underwent renovations. It expects to reopen in 2006, but call ahead before visiting.

Crowne Plaza Golf Resort & Casino at the Royal Oasis, the Mall at W. Sunrise Hwy. ✆ **242/350-7000.** Buffet lunch $18–$19 daily; buffet dinner $23 daily. AE, DC, MC, V. Call for hours.

Palm Grill & Coconut Bar BAHAMIAN/INTERNATIONAL/SEAFOOD Off the lobby at the Royal Oasis resort, this eatery offers two distinct dining experiences. The Palm Grill is a fashionable bistro with tables inside or out; the kitchen serves a beautifully roasted prime rib at whatever doneness you prefer, fettuccine Alfredo with the tantalizing addition of fresh shrimp, and Bahamian snapper cooked just right— still moist—and served with grilled vegetables. At the more convivial Coconut Bar, you can order your fill of well-stuffed sandwiches, juicy burgers and fries, freshly made salads, and, of course, conch and other main courses from the same kitchen.

Crowne Plaza Golf Resort & Casino at the Royal Oasis, the Mall at W. Sunrise Hwy. ✆ **242/350-7000.** Palm Grill main courses lunch $6.25–$12, dinner $12–$22. Coconut Bar main courses $7.50–$18. AE, DC, DISC, MC, V. Palm Grill daily 6:30–11:30am, noon–3pm, and 5:30–11pm. Coconut Bar daily 10am–1am.

Paradiso ⭐ ITALIAN Set among dark woods and high booths both elegant and tasteful, you'll find yourself in an oasis of fine Italian dining here. As you enjoy an aperitif, peruse the menu of selections representing some of the best recipes from the Italian kitchen. Veal saltimbocca (the word literally means "jump in your mouth") is a concoction with cheese and ham, and is most rewarding, as is the marinated filet mignon wrapped in pancetta. Nothing is finer nor more expensive than the lobster al Sardinia (with fresh tomatoes and vegetables). Dishes for the most part, are spiced, flavored, and sauced, especially the tender cutlets of oregano-flavored scaloppine and the fettuccine with "fruits of the sea," including Bahamian conch, scallops, lobster, and shrimp (among other seafood). Waiters are prompt and attentive, and there's a good wine list.

Crowne Plaza Golf Resort & Casino at the Royal Oasis, the Mall at W. Sunrise Hwy. ✆ **242/352-7000.** Reservations required. Main courses $18–$22. AE, DC, DISC, MC, V. Tues, Thurs–Sun 5:30–11pm.

Prop Club AMERICAN/INTERNATIONAL With a name like Prop Club, you expect a kind of laid-back airplane hangar decor. Instead, you get parts of aircraft that crashed off the coast of Grand Bahama Island. When the weather's right, which it is most of the time, large doors open to bring the outdoors inside, and the party overflows onto the beach. You won't find the most enticing menu on the island here, but the place is a lot of fun—and the offerings far exceed most pub grub. Dig into a "mountain of ribs," or else savor the crab cakes (which actually contain a lot of crab, not just stuffing). Ever had a grilled margarita chicken sandwich? You can order one here, along with juicy burgers, fajitas, and the like.

At the Westin & Sheraton at Our Lucaya, Royal Palm Way. ✆ **242/373-1333.** Main courses $12–$23. AE, DC, MC, V. Lunch noon–5pm. Dinner 5–10pm. Bar noon–1am on weeknights; noon–2am on weekends.

AT PORT LUCAYA MARKETPLACE
EXPENSIVE

Luciano's ✿ FRENCH/CONTINENTAL   With its tables usually occupied by local government officials and deal makers, Luciano's is the grande dame of Freeport restaurants, with a very European atmosphere. It's the only restaurant in Port Lucaya offering caviar, foie gras, and oysters Rockefeller, all served with a flourish by a formally dressed waitstaff wearing black and white. You can go early and enjoy a cocktail in the little bar inside or on the wooden deck overlooking the marina. Lightly smoked and thinly sliced salmon makes a good opener, as do snails in garlic butter. Fresh fish and shellfish are regularly featured and delicately prepared, allowing their natural flavors to shine through, with no heavy, overwhelming sauces. Steak Diane is one of Luciano's classics, along with an especially delectable veal medallion sautéed with shrimp and lobster.

Port Lucaya Marketplace. ✆ 242/373-9100. www.portlucaya.com/lucianos. Reservations required in winter. Main courses $27–$44. AE, MC, V. Daily 5:30–9:45pm (last order).

Ferry House ✿ CAJUN/SEAFOOD   This restaurant's bar floats on pontoons, beneath a canvas canopy, above the waters of Bell Channel, the waterway that funnels boats from the open sea into the sheltered confines of Port Lucaya Marina. Lunches are relatively simple affairs, consisting of pastas, catch of the day, and meal-size salads. Dinner might feature a seafood platter laden with calamari, fish, and shrimp; a delectable duck breast with potatoes and vegetables; fresh salmon with hollandaise sauce; and savory grilled rack of lamb. But our favorite meal here is the ginger-and-honey-glazed tiger shrimp, served with a lobster bisque.

Beside Bell Channel, Port Lucaya. ✆ 242/373-1595. Reservations recommended for dinner. Lunch platters $15–$19; dinner main courses $27–$39. AE, MC, V. Mon–Fri noon–2pm; Tues–Sun 6–9pm.

MODERATE

Fatman's Nephew ✿ BAHAMIAN   In another location, "Fatman" became a legend on Grand Bahama Island. Although he's no longer with us, the Fatman must have left his recipes and cooking skills to another generation of cooks. Today the place, which used to cater mainly to locals, has gone touristy, but much of the same traditional fare is still served with the same unflagging allegiance to Bahamian ways. The restaurant overlooks the marina at Port Lucaya from an eagle's-nest position on the second floor. You can enjoy drinks or meals inside, but we like to head out to an outdoor covered deck to watch the action below. At least eight kinds of game fish—including both wahoo and Cajun blackened kingfish—plus curried chicken, mutton, or beef are usually offered. Bahamian-style shark soup, made from the flesh of hammerheads ("little tender ones," according to the chef), is sometimes featured on the menu. Most dishes, except for expensive shellfish, fall at the lower end of the price scale. Beware, as the local staff can be flighty.

Port Lucaya Marketplace. ✆ 242/373-8520. Main courses $10–$40. AE, DISC, MC, V. Wed–Mon 5–11pm.

Giovanni's Cafe ✿ ITALIAN/SEAFOOD   Tucked away into one of the pedestrian thoroughfares of Port Lucaya Marketplace, you'll find a yellow-sided clapboard house that opens into a charming 38-seat Italian trattoria. The chefs (including head chef Giovanni Colo) serve Italian-influenced preparations of local seafood, specializing in seafood pasta (usually prepared only for two diners) and a lobster special. Giovanni stamps each dish with his Italian verve and flavor, whether it be Bahamian conch, local seafood, or scampi. Dishes show off his precision and rock-solid technique, exemplified by sirloin steak with fresh mushrooms, delectable shrimp scampi, and fattening, but extremely good, spaghetti carbonara.

Port Lucaya Marketplace. (€) 242/373-9107. Reservations recommended. Main courses lunch $8–$12, dinner $13–$33. AE, MC, V. Mon–Sat 8:30am–10pm; Sun 5–10pm.

La Dolce Vita ☂ ITALIAN   Next to the Pub at Lucaya (see listing below), this small upscale Italian restaurant has a modern decor and traditional food. Enjoy freshly made pastas and Italian-style pizzas on a patio overlooking the marina or in the 44-seat dining room. Start with portobello mushrooms, fresh mozzarella with tomatoes, and a vinaigrette, or else carpaccio with arugula and spices. Homemade ravioli appears with different fillings such as cheese, lobster, or spinach. An excellent risotto flavored with black ink is served, or else you can order roast pork tenderloin or a crisp and perfectly flavored rack of lamb.

Port Lucaya Marketplace. (€) **242/373-8652.** Reservations recommended. Main courses $11–$31. AE, MC, V. Daily 5:30–11pm. Closed Sept.

Pisces ☂ INTERNATIONAL   This is our favorite among the many restaurants in the Port Lucaya Marketplace, and we're seconded by a healthy mix of locals and yacht owners who pack the place every weekend. Decorated with Tiffany-style lamps and captain's chairs, it boasts the most charming waitstaff on Grand Bahama Island. Pizzas are available and come in 27 different varieties, including a version with conch, lobster, shrimp, and chicken as well as one with Alfredo sauce. Dinners are more elaborate, with a choice of curries (including a version with conch); lobster in cream, wine, and herb sauce; all kinds of fish and shellfish; and several kinds of pasta.

Port Lucaya Marketplace. (€) 242/373-5192. Reservations recommended. Pizzas $12–$28; dinner main courses $9–$30. AE, DISC, MC, V. Mon–Sat 5pm–1:30am.

Pub at Lucaya ENGLISH/BAHAMIAN   Opening onto Count Basie Square, this restaurant and bar lies at the center of the Port Lucaya Marketplace. Returning visitors might remember the joint when it was called Pusser's Pub, named after that popular brand of rum.

You can come here to eat, but many patrons visit just for the drinks, especially rum-laced Pusser's Painkillers. You can order predictable pub grub such as shepherd's pie or steak-and-ale pie. Juicy American-style burgers are another lure. But you can also dine on substantial Bahamian fare at night, especially Bahamian lobster tail, cracked conch, chicken breast with herbs, or the fresh grilled catch of the day. The tables outside overlooking the water are preferred, or else you can retreat inside under a wooden beamed ceiling, where the rustic tables are lit by *faux* Tiffany-style lamps.

Port Lucaya Marketplace. (€) **242/373-8450.** Sandwiches and burgers $8–$9; main courses $13–$40. AE, MC, V. Daily 11am–11pm (bar until 1am).

Shenanigan's Irish Pub CONTINENTAL   Dark and beer-stained from the thousands of pints of Guinness, Harp, and Killian's that have been served and spilled here, this is the premier Irish or Boston-Irish hangout on Grand Bahama Island. Many visitors come just to drink, sometimes for hours at a time, soaking up the suds, and perhaps remembering to eventually order some food. If you get hungry, there's surf and turf, French-style rack of lamb for two, seafood Newburg, and several preparations of chicken. Most dishes, except for lobster, are at the low end of the price scale.

Port Lucaya Marketplace. ✆ 242/373-4734. Main courses $9–$43. AE, DISC, MC, V. Mon–Thurs 5pm–midnight; Fri–Sat 5pm–2am (last order at 9:45pm).

INEXPENSIVE

Georgie's BAHAMIAN/AMERICAN   This laid-back, informal restaurant allows you to dine harborside at Port Lucaya for breakfast, lunch, or dinner. It gets particularly busy at happy hour in the late afternoon when prices on drinks are reduced. Service shows more effort than polish, but dishes do arrive and they are quite flavorful time-tested recipes, a repertoire of old favorites like cracked conch (similar to breaded veal cutlet) served with tasty coleslaw. The catch of the day is usually pan-fried grouper or snapper served with peas 'n' rice. The chef almost daily prepares hot roast beef, serving it with mashed potatoes and mixed vegetables; for lunch, try one of the island's better chef's salads, loaded with turkey, ham, fresh tomatoes, cheese, and other good things. Other favorites here include fresh lobster, conch fritters, and barbecue chicken.

Port Lucaya Marketplace. ✆ 242/373-8513. Breakfast $5; main courses lunch $6–$19, dinner $8–$19. DC, MC, V. Thurs–Tues 7am–11pm.

Outrigger's Native Restaurant/White Wave Club BAHAMIAN   Cement-sided and simple, with a large deck extending out toward the sea, this restaurant was here long before the construction of the nearby Port Lucayan Marketplace, which lies only 4 blocks away. The restaurant area is the domain of Gretchen Wilson, whose kitchens produce a rotating series of dishes that include such lip-smacking dishes as lobster tails, minced lobster, steamed or cracked conch, pork chops, chicken, fish, and shrimp, usually served with peas 'n' rice and macaroni. Every Wednesday night, from 5pm to 2am, the restaurant is the venue for Outrigger's Famous Wednesday Night Fish Fry, when as many as a thousand diners will line up for platters of fried or steamed fish, priced at $10 each, which are accompanied by a DJ and dancers. Drinks are served within the restaurant, but at any time of the week, you might consider stepping into the nearby ramshackle bar, the White Wave Club, which serves only drinks.

Smith's Point. ✆ 242/373-4811. Main courses $10–$16. No credit cards. Sun–Fri 4pm–midnight; Sat 11am–midnight.

Zorba's BAHAMIAN/GREEK   First thing in the morning, you'll see locals standing in line for the Bahamian breakfasts served at Zorba's. From chicken souse to corned beef and grits, all the island eye-openers are on the menu. Eggs snag less daring early risers. Lunch could be a fat gyro or a souvlakia kabob. Dinner can begin with a Greek salad and then move on to moussaka, with baklava for a sweet finish. We won't pretend the food here is like a trip to the Greek isles, but it's satisfying and filling. At this casual dining spot, you can eat either inside or enjoy your meal alfresco.

Port Lucaya Marketplace. ✆ 242/373-6137. Main courses lunch $4–$13, dinner $11–$24. AE, DISC, MC, V. Daily 7am–10:30pm.

OUTSIDE FREEPORT/LUCAYA

Bishop's Restaurant ★ Finds BAHAMIAN   This eatery, known mainly to East End locals, is patronized for its real down-home cooking. Just over 50km (32 miles) east of Lucaya, the restaurant opens onto views of the sea. Far from the high-rise hotels, this little restaurant and lounge looks the way they did in The Bahamas of the 1920s and 1930s. Some of the best cracked conch we've sampled on Grand Bahama Island is served here, rolled in a light batter and fried in piping hot oil so that its crust is slightly crunchy. Another favorite, always on the menu, is fried grouper with classic peas 'n' rice. Or, for a savory dish, order the chicken barbecued in zesty sauce.

High Rock. ℂ **242/353-4515.** Main courses $10–$15. MC, V. Daily 9am–5pm.

Club Caribe AMERICAN/BAHAMIAN   Set about 11km (7 miles) east of the International Bazaar, beside a beach and an offshore reef, this restaurant is a funky and offbeat charmer. You can spend a day on the beach here, renting the club's snorkeling equipment, sunbathing or swimming, and perhaps enjoying one of the house-special cocktails (try a Caribe Delight, made with bananas, banana-flavored liqueur, and rum). When it's lunchtime, you might order up a heaping platter of cracked conch; barbecued ribs; snapper or wahoo that's fried, steamed, or grilled; or a sandwich or salad. This place is simple, outdoorsy, and a refreshing change from the more congested parts of Grand Bahama. On Friday, they're usually open until 9pm or later, with live music. Oysters on the half shell, mussels, and clams are all bought fresh on Friday for a tasty weekend treat.

Churchill Beach, Mather Town, off Midshipman Rd. ℂ **242/373-6866.** Main courses $5–$25. AE, MC, V. Tues–Sun 11am–6pm (or later, depending on business).

Margarita Villa Sand Bar BAHAMIAN/AMERICAN   Known for making the island's best Bahama Mama drink, this funky little local hangout with a rustic deck sits under coconut palms overlooking the ocean. It's an extremely casual place, with handmade barrel tables, and sand on the floor, a small menu, and an offbeat location in the little island settlement of Mather Town. When not downing some of the best margaritas and burgers in the area, patrons can be seen on the beach sunning, snorkeling, or swimming. Dig into a basket of conch fritters, a "cheeseburger in paradise," fish and chips, or steak and fries. The big event of the week is the bonfire on the beach, Tuesday from 6:30 to 10pm. A full dinner and all the activities, including music, dancing, and games, goes for $41 per person.

Mather Town. ℂ **242/373-4525.** Reservations required for bonfire night. Main courses $5–$14. DISC, MC, V. Daily 11am–10:30pm (or later, depending on business).

5 Beaches, Watersports & Other Outdoor Pursuits

HITTING THE BEACH

Grand Bahama Island has enough beaches for everyone, the best ones opening onto Northwest Providence Channel at Freeport and sweeping east for some 97km (60 miles) to encompass Xanadu Beach, Lucayan Beach, Taíno Beach, and others, eventually ending at such remote eastern outposts as Rocky Creek and McLean's Town. Once you leave the Freeport/Lucaya area, you can virtually have your pick of white sandy beaches all the way east. Once you're past the resort hotels, you'll see a series of secluded beaches used mainly by locals. If you like people, a lot of organized watersports, and easy access to hotel bars and rest rooms, stick to Xanadu, Taíno, and Lucayan beaches.

Though there's fine snorkeling offshore, you should book a snorkeling cruise aboard one of the catamarans offered by Paradise Watersports (see below) to see the most stunning reefs.

Xanadu Beach 🐟🐟 is one of our favorite beaches, immediately east of Freeport and the site of the famed Xanadu Beach Resort. The 1.6km-long (1-mile) beach may be crowded at times in winter, but that's because of those gorgeous, soft, powdery white sands, which open onto tranquil waters. The beach is set against a backdrop of coconut palms and Australian pines. You can hook up here with some of the best watersports on the island, including snorkeling, boating, jet-skiing, and parasailing.

Immediately east of Xanadu is **Silver Point Beach,** a little white-sandy beach, site of a timeshare complex where guests are out riding the waves on water bikes or playing volleyball on the beach. You'll see horseback riders from Pinetree Stables (see below) taking beach rides along the sands.

Most visitors will be found at **Lucayan Beach,** right off Royal Palm Way and immediately east of Silver Point Beach. This is one of the best beaches in The Bahamas, with kilometers of white sand. It might be crowded for a few weeks in winter, but most of the time you can find beach-blanket space. At any of the hotel resorts along this beach, you can hook up with an array of watersports or get a frosty drink from a hotel bar. It's not for those seeking seclusion, but it's a fun beach-party scene.

Immediately to the east of Lucayan Beach is **Taíno Beach,** a family favorite and a good place for watersports. This, too, is a fine, wide beach of white sands, opening onto generally tranquil waters.

Another choice not too far east is **Gold Rock Beach,** a favorite picnic spot with locals on weekends, although you'll usually have this beach to yourself on weekdays. Gold Rock Beach is a 19km (12-mile) drive from Lucaya. At Gold Rock you are at the doorstep to the **Lucayan National Park** (see below), a 16-hectare (40-acre) park filled with some of the longest, widest, and most fabulous secluded beaches on the island.

BIKING

A guided bike trip is an ideal way to see parts of Grand Bahama that most visitors miss. Starting at **Barbary Beach,** you can pedal a mountain bike along the southern coast parallel to the beach. Stop for a snack, lunch, and a dip. Finally, you reach **Lucayan National Park,** some 19km (12 miles) away. Explore the cave were the Indians buried their dead in the days when Grand Bahama was theirs, centuries before the coming of Columbus. Crabs here have been known to come up through holes in the ground carrying bits of bowls once used by the Lucayans. **Kayak Nature Tours** (✆ **242/373-2485**), the company that sponsors these trips, transports you home to your hotel by van, so you don't have to exhaust yourself in the heat cycling back. The cost is $79 for adults, half price for children ages 10 to 16. All equipment, sustenance, and round-trip transportation from your hotel is included.

Moments Private White Sands for You Alone

Once you head east from Port Lucaya and Taíno, you'll discover so many splendid white sandy beaches that you'll lose count. Although these beaches have names, you'll never really know what beach you're on, unless you ask a local, because they are unmarked. If you like seclusion and don't mind the lack of any facilities, you'll find a string of local favorites. Directly east of Taíno is **Churchill's Beach,** followed by **Smith's Point, Fortune Beach,** and **Barbary Beach.** Fortune Beach is a special gem because of its beautiful waters and white sands.

BOAT CRUISES

Ocean Wonder, Port Lucaya Dock (© 242/373-5880), run by Reef Tours, is a gargantuan 18m (60-ft.) Defender glass-bottom boat. Any tour agent can arrange for you to go out on this vessel. You'll get a panoramic view of the beautiful underwater life that lives off the coast of Grand Bahama. Cruises depart from Port Lucaya behind the Straw Market on the bay side at 9:30am, 11:15am, 1:15pm, and 3:15pm, except Friday, when only two tours leave at 9:30 and 11:15am. The tour lasts 1½ hours, costs $25 for adults and $15 for children 6 to 12, and is free for children 5 and under. Make reservations a day or two ahead, as the boat does fill up quickly.

Superior Watersports (P.O. Box F-40837, Freeport; © 242/373-7863; www. superiorwatersports.com), offers trips on its *Bahama Mama,* a two-deck 22m (72-ft.) catamaran. Its Robinson Crusoe Beach Party, offered daily from 11am to 4pm from October through March, but from noon to 5pm from April through September, costs $59 per person and $39 for children under 12. There's also a shorter sunset booze cruise that goes for $29. (From Apr–Sept, these cruises are on Tues, Thurs, and Sat night from 6:30–8:30pm, and from Oct–Mar the same nights, but from 6–8pm.) Call for information about how to hook up with this outfitter.

For an underwater cruise, try the company's quasi-submarine, the *Seaworld Explorer.* The sub itself does not descend; instead, you walk down into the hull of the boat and watch the sea life glide by. The "semisub" departs daily at 9:30 am, 11:30am, and 1:30pm, and the two-hour ride costs $39 for adults and $25 for children age 2 to 12.

THE DOLPHIN EXPERIENCE

A pod of bottle-nosed dolphins is involved in a unique dolphin/human familiarization program at Dolphin Experience, located at **Underwater Explorers Society (UNEXSO),** next to Port Lucaya, opposite Lucayan Beach Casino (© 800/992-DIVE or 242/373-1244; www.unexso.com). This "close encounter" program allows participants to observe these intelligent and friendly animals close up and to hear an interesting talk by a member of the animal-care staff. The world's largest dolphin facility, the conditions aren't cramped here, and dolphins can swim out to sea. You can step onto a shallow wading platform and interact with the dolphins; the experience costs $75 and is an educational, fun adventure for all ages. Children under 3 participate free, while it costs $38 for those aged 4 to 12. You'll want to bring your camera. Dolphins also swim out from Sanctuary Bay daily to interact with certified scuba divers in a "dolphin dive" program, costing $159.

Swimming with dolphins has its critics and supporters. You may want to visit the Whale and Dolphins Conservation Society's website at www.wdcs.org. For more information about responsible travel in general, check out these websites: Tread Lightly (www.treadlightly.org) and the International Ecotourism Society (www.ecotourism.org).

FISHING

In the waters off Grand Bahama, you can fish for barracuda, snapper, grouper, yellowtail, wahoo, and kingfish, along with other denizens of the deep.

Reef Tours, Ltd., Port Lucaya Dock (© 242/373-5880 or 242/373-5891; www.bahamasvg.com/reeftours), offers one of the least expensive ways to go deep-sea fishing around Grand Bahama Island. Adults pay $90 if they fish, $45 if they only go along to watch. Four to six people can charter the entire 13m (42-ft.) craft for $540 per half-day or $1,050 per whole day. The 9.6m (32-ft.) boat can be chartered for

---

Moments Land & Sea Eco-Tours

If you're a nature lover, escape from the casinos and take one of the **East End Adventures** (© **242/373-6662;** www.bahamasecotours.com) bush and sea safaris. You're taken through dense pine forests and along deserted beaches, going inland on hikes to such sites as blue holes, mangrove swamps, and underground caverns. You may even learn how to crack conch. A native lunch is served on a serene beach in Lightbourne's Cay, a remote islet in the East End. Most of the tour is laid-back, as you can snorkel in blue holes or shell hunt. Safaris are conducted daily between 8am and 5:30pm; the cost is $110 for adults and $55 for kids ages 2 to 12.

$375 half-day and $720 for a whole day. Departures for the 4-hour half-day excursions are daily at 8:30am and 1pm, while the 8-hour full-day excursions leave daily at 8:30am. Bait, tackle, and ice are included in the cost.

GOLF

This island boasts more golf links than any other in The Bahamas. The courses are within 11km (7 miles) of one another, and you usually won't have to wait to play. All courses are open to the public year-round, and clubs can be rented from all pro shops on the island.

Emerald Golf Course, the Mall South, at Crowne Plaza Golf Resort & Casino at the Royal Oasis (© **242/350-7000**), was the site of The Bahamas National. Open some years back, and more recently, in conjunction with the Ruby course (see below), it's the site of the annual January Grand Bahama Pro-Am Tournament. The course has plenty of trees along the fairways, as well as an abundance of water hazards and bunkers. The toughest hole is the 9th, a par 5 with 545 yards from the blue tees to the hole. In winter, greens fees to either of these courses are $95 per day, reduced to $85 in summer.

The championship **Ruby Golf Course,** Sunrise Highway, also at Crowne Plaza Golf Resort & Casino at the Royal Oasis (© **242/350-7000**), received a major upgrade in 2001 by Jim Fazio Golf Design, Inc. The Ruby course was lengthened to increase the rating and to enhance play. A fully automated irrigation system was also installed. For greens fees, see the Emerald Golf Course, above. It's a total of 6,750 yards if played from the championship blue tees.

Fortune Hills Golf & Country Club, Richmond Park, Lucaya (© **242/373-2222**), was originally intended to be an 18-hole course, but the back 9 were never completed. You can replay the front 9 for 18 holes and a total of 6,916 yards from the blue tees. Par is 72. Greens fees are $26 for 9 holes, $35 for 18. Electric 2-seater carts cost $38 for 9 and $48 for 18 holes. Club rental costs $18 for 18 holes and $14 for 9 holes.

The best-kept and most-manicured course on Grand Bahama is the **Lucayan Park Golf & Country Club,** Lucaya Beach at Our Lucaya (© **242/373-1333**). Made over after hurricane Jeanne of 2004, this beautiful course is known for the hanging boulder sculpture at its entrance. Greens are fast, with a couple of par 5s more than 500 yards long, totaling 6,824 yards from the blue tees and 6,488 from the whites. Par is 72. Greens fees are $120 for 18 holes, including a mandatory shared golf cart. We'll let you in on a secret: Even if you're not a golfer, sample the food at the club restaurant—everything from lavish champagne brunches to first-rate seafood dishes is delicious.

The first golf course to open in The Bahamas since 1969 made its premiere late in 2000. **The Reef Course** ✸✸ Royal Palm Way, at Our Lucaya (© **242/373-1333;** www.ourlucaya.com/reef_course.asp), was designed by Robert Trent Jones, Jr., who called it "a bit like a Scottish course but a lot warmer." This course requires precise shot-making to avoid its numerous lakes. You'll find water on 13 of the 18 holes and various types of long grass swaying in the trade winds. The course boasts 6,920 yards of links-style playing grounds. Residents of Our Lucaya, with which the course is associated, pay $110 for 18 holes or $50 for 9 holes. Nonresidents are charged $120 for 18 holes, $65 for 9 holes.

HORSEBACK RIDING

Pinetree Stables, Beachway Drive, North, Freeport (© **242/373-3600** or 305/433-4809; www.pinetree-stables.com), are the best riding stables in The Bahamas, superior to rivals on New Providence Island (Nassau). Pinetree offers trail rides to the beach in winter Tuesday through Sunday at 9 and 11:30am, 9 and 11am off season. The cost is $75 per person for a ride lasting 2 hours. No children under 8 are allowed. The weight limit per person is 200 pounds.

SEA KAYAKING

If you'd like to explore the waters off the island's north shore, call **Kayak Nature Tours** (© **242/373-2485**), who'll take you on trips through the mangroves, where you can see wildlife as you paddle along. The cost is $79 per person (children half-price), with lunch included. Double kayaks are used on these jaunts, and children must be at least 3 years of age. For the same price, you can take a 30-minute trip by kayak to an offshore island, with 1½ hours of snorkeling included along with lunch. Call ahead for reservations for either of these tours. A van will pick you up at your hotel at 9am and deliver you back at the end of the tours at 3pm.

⟨Finds⟩ The Ultimate in Relaxation

The ideal place to relieve the stresses of everyday life can be found at the **Sheraton at Our Lucaya's Senses Spa** (p. 149). The spa boasts an exercise facility with health checks, personal trainers, and yoga classes. A cafe serves fresh, natural food and elixirs. During one of their signature treatments, the Total Senses Massage, two massage therapists work in sync to relieve your tension. Throughout the Salt Glo body polish treatment, a therapist buffs away dead-skin cells and polishes your skin with natural elements from The Bahamas.

At the **Crowne Plaza Golf Resort & Casino at the Royal Oasis** (p. 145), the **Serenity Spa** offers exotic spa treatments to reflect the beauty, spirit, and traditions of the island. You can try individual body treatments, facials, massages, and manicures/pedicures, or choose from a wide selection of spa packages—including the Golfer's/Sports Package, which includes a mineral scrub, massage, and pedicure. Get ready to relax.

SNORKELING & SCUBA DIVING

Serious divers are attracted to such Grand Bahama sites as the Wall, the Caves, Theo's Wreck, and Treasure Reef. **Theo's Wreck** ★★ is the most evocative site; it was a freighter that was deliberately sunk off Freeport to attract marine life. Today it does just that, as it teems with everything from horse-eyed jacks to moray eels. Other sites frequented by UNEXSO include Spit City, Ben Blue Hole, Pygmy Caves, Gold Rock, Silver Point Reef, and the Rose Garden. Keep in mind that UNEXSO's specialty is diving, while Paradise Watersports primarily entertains snorkelers.

Underwater Explorers Society (UNEXSO) ★★★ (© **800/992-DIVE** or 242/373-1250; www.unexso.com), one of the premier dive outfitters in The Bahamas and the Caribbean, offers seven dive trips daily, including reef trips, shark dives, wreck dives, and night dives. Divers can even dive with dolphins in the open ocean here—a rare experience offered by very few facilities in the world (see "The Dolphin Experience," above).

A popular 3-hour learn-to-dive course is offered daily. Over UNEXSO's 30-year history, more than 50,000 people have successfully completed this course. For $85, students learn the basics in UNEXSO's training pools and dive the beautiful shallow reef with their instructor.

TENNIS

Crowne Plaza Golf Resort & Casino at the Royal Oasis ★★, at the Mall at West Sunrise Highway (© **242/350-7000;** www.theroyaloasis.com), has a near monopoly on tennis courts on Grand Bahama. Guests and nonguests are charged $10 per hour, and lessons are also available. Their 11 courts are open daily from 7am to 9pm. If you want to play at night, you have to call and reserve a special time. It costs $12 for the courts to be lighted.

WATERSPORTS IN GENERAL

Ocean Motion Water Sports Ltd., Sea Horse Lane, Lucaya Beach (© **242/374-2425;** www.oceanmotionbahamas.com), is the largest watersports company on Grand Bahama, offering a wide variety of activities daily, weather permitting, from 9am to 5pm, including snorkeling, parasailing, Hobie Cats, banana boats, water-skiing, jet skis, windsurfing, and other activities. Parasailing, for example, costs $60 per person; snorkeling trips $35 ($18 for kids under 12) for 1½ hours; water-skiing, $40 per 2-mile (3.2km) pull, $50 for a 30-minute lesson; Hobie Cats $50 for the 14-foot (4.2m), $75 for the 16-foot (4.8m), $20 for a lesson; windsurfing $30 per hour, $100 for a 2-hour lesson; kayaking, $20 for a single kayak, $25 for a double; water trampoline, $20 full day, $10 half-day; and banana boating $10 per person for a 2-mile (3.2km) ride along a white-sandy beach. Call for reservations, especially for windsurfing.

Lucaya Watersports, Taíno Beach (© **242/373-6375**), also offers various options for fun in the surf, including WaveRunners rented at $60 per 30 minutes or double kayaks costing $20 per hour for two passengers. The outfitter also offers double paddle boats, holding four people, for $20 per hour. The sunset cruises—a 2-hour tour offered Wednesday between 5 and 7pm, costing $45 per person—are especially popular. Glass-bottom boat tours, snorkeling, and a night cruise are also available. You can bring out your inner Bahamian during the night cruise at its all-you-can-eat buffet for $50 per person, Tuesday 6 to 9pm.

6 Seeing the Sights

Several informative tours of Grand Bahama Island are offered. One reliable company is **H. Forbes Charter Services Ltd.,** the Mall at West Sunrise Highway, Freeport (© **242/352-9311;** www.forbescharter.com). From headquarters in the International Bazaar, this company offers half- and full-day bus tours. The most popular option is the half-day Super Combination Tour, priced at $25 per adult and $20 per child age 5 to 12. It includes drive-through tours of residential areas and the island's commercial center, stops at the island's deep-water harbor, shopping, and a visit to a wholesale liquor store. Departures are Monday through Saturday at 9am and 1pm; the tour lasts 3½ hours.

See also "Beaches, Watersports & Other Outdoor Pursuits," above, for details on UNEXSO's Dolphin Experience, and "Shopping," below, for coverage of the International Bazaar and the Port Lucaya Marketplace.

Lucayan National Park   This 16-hectare (40-acre) park, filled with mangrove, pine, and palm trees, contains one of the loveliest, most secluded beaches on Grand Bahama, a long, wide, dune-covered stretch of sandy beach that you'll reach by following a wooden path winding through the trees. Bring your snorkeling gear so you can glimpse the colorful creatures living beneath the turquoise waters of a coral reef offshore. As you wander through the park, you'll cross Gold Rock Creek, fed by a spring from what is said to be the world's largest underground freshwater cavern system. There are 36,000 entrances to the caves—some only a few feet deep. Two of the caves can be seen, because they were exposed when a portion of ground collapsed. The pools in the caves are composed of 2m (6½ ft.) of freshwater atop a heavier layer of saltwater. Spiral wooden steps have been built down to the pools.

The freshwater springs once lured native Lucayans, those Arawak-connected tribes who lived on the island and depended on fishing for their livelihood. They would come inland to get fresh water for their habitats on the beach. Lucayan bones and artifacts, such as pottery, have been found in the caves, as well as on the beaches.

Settlers Way, eastern end of East Sunrise Hwy. © 242/352-5438. Admission $3; tickets available only at the Rand Nature Centre (see below). Daily 9am–4pm. Drive east along Midshipman Rd., passing Sharp Rock Point and Gold Rock.

Parrot Jungle's Garden of the Groves *(Kids*   One of the island's major attractions is this 12-acre (4.8 hectares) garden, which honors its founder, Wallace Groves, and his wife, Georgette. Eleven kilometers (7 miles) east of the International Bazaar, this scenic preserve of waterfalls and flowering shrubs has some 10,000 trees, free-form lakes, footbridges, ornamental borders, lawns, and flowers. Tropical birds flock here, making this a lure for bird-watchers and ornithologists. The new managers—Parrot Jungle of Miami—have introduced a number of animals to the site, including macaws, cockatoos, pygmy goats, potbelly pigs, and American alligators. Other species introduced include the park's first Bahamian raccoons and the white-crowned pigeon, the latter on the endangered species list. The park also has a children's playground. A lovely little nondenominational chapel, open to visitors, looks down on the garden from a hill. **The Palmetto Café** serves snacks and drinks, and a Bahamian straw market is located at the entrance gate. At press time, the garden was closed due to renovations. Please call ahead or check the website for updates.

Midshipman Rd. and Magellan Dr. © 242/373-5668. www.gardenofthegroves.com. Admission $10 adults, $7 children 3–10, free for children under 3. Garden and cafe daily 9am–4pm.

Finds **A Sudsy Look at Grand Bahama**

You don't think of Freeport as brewery country, but the island is known for its Hammerhead Ale, a favorite of connoisseurs. The **Grand Bahama Brewing Co.,** Logwood Road, Freeport (© **242/351-5191**), offers tours Monday to Friday of its brewery at 10am, 12:30pm, and 4:40pm. In addition to Hammerhead Ales, Lucayan Lager is also made here. Tours cost $5, but the fee is credited to any lager or ale purchases you might make.

Pirates of The Bahamas Beach Theme Park *(Kids)*   Islanders think of this amusement park as their Disney World. One of the largest watersports centers in The Bahamas, it features pools for diving and swimming, along with an array of activities such as parasailing, banana boating, snorkeling, kayaking, paddle-boating, and jet-skiing. Children have their own Captain Kidd's Camp with a supervised playground. Something's always happening here, including beach or bonfire parties along with such attractions as an 18-hole minigolf course. Although you don't pay a general admission fee, you are charged for some of the attractions, such as $6 for the minigolf and varying fees for the watersports. The Bonfire Party Night on Thursday and Sunday, lasting from 5 to 9pm, costs adults $50, children $40, including free transportation from your hotel, live entertainment, and an all-you-can-eat buffet dinner. A restaurant and bar are housed on-site here in a wooden structure that evokes a Spanish galleon.

Jolly Roger Dr., Taíno Beach. © **242/373-8456**. Daily 9am–9pm.

Rand Nature Centre   This 100-acre (40-hectare) pineland sanctuary, located 3km (2 miles) east of the center of Freeport, is the regional headquarters of The Bahamas National Trust, a nonprofit conservation organization. Nature trails highlight native flora and "bush medicine" and provide opportunities for bird-watching; as you stroll, keep your eyes peeled for the lush blooms of tropical orchids or the brilliant flash of green and red feathers in the trees. Wild birds abound at the park. You can join a bird-watching tour on the first Saturday of every month at 8am. Other features of the nature center include native animal displays, an education center, and a gift shop selling nature books and souvenirs.

E. Settlers Way. © **242/352-5438**. Admission $5 adults, $3 children 5–12, free for children under 5. Mon–Fri 9am–4pm.

7 Shopping

Shopping hours in Freeport/Lucaya are generally Monday to Saturday 9am to 6pm. However, in the International Bazaar, hours vary widely. Most places are open Monday through Saturday. Some begin business daily at 9:30am; others don't open until 10am, and closing time ranges from 5:30 to 6pm.

THE INTERNATIONAL BAZAAR

One of the world's most unusual shopping complexes, the International Bazaar, at East Mall Drive and East Sunrise Highway, covers 4 hectares (10 acres) in the heart of Freeport. Although it remains one of the most visited sites in The Bahamas, it frankly is a bit tarnished today and is due for a makeover. Its rising competitor, the Port

Lucaya Marketplace (see below), is looking better every day. Buses at the entrance of the complex aren't numbered, but those marked INTERNATIONAL BAZAAR will take you right to the gateway at the Torii Gate on West Sunrise Highway. The fare is $1. Visitors walk through this much-photographed gate, a Japanese symbol of welcome, into a miniature World's Fair setting (think of it as a kitschy Bahamian version of Epcot). Continental cafes and dozens of shops loaded with merchandise await visitors. The bazaar blends architecture and cultures from some 25 countries, each recreated with cobblestones, narrow alleys, and authentically reproduced architecture. True, it's more theme-park-style shopping than authentic Bahamian experience, but it's fun nevertheless. In the nearly 100 shops, you're bound to find something that is both unique and a bargain. You'll see find African handcrafts, Chinese jade, British china, Swiss watches, Irish linens, and Colombian emeralds—and that's just for starters.

On a street patterned after the Ginza in Tokyo, just inside the entrance to the bazaar, is the Asian section. A rich collection of merchandise from the Far East can be found here, including cameras, handmade teak furniture, fine silken goods, and even places where you can have clothing custom-made.

To the left, you'll find the Left Bank of Paris, or at least a reasonable facsimile, with sidewalk cafes where you can enjoy a café au lait and perhaps a pastry under shade trees. In the Continental Pavilion, you can find leather goods, jewelry, lingerie, and gifts at shops with names such as Love Boutique.

A narrow alley leads you from the French section to East India, where shops sell such exotic goods as taxi horns and silk saris. Moving on from the India House, past Kon Tiki, you arrive in Africa, where you can purchase carvings or a colorful dashiki.

For a taste of Latin America and Iberia, make your way to the Spanish section, where serapes and piñatas hang from the railings, and imports are displayed along the cobblestone walks.

Many items sold in the shops here are said to cost 40% less than if you bought them in the United States, but don't count on that. If you were contemplating a big purchase, it's best to compare prices before you leave home. You can have purchases sent anywhere you wish.

The **Straw Market,** next door to the International Bazaar, contains items with a special Bahamian touch—colorful baskets, hats, handbags, and place mats—all of which make good gifts or souvenirs from your trip. (Be aware that some items sold here are actually made in Asia.)

Here's a description of the various shops in the bazaar.

ART
Flovin Gallery This gallery sells original Bahamian and international art, frames, lithographs, posters, and Bahamian-made Christmas ornaments and decorated coral. It also offers handmade Bahamian dolls, coral jewelry, and other gift items. Another branch is at the Port Lucaya Marketplace (see below). In the Arcade section of the International Bazaar. ✆ 242/352-7564.

CRYSTAL & CHINA
Island Galleria There's an awesome collection of crystal here. Fragile, breakable, and beautiful, it includes works of utilitarian art in china and crystal by Waterford,

Aynsley, Lenox, Dansk, and Swarovski. Anything you buy can be carefully packed and shipped. Another branch is located in the Port Lucaya Marketplace (© 242/373-4512). International Bazaar. © **242/352-8194.**

FASHION

Cleo's Boutique   This shop offers everything from eveningwear to lingerie. A warm and inviting destination, Cleo's prides itself on capturing the Caribbean woman in all of her moods. You can also find a wide array of costume jewelry beginning at $25 per piece. International Bazaar. © **242/352-3340.**

HANDCRAFTS & GIFTS

Caribbean Cargo   One of the island's best, this gift shop specializes in such items as picture frames, T-shirts that change color in sunlight, and a variety of other clothes. Another branch of this store is at the Port Lucaya Marketplace (© 242/373-7950). In the Arcade section of the International Bazaar. © **242/352-2929.**

Far East Traders   Look for Asian linens, hand-embroidered dresses and blouses, silk robes, lace parasols, smoking jackets, and kimonos here. A branch is located inside the Island Galleria at the Port Lucaya Marketplace (© 242/373-8697). International Bazaar. © **242/352-9280.**

Paris in The Bahamas   This shop contains the biggest selection of luxury goods under one roof in the International Bazaar. The staff wears couture black dresses like you might have expected in Paris, and everywhere there's a sense of French glamour and conspicuous consumption. You can find both Gucci and Versace leather goods for men and women; crystal from Lalique, Baccarat, Daum, and Kosta Boda, and a huge collection of cosmetics and perfumes. International Bazaar. © **242/352-5380.**

Unusual Centre   Where else can you get a wide array of items made of walrus skin or goods made from exotic feathers such as peacock? There's another branch at the Port Lucaya Marketplace (© **242/373-7333**). International Bazaar. © **242/352-3994.**

JEWELRY

Colombian Emeralds International   This branch of the world's foremost emerald jeweler offers a wide array of precious gemstone jewelry and one of the island's best watch collections. Careful shoppers will find significant savings over U.S. prices. The outlet offers certified appraisals and free 90-day insurance. Two more branches are at the Port Lucaya Marketplace (© 242/373-8400). South American Section of the International Bazaar. © **242/352-1138.** www.dutyfree.com.

LEATHER GOODS

The Leather Shop   Along with carrying the designer Land, this outlet carries a variety of leather goods including backpacks, coats, shoes, and gift items. An additional location is in the RND Plaza (© 242/352-2895). International Bazaar. © **242/352-5491.**

PERFUMES & FRAGRANCES

The Perfume Factory Fragrance of The Bahamas   This is the top fragrance producer in The Bahamas. The shop is housed in a model of an 1800s mansion, in which visitors are invited to hear a 5-minute commentary and to see the mixing of fragrant oils. There's even a "mixology" department where you can create your own fragrance from a selection of oils. The shop's well-known products include Island Promises, Goombay, Paradise, and Pink Pearl (with conch pearls in the bottle). The shop also sells Guanahani, created to commemorate the 500th anniversary of Columbus's first landfall, and Sand, the leading Bahamian-made men's fragrance. At the rear of the International Bazaar. $\mathcal{C}$ 242/352-9391. www.perfumefactory.com.

STAMPS & COINS

Bahamas Coin and Stamp Ltd.   This is the major coin dealer on the island, specializing in Bahamian coin jewelry, ancient Roman coins, and relics from sunken Spanish galleons. It also carries a vast selection of antique U.S. and English coins and paper money, as well as collectible stamps. International Bazaar. $\mathcal{C}$ 242/352-8989.

PORT LUCAYA MARKETPLACE

Port Lucaya Marketplace on Seahorse Road is a shopping and dining complex set on 2.4 hectares (6 acres). Free entertainment, such as steel-drum bands and strolling musicians, adds to a festival atmosphere. A boardwalk along the water makes it easy to watch the frolicking dolphins.

The complex rose on the site of a former Bahamian straw market, but the craftspeople and their straw products are back in full force after having been temporarily dislodged.

The waterfront location is a distinct advantage. Many of the restaurants and shops overlook a 106-slip marina, home of a "fantasy" pirate ship featuring lunch and dinner/dancing cruises. A variety of charter vessels are also based at the Port Lucaya Marina, and dockage at the marina is available to visitors coming by boat to shop or dine.

Androsia   This is the Port Lucaya outlet of the famous batik house of Andros Island. Its designs and colors capture the spirit of The Bahamas. Fabrics are handmade on the island of Andros. The store sells quality, 100%-cotton resort wear, including simple skirts, tops, jackets, and shorts for women, and it also offers a colorful line of children's wear. Port Lucaya Marketplace. $\mathcal{C}$ 242/373-8387.

Bandolera   The staff can be rather haughty here, but despite its drawbacks, the store carries a collection of chic women's clothing that's many cuts above the usual run of T-shirts and tank tops that are the norm within many of its competitors. Port Lucaya Marketplace. $\mathcal{C}$ 242/373-7691.

Flovin Gallery II   This branch of the art gallery located in the Port Lucaya Marketplace sells a collection of oil paintings (both Bahamian and international), along with lithographs and posters. In its limited field, it's the best in the business. It also features a number of gift items, such as handmade Bahamian dolls, decorated corals, and Christmas ornaments. Port Lucaya Marketplace. $\mathcal{C}$ 242/373-8388.

Harley-Davidson of Freeport   This is one of only two registered and licensed Harley outlets in The Bahamas. You can special order a motorcycle if you feel flush with funds from a casino, but it's more likely that you'll content yourself with T-shirts, leather vests, belts, caps, sunglasses, and gift items. Port Lucaya Marketplace. $\mathcal{C}$ 242/373-8269.

Jeweler's Warehouse   Bargain hunters looking for good buys on discounted, closeout 14-karat gold and gemstone jewelry should come here. Discounts range up to 50%, but the quality of many of these items remains high. Guarantees and certified appraisals are possible. Port Lucaya Marketplace. $\mathcal{C}$ 242/373-8401.

Les Parisiens   This outlet offers a wide range of fine jewelry and watches. It also sells crystal, Versace wear, and perfumes, including the latest from Paris. Port Lucaya Marketplace. ✆ **242/373-2974.**

UNEXSO Dive Shop   This premier dive shop of The Bahamas sells everything related to the water—swimsuits, wet suits, underwater cameras, video equipment, shades, hats, souvenirs, and state-of-the-art diver's equipment. Port Lucaya Marketplace. ✆ **800/992-3483** or 242/373-1244.

8 Grand Bahama After Dark

Many resort hotels stage their own entertainment at night, and these shows are open to the general public.

ROLLING THE DICE

Royal Oasis Casino   Most of the nightlife in Freeport/Lucaya centers around this glittering, giant, Moroccan-style palace, one of the largest casinos in The Bahamas and the Caribbean. Under this Moorish-domed structure, visitors play games of chance and attend Las Vegas–inspired floor shows. Open daily 10am to 2am. Entrance is free. In the Crowne Plaza Golf Resort & Casino at the Royal Oasis, the Mall at W. Sunrise Hwy. ✆ **242/350-7000.**

Casino at Westin & Sheraton at Our Lucaya   We call this casino the best on the island. It far exceeds the glamour of its rival casino in Freeport. The casino's 30 tables offer guests their choice of games, ranging from baccarat to Caribbean stud poker. Blackjack and roulette are also popular games of chance here; for the frugal gambler, some 400 slot machines await. The casino is open daily from 10am to 2am or later. Entrance is free. The Westin & Sheraton at Our Lucaya, Royal Palm Way. ✆ **242/373-1333.**

THE CLUB & BAR SCENE

Located in the center of the **Port Lucaya Marketplace** waterfront restaurant and shopping complex, **Count Basie Square** contains a vine-covered bandstand where the best live music on the island is performed on Tuesday, Friday, and Saturday evenings from about 7:30 to 8pm. And it's free! The square honors the "Count," who used to have a grand home on Grand Bahama. Steel bands, small Junkanoo groups, and even gospel singers from a local church are likely to be heard performing here, their voices or music wafting across the 50-slip marina. You can sip a beer or a tropical rum concoction at one of the bars in the complex. (See "Where to Dine," earlier in this chapter, for details on a few of these, including **Fatman's Nephew** and **Shenanigan's Irish Pub.**)

Finds Bahamian Theater

Instead of one of those Las Vegas leggy showgirl revues, you can call the 450-seat **Regency Theater,** W. Sunrise Hwy. (✆ **242/352-5533**), and ask if one of its performances is being scheduled. This is the home of two nonprofit companies, The Freeport Players' Guild and Grand Bahama Players. The season runs from September to June, and you are likely to see works by both Bahamian and Caribbean playwrights. Some really intriguing shows are likely to be staged every year by both groups, which are equally talented. Tickets cost from $10 to $15.

John B. Lounge   Inside a formidable pile, this club offers some of the best live entertainment on the island. At the outdoorsy John B. Lounge, live music is presented Friday to Sunday. The bar lounge and adjoining dance club are open nightly from 9pm to 2am. Most visitors attend, however, for the Goombay production on Tuesday and Saturday. If you want dinner and a show, arrive at 6:30pm; otherwise, showtime is at 7:30pm. The cost of both is $45. Or you can attend just to see the show, paying from $5 per drink. In the Crowne Plaza Golf Resort & Casino in the Royal Oasis, the Mall at W. Sunrise Hwy. ☎ 242/350-7000.

Prop Club   This sports bar and dance club is the most action-oriented of them all at Lucaya, and you can also dine here on hearty fare. Each night something different is happening: karaoke on Tuesday and Thursday, sumo wrestling on Wednesday, cultural show nights on Thursday, island "jam nights" on Friday, and '70s revival nights on Saturday. But also expect a "get down with the DJ" snooze-a-thon on Sundays, and game nights on slow Mondays. The highlight is the cultural show with a live Junkanoo finale. You can also dine here, enjoying the likes of coconut shrimp, blackened grouper, and sirloin steak, paying from $10 for a full meal. For decor, as the name suggests, remnants of an old airplane and antique propellers adorn the walls. The kitchen is open daily from noon to 10pm, but the bar is open noon to 1am. The DJ arrives at 10pm every night. The Sheraton at Our Lucaya, Royal Palm Way. ☎ 242/373-1333.

9 A Side Trip to West End

If you're looking for a refreshing escape from the plush hotels and casinos of Freeport/Lucaya, head to West End, 45km (28 miles) from Freeport. At this old fishing village, you'll get glimpses of how things used to be before package-tour groups began descending on Grand Bahama.

To reach West End, you head north along Queen's Highway, going through Eight Mile Rock, to the northernmost point of the island.

A lot of the old village buildings are now dilapidated, but they still have some charm and some legend. Many old-timers remember when rum boats were busy and the docks buzzed with activity day and night. This was from about 1920 to 1933, when Prohibition rather unsuccessfully reigned in the United States. West End was so close to the U.S. mainland that rumrunning became a lucrative business, with booze flowing out of West End into Florida at night. Al Capone was reputed to have been a frequent visitor.

Villages along the way to West End have colorful names, such as **Hawksbill Creek.** For a glimpse of local life, try to visit the fish market along the harbor here. You'll pass some thriving harbor areas, too, but the vessels you'll see will be oil tankers, not rumrunners.

Eight Mile Rock is a hamlet of mostly ramshackle houses that stretches along both sides of the road. At **West End,** you come to an abrupt stop. You can enjoy a meal here at the Buccaneer Club or Pier One before heading back to Freeport/Lucaya to catch the last show at the casino.

WHERE TO DINE ON WEST GRAND BAHAMA
EXPENSIVE
Buccaneer Club ✦ *Finds* CONTINENTAL/BAHAMIAN   The Buccaneer Club is a tropical version of a German beer garden and is the best place to eat on the way to

the West End. Heinz Fischbacher and his Bahamian wife, Kitty, created the whimsical decor. The compound is ringed with stone walls; inside it, palm-dotted terraces and foot-stomping alpine music provide lots of fun for the yachting crowd that always packs this place. The collection of inner rooms contains mismatched crystal chandeliers and a beer-hall ambience that's unique in The Bahamas. Artwork and rare Lucayan artifacts (discovered by the owner in 1996) are showcased throughout the club. Many of the dishes are from eastern Europe, including a decent Wiener schnitzel and an excellent veal Oskar. On the occasional Tuesday, the Fischbachers host Junkanoo beach parties, which cost $40 per person. The price includes transportation from hotels, an hour-long open bar, a buffet, a tequila-drinking contest, and limbo dancing.

Deadman's Reef. ℂ **242/349-3794**. Reservations required. Main courses $16–$35. AE, MC, V. Tues–Sun 5pm until closing.

MODERATE

Pier One BAHAMIAN/INTERNATIONAL   Many people head to this restaurant because it's close to the cruise-ship dock. It's also an ideal place to sample some fresh seafood before you head up Queen's Highway to the West End. It rises on stilts a few steps from the water's edge, and a footbridge leads to an interior loaded with nautical artifacts. The high-ceilinged bar is a nice spot for a round of drinks before your meal. The most desirable dining room, of the several here, overlooks schools of fish. The lunch fare includes a delectable cream-based clam chowder, and fresh oysters are also available. The house specialty is actually baby shark, prepared in a number of ways. (There's a shark pool on-site.) We prefer ours sautéed with garlic; the stuffed version, with cheese and crabmeat, tends to overpower the natural shark flavor. A fresh fish of the day is also featured.

Freeport Harbour. ℂ **242/352-6674**. Reservations recommended for dinner. Main courses lunch $5.95–$22, dinner $18–$45. AE, DISC, MC, V. Mon–Fri 10am–4pm; daily 5:30–10pm.

INEXPENSIVE

Star Restaurant & Bar *Finds* BAHAMIAN   At the very western tip of Grand Bahama, about a 45-minute drive from the center of Freeport, this battered old restaurant and bar is housed in the island's oldest hotel. Since 1946 this two-structure building has welcomed the likes of everyone from Ernest Hemingway to Martin Luther King, Jr. Conch, done in many lovely forms, is the specialty: The conch chowder and the fresh conch salad are the island's best. You can also order fried chicken and fish and chips, plus various seafood platters; just tell the cook how you like them cooked. And surely no one serves a better Bahama Mama!

Bayshore Rd., West End. ℂ **242/346-6207**. Main courses $8–$15. No credit cards. Daily 9am–3am.

6

Bimini, the Berry Islands & Andros

In this chapter, we begin a journey through the Out Islands—a very different place from the major tourist developments of Nassau, Cable Beach, Paradise Island, and Freeport/Lucaya.

Bimini, the Berry Islands, and Andros are each unique. Bimini is famous and overrun with tourists, particularly in summer, but visitors will have the Berry Islands practically to themselves. These two island chains to the north and west of Nassau could be called the "westerly islands," because they, along with Grand Bahama, lie at the northwestern fringe of The Bahamas. They are the closest islands to the Florida coastline.

In contrast, much larger Andros is located southwest of Nassau. In many ways Andros is the most fascinating. The story goes that mysterious creatures once inhabited this series of islands laced with creeks and dense forests.

Each of the three island chains attracts a different type of visitor. **Bimini,** just 81km (50 miles) off the east coast of Florida (and the setting for Hemingway's *Islands in the Stream*) lures the big-game fisher, the yachter from Miami, and even the drug dealer from south Florida. (The proximity to the Florida mainland helps make drug smuggling big business here.) Bimini is home to world-famous sportfishing, excellent yachting and cruising, and some good scuba diving. Anglers will find seas swarming with tuna, dolphin-

fish, amberjack, white and blue marlin, swordfish, barracuda, and shark, along with many other varieties. Bonefish are also plentiful around the flats off the coast of Alice Town, the capital, but the blue marlin is the prize. (Bahamians think so highly of this fish that they even put it on their $100 bill.) Scuba divers can see black coral trees over the Bimini Wall and reefs off Victory Cay.

The **Berry Islands** might attract the weary Bill Gates or Steve Forbes types. It also draws fishermen, but this string of islands, which has only 700 residents, is mainly for escapists—*rich* escapists. The islands' very limited accommodations (some of which used to be private clubs) lie near the Tongue of the Ocean, home of the big-game fish.

Andros, the largest island in the nation, is mainly uninhabited. If The Bahamas still has an unexplored wilderness, this is it. The island's forest and mangrove swamps are home to a wide variety of birds and animals, including the nonpoisonous Bahamian boa constrictor and the 2m-long (6½-ft.) iguana. The Bahamian national bird, the West Indian flamingo, can also be spotted during migration in late spring and summer. The waters off Andros are home to a wondrous barrier reef, the third largest in the world and a diver's dream. The reef plunges 167km (104 miles) to a narrow drop-off known as the Tongue of the

Ocean. Andros's mysterious blue holes, another diver's delight, are formed when subterranean caves fill with seawater, causing the ceiling to collapse and expose clear, deep pools. Few come here anymore looking for Sir Henry Morgan's pirate treasure, said to be buried in one of the caves off Morgan's Bluff on the north tip of the island. But Andros does attract anglers, mostly because it is known for its world-class fishing for marlin and the bluefin tuna, and its bonefishing is perhaps the best in the world.

1 Bimini ⋆

Bimini is still known as the big-game fishing capital of the world, and fishermen still come here throughout the year to fish in flats, on the reefs, and in the streams. Ernest Hemingway came to write and fish, and here, he wrote much of *To Have and Have Not*. His novel *Islands in the Stream* put Bimini on the map. Regrettably, fishing isn't what it used to be in Papa's day, and such species as marlin, swordfish, and tuna have been dangerously overfished by commercial longline boats.

Located 81km (50 miles) east of Miami, Bimini consists of a number of islands, islets, and cays, including North and South Bimini, the main tourist areas. You'll most often encounter the word "Bimini," but it might be more proper to say "The Biminis," since North Bimini and South Bimini are two distinct islands, separated by a narrow ocean passage. Ferry-service shuttles between the two. The major development is on North Bimini, mostly in Alice Town. The western side of North Bimini is a long stretch of lovely beachfront.

Off North Bimini, in 9m (30 ft.) of water, are some large hewn-stone formations that some people say came from the lost continent of Atlantis. Divers find the reefs laced with conch, lobster, coral, and many tropical fish.

Bimini's location off the Florida coastline is at a point where the Gulf Stream meets the Bahama Banks. This fact has made Bimini a favorite cruising ground for America's yachting set, who follow the channel between North and South Bimini into a spacious, sheltered harbor, where they can stock up on food, drink, fuel, and supplies at well-equipped marinas. From here, they can set off to cruise the cays that begin south of South Bimini. Each has its own special appeal, beginning with Turtle Rocks and stretching to South Cat Cay (the latter of which is uninhabited). Along the way, you'll pass Holm Cay, Gun Cay, and North Cat Cay.

Hook-shaped North Bimini is 12km (7½ miles) long, and combined with South Bimini, it makes up a landmass of only 23 sq. km (9 sq. miles). That's why Alice Town looks so crowded. Another reason is that a large part of Bimini is privately owned; despite pressure from the Bahamian government, the landholders have not sold their acreage, and Bimini can't "spread out" until they do. At Alice Town, the land is so narrow that you can walk "from sea to shining sea" in just a short time. Most of Bimini's population of some 1,600 people lives in Alice Town; other hamlets include Bailey Town and Porgy Bay.

Although winter is usually high season in The Bahamas, visitors flock to Bimini's calmer summer waters, which are better for fishing. Winter, especially from mid-December to mid-March, is quieter, and Bimini has never tried to develop a resort structure that would attract more winter visitors. If you go to Bimini, you'll hear a lot of people mention **Cat Cay** (not to be confused with Cat Island, in the Southern Bahamas). You can stay overnight at Cat Cay's marina, which lies 13km (8 miles) off South Bimini.

Transient slips are available to mariners. The island is the domain of **Cat Cay Yacht Club** (© 242/347-3565), whose initiation fee is a cool $25,000. This privately owned island—attracting titans of industry and famous families—is for the exclusive use of Cat Cay Club members and their guests. At their leisure, they can enjoy the golf course, tennis, a large marina, white-sand beaches, and club facilities such as restaurants and bars. Many wealthy Americans have homes on the island, which has a private airstrip.

GETTING THERE

Note: A passport or a birth certificate with picture ID is required of *everyone* for entry to Bimini (bring your passport to be on the safe side), and an outbound (return) ticket also must be presented to Bahamian Customs before you will be allowed entry. A departure tax is included in all airfares.

BY PLANE   The island's only airstrip is at the southern tip of South Bimini, a time-consuming transfer and ferryboat ride away from Alice Town on North Bimini, site of most of the archipelago's hotels and yacht facilities.

The best way to avoid this transfer is to fly for 20- to 30-minutes via the small **Chalk's Ocean Airways,** (© 800/424-2557; www.chalksoceanairways.com). The airline has a fleet of 17-passenger amphibious aircraft that depart from the runway at Ft. Lauderdale/Hollywood International Airport and land in the waters near Alice Town. The baggage allowance per passenger is 30 pounds; if you're carrying heavy travel or fishing gear, you'll be hit with overweight charges. ***Note:*** Chalk's doesn't allow any hand luggage on board—every piece of your luggage must be weighed and checked in.

Also, **Island Air** (© 800/444-9904 or 954/359-9942; www.islandaircharters.com) flies four times a week from Fort Lauderdale to South Bimini. Finally, **Western Air** (© 242/347-4100; www.westernairbahamas.com) wings in from Nassau's domestic air terminal.

BY BOAT   In the olden days, the traditional way to get from Nassau to Bimini was by a slow-moving boat; you can still do it, and it'll take you 12 hours. You can go by sea on the MV *Bimini Mack,* which leaves from Potter's Cay Dock in Nassau and stops at Cat Cay and Bimini. The vessel leaves Nassau Thursdays at 2am. For details about departure, call the dockmaster at **Potter's Cay Dock** in Nassau (© 242/393-1064).

GETTING AROUND

If you've taken our advice and traveled lightly to Bimini, you can walk to your hotel from the point where the seaplanes land in Alice Town. If not, a small minibus will transport you for $3 per person. If you arrive at the small airport on South Bimini, you'll need to pay for a $5 taxi and ferry ride to Alice Town.

You won't need a car on Bimini—and in fact, you won't find a car-rental agency here. Most people walk to where they want to go (though your hotel may be able to arrange a minibus tour or rent you a bike or golf cart). The walk is up and down King's Highway, which has no sidewalks. It's so narrow that two automobiles have a tough time squeezing by. Be careful walking along this highway, especially at night when drivers might not see you.

This highway, lined with low-rise buildings, splits Alice Town on North Bimini. If you're a beachcombing type, stick to the side bordering the Gulf Stream. It's here you'll find the best beaches. The harborside contains a handful of inns (most of which are reviewed below), along with marinas and docks where supplies are unloaded. You'll see many Floridians arriving on yachts.

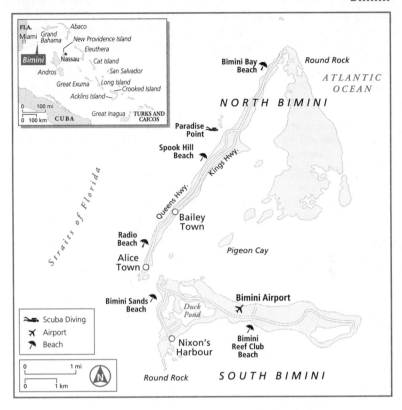

FAST FACTS: Bimini

Banks **The Royal Bank of Canada** has a branch office in Alice Town (*☎* **242/ 347-3031**), with an **ATM,** open Monday and Friday 9:30am to 3pm and Tuesday, Wednesday, and Thursday 9:30am to 1pm.

Clothing If you're going to Bimini in the winter months, take along a windbreaker for those occasional chilly nights.

Customs & Immigration The Chalk's flight from Miami stops right near the Alice Town office of **Customs and Immigration** (*☎* **242/347-3100** for Customs; **242/347-3446** for Immigration) for The Bahamas. There's only one Immigration officer, plus another Customs official.

In Miami you will have been handed a Bahamian Immigration Card to fill out, and you must carry proof of your citizenship. Though it may be possible to use your voter-registration card or a birth certificate plus photo ID, we recommend that you bring your passport to be on the safe side. Regrettably, many passengers cross over from Miami with only a driver's license, which will not be accepted by Immigration. Customs may examine your baggage.

Drugs The rumrunners of the Prohibition era have now given way to those smuggling illegal drugs into the United States from The Bahamas. Because of its proximity to the U.S. mainland, Bimini, as is no secret to anyone, is now a major drop-off point for drugs, many on the way from Colombia. If not intercepted by the U.S. Coast Guard, these drugs find their way to Florida and eventually to the rest of the United States.

Buying and/or selling illegal drugs, such as cocaine and marijuana, is an extremely risky business in The Bahamas. You may be approached by dealers on Bimini, some of whom are actually undercover agents. If caught with illegal drugs, you face immediate imprisonment.

Emergencies To call the police or report a fire, dial © **919.**

Medical Care Nurses, a doctor, and a dentist are on the island, as well as the **North Bimini Medical Clinic** (© **242/347-2210**). However, for a serious medical emergency, patients are usually airlifted to either Miami or Nassau. Helicopters can land in the well-lit baseball field on North Bimini.

Visitor Information There's a branch of **The Bahamas Ministry of Tourism** in Bimini, located in the Government Building, Queens Highway, Alice Town (© **242/347-3529**). It's open Monday to Friday 9am to 5pm.

WHERE TO STAY

Accommodations in Bimini are extremely limited, and it's almost impossible to get a room during one of the big fishing tournaments unless you've reserved way in advance. Inns are cozy and simple; many are family-owned and -operated (chances are, your innkeeper's name will be Brown). Furnishings are often timeworn, the paint chipped. No one puts on airs here; the dress code, even in the evening, is very simple and relaxed. From wherever you're staying in Alice Town, it's usually easy to walk to another hotel for dinner or drinks.

Bimini Big Game Resort & Marina ★★ The chosen "watering hole" of big-game fishermen since the 1950s, this resort is better than ever following multimillion-dollar renovations. Its 81-slip marina often makes it a favorite stopover with the yachting crowd from Florida's east coast. The resort's restoration has been called a rebirth, and its patrons—mainly boaters, divers, eco-adventurers, and the deep-sea and bonefishing elite—have remained loyal. Both the resort and marina facilities have been improved. The guest rooms and the dining and drinking facilities were completely overhauled. Accommodations are now well furnished, both the guest units in the main building and those in surrounding cottages. All rooms have patios or porches opening onto the marina and the club's swimming pool; the ground-floor cottages are more spacious than the standard bedrooms and have tiny kitchenettes and refrigerators. The small bathrooms are well maintained and come with shower stalls.

If you want to charcoal-broil your catch at the end of the day (hotel staff can arrange all sorts of fishing charters), you can use one of the outdoor grills. This hotel is also the best place for food and entertainment on the island (see "Where to Dine" and "Bimini After Dark," later in this chapter).

King's Hwy. (P.O. Box 699), Alice Town, Bimini, The Bahamas. © **800/737-1007** in the U.S. or 242/347-3391. Fax 242/347-3392. www.biminibiggame.com. 47 units (12 cottages, 35 rooms). Year-round $135–$185 double; $175–$225 cottage. Extra person $25. MC, V. **Amenities:** Restaurant; 3 bars; pool; all nonsmoking rooms. *In room:* A/C, TV, kitchenette (in some), minibar (in some), fridge (in some), hair dryer, no phone.

Bimini Blue Water Resort Ltd. ⭐ *(Finds)*   This is essentially a resort complex for sportfishermen, with complete dockside services, containing 32 modern slips. It's one of the finest places of its kind in The Bahamas. The main building is a white-frame waterfront Bahamian guesthouse, the Anchorage, where Michael Lerner, the noted fisherman, used to live. It's at the top of the hill, with a dining room and bar from which you can look out onto the ocean (see "Where to Dine," below). The regular mid-size bedrooms contain double beds, wood-paneled walls, white furniture, and picture-window doors that lead to private balconies. Bathrooms are small with shower units.

The Marlin Cottage, although much altered, was one of Hemingway's retreats in the 1930s. He used it as a main setting in *Islands in the Stream*. It has three bedrooms, three bathrooms, a large living room, and two porches.

King's Hwy. (P.O. Box 601), Alice Town, Bimini, The Bahamas. ℰ **242/347-3166.** Fax 242/347-3293. 13 units. Year-round $90 double; $190 suite; $285 cottage. AE, MC, V. **Amenities:** Restaurant; bar; pool; babysitting. *In room:* A/C, TV, fridge, iron/ironing board, no phone.

Bimini Sands Beach Club Hotel   Two distinctly different aspects of this complex both lie at the edge of a sandy beach, a 5-minute drive from South Bimini's international airport. The less well accessorized and comfortable of the two is the two-story hotel, half of whose rooms overlook the sea, the other half of which front a marina. Originally built in the 1970s, it was radically reconstructed in 2005. Expect something akin to a roadside motel in Florida, except with a sandy beach a few steps away. The condo complex is more elaborate, again with many of the features you'd expect (kitchens, balconies, patios, contemporary furniture, and so on) of a generic-looking apartment complex somewhere in south Florida. Like the hotel section, half the rooms overlook the sea, the other half overlook a marina. Rooms in each of the two complexes do feature well-maintained bathrooms with tub and shower combinations.

Island in the Stream

Nevil Norton Stuart, a Bahamian, came to Bimini in the late 1920s and purchased the Fountain of Youth, a Prohibition-era bar, renaming it the **Bimini Big Game Resort & Marina.** In 1940, Stuart reclaimed land in Bimini Harbor, constructed a marina, and added several cottages along with a desalination plant. Thus began the legend of one of the most highly publicized sportfishing meccas in the world.

Film stars, including Judy Garland and Sir Anthony Hopkins, among others, have lodged at the club, and Martin Luther King, Jr., visited twice. Of course, no one immortalized the island as much as Hemingway, who called it "My Island in the Stream."

Today the complex has grown to more than 50 rooms, including cottages and penthouses, and it's owned by the rum maker Bacardi International. In the 100-slip marina, you'll find enormous sportfishing boats, costing more than several million dollars, proudly standing alongside simple outboard-powered runabouts.

South Bimini. ℂ **242/347-3500.** Fax 242/347-3501. www.biminisands.com. 208 units. Year-round $130–$150 double; $235–$260 1-bedroom apt; $375–$385 2-bedroom apt. 2-night minimum required in condo complex. AE, MC, V. **Amenities:** 2 restaurants; 4 bars; 2 pools; tennis court; laundry service. *In room:* A/C.

Compleat Angler Hotel Right on the main street, and affiliated with the Bimini Blue Water Resort, this small timeworn hotel was built in the 1930s, when big-game fishing was at its peak. The building is designed like an old country house, with Bahamian timber. The wood on the face of the building is from rum barrels used during the Prohibition era. Don't expect anything too fancy, but the Compleat Angler is loaded with island atmosphere. Ernest Hemingway made the hotel his headquarters on and off from 1935 to 1937 while he was stalking marlin, and the room in which he stayed is still available to guests. He penned parts of *To Have and Have Not* here. The small to midsize rooms are tidily maintained and comfortable, with cramped bathrooms containing shower stalls. The best units are those in the front opening onto the encircling veranda, overlooking the courtyard bar and the street. You can swim, dine, shop, or fish right at your doorstep, and book fishing charters at the hotel. *Note:* Because of the famously noisy bar on the premises (see "Bimini After Dark," below), this hotel is most suitable for night owls.

King's Hwy. (P.O. Box 601), Alice Town, Bimini, The Bahamas. ℂ **242/347-3122.** Fax 242/347-3293. 12 units. Year-round $70–$85 double. AE, MC, V. **Amenities:** 3 bars; pool. *In room:* A/C, iron/ironing board, no phone.

Sea Crest Hotel and Marina *(Kids* Built in 1981 and upgraded every year since, this hotel lies right on the main highway and was the first place to give the Bimini Big Game Resort & Marina some real competition. It's still not as good as that traditional leader, but the price is right. Rooms in this three-story hotel, which looks like a motel, are at their best on the third floor due to the better ocean or bay views there. Rooms don't have phones, and many are small, with rather cramped bathrooms, each with a shower stall, but they're comfortably furnished in a simple, traditional way. Accommodations open onto small balconies. Since the location is right in the heart of Alice Town, you can generally walk where you want to go. The Sea Crest is a family favorite, and children under 12 stay free. There's an on-site restaurant, Captain Bob's, which is independently operated and serves good seafood. The hotel is also a favorite of the boating crowd, because it offers a small 18-berth marina.

King's Hwy. (P.O. Box 654), Alice Town, Bimini, The Bahamas. ℂ **242/347-3071.** Fax 242/347-3495. www.seacrest bimini.com. 14 units. Year-round $99–$125 double; $220 2-bedroom suite; $320 3-bedroom suite. MC, V. **Amenities:** Marina. *In room:* A/C, TV, no phone.

WHERE TO DINE

Anchorage Dining Room SEAFOOD/BAHAMIAN/AMERICAN This dining room overlooks the harbor of Alice Town; you can see the ocean through picture windows. The modern, paneled room is filled with captain's chairs and Formica tables. You might begin your dinner with conch chowder, then follow with one of the tempting seafood dishes, including spiny broiled lobster or perhaps a chewy cracked conch. They also do a good fried Bahamian chicken and a tender New York sirloin. The cooking is straightforward and reliable, and never pretends to be more than just that.

In the Blue Hole Water Resort, King's Hwy., Alice Town. ℂ **242/347-3166.** Main courses $13–$25. AE, MC, V. Wed–Mon 6–10pm.

Red Lion Pub BAHAMIAN This centrally located restaurant is far larger than its simple facade would indicate. In a relaxed, friendly atmosphere, it's one of the best places on the island to retreat to after a day of fishing and sailing. It's one of the few nonsmoking restaurants in the Out Islands. The dining room is in a large extension of the original pub and overlooks the marina in back. The well-prepared meals are local home cooking: the local fish of the day, cracked conch, barbecued ribs, baked grouper in foil, followed by either Key lime pie or banana cream pie. The price of the main course practically gets you a dinner unto itself.

King's Hwy., Alice Town. ℂ 242/347-3259. Main courses $15–$28. No credit cards. Tues–Sun 6–10pm; pub Tues–Sun until 10:30pm.

The Tackle Box BAHAMIAN/INTERNATIONAL   Set in the annex of the Bimini Big Game Resort & Marina (p. 180), this restaurant is the one most likely to be open at the time of your visit. Expect fine views, as it's located directly adjacent to the marina with dozens of world-class fishing boats. Don't expect grand or even particularly esoteric cuisine, as the menu might remind you of what's available at a bar and grill in neighboring Florida. Lunches are simpler than dinners, with salads, simple grills, burgers, chicken fingers, soups, and stews. Lunches are leisurely, dinners are even more so, but with a wider choice of steaks, grills, lobster dishes, pastas, and fresh fish, especially wahoo, mahimahi, swordfish, and tuna. Bear in mind that the offerings here might (or might not, depending on a seemingly whimsical collection of factors) be supplemented with a slightly more expensive on-site restaurant, The Clubhouse, which lies in a building of its own a few paces away.

In the Bimini Big Game Resort & Marina, King's Hwy., Alice Town. ℂ 242/347-3391. Reservations recommended. Main courses lunch $4.75–$9, dinner $19–$30. MC, V, AE. Daily 10am–10pm.

WATERSPORTS & OTHER OUTDOOR ACTIVITIES
BEACHES
The beaches on Bimini are all clearly marked and signposted from the highways.

The beach that's closest to Alice Town is **Radio Beach,** the only one on Bimini with toilets, vendors, and snack bars. It's set adjacent to the piers and wharves of Alice Town, and consequently, it's the most popular and crowded beach on the island.

About 3km (2 miles) north of Alice Town, facing west, is **Spook Hill Beach.** Both it and its cousin, **Bimini Bay Beach,** about 4km (2½ miles) north of Alice Town, offer fewer crowds, good snorkeling, and lots of sunshine. Both are sandy bottomed and comfortable on your feet. Above all, many local residents prefer **Bimini Bay Beach,** which is wider than any other on the island.

On South Bimini, the two favorites are the west-facing **Bimini Sands Beach,** a sandy-bottomed stretch that's immediately south of the channel separating North from South Bimini; and the **Bimini Reef Club Beach,** south of the airport, where offshore snorkeling is especially worthwhile, thanks to very clear waters.

FISHING
Ernest Hemingway made fishing here famous. But Zane Grey came this way, too, as did Howard Hughes. Richard Nixon used to fish here aboard the posh cruiser of his friend Bebe Rebozo. In the trail of Hemingway, fishermen still flock to cast lines in the Gulf Stream and the Bahama Banks.

Of course, everyone's still after the big one, and a lot of world records have been set in this area for marlin, sailfish, swordfish, wahoo, grouper, and tuna. But these fish are becoming evasive and their dwindling numbers are edging them close to extinction. Fishing folk can spin cast for panfish and boat snapper, yellowtail, and kingfish. Many experts consider stalking bonefish, long a pursuit of baseball great Ted Williams, to be the toughest challenge in the sport.

⸝Finds⸍ Ruins of the Roaring '20s

A major attraction for both snorkelers and divers, not to mention rainbow-hued fish, is the *Sapona,* lying hard aground in 4.5m (15 ft.) of water between South Bimini and Cat Cay ever since it was blown here by a hurricane in 1929. In the heyday of the Roaring Twenties, the ship, which was built by Henry Ford, served as a private club and speakeasy. You'll have to take a boat to reach the wreck site. Spearfishermen are attracted to the ruins, looking for the giant grouper, and dive operators on Bimini include the site in their repertoire. It's shallow enough that even snorkelers can see it.

Five charter boats are available in Bimini for big-game and little-game fishing, with some center-console boats rented for both bottom and reef angling. At least eight bonefishing guides are available, and experienced anglers who have made repeated visits to Bimini know the particular skills of each of these men who will take you for a half- or full day of "fishing in the flats." Most skiffs hold two anglers, and part of the fun in hiring a local guide is to hear his fish tales and other island lore. If a guide tells you that 16-pound bonefish have turned up, he may not be exaggerating—catches that large have really been documented.

Reef and bottom-fishing on Bimini are easier than bonefishing and can be more productive. Numerous species of snapper and grouper can be found, as well as amberjack. This is the simplest and least expensive boat fishing, because you need only a local guide, a little boat, tackle, and a lot of bait. Sometimes you can negotiate to go out bottom-fishing with a Bahamian, but chances are he'll ask you to pay for the boat fuel for his trouble. That night, back at your Bimini inn, the cook will serve you the red snapper or grouper you caught that day.

Most hotel owners will tell you to bring your own fishing gear to Bimini. A couple of small shops sell some items, but you'd better bring major equipment with you if you're really serious. Bait, of course, can be purchased locally.

At the **Bimini Big Game Resort & Marina,** King's Highway, Alice Town (② 242/347-3391), you can charter a 12m (39-ft.) Hatteras at $700 to $800 for a full day of fishing, or $400 to $600 for a half-day. A Bertram, either 8.5 or 9.5m (28 or 31 ft.), will also cost $800 to $900 for a full day or $400 to $500 for a half-day. Although this outfitter is your best bet, you can also pick up a list of locals whose boats are available for charter at **Bimini Blue Water Marina,** King's Highway, Alice Town (② 242/347-3166). The average rate is around $450 to $500 per half-day or $600 to $900 for a full day.

SCUBA DIVING & SNORKELING

Explore the black coral gardens and reefs here, plus wrecks and blue holes, plus a mysterious stone formation on the bottom of the sea that some people claim is part of the lost continent of Atlantis (it's 457m/1,500 ft. offshore at Bimini Bay, under about 6m/20 ft. of water). Bimini waters are known for a breathtaking drop-off at the rim of the continental shelf, a cliff extending 600m (1,368 ft.) down, a veritable underwater mountain.

The finest and most experienced outfitter is **Bimini Undersea,** King's Highway, Alice Town (② 242/347-3089; www.biminiundersea.com).

The people to see here are Bill and Nowdla Keefe. Half-day snorkeling trips cost $29. Scuba rates are $49 for a one-tank dive, $89 for a two-tank dive, and $119 for a three-tank dive. Night dives, which vary weekly, go for $49. All-inclusive dive packages are also available. For further information or reservations, the Keefes can be reached at © 800/348-4644 or 305/653-5572.

You can also swim with dolphins in the wild two or three times a week, depending on demand. Most excursions take from 3 to 4 hours and cost $119 for adults or $89 for children 12 and under. Swimming with dolphins has its critics and supporters. You may want to visit the Whale and Dolphins Conservation Society's website at www.wdcs.org. For more information about responsible travel in general, check out these websites: Tread Lightly (www.treadlightly.org) and the International Ecotourism Society (www.ecotourism.org).

TRACING THE FOOTSTEPS OF PONCE DE LEON & PAPA

At the southern tip of North Bimini, ramshackle **Alice Town** is all that many visitors ever see of the islands, since the major hotels are found here. You can see the whole town in an hour or two. The **Bimini Big Game Resort & Marina,** King's Highway, has some of the best duty-free liquor buys in town. If you're a souvenir collector, ask at the front office for T-shirts, sunglasses, coffee mugs, and Big Game hats.

If you're on the trail of Papa Hemingway, you'll want to visit the **Compleat Angler,** King's Highway in Alice Town (© 242/347-3122), where you'll find a museum of Hemingway memorabilia. The collection of prints and writings describes the times he spent in Bimini, mainly from 1935 to 1937. The prints are posted in the sitting room downstairs, and much of this memorabilia makes interesting browsing. Many books by Hemingway are in the library collection.

As you're exploring the island, you may want to stop off at the **Bimini Straw Market,** strike up a conversation with some islanders, and perhaps pick up a souvenir. Next door to the Bahamas Customs Building, you'll usually find two dozen vendors here.

If you're curious, drop into the little **Bimini Museum** (© 242/347-3038) on King's Highway, a sort of grab bag of mementos left behind by visiting celebrities. The museum owns the 1964 immigration card of Martin Luther King, Jr., a domino set left by frequent visitor Adam Clayton Powell (the congressman from New York), and

---

Fun Fact   Myths of Bimini

Bimini has long been shrouded in myths, none more far-fetched than the one claiming that the lost continent of **Atlantis** lies off the shores of North Bimini. This legend grew because of the weirdly shaped rock formations that lie submerged in about 6m (20 ft.) of water near the shoreline. Pilots flying over North Bimini have reported what they envision as a "lost highway" under the sea. This myth continues, and many scuba divers are attracted to North Bimini to explore these rocks.

Ponce de León came to South Bimini looking for that legendary **Fountain of Youth.** He never found it, but people still come to South Bimini in search of it. Near the end of the 19th century, a religious sect reportedly came here to "take the waters"—supposedly a bubbling fountain or spring. If you arrive on South Bimini and seem interested enough, a local guide (for a fee) will be only too happy to show you "the exact spot" where the Fountain of Youth once bubbled.

Moments **A Drink at the End of the World**

Everybody eventually makes his or her way to the **End of the World Bar** (no phone) on King's Highway in Alice Town. When you get here, you may think you're in the wrong place—it's just a waterfront shack with sawdust or sand on the floor and graffiti everywhere. The late New York congressman Adam Clayton Powell put this bar on the map in the 1960s. Between stints in Washington battling Congress and preaching at the Abyssinian Baptist Church in Harlem, the controversial congressman could be found sitting at a table here. While the bar doesn't attract the media attention it did in Powell's heyday, it's still a local favorite. Open daily from 9am to 3am.

Ernest Hemingway's fishing log and vintage fishing films. Other island artifacts such as rum kegs are also exhibited. The location in a two-story 1920s house is a 4-minute walk from the seaplane ramp. Charging $2, the museum is open Monday to Saturday 9am to 9pm. Elementary-school-age children are admitted free.

The **Queen's Highway** runs up the western side of North Bimini, and as you head north along it, you'll find it lined with beautiful beachfront. **King's Highway** runs through the town and continues north. It's lined with houses painted gold, lime, buttercup yellow, and pink that gleam in the bright sunshine.

At some point, you may notice the ruins of Bimini's first hotel, the **Bimini Bay Rod and Gun Club,** sitting unfinished on its own beach. Built in the early 1920s, it did a flourishing business until a hurricane wiped it out later in that decade. It was never rebuilt, though developers once made a never-finished attempt.

If you want to visit **South Bimini,** you can rent a taxi to see the island's limited attractions for about $17, which, regrettably, at least to our knowledge, does not include Ponce de León's legendary Fountain of Youth, as once rumored. There's not a lot to see, but you are likely to hear some tall tales worth the cab fare. You can also stop off at some lovely, uncrowded beaches.

BIMINI AFTER DARK

You can dance to a Goombay drum beat or try to find some disco music. Most people have a leisurely dinner, drink a lot in one of the local watering holes, and go back to their hotel rooms by midnight so they can get up early to continue pursuing the elusive "big one" the next morning. Every bar in Alice Town is likely to claim that it was Hemingway's favorite. He did hit quite a few of them, in fact. There's rarely a cover charge anywhere unless some special entertainment is being offered.

Beginning at midmorning and lasting until midnight at least, the bars at the **Bimini Big Game Resort & Marina,** King's Highway, Alice Town (© 242/347-3391), are the place to hang out. Tall fish tales of the big one that got away fill the air. **The Tackle Box** (p. 183) starts serving its famed conch pizza at noon. You can play a hand of cards here, or tune in to one of the TV sets positioned for your favorite sports program; it's the best place to entertain yourself during a lazy day in Bimini. The poolside **Barefoot Bar,** open from midmorning to late afternoon, serves favorite island drinks and ice-cold beer. Off the main dining room is the **Clubhouse,** featuring live bands on occasion.

Constructed of Prohibition-era rum kegs, the bar at the **Compleat Angler Hotel,** King's Highway, Alice Town (© 242/347-3122), hosts an eclectic clientele who come to dance to the nightly calypso band and drink Goombay Smashes. The bartender makes the best planter's punch in The Bahamas, challenging anyone to make it better. The place, as mentioned, is filled with Hemingway memorabilia, and it's open daily from 8am "until it closes."

2 The Berry Islands *

A dangling chain of cays and islets on the eastern edge of the Great Bahama Bank, the unspoiled and serene Berry Islands begin 56km (35 miles) northwest of New Providence (Nassau), 242km (150 miles) east of Miami. This 30-island archipelago is known to sailors, fishermen, yachtspeople, Jack Nicklaus, and a Rockefeller or two, as well as to the beachcombers who love its pristine sands.

As a center of fishing, the Berry Islands are second only to Bimini. At the tip of the Tongue of the Ocean, aka TOTO, world-record-setting big-game fish are found, along with endless flats (the shallow bodies of water near the shore where bonefish congregate). In the "Berries," you can find your own tropical paradise islet, and enjoy—sans wardrobe—totally isolated white-sand beaches and palm-fringed shores. Some of the best shell collecting in The Bahamas is found on the beaches of the Berry Islands and in their shallow-water flats.

The main islands are, beginning in the north, Great Stirrup Cay, Cistern Cay, Great Harbour Cay, Anderson Cay, Haines Cay, Hoffmans Cay, Bond's Cay, Sandy Cay, Whale Cay, and Chub Cay. One of the very small cays, lying north of Frazer's Hog Cay and Whale Cay, has, in our opinion, the most unappetizing name in the Bahamian archipelago: Cockroach Cay.

The largest island within the Berry Islands is **Great Harbour Cay,** which sprawls over 1,520 hectares (3,754 acres) of sand, rock, and scrub. Development here received a great deal of publicity when Douglas Fairbanks, Jr., was connected with its investors. It became a multimillion-dollar resort for jet-setters who occupied waterfront town houses and villas overlooking the golf course or marina. Cary Grant, Brigitte Bardot, and other stars have all romped on the 12km (7½ miles) of almost-solitary beachfront you can still find here.

Bond's Cay, a bird sanctuary in the south, and tiny Frazer's Hog Cay (stock is still raised here) are both privately owned. An English company used to operate a coconut and sisal plantation on Whale Cay, also near the southern tip. Sponge fishermen and their families inhabit some of the islands.

BERRY ISLANDS ESSENTIALS

GETTING THERE   Great Harbour Cay is an official point of entry for The Bahamas if you're flying from a foreign territory such as the United States.

You can get here only via charter flights from South Florida, making these some of the most inconvenient islands to reach in all The Bahamas. **Tropical Diversions** (© **954/921-9084**) flies from Fort Lauderdale to Great Harbour Cay, usually in a small twin-engine Aztec Cessna 402; and **Island Express** (© **954/359-0380**) also operates charters from Fort Lauderdale, winging in to Chub Cay Airport.

If you're contemplating the **mail-boat** sea-voyage route, the **MV** *Captain Gurthdean* leaves Potter's Cay Dock in Nassau once a week on Tuesday at 7pm, heading for the Berry Islands. Inquire at the **Potter's Cay Dock** for an up-to-the-minute report (contact the dockmaster at © **242/393-1064**).

FAST FACTS The **Great Harbour Cay Medical Clinic** is located at Bullock's Harbour on Great Harbour Cay (𝒞 **242/367-8400**). The **police station** is also at Bullock's Harbour (𝒞 **242/367-8344** and -8104).

GREAT HARBOUR CAY

An estimated 700 residents live on Great Harbour Cay, making it the most populated island of the Berry chain. Its main settlement is **Bullock's Harbour,** which might be called the "capital of the Berry Islands." The cay is about 2.5km (1½ miles) wide and some 13km (8 miles) long. A grocery store and some restaurants are about all you'll find in town. Most visitors arrive to stay at the **Great Harbour Cay Yacht Club & Marina,** which for 2005 or 2006 is being turned into a posh and much bigger resort. Check its status before coming here.

Great Harbour Cay lies between Grand Bahama Island and New Providence (Nassau). It's 97km (60 miles) northwest of Nassau and 242km (150 miles) east of Miami, about an hour away from Miami by plane or half a day by powerboat. Unlike most islands in The Bahamas, the island isn't flat but contains rolling hills.

Deep-sea fishing possibilities abound here, including billfish, dolphinfish, king mackerel, and wahoo. Light-tackle bottom-fishing is also good. You can net yellowtail, snapper, barracuda, triggerfish, and plenty of grouper. Bonefishing here is among the best in the world. The Great Harbour Cay marina is an excellent facility, with some 80 slips and all the amenities. Some of Florida's fanciest yachts pull in here.

When you tire of fishing, you can relax on 13km (8 miles) of gorgeous white-sand beaches, play the 9-hole golf course designed by Joe Lee, or try your backhand on one of the four clay tennis courts.

WHERE TO STAY & DINE

Tropical Diversions Resort ⌖   On the northern tip of the Berry Island chain, this is not actually a resort but a booking agency for a series of beach villas, town houses, and private homes. Each of these rentals is privately owned but rented by Tropical Diversions when the owners aren't on island. Accommodations, of course, depend on the taste of the individual owners, but all are inspected and well maintained. Rentals can be either on a daily or weekly basis. Although the furnishings are different, most of the rentals have full kitchens along with sundecks and maid service. The beach villas lie on the eastern shore, and come with anywhere from one to three bedrooms. The light, open architecture makes for a breezy ambience. All these villas open onto the beach. On the other hand, the town houses lie at the marina, offering spacious living in two-story layouts with private dockage facilities for boats and yachts. Most of these are two-or three-bedrooms rentals. The beach homes, though more expensive, are for those seeking complete privacy. Guests can partake of various dining facilities such as the Tamboo Club, which presents fish-and-seafood buffets twice weekly. Other choices include the Wharf Restaurant at the marina for complete dinners or else the Beach Club for light lunches.

Great Harbour Cay, The Berry Islands, The Bahamas. 𝒞 **800/342-7256** or 954/921-9084. www.tropicaldiversions.com. 13 beach villas and private homes, 4 town houses. Year-round $90–$600 beach villas; $180–$240 town house; from $600 private home. AE, MC, V. **Amenities:** 3 restaurants; 3 bars; beach; boating; dock; fishing; snorkeling. *In room:* A/C, kitchen, washer/dryer (in some), coffeemaker, no phone.

CHUB CAY

Named after a species of fish that thrives in nearby waters, Chub Cay is well known to sportfishing enthusiasts. A self-contained hideaway with a devoted clientele, it's the southernmost of the Berry Islands, separating the mainland of South Florida from the commercial frenzy of Nassau.

Chub Cay's development began in the late 1950s as the strictly private (and rather spartan) enclave of a group of Texas-based anglers and investors. It was originally uninhabited, but over the years a staff was imported, dormitory-style housing was built, and the island's most famous man-made feature (its state-of-the-art 90-slip marina) was constructed in the 392-hectare (968-acre) island's sheltered lagoon.

Chub Cay is today a tranquil, scrub-covered sand spit with awesome amounts of marine hardware, a dozen posh private homes, the marina, and a complex of buildings devoted to the **Chub Cay Resort & Marina** (see below). Today, membership in the club begins at around $2,500 a year and grants reduced rates for marina slip rental, boat repairs, and hotel-room and villa rental. Nonmembers, however, are welcome to use the facilities, and rent rooms at the rates listed below.

A liquor store and a yachties' commissary are on the island, an outlet for the sale of marine supplies, and a concrete runway for landing anything up to and including a 737. Most visitors reach Chub Cay by private yacht from the Florida mainland, but if you prefer to charter your fishing craft on Chub Cay, you'll find a miniarmada of suitable craft at your disposal. **Island Express Airlines** (*©* **954/359-0380**) flies charter flights to Chub Cay from Fort Lauderdale. Charter flights can be arranged with the help of the Chub Cay Resort & Marina's desk staff. If you opt to fly here, travel light; no more than 40 pounds of baggage is allowed per passenger.

The water temperature around Chub Cay averages a warm 80°F to 85°F (27°C–29°C) year-round, even at relatively deep depths. There's only a small tidal change, and under normal conditions, no swell or noticeable current in offshore waters. The waters are incredibly clear, making for great snorkeling.

WHERE TO STAY & DINE

Chub Cay Resort & Marina *⭐ Finds* Breezy and comfortable, these air-conditioned accommodations are the only available option on all of Chub Cay. During the life of this edition, the resort will be undergoing a massive expansion to include more rooms and amenities. Check on any changes due to the construction before booking here. The place prides itself on its marina, freshwater swimming pools, and many nearby sandy beaches. Throughout the resort, there's a nautical, laid-back kind of feeling and a clubby atmosphere. Don't expect inspired architecture. None of the rooms has a phone, although a phone is available at the reception desk. The decor consists of modern wicker with firm beds, plus small, well-organized bathrooms with shower/tub combinations. The remote feeling here is a welcome relief to many guests.

There's a restaurant, the Harbour House, with its own bar, and the Hilltop Bar on the island's highest elevation. The latter offers a TV for sports broadcasts and pool tables.

Chub Cay, Berry Islands, The Bahamas (mailing address: Chub Cay Resort & Marina, P.O. CB-13746, Nassau, The Bahamas). *©* **800/662-8555** or 242/325-1490. Fax 242/322-5199. www.chubcay.com. 44 units (subject to change). Year-round $135–$170 double; $400 2-bedroom villa; $600 3-bedroom villa; $800 4-bedroom villa. Discounts available for stays of 10 days or more. AE, MC, V. **Amenities:** Restaurant; 3 bars; 2 pools; 2 tennis courts; babysitting; laundry service. *In room:* A/C, TV, kitchenette (in some), beverage maker (in some), hair dryer, iron/ironing board (in some), no phone.

3 Andros (★(★

The largest island in The Bahamas, Andros is an excellent budget destination. One of the biggest unexplored tracts of land in the Western Hemisphere, it's still quite mysterious. Mostly flat, its 5,957 sq. km (2,323 sq. miles) are riddled with lakes and creeks, and most of the local residents—who still indulge in fire dances and go on wild boar hunts on occasion—live along the shore.

Andros is 161km (100 miles) long and 64km (40 miles) wide. Its interior consists of a dense, tropical forest, really rugged bush, and mangrove country. The marshy and relatively uninhabited west coast is called the "Mud," and the east coast is paralleled for 193km (120 miles) by the third-largest underwater barrier reef in the world. The reef drops more than 167km (104 miles) into the Tongue of the Ocean, or TOTO. On the eastern shore, this "tongue" is 229km (142 miles) long and 1,000 fathoms (1⅛ miles or .38 leagues) deep.

Lying 274km (170 miles) southeast of Miami and 48km (30 miles) west of Nassau, Andros is actually three major land areas: North Andros, Middle Andros, and South Andros. In spite of its size, Andros is very thinly populated (its residents number only around 5,000), although the tourist population swells it a bit. The temperature range here averages from 72°F to 85°F (22°C–29°C).

You won't find the western side of Andros written about much in yachting guides, because tricky shoals render it almost unapproachable by boat. The east coast, however, has kilometers of unspoiled beaches and is studded with little villages. Hotels that range from simple guest cottages to dive resorts to fishing camps have been built here. "Creeks" (we'd call them rivers) intersect the island at its midpoint. Also called *bights,* they range in length from 8 to 40km (5–25 miles), and they are dotted with tiny cays and islets.

The fishing at Andros is famous, establishing records for blue marlin caught offshore. Divers and snorkelers find that the coral reefs are among the most beautiful in the world, and everyone loves the pristine beaches.

Warning: Be sure to bring along plenty of mosquito repellent.

ANDROS ESSENTIALS

GETTING THERE   Reaching Andros is not that difficult. **Western Air** (© **242/377-2222** in the U.S.; www.bahamasair.com) has twice-daily 15-minute flights from Nassau to the airport at Andros Town in Central Andros (© 242/368-2759). Airports are also at San Andros in the north (© 242/329-4000); at Mangrove Cay (© 242/369-0003); and at Congo Town in South Andros (© 242/369-2222). **Lynx Air International** (© **888/596-9247**) flies from Fort Lauderdale to Congo Town three times a week.

Make sure you know where you're going in Andros. For example, if you land at Congo Town on South Andros and you've booked a hotel in Nicholl's Town, you'll find connections nearly impossible at times (involving both ferryboats and a rough haul across a bad highway).

Andros's few available taxis know when the planes from Nassau are going to land, and they drive out to the airports, hoping to drum up some business. Taxis are most often shared. A typical fare from Andros Town Airport to Small Hope Bay Lodge is about $30.

Many locals, along with a few adventurous visitors, use **mail boats** to get to Andros; the trip takes 5 to 7 hours across some beautiful waters. North Andros is serviced by the **MV *Lisa J. II,*** a mail boat that departs Potter's Cay Dock in Nassau heading for Morgan's Bluff, Mastic Point, and Nicholl's Town. It departs Nassau on Wednesday, returning to Nassau on Tuesday. The **MV *Captain Moxey*** departs Nassau on Monday, calling

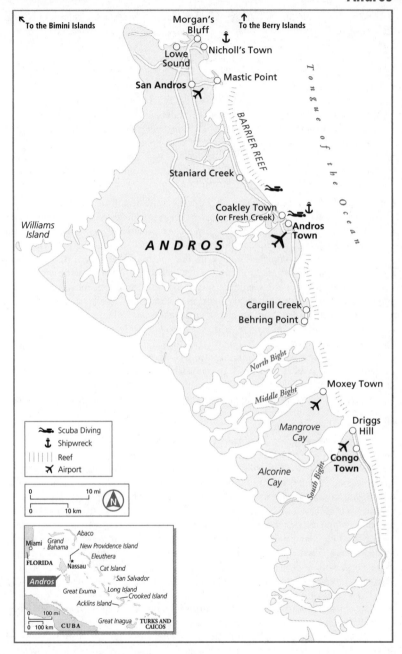

Andros

To the Bimini Islands

To the Berry Islands

Morgan's Bluff

Nicholl's Town

Lowe Sound

Mastic Point

San Andros

Tongue of the Ocean

BARRIER REEF

Staniard Creek

Coakley Town (or Fresh Creek)

Andros Town

Williams Island

A N D R O S

Cargill Creek

Behring Point

North Bight

Moxey Town

Middle Bight

Mangrove Cay

Driggs Hill

Alcorine Cay

Congo Town

South Bight

Scuba Diving
Shipwreck
Reef
Airport

0   10 mi
0   10 km

N

Abaco
Grand Bahama
Miami
New Providence Island
FLORIDA
Nassau
Eleuthera
Andros
Cat Island
San Salvador
Great Exuma
Long Island
Crooked Island
Acklins Island
0   100 mi
0   100 km
Great Inagua
CUBA
TURKS AND CAICOS

at Long Bay Cays, Kemps Bay, and the Bluff on South Andros. It heads back to Nassau on Wednesday. The **MV *Mangrove Cay Express*** departs Nassau Wednesday night for Lisbon Creek, the trip taking 5½ hours. It sails back to Nassau on Monday afternoon. Finally, **MV *Lady D*** departs Nassau on Wednesday for Fresh Creek, stopping at Spaniard Creek, Blanket Sound, and Browne Sound. The trip takes 5½ hours. The return voyage to Nassau is on Sunday. For details about sailing and costs, contact the dockmaster at **Potter's Cay Dock** in Nassau (© **242/393-1064**).

A far more luxurious way to go over the waters is aboard *Sea Link* or *Sea Wind* (© **242/323-2166;** fax 242/322-8185; www.bahamasferries.com). The *Sea Link* carries 250 passengers, and the *Sea Wind* seats 180, with another 100 seats available on the open-air decks of both vessels. Depending on where you dock on Andros, trip time from Nassau to Fresh Creek takes 1 hour and 45 minutes. From Nassau to Driggs Hill on Andros, however, takes 2 hours and 30 minutes.

ORIENTATION　Chances are your hotel will be in **North Andros,** in either Andros Town or Nicholl's Town. North Andros is the most developed of the three major Andros islands. **Nicholl's Town** is a colorful old settlement with some 600 people and several places serving local foods. Most visitors come to Nicholl's Town to buy supplies at a shopping complex. Directly to the south is **Mastic Point,** which was founded in 1781. If you ask around, you'll be shown to a couple of concrete-sided dives that offer spareribs and Goombay music. To the north of Nicholl's Town is **Morgan's Bluff,** namesake of Sir Henry Morgan, a pirate later knighted by the British monarch. **Andros Town,** with its abandoned docks, is another village, about 47km (29 miles) south of Nicholl's Town. Most visitors come to Andros Town to stay at the **Small Hope Bay Lodge** (p. 195) or to avail themselves of its facilities. The biggest retail industry, Androsia batik, is in the area, too. The scuba diving—minutes away on the barrier reef—is what lures much of the world to this tiny place; others come here just for the shelling. On the opposite side of the water is **Coakley Town.** If you're driving, before you get to Andros Town, you may want to stop and spend some restful hours on the beach at **Staniard Creek,** another old settlement on Andros that feels like it drifted from the South Seas.

Moving south to the second major landmass, **Central Andros** is smaller than either North or South Andros. The least developed of the three, the island is studded with hundreds upon hundreds of palm trees. The Queen's Highway runs along the eastern coastline, but the only thing about this road that's regal is its name. In some 7km (4⅓ miles), you can practically travel the whole island. It's truly sleepy, and for that very reason, many people come here to get away from it all. You won't find much in the way of accommodations, but you'll find some.

The third and last major land area, **South Andros** is the home of the wonderfully named **Congo Town,** where life proceeds at a snail's pace. The Queen's Highway, lined in part with pink-and-white conch shells, runs for about 40km (25 miles) or so. The island, as yet undiscovered, has some of the best beaches in The Bahamas, and you can enjoy them almost by yourself.

Another tiny island, undeveloped **Mangrove Cay,** is an escapist's dream, attracting naturalists and anglers, as well as a few divers. It's separated from the northern and southern sections of Andros by bights. The settlements here only got electricity and a paved road in 1989. The best place for snorkeling and diving on Mangrove Cay is **Victoria Point Blue Hole** (any local can point you there if you're interested). Another village (don't blink as you pass through or you'll miss it) is **Moxey Town,** where you are likely to see fishermen unloading conch from the fishing boats. Ferries, operated free by the Bahamian government, ply back and forth over the waters separating Mangrove Cay from South Andros. At the end of the road in North Andros, private arrangements can be made to have a boat take you over to Mangrove Cay.

GETTING AROUND   Transportation can be a big problem on Andros. If you have to go somewhere, try to use one of the local taxi drivers, though this can be a pricey undertaking.

The few rental cars available are in North Andros. These are few and far between, owing to the high costs of shipping cars to Andros. The weather also takes a great toll on the cars that are brought in (the salt in the air erodes metal), so no U.S. car-rental agencies are represented. Your best bet is to ask at your hotel to see what's available. It's not really recommended that you drive on Andros because roads are mainly unpaved and in bad condition, and gasoline stations are scarce. Outlets for car rentals come and go faster here than anybody can count. Renting a car is less formal, and less organized, than you might be used to, and you won't find organized links to any toll-free company stateside. The concierge at Andros's most upscale hotel, Kamaleme Cay, will arrange a cab or a rental car for you, but frankly, it's all word of mouth and terribly unlicensed and informal, with no options for purchase of additional insurance. Taxi drivers and owners of a handful of battered cars that can be rented will be at the airport in time for the landing of most flights from the U.S. mainland or from Nassau. You can negotiate a car rental on-site or—perhaps more safely and conveniently—you can hire one of the local taxis for access to wherever you want to go. Rates go for between $85 and $100 a day, plus gas. Be warned that signpostings and road conditions are horrible, but it's hard to get lost because the only road is the north-south much-rutted thoroughfare known as Queen's Highway.

You may want to rent a bike, but you'll experience the same bad roads you would in a rental car. Guests of the Small Hope Bay Lodge, Chickcharnie, and Mangrove Cay Inn can rent bikes at their hotels.

VISITOR INFORMATION   The **Ministry of Tourism** is located in Andros Town (© **242/368-2286**). It is open Monday to Friday 9am to 5pm.

FAST FACTS   Banks are rare on Andros. There's one, **ScotiaBank** (© **242/329-2700**), in Nicoll's Town, with an **ATM,** open Monday to Thursday 9:30am to 3pm, and Friday 9:30am to 4pm.

The island's post office is in Nicholl's Town on North Andros (© **242/329-2034**). Hours are Monday through Friday from 9am to 4:30pm. Hotel desks will also sell you Bahamian stamps. Make sure you mark cards and letters as airmail; otherwise, you'll return home before they do. Each little village on Andros has a store that serves as the post office.

Government-run clinics are at **North Andros** (© **242/329-2055**) and at **Central Andros** (© **242/368-2038**). Bring with you whatever medicines you'll need while visiting Andros, because local supplies are very limited.

Call the **police** on **North Andros** at © **919;** on **Central Andros** at © **242/368-2626;** and on **South Andros** at © **242/369-4733.**

WHERE TO STAY

At the hotels listed below with no phone in room, phone service is available only at the front desks.

IN STANIARD CREEK

Kamalame Cay ★★★ *Finds* In 1995, a group of international investors created one of the most exclusive resorts in the Out Islands from the scrub-covered 38-hectare (94-acre) landscape of a private cay off the east coast of Andros Island. Since then, it has discreetly and quietly attracted a clientele of banking moguls and financial wizards from Europe and North America, all of whom come for the superb service, escapist charm, 5km (3 miles) of white-sand beaches, and a series of waterborne adventures that are among the best of their kind in The Bahamas. A staff from 30 to 50, some of whom were imported from other parts of The Bahamas, includes six full-time gardeners, an army of chambermaids and cooks, and a sporting-adventure staff that's ready, willing, and able to haul groups of urban refugees out for scuba, windsurfing, snorkeling, deep-sea, and bonefishing excursions above one of the largest barrier reefs in the world.

Accommodations include a few smaller rooms, tasteful and very comfortable, located next to the marina. More opulent are the cottages and suites, all of which lie adjacent to the beach; these are mainly crafted from local coral stone, cedar shingles, tropical-wood timbers, tile, and, in some cases, thatch. Each is outfitted in a breezy but stylish tropical motif that evokes a decorator's journal. Food is superb, focusing on fresh fish, lobster, local soups, homemade breads, and surprisingly good wines.

Staniard Creek, Andros, The Bahamas. © 242/368-6281. Fax 242/368-6279. www.kamalame.com. Winter $740–$940 double, $1,100 cottage suite, $1,250–$2,380 villa suite, $3,620 silvertop suite; off season $561–$649 double, $770 cottage suite, $880–$1,628 villa suite, $2,489 silvertop suite. Rates all-inclusive, including a boat ride from Kamalame Cay. Discounts of up to 20% June–Oct. MC, V. **Amenities:** Restaurant; bar; pool; tennis court; watersports equipment/rentals; room service (upon request); babysitting; laundry service. *In room:* A/C, minibar, beverage maker, hair dryer, iron/ironing board, safe, no phone.

IN ANDROS TOWN

Andros Lighthouse Yacht Club & Marina At the mouth of Fresh Creek with an 18-slip marina, this complex is a favorite of the yachting crowd. The hotel rents comfortably furnished villas, each with a certain flair enhanced by Caribbean fabrics and ceiling fans. Accommodations open onto private patios and come with well-maintained private bathrooms with shower units. Scuba divers, snorkelers, and fishermen make ample use of the beach and the offshore waters, because the hotel lies near one of the world's largest barrier reefs and the deep Tongue of the Ocean.

The hotel has a good restaurant serving Bahamian and American dishes. Fishing charters are readily available, and scuba diving and snorkeling can easily be arranged through the hotel. The package rates offered by the hotel, in addition to room and meals, include airport pickup.

Andros Town, Andros, The Bahamas. © 242/368-2305 or -2306. Fax 242/368-2300. www.androslighthouse.com. 20 units. Year-round $110–$140 double; $130–$170 villa. MAP (breakfast and dinner) add $40 per extra per person. Ask about dive packages. AE, DC, DISC, MC, V. **Amenities:** Restaurant; 2 bars; pool; 2 tennis courts; limited room service; coin-operated laundry; nonsmoking room; rooms for those w/limited mobility. *In room:* A/C, TV, kitchenette, fridge, hair dryer, iron/ironing board, safe.

IN BEHRING POINT

Tranquility Hill Fishing Lodge At the eastern entrance to North Bight, this is a fisherman's haven, lying just a short drive from Middle and South Bights. The rustic inn lies near miles and miles of virgin flats teaming with trophy-size bonefish. Numerous creeks and lakes are in the area where record catches have been made of gray snapper, tarpon, and jacks. Three "Sunken Rocks"—with large colonies of barracuda, Spanish mackerel, and mutton snapper—are here, too. Nearby is the third-largest reef in the world, with a sea of dolphins, kingfish, wahoo, marlin, and tuna. Bedrooms are spacious and well furnished with comfortable beds and bathrooms with shower units. Meals are prepared Bahamian-style, and guess what's on the menu? Enough fish and seafood to delight, although the cook will also prepare special requests. Meals are served family-style.

Behring Point, Andros, The Bahamas. ©/fax **242/368-4132.** www.bahamas-mon.com/hotels/tranquil. 11 units. Year-round $378–$400 double. Rates include meals. MC, V. **Amenities:** Bar; laundry service; nonsmoking rooms; rooms for those w/limited mobility. *In room:* A/C, TV, no phone.

IN CARGILL CREEK

Andros Island Bonefishing Club ★ *Finds*   If Hemingway were around today and wanted to go bonefishing, we'd invite him here. This rustic lodge lies at the confluence of Cargill Creek, the Atlantic Ocean, and the eastern end of North Bight. It fronts a small protected creek, a short distance from a wadeable flat, and fishing boats can dock directly in front of the lodge. Constructed in 1988, this is a modern but rather bare-bones facility that draws more repeat guests than any other hostelry in The Bahamas. More than two dozen fishermen can stay here at any time in accommodations with queen-size beds, ample dresser and closet space, bathrooms equipped with shower/tub combinations, and ceiling fans. The club is the domain of Captain Rupert Leadon, who knows more fishing stories than anybody else in Andros.

Hearty and plentiful food, with an emphasis on fresh seafood, including Bahamian lobster and conch, is served at communal tables.

Cargill Creek, Andros, The Bahamas. © **242/368-5167.** Fax 242/368-5235. www.androsbonefishing.com. 12 units. Year-round $1,119 per person 3 nights; $1,958 per person 5 nights; $2,797 per person 7 nights. Rates include tax, all meals, all-day fishing w/boat and guide, transportation to and from Andros Town. Room only, $210 per person. MC, V. **Amenities:** Restaurant; bar; babysitting; laundry service; rooms for those w/limited mobility. *In room:* A/C, ceiling fan, fridge.

IN FRESH CREEK

Small Hope Bay Lodge ★★ *Kids*   This is the premier diving and fishing resort of Andros, and one of the best in the entire Bahamas, with a white-sandy beach right at its doorstep. It's an intimate and cozy beachside cottage colony, where tall coconut palms line a lovely beach and a laid-back atmosphere always prevails. And, because this place is all-inclusive, the price you pay includes all accommodations, meals, drinks, taxes, service charges, airport taxi transfers, even the use of kayaks, windsurfers, and other boats, as well as bicycles and scuba lessons.

Its name comes from a prediction (so far, accurate) from pirate Henry Morgan, who claimed there was "small hope" of anyone finding the treasure he'd buried on Andros. For conversations and meals, guests congregate in a spacious living and dining room. Andros Town Airport is a 10-minute taxi ride from the lodge. Spacious cabins, cooled by ceiling fans, are made of coral rock and Andros pine and are decorated with Androsia batik fabrics. Honeymooners like to order breakfast served in (their water) bed.

For groups of three or more, the resort has a limited number of family cottages, featuring two separate rooms connected by a single bathroom. Single travelers have a choice of staying in a family cottage with private accommodations (which is the same as per-person double occupancy) or staying in a regular cottage with private bathroom. All bathrooms are neatly kept.

The bar is an old boat, dubbed the *Panacea*. The food is wholesome, plentiful, and good—including favorites such as conch chowder, lobster, and hot johnnycake. The chef will even cook your catch for you or make up a picnic lunch. Lunch is a buffet; dinner, a choice of seafood and meat every night. Children under 10 dine in the game room. Drinks are offered on a rambling patio built out over the sea. Nightlife is spontaneous—with dancing in the lounge or on the patio, and water slides. Definitely do not wear a tie at dinner.

Diving is the lodge's specialty. The owners have been diving for more than 3 decades, and their well-respected dive shop has sufficient equipment, boats, and flexibility to give guests any diving experience they want, including a resort course for beginners. If you'd rather fish, the lodge can hook you up with an expert guide, especially for bonefishing.

Fresh Creek, Andros, The Bahamas (mailing address: P.O. Box CB11817, Nassau, Bahamas). © **800/223-6961** in the U.S. and Canada, or 242/368-2014. Fax 242/368-2015. 21 units. www.smallhope.com. Depending on the season $175–$209 adult nondiver, $100-120 child (10–15) nondiver, $75 child (2–9), $235–$279 adult diver, $190 child (10–15) diver. Rates include tax, all meals, drinks, tips, airport transfers, and most activities. AE, MC, V. **Amenities:** Restaurant; bar; Jacuzzi; kayak; children's programs; massage; babysitting; laundry service; nonsmoking rooms. *In room:* Ceiling fan, no phone.

IN NICHOLL'S TOWN

Conch Sound Resort Inn   This simple little inn doesn't open onto the sands, but the hotel's free shuttle will take you to a good beach just a 10-minute walk away. Bedrooms are no better than those in a low-cost motel, but they are comfortable, fairly spacious, and well maintained, attracting divers and bonefishermen. The rooms are furnished with private bathrooms with showers. The most expensive units here are the four suites, with two bedrooms and an equipped kitchen each.

Conch Sound Hwy., Nicholl's Town, Andros, The Bahamas. © **242/329-2060**. Fax 242/329-2341. 10 units. Year-round $90 double; $200 suite. No credit cards. **Amenities:** Restaurant; bar; pool; watersports equipment/rentals; car-rental desk; limited room service; babysitting; laundry service; nonsmoking rooms. *In room:* A/C, TV, kitchenette, iron, no phone.

Green Windows Inn   Kenny Robinson and her husband, Patrick, run this small, laid-back hotel set in a landscape of fruit trees and palms, where guests like to take their after-meal walks. The small rooms are on the second floor of the two-story inn, over the restaurant and bar. One recent improvement at the inn is the installation of tiny private bathrooms with shower/tub combinations in every bedroom along with both ceiling fans and air-conditioning. The restaurant caters only to hotel guests, with mainly seafood and local food cooked to order. The beach is a 10-minute walk from the inn, and the Robinsons can arrange bonefishing and snorkeling trips.

Rawfon St. (P.O. Box 23076), Nicholl's Town, Andros, The Bahamas. © **242/329-2194**. Fax 242/329-2016. androsfishing@hotmail.com. 10 units. Year-round $90 double. AE, MC, V. **Amenities:** Restaurant; bar; nonsmoking room. *In room:* A/C, TV, beverage maker, iron/ironing board, no phone.

ON SOUTH BIGHT

Tiamo Lodge ★ *(Finds)*   One of the most ecologically aware places in the entire Bahamas, this lodge was built in stages between 1999 and 2003. It's nestled on 4.8 hectares (12 acres) of land that's studded with copses of unusually large trees, directly beside the bight (inland waterway) that runs along the midsection of Andros. About 30% of the guests here come for the fishing, and if that's your interest, a boat rental (without fishing equipment included) goes for $375 a day. Accommodations are within wood-framed, plank-sided bungalows, each with a screened-in, wraparound porch, a sense of privacy, and a handful of "rustically elegant" amenities that are limited by the eco-sensitive nature of the resort. This lack of plush hugely appeals to the nature-loving clients who come here. Days are spent reading, swimming off the white-sand beach that flanks one side of the resort, and generally reflecting on one's life. It's strongly advised that you bring your own company to this place, since many of the activities are engineered for couples.

Drigg's Hill, South Bight, Andros Island. © **800/201-4356** or 242/357-2489. www.tiamoresorts.com. 11 units. Year-round $275–$295 double. Rates include meals, airport transfers, and almost all activities. AE, DC, DISC, MC, V. **Amenities:** Restaurant; bar; kayaking; snorkeling; laundry service; hiking. *In room:* No phone.

ON MANGROVE CAY

The Mangrove Cay Inn   This pleasant, well-managed inn belongs to a native son, Elliott Greene, who returned with his wife Pat after years of cold-weather life in Syracuse, New York, to establish this breezy motel a short walk from the center of Grants, the third-largest village on Mangrove Cay (Moxey Town and Burnt Rock, though tiny, are still larger). Positioned amid scrubland, in the geographic center of the 14km-long (8¾-mile) island, the hotel was built in the early 1990s, 2 years after the inn was established as an easygoing and affable restaurant.

Separated from Grant's Beach by a brackish lake that's stocked with fish, with a mysterious blue hole positioned beside the path connecting the hotel to the beach, the accommodations have cozy but completely unpretentious furnishings. Each unit contains a small bathroom with a shower/tub combination. How do guests spend their time here? Veranda sitting on a porch that runs the length of the building and overlooks the water; riding on any of the bicycles that the hotel rents for a fee of around $10 a day; snorkeling with the hotel's equipment on the outlying reef (waters offshore are particularly rich in natural sponges and spiny Caribbean lobster); hiking; hill climbing; and looking for chickcharnies (mythical red-eyed, three-toed, birdlike creatures). And if you're interested in fishing excursions, the Greenes can hire a local fishing guide for a full-day outing (about $300 a day for up to four).

The wing that contains the bedrooms is attached to a restaurant that serves a combination of Bahamian and American food with specialties of cracked conch, grilled grouper and snapper, burgers, and steaks.

c/o General Post Office, Grants, Mangrove Cay, Andros, The Bahamas. © **242/369-0069.** Fax 242/369-0014. www.batelnet.bs/mangrove_cay. 14 units. Year-round $105 double; 1-bedroom cottage $175, 2-bedroom cottage $300. No credit cards. **Amenities:** Restaurant; bar; bike rentals; limited room service; laundry service; nonsmoking rooms; rooms for those w/limited mobility. *In room:* A/C, ceiling fan, TV (in some), kitchens (in some), beverage maker (in some), hair dryer, iron/ironing board, no phone.

Seascape Inn ★ *Finds*   Joan and Mickey McGowan are some of the most welcoming innkeepers in the Andros chain of islands. They took several cottages with private decks opening onto the ocean and turned them into secluded retreats for discerning guests. The cabins here are handsomely furnished with handmade mahogany pieces along with original Bahamian art. Each cottage is spacious and well maintained, with neat, shower-only bathrooms. Included in the price is one of the best breakfasts you'll get on Andros: Mrs. McGowan is an excellent baker, turning out such early morning delights as banana bread. Fellow guests meet in the elevated dining room to dine on excellent American and Bahamian cuisine. The McGowans will also help arrange scuba diving and snorkeling trips if you wish.

Mangrove Cay, Andros, The Bahamas. ©/fax **242/369-0342.** www.seascapeinn.com. 5 cottages. Year-round $132–$143 double. Rates include breakfast and use of kayaks and bikes. AE, MC, V. **Amenities:** Restaurant; bar; bikes; kayaks; watersports equipment/rentals; laundry service; all nonsmoking rooms. *In room:* Ceiling fan, no phone.

SOUTH ANDROS

Emerald Palms Resort ★   Lodging at this laid-back place, 3km (2 miles) from the Congo Town airport, is a lot like staying at a beachside ranch. The accommodations are set on 8km (5 miles) of beachfront on an island that contains 10,000 palm trees. The hotel is casual—a place to get away from urban life and rest your jangled nerves on a white-sand beach. Guests are treated like members of the family.

The rooms are large and comfortable, with well-laid-out bathrooms with adequate shelf space and shower stalls. All in all, it's a relaxed, tropical ambience.

Scattered over the palm-studded property are hammocks and a freshwater swimming pool. The dining room features Bahamian seafood, and outdoor steak barbecues and seafood buffets are sometimes held. South Bight marina is 2.5km (1½ miles) away, serving as a yacht anchorage for anyone who arrives by boat. The hotel will also rent you a car or bike if you need one.

Driggs Hill (P.O. Box 800), South Andros, The Bahamas. © 242/369-2661. Fax 242/369-2711. 42 units. Winter $185–$285 double, $395–$495 1-bedroom villa, $495–$595 2-bedroom villa; off season $135–$165 double, $315 1-bedroom villa, $395–$495 2-bedroom villa. MAP (breakfast and dinner) $40 extra person. AE, MC, V. **Amenities:** Restaurant; 2 bars; pool; Jacuzzi; car-rental desk; limited room service; nonsmoking rooms; rooms for those w/limited mobility. *In room:* A/C, TV, minibar, kitchenette (in some), beverage maker, hair dryer, safe.

WHERE TO DINE

Andros follows the rest of The Bahamas in its cuisine. Conch, in all its many variations, is the staple of most diets, along with heaping portions of peas 'n' rice, johnnycake, and pig or chicken souse.

Almost everyone on Andros knows about **Hank's Place,** outside of Andros Town in Fresh Creek (© **242/368-2447**). Owned and operated by native-born Androsians Hank and Eva Thompson, this brown-painted wood-sided restaurant in Fresh Creek includes a dining room set on piers above the sea, and a white-sided kitchen building that's firmly planted on shore. Come here for rib-sticking portions of the kind of food that many Bahamians remember from their childhood. Or try the steaming portions of conch chowder and fritters; fish such as snapper, wahoo, and especially grouper; beefsteaks; and several types of chicken, both fried and stewed. Everything here tastes better when accompanied by the frothy, pink-colored, rum-based cocktail called a Hanky-Panky. In addition to the meals served here, the place offers two simple but clean bedrooms, each with phone, air-conditioning, and TV. They're priced, year-round, at $70 for up to two occupants. You'll find this place prominently signposted within a 5-minute drive north of the Andros Town airport.

Emerald Palms Resort, outside Congo Town (© **242/369-2661**), is the best place to dine in South Andros. Most guests book into these hotels on the Modified American Plan (MAP), which takes care of breakfast and dinner but frees them to shop around for lunch. At any of these hotels, a dinner will run around $25 to $40 per person.

If you're touring the island during the day, you'll find some local spots that serve food. If business has been slow at some of these little places, however, you might find nothing on the stove. You take your chances. On Mangrove Cay, try **Dianne Cash's Total Experience,** Main Road (© **242/369-0430**), where you can sample Dianne's version of baked crab backs served with peas 'n' rice. Don't plan on dropping by this place without some kind of advance notification, though.

BEACHES, WATERSPORTS & OTHER OUTDOOR PURSUITS

Golf and tennis fans should go elsewhere, but if you want some of the best bonefishing and scuba diving in The Bahamas, head to Andros.

HITTING THE BEACH

The eastern shore of Andros, stretching for some 161km (100 miles), is an almost uninterrupted palm grove opening onto beaches of white or beige sand. Several dozen

---

(*Fun Fact* **The Bahamian Loch Ness Monster**

When the Atlantic Undersea Testing and Evaluation Centre (AUTEC) first opened, Androsians predicted that the naval researchers would turn up "Lusca." Like the Loch Ness Monster, Lusca reportedly had been sighted by dozens of locals. The sea serpent was accused of sucking both sailors and their vessels into the dangerous blue holes around the island's coastline. No one has captured Lusca yet.

---

access points lead to the beach along the eastern shore. The roads are unmarked but clearly visible. The clear, warm waters offshore are great for snorkeling.

FISHING

Andros ✿✿✿ is called the "Bonefish Capital of the World." The actual capital is Lowe Sound Settlement, a tiny hamlet with only one road, 6.5km (4 miles) north of Nicholl's Town. Anglers come here to hire bonefish guides. **Cargill Creek** is one of the best places for bonefishing on the island; nearby, anglers explore the flats in and around the bights of Andros (some excellent flats, where you can wade in your boots, lie only 68–113m/223 ft.–371 ft. offshore).

Whether you're staying in North, Central, or South Andros, someone at your hotel can arrange a fishing expedition with one of the many local guides or charter companies. In particular, the **Small Hope Bay Lodge,** in Andros Town on North Andros (© **242/ 368-2013**), is known for arranging fishing expeditions for both guests and nonguests; a guide will take you out for superb bonefishing. They also offer fly-, reef-, and deep-sea fishing, and provide tackle and bait.

SCUBA DIVING & SNORKELING

Divers from all over the world come to explore the **Andros barrier reef** ★★★, which runs parallel to the eastern shore of the island. It's one of the largest reefs in the world, but unlike Australia's Great Barrier Reef, which is kilometers off the coast, the barrier reef of Andros is easily accessible, beginning a few hundred yards offshore.

One side of the reef is a peaceful haven for snorkelers and novice scuba divers, who report that the fish are tame (often a grouper will eat from your hand, but don't try it with a moray eel). The water here is from 2.5 to 4.5m (8¼–15 ft.) deep.

On the other side of the reef it's a different story. The water plunges to a depth of 167km (104 miles) into the awesome **TOTO (Tongue of the Ocean)** ✿✿✿. One diver reported that, as an adventure, diving in the ocean's "tongue" was tantamount to a flight to the moon.

Myriad, multicolored marine life thrives on the reef, and it attracts nature lovers from all over the world. The weirdly shaped coral formations alone are worth the trip. This is a living, breathing garden of the sea, and its caves feel like cathedrals.

For many years the U.S. Navy has conducted research at a station on the edge of TOTO. The research center—devoted to oceanographic, underwater weapons, and antisubmarine research—is at Andros Town. Called **AUTEC (Atlantic Undersea Testing and Evaluation Centre),** this is a joint U.S. and British undertaking.

Among other claims to fame, Andros is known for its **"blue holes,"** which rise from the brine. Essentially, these are narrow, circular pits that plunge as much as 60m (197 ft.) straight down through rock and coral into murky, difficult-to-explore depths.

Most of them begin under the level of the sea, although others appear unexpectedly—and dangerously—in the center of the island, usually with warning signs placed around the perimeter. Scattered at various points along the coast, they can be reached either in rented boats or as part of a guided trip. The most celebrated blue hole is Uncle Charlie's Blue Hole, mysterious and fathomless, and once publicized by Jacques Cousteau. The other blue holes are almost as incredible.

One of these blue holes, called **Benjamin's Blue Hole** ⟨, is named after its discoverer, George Benjamin. In 1967, he found stalactites and stalagmites 360m (1,181 ft.) below sea level. What was remarkable about this discovery is that stalactites and stalagmites are not created underwater. This has led to much speculation that The Bahamas are actually mountaintops, and all that remains of a mysterious continent that sank beneath the sea (perhaps Atlantis?). Although Cousteau made a film—making the Blue Holes of Andros internationally famous—most of the blue holes, like most of the surface of the island itself, remain unexplored. Tour boats leaving from Small Hope Bay Lodge will take you to these holes.

As for snorkeling, you might head a few kilometers north of Nicholl's Town, where you'll find a crescent-shaped strip of white-sand beach, along with a headland, **Morgan's Bluff,** honoring the notorious old pirate himself. If you're not a diver, and can't go out to the Andros Barrier Reef off the shorefront at Fresh Creek and Andros Town, you can do the second-best thing and snorkel near a series of reefs known as "The Three Sisters." Sometimes, if the waters haven't turned suddenly murky, you can see about 3.5m (11 ft.) down—all the way to the sandy bottom. The schools of elkhorn coral are especially dramatic here.

Since **Mangrove Cay** is very underdeveloped, rely on the snorkeling advice and gear rentals you'll get from the dive shop at the **Seascape Inn** (② 242/369-0342). A two-tank dive costs $65 for guests of the hotel, or $85 for nonguests. Night dives are also possible once or twice a month ($60 for guests; $85 for nonguests).

Small Hope Bay Lodge, Fresh Creek, Andros Town, Central Andros (② 800/223-6961 in the U.S. and Canada or 242/368-2013; www.smallhope.com), lies a short distance from the barrier reef, with its still-unexplored caves and ledges. A staff of trained dive instructors at the lodge caters to beginners and experienced divers alike. Snorkeling expeditions can be arranged, as well as scuba outings (visibility underwater exceeds 30m/98 ft. on most days, with water temperatures ranging from 72°F–84°F/22°C–29°C). You can also rent gear here. To stay at the hotel here for 7 nights and 6 days, all-inclusive (meals, tips, taxes, airport transfers, and three dives a day), costs adults $1,585 to $1,883. (For children aged 10–17, the cost is $1,240–$1,260.) All guests are allowed access to the beachside hot-tub whirlpool, as well as to all facilities, such as free use of sailboats, windsurfers, and bicycles.

EXPLORING THE ISLAND

Andros is largely unexplored, and with good reason—getting around takes some effort. With the exception of the main arteries, the few roads that exist are badly maintained and full of potholes. Sometimes you're a long way between villages or settlements, and if your car breaks down, all you can do is wait and hope that someone comes along to give you a ride to the next place, where you'll hope to find a skilled mechanic. If you're striking out on your own, make sure you have a full tank, because service stations are few and far between.

At present, not all of Andros can be explored by car. We hope that as Andros develops, it will be easier to get around, connected by a road and causeways stretching some

---

Moments **What Would Tennessee Have Thought?**

One custom in Andros is reminiscent of the Tennessee Williams drama *Suddenly, Last Summer:* Catching **land crabs,** which leave their burrows and march relentlessly to the sea to lay their eggs. The annual ritual occurs between May and September. However, many of the hapless crabs will never have offspring; both visitors and Androsians walk along the beach with baskets and catch the crustaceans before they reach the sea. Later, they clean them, stuff them, and bake them for dinner.

161km (100 miles) or more. Most of the driving and exploring is currently confined to North Andros, and there, only along the eastern sector, going by Nicholl's Town, Morgan's Bluff, and San Andros.

If you're driving on Central or South Andros, you must stay on the rough **Queen's Highway.** The road in the south is paved and better than the one in Central Andros, which should be traveled only in an emergency or by a local.

Near Small Hope Bay at Andros Town, you can visit the workshop where **Androsia batik** is made (the same Androsia batik sold in the shops of Nassau and other towns). Androsia's artisans create their designs using hot wax on fine cotton and silk fabrics. The fabrics are then made into island-style wear, including blouses, skirts, caftans, shirts, and accessories. All hand-painted and hand-signed, the resort wear comes in dazzling red, blue, purple, green, and earth tones. You can visit the factory in Andros Town (© **242/368-2080;** www.androsia.com) Monday to Friday from 8am to 5pm, and Saturday 9am to 2pm.

Morgan's Bluff, at the tip of North Andros, lures men and women hoping to strike it rich. The pirate Sir Henry Morgan is supposed to have buried a vast treasure here, but it has eluded discovery to this day, although many have searched for it.

Bird-watchers are attracted to Andros for its varied **bird population.** In the dense forests, in trees such as lignum vitae, mahogany, Madeira, "horseflesh," and pine, lives a huge feathered population: many parrots, doves, and marsh hens. Ever hear a whistling duck?

Botanists are lured here by the **wildflowers** of Andros. Some 40 to 50 species of wild orchids are said to thrive here, some of which can be found nowhere else. New discoveries are always being made, as more and more botanists study the rich vegetation of Andros.

Red Bay Village is the type of discovery that continues to make Andros seem mysterious. An ancient tribe, headed by a chief and religiously following old rituals, was found living here as recently as a quarter of a century ago. The passage of time has made little difference to these people. Now the world comes to their door, and changes are inevitable; although the people still follow their ancient customs of fishing. The village is believed to been settled sometime in the 1840s by Seminoles and blacks fleeing slavery in Florida. Located off the northwestern coast of Andros, a causeway now connects it to the mainland, and tourists can visit. You can reach Red Bay Village by road from Nicholl's Town and San Andros. You should be polite and ask permission before indiscriminately photographing the people who live here.

7

The Abacos

Called the "top of The Bahamas," the Abacos compose the northernmost portion of the nation. This boomerang-shaped mini-archipelago is 209km (130 miles) long and consists of Great Abaco and Little Abaco, as well as a sprinkling of cays. The islands are about 322km (206 miles) east of Miami and 121km (75 miles) north of Nassau.

People come here mainly to explore the outdoors. The **sailing** ★★ and **fishing** ★★ are spectacular, and the diving is excellent, too. There are also many lovely, uncrowded beaches. The Abacos are definitely a world apart from the glitzy pleasures of Freeport/Lucaya, Nassau, or Paradise Island.

Many residents of the Abacos descend from Loyalists who left New England after the American Revolution. Against a backdrop of sugar-white beaches and turquoise water, their pastel-colored clapboard houses and white-picket fences retain the Cape Cod architectural style of the first settlements on Abacos. One brightly painted sign in Hope Town says it all: SLOW DOWN. YOU'RE IN HOPE TOWN. The same could be said for all the Abacos.

The weather is about 10°F (12°C) warmer here than in southern Florida, but if you visit in January or February, remember that you're not guaranteed beach weather every day (Miami and Fort Lauderdale, even Key West, can get chilly at times). When winter squalls hit, temperatures can drop to the high 40s °F (high single digits Celsius) in severe cases. Spring in the Abacos, however, is one of the most glorious and balmy seasons in all the islands. In summer, it gets very hot around noon, but if you act as the islanders do and find a shady spot to escape the broiling sun, the trade winds will cool you off.

Some yachters call the Abacos the world's most beautiful cruising grounds. Excellent marine facilities, with guides, charter parties, and boat rentals, are available here; in fact, Marsh Harbour is the bareboat-charter center of the northern Bahamas. There you can rent a small boat, pack a picnic, and head for one of many uninhabited cays just big enough for two.

Anglers from all over the world come to test their skill against blue marlin, kingfish, dolphinfish, yellowfin tuna, sailfish, wahoo, amberjack, and grouper. Like fishing tournaments? They abound at Walker's Cay.

Finally, scuba divers can plumb the depths and discover caverns, inland "blue holes," coral reefs, and gardens, along with marine preserves and wrecks. Some scuba centers even feature night dives.

ABACOS ESSENTIALS
GETTING THERE

BY PLANE   Three airports are found in the Abacos: **Marsh Harbour** (the major one, on Great Abaco Island), **Treasure Cay,** and **Walker's Cay.** The official points of entry are by water at Marsh Harbour, Treasure Cay, Walker's Cay, and Green Turtle

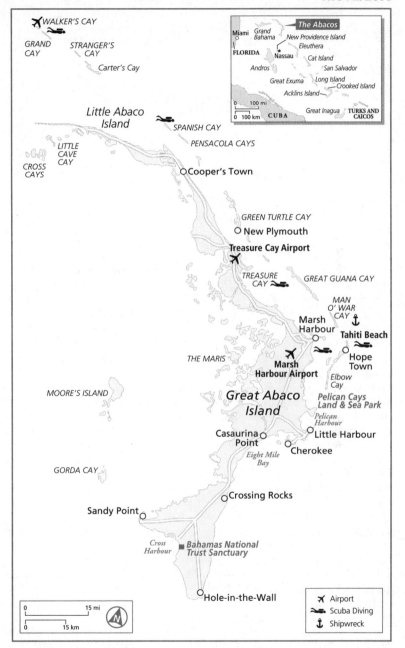

The Abacos

Miami
Grand Bahama
New Providence Island
Eleuthera
FLORIDA
Nassau
Cat Island
Andros
San Salvador
Great Exuma
Long Island
Crooked Island
Acklins Island
Great Inagua
CUBA
TURKS AND CAICOS

WALKER'S CAY

GRAND CAY
STRANGER'S CAY
Carter's Cay

Little Abaco Island
SPANISH CAY
PENSACOLA CAYS
LITTLE CAVE CAY
CROSS CAYS
Cooper's Town

GREEN TURTLE CAY
New Plymouth
Treasure Cay Airport
TREASURE CAY
GREAT GUANA CAY

MAN O' WAR CAY
Marsh Harbour
Tahiti Beach
THE MARIS
Marsh Harbour Airport
Hope Town
Elbow Cay

MOORE'S ISLAND
Great Abaco Island
Pelican Cays Land & Sea Park
Pelican Harbour

Casaurina Point
Little Harbour
Cherokee
Eight Mile Bay

GORDA CAY

Crossing Rocks

Sandy Point

Cross Harbour
Bahamas National Trust Sanctuary

Hole-in-the-Wall

| 0 | 15 mi |
| 0 | 15 km |

✈ Airport
≈ Scuba Diving
⚓ Shipwreck

Cay (New Plymouth). Green Turtle Cay doesn't have an airstrip, but many members of the yachting crowd clear Customs and Immigration there.

Many visitors arrive from Nassau or Miami on **Bahamasair** (© **800/222-4262** or 242/367-2095;www.bahamasair.com). Flight schedules change frequently in The Bahamas, but you can usually get two to three flights out of Nassau on Fridays and Sundays, going first to Marsh Harbour, then on to Treasure Cay. If you're in West Palm Beach, you can often take a direct morning flight to Marsh Harbour and Treasure Cay.

Other connections include **American Eagle** (© **800/433-7300** or 242/367-2231; www.aa.com), with flights from Miami to Marsh Harbour once daily; and **Continental Connection** (© **800/231-0856** or 242/367-3415 in Marsh Harbour, 242/365-8615 in Treasure Cay; www.continental.com), which flies to Marsh Harbour and Treasure Cay two to three times daily from several Florida locales. A smaller carrier is **Twin Air** (© **954/359-8266;** www.flytwinair.com), flying from Fort Lauderdale to Treasure Cay on Mondays, Wednesdays, and Fridays.

BY BOAT   The mail boat **MV *Legacy*** sails on Tuesday from Nassau to Hope Town, Marsh Harbour, Turtle Cay, and Green Turtle Cay. It returns to Nassau on Friday. Trip time is 12 hours. The **MV *Legacy*** leaves Nassau on Tuesday, with stops at Green Turtle Cay, Hope Town, Marsh Harbour, and Turtle Cay, going back to Nassau on Thursday. Each trip takes 12 hours. For details on sailings (subject to change) and costs, contact the dockmaster at **Potter's Cay Dock** in Nassau (© **242/393-1064**).

Bahamas Ferries now operates a direct service from Nassau aboard the *Sea Wind*. A one-way fare costs $50 per adult and $35 for children and round-trip is $90 per adult and $55 for children (ages 2 and under free). For more information and for bookings, call © **242/323-2166.** The trip from Nassau to Sandy Point in the Abacos takes 1 hour and 50 minutes.

GETTING AROUND

BY TAXI   Unmetered taxis, which you often have to share with other passengers, meet all arriving flights. They will take you to your hotel if it's on the Abaco "mainland"; otherwise, they will deposit you at a dock where you can hop aboard a water taxi to one of the neighboring offshore islands, such as Green Turtle Cay or Elbow Cay. Most visitors use a combination taxi and water-taxi ride to reach the most popular hotels. From Marsh Harbour Airport to Hope Town on Elbow Cay, the cost is about $12 for the transfer. From the Treasure Cay Airport to Green Turtle Cay, the charge is about $15. Elbow Cay costs about $11 for the transfer.

It's also possible to make arrangements for a taxi tour of Great or Little Abaco. These, however, are expensive, and you don't really see much.

BY FERRY   Mostly, you'll get around with **Albury's Ferry Service** (© **242/367-3147;** www.oii.net/alburysferry), which provides several ferry connections between Marsh Harbour and both Elbow Cay (Hope Town) and Man-O-War Cay, a 20-minute trip to either destination. The one-way fare is $15 adults, $7.50 for children 11 and younger. (Ferries also go to Guana Cay.) The ferry docks are not far from the Marsh Harbour Airport; it's about a 10-minute, $13 to $14 cab ride for two passengers (plus $3 for each additional passenger).

For car-ferry service to Green Turtle Cay, see the section, "Green Turtle Cay (New Plymouth)," later in this chapter. Ferries go from Great Abaco Island to Green Turtle Cay, but those docks are a 35-minute $70 cab ride for up to four passengers from the Marsh Harbour Airport. It's better to fly to Treasure Cay rather than Marsh Harbour to do this, and then take a taxi to the ferry docks.

1 Marsh Harbour (Great Abaco Island)

The largest town in the Abacos, and the third largest in The Bahamas, Marsh Harbour lies on Great Abaco Island and is the major gateway to this island group.

Marsh Harbour is also a shipbuilding center, but tourism accounts for most of its revenues: A number of good inns are here. Although the town doesn't have the quaint New England charm of either New Plymouth or Hope Town, it does have a shopping center and various other facilities not found in many Out Island settlements. Good water-taxi connections, too, make this a popular place from which to explore offshore cays, including Man-O-War and Elbow. Several hotels will also rent you a bike if you want to pedal around town.

MARSH HARBOUR ESSENTIALS

GETTING THERE See "Abacos Essentials," above. Marsh Harbour is the most easily accessible point in the Abacos from the U.S. mainland, with daily flights from Florida.

GETTING AROUND You won't need a car to get around the town itself, but if you want to explore the rest of the island on your own, you can rent a car, for $70 a day or $350 per week (be prepared for bad roads, though). In Marsh Harbour, call **A&P Rentals** at © **242/367-2655** to see if any vehicles are available.

Rental Wheels of Abaco at Marsh Harbour (© **242/367-4643**) will rent bikes at $10 a day or $45 a week, and also mopeds at $45 per day or $200 a week.

VISITOR INFORMATION The **Abaco Tourist Office** is at Queen Elizabeth Drive in the commercial heart of town (© **242/367-3067**). It's open Monday to Friday from 9am to 5pm.

FAST FACTS There's a **First Caribbean International Bank** on Don MacKay Boulevard (© **242/367-2152**), plus several other banks and a **post office** (© **242/367-2571**).

For medication, go to the **Chemist Shop Pharmacy,** Don MacKay Boulevard (© **242/367-3106**), open Monday through Saturday 8:30am to 5:30pm.

Dial **911** if you need the **police.**

SPECIAL EVENTS In July, Marsh Harbour hosts **Regatta Week,** the premier yachting event in the Abacos, attracting sailboats and their crews from around the world. It's held sometime around the U.S. and Bahamian Independence Days (July 4 and July 10). Many of the yachters participating in this event stay at the Green Turtle Club (p. 226). For registration forms and more information, write to **Regatta Time in Abaco,** P.O. Box AB20551, Marsh Harbour, Abaco, The Bahamas, or call David Ralph at © **242/367-2677.**

WHERE TO STAY

Abaco Beach Resort & Boat Harbour ⭐ This beachfront resort—the biggest and best in Marsh Harbour—is a good choice, especially if you're serious about diving or fishing. Extending over a sprawling acreage at the edge of town and fronting a small but lovely beach, it's a business with several different faces: the hotel, with handsomely furnished rooms that overlook the Sea of Abaco; the well-managed restaurant and bar; the Boat Harbour Marina, which has slips for 180 boats and full docking facilities; and a full-fledged dive shop.

Angler's Restaurant is one of Marsh Harbour's best (see listing under "Where to Dine," below). There's a swim-up bar and a beachfront bar serving light snacks and grog. To reach the resort from Marsh Harbour Airport, take a taxi ($14, but be sure to agree on the price first with the driver; 6.5km/4 miles).

P.O. Box AB20669, Marsh Harbour, Abaco, The Bahamas. © 800/468-4799 in the U.S., or 242/367-2158. Fax 242/367-2158. www.abacoresort.com. 82 units. Year-round $205–$295 double; $400 suite; $550 cottage. AE, DISC, MC, V. **Amenities:** Restaurant; 2 bars; 2 pools; 2 tennis courts; fitness room; bike rentals; free use of watersports equipment; boat rentals; dive shop; gift shop; massage; coin-operated laundry; nonsmoking rooms; rooms for those w/limited mobility. *In room:* A/C, TV, dataport, kitchen (in some), minibar, beverage maker, hair dryer, iron, safe.

Conch Inn Marina & Hotel   Set at the southeastern edge of the harbor, this is a casual, one-story hotel leased on a long-term basis by one of the world's largest yacht-chartering companies, The Moorings. A number of small sandy beaches are within walking distance. Its motel-style, midsize bedrooms are small, each with two double beds (rollaways are available for extra occupants). Bathrooms are small but neatly kept with shower/tub combinations. All units overlook the yachts bobbing in the nearby marina.

On the premises are an open-air swimming pool, fringed with palm trees, and a nearby branch of the Dive Abaco scuba facility. The on-site restaurant and bar (Conch Crawl), is under independent management.

E. Bay St. (P.O. Box AB20469), Marsh Harbour, Abaco, The Bahamas. © 242/367-4000. Fax 242/367-4004. www.go-abacos.com/conchinn/conchhm/ci_marina.html. 9 units. Year-round $160 double. Extra person $20 per day. AE, MC, V. **Amenities:** Restaurant; bar; pool; nonsmoking rooms. *In room:* A/C, TV, fridge, beverage maker, iron.

Lofty Fig Villas   This family-owned bungalow colony across from the Conch Inn overlooks the harbor. It doesn't have the services of a full-fledged resort, but it's good for families and self-sufficient types. Built in 1970, it stands in a tropical landscape with a freshwater pool and a gazebo where you can barbecue. Rooms have one queen-size bed and a queen-size hide-a-bed sofa, a fully tiled bathroom with shower, a dining area, a kitchen, and a private screened-in porch. Maid service is provided Monday through Saturday.

You're about a 10-minute walk from a supermarket and shops, and restaurants and bars lie just across the street. Marinas, a dive shop, and boat rentals are also close at hand. From the Lofty Fig, walk, bike, or drive 1.5km (1 mile) east to a point near the Marsh Harbour ferryboat docks for access to a sandy beach and a snorkeling site (many visitors opt to go to Guana Cay for their day at the beach, via ferryboat).

P.O. Box AB20437, Marsh Harbour, Abaco, The Bahamas. ©/fax 242/367-2681. http://go-abacos.com/theabs/marsh/mh_fig.html. 6 villas. Dec 15–Sept 15 $130 daily, $845 weekly, extra person $30 per day; Sept 16–Dec 14 $105 double, $683 weekly, extra person $20 per day. MC, V. **Amenities:** Outdoor pool. *In room:* A/C, kitchen, beverage maker, no phone.

WHERE TO DINE

If you'd like to go really casual, try **Island Bakery,** Don McKay Boulevard (© 242/367-2129), which has the best Bahamian bread and cinnamon rolls on the island, often emerging fresh from the oven. You might even pick up the makings for a picnic.

The best pizzas are sold at **Sapodilly's Bar & Grill,** Bay Street (© 242/367-3498); see below.

Angler's Restaurant ⭐ BAHAMIAN/INTERNATIONAL   At the Boat Harbour, overlooking the Sea of Abaco, this is the main restaurant of the town's major resort. The interior features a nautical theme and Bahamian decor. Within a few steps of your seat, dock pilings rise from the water, yachts and fishing boats come and go, and the place is open and airy. The menu changes daily, but fresh seafood, which the chef prepares with finesse, is always featured, along with a well-chosen selection of meat and poultry dishes. Begin with crab cakes served with a Caribbean salsa and garnished with Mesculan greens, or perhaps the sesame seed–encrusted tuna steak, accompanied with sweet soy sauce. Main dishes dance with flavor, notably the island cracked conch marinated in a coconut-lime sauce; grilled baby lamb chops seasoned with Herbes de Provence; and freshly caught grouper seared and basted in a lemon-and-caper sauce.

In the Abaco Beach Resort & Boat Harbour, Marsh Harbour. (C) 242/367-2158. Reservations recommended for dinner. Main courses $6–$29. AE, DISC, MC, V. Daily 7am–2:30pm and 6–9:30pm.

Conch Crawl BAHAMIAN   Adjacent to the Conch Inn and the upscale facilities of the Moorings, the eatery attracts a lot of yachties and visiting professional athletes. The cooks use local ingredients, such as freshly caught grouper and snapper, whenever they can. They also know every conceivable way to prepare conch. The regulars don't even have to consult the menu; they just ask, "What's good?" Diners also look for daily specials, such as curried chicken or steamed chicken. Fish and seafood are always on the menu. If you're frittering away a few hours, drop in for a Conch Crawl, a rum-based drink with secret ingredients. The bar, set beneath an octagon gazebo near the piers, is a fine place to meet people.

At the Conch Inn (The Moorings), Bay St. (C) 242/367-4444. Reservations not required. Main courses $18–$28. MC. Daily 7:30am–10pm.

The Jib Room BAHAMIAN/AMERICAN   This funky restaurant/bar is a hangout for local residents and boat owners who savor its welcoming spirit. If you want the house-special cocktail, a Bilge Burner, get ready for a head-spinning combination of apricot brandy, rum, coconut juice, and Kahlua. Saturday night brings Jib's steak barbecue, when as many as 300 1-lb. New York strip steaks are served. The only other dinner option is Wednesday, when grilled baby back ribs might be the featured dish of the day. Other choices include a seafood platter, grilled chicken, and broiled lobster—and yes, you've probably had it all before in better versions, but the dishes are well prepared. Go for the convivial atmosphere rather than the food.

Marsh Harbour Marina, Pelican Shores. (C) 242/367-2700. Lunch platters $8.50–$12; fixed-price dinners $23. MC, V. Wed–Sat 11:30am–2:30pm; dinner Wed and Sat 8–11pm.

Mangoes Restaurant ⭐ BAHAMIAN/INTERNATIONAL   Near the harbor in one of the town's most distinctive buildings, Mangoes is the best, and certainly the most popular, restaurant on the island, attracting both yachties and locals. It boasts a cedar-topped bar and a cathedral ceiling that soars above a deck jutting out over the water. Somehow the chefs seem to try a little harder here, offering a typical menu adding a hint of island spirit. Our faithful friend, grilled grouper, is dressed up a bit with mango and tomatoes, and cracked conch makes an appearance as well. Your best bet, as in nearly all Bahamian restaurants, is usually the fresh catch of the day and Mangoes is no exception. At lunch you can sample their locally famous "conch burger."

Front St. (C) 242/367-2366. Reservations recommended. Main courses lunch $12–$15, dinner $14–$32. AE, MC, V. Mon–Sat 11:30–2:30am; daily 6–10pm.

Mother Merle's Fishnet ⭐ *Finds* BAHAMIAN   Many of the meals eaten aboard the yachts and sailing craft in the nearby harbor are prepared here. There's no dining room on the premises, so don't expect a place to sit and linger, although the well-prepared food, if you don't mind hauling it off to another venue, makes the limitations most palatable. The setting is a cement house on the town's main street. Inside, you'll find the gentle but aging matriarch Merle Williams, who is assisted by her able-bodied daughters, Angela and Shirley. As Mother Merle tells it, all Bahamian women are good cooks, a bit of an exaggeration, but you'll believe her words when you taste her family's three different preparations of chicken, all prepared by secret family recipes. Locals swear that Mother Merle makes the best cracked conch in the Abacos, and she's also known for her different preparations of grouper. Happy hour with live music is every Friday from 5:30 to 7:30pm.

Dundas Town. ✆ **242/367-2770.** Takeout service only. Main courses $9–$17. No credit cards. Tues–Sat 6:30–11pm.

Sapodilly's Bar & Grill BAHAMIAN   This restaurant occupies an open-air pavilion across the road from the harborfront, in an area of town known as "the tourist strip." Even if you eventually head into the high-raftered interior dining room, take time out for a drink or two on the covered open-air deck, surrounded by vibrant Junkanoo colors and a crowd of local hipsters, yacht owners, marina workers, and businessmen visiting from other parts of The Bahamas. Lunch might consist of grilled fish sandwiches, burgers, salads, and quiche. Dinners are more elaborate, with 12-ounce New York strip steak, a flavor-filled shrimp kabob in teriyaki sauce, and zesty curried filets of grouper. There's a happy hour with live music every Friday from 5:30 to 7:30pm.

E. Bay St. ✆ **242/367-3498.** Reservations recommended. Lunch platters and sandwiches $8–$13; dinner main courses $18–$26. MC, V. Daily 11:30am–3pm and 6–9pm.

Wally's ⭐ BAHAMIAN/INTERNATIONAL   Across the street from the water, this eatery occupies a tidy pink colonial villa on a lawn dotted with hibiscus. You'll find here an outdoor terrace, a boutique, and an indoor bar and dining area filled with Haitian paintings. The special drink of the house is a Wally's Special, containing four kinds of rum and a medley of fruit juices. The chef prepares the best Bahamian cracked conch at Marsh Harbour, as well as tender filet mignon, lamb chops, tarragon chicken, and an excellent version of smothered grouper. Main dishes come with a generous house salad and vegetables. The place really shines at lunchtime, when things tend to get very busy as hungry diners devour dolphinfish burgers, several kinds of chicken platters, and some well-stuffed sandwiches. Part of the style here comes courtesy of sisters Barbara and Maureen Smith, who head to Paris every fall and bring culinary discoveries back to their enterprise in Marsh Harbour.

E. Bay St. ✆ **242/367-2074.** Reservations recommended for dinner. Lunch sandwiches and platters $9–$15; dinner main courses $27–$30. AE, DISC, MC, V. Mon–Sat 11:30am–3pm; Fri–Sat 6–9pm. Closed 6 weeks Sept–Oct.

BEACHES, WATERSPORTS & OTHER OUTDOOR PURSUITS

Whatever sport you want to pursue—whether snorkling or a full-day's fishing charter—the innkeepers at Marsh Harbour can set you up with the right people or equipment. For variety, you can also take the ferry over to Hope Town and check out the facilities and outfitters there.

Of the major towns of the Out Islands, Marsh Harbour has some of the least appealing beaches. You can try one of three private beaches, but none is very enticing, and none really want outsiders. The easiest to circumvent is the one at the Abaco Beach Resort, but it's small, not really fabulous, and, again, private. Buy a drink for a local at the hotel bar, and you're in, but that, at best, is a somewhat uncomfortable arrangement.

To compensate, beachgoers get into their cars and head south of Marsh Harbour. After 15 to 20 minutes of southbound driving, and at points south of Little Harbour, lots of good beaches begin to appear. The beaches near the hamlet of **Casuarina Point** benefit from some battered, all-Bahamian restaurants in the vicinity.

Some swimmers heading south from Marsh Harbour make it a point to go eastward from the main highway whenever an offshoot road appears, usually at points near Little Harbour or at points south of Little Harbour. Other times, they simply stop their cars wherever they feel like it.

None of the beaches on Great Abaco Island has facilities or lifeguards. Guard your valuables and stay alert to be safe.

BOAT CHARTERS

Ask about the depth of the harbor before you rent a boat, and even more importantly, before you attempt to navigate your way in or out of Marsh Harbour, since Hurricane Floyd changed the configuration of the channel. Yachts with deep drafts have reported trouble getting in and out of the port at times.

If you'd like to try bareboating in The Bahamas—seagoing without captain or crew— **Abaco Bahamas Charters,** Hopetown, Abaco (C 800/626-5690; fax or local phone 242/366-0151; www.abacocharters.com), can set you up; weekly charters with a choice of eight boats begin at $1,625 (and can go as high as $4,200 during high season), with a $1,500 deposit required. Only experienced sailors can rent.

The Moorings (C 800/535-7289 or 242/367-4000; www.moorings.com) is one of the leading charter sailboat outfitters in the world. It operates from an eagle's nest perch behind the Conch Inn Resort and Marina, overlooking a labyrinth of piers and wharves—at least 80 berths, with more on the way—where hundreds of upscale water-craft are tied up (many of them are for rent). With one of its vessels, you can enjoy short sails between the islands, stopping at white sandy beaches and snug anchorages. Yacht rentals generally range from $455 to $1,280 a day, with a skipper costing another $144 per day, and an onboard cook (if you want one) priced at an additional $124 per day.

For the more casual boater, **Sea Horse Boat Rentals,** at the Abaco Beach Resort (C 242/367-2513), offers some of the best rentals. A 5.5m (18-ft.) Boston Whaler rents for $170 per day, and you can also book a 6.5m (21-ft.) Privateer for $200 per day. Other vessels are for rent, too, and all boats are equipped with a Bimini top, coolers, a compass, and a swimming platform, along with life jackets, a paddle, docking lines, and other equipment. Sea Horse is open daily from 8am to 5pm.

SNORKELING & SCUBA DIVING

Divers swim to the **Abacos Train Wreck,** which can be explored in 4.5 to 6m (15–20 ft.) of water, the wreck consisting of two almost intact locomotives lying on their sides. Yet another wreck nearby, *Adirondack,* lies in shallow water some 3 to 7.5m (10–25 ft.) deep. Many divers also come here to explore the government-protected **Sea Preserve and Fowl Cay Land,** which teems with multicolored sea life in shallow reefs.

The best place to snorkel is **Mermaid Reef and Beach,** with its colorful reef, moray eels, and plethora of beautiful rainbow-hued fish. The reef and beach lie on Pelican Shores, the northernmost edge of the Marsh Harbour waterfront directly west of the Marsh Harbour Marina. From the center of Marsh Harbour at East Bay Street, walk east along the harbor and then head northwest until you reach the marina. Once at the marina, continue to walk west to Pelican Shores across the stretch of scrub and sand until you reach Mermaid Reef and Beach where you can enjoy the beach or else go snorkel-ing in the clear waters. **Sea Horse Boat Rentals** at the Abaco Beach Resort & Boat Har-bour marina (C 242/367-2513) rents snorkel gear.

Scuba divers might want to check out the nearby **Pelican Cays Land and Sea Park** 🐾. You won't find any organized excursions here, but Dive Abaco (see below) is the best source of information and might arrange a trip. You can also drive down to the park by following the road immediately south of Marsh Harbour and then turning east at the sign leading toward the park. Several small beaches are suitable for swimming. The easiest jumping-off point is at Pelican Harbour.

Dive Abaco, Marsh Harbour (© **800/247-5338** in the U.S., or 242/367-2787; www.diveabaco.com), rents snorkel gear and offers full dive trips to tunnels and caverns in the world's third-longest barrier reef. Resort courses for uncertified novice divers are all-inclusive for $152. Two-tank dives, including tanks and weights for certified divers, are $82. Snorkeling is $52. Trips depart daily at 9:30am, and afternoon trips are dictated by demand. Shop hours are daily from 8:30am to 5pm; ask for owner-operator Keith Rogers.

ATTRACTIONS ON LAND

Marsh Harbour is the best center for exploring the nature-created attractions of both Great Abaco and Little Abaco.

A fully graded and tarred main highway links all the settlements on the "mainland," with such colorfully named hamlets as Fire Road, Mango Hill, Coopers Town, Joe Creek, Red Bays, Snake Cay, Little Harbour, Sandy Point, Cherokee Sound, and our favorite, Hole-in-the-Wall, which lies at the "bottom" of Great Abaco.

Driving south for 40km (25 miles) from Marsh Harbour along the Great Abaco Highway, you come first to **Cherokee Sound,** with a population of 150 dwellers, at the end of a peninsula jutting out into Cherokee Sound. Residents are descended from Loyalists who fled mainland U.S. in 1783 and remained faithful to the British Crown. These people faced an inhospitable land and for 2 centuries have tried to make a living as best they can. The men dive for lobsters or go out at night "sharking." The jaws of the sharks are sold in Marsh Harbour. They also hunt down tiniki crabs, as well as pigeon and wild boar in the remote pinelands of the Abacos.

This unhurried routine in the remote village of Cherokee Sound—surrounded by several deserted Atlantic beaches and a section of salt marshes with panoramic views—may one day change, as a new vacation home community is going to be built in the area with an 18-hole golf course. There will even be a spa and equestrian center, though no date has been set for the opening. Stay tuned or else head for Cherokee Sound now before its sleepy way of life is forever altered.

Forty-eight kilometers (30 miles) south of Marsh Harbour takes you to **Little Harbor,** a cay shaped like a circle with a white-sandy beach running along most of its waterfront. The location is to the immediate each of Cherokee Sound. At Little Harbour, you can visit **Pete Johnston's Foundry** (© 242/367-2720), the only bronze foundry in The Bahamas. Settling here in 1951, the Johnston family achieved international fame as artists and sculptors. They use an old "lost-wax" method in the casting of their bronze sculptures, many of which are sold in prestigious art galleries in America, although you can also buy them directly from the foundry itself. Mrs. Johnston creates porcelain figurines of island life such as birds, fish, boats, and even fishermen. The Johnstons welcome visitors at their studio daily from 10 to 11am and 2 to 3pm. You can also purchase a remarkable book here, *Artist on His Island,* detailing the true-life adventures of Randolph and Margot Johnston, who lived a Swiss Family Robinson adventure when they first arrived at Little Harbour with their three sons.

Sailing in an old Bahamian schooner, the *Langosta,* they stayed in one of the local caves until they eventually erected a thatched dwelling for themselves.

After a visit to the foundry, you can stop in for a drink at the laidback **Pete's Pub and Gallery** nearby (© **242/367-2720;** www.petespubandgallery.com). At the pub, you'll think you've arrived in *Gilligan's Island* (remember the old TV sitcom?). The beer is cold and the art on the walls is for sale. The pub was constructed in part from the timbers of the *Langosta.* You can also order lunch here daily costing from $20. Fresh seafood such as mango-glazed grouper or lemon-pepper dolphin is served along with burgers. A wild boar roast is offered every Saturday from April to July. In the evening, Pete Johnston might sing a medley of sea chanties, accompanying himself on his guitar. The pub is open daily from 11am "until everyone leaves at night." It is closed September and October.

After leaving Cherokee and Little Harbour, you can return to the Great Abaco Highway, heading south once again to reach the little fishing village of **Casuarina Point** west of Cherokee Sound. Here you'll find a lovely stretch of sand and some jade-colored boneflats. If you keep going south, you come to **Crossing Rocks,** a little fishing village 64km (40 miles) to the south of Marsh Harbour, noted for its kilometer-long beach of golden sand. The hamlet where locals barely eke out a living takes its name from the isthmus where Great Abaco Island narrows to its thinnest point.

From here, if you continue traveling south, you come to a fork in the road, the southern road going to the **Abaco National Park** (also called Bahamas National Trust Sanctuary; © **242/393-1317**) and the aptly named **Hole-in-the-Wall,** the end of the line for Great Abaco. Hole-in-the-Wall is a poor little hamlet with a few settlers, which marks the end of the line for drives along the Abacos.

Protected by the government, the 8,296-hectare (20,491-acre) Abaco National Park, established in 1994, sprawls across the southeastern portion of Grand Abaco Island. Some 2,023 hectare (4,997 acres) of it is pine forest, with a lot of wetlands that are home to native bird life, including the endangered Bahama parrot. Hardwood forests, sand dunes, and mangrove flats fill the area. Rangers, under the sponsorship of the Bahamas National Trust, operate occasional tours of the sanctuary and protect the area.

Touring on your own can be extremely difficult, and most private outfitters in the area aren't very well organized. An exception is **Ron and Erin Lowe-Pagliaro** (www.abacooutback.com), who offer sea-kayaking, snorkeling, land tours, and birding excursions. A half-day kayak trip costs $55 per adult or $35 for children 11 and under; a full day costs $85 for adults and $45 for children. They also offer a tour that goes 2½ hours south of Marsh Harbour through the Abaco National Park to Hole-in-the-Wall; these trips cost $95 per adult or $55 per child.

SHOPPING

Bahama Dawn, Engar Gottlieb Boulevard, next to the public library (© **242/367-4648**), carries a collection of Androsia batik clothing, along with some local crafts. For souvenir items, try **Iggy Biggy,** Main Street, across from Conch Inn (© **242/367-3596**).

MARSH HARBOUR AFTER DARK

The **Sand Bar,** opening onto the Sea of Abaco at the Abaco Beach Resort & Boat Harbour (© **242/367-2158**), is the most popular gathering spot in town. The yachting crowd, often from Miami, hangs out here, swapping tall tales of the sea while downing strong rum punches. Another good hangout is **Wally's,** East Bay Street (✆ **242/ 367-2074**). You can enjoy the special punch on an outdoor terrace or inside a cozy bar. On Wednesday and Saturday, live entertainment is often presented. **Sapodilly's Bar & Grill,** East Bay Street (✆ **242/367-3498**), attracts an interesting blend of locals and visitors, some of whom play at its pool table, others preferring to mix and mingle at the bar.

2 Elbow Cay (Hope Town) ⭐

Elbow Cay is well known for its spectacular white-sand beaches. One of The Bahamas's best, **Tahiti Beach** lies in splendid isolation at the far end of Elbow Cay, with sparkling waters and powdery white sands. Access is possible only on foot, by riding a rented bicycle across sand and gravel paths from Hope Town, or by private boat.

The cay's largest settlement is **Hope Town,** a little village with a candy-striped, 36m (118-ft.) lighthouse—the most photographed attraction in the Out Islands. Hope Town seems frozen in time. Like other offshore cays of the Abacos, it was settled by Loyalists who left the new United States and came to The Bahamas to remain subjects of the British Crown. Its clapboard, saltbox cottages are weathered to a silver gray or painted in pastel colors, with white-picket fences setting them off. The buildings may remind you of New England, but this palm-fringed island has South Seas flavor.

The island is almost free of cars. In exploring Hope Town, you can take one of two roads: "Up Along" or "Down Along," which both run along the water.

ELBOW CAY ESSENTIALS

GETTING THERE   You can reach Elbow Cay in about 20 minutes, via regularly scheduled ferry service from Marsh Harbour on Great Abaco. A one-way fare is $10, same-day round-trip is $15, and service is three times daily. For more information, call **Albury's Ferry Service** at ✆ **242/365-6010** or visit www.oii.net/Information/ Ferry.html.

GETTING AROUND   Many visitors rent boats to get around the island, explore nearby cays, and go fishing and snorkeling. But if you're not interested in playing sea captain, you can still move easily around Elbow Cay. The quiet, narrow streets of Hope Town are reserved for pedestrians, and you can walk to many other parts of tiny Elbow Cay. You can't rent a car on Elbow Cay, but it isn't a problem. Hope Town, the scenic seaside village, bans all motor vehicles. If you'd like a golf cart delivered to your hotel, call **Island Cart Rental** (✆ **242/366-0448;** www.islandcarrentals.com); these gas or electric carts cost $40 to $45 a day or $240 to $270 week. Hotels provide shuttle vans to and from town. Some dining rooms offer pick-up and drop-off service at dinnertime if you call ahead. Bicycles—often free for hotel guests—are available at or near most accommodations. Taxis meet incoming flights at the Marsh Harbour airport, and they greet arriving ferries as well. During your stay, the staff at your hotel can call one for you when you need it.

FAST FACTS   If you're in need of medical attention, you must go to Marsh Harbour. A local **post office** (✆ **242/366-0098**) is at the head of the upper public dock, but expect mail sent from here to take a long time. Hours are Monday to Friday from 9am to noon and from 1 to 5pm.

WHERE TO STAY

Elbow Cay's long and secluded white-sand shores, some backed by sandy dunes, are some of The Bahamas' most stunning locales. Although accommodations are on or near sandy shores, beaches remain virtually vacant but because the hotels are small and few in number.

Abaco Inn ⚡ *(Finds)*   A sophisticated little hideaway about 3km (2 miles) south of Hope Town, the Abaco Inn faces a lovely sandy beach on White Sound. Compared to its main rival, Club Soleil Resort, Abaco Inn is actually more of a resort. An informal barefoot elegance and a welcoming spirit prevail here on the narrowest section of Elbow Cay, between the crashing surf of the jagged eastern coast and the sheltered waters of White Sound and the Sea of Abaco to the west. From the cedar-capped gazebo, you can gaze out over the rocky tidal flats of the Atlantic. Excellent snorkeling is close.

The midsize accommodations are arranged in a crescent facing the beach. They're set amid palms and sea grapes, and each has its own hammock placed conveniently nearby for quiet afternoons of reading or sleeping. Each comfortable unit has a ceiling fan, a bathroom with a shower/tub combination, white-tile floors, sliding-glass doors, and traditional furniture.

A modern, rambling clubhouse with a fireplace is both the social center and the most appealing restaurant/bar on the island (see "Where to Dine," below). Shuttle service is available from the airport. Boating and fishing can be arranged through the hotel.

White Sound, Hope Town, Elbow Cay, Abaco, The Bahamas. (C) 800/468-8799 in the U.S., or 242/366-0133. Fax 242/366-0113. www.abacoinn.com. 22 units. Year-round $126–$165 double; $240 villa for 2. Extra person $50 per day. AE, DISC, MC, V. **Amenities:** Restaurant; bar; pool; bike rentals; babysitting; laundry service; nonsmoking rooms; rooms for those w/limited mobility. *In room:* A/C, beverage maker, hair dryer, iron, no phone.

Club Soleil Resort   Abaco Inn (see listing above) may have better accommodations, but nothing surpasses the tranquillity of this inn. Because of its isolated position near the lighthouse on the western edge of Hope Town's harbor, the only way to get to this Spanish-style resort is by boat. Once there, you're just a short walk from some lovely sandy beaches. If you bring your own boat, you can moor it at this hotel's marina, but if you just happen to have left your boat at home, call the owners. They will arrange a free waterborne transfer from any nearby coastline you designate. Midsize rooms with shower units are contained in a two-story, Mediterranean-inspired annex, and they overlook a swimming pool and the boats in the harbor. Each room contains two double beds and a clean and tasteful decor. The restaurant is covered separately under "Where to Dine," below.

Western Harbourfront, Hope Town, Elbow Cay, The Bahamas. (C) 242/366-0003. Fax 242/366-0254. www.clubsoleil.com. 7 units. Year-round $130 nightly double; $160 nightly 2-bedroom apt; $1,000 weekly 2-bedroom apt. AE, MC, V. Closed Sept. **Amenities:** Restaurant; bar; pool; laundry service; all nonsmoking rooms. *In room:* A/C, TV, kitchen (in apt), minibar, coffeemaker, hair dryer, no phone.

Hope Town Hideaways   Staying here is like living in your own "second home" in The Bahamas. Five gingerbread-trimmed villas lie across the harbor from where the ferryboats arrive from Marsh Harbour. On 4.5 hectares (11 acres) of grounds, which are reached by boat, this hideaway lives up to its name. The accommodations are part of a larger complex of privately owned homes, surrounded by grounds handsomely landscaped with orange trees, mangoes, and flamboyant bougainvillea. One or two couples—the maximum is six guests—can sleep comfortably in the units, each of which includes a large kitchen, dining room, a living area with two single daybeds, and two bedrooms. Furnishings are custom built, and each private bathroom comes with a tub/shower. You're not on the beach but you can enjoy the freshwater pool here. Hideaways is also a management company featuring more than 75 privately owned cottages and villas to rent on island.

1 Purple Porpoise Plaza, Hope Town, Elbow Cay, Abaco, The Bahamas. ℭ **242/366-0224.** Fax 242/366-0434. www. hopetown.com. 5 villas. Year-round $250 cottage for 2, $370 cottage for 3–4, $420 cottage for 5–6. DISC, MC, V. **Amenities:** Freshwater pool, kitchen. *In room:* A/C, no phone.

Sea Spray Resort and Villas ℛ

On 2.4 hectares (6 acres) of landscaped grounds, 5.5km (3½ miles) south of Hope Town and near the southernmost tip of Elbow Cay, these beachfront villas are owned and operated by Ruth Albury, who runs them in a welcoming, personal way. Rented villas include full kitchens and decks that overlook the water. Accommodations are spacious and comfortably furnished, each with a small bathroom containing a shower/tub combination. The Alburys and their hardworking staff are happy to share their vast experience of what to see and do on Elbow Cay and in the Abacos: You can bike, sail, go deep-sea fishing, snorkel, go bonefishing, or explore nearby deserted islands.

Sea Spray also operates a restaurant serving well-prepared food at all three meals while diners enjoy a view of the crashing surf and a weathered gazebo. Nonguests are welcome, too; if you phone in advance for a reservation, management will send a van to collect you from Hope Town.

White Sound, Elbow Cay, Abaco, The Bahamas. ℭ **242/366-0065.** Fax 242/366-0383. www.seasprayresort.com. 5 units. Year-round $180–$260 per night or $950–$1,500 per week 1-bedroom apt, $350 per night or $1,950 per week 2-bedroom apt, $350–$430 per night or $1,950–$2,450 per week 3-bedroom apt. Extra person $100 per day. AE, MC, V. **Amenities:** Restaurant; bar; pool; watersports equipment/rentals. *In room:* A/C, TV, dataport, kitchen, no phone.

Turtle Hill Vacation Villas ℛ

On the outskirts of Hope Town, a trio of luxury villas lie just steps from a vast secluded beach where sea turtles return to nest. Fruit trees and other tropical foliage make this a secluded getaway. Each house sleeps six persons comfortably in two large bedrooms, with a queen-size sleeper sofa in the living room, a full bathroom, a well-equipped kitchen, a spacious living and dining area, and both central air-conditioning and ceiling fans. Linen is provided, and a Caribbean-style cabana bar serves drinks and finger foods daily.

Between Abaco Sea and Hope Town, Hope Town, Abaco, The Bahamas. ℭ **800/339-2124** in the U.S., or 242/366-0557. Fax 242/366-0557. www.turtlehill.com. 6 units. Winter $1,850–$2,050 per week; off-season $1,450–$1,650 per week. AE, MC, V. **Amenities:** Restaurant; bar; 2 pools; babysitting; laundry service; dry cleaning; nonsmoking rooms. *In room:* A/C, ceiling fans, TV, kitchen, beverage maker, hair dryer (in some), iron, no phone.

WHERE TO DINE

Abaco Inn ℛ BAHAMIAN/INTERNATIONAL

Flavor-filled food is served in a breezy, almost elegant waterfront setting. The chef prepares lunch dishes such as conch chowder, pasta primavera, and salads with delectable homemade dressings featuring tarragon and other herbs. The dinner menu changes frequently but usually offers seafood, vegetarian, and meat dishes, each expertly seasoned and well prepared. Typical meals are likely to begin with seafood bisque or vichyssoise, followed by coconut grouper (a house specialty), spinach fettuccine Alfredo, roasted lamb with herbs and mint sauce, or, our favorite, broiled red snapper with a light salsa. The crème brûlée and Key lime, coconut, and chocolate silk pies are delectable. The inn will send a minivan to pick you up from other parts of the island if you phone in advance.

About 4km (2½ miles) south of Hope Town. ℭ **242/366-0133.** Reservations required for dinner. Lunch sandwiches, salads, and platters $6–$12; dinner main courses $15–$32. AE, DISC, MC, V. Daily 8–10:30am, noon–3pm, and 6:30–8:30pm.

Cap'n Jacks BAHAMIAN

Depending on when you come, you may find turtle burgers or crawfish on the menu at this casual alfresco dining spot at the edge of the harbor. Any time of year, the grouper and conch are well prepared and the freshest food on the menu. Landlubbers gravitate toward the more routine fried chicken and burgers. The Key lime and chocolate silk pies are justifiably popular dessert choices. Try Cap'n Jacks' version of the omnipresent Goombay Smash. Come on Wednesday or Friday for live local music in the evening between 8 and 11pm.

On the harbor in Hope Town. ✆ 242/366-0247. Main courses: $8.25–$22. MC, V. Mon–Sat 8am–9pm.

Harbour's Edge ✰ BAHAMIAN   Hope Town's best and most popular restaurant is set on piers above the water in a clapboard house. It's the island's lighthearted social center. The bar has an adjacent waterside deck where you can moor if you arrive by boat, as many visitors do. Here and in the dining room as well, the crackle of VHF radio is always audible—boat owners and local residents often reserve tables on short-wave radio, channel 16.

Lunch includes such typical yet flavor-filled dishes as conch fritters, conch chowder, hamburgers, sandwiches, and conch platters. In the evening, dinners are also well-prepared—generous portions of chicken in white wine with potatoes, Greek or Caesar salad, pan-fried pork chops, chargrilled grouper, New York strip steak, fish in coconut milk, and more.

Hope Town, next to the post office. ✆ 242/366-0087. Reservations recommended. Main courses lunch $9–$18, dinner $15–$38. MC, V. Wed–Mon 11:30am–11pm; bar Wed–Mon 10am–2am. Closed mid-Sept–mid-Oct.

Hope Town Harbour Lodge ✰ BAHAMIAN   One of the first lodges or inns ever built in Hope Town, this restaurant is still winning new friends. At night, loving couples opt for a table on the cozy terrace with views of the harbor and the lights from the yachts. Begin the evening with a rum punch in Wrecker's Bar overlooking the water. The menu here is hardly inventive, but it's good, featuring the usual array of chicken, steak, and pork chops. Occasionally, a fisherman will bring in a big marlin that the chef grills to perfection. Bahamian lobster appears delightfully in a creamy fettuccine and the local grouper is fashioned into spring rolls, Chinese-style, and served with a mustard-laced chutney sauce. In the main dining area are picture windows, rattan chairs, and nautical prints. During lunch, diners gravitate to the Reef Bar and Grill fronting the water.

Don't overlook the lodge as a possibility for rooms. It rents 20 comfortably furnished and air-conditioned doubles, with prices going from $170 to $180 all year. Accommodations lie on any of three floors, each with a patio or balcony, sliding glass doors, a small bathroom with shower stall, and wicker furnishings.

Hope Town. ✆ 242/366-0095. Reservations recommended for dinner. Main courses lunch $7–$12, dinner $20–$38. MC, V. Daily 11:30am–2:30pm; Tues–Sun 6:30–8pm.

Rudy's Place ✰ *Finds* BAHAMIAN/AMERICAN   Because of its isolated position—in a wooden house in a valley in the center of the island—this restaurant provides free transportation before and after dinner. Owner Rudy Moree prepares recipes handed down from his Bahamian grandmother. These, adapted to the tastes of his international clientele, might include crawfish tails baked with Parmesan and butter, a delectable broiled shrimp in a white wine–and-garlic sauce, or even a passable roasted duck in an orange sauce. Rudy's has added six comfortably furnished cottages, three of which have an ocean view. Year-round a double rents for $225 to $250 per night.

Center Line Rd. ✆ 242/366-0062. Reservations recommended. Fixed-price dinners $20–$30. MC, V. Mon–Sat 6:30–8:30pm (last order). Closed Sept–Oct.

BEACHES, WATERSPORTS & OTHER OUTDOOR PURSUITS

In Hope Town, you'll find sandy beaches right at your doorstep, and more beaches in the south are only about a 15-minute ride away. **Garbanzo Beach,** near Sea Spray Resort, lures many surfers. Isolated **Tahiti Beach** ★★, at the southern end of the island (a little more than .6km/a mile from Sea Spray), got its name from the thick wall of palms there. At low tide, the shelling can be excellent along this gorgeous curve of sand, and the shallow waters make for good bonefishing, too. Across the way, you can see uninhabited **Tilloo Cay** and the Atlantic's crashing waves in the distance.

Tahiti Beach is about a 10-minute bike ride from Sea Spray and about 20 minutes from Abaco Inn, both in the White Sound area. To get here, you have to walk your bike up and down a few small, but rocky, rises.

Along the way, you'll pass sea-grape trees, fluffy long-needled pines, and other varied roadside vegetation. Turn left when you come to the first major left (by the white house on the bluff). Turn right when you see two stone pillars. Go downhill and turn left at the end of the road at the wire fences. Take this path to the end. Walk along the dense palm grove to the beach. Because you're heading for the shore, which is public, ignore the PRIVATE—NO TRESPASSING signs.

Irresistible deserted beaches lie to the south of Elbow Cay on pencil-thin **Tilloo Cay** (see above) and the tiny **Pelican Cays.** They make excellent targets for a day's sail. The waters around Tilloo Cay, packed with grouper and conch, are particularly good for both fishing and swimming. In the Pelican Cays Land and Sea Park, **Sandy Cay Reef** is one of the most colorful dive sites around. Line fishing, spear fishing, and shelling, however, are all taboo in this protected area.

The waves and breezes at **Garbanzo Beach,** in the **White Sound** area, make it prime hang-ten territory. If you don't bring your own surfboard, the staff at nearby **Sea Spray Resort** (✆ 242/366-0065) can help you get one.

The waters off the coast of Elbow Cay are a popular spot for boating and fishing. Head to the marina to join the fun.

Set about 20 steps south of Hope Town's post office, **Froggie's Out Island Adventures,** Harbour Road (✆ 242/366-0431; www.froggiesabaco.com), is the largest dive outfitter in the Abacos, with three boats (ranging from 11–17m/36–56 ft. in length)

Finds **Exploring the Abacos by Boat**

The ideal way to explore the Abacos is by boat. **Island Marine,** Parrot Cay in Hope Town (✆ 242/366-0282; fax 242/366-0281), will set you up with one of its rental boats. You can then cruise to the boat-building settlement of Man-O-War Cay, to artist Pete Johnson's bronze foundry/gallery/pub in Little Harbour (see section 1, "Marsh Harbour [Great Abaco Island]," earlier in this chapter), and to many uninhabited cays and deserted beaches where you can go shelling, exploring, and picnicking in peace.

Small-boat rentals range from a 5m (16-ft.) Boston Whaler to 7m (23-ft.) Man-O-War boats, or even 6.5m (21-ft.) Aquasports. Prices run from $90 to $135 per day or $500 to $800 per week.

that owner Theresa Albuery uses to haul divers out to fabulous local dive sites. Beginners pay $140 for a full day, $120 for a half-day, with a lesson included in both rates. Experienced divers are charged $90 for a half-day one-tank excursion, $100 for a full-day two-tank excursion, gear included.

The company also organizes tours, from snorkel cruises to dolphin-watching trips. A full-day cruise out to Great Guana Cay costs $70 per person. An equivalent tour to Little Harbour, near the southernmost point of the Abacos, including visits to selected restaurants, bars, and an art gallery, also costs $50 per person. Froggie's Sunset Cruise (seasonal), departing an hour before sunset and returning an hour after it's dark, costs $35 per person.

LAND ATTRACTIONS

No cars are allowed in the heart of **Hope Town,** so bikers and pedestrians have the narrow paved streets, with names like Loves' Lane, to themselves. As you wander through the town, you see harbor-side restaurants and pastel-painted saltbox cottages with purple and orange bougainvillea tumbling over stone and picket fences. Amid the usual island fare at the handful of souvenir shops is resort wear made from Androsia, the fabric produced on the Bahamian island of Andros. See "Shopping," below.

To find out why Malone is such a common surname, stop by the **Wyannie Malone Museum** (officially open most days from 10am–noon, but unofficially open "whenever"). This small collection of island lore is in tribute to the South Carolinian widow and mother of four who founded Hope Town around 1783.

Before **Hope Town's red-and-white striped lighthouse** was erected in 1838, many of Hope Town's residents made a good living luring ships toward shore to be wrecked on the treacherous reefs and rocks turn the salvaged cargoes into cash. To protect this livelihood, some people tried in vain to destroy the beacon while it was being built. Today, you can climb to the top of the 36m (118-ft.) tower for panoramic views of the harbor and town. Most weekdays between 10am and 4pm, the lighthouse keeper will be happy to give you a peek. The lighthouse is within walking distance of **Club Soleil** and **Hope Town Hideaways.** If you're staying elsewhere, you can make arrangements through your hotel for a visit.

SHOPPING

Of course, no one comes to Hope Town just to shop, but once you're here, you might want to pick up a souvenir. The **Ebb Tide Gift Shop** (② 242/366-0088), the best-stocked gift shop in town, lies in a white clapboard house with aqua trim 1 block from the harbor. Inside, you'll find many treasures, including Androsia batiks made on Andros, costume jewelry, T-shirts, original watercolors, and fabrics sold by the yard. It's open 9am to 5pm Monday to Saturday.

ELBOW CAY AFTER DARK

On Saturday nights, a young party crowd gathers at **Harbour's Edge** (② 242/366-0087), a Hope Town bar and restaurant with the island's only pool table. On Monday night, Bahamian barbecues draw many people to **Sea Spray Resort** (② 242/366-0065), about 4.8km (3 miles) from Hope Town. The food is good considering the low prices, and you can hear live music. Other evenings, people hang out at the bars of hotels and restaurants—or they turn in early to rest up for yet another day of exploring.

3 Man-O-War Cay

Visiting here is like going back in time. The island has some lovely beaches, and many visitors come here to enjoy them—but it's best to leave your more daring swimwear at home. The people who call this island home are deeply religious and conservative. You won't find any crime—unless you bring it with you. No alcoholic beverages are sold on the island, although you can bring your own supply.

Like New Plymouth on Green Turtle Cay or Hope Town on Elbow Cay, Man-O-War is a Loyalist village, with similarities to a traditional New England town. The pastel clapboard houses, built by ships' carpenters and trimmed in gingerbread, are set off by freshly painted white-picket fences intertwined with bougainvillea.

The people here are shy, but they do welcome outsiders to their remote, isolated island. They are proud of their heritage, which includes a proud boat-building tradition, and many, especially the old-timers, have known plenty of hard times. Many of them are related to the "conchs" of Key West and, like them, are a tough, insular people who have exhibited a proud independence for many years.

Tourism has only just begun to infiltrate Man-O-War Cay. Because of the relative lack of hotels and restaurants, many visitors come over just for the day, often in groups from Marsh Harbour. If you do stay for a while, stop by the Man-O-War Marina to arrange your boat rentals and watersports; there's also a dive shop there.

GETTING THERE & GETTING AROUND

To reach Man-O-War Cay, you must cross the water from Marsh Harbour. **Albury's Ferry Service** (*℗* **242/367-3147** in Marsh Harbour or 242/365-6010 in Man-O-War; www.oii.net/Information/Ferry.html) leaves from a dock near the Abaco Beach Resort. The round-trip same-day fare is $15 for adults and $8 for children ages 6 to 12. The ride takes about 20 minutes.

Except for a few service vehicles, Man-O-War Cay has almost no cars. If you want to explore farther than your own two feet will carry you, ask around and see if one of the locals will rent you a golf cart.

WHERE TO STAY

Schooner's Landing Set in isolation on Man-O-War Cay's northeastern edge, this four-unit apartment complex is the only officially designated place to stay on the island. A seawall separates its lawns and hibiscus shrubs from the crashing surf, so swimmers and snorkelers meander a short distance down to the sands of a nearby beach. Each two-story unit contains a kitchen, ceiling fans, two private bathrooms, a TV, and a summery decor of wicker and rattan furniture. Each comes with a small, tidily kept bathroom with a shower/tub combination. There's no bar or restaurant, but either of two grocery stores on the island will deliver; most visitors opt to cook in, anyway.

Man-O-War Cay, Abaco, The Bahamas. *℗* **242/367-4469** or 242/365-6072. Fax 242/365-6285. www.schooners landing.com. Year-round $275 daily or $1,875 weekly. 3-day minimum stay required. MC, V. **Amenities:** Pool; laundry service; nonsmoking rooms; rooms for those w/limited mobility. *In room:* A/C, ceiling fan, TV, kitchen, microwave, barbecue grill, beverage maker, iron.

WHERE TO DINE

Man-O-War Marina Pavilion ★ *(Finds* AMERICAN/BAHAMIAN The sides of this wooden pavilion are open to the breezes and a view of the boats bobbing at the nearby harbor. A crowd of loyal boat owners and local residents is always here, enjoying the simple but savory cuisine of Marjorie Eldon. Monday to Thursday, the focus is on such time-favored staples as roasted chicken fingers, grilled fish, burgers, fried conch with peas 'n' rice, and steaks. On Friday and Saturday nights, however, many locals arrive for grilled lamb, fish, steaks, or chicken, and the place is practically transformed into a neighborhood block party. Though liquor isn't served, you can BYOB.

Man-O-War Marina, Man-O-War Cay. *C* 242/365-6185. Main courses lunch $3–$11, dinner $11–$26. No credit cards. Mon–Thurs 11am–2pm; Fri–Sat 5:30–8:30pm. Closed Aug 15–Sept 30.

SHOPPING

The most unusual store and studio on the island, **Albury's Sail Shop** (*C* **242/365-6014,** located at the Man-O-War marina) occupies a house overlooking the water at the eastern end. The floor space is devoted to the manufacture and display of an inventory of brightly colored canvas garments and accessories. The 8-ounce cotton duck fabric once served as sailcloth for the community's boats. When synthetic sails came into vogue, four generations of Albury women put the cloth and their talents to use. Don't stop without chatting with them. Hours are Monday through Saturday from 7am to 5pm.

4 Great Guana Cay ⟨★⟩

The longest of the Abaco cays, Great Guana, on the east side of the chain, stretches 11km (7 miles) from tip to tip and lies between Green Turtle Cay and Man-O-War Cay. The beachfront running the length of the cay is spectacular, one of the loveliest in The Bahamas. The reef fishing is superb, and bonefish are plentiful in the shallow bays.

The settlement stretches along the beach at the head of the palm-fringed Kidd's Cove, named after the pirate, and the ruins of an old sisal mill near the western end of the island make for an interesting detour. The island has about 150 residents, most of them descendants of Loyalists who left Virginia and the Carolinas to settle in this remote place, often called the "last spot of land before Africa."

As in similar settlements in New Plymouth and Man-O-War Cay, houses here resemble those of old New England. Over the years the traditional pursuits of the islanders have been boat-building, carpentry, farming, and fishing. It won't take you long to explore the village; it has only two small stores, a one-room schoolhouse, and an Anglican church—and that's about it.

GETTING THERE & GETTING AROUND

Albury's Ferry Service, Marsh Harbour (*C* **242/365-6010** http://oii.net/Information/Ferry.html), runs a four-times-a-day service to Great Guana Cay. A round-trip ticket costs $15 for adults, $8 for children under 11.

Instead of driving around the island, most people get around in small boats. On the cay, boats are available to charter for a half-day or a full day (or a month, for that matter). For example, a 7m (23-ft.) sailboat, fully equipped for living and cruising, is available for charter, and deep-sea fishing trips can be arranged. Try **Island Marine Boat Rentals** (*C* **242/366-0282;** www.islandmarine.com), which rents 5m (17-ft.) Boston Whalers at $100 per day, $90 per day for 3 days, or $560 per week. **Sea Horse Boat Rentals** (*C* **242/367-2513;** www.sea-horse.com), rents 5.4m (18-ft.) Privateers at $150 per day (for rentals of 7 days or more, the cost is $95 per day or $665 for the week). Both establishments are open Monday to Saturday 8am to 5pm. Island Marine is also open on Sunday 8am to noon.

WHERE TO STAY

Dolphin Beach Resort ⚘   Set directly astride one of the best beaches in The Bahamas, a 15-minute walk north of Guana Cay's largest settlement (Guana Village), with miles of powder-soft sand in front of you, this resort offers informal but very comfortable lodgings. Four of the units are in the main house and have queen-size beds and ceiling fans, TVs, small refrigerators, and microwaves; three of them have private screened-in decks with teakwood furniture. The oceanfront cottages (nine in all) also have queen-size beds, ceiling fans, air-conditioning, and full-size kitchenettes with stoves and charcoal grills. Cottages can accommodate between two and four guests, depending on their size. The showers are placed outside but are secluded and screened off by island flora. The place is private, intimate, and laid-back.

There's a restaurant on the premises, Bluewater Grill, with a "conch crawl," a Bahamian take on a lobster tank. Nippers, a beachfront bar and grill, is within a 5-minute walk.

Great Guana Cay, Abaco, The Bahamas (Mailing address: General Delivery, Great Guana Cay, Abaco, Bahamas). ℭ 800/ 222-2646 or 242/365-5137. www.dolphinbeachresort.com. 13 units. Year-round $120–$195 double; $170–$350 cottage. AE, MC, V. **Amenities:** Restaurant; bar; pool; watersports equipment/rentals; limited room service. *In room:* A/C, TV, kitchen, microwave, beverage maker, hair dryer, no phone.

WHERE TO DINE

For fun on the beach, head for **Nippers Beach Bar & Grill,** Great Guana Cay (ℭ **242/ 365-5143;** www.nippersbar.com), a dive where visitors hang out with the locals. Right on the sands, you sit in split-level gazebos and take in the surf, the most stunning seascape in the Abacos, with a snorkeling reef just 11m (36 ft.) offshore. Burgers and well-stuffed sandwiches satisfy your hunger at lunch. But the best time to go is on a Sunday afternoon, for a pig roast with 900 to 1,000 people who gather for food, drinks, and dancing on the beach. One guest is said to have consumed five "Nipper Trippers"—and lived to tell about it. This is the bartender's specialty, a mix of five different rums along with tropical juices. It's lethal. The Sunday pig roast is from 12:30 to 4:30pm and costs $20; other menu items range in price from $9 to $16. The grill is open daily 11:30am to 10pm, the bar 7am to 10pm. American Express, Discover, MasterCard, and Visa are accepted.

5 Treasure Cay ⚘

Treasure Cay now contains one of the most popular and elaborate resorts in the Out Islands. On the east coast of Great Abaco, it boasts not only 5.5km (3½ miles) of spectacular sandy beach, widely recognized as one of the top 10 beaches in The Bahamas, but also one of the finest marinas in the Commonwealth, with complete docking and charter facilities.

Before the tourist complex opened, the cay was virtually unsettled. As a result, the resort has become the "city," providing its visitors, who number in the thousands, with everything they need, including medical supplies, grocery-store items (liquor, naturally), and even bank services. But don't count on these services when you need them. There are no ATMs on the island, and the bank is only open Tuesday and Thursday (and Thurs is payday on the island, so it's impossibly overcrowded). Medical supplies, even solutions for contact lenses, aren't available on the weekends. The real-estate office peddles condos, and the builders predict that they will one day reach a capacity of 5,000 guests. They're hoping that many visitors will like Treasure Cay enough to buy into it.

See "Getting There" under "Abacos Essentials," at the beginning of this chapter, for details on flying to Treasure Cay. Some direct service is available to the island from Florida. You could also fly into Marsh Harbour (see section 1, "Marsh Harbour [Great Abaco Island]," earlier in this chapter) and take a 32km (20-mile) taxi ride north along the paved but bumpy Sherben A. Boothe Highway.

Treasure Cay also hosts one of the most popular fishing tournaments in The Bahamas: the **Treasure Cay Billfish Championship** in May.

GETTING AROUND

Renting a car isn't necessary. To get where you're going, you can walk, bike, take a golf cart or a taxi. Some restaurants outside the resort will even send a shuttle to pick you up from your hotel. Except for moving between the airport or ferry dock and your hotel, you won't need a cab. For details about taxi fares, call the **Treasure Cay Airport Taxi Stand** (© **242/365-8661**). For a special occasion when you need airport pickups or a trip to dinner in style, call **Elegante Limo Service** (© **242/365-8248** or 242/365-8053; $115 an hour for up to 10 passengers); this company also rents golf carts.

The only real reason to rent a car is for the 35-minute drive to **Marsh Harbour** to catch the ferries to **Elbow Cay** and **Man-O-War Cay,** two offshore islands (see above). If you decide you want to do so, you can rent a car for $75 a day at the **Cornish Car Rental** (© **242/365-8623** at the Treasure Cay Airport).

Through **Wendell's Bicycle Rentals** (© **242/365-8687**), across from the bank in the Treasure Cay shopping center, you can rent beach cruisers (single-gear bikes with wide wheels) or mountain bikes (wide-wheeled bikes with multiple gears) for $7 a day or $42 a week. Four-seater electric golf carts go for $40 a day or $245 a week through Wendell's or **Claridge Golf Carts** (© **242/365-8248** or 242/365-8053), just outside town.

WHERE TO STAY

Rooms can be scarce in May when the place is packed with anglers trying to achieve fame in the Treasure Cay Billfish Championship.

In addition to the cay's two main hotels, you can also arrange condo rentals. The best agency for this service is **Bahama Beach Club** (© **800/563-0014** in the U.S. or Canada). A 3-night minimum stay is required, and prices are $300 per night for a two-bedroom unit, $350 a night for a three-bedroom unit, and $400 a night for a four-bedroom unit.

Banyan Beach Club Resort   Heavily damaged by Hurricane Francis in 2004, this resort was closed for most of 2005, but is expected to bounce back and begin receiving guests again in 2006. However, check its status before trying to book here. It doesn't, of course, have the amenities of the much larger Treasure Cay Resort 1km (⅔ mile) away, but it does have a slightly lower price tag and an idyllic location on the white sands of a stunning beach. Each apartment here comes with a kitchenette, streamlined furnishings, and small bathrooms equipped with shower/tub combinations. When it's open and running again, this should be a good place for a tranquil vacation devoted to swimming, reading, and relaxing.

P.O. Box AB 22158, Treasure Cay, Abaco, The Bahamas. © **888/625-3060** or 242/365-8111. Fax 242/365-8112. www.banyanbeach.com. 21 units. Year-round $130–$250 1-bedroom suite; $215–$350 2-bedroom suite. AE, DISC, MC, V. **Amenities:** Bar; 2 pools; watersports equipment/rentals; golf carts for rent; coin-operated laundry; nonsmoking rooms; rooms for those w/limited mobility. *In room:* A/C, TV, ceiling fan, kitchenette, beverage maker, hair dryer, iron.

Treasure Cay Hotel Resort & Marina ⭐   One of the biggest of the Out Island resorts, this property attracts boaters, golfers, fishermen, and divers, as well as yachties and escapists seeking a remote, yet rather luxurious, retreat. The foundation for this resort was laid in 1962, when a group of international investors recognized the potential of the property. The vast majority of the peninsula, as well as the marina facility, all of the villas, 80 privately owned condominiums, the tennis courts, and several blocks of other housing, remains under the ownership of the original investors. Guests can rent electric golf carts (around $35 a day) or bicycles to explore the far-flung palm and casuarina groves of the sprawling compound.

Along with architecture that looks like it jumped off the pages of *House and Garden,* the setting here includes tropical plantings, a spectacular beachfront, an excellent golf course, and marina facilities. Simply furnished in conservatively modern tropical motifs, most accommodations overlook the dozens of sailing craft moored in the marina. The renovated rentals are very attractive, with full kitchens, two bedrooms, and washer/dryers, plus a midsize bathroom with a shower/tub combination.

The restaurant, the Spinnaker, serves standard fare, and two bars dispense tropical drinks.

Treasure Cay, Abaco, The Bahamas. (C) **800/327-1584** or 242/365-8535. Fax 242/365-8801. (Reservations: Treasure Cay Services, Inc., 2301 S. Federal Hwy., Fort Lauderdale, FL 33316; (C) 954/525-7711.) www.treasurecay.com. 96 units. Winter $170–195 double, $315–$385 suite; off season $140–$160, $260–$330 suite. Full board. $60 extra per person per day. AE, DISC, MC, V. **Amenities:** Restaurant; 2 bars; pool; golf course; 6 tennis courts; watersports equipment/rentals; nonsmoking rooms; rooms for those w/limited mobility. *In room:* A/C, TV, dataport, kitchenette, beverage maker, hair dryer, iron.

WHERE TO DINE

Many vacationers stay in accommodations with kitchens or kitchenettes. However, if you know you're never going to feel like cooking, consider purchasing your hotel's meal plan or dine at nearby local restaurants, some of which provide transportation.

You can find rather standard food at the **Beach Bar & Grill** at the Banyan Beach Club ((C) **242/365-8111**), which opens daily from 11:30am to 6pm. Platters of food cost $4 to $8. Another eatery worth checking out is the roadside **Coconut's** on Queen's Highway ((C) **242/365-8885**), which serves typically Bahamian fare, such as grouper and conch along with a few Italian specialties. Main courses range from $15 to $26, and it's open daily from 6 to 9:30pm.

The Spinnaker Restaurant AMERICAN/BAHAMIAN   Serving reliable seafood, steak, pasta, and Bahamian specialties, this resort restaurant at the Treasure Cay Marina has a prime waterside spot. For lunch, the cracked conch makes a good choice. At night, the portions of meat and potatoes or fresh fish (prepared in a variety of ways, from steamed to blackened) are generous. Guests of the Banyan Beach Club, about a half-mile away, usually arrive by golf cart.

On the water in Treasure Cay Marina. (C) **242/365-8469.** Reservations suggested for dinner. Main courses $17–$30. AE, DC, MC, V. Daily 7am–9:30pm. Limited hours in autumn and early winter.

Touch of Class BAHAMIAN   Call ahead for this popular local eatery to send a courtesy van to pick you up at your hotel. Come here when you're ready to try some real Bahamian food, such as fried freshly caught grouper filet with a sauce of tomatoes, sweet peppers, and onions, or tender cracked conch served with a mound of peas 'n' rice. If you can't decide what to order, try to seafood plate, which offers a sampling of grouper, lobster, and conch. Both the Key lime pie and the banana cream pie are luscious desserts.

On Queen's Hwy., a 10-minute drive from Treasure Cay resort. (C) **242/365-8195.** Main courses $16–$28. MC, V. Daily 6–9pm.

BEACHES, WATERSPORTS & OTHER OUTDOOR PURSUITS

The beaches here are blissfully tranquil. Watersports in Treasure Cay are lots of fun, especially highlighted during the Treasure Cay Billfish Championship each spring. And although this area is far less developed than the more popular islands, golfers don't have to head to Nassau or Freeport for a great game. The course here is a big draw.

If you desire a beach with some of the softest, whitest sand you can imagine and water in some of the most amazing shades of blue and green, then **Treasure Cay Beach** 🎖️🎖️ is it. What's especially alluring about this beach is that—unlike eye-catching stretches on busier, more built-up islands—this 5.5km (3½ miles) shore is never crowded.

Treasure Cay Golf Club (☎ 242/365-8535), designed by Dick Wilson, offers 6,985 yards of fairways, though it's hardly the best course this famed golf architect ever designed. Greens fees for hotel guests are $42 for 9 holes and $63 for 18 holes; for nonguests, it costs $58 for 9 holes for and $90 for 18 holes. This is the only golf course in the Abacos, and it lies 1km (⅝ mile) from the center of the resort.

Treasure Cay Marina (☎ 242/365-8250) offers full-service facilities for a variety of watersports. Fishing boats with experienced skippers will guide anglers to tuna, marlin, wahoo, dolphinfish, barracuda, grouper, yellowtail, and snapper. Treasure Cay's own bonefish flats are just a short cruise from the marina. A full day of bonefishing costs $325. A sportfishing boat goes for $425 for a half-day, $550 for a full day. In addition, you can arrange to rent a sailboat, a Hobie Cat, windsurfing boards, and snorkeling gear. The marina has showers, fish-cleaning facilities, daily laundry service, and water and electricity hookups.

Deep-sea fishing is arranged through the reception desk of the **Treasure Cay Hotel Resort & Marina** (☎ 242/365-8535), which will also arrange for you to hire a bonefishing guide. The same resort has six of the best tennis courts in the Abacos, four of which are lit for night games. Fees are $16 hourly for the hard courts or $18 hourly for the clay courts.

Treasure Cay Hotel Resort & Marina (☎ 242/365-8801) also offers six tennis courts—three clay surfaces ($16 an hr.) and three hard surfaces ($14 an hr.)—all lit for night play. Check with the hotel to make arrangements to play.

The best diving is provided by **J.I.C. Boat Rentals & Treasure Divers** (☎ 242/365-8465), which rents equipment and takes scuba divers to some of the best sites in the Abacos with spectacular marine life in all its rainbow-hued glory. Guana Cay, Whale Cay, and No Name Cay are some of the best sites for viewing Bahamian marine life. Divers can also visit the site of the 1865 wreck of *San Jacinto,* a steamship freighter that went down. The cost for any dive is $83. If you're not a serious diver but want a close encounter with the water, call **Rich's** (☎ 242/365-8582) which can take you on $68 snorkeling and island-exploring trips that include a cookout on the beach.

TREASURE CAY AFTER DARK

Fishermen, yachties, and hotel guests head nightly to the **Tipsy Seagull Bar,** Treasure Cay (☎ 242/365-8535), which presents live music sometime after 7pm in winter (off season only on Fri and Sat nights). When there's a fishing tournament on island, this bar is jam-packed. The setting is an A-frame and the decor is nautical memorabilia. Bar patrons who want to hang out can order such treats as pizza and lobster from the resort's adjoining Spinnaker restaurant, which can then be eaten at the bar here. Happy hour is nightly from 5 to 7pm. It's closed in autumn and early winter.

6 Green Turtle Cay (New Plymouth) ★★

Five kilometers (3 miles) off the east coast of Great Abaco, Green Turtle Cay is the jewel of the archipelago, a little island with an uneven coastline, deep bays, sounds, and good beaches, one of which stretches for 1,080m (3,542 ft.). You can roam through green forests, gentle hills, and secluded inlets. The island is 5.5km (3½ miles) long and 1km (⅔ mile) across, lying some 274km (170 miles) due east of Palm Beach, Florida.

Water depths seldom exceed 4.5 to 6m (15–20 ft.) inside the string of cays that trace the outer edge of the Bahama Bank. Coral gardens teem with colorful sea life, making for fabulous snorkeling. Shelling on the lovely beaches and offshore sandbars is among the finest in The Bahamas. If you have a boat, you can explore such deserted islands as Fiddle Cay to the north and No Name Cay and Pelican Cay to the south of Green Turtle Cay.

New Plymouth, at the southern tip of the cay, is an 18th-century settlement that has the flavor of an old New England sailing port. Much of the original masonry was made from lime that was produced when conch shells were broken up, burned, and sifted for cement (records say that the alkali content was so high that it would burn the hands of the masons who used it). Clapboard houses with gingerbread trim line the narrow streets of the little town, which once had a population of 1,800 people, now shrunk to 400. Green Turtle Cay became known for the skill of its shipbuilders, although the industry, like many others in the area, failed after slaves were totally emancipated in The Bahamas in 1838.

Parliament is the village's main street, and you can walk its length in just 10 minutes, passing only by a few clucking hens. Many of the houses have front porches, occupied in the evening by locals enjoying the breezes.

GREEN TURTLE CAY ESSENTIALS

GETTING THERE   Fly to **Treasure Cay Airport,** where a taxi will take you to the ferry dock for departures to Green Turtle Cay (New Plymouth). At the dock, you may have to wait a while for the ferry. It's about a 15- to 20-minute ride to Green Turtle Cay from the dock. The ferry will take you directly to the Green Turtle Club, if you're staying there, or to New Plymouth. This land-and-sea transfer costs $16 per person round-trip.

GETTING AROUND   Although you can walk to many parts of Green Turtle Cay, water is the most common mode of transportation. Many vacationers rent boats, but if you'd rather not, you still have other choices for getting around. Some hotels provide water transport to town or to weekly hotel parties. Most of the island is accessible by foot. The virtually car-free streets of New Plymouth, the quiet 18th-century village by the sea, are prime walking territory. On Green Turtle Cay, golf carts stand in for rental cars. **D & P Rentals** (✆ 242/365-4655) at the Green Turtle Club marina rents theirs for $45 for 8 hours or $60 per day. You can bike all over the island, and pedaling is especially scenic in historic New Plymouth. For $12 a day, **Brendal's Dive Center** (✆ 242/365-4411), at the Green Turtle Club marina, rents cruisers and 10-speeds.

FAST FACTS   First Caribbean International Bank operates a branch (✆ 242/365-4144) open only from 10am to 2pm on Tuesday and Thursday. There is an **ATM** here.

If you need medical attention on **Green Turtle Cay,** visit the government clinic (✆ 242/365-4028) run by a nurse.

You enter Green Turtle Cay's **post office** (🕾 **242/365-4242**) through a pink door on Parliament Street. It has a public telephone. Hours are Monday to Friday from 9am to 5pm.

As for safety, there's no crime in New Plymouth, unless you import it yourself. The little stone jail here makes visitors chuckle. No one can remember when, if ever, it held a prisoner.

SPECIAL EVENTS   One event that draws visitors in droves is the **Green Turtle Club Fishing Tournament,** held in May. In 1984, the winner hooked a 226kg (500-lb.) blue marlin; it was so heavy that the competing participants from other boats generously climbed aboard the winning craft to bring the fish in. For more information, contact one of the Bahamian Tourist Offices or the **Green Turtle Club Hotel** (🕾 **242/365-4271**), which is more or less the official headquarters, when the tournament is held.

WHERE TO STAY

The Bluff House Beach Hotel 🎯

One of the most famous and legendary hotels in the Out Islands, Bluff House originated in the 1950s when it was the private home of C. Pearce Cody III and his wife, Kitty. When friends of their friends asked if they could pay for a few days' stay, the Codys reinvented their home as the first hotel in the Out Islands. They've welcomed some extremely famous guests in the intervening years, including a well-heeled "same time next year" group. Bluff House occupies one of the most desirable pieces of real estate in The Bahamas, 4 hectares (10 acres) on the highest point in the Abacos with panoramic views; it fronts the Sea of Abaco on one side and the sheltered harbor of White Sound on the other. A romantic spot, it has a lovely nautical charm with British colonial overtones. Against a backdrop of palm, oak, and pine-forested jogging trails, it lies within a 5-minute boat ride from the village of New Plymouth.

The hotel offers villas and hotel rooms in a variety of configurations and sizes, either set beside the beach or cantilevered into the steep hillside facing the sheltered harbor; all have lovely views and some have kitchens. The best accommodations are the spacious colonial-style suites, with cathedral ceilings and balconies that overlook the Sea of Abaco. Inside, decor includes floral bed covers and tropical furniture.

Breakfast and dinner are served in the main Club House (p. 227), where drinks and fresh hors d'oeuvres are offered before a candlelit dinner that features local conch, grouper, snapper, and lobster, as well as roast duck a l'orange. The bar/lounge in the hotel's main building is one of our favorite rooms in The Bahamas, with sweeping vistas out across Green Turtle Cay; the blue-and-white, cypress-paneled interior is cozy and comfortable, with simple good taste. Peace and prosperity prevail among nautical memorabilia and a flickering fire within an iron stove as slow-whirling tropical fans, wicker furnishings, and polished wooden floors create an upscale and highly appealing ambience. The bar and grill, the Jolly Roger Bistro, specializes in light meals. Most Thursdays, dinner is served as part of an elaborate beachfront barbecue that's accompanied by music from a live local band (Tues nights only).

Green Turtle Cay, Abaco, The Bahamas. 🕾 **800/745-4911** or 242/365-4247. Fax 242/365-4248. www.bluffhouse.com. 30 units. Year-round $160–$215 double; $150–$265 suite; $225–$340 1-bedroom villa; $315–$445 2-bedroom villa; $415–$565 3-bedroom villa; $500–$800 cottage. MAP (breakfast and dinner) $20 extra per person. AE, DISC, MC, V. **Amenities:** 2 restaurants; 2 bars; pool; tennis court; nonsmoking rooms; rooms for those w/limited mobility. *In room:* A/C, beverage maker, hair dryer, no phone.

Coco Bay Cottages   On the north end of Green Turtle Cay, at a point where 150m (492 ft.) of land separate the Atlantic from the Sea of Abaco, this cottage complex opens onto a beach on the Atlantic side of the island and another sandy beach on the more tranquil bay. It's ideal for those who'd like to anchor in for a while (literally—lots of folks arrive by private boat, which you can moor here free, and otherwise you arrive directly by water taxi from the airport dock). The cottages enjoy a 70% repeat clientele. On 2 hectares (5 acres), dotted with some 50 tropical fruit trees, this ocean-front property features Caribbean furnishings and refreshing pastel colors. The small-est, the honeymoon cottage, sleeps only two in one bedroom. The largest cottage, which can sleep five comfortably, is a two-bedroom, two-bathroom unit with a living room, a dining room, and a fully equipped kitchen with microwave.

The spacious cottages have improved over the years. Linens and kitchen utensils are provided (you can stock up on food and beverages at one of the three grocery shops in New Plymouth), and air-conditioning, ceiling fans, and trade winds cool the rooms. A 1-week minimum stay is required.

P.O. Box AB22795, Green Turtle Cay, Abaco, The Bahamas. ✆ **800/752-0166** or 242/365-5464. Fax 242/365-5465. www.cocobaycottages.com. 4 cottages. Year-round $200–$250. Weekly $1,400–$1,700. MC, V. **Amenities:** Exercise equipment; laundry service; nonsmoking rooms. *In room:* A/C, kitchen, beverage maker, hair dryer, no phone.

Green Turtle Club 🐢🐢   An outstanding place for laid-back luxury, and a bit more elegant than Bluff House, this resort attracts honeymooners and snorkelers. The excel-lent full-service marina and the dive shop on its premises draw serious anglers, boaters, and divers as well. Although the Green Turtle Club sustained heavy damage during the 1999 hurricanes, it immediately undertook major renovations and repair work, emerging in tip-top shape. The waters around the resort are shallow enough to spot schools of fish from the shore—and sometimes you'll even see a green turtle paddling along above the sandbanks. Spread across 32 hectares (79 acres) of low-lying scrub-land, the inn's ambience is very much that of a clubhouse, lodge, and country club. The courteous staff offers assistance yet doesn't intrude on anyone's peace and privacy.

The Green Turtle Yacht Club, host of the prestigious Bahama Cup Around the Island Race, has its base here. It's associated with the Birdham Yacht Club, one of the oldest in England, and with the Palm Beach Yacht Club. Members have their own vil-las right on the water, often with private docks, although temporary guests will be lodged in spacious bungalows (usually two accommodations to a building) set within a gently sloping, carefully landscaped garden. Rooms are among the most upscale and luxurious in the Out Islands. Think England in the Tropics, for the bedrooms boast Sheraton-style mahogany furniture, four-poster beds, French-inspired draperies, oak floors, terra-cotta-tiled patios, and wicker or rattan furniture. Each comes with an immaculate midsize bathroom and almost all contain shower/tub combinations plus generous shelf space.

The flag-festooned bar is the social center of the resort, where there's occasionally live music. There's an unmistakable British note to evenings here, beginning with predinner cocktails beside a roaring fire in the bar's iron stove (in chilly weather only, of course), before everyone adjourns to the pine-paneled dining room for well-pre-pared dinners. Breakfast and lunch are usually served on the veranda.

Green Turtle Cay, Abaco, The Bahamas. ✆ **800/963-5450** or 242/365-4271. Fax 242/365-4272. www.greenturtle club.com. 34 units. Year-round $170–$295 double; $240–$370 suite. Prices higher at Christmas. Children under 12 stay free in parent's room. Extra person $20 per day. MAP (breakfast and dinner) $41 extra per adult, $26 for children under

12. AE, DISC, MC, V. Take a taxi from Treasure Cay Airport to the ferry dock, transfer to a water taxi to the club for a fee of about $10 each way. **Amenities:** Restaurant; 2 bars; pool; watersports equipment/rentals; bike rentals; babysitting; coin-operated laundry; nonsmoking rooms. *In room:* A/C, TV, fridge, beverage maker, hair dryer, iron, no phone.

New Plymouth Inn ⭐ Renovated in 2004, this two-story inn, a mix of New England and Bahamian styles, stands next door to the former home of Neville Chamberlain, the prime minister of Great Britain on the eve of World War II. It's more like a guesthouse or a big B&B than either the Green Turtle Club or Bluff House. In the heart of New Plymouth Village, the inn has colonial charm, a Loyalist history, cloistered gardens, and a patio pool. It was one of the few buildings in town to survive the 1932 hurricane. The inn is run by Wally Davies, an expert diver and swimmer, who has turned New Plymouth Inn into a charming oasis, refurbishing the 120-year-old building with taste and care.

The inn has wide, open verandas, intricate cutout wooden trim, and an indoor A-frame dining room. The comfortable hammock on the front porch is constantly in high demand. The light and airy rooms are kept spotlessly clean; some units are air-conditioned, and each comes with a bathroom containing a shower unit. Many of the same guests have come back every year since the inn opened in 1974.

Out on the veranda, you can smell night-blooming jasmine mixing with fresh-baked island bread. Dinners of fresh native lobster, snapper, conch, and vintage wines are served by candlelight. Roasts, steaks, chops, and imported beer in frosty steins are also part of the menu. The bar and lounge are the social center. Sunday brunch is the most popular on the island.

New Plymouth, Green Turtle Cay, Abaco, The Bahamas. ℂ 242/365-4161. Fax 242/365-4138. 9 units. Year-round $150 double. MAP $25 (breakfast and dinner). MC, V. Closed Sept–Oct. **Amenities:** Restaurant; pool; watersports equipment/rentals; laundry service; rooms for those w/limited mobility. *In room:* A/C, hair dryer, iron, no phone.

WHERE TO DINE

The previously recommended hotels have the best food on the island, but consider one of these local spots as well.

The Club House Restaurant ⭐ INTERNATIONAL You can drop in here at midday for a burger, sandwich, or salad, but a note of elegance emerges at dinner. Start an evening meal off with the cocktail hour at the bar here, which we think is one of the most beautiful and appealing in the Out Islands. Lined with limed cypress, trimmed in cerulean blue, and beautifully proportioned, it includes sweeping views out over two shorefronts from the highest point in the Abacos. Dinner is served within a Queen Anne–style dining room. It's always a set menu, with items that change every night, but the cuisine is invariably excellent. You might start with something like Waldorf salad or smoked salmon, followed by grilled and mango-flavored chicken breast or lobster tail that's simply broiled with lemon and butter. Triple chocolate cheesecake or Key lime pie makes a soothing dessert.

At the Bluff House Club Beach Hotel, Green Turtle Cay. ℂ **242/365-4247.** Reservations required. Lunch platters $8–$20; fixed-price dinners $33 per person. AE, MC, V. Daily 11:30am–2:30pm; hors d'oeuvre service (included in the dinner price) begins at 6:30pm, dinner begins at 7:30pm.

Laura's Kitchen BAHAMIAN/AMERICAN On the main street of town, across from the Albert Lowe Museum, this family-owned spot occupies a well-converted white Bahamian cottage. Laura Sawyer serves up lunch and dinner in a simple, homey decor. The menu changes nightly, depending on what's at the market, but she always serves the old reliables her family has eaten for generations: fried grouper, fried chicken, and a tasty cracked conch. The eatery is mainly known for its burgers: fish burgers, conch burgers, hamburgers, cheeseburgers, and bacon-and-cheese burgers.

King St. © 242/365-4287. Reservations recommended for dinner. Lunch $4–$10; dinner $13–$25. MC, V. Mon–Sat 11am–3pm; daily 6–9pm. Closed Sept and Christmas Day.

Plymouth Rock Liquors & Café BAHAMIAN/AMERICAN   This place has the best selection of wines and liquors for sale in New Plymouth, including at least 70 kinds of rum, plus Cuban cigars. Part of its space is set aside for a pleasant and attractive luncheonette run by hardworking co-owners Kathleen and David Bethell. They serve up tasty sandwiches, split-pea soup, beef souse, and cracked conch with cucumber slices and potato salad. There's also an art gallery on the premises, featuring works by about 50 artists, many of whom specialize in local themes.

Parliament St. © 242/365-4234. Sandwiches and platters $4–$8.50. DISC, MC, V. Cafe Mon–Sat 9am–3:30pm; liquor store Mon–Thurs 9am–6pm, Fri–Sat 9am–7pm.

Rooster's Rest Pub & Restaurant BAHAMIAN   This local dive just beyond the edge of town serves good Bahamian food, including lobster, conch, and your best bet, fresh fish. It's casual through and through, the way The Bahamas used to be; nouvelle cuisine hasn't washed up on these shores yet. All main courses in the evening are served with peas 'n' rice, coleslaw, and potato salad. The cook also prepares some tasty ribs. Live music is offered at least 2 nights a week.

Gilliam's Bay Rd. © 242/365-4066. Reservations recommended for dinner. Lunch burgers and snacks $8–$12; main courses $10–$20. MC, V. Mon–Sat 11:30am–9:30pm.

The Wrecking Tree Bar & Restaurant BAHAMIAN   This funky wooden place is recognized by its coral and terra-cotta colors, and by the much-mangled casuarinas tree that grows next to its foundation. The hearty menu is as simple as can be, featuring mostly peas 'n' rice, conch, grouper fingers, chicken souse, and burgers. Come here for a simple lunch, a midday beer, and a view over the boats in the nearby harbor.

The Harbourfront. No phone. Main courses $13–$15. No credit cards. Mon–Sat 11am–9pm.

BEACHES, WATERSPORTS & OTHER OUTDOOR PURSUITS

Along with sampling Green Turtle Cay's aquatic diversions, you can visit a museum and wander the streets of New Plymouth, the historic waterfront village.

About a 10-minute walk from **Bluff House** and 5 minutes from the **Green Turtle Club, Coco Bay** ✸✸ is one of the most beautiful crescents in The Bahamas. Shaded by casuarina pine trees and lapped by lazy waves, this long beach is often empty. The rougher **Ocean Beach,** about a 10-minute stroll from either Bluff House or the Green Turtle Club, is another stunner. Frothy waves thrash the stark white sand, set off by the intense blue of the Atlantic.

You can take a boat trip to one of the nearby uninhabited islands that are ringed with even more pristine beaches. On **Manjack Cay,** for example, the expanse of sugar-white sand seems to go on forever, and the shallow, clear water is a brilliant shade of turquoise. There's no regular service from the ferry dock; negotiate with one of the local boatmen or hook up with one of the trips offered by **Captain Ray** (© 916/933-3766).

With one of the world's largest barrier reefs, the **Abacos** offers some of The Bahamas' most varied and least crowded (also known as best) snorkeling and diving sites. You can get an eyeful at reefs starting in depths of just 1.5m (5 ft.) and ranging to 18m (59 ft.) and more. Like sheets on a clothesline, sprawling schools of fish billow by coral caverns, huge tube and barrel sponges, and fields of elk and staghorn coral. Sea turtles and large groupers are common sights. In fact, the waters are so clear that you can often see farther than 30m (98 ft.).

Scuba divers can poke around the wreck of the *San Jacinto.* At this American steamship that was built in 1847 and sank 2 decades ago, you can feed the resident bright-green moray eel. Plan to spend about $135 for a scuba resort course, $500 for full certification, $55 for a one-tank dive, and $75 for a two-tank dive.

If you like small groups and big fun, try **Brendal's Dive Center** (© 242/365-4411; www.brendal.com) at the **Green Turtle Club Marina.** Whether you're an experienced diver or snorkeler or you're just getting your feet wet, the personal attention makes the difference here. Originally from **Acklins,** a small Bahamian island to the south, Brendal has more than 2 decades of underwater experience. A special treat for snorkelers is the wild dolphin encounter trip ($75 per person), which includes stops at undisturbed islands. This company also rents kayaks ($10 per hour for singles, $12 per hour for doubles, or $190 a week for the single, $250 for the double). You can also hook up with this activity at **Green Turtle Divers** (© 242/365-4271), which has a full-service dive shop right at the hotel. Both divers and snorkelers get a 15% discount if registered at the hotel.

Call Lincoln Jones at © 242/365-4223, and he'll arrange a snorkeling adventure for you—probably on some deserted beach that only he knows about. Prices are to be negotiated, of course, but a lunch of fresh conch or lobster is a fine addition to any day.

If you've had enough of sitting on the beach and relaxing, you can explore the ocean. From boat rentals to fishing expeditions, Green Turtle Cay offers an array of things to do.

Based at the Green Turtle Club marina, **Brendal's Dive Center** (© 242/365-4411) can take you on a group sunset cruise (complete with rum punch) on a 8.8m (29-ft.) sailboat for $60 per person (up to eight passengers). To see the coral without getting wet, Brendal's hosts glass-bottom boat trips for $50 per person.

Contact **Donny's Boat Rentals** (© 242/365-4119) in **Black Sound** for speedboats. This company rents Whalers and Makos (types of motorboats) starting at $65 a day for a 4.2m (14-ft.) boat. Or try **Reef Rentals** (© 242/365-4145), directly across from the ferry dock in **New Plymouth.** This fleet includes a sleek motorboat made on **Man-O-War Cay,** the nearby island long known for its excellent boat building. Rentals start at $265 for 3 days for a 5.7m (19-ft.) Wellcraft.

Reserving a boat when you make your hotel and airline reservations is a good idea, particularly during the busy spring and summer.

If you want to go deep-sea fishing, the people to see are the Sawyer family, two cousins. Referrals are usually made through the **Green Turtle Club** (© 242/365-4070), or you can call directly at © 242/365-2461. A half-day of fishing costs $250; a full day is $350. These costs can be divided among four people. If you want to go bonefishing, the charge is $140 per half-day or $240 for a full day.

Fishermen from all over the world visit Green Turtle Cay, seeking yellowfin, dolphin (not the mammal), and big game wahoo, among other catches.

The annual **Green Turtle Club Fishing Tournament** (© 800/688-4752 or 242/365-4271) was on hold at press time, but call for information to see whether it's on when you're visiting in May. There's a tennis court at **Bluff House** (© 242/365-4247), where guests play free.

EXPLORING THE ISLAND: A JOURNEY TO THE 18TH CENTURY

New Plymouth celebrated its bicentennial in 1984 by establishing a memorial that honors American Loyalists and also some of their notable descendants, including Albert Lowe, a pioneer boat-builder and historian.

Across from New Plymouth Inn on Parliament Street, the **Memorial Sculpture Garden** honors residents of the Abacos, both living and dead. What blooms at this garden are busts of island notables on stone pedestals. Read about some of the American loyalists who came to The Bahamas from New England and the Carolinas. Statues are also dedicated to their descendants and to those people who were enslaved in these islands. You can see everyone from Albert Lowe (see below)—whose forebears were among New Plymouth's original European American settlers—to African-Bahamian Jeanne I. Thompson, the second woman to practice law in The Bahamas. This garden is laid out in the pattern of the Union Jack flag.

There isn't much shopping here, but consider a visit to the **Ocean Blue Gallery,** adjoining the Plymouth Rock Café on Parliament Street (© **242/365-4234**). This two-room outlet has one of the best collections of local artwork in the Abacos, including some sculptures and some paintings, all originals.

Albert Lowe Museum ★★   More than anything else we've seen in The Bahamas, this museum gives a view of the rawboned and sometimes difficult history of the Out Islands. You can easily spend a couple of hours reading the fine print of the dozens of photographs that show the hardship and the valor of citizens who changed industries as often as the economic circumstances of their era dictated.

There's a garden in the back of this beautifully restored Loyalist home; the caretaker will give you a guided tour of the stone kitchen, which occupants of the house used as a shelter when a hurricane devastated much of New Plymouth in 1932. Inside the house, a narrow stairway leads to three bedrooms that reveal the simplicity of 18th-century life on Green Turtle Cay. Amid antique settees, irreplaceable photographs, and island artifacts, you'll see a number of handsome ship models, the work of Albert Lowe, for whom the museum was named.

The paintings of Alton Lowe, son of the former boat-builder and founder of the museum, are also on display. Cherub-faced and red-haired, Alton is—and has been for a while—one of the best-known painters in The Bahamas. His works hang in collections all over the world; some appears on Bahamian postage stamps, blowups of which are displayed here. Your tour guide might open the basement of the house, as well, where you'll find some of Alton's paintings for sale alongside work by other local artists.

Parliament St. © **242/365-4094**. Admission $5 adults, $2.50 students, free for children 5 and under. Mon–Sat 9–11:45am and 1–4pm.

GREEN TURTLE CAY AFTER DARK

Ask at your hotel if the local Junkanoo band, the **Gully Roosters,** are playing their reggae- and calypso-inspired sounds. They're the best in the Abacos and often appear at various spots on island. Also make sure to visit **Miss Emily's Blue Bee Bar** (described below). You might catch a live band and you'll certainly enjoy a wonderful setting for a drink in the bars at the **Bluff House** and the **Green Turtle Club** (see "Where to Stay," above). **Rooster's Rest Pub & Restaurant** (see "Where to Dine," above) is yet another option.

A much more upscale bar than Miss Emily's is the **Yacht Club Pub** (© **242/365-4271**), at the Green Turtle Club. Along with sailors and fisherman, some of the captains (and the owners) of the world's most expensive yachts stop off here to enjoy the lively

---

Finds **Miss Emily's Blue Bee Bar**

Our favorite bar in the Out Islands is **Miss Emily's Blue Bee Bar,** on Victoria Street in New Plymouth (✆ **242/365-4181**). This simple bar is likely to be the scene of the liveliest party in the Out Islands at any time of day; even normally buttoned-up types find themselves flirting or dancing before long. You never know what will be going on here. Until rising waters from the 1999 hurricanes washed some of them away, most of its walls were covered with the business cards of past guests and celebrities. Only some now remain, but stop by and see how many replacements have been plastered up. The Goombay Smash, a specialty here, has been called "Abaco's answer to atomic fission." Its recipe includes secret proportions of coconut rum, "dirty" rum, apricot brandy, and pineapple juice. Miss Emily (Mrs. Emily Cooper) was a legend in these parts. She's gone now, but her memory lives on: Her daughter, Violet Smith, knows her secret recipe for the Goombay Smash, and makes a potent rum punch. Tips at the bar go to St. Peter's Anglican Church. No food is ever served here, but the bar is open Monday to Saturday from 11am until late.

---

atmosphere and the bartender's special, a Tipsy Turtle, made by the gallon (orange juice, pineapple juice, vodka, coconut rum, banana rum, and grenadine). Appetizers are served nightly from 6:30 to 7:30pm. Live bands are featured on Monday, Wednesday, and Friday nights.

7 Spanish Cay

Set 19km (12 miles) northwest of Green Turtle Cay, this island was named after a pair of Spanish galleons that sank offshore during the 17th century. Originally owned by Queen Elizabeth II, the island was purchased in the 1960s by Texas-based investor (and former owner of the Dallas Cowboys) Clint Murchinson. After his death in the early 1980s, two successive Florida conglomerates poured time, money, and land-scaping efforts into developing the island as a site for upscale private homes. Today, guests of the inn (see below) and local residents putter along the island's paved roads in electric-powered golf carts.

Most visitors arrive by private boat or chartered aircraft from Fort Lauderdale. You can also fly to Treasure Cay from Palm Beach on **Bahamasair** (✆ **800/222-4262** or 242/365-8601; www.bahamasair.com) and have the inn arrange water transportation. Two daily flights arriving here take off from Nassau.

WHERE TO STAY & DINE

The Spanish Cay Resort & Marina ☆   Renovations and improved transportation have made this property better and more accessible than ever. Bedrooms have been improved and completely refurbished to accommodate more than two guests per room. All the suites are roomy and spacious, with a double bed, a foldout sofa bed, and a small refrigerator, plus a tidy bathroom with a shower stall. The apartments, of course, are even more spacious, with both king-size beds and twins in their two bedrooms, plus a full kitchen, living room, dining room, and deck overlooking the marina. A one-bedroom apartment can sleep up to four people; a two-bedroom accommodates six.

Two on-site restaurants (Point House, open daily, and Wrecker's Bar, open in high season) serve conch, chicken, always some kind of fresh fish, steak, and occasionally lobster. Dinners are reasonably priced. You can also get food and drinks at the poolside Tiki Bar.

Cooper's Town, Abaco, The Bahamas. © **888/722-6474** or 954/926-7771. Fax 954/925-8082. www.spanishcay.com. 22 units. Winter $250–$300 double, $450 2-bedroom condo; off season $200–$210 double, $375 2-bedroom condo. MC, V. **Amenities:** 2 restaurants; bar; 4 tennis courts; watersports equipment/rentals. *In room:* A/C, TV, fridge, no phone.

8 Walker's Cay

Lying at the edge of the Bahama Bank, this is the northernmost, the outermost, and one of the smallest islands in the Abaco chain. The cay produces its own fresh water and electricity. Coral reefs surround this island, dropping off to depths of some 300m (984 ft.). It's known around the world as one of the best deep-sea fishing resorts.

Ponce de León reportedly stopped here in 1513 in search of fresh water—just 6 days before he "discovered" Florida. From the 17th century, this was a place known to pirates, who stored their booty here. It became a bastion for blockade-runners during the American Civil War, and later it was a hideout for rumrunners in the days of U.S. Prohibition.

To get here, prospective guests should call the Walker's Cay Hotel and Marina at © **800/WALKERS** and make arrangements for a flight from Fort Lauderdale.

WHERE TO STAY & DINE

Walker's Cay Hotel & Marina ⚓   Established in the 1930s and a legend among sportfishermen ever since, this resort occupies all 41 hectares (101 acres) of a private island that contains the largest and most elaborate full-service marina in the Abacos. Each year, it runs at least two of the country's biggest deep-sea fishing tournaments. Come here for the fishing, for the marina and its charter boats, and for the way that sports permeate the air, but not necessarily for the luxury of the accommodations. Although they benefited from a renovation, these are rather-standard motel-style units. Each accommodation contains a small bathroom with a shower stall. Meals are generally adequate, served in the Lobster Trap and Conch Pearl restaurants; both have bars and offer American/Bahamian fare, chiefly steak and fresh fish.

Walker's Cay, Abaco, The Bahamas (Mailing address: 700 SW 34th St., Fort Lauderdale, FL 33315). © **800/WALKERS** in the U.S. and Canada, or 242/353-1252. Fax 954/359-1414. www.walkerscay.com. Mar 1–Sept 3 $160–$170 double, $425–$475 2-bedroom villa; Sept 4–Feb 28 $130–$140 double, $425–$475 2-bedroom villa; year-round $675 Harbour House. MAP (breakfast and dinner) $40 extra per person. AE, DISC, MC, V. **Amenities:** 2 restaurants; 2 bars; tennis court; babysitting. *In room:* A/C, no phone.

8

Eleuthera

A sort of Bahamian Plymouth Rock, Eleuthera Island was the first permanent settlement in The Bahamas, founded in 1648. A search for religious freedom drew the Eleutherian Adventurers from Bermuda here, to the "birthplace of The Bahamas." The long narrow island they discovered and colonized still bears the name "Eleuthera"—Greek for freedom. The locals call it "Cigatoo."

These adventurers found an island of white- and pink-sand beaches framed by casuarina trees, high, rolling green hills, sea-to-sea views, dramatic cliffs, and sheltered coves, and they're still here, unspoiled, waiting for you to discover today. More than 161km (100 miles) long but merely 3km (2 miles) wide (guaranteeing that you're never far from the beach), Eleuthera is about 113km (70 miles) east of Nassau (a 30-min. flight). The population of 10,000 is largely made up of farmers, shopkeepers, and fishermen who live in old villages of pastel-washed cottages. The resorts here are built around excellent harbors, and roads run along the coastline, though some of them are inadequately paved.

Eleuthera and its satellite islands, **Spanish Wells** and **Harbour Island,** offer superb snorkeling and diving amid coral gardens, reefs, drop-offs, and wrecks. Anglers come to Eleuthera for bottom-, bone-, and deep-sea fishing, testing their skill against the dolphinfish, the wahoo, the blue and the white marlin, the Allison tuna, and the amberjack. Charter boats are available at Powell Point, Rock Sound, Spanish Wells, and Harbour Island. You can also rent Sunfish, sailboats, and Boston Whalers for reef fishing.

Eleuthera rivals the Abacos in terms of popularity among foreign visitors, although boaters are more drawn to the Abacos and the Exumas. Along with the Abacos, Eleuthera has the largest concentration of resort hotels outside of the major developments of Nassau/Paradise Island and Freeport/Lucaya.

We love gorgeous **Harbour Island,** with its charming Dunmore Town, even more than New Plymouth or Hope Town in the Abacos; it's almost a Cape Cod in the Tropics. Of the 10 destinations recommended in this chapter, Harbour Island gets our vote as the number-one choice.

Spanish Wells is another small island just off the north end of Eleuthera. Spanish galleons put sailors ashore to fill the ships' casks with fresh water after long sea voyages—hence the present-day name of the island.

ELEUTHERA ESSENTIALS
GETTING THERE

BY PLANE   Eleuthera has two main airports. **North Eleuthera Airport** (© **242/ 335-1242**), obviously, serves the north along with the two major offshore cays, Harbour Island and Spanish Wells. **Governor's Harbour Airport** (© **242/332- 2321**) serves the center of the island.

Bahamasair (© 800/222-4262; www.bahamasair.com) offers daily flights between Nassau and the three airports, North Eleuthera, Governor's Harbour, and Rock Sound.

In addition, several commuter airlines, with regularly scheduled service, fly from the Florida mainland with either nonstop or one-stop service. Many private flights use the North Eleuthera Airport, with its 1,350m (4,428-ft.) paved runway. It is an official Bahamian port of entry, and a Customs and Immigration official is on hand. **USAir Express** (© 800/428-4322; www.usairways.com) operates what may be the most popular way of reaching two of Eleuthera's airports directly from the mainland of Florida. Flights depart once a day from Miami flying nonstop to North Eleuthera and then continue on, after briefly unloading passengers and baggage, to Governor's Harbour.

Other small carriers include **Twin Air** (© 954/359-8266; www.flytwinair.com), flying from Fort Lauderdale three times a week to Rock Sound and Governor's Harbour and Thursday to Tuesday to North Eleuthera.

BY FERRY   An interisland link, **Bahamas Fast Ferries** (© 242/323-2166; www.bahamasferries.com), originates in Potter's Cay, beneath the Paradise Island Bridge, and fans out at regular intervals to Harbour Island, North Eleuthera, and Governor's Harbour. Round-trip fares are $110 for adults, $70 for children under 12.

BY MAIL BOAT   Several mail boats visit Eleuthera from Nassau, leaving from Potter's Cay Dock. Weather conditions often cause their schedules to change. For details about sailings, consult the dockmaster at **Potter's Cay Dock** in Nassau (© 242/393-1064).

The **MV** *Current Pride* goes from Nassau to Current Island, serving lower and upper Bogue. It departs Nassau every Thursday and returns on Tuesday.

The *Bahamas Daybreak III* departs on Monday for South Eleuthera, stops at Rock Sound, and returns to Nassau on Tuesday. It then leaves from Nassau on Thursday for the Bluff and Harbour Island, with a Sunday return scheduled. The *Eleuthera Express* sails from Nassau to Spanish Wells and Governor's Harbour on Monday and Thursday, and returns to Nassau on Sunday and Tuesday.

GETTING AROUND

It's virtually impossible to get lost on Eleuthera—there's only one road that meanders along the entire length of its snake-shaped form, and you'll stray from it only very rarely. Most visitors take a taxi only when they arrive at one of the local airports or when they have to return to that airport to go home. Taxis meet all incoming flights and are also available at ferry docks. Because cabbies are independent operators on Eleuthera, you can't call one central number. If you need to call a taxi, your hotel staff can summon one for you, but you may have to wait a while, so plan ahead.

You can easily traverse all the settlements—really, hamlets, in most cases—on foot. With little traffic on the island, walking is an enjoyable experience here.

You don't find any American car-rental agencies on the island. Usually, your hotel staff can arrange for a car rental (prices are around $80 a day). Often, we've ended up with someone's private car. The best bet for car rentals is the North Eleuthera-based **Fine Threads Taxi, Rental Cars & Tours** (© 242/359-7780 or 242/335-1556). Here, owner Frederick Neely (nicknamed "Fine Threads" because of his well-tailored clothes) either rents you a car or takes you on a private island tour. An 8-hour experience for two or three people will cost $200, 8 to 12 people, $300. Tours usually begin at 9am and take in a series of bars, restaurants, and geological or historical attractions in Rock Sound, Lower Bogue, Palmetto Point, and Gregory Town. If you negotiate with your driver, you may also visit Preacher's Cave.

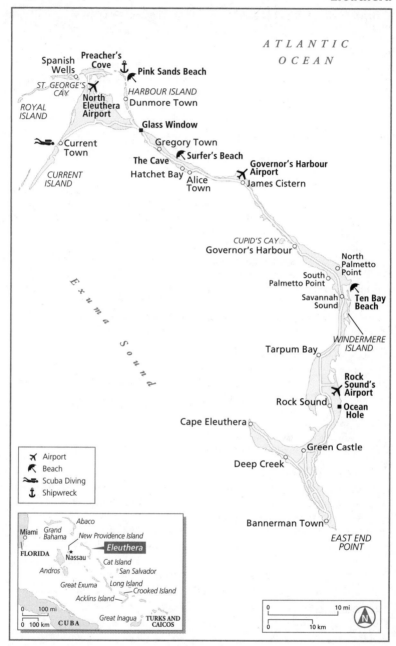

Eleuthera

ATLANTIC OCEAN

Spanish Wells
Preacher's Cove
Pink Sands Beach
ST. GEORGE'S CAY
ROYAL ISLAND
HARBOUR ISLAND
Dunmore Town
North Eleuthera Airport
Glass Window
Current Town
Gregory Town
CURRENT ISLAND
The Cave
Surfer's Beach
Hatchet Bay
Governor's Harbour Airport
Alice Town
James Cistern

E x u m a   S o u n d

CUPID'S CAY
Governor's Harbour
North Palmetto Point
South Palmetto Point
Savannah Sound
Ten Bay Beach
WINDERMERE ISLAND
Tarpum Bay
Rock Sound's Airport
Rock Sound
Ocean Hole
Cape Eleuthera
Green Castle
Deep Creek
Bannerman Town
EAST END POINT

Airport
Beach
Scuba Diving
Shipwreck

Abaco
Miami
Grand Bahama
New Providence Island
FLORIDA
Eleuthera
Nassau
Cat Island
Andros
San Salvador
Great Exuma
Long Island
Crooked Island
Acklins Island
Great Inagua   TURKS AND CAICOS
C U B A

0   100 mi
0   100 km

0   10 mi
0   10 km

1 Rock Sound

Located in South Eleuthera, Rock Sound is a small shady village, the island's main town and once its most exclusive enclave. The closing of two old-time landmark resorts, the Cotton Bay Club and the Windermere Club, has at least for now halted the flow of famous visitors, who once included everybody from the late Princess Diana to a parade of CEOs. No reopenings are yet in sight, but at least that means that you can have many of South Eleuthera's best beaches practically to yourself.

Rock Sound opens onto Exuma Sound and is located to the south of Tarpum Bay. The town is at least 2 centuries old, and it has many old-fashioned homes with picket fences out front. Once notorious for wreckers who lured ships ashore with false beacons, it used to be known as "Wreck Sound."

After leaving Rock Sound, head south, bypassing the Cotton Bay Club, and continue through the villages of Green Castle and Deep Creek. At this point, you take a sharp turn northwest along the only road leading to **Cape Eleuthera.** Locals call this Cape Eleuthera Road, though you won't find any markings other than a sign pointing the way. If you continue to follow this road northwest, you'll reach the end of the island chain, jutting out into Exuma Sound.

Now relatively deserted, Cape Eleuthera was once home to a chic resort and yacht club that drew some of the movers and shakers from America's East Coast, including Richard Nixon and his pal Bebe Rebozo; some of the top golfers in America played its Bruce Devlin–Bob van Haage 18-hole course, which winds its way along the water. They're all gone now, but the splendid **white-sand beaches**—three of them—remain the same, and locals claim the deep-sea fishing is as fine as it ever was.

ROCK SOUND ESSENTIALS

Rock Sound itself boasts a shopping center and a bank—with an ATM—in addition to its airport, but not a lot else. Many residents who live in South Eleuthera come here to stock up on groceries and supplies.

A doctor and four resident nurses form the staff of the **Rock Sound Medical Clinic** (© **242/334-2226**). Office hours are Monday to Friday from 9am to 4:30pm; after that, the doctor is always available to handle emergency cases.

If you need the police, call © **242/334-2244.**

OUTDOOR ACTIVITIES

The only place to play golf in Eleuthera is at the **Cotton Bay Golf Course** designed by Robert Trent Jones, Jr., on the site of the now defunct Cotton Bay Club, Rock Sound (© **242/334-6156;** www.eleu.net/golf.html). This 18-hole, 7,068-yard, par-72 course has attracted some of the most famous players in the world. Even though the Cotton Bay Club is closed itself, many Americans who maintain second homes at Rock Sound

---

Fun Fact **A "Hole" in the Ocean**

The **Ocean Hole,** which is about 2km (1¼ miles) east of the heart of Rock Sound, is said to be bottomless. This saltwater lake that eventually meets the sea is one of the most attractive spots on Eleuthera. You can walk right down to the edge of the water. Many tropical fish can be seen here; they seem to like to be photographed—but only if you feed them first.

still use the course. Regrettably, golf course maintenance isn't what is used to be in the heyday of the resort. Many fairways aren't marked properly, and the restaurant and clubhouse are long gone. The club still has caddies but no more golf carts. The greens fees are $70 for 9 holes or $100 for 18 holes. Reservations are necessary.

WHERE TO STAY & DINE

Sammy's Place BAHAMIAN   Hot gossip and cheap, juicy burgers make Sammy's the most popular hangout in Rock Sound—come here for a slice of local life. Sammy's is on the northeastern approach to the settlement, in a neighborhood that even the owner refers to as "the back side of town." Sammy Culmer (who's assisted by Margarita, his daughter) will serve you drinks (including Bahama Mamas and rum punches), conch fritters, Creole-style grouper, breaded scallops, pork chops, and lobster. If you drop in before 11am, you might be tempted by the selection of egg dishes or omelets.

This is primarily a restaurant and bar, but Sammy does rent four rooms with air-conditioning and cable TV, plus two efficiency cottages containing two bedrooms with a kitchen. The double occupancy accommodations can be yours for $66 per night; cottages cost $100 per night.

Albury's Lane, Rock Sound. ⓒ **242/334-2121.** Breakfast $5–$11; lunch $5–$14; main courses $9–$25. No credit cards. Daily 7:30am–10pm.

2 Tarpum Bay

If you're looking for an affordable vacation on high-priced Eleuthera, head here. This charming waterfront village, some 15km (9⅓ miles) north of Rock Sound, is good for fishing and has a number of simple, inexpensive guesthouses. This tiny settlement with its many pastel-washed, gingerbread-trimmed houses is a favorite of artists, who have established a small colony here with galleries and studios.

Gaulding's Cay, north of town, has a lovely beach with exceptional snorkeling.

WHERE TO STAY

Cartwright's Ocean Front Cottages   Cartwright's is a cluster of simple cottages right by the sea, with fishing, snorkeling, and swimming at your door. This is one of the few places where you can sit on your patio and watch the sunset. The small cottages, most recently renovated in 1996, are fully furnished, with utensils, stove, refrigerator, pots and pans, and maid service provided. Each unit comes with a small bathroom containing a shower stall. You'll be within walking distance of stores and local eateries.

Bay St., Tarpum Bay, Eleuthera, The Bahamas. ⓒ **242/334-4215.** cartwrights@hotmail.com. 3 units. Year-round $100 1-bedroom cottage; $150 2-bedroom cottage; $180 3-bedroom cottage. No credit cards. **Amenities:** Babysitting; laundry service. *In room:* A/C, TV, kitchenette, coffeemaker, iron, no phone.

3 Windermere Island

Windermere is a very tiny island, connected by ferry to "mainland" Eleuthera. It is midway between the settlements of Governor's Harbour and Rock Sound.

This island couldn't be more discreet. "We like to keep it quiet around here," one of the staff at the presently closed Windermere Island Club once told us. Regrettably, that wasn't always possible for this once-deluxe and snobbish citadel. When Prince Charles first took a pregnant Princess Diana here in the 1980s, she was photographed by paparazzi in her swimsuit. Much to the horror of the club, the picture gained worldwide notoriety.

Even without its posh hotel, Windermere Island is worth a day trip. **Savannah Sound,** with its sandy sheltered beaches and outstanding snorkeling, is particularly appealing (bring your own gear). The beaches here are excellent for shelling and picnicking, and offer good bonefishing, with some catches more than 10 pounds.

West Beach, a good place for sunning and swimming (great for children), is about a 10-minute walk from the shutdown Windermere Island Club. The beach is on Savannah Sound, the body of calm, protected water separating Windermere from the main island of Eleuthera.

Visitors can enjoy a number of activities, from bonefishing to windsurfing. The dockmaster at West Beach is well qualified to guide and advise about bonefishing, or perhaps you'd like to go deep-sea fishing for white marlin, dolphinfish, grouper, wahoo, Allison tuna, and amberjack. Since there is no permanent outfitter, you have to ask around locally about who can take you out.

4 Palmetto Point

On the east side of Queen's Highway, south of Governor's Harbour, North Palmetto Point is a little village where visitors rarely venture (although you can get a meal there). This laid-back town will suit you if you want peace and quiet off the beaten track.

Ten Bay Beach ★★ is one of the best beaches in The Bahamas, with its sparkling turquoise water and wide expanse of soft white sand. The beach lies a 10-minute drive south of Palmetto Point and just north of Savannah Sound. There are no facilities, only idyllic isolation.

WHERE TO STAY

Palmetto Shores Vacation Villas   This is a good choice if you want your own apartment and value independence and privacy over hotel services. Asa Bethel rents villas suitable for two to four guests. Units are built in a plain Bahamian-style, with living rooms, kitchens, small bathrooms with shower/tub combinations, and wraparound balconies that open directly onto your own private beach. Furnishings are simple but reasonably comfortable, VCRs are included, and the villas lie within walking distance of local shops and tennis courts.

P.O. Box EL25131, Governor's Harbour, Eleuthera, The Bahamas. ✆ **888/688-4752** or 242/332-1305. Fax 242/332-1305. 15 units. Winter $100–$120 1-, 2-, and 3-bedroom villa; off season $90–$110 1-, 2-, and 3-bedroom villa. Extra person $20–$30 per day summer, $30 per day winter. MC, V. **Amenities:** Watersports equipment/rentals; car-rental desk; babysitting; laundry service; dry cleaning; rooms for those w/limited mobility. *In room:* A/C, TV, kitchen, coffeemaker, iron.

Unique Village   Located on a steep rise above the Atlantic coast of Eleuthera, this hotel is the creative statement of a Palmetto Point businessman who also owns the local hardware store (Unique Hardware). Built in 1992, the hotel offers accommodations in several configurations (everything from conventional single or double rooms to a one-bedroom apartment with a kitchenette to two-bedroom villas with full kitchens). Each comes with a small bathroom with a shower/tub combination. A flight of wooden steps will bring you to the beach, where a reef breaks up the Atlantic surf and creates calm waters on this sandy cove. There's a bar and restaurant, also called Unique Village, on-site (see "Where to Dine," below), but few other luxuries. Although you won't find sailing, scuba, or tennis on-site, the staff can direct you to other facilities that lie within a reasonable drive (you'll probably want a car here).

N. Palmetto Point, The Bahamas. ✆ **800/820-8471** or 242/332-1830. Fax 242/332-1838. www.uniquevillage.com. 15 units. Winter $120–$130 double, $160 1-bedroom apt, $190 2-bedroom apt; off season $90–$100 double, $140 1-bedroom apt, $180 2-bedroom apt. Extra person $25 per day. MAP (breakfast and dinner) $38 per person. FAP $50 per person. MC, V. **Amenities:** Restaurant; bar; free snorkeling equipment; laundry service. *In room:* A/C, TV, kitchenette, coffeemaker, iron.

WHERE TO DINE

Mate & Jenny's Pizza Restaurant & Bar BAHAMIAN/AMERICAN   This restaurant, known for its conch pizza, has a jukebox and a pool table. It's the most popular local joint, completely modest and unassuming. In addition to pizza, the Bethel family will prepare pan-fried grouper, cracked conch, or light meals, including snacks and sandwiches. Lots of folks come here just to drink. Try their Goombay Smash, Rumrunner, piña colada, or just a Bahamian Kalik beer.

S. Palmetto Point, right off Queen's Hwy. (C) 242/332-1504. Pizza $7–$27; main courses $4–$25. MC, V. Mon–Tues and Thurs–Sat 11am–9pm.

Muriel's Bakery ⭐ *Finds* BAHAMIAN   Muriel Cooper's operation runs a bakery and a takeout food emporium. Her rich and moist pineapple and coconut cakes are some of the best you'll find in the Out Islands. Try the rich, moist coconut tarts, pineapple tarts, and lemon pies. Muriel's cakes, including birthday and wedding cakes, cost $20 and up.

N. Palmetto Point. (C) 242/332-1583. No credit cards. Mon–Sat 10am–5pm.

Unique Village Restaurant & Lounge BAHAMIAN/AMERICAN   This is the best place for food in the area, offering the widest selection. You can drop in for a Bahamian breakfast of boiled or stewed fish served with johnnycake, or steamed corned beef and grits ("regular" breakfasts, including hearty omelets, are also available). Lunch offerings include zesty conch chowder and an array of salads. Burgers are served, along with what the kitchen calls "Bahamian belly pleasers," including the steamed catch of the day. At night the choices grow, and you'll find the best New York sirloin available in mid-Eleuthera, ranging in size from 8 to 16 ounces. Cracked conch fried in a light beer batter is one of the better renderings of this dish on the island.

In the Unique Village, N. Palmetto Point. (C) 242/332-1830. Main courses $15–$36. MC, V. Daily 7:30–11am, 11:30am–5pm, and 6–8:30pm.

5 Governor's Harbour

At some 300 years old, Governor's Harbour is the island's oldest settlement, reportedly the landing place of the Eleutherian Adventurers. The largest town on Eleuthera after Rock Sound, it lies midway along the 161km-long (100-mile) island; its airport is likely to be your gateway to the island.

The town today has a population of about 1,500, with some bloodlines going back to the original settlers, the Eleutherian Adventurers, and to the Loyalists who followed some 135 years later. Many old homes line the streets amid the bougainvillea and casuarina trees.

GOVERNOR'S HARBOUR ESSENTIALS

GETTING THERE   See "Eleuthera Essentials: Getting There," at the beginning of this chapter, for details. The town airport is one of the island's major gateways, with daily flights arriving from Nassau and Florida.

VISITOR INFORMATION   The **Eleuthera Tourist Office** is on Queens Highway ((C) 242/332-2142); it's generally open Monday to Friday 9am to 5pm.

FAST FACTS   If you're staying outside the town in a cottage or an apartment, you may find services and supplies in Governor's Harbour or at nearby Palmetto Point.

Governor's Harbour has a branch of **First Caribbean International Bank** on Queen's Highway (📞 **242/332-2300**) with an **ATM.** Hours are Monday to Thursday 9:30am to 3pm and Friday 9:30am to 4:30pm.

The Governor Harbour's Medical Clinic (📞 **242/332-2001**), located on Queen's Highway, is open Monday to Friday from 9am to 5:30pm. The clinic is also the site of a dentist's office. The dentist is here from 9:30am to 3pm, Monday to Wednesday and Friday only. Call for an appointment before going. The Governor Harbour's Medical Clinic also fills prescriptions.

Check with your hotel for Internet access. An Internet cafe has opened on the second floor of the Haynes Library (📞 **242/332-2877**) at Governor's Harbour. The charge is $10 per hour, and the library is open Monday to Saturday 9am to 5pm.

If you need the police, call 📞 **242/332-2111,** Queen's Highway, governor's Harbor police station.

There's a **post office** on Haynes Avenue (📞 **242/332-2060**); hours are Monday to Friday 9am to 4:30pm.

WHERE TO STAY

The Cigatoo Resort 🌟 *Finds*   Yes, that was the Duchess of York ("Fergie") that we spotted on the beach. How did she find this remote tropical complex? Two world travelers, Franco and Katherine Ostini, opened this inn on a hill with panoramic views of the ocean. They try to bring some of the polish of Europe to the laid-back aura of Eleuthera. Nothing much happens here; you create your own amusement. That might be lounging in a deck chair by the freshwater pool or else taking in a view of the tropical gardens. A good sandy beach, ideal for both beachcombing and swimming, is a 5-minute walk away.

Although comfortable and well maintained, the decor of the bedrooms would not seem out of place in Miami in the '60s. Built around the pool, the bedrooms open onto ocean or garden views. Each has a private balcony with chairs. If you're just passing through, consider a stopover here for lunch, as the Bahamian style food is good.

Governor's Harbor (P.O. Box EL25086), Governor's Harbor, Eleuthera, The Bahamas. 📞 800/688-4752 or 242/332-3060. Fax 242/332-3061. 22 units. Winter $113 double; off season $103 double. MC, V. **Amenities:** Restaurant; bar; pool; tennis court; limited room service (7am–10pm); babysitting; self-service laundry. *In room:* A/C, TV, dataport, hair dryer, iron.

Cocodimama Charming Resort 🌟 *Finds*   This charmingly named and private hideaway is set by the water 9.5km (6 miles) north of Governor's Harbour. Built in a modern Bahamian style with verandas, the property opens onto a beach where you can enjoy such sports as kayaking, Hobie Catting, snorkeling, and windsurfing. Scuba-diving trips and deep-sea fishing can also be arranged. The spacious and handsomely furnished bedrooms are spread over a trio of pastel-painted cottages in a tropical garden. Opening onto views, the accommodations are furnished with teak from Bali and Italian ceramics. Each unit is a suite unto itself with a hammock-hung patio. Some of the bedrooms have a comfortable sofa that can be used as a third bed. The owners of the hotel are expatriates from Italy, and the menu reflects their origin along with many Bahamian dishes.

Alabaster Bay (P.O. Box 122), Governor's Harbour, Eleuthera, The Bahamas. 📞 242/332-3150. Fax 242/332-3155. www.cocodimama.com. 12 units. Winter $200–$210 double; off season $170 double. MAP (breakfast and dinner) $60 per person, free for children under 9. MC, V. **Amenities:** Restaurant; bar; watersports equipment/rentals; limited room service; rooms for those w/limited mobility. *In room:* A/C, TV, kitchenette, coffeemaker, hair dryer, iron.

Duck Inn and Orchid Gardens 🌟 *Finds*   The accommodations you'll rent here are larger, plusher, more historic, and more charming than what you'd expect in a conventional hotel. All come with kitchenettes. The complex consists of three clap-board-sided houses, each built between 80 and 175 years ago, and each almost adja-cent to another, midway up a hillside overlooking the sea. Nassau-born John (J.J.) Duckworth and his Michigan-born wife, Katie, along with their son John Lucas, are your hosts. Much of their time is spent nurturing a sprawling collection of beautiful orchids being cultivated for export to Europe and the U.S. Their collection of orchids, some 4,000 strong, is one of the largest in North America.

Queen's Hwy., Governor's Harbour, Eleuthera, The Bahamas. © 242/332-2608. www.duckinncottages.com. 3 units. Year-round $110–$220 cottage. AE, DISC, MC, V. **Amenities:** Babysitting; nonsmoking rooms. *In room:* A/C, TV, kitch-enette, coffeemaker, iron, no phone.

WHERE TO DINE
Pammy's BAHAMIAN   Tile-floored and Formica-clad, this is just a little cubbyhole with a few tables. Lunchtime brings sandwiches, or platters of cracked conch, pork chops, and either broiled or fried grouper. Don't expect anything fancy, because this def-initely isn't. It's a true local joint serving up generous portions of flavor-filled food.

Queen's Hwy. at Gospel Chapel Rd. © 242/332-2843. Reservations accepted only for dinner. Breakfast $3.50–$7; light lunch $5–$10; main courses $14–$20. No credit cards. Mon–Sat 8am–5pm.

HITTING THE BEACH
Near the center of town are two sandy beaches known locally as the **Buccaneer Public Beaches;** they're adjacent to the Buccaneer Club, on the sheltered western edge of the island, facing Exuma Sound. Snorkeling is good here—it's best at the point where the pale turquoise waters near the coast deepen to a dark blue. Underwater rocks shelter lots of marine flora and fauna. The waves at these beaches are relatively calm.

On Eleuthera's Atlantic (eastern) side, about 1km (⅔-mile) from Governor's Harbour, is a much longer stretch of mostly pale pink sand, similar to what you'll find in Harbour Island. Known locally as the **Club Med Public Beach,** it's good for bodysurfing and, on days when storms are surging in the Atlantic, even conventional surfing.

Don't expect any touristy kiosks selling drinks, snacks, or souvenirs at any of these beaches, because everything is very pristine and undeveloped.

GOVERNOR'S HARBOUR AFTER DARK
Ronnie's Smoke Shop & Sports Bar, Cupid's Cay (© 242/332-2307), is the most happening nightspot in central Eleuthera, drawing folks from miles away. You'll find it adjacent to the cargo depot of Cupid's Cay, in a connected cluster of simple buildings painted in combinations of black with vivid Junkanoo colors. Most folks come here just to drink Kalik beer and talk at either of the two bars. But if you want to dance, there's an all-black room just for disco music on Friday and Saturday nights. There's also the only walk-in cigar humidor on Eleuthera. If you get hungry, order up a plate of barbe-cue, a pizza, chicken wings, or popcorn. The place is open daily from 9am until at least 2am, and sometimes 5am, depending on business.

6 Hatchet Bay

Forty kilometers (25 miles) north of Governor's Harbour, Hatchet Bay was once known for a sprawling British-owned plantation that had 500 head of dairy cattle and thousands of chickens. Today, that plantation is gone, and this is now one of the sleepiest villages on Eleuthera, as you can see if you veer off Queen's Highway onto one of the town's ghostly main streets, Lazy Shore Road or Ocean Drive.

WHERE TO STAY & DINE

Rainbow Inn Three kilometers (2 miles) south of Alice Town, and near a sandy beach, the Rainbow Inn is a venerable survivor in an area where many competitors have failed. Quirky and appealing to guests who return for quiet getaways again and again, it's an isolated collection of seven cedar-sided octagonal bungalows. The accommodations are simple but comfortable, spacious, and tidy; each has a kitchenette, lots of exposed wood, a ceiling fan, a small bathroom with a shower unit, and a porch. A sandy beach is just steps away.

One of the most appealing things about the place is its bar and restaurant, a destination for residents far up and down the length of Eleuthera. It's an octagon with a high-beamed ceiling and a thick-topped woodsy-looking bar where guests down daiquiris and piña coladas amid nautical trappings. It has live Bahamian music twice a week and one of the most extensive menus on Eleuthera. The owners take pride in the fact that the menu hasn't changed much in 20 years, a fact that suits its loyal fans just fine. Local Bahamian food includes fish, conch chowder, fried conch, fresh fish, and Bahamian lobster. International dishes feature French onion soup, escargot, and steaks, followed by Key lime pie for dessert. Table no. 2, crafted from a triangular teakwood prow of a motor yacht that was wrecked off the coast of Eleuthera in the 1970s, is a perpetual favorite.

(P.O. Box EL25053), Governor's Harbour, Eleuthera, The Bahamas. © **800/688-0047** in the U.S. or 242/335-0294. Fax 242/335-0294. www.rainbowinn.com. 5 units. Year-round $115–$140 studio; $175–$200 2- or 3-bedroom villa. MAP (breakfast and dinner) $45 extra per person. MC, V. **Amenities:** Restaurant; bar; pool; tennis court; watersports equipment/rentals; car-rental desk; babysitting; laundry service. *In room:* A/C, kitchenette, fridge, coffeemaker.

7 Gregory Town

Gregory Town stands in the center of Eleuthera against a backdrop of hills, which break the usual flat monotony of the landscape. A village of clapboard cottages, it was once famed for growing pineapples. Though the industry isn't as strong as it was in the past, the locals make good pineapple rum out of the fruit, and you can visit the Gregory Town Plantation and Distillery, where it's produced. You're allowed to sample it, and we can almost guarantee you'll want to take a bottle home with you.

WHERE TO STAY

The Cove Eleuthera On a private sandy cove 2.5km (1½ miles) northwest of Gregory Town and 5km (3 miles) southeast of the Glass Window, this year-round resort is set on 11 hectares (27 acres) partially planted with pineapples; it consists of a main clubhouse and seven tropical-style buildings, each containing four units, nestled on the oceanside. In 2004 and 2005, under the leadership of a new owner, all the rooms were upgraded and vastly improved with new decor. Each one has tile floors and a porch, with no TVs or phones to distract you. All accommodations are equipped with a small bathroom that includes a shower stall.

The restaurant (see listing below) serves three meals a day, and the lounge and poolside patio are open daily for drinks and informal meals. Kayaks, bicycles, two tennis courts, and a small freshwater pool compete with hammocks for your time. There's fabulous snorkeling right off the sands here, with colorful fish darting in and out of the offshore reefs.

Queen's Hwy. (P.O. Box GT1548), Gregory Town, Eleuthera, The Bahamas. © **800/552-5960** in the U.S. and Canada or 242/335-5142. Fax 242/335-5338. www.thecoveeleuthera.com. 23 units. Year-round $165–$195 double; $295–$395 suite. MC, V. **Amenities:** Restaurant; bar; pool; 2 tennis courts; watersports equipment/rentals; laundry service; non-smoking rooms. *In room:* A/C, hair dryer, kitchenettes (in some), no phone.

Finds **For a Drop-Dead Pineapple Tart**

Follow the smell of fresh-baked goods to **Thompson's Bakery,** Johnson Street (© **242/335-5053**), which is open Monday to Saturday 8:30am to 6pm. Run by two local sisters, Monica and Daisy Thompson, this simple bakery occupies a wooden lime-green building near the highest point in town. Although it churns out lots of bread—including raisin, whole-wheat, and coconut—every day, its fresh pineapple tarts, priced at $1 each, are among the best we've ever tasted. You might also find fresh-baked doughnuts and cinnamon rolls.

WHERE TO DINE

Cambridge Villas BAHAMIAN   This is one of the few choices in town, occupying a large cement-sided room on the ground floor of a battered hotel (the accommodations aren't as appealing as the restaurant). Harcourt and Sylvia Cambridge, the owners, serve conch burgers, conch chowder, and sandwiches, usually prepared by Sylvia herself. It's just a simple spot, where you might be entertained by the continually running soap operas broadcast from a TV over the bar.

Main St. © **242/335-5080.** Reservations not required. Sandwiches and platters $5–$10. AE, MC, V. Mon–Sat 8am–9pm; Sun 10am–9pm.

The Cove BAHAMIAN/CONTINENTAL   In the previously recommended hotel 2.5km (1½ miles) north of Gregory Town, this spacious dining room is your best bet in the area. It's nothing fancy but good homemade local fare. The restaurant is decorated in a light, tropical style. Lunch begins with the inevitable conch chowder. We recommend you follow it with a conch burger, a generous patty of ground conch blended with green pepper, onion, and spices. Conch also appears several times in the evening, and we think this is the best cracked conch in town, tenderized, dipped in a special batter, and fried to a golden perfection. The kitchen serves the best fried chicken in the area, too.

Queen's Hwy. © **242/335-5142.** Breakfast $6–$8; lunch $8–$18; main courses $16–$30. MC, V. Daily 8–10:30am, 11:30am–2:30pm, and 5:30–9pm.

EXPLORING THE AREA: THE GLASS WINDOW & BEYOND

On Queen's Highway in the heart of town, behind a colorful facade, is the **Island Made Gift Shop** (© **242/335-5369**), with an outstanding inventory that owes its quality to the artistic eye and good taste of owner Pamela Thompson. Look for one-of-a-kind paintings on driftwood or crafted on the soles of discarded shoes, handmade quilts from Androsian fabrics, Abaco ceramics, and jewelry made from pieces of glass found on the beach. There are extraordinary woven baskets from the descendants of Seminole Indians and escaped slaves living in remote districts of Andros Island. Especially charming are bowls crafted from half-sections of conch shells.

Dedicated surfers have come here from as far away as California and Australia to test their skills at **Surfer's Beach,** a couple of kilometers south of town on the Atlantic side. The waves are at their highest in winter and spring; even if you're not brave enough to get out there, it's fun to watch.

South of town on the way to Hatchet Bay are several caverns worth visiting, the largest of which is called simply **the Cave.** It has a big fig tree out front, which the people of Gregory Town claim was planted long ago by area pirates who wanted to conceal the cave because they had hidden treasure in it.

Local guides (you have to ask around in Gregory Town or Hatchet Bay) will take you into the interior of the cave, where the resident bats are harmless (even though they must resent the intrusion of tourists with flashlights). At one point the drop is so steep—about 3.5m (11 ft.)—you have to use a ladder to climb down. Eventually, you reach a cavern studded with stalactites and stalagmites. At this point, a maze of passageways leads off through the rocky underground recesses. The cave comes to an abrupt end at the edge of a cliff, where the thundering sea is some 27m (89 ft.) below.

After leaving Gregory Town and driving north, you come to the famed **Glass Window,** Eleuthera's chief sight and narrowest point. Once a natural rock arch bridged the land, but it's gone now, replaced by an artificially constructed bridge. As you drive across it, you can see the contrast between the deep blue ocean and the emerald green shoal waters of the sound. The rocks rise to a height of 21m (69 ft.). Often, as ships in the Atlantic are being tossed about, the crew looks across the narrow point to see a ship resting quietly on the other side. Hence the name Glass Window. Winslow Homer was so captivated by this spot that he once captured it on canvas.

GREGORY TOWN AFTER DARK

The place to be in Gregory Town, especially on a Saturday night, is **Elvina** on Main Street (✆ **242/335-5032**). Owners Ed and Elvina Watkins make you feel right at home and practically greet you at the door with a cold beer. Surfers and locals alike flock here to chow down on burgers, Bahamian dishes, and Cajun grub, served daily from 10am to "whenever we close." Elvina's husband, "Chicken Ed," is from Louisiana and makes great jambalaya. Live music is played on Tuesday and Friday nights.

8 The Current

The inhabitants of the Current, a settlement in North Eleuthera, are believed to have descended from a tribe of Native Americans. A narrow strait separates the village from Current Island, where most of the locals make their living from the sea or from plaiting straw goods.

This is a small community where the people often welcome visitors. You won't find crowds or artificial attractions. Everything focuses on the sea, a source of pleasure for the visiting tourists, but a way to sustain life for the local people.

From the Current, you can explore some interesting sights in North Eleuthera, including **Preacher's Cave,** where the Eleutherian Adventurers found shelter in the mid–17th century when they were shipwrecked with no provisions. (Note that your taxi driver may balk at being asked to drive there; the road is hard on his expensive tires.) If you do reach it, you'll find a cave that seems like an amphitheater. The very devout Eleutherian Adventurers held religious services inside the cave, which is pierced by holes in the roof, allowing light to intrude. The cave is not far from the airport, in a northeasterly direction. Another sight is **Boiling Hole,** which is in a shallow bank that seems to boil at changing tides.

WHERE TO STAY

Sandcastle Apartments For escapists seeking a location far removed from the usual tourist circuit, this utterly plain but airy accommodation is a good bet. The on-site kitchen, the easy access to a simple grocery store within a 5-minute walk, and the self-contained nature of this extremely modest accommodation often appeal to families. Each bedroom has a double bed, a queen-size pullout bed in the living room, and a view over shallow offshore waters, where children can wade safely for a surprisingly long distance offshore. The accommodations each have a small bathroom with a shower stall and lie just across the road from the sea; if you want to explore, bicycles are available for $5 per day.

The Current, Eleuthera, The Bahamas. © 242/335-3244. Fax 242/393-0440. 2 units. Year-round $75–$90 double. Extra person $8 per day. No credit cards. **Amenities:** Nonsmoking rooms. *In room:* A/C, coffeemaker.

9 Harbour Island ★★★

One of the oldest settlements in The Bahamas, founded before the United States was a nation, Harbour Island lies off the northern end of Eleuthera, some 322km (200 miles) from Miami. It is 5km (3 miles) long and 1km (⅔-mile) wide. The media have hailed this pink-sand island as the new St. Bart's, a reference to how chic it has become. If you're jogging along the beach, you might trip over a movie star.

Affectionately called by its original name, "Briland," Harbour Island is studded with good resorts. The spectacular **Pink Sands Beach** ★★★ runs the whole length of the island on its eastern side. The famous beach is protected from the ocean breakers by an outlying coral reef, which makes for some of the safest swimming in The Bahamas. Except for unseasonably cold days, you can swim and enjoy watersports year-round. The climate averages 72°F (22°C) in winter, 77°F (25°C) in spring and fall, and 82°F (28°C) in summer. Occasionally, evenings are cool, with a low of about 65°F (18°C) from November to February.

HARBOUR ISLAND ESSENTIALS

GETTING THERE   To reach Harbour Island, take a flight to the **North Eleuthera airstrip,** which is only a 1½-hour flight from Fort Lauderdale or Miami and a 30-minute flight from Nassau (see "Eleuthera Essentials," at the beginning of this chapter, for details on which airlines provide service). From there, it's a 1.5km (1-mile) taxi ride to the ferry dock. The taxi costs about $4 per person if you share the expense with other passengers. From the dock, you'll take a 3km (2-mile) motorboat ride to Harbour Island. There's usually no waiting, because a flotilla of high-powered motorboats makes the crossing whenever at least two customers show up, at a cost of around $5 per person. (If you're traveling alone and are willing to pay the $8 one-way fare, the boat will depart immediately, without waiting for a second passenger.)

Another way you can get to Harbour Island is to board a speedy 177-passenger catamaran in Nassau. Contact **Bahamas Fast Ferries** (© 242/323-2166). You can begin this 2-hour trip at **Potter's Cay Dock,** which is under the bridge leading from Paradise Island to downtown Nassau. The fare for one of these daily excursions is $110 round-trip or $65 one-way for adults, and $70 round-trip or $45 one-way for children ages 2 to 11. This ferry pulls up to Harbour Island's Government Dock, where taxis wait to take you to your hotel.

GETTING AROUND   Once they reach Harbour Island, most people don't need transportation. They walk to where they're going, rent a bicycle (check your equipment carefully before you rent it, because some bicycles rented to tourists on Harbour Island are way past their prime), or putt-putt around the island on an electric golf cart. Most hotels offer these for rent, or at least will arrange for a cart or bicycle; usually, they'll be delivered directly to your hotel.

Michael's Cycles on Colebrook Street (© 242/333-2384) is the best place to go if you want some mobility other than your own two feet. The shop is open daily from 8am to 6pm. Bikes rent for $12 per day, and you can also rent two-seater motorbikes for $30 a day, or even a four-seater golf cart for $48 per day. You can also rent kayaks for $40 per day, paddle boats for $40 per day (or $10 per hour), or jet skis for $85 per hour.

VISITOR INFORMATION   The **Harbour Island Tourist Office** is on Dunmore Street (© **242/333-2621**); it's generally open Monday to Friday 9am to 5pm.

FAST FACTS   The Royal Bank of Canada is on Dunmore Street (© **242/333-2250**). Hours are Monday to Thursday 9:30am to 3pm and Friday 9:30am to 4:30pm.

The Harbour Island Health Centre, South Street, Dunmore Town (© **242/333-2227**), handles routine medical problems. Hours are Monday through Friday from 9am to 5pm. The on-call doctor can be reached at © **242/333-2822.**

Resorts usually have Internet access. Arthur's Bakery, located in the center of town, also offers it. You can use the computer there or bring your own laptop. Hours are Monday to Saturday 8am to 2pm, costing $10 for 15 minutes.

You can get prescriptions filled at **Briland's Pharmacy** (© **242/333-3427**), located at Johnson's Plaza, Dunmore Street. Hours are Monday to Saturday 9am to 5pm.

The post office (© **242/333-2215**) is on Gaol Alley, and it's open Monday to Friday 9am to 5:30pm.

The police can be reached at either © **919** or © **242/333-2111.**

WHERE TO STAY
VERY EXPENSIVE
Dunmore Beach Club ⭐   This formal and exclusive colony of cottages is the quintessentially elegant hideaway, with 3.2 hectares (8 acres) of well-manicured grounds along the island's legendary 5km (3-mile) pink-sand beach. It's not as elaborate or sleek as its nearest rival, Pink Sands, but it's cozier if not in a bit of decline. Renovations brought some of the units up to standard with huge showers and whirlpool tubs. The Bahamian-style bungalows attractively combine traditional furnishings and tropical accessories, with no phones or TVs to distract you. The Dunmore's heyday may have come and gone, but the feeling here is still dignified, comfortable, and pleasant.

Breakfast is offered on a garden terrace under pine trees with a view of the beach. Dinner is served, at one sitting, at 8pm; men must wear jackets (ties are optional). Bahamian and international cuisine is served formally in a dining room with a beamed ceiling, louvered doors, expensive china, and windows with views over the blue Atlantic. A clubhouse is the focal point for socializing; a living room with a library and fireplace provides additional cozy nooks, as does an oceanview bar.

Colebrook Lane (P.O. Box EL27122), Harbour Island, The Bahamas. © **877/891-3100** or 242/333-2200. Fax 242/333-2429. www.dunmorebeach.com. 15 units. Winter $499–$579 double, $649–$749 suite, $1,500–$1,600 house. Off season $470–$530 double, $599–$699 suite, $1,000–$1,500 house. Winter rates include all meals. MC, V. **Amenities:** Restaurant; bar; tennis court; bike rentals; babysitting; laundry service; nonsmoking rooms; rooms for those w/limited mobility. *In room:* A/C, minibar, hair dryer, safe, no phone.

Pink Sands ⭐⭐⭐   This is a posh and sophisticated hideaway, just the place to sneak away to with that special (wealthy) someone, adjacent to a 5km (3-mile) stretch of pink-sand beach, sheltered by a barrier reef. Yes, that was Julia Roberts in a bikini we spotted leaving the cottage next door. It's an elegant, relaxed retreat on an 11-hectare (27-acre) beachfront estate; it feels a bit like a pricey private club, but it's less snobbish and a lot more hip than the Dunmore Beach Club. Its owner is Chris Blackwell, the founder of Island Records, who is increasingly known as a hotel entrepreneur and who spared no expense here. The resort's outrageous clubhouse is the most beautifully and imaginatively decorated room in the Out Islands.

The airy, spacious bedrooms have either an ocean or a garden view. Smaller units contain Art Deco touches straight out of Miami's South Beach; larger, more expensive units have Indonesian (especially Balinese) furnishings and art, and huge decks. All rooms have kitchenettes or kitchens, central air-conditioning, pressurized water systems, walk-in closets, satellite TVs, CD players and a CD selection, wet bars, private patios with teak furnishings, and beautifully tiled bathrooms with tubs and showers. The interior design features marble floors with area rugs, oversize Adirondack furnishings, local artwork, and batik fabrics. The rooms have dataports, and fax machines and cellular phones can be supplied if you need them.

Hotel guests get some of the best meals on the island, an ABC fusion of Asian, Bahamian, and Caribbean cuisine. Dinner is a four-course nightly affair, included in the MAP (breakfast and dinner) price for guests and priced at $70 per person, without drinks, for nonguests who phone ahead for reservations. Lunches are much less formal, served in the Blue Bar, a postmodern pavilion beside the beach.

Chapel St., Harbour Island, The Bahamas. © **800/OUTPOST** or 242/333-2030. Fax 242/333-2060. www.islandout post.com/PinkSands. 25 units. Winter $655–$765 1-bedroom cottage, $1,150–$2,100 2-bedroom cottage; off season $525–$635 1-bedroom cottage, $975–$1,400 2-bedroom cottage. Rates include MAP (breakfast and dinner). AE, MC, V. **Amenities:** 2 restaurants; 2 bars; pool; 3 tennis courts; health club; limited room service; babysitting; laundry service; nonsmoking rooms. *In room:* A/C, TV, dataport, kitchenette or kitchen, minibar, wet bar, coffeemaker, hair dryer, iron/ironing board, safe, CD player (and CDs).

EXPENSIVE

Coral Sands 𝘢𝘢 *Kids*   The hotel, whose exterior is painted a soft coral pink, stands on 3.6 hilly hectares (9 acres) overlooking the beach and within walking distance of the center of Dunmore Town, which is in a British Colonial style. This is one of the most consistently reliable hotels on island, avoiding the glitter of some of the more volatile properties. It also opens onto one of the best beach locations, and is a favorite of families, whereas some of the posher resorts don't really cater to children. Coral Sands is a longtime favorite that does a big business with happy repeat visitors. Originally built with an airy design that featured big-windowed loggias and arcades, it opens directly onto the 5km (3-mile) pink-coral-sand beach for which the town is famous. Casual elegance, with ample doses of personal charm and friendliness, permeates every aspect of this hotel. Improvements have revitalized the property and freshened up the decor. Many rooms have private verandas or terraces, all are eminently comfortable, and all allow you to fall asleep to the soothing sounds of waves breaking on the shore. Bathrooms are midsize and well kept, mostly with shower/tub combos. The latest series of restored rooms are on the second floor of the complex in the Caribe building. They have been converted into luxury one-bedroom deluxe oceanview suites, some with two bathrooms, others with one bathroom. All of these suites have a bedroom facing the ocean plus a separate living room with sofa.

The hotel's restaurant, The Poseidon, offers fine cuisine. Simpler, less elaborate food is also offered at the beachfront Commander's Beach Bar & Restaurant, which is dramatically cantilevered high above the pale pink sands.

Chapel St., Harbour Island, The Bahamas. © **800/468-2799** in the U.S. and Canada or 242/333-2350. Fax 242/333-2368. www.coralsands.com. 39 units. Winter $235–$560 double, $585 1-bedroom suite; off season $175–$470 double, $525–$535 1-bedroom suite. MAP (breakfast and dinner) $55 extra per person. 3-night minimum stay. AE, MC, V. **Amenities:** Restaurant; bar; pool; tennis court; watersports equipment/rentals; babysitting; laundry service; nonsmoking rooms; rooms for those w/limited mobility. *In room:* A/C, TV (in some), kitchen, coffeemaker, hair dryer, safe.

Rock House Hotel ★★★ *Finds*   After months of rebuilding, this hotel (originally an unpretentious B&B) reopened in a lavishly augmented format that thrust it into the spotlight as one of Harbour Island's most glamorous and stylish inns. The force behind the restoration was two partners who included J. Wallace Tutt, a building contractor who had designed buildings, for among others, Cher and Versace.

Set on a low bluff above the harbor, in the center of Harbour Island's only village, and painted a pale shade of yellow, it combined the original, 1940s-era B&B and an adjoining site that had functioned for several decades as a Catholic schoolhouse. Today, the complex combines the kind of aesthetic you might have expected in a hip enclave of Miami, and incorporates a stylish (and separately recommended) restaurant. Nine of the most whimsical accommodations on Harbour Island are found here. Each is outfitted with a name and a decorative style that's unique from each of its neighbors. Examples include the Monkey Room, the Palm Room, the Asian Suite, the Citrus Room, the Pineapple Room, and the Parrot Room. The resort's social center is its bar, and the lavishly landscaped confines of its swimming pool, which is lined with the kind of tentlike cabanas that you might have expected along the coast of Sardinia.

Bay and Hill sts., Harbour Island, Eleuthera, The Bahamas. © 242/333-2053. Fax 242/333-3173. www.rockhouse bahamas.com. 9 units. Year-round $275–$395 double; $480–$655 suite. AE, DC, MC, V. No children under 18 accepted. **Amenities:** 2 restaurants; 2 bars; pool; gym/exercise room; limited room service (7am–10:30pm); laundry service; all nonsmoking rooms. *In room:* A/C, TV, dataport, minibar, safe.

Runaway Hill Club   Small and intimate, this conservative, comfortable hotel overlooks acres of pink sandy beachfront. It has a huge lawn and is separated from Colebrook Street by a wall. The building's original English colonial dormers are still prominent, as are many of its original features. In winter, a crackling fire is sometimes built in the hearth near the entrance. The social center is a cheerfully decorated lounge/dining room/bar/reception area painted in joyful island colors with a sense of Bahamian whimsy. Each of the bedrooms is different, giving the impression that you are lodging in a private home—as indeed this used to be. Only two of the rooms at this place are in the original house, and these are accessible via the building's original 18th-century staircase. The others are within comfortable annexes built during the '70s and '80s. Bathrooms are small but well maintained, and seven contain tub/shower combos, the rest showers.

Dinners are served on the breeze-filled rear porch overlooking the swimming pool, and nonguests are welcome (see "Where to Dine," below).

Colebrook St. (P.O. Box EL27031), Harbour Island, The Bahamas. © 800/728-9803 in the U.S., or 242/333-2150. Fax 242/333-2420. www.runawayhill.com. 10 units. Year-round $375–$425 double; $450 villa. MAP (breakfast and dinner) $120 extra per person. MC, V. Closed Sept 5–Nov 15. **Amenities:** Restaurant; bar; pool; watersports equipment/rentals; bike rentals; laundry service. *In room:* A/C, hair dryer, safe, no phone.

MODERATE

The Landing ★★   This intimate inn is understated, tasteful, and lovely. Virtually destroyed by a hurricane in 1999, it was well restored by its owners. India Hicks, the daughter of the famed London decorator, David Hicks, has taken over, drawing much of England to Harbour Island. She is the granddaughter of Lord Mountbatten of Burma (grandson of Queen Victoria), and was a bridesmaid to the Princess of Wales at her wedding to Charles. The first doctor on Harbour Island built the house in the 1850s as his private residence. It's set within a pair of stone- and clapboard-sided buildings constructed in 1800 and 1820, respectively, very close to the piers where ferryboats arrive from Eleuthera. A veranda looks out over the harbor. Accommodations

---

Finds Ma Ruby's Conch Burger

If you'd like to sample some real local fare, head to **Ma Ruby's** on Colebrook Street (© **242/333-2161**). Some islanders claim you will get the best meal in Eleuthera if Ma Ruby (the cook and owner) is personally in the kitchen. Her conch burger is certainly worthy of an award. She's been stewing chicken, baking grouper, and serving hearty meals in a trellised courtyard for a long time, and she's got a lot of devoted fans. The place is well known for its cheeseburgers, which the manager says were ranked as one of the 10 best in the world by "Mr. Cheeseburger in Paradise" himself, Jimmy Buffett. The prices range from $5 to $15 for the a la carte menu; a four-course fixed-price Bahamian dinner costs $15 to $45. The restaurant is open daily 8am to midnight.

---

are breezy, airy, and high ceilinged, and they open onto wraparound verandas, which seem to expand the living space within. Expect bold, cheerful island colors, and design touches that evoke the seafaring days of old Harbour Island. The bathrooms are large and tiled, with tubs and showers.

Bay St. (P.O. Box 190), Harbour Island, The Bahamas. © **242/333-2707**. Fax 242/333-2650. www.harbourisland landing.com. 7 units. Winter $226–$325 double; off season $198–$275 double. Rates include breakfast. MC, V. **Amenities:** Restaurant; bar; babysitting; nonsmoking rooms. *In room:* A/C, hair dryer, no phone.

INEXPENSIVE

Bahama House Inn ★ *Finds*   This is the only authentic B&B, with the owners living on-site, on Harbour Island. The setting is a pink-sided clapboard house that was built between 1798 and 1800 by the island's first justice of the peace, Dr. Johnson. In 1999, Denver-born owners John and Joni Hersh bought a 1950s-era house next door for future expansions. Midsize rooms are artfully old-fashioned, low-key, and comfortable, and they are usually accessible via gracious verandas that wrap around the upper and lower floors. Bathrooms are tiled, beautifully maintained, and come with shower stalls. Everything shows a personal touch here, including the beautiful gardens. The beach is a 5-minute walk away, and the house's living room has satellite TV.

At the corner of Dunmore and Hill sts., Harbour Island, The Bahamas. © **242/333-2201**. Fax 242/333-2850. www. bahamahouseinn.com. 7 units. Winter $140–$185 double; off season $115–$160 double. Rates include breakfast. MC, V. Closed Aug–Sept. Children under 12 not accepted. **Amenities:** Restaurant; bar; laundry service; rooms for those w/limited mobility. *In room:* A/C, hair dryer, safe, no phone.

Tingum Village   This is a simple, no-frills choice, but it does the trick at bargain prices and draws a loyal repeat business. It lies just off the main street, a 3-minute walk to the beach. Set in a steamy tropical garden, Tingum Village offers basic accommodations in small cement-sided bungalows. Each of the rooms has air-conditioning, ceiling fans, and a patio with plastic furniture, plus a small bathroom with a shower stall. Rooms aren't the most comfortable, and you'll really wish they'd improve the wattage in the reading lamps, and that the ceiling fans wouldn't squeak. But it has its charming moments as well. The cottage is meant for six to eight people, though it can hold up to 10 (but that would be very cramped).

The hotel's restaurant, Ma Ruby's, overlooks the garden and offers standard Bahamian and American food (see listing below).

Colebrook St. (P.O. Box 61), Harbour Island, Eleuthera, The Bahamas. © **242/333-2161**. Fax 242/333-2161. 19 units. Winter $115–$150 double, $135 triple, $160–$175 1-bedroom suite, $200–$250 2-bedroom suite, $250–$300 cottage;

off season $100–$135 double, $120 triple, $145–$160 1-bedroom suite, $185–$235 2-bedroom suite, $235–$285 cottage. MC, V. **Amenities:** Restaurant; bar; limited room service; babysitting; laundry service; nonsmoking rooms; rooms for those w/limited mobility. *In room:* A/C, kitchenettes, coffeemaker (in some), hair dryer (in some), no phone.

WHERE TO DINE

If you don't want to dress up for lunch, you can head for **Seaview Takeaway** (© 242/ 333-2542), at the foot of the ferry dock. Here you can feast on all that good stuff: pig's feet, sheep-tongue souse, and most definitely cracked conch. Everything tastes better with peas 'n' rice. Daily specials range from $3 to $8, and service is Monday to Saturday 8am to 5pm.

EXPENSIVE

The Landing ★ AUSTRALIAN/INTERNATIONAL   This restaurant occupies the ground floor and most of the garden of the previously recommended hotel, a stately looking antique building that's just to the right of the dock as your ferryboat pulls into Harbour Island. Designed and built with a combination of thick stone walls and clapboards in 1800, with an annex that's only 20 years younger, it's the domain of India Hicks (see listing above).

The menu changes with the availability of fresh ingredients. You might begin with an arugula salad with shaved Parmesan cheese, or else steamed stone crab and shrimp wrapped in a lettuce leaf with a tamarind-flavored broth. Among the more delectable main courses are seared scallops with cucumber and chilled rice noodles, or else braised pork belly with soy, ginger, and star anise flavors. A spicy Thai-inspired green chicken curry is served with jasmine-scented rice.

Bay St. © 242/333-2707. www.harbourislandlanding.com Reservations recommended. Main courses lunch $12–$24, dinner $20–$40. MC, V. Sun 8am–2pm; Thurs–Tues 6:30–10:30pm.

Rock House Restaurant ★★ INTERNATIONAL   Set on a covered terrace that overlooks the boats bobbing at anchor in the harbor, within the previously recommended hotel, this restaurant is the showcase of Harbour Island's newest and perhaps most stylish hotel. Inside, there's a feeling of a hip bodega in Miami, lots of varnished mahogany, pale yellow walls, spinning ceiling fans, and in addition to the table groupings for groups of two and four diners at a time, a very large "chef's table" with 16 chairs, originally reputed to have been among the furnishings in Washington, D.C.'s White House before a long-ago refurbishment. Lunches are charming but, at least in terms of gastronomy, rather simple affairs, with dishes that include burgers, rock lobster salad sandwiches, and conch chowders. Dinners are more elaborate and more of a showcase for the chef. The best menu items include "Ying-yang" soup, crafted from roasted red and yellow peppers with smoked mozzarella and chili oil; chicken with Asian noodles and a tahini-flavored aioli; crab cakes served with a confit of sweet peppers and Béarnaise sauce; grilled lobster tail with clarified butter; and tiger-shrimp spaghetti with local goat cheese, peppers, and parsley. Especially flavorful is a crispy pan-fried "almost de-boned" chicken breast with a citrus-flavored herb sauce.

In the Rock House Hotel, Bay and Hill sts. © 242/333-2053. www.rockhousebahamas.com. Reservations recommended. Main courses lunch $15–$24, dinner $36–$55; Fri night buffet $35. AE, DC, MC, V. Daily noon–4pm and 6:30–10pm.

Runaway Hill Club ★ BAHAMIAN/AMERICAN/INTERNATIONAL   The dining room here enjoys a sweeping view over the beachfront. Inside, the decor is brightly painted in strong, whimsical colors, with wicker and rattan furniture and a fine collection of watercolors the owner has spent years collecting. The kitchen is known for such well-prepared dishes as rack of veal with a sherry-flavored caper sauce and noodles, conch marinara, crabmeat soup with scotch, scallops in sherry sauce, spicy lobster bisque, beef tenderloin, and many versions of local fish.

Colebrook St. ✆ 242/333-2150. www.runawayhill.com. Reservations required. Fixed-price dinner from $60. AE, MC, V. Mon–Sat dinner at 8pm. Closed Sept 5–Nov 15.

MODERATE

The Harbour Lounge
INTERNATIONAL   This old clapboard-sided building is the first place you're likely to see as you step off the ferryboat arriving from the "mainland" of Eleuthera. Built in the early 1800s, it's one of the most satisfying and authentic choices on the island. Sometimes dining here is like attending an island dinner party. The menu has included such items as marinated blackened grouper, soft-shell or stone crabs, lobster tail, different preparations of conch, and a combination of feta cheese and shrimp marinara. Overall, it's a charming place, and the veranda will give you a front-row seat for all the goings-on of Harbour Island.

Bay St. ✆ 242/333-2031. Reservations recommended for dinner. Lunch salads, sandwiches, platters $10–$22; dinner main courses $10–$38. MC, V. Tues–Sun 11:30am–3pm and 6–9:15pm.

Restaurant Sip Sip ★ Finds
BAHAMIAN/MEDITERRANEAN   The only problem with this restaurant is that it's locked tight, except for large parties, every evening, preferring to focus on lunch instead. Set on a dune, close to both the Ocean View Guest House and the Dunmore Beach Club, it was built in 2003 in a traditional, green-painted clapboard-sided design evocative of Harbour Island buildings that are a lot older. Inside, the cuisine is the product of the Bahamian/American couple Jim Black and Julie Lightbourne, who met in Africa while Jim was working in the safari business. Within a brightly painted blue and mostly green interior, with mahogany doors, windows, and bartops, you'll find a changing menu that, depending on the whim of the owners, might focus on Bahamian, Italian, French, Thai, or Pacific Rim cuisine. The menu might include, for example, hummus with grilled pita bread; conch chili (a welcome variation on conch chowder), fresh salads made with tomatoes and buffalo mozzarella, baba ganoush, the eggplant specialty that originated in Lebanon; quesadillas, including a version stuffed with lobster, shrimp, and tropical fruit salsa, and a flavorful version of curried chicken salad studded with chunks of apple and served with mango chutney. Grouper filets, prepared in at least two different ways, are usually available as well. The restaurant's name, incidentally, translates from local patois as "gossip."

Court St. ✆ 242/333-3316. Reservations not necessary. Main courses $11–$15. MC, V. Wed–Mon 11:30am–4pm. Closed Wed June–Nov.

INEXPENSIVE

Angela's Starfish Restaurant
BAHAMIAN/AMERICAN   This is the local joint where many of the islanders go themselves, and it serves the most authentic Eleutherian cuisine. Residents as well as visitors plan their Sunday around an evening meal here, although it's equally crowded on other nights. Run by Bahamians Angela and Vincent Johnson, the house sits on a hill above the channel in a residential section somewhat removed from the center of town. Angela can often be seen in the kitchen baking. Cracked conch and an array of seafood are specialties, and chicken potpie and pork chops are also favorites. You can dine on the palm-dotted lawn with its simple tables and folding chairs, although for chilly weather there's an unpretentious dining room inside near the cramped kitchen. It can get quite festive at night, after the candles are lit and the crowd becomes jovial.

Dunmore and Grant sts. ℂ **242/333-2253**. Reservations required. Breakfast $6–$12; lunch $5–$10; dinner main courses $13–$25. No credit cards. Daily 7:30am–8:30pm.

Avery's Restaurant & Grill BAHAMIAN/AMERICAN   From the moment you enter, you get the sense that this is a simple, friendly, family-run restaurant. It occupies a tiny wooden house, painted in tones of orange and yellow, near Tingum Village. Inside, you'll find a clean, white-tiled room with no more than four tables, and a deck with three more. Mariah Campbell and her daughter, Murieta, are the owners. Their breakfasts provide nourishment to city employees around town. The rest of the day, sandwiches and platters of seafood and steaks emerge steaming from the kitchens in an unending stream.

Colebrook St. ℂ **242/333-3126**. Reservations not accepted. Breakfast and lunch platters $7–$18; dinner main courses $25–$30. No credit cards. Daily 6:30am–3pm and 6–10pm.

BEACHES, WATERSPORTS & OTHER OUTDOOR PURSUITS

Pink Sands Beach ✵✵✵ is our favorite beach in all The Bahamas; its sands stretch for 5 uninterrupted kilometers (3 miles). Although the beach is set against a backdrop of low-rise hotels and villas, it still feels tranquil and pristine. The sun is best in the morning (afternoons start to become shadowy), and waves are generally gentle, owing to an offshore reef that breaks the waves coming in from the Atlantic. Many places are good for snorkeling, and this beach is also the best place on the island for a long, leisurely morning stroll.

The **diving** in this part of The Bahamas is among the most diverse in the region. The most spectacular dive site, judged among the 10 top dives in the world, is the **Current Cut Dive** ✵✵✵. One of the fastest (9 knots) drift dives in the world, it involves descending into the fast-moving current racing between the rock walls that define the underwater chasm between Eleuthera and Current Island. Swept up in the currents with schools of stingrays, mako sharks, and reef fish, divers are propelled along 1km (⅔ mile) of underwater distance in less than 10 minutes. The dive may be one of the highlights of your whole life.

Valentine's Dive Center, Harbourfront (ℂ **242/333-2080;** www.valentines dive.com), maintains a full range of dive activities. The dive center is in a wooden building near the entrance to Valentine's Marina. Lessons in snorkeling and scuba diving for beginners are given daily at 10am. Snorkeling from a boat costs $35 for a half-day tour. A full certification course for scuba is taught for $650. Single-tank dives, daily at 1:30pm, cost $55; two-tank dives go for $75 daily at 9:30am; and night dives (four divers minimum) are $70 per person.

You can rent a motorboat through **Michael's Cycles** (ℂ **242/333-2384** or 242/464-0994) on Colebrook Street near Seagrapes nightclub. Plan to spend about $65 for a half-day or $75 for a full day on a 4m (13-ft.) boat and $100 for a half-day or $150 for a full day on a 5m (16-ft.) boat. Kayaks here go for $40 a day.

You can make arrangements for fishing guides and charters through your hotel or by contacting **Valentine's Dive Center** (ℂ **242/333-2080**), on the harbor side of the island in Dunmore Town. Deep-sea fishing trips start at $550 for a half-day or $750 for a full day.

EXPLORING THE ISLAND

Dunmore Town, located on the harbor side of Harbour Island, was named for the 18th-century royal governor of The Bahamas who helped develop it and had a summer home here. You can walk around the narrow, virtually car-free lanes here in less than

20 minutes, or stroll slowly to savor the sight of the old gingerbread cottages that line the waterfront. Overhung with orange, purple, and pink bougainvillea, white picket fences enclose wooden houses painted pastel blue, green, and lilac. Wind chimes tinkle in front of shuttered windows. Coconut palms and wispy casuarina pines shade grassy yards.

Americans and Canadians own some of these houses, which have whimsical names, such as "Up Yonder" and "Beside the Point," instead of house numbers. One of the oldest, **Loyalist Cottage,** was built in 1797. It survives from the days when the original settlers, loyal to the British Crown, left the American colonies after the Revolutionary War. The porches along the harbor make for prime sunset watching. Lucky for you, some porches aren't connected to private homes. The terrace at Harbour Lounge Bar and Restaurant is an idyllic perch. Just across the road from Loyalist Cottage, you can browse through straw goods, T-shirts, and fruits and vegetables at the vendors' stalls.

On Sundays, dressed-up residents stand in sociable clusters outside churches before and after services. Two of The Bahamas' first churches are found in Dunmore Town and are still going strong: **St. John's,** The Bahamas' oldest Anglican church, established in 1768, and **Wesley Methodist Church,** built in 1846.

Spend some time wandering the streets—some hilly, some flat—away from the heart of town. You can see roosters doing their jerky marches through front yards and horses grazing in small fields. You'll find unassuming but perfectly good Bahamian restaurants, bars, and nightclubs in this locals' area.

SHOPPING

Miss Mae's, Dunmore Street (© 242/333-2002), lives up to its billing. It's one of the island's finest clothing boutiques.

Briland's Androsia, King Street (© 242/333-2342) sells the best selection of bathing suits, with bright batik fabrics printed on the island of North Andros.

Blue Rooster, in the center (© 242/333-2240), along with the Shop at the Landings (see below) offers what might be the most upscale and stylish collection of men's and women's clothing and (casual) evening wear on the island. Come here for something sporty and trim-looking to wear into a posh hotel's dining room, especially if the New Englandish, button-down look appeals to you. **The Shop at the Landing,** at the Landing Resort (© 242/333-2707), usually wins as the most stylish clothing store on the island. It focuses on stylish and wearable sportswear and things you might wear to a casual island cocktail party, a posh brunch, or a buffet dinner aboard a yacht.

Finally, check out **Princess Street Gallery** (© 242/333-2788), where Charles Carey has restored an ancestral home and uses it as a showcase to display works by local artists.

HARBOUR ISLAND AFTER DARK

Unpretentious **Gusty's,** Coconut Grove Avenue (© 242/333-2165), boasts sweeping sea and sunset views. Inside, you'll find a sand-covered floor, while the outdoor veranda is sometimes the scene of fashion shows of local dressmakers. Live music by a DJ is featured every night.

Seagrapes, Colebrook Street (no phone), is another favorite place of the locals, where you can boogie down to the sounds of disco or catch a live band. Expect to be jostled and crowded on a Saturday night, because everyone on the island comes here for a wild Bahamian hoedown.

Vic-Hum Club, Barracks Street (© 242/333-2161), established in 1955, is the quintessential Harbour Island dive. Walls have been layered with the covers of hundreds of record albums and sports posters that music-industry and basketball buffs find fascinating. The Vic-Hum is open 24 hours a day, catering to breakfasting construction workers in the morning, and locals meeting friends for a beer all afternoon. Some of them play basketball on an indoor court that's transformed later in the evening into a dance floor (disco music begins at 10pm every Fri and Sat).

10 Spanish Wells

Called a "quiet corner of The Bahamas," Spanish Wells is a colorful cluster of houses on St. George's Cay, 1km (⅔ mile) off the coast of northwest Eleuthera. Here, you'll find sparkling bays and white beaches, sleepy lagoons, excellent diving, and fine fishing colony.

You can walk or bicycle through the village, looking at the houses, some more than 200 years old, which have New England saltbox styling but bright tropical coloring. You can see handmade quilts in many colors, following patterns handed down from generations of English ancestors. Homeowners display these quilts on their front porches or out their windows, and they are for sale. No one locks doors or removes ignition keys from cars.

GETTING THERE

To reach the island, you can fly to the **airstrip on North Eleuthera,** from which taxis will deliver you to the ferry dock. Regardless of the time of day you arrive, a ferryboat will be either waiting for passengers or about to arrive with a load of them.

A ferry (© **242/554-6268**) runs between Gene's Bay in North Eleuthera to the main pier at Spanish Wells. The ferries depart whenever passengers show up, and the cost is $10 per person round-trip.

WHERE TO STAY

The Adventurer's Resort   This is your only choice for lodging in Spanish Wells. It occupies a two-story, pale lavender-colored building in a well-tended garden about .5km (⅛ mile) west of the town center. A staff member will direct you to the beach, which lies about 1km (⅔ mile) away. The small bedrooms have simple, durable furniture with tropical upholstery; six of the units are apartments with kitchenettes. Each comes with a shower/tub combination. Maid service is provided when you rent the regular double room, but not the apartments.

Harbourfront (P.O. Box El 27498), Spanish Wells, The Bahamas. © **242/333-4883.** Fax 242/333-5073. www.bahamas vg.com/adventurers.html. 22 units. Year-round $75 double; $130 1-bedroom apt, $190 2-bedroom apt. MC, V. **Amenities:** Watersports arrangements; room service; coin-operated laundry; nonsmoking rooms. *In room:* A/C, TV, kitchenette, coffeemaker, iron, no phone.

WHERE TO DINE

Anchorage BAHAMIAN   Although you won't find Spanish Wells written up in any gourmet books, you can dine well here if you stick to locally caught fish and the like. The island is known for its *langoustes* (small Bahamian lobsters), and this is what you should order if featured on the menu. Locals also grow their own tomatoes, onions, and pineapples. Decent, unpretentious, and well scrubbed, this little eatery serves such home-cooked Bahamian style items as cracked conch or grouper fish fingers. For dessert, try one of the cook's mud pies.

Along the waterfront at the port in Spanish Wells. **242/333-4023.** Reservations required Sat–Sun. Main courses $12–$22. No credit cards. Mon–Sat 9am–1:30pm; daily 5–10pm.

9

The Exumas

The Exumas are some of the prettiest islands in The Bahamas. Shades of jade, aquamarine, and amethyst in deeper waters turn to transparent opal near sandy shores: The water and the land appear almost inseparable. Sailors and their crews like to stake out their own private beaches and tropical hideaways, and several vacation retreats have been built by wealthy Europeans, Canadians, and Americans.

A spiny, sandy chain of islands, the Exumas begin just 56km (35 miles) southeast of Nassau and stretch more than 161km (100 miles) from Beacon Cay in the north to Hog Cay and Sandy Cay in the south. These islands have not been developed like the Abacos and Eleuthera, so they are relatively inexpensive. But they still have much to offer, with crystal-clear waters on the west around the Great Bahama Bank, the 1,500m-deep (4,920-ft.) Exuma Sound on the east, uninhabited cays ideal for picnics, rolling hills, ruins of once-great plantations, and coral formations of great beauty. Although they're crossed by the Tropic of Cancer, the islands have average temperatures ranging from the mid-70s to the mid-80s (mid- to upper 20s Celsius).

Most of our resort recommendations are in and around George Town, the pretty, pink capital of the Exumas, on Great Exuma. A community of some 900 residents, it was once considered a possible site for the capital of The Bahamas because of its excellent **Elizabeth Harbour** (see "Exploring George Town," later).

Nearly all the other cays are uninhabited or sparsely populated. Over the years, remote accommodations have come and gone on these islands. Today, the only resort hotels, which attract mostly the yachting set, are found at Staniel Cay and Sampson Cay.

The cruising grounds around the Exumas, which are scattered over an ocean area of 233 sq. km (91 sq. miles), are among the finest to be found in the Western Hemisphere, if not in the world, for both sail- and powerboats. The **sailing** rivals both those of the Grenadines in the Caribbean and the Abacos in The Bahamas. Which yachters prefer depends on personal taste; each is paradise if you're a boater. If you don't come in your own craft, you can rent one here, from a simple little Daysailer to a fishing runabout, with or without a guide. The annual regatta in April in Elizabeth Harbour has attracted such notables as Prince Philip and the ex-king of Greece, Constantine. The Exumas are often referred to by yachting people as "where you go when you die if you've been good."

Snorkeling and scuba-diving opportunities draw aficionados from around the world to the **Exuma Cays National Land and Sea Park** ★★★, a vast underwater preserve, and to the exotic limestone and coral reefs, blue holes, drop-offs, caves, and night dives. Dive centers in George Town and Staniel Cay provide air fills and diving equipment.

Fishing is superb here, and the "flats" on the west side of Great Exuma are famous for bonefishing. You can find (if you're lucky) blue marlin on both sides of Exuma Sound, as well as sailfish, wahoo, and white marlin, plus numerous others.

> **Finds Saddle Cay: The Perfect Beach**
>
> For years boaters have known of a special beach, **Saddle Cay,** whose horseshoe-shaped curve lies near the northern tip of the small archipelago. The only way to reach it is by private boat; there are no organized excursions or tours (the Exumas are much too laid-back for that). However, if you own a boat, head for Saddle Cay, and you won't be disappointed when you see this totally unspoiled beach of white sands and tranquil waters. The cay is perfect for beachcombers, bird-watchers, and snorkelers—but don't expect facilities.

The Exumas are among the friendliest islands in The Bahamas; the people are warmhearted and not (yet) spoiled by tourism. They seem genuinely delighted to receive and welcome visitors to their shores. They grow a lot of their own food, including cassava, onions, cabbages, and pigeon peas, on the acres their ancestors worked as slaves. Many fruits grow on the cays, including guavas, mangoes, and avocados. At Government Wharf in George Town, you can watch these fruits being loaded for shipment to Nassau. The sponge industry is being revived locally; this product of the sea is found in shallow waters and creeks to the south side of the Exumas.

EXUMAS ESSENTIALS
GETTING THERE

BY PLANE   The Exumas' major commercial airport—the **Exuma International Airport**—is 16km (10 miles) from George Town, the capital. The most popular way to visit the Exumas is to fly there aboard **Bahamasair** (© 800/222-4262; www.bahamasair.com), which has twice daily service from Nassau to George Town. The first flight usually leaves Nassau in the morning sometime around 6:20am, depending on the day. The second flight is at 4pm. Be sure and call ahead because flight schedules are subject to change.

American Eagle (© 800/433-7300; www.aa.com) serves Exuma from Miami three times a day.

Other minor carriers servicing the archipelago include **Lynx Air International** (© 888/596-9247; www.lynxair.com), on Thursday, Friday, and Sunday, with air links from Fort Lauderdale.

For flights to the private airstrip at Staniel Cay, refer to section 3 of this chapter.

BY BOAT   There is now a motorized catamaran making the 8-hour transit from Nassau. It arrives in George Town every Monday and Wednesday at 7:30pm. It departs Georgetown on Tuesday and Thursday. The cost of a round trip is $90 per person. Technically designed for the transport of building supplies and freight, it nonetheless allows passengers as well, many of whom stretch out on the deck in sleeping bags. There are no sleeping compartments on board. For information, call **Bahamas Fast Ferry** at © 242/323-2166.

Several **mail boats** leave from Potter's Cay Dock in Nassau, stopping at various points along the Exumas.

Two separate mail steamers, the **MV Grand Master** and the **Captain C,** sail from Nassau several days a week, stopping at Big Farmer's Cay, Staniel Cay, Black Point, George Town, and Barraterre. Stopovers including George Town last no more than a few hours.

The Exumas

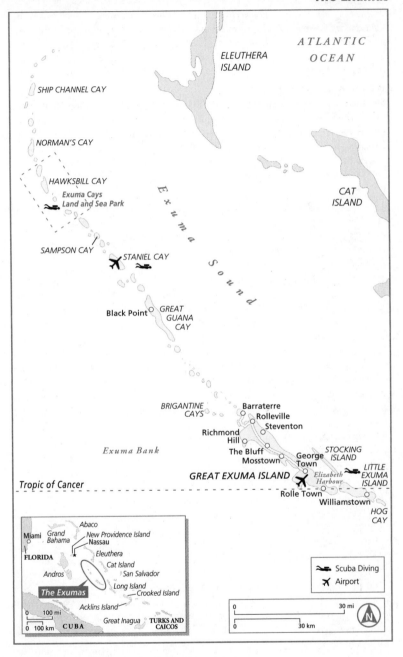

ATLANTIC OCEAN

ELEUTHERA ISLAND

SHIP CHANNEL CAY

NORMAN'S CAY

HAWKSBILL CAY

Exuma Cays Land and Sea Park

CAT ISLAND

SAMPSON CAY

STANIEL CAY

E x u m a   S o u n d

Black Point

GREAT GUANA CAY

BRIGANTINE CAYS

Barraterre

Rolleville

Steventon

Richmond Hill

Exuma Bank

The Bluff

Mosstown

George Town

STOCKING ISLAND

GREAT EXUMA ISLAND

Elizabeth Harbour

LITTLE EXUMA ISLAND

Tropic of Cancer

Rolle Town

Williamstown

HOG CAY

Abaco

Miami Grand Bahama New Providence Island

Nassau

FLORIDA

Eleuthera

Cat Island

San Salvador

Andros

Long Island

The Exumas

Crooked Island

Acklins Island

Great Inagua **TURKS AND CAICOS**

0 100 mi

0 100 km **CUBA**

Scuba Diving

Airport

0   30 mi

0   30 km

N

Passengers as well as small amounts of freight are allowed on board. It usually takes about 21 hours for either of the ships to make the full-circuit itinerary described above.

Since hours and sailing schedules are subject to change because of weather conditions, it's best to check with the dockmaster at **Potter's Cay Dock** in Nassau (© **242/393-1064**).

GETTING AROUND

After your arrival at the airport in George Town, chances are you'll meet Kermit Rolle. Kermit, who runs things up in Rolleville, knows as much about the Exumas as anyone else (maybe more). You can stop in at **Kermit's Airport Lounge,** from 7am to 5:30pm, Exuma International Airport (© **242/345-0002**), which is just across from the airport terminal building. If you're lucky, Kermit will be free, and you can negotiate a deal with him to take you in his car for a tour.

BY TAXI If your hotel is in George Town, it will cost about $25 to get there in a taxi from the airport. Rides often are shared. If you're going on to **Stocking Island,** an islet in Elizabeth Harbour, make prior arrangements with your hotel for boat transfers. The island has only a few taxis, and most of them wait at the airport. Hotels can usually get you a taxi if you need to go somewhere and don't have a car. Otherwise, for a taxi, call **Leslie Dames** at © **242/357-0015.**

BY CAR It's also possible to rent a car during your stay, though the major North American companies aren't represented here. Try **Exuma Transport,** Main Street, George Town (© **242/336-2101**). They have cars to rent for $60 per day and up, or $300 per week. A $200 deposit is required. Your hotel can also usually arrange a rental car for you through a local firm.

The George Town area has two gas stations: one near Exuma International Airport and the other in Farmers Hill. They're generally open Monday to Saturday 8am to 5pm, Sunday 8am to noon, and on holidays 8 to 10am.

BY BOAT For ferries between George Town and the beaches on Stocking Island, call **Club Peace & Plenty** at © **242/336-2551.** With departures twice a day, the ferries are complimentary to Club Peace & Plenty guests. If you're not staying at that hotel, the cost is $8 round-trip and free for children under age 10.

BY BIKE A bicycle is a pleasant way to get around Exuma. To rent one, contact **Starfish Activity Center** in George Town (© **242/336-3033**). Mountain and cruiser bikes run $10 for 2 hours, $15 for a half-day, $20 for a full day, and $100 per week. Those rates include a helmet and a map. Starfish Activity Center also hosts guided bike tours.

BY FOOT George Town is designed for strolling, but don't expect sights that scream tourist attraction. This is a handsome little waterfront village where browsing at the tree-shaded straw market, sampling fresh conch salad at the dock, and mingling with residents and fellow vacationers over drinks and home-style meals are the big draws. The most idyllic walk is around **Lake Victoria.**

Shuttle service is provided to town from **Peace & Plenty Beach Inn,** or you can walk the scenic mile. If you don't succumb to wheels, you can leisurely enjoy glimpses of the turquoise and neon blue water through the wispy casuarina pines and bushy coconut palms lining **Queen's Highway.** "Highway" is a serious overstatement, so walking here is fine as traffic is sparse.

1 George Town

The Tropic of Cancer runs directly through George Town, the capital and principal settlement of the Exumas, located on the island of Great Exuma. This tranquil seaport village opens onto a 24km-long (15-mile) harbor. George Town, partly in the Tropics and partly in the temperate zone, is a favorite port of call for the yachting crowd.

If you need to stock up on supplies, George Town is the place to go, as it has more stores and services than any other spot in the Exumas. There are dive centers, marinas, markets, a doctor, and a clinic. The town often doesn't bother with street names, but everything's easy to find.

GEORGE TOWN ESSENTIALS

GETTING THERE   Flights from Nassau and Miami come into nearby Exuma International Airport, 16km (10 miles) away. See the beginning of this chapter for details on airlines and taxis.

FAST FACTS   A branch of the **Bank of Nova Scotia,** Queen's Highway (© **242/336-2651**), is open Monday to Thursday 9:30am to 3pm, on Friday 9:30am to 4:30pm. It has an ATM.

For information about the Exumas, go to the Ministry of Tourism Office in Exuma (© **242/336-2457**), on Queens Highway, across from the Exuma Market. It is open daily from 9am to 5pm.

If you come to the Exumas aboard your own boat, **Exuma Docking Services,** Main Street, George Town (© **242/336-2578**), has slips for 52 boats, with water and electricity hookups. There's a restaurant on the premises, and you can replenish your liquor stock from the store here. They also have a laundromat, fuel dock, fuel pumps, and a store with supplies for boats and people.

The government-operated **medical clinic** can be reached by phone at © **242/336-2088.** Go here to have a prescription filled. To call the **police** in George Town, dial © **242/336-2666,** but only for an emergency or special services.

The **Post Office** lies in the Government Building in George Town and is open Monday to Friday 9am to 4:30pm. For **Internet access,** check with your hotel. You can also go to the **ABC Exuma Internet Café** at the Exuma International Airport (© **242/345-6038**).

SPECIAL EVENTS   In April, the **Family Island Regatta** (© **954/475-8315** for more information) draws a yachting crowd from all over the world to Elizabeth Harbour. It's a rollicking week of fun, song, and serious racing when the island sloops go all out to win. It's said that some determined skippers bring along extra crewmen to serve as live ballast on windward tacks, and then drop them over the side to lighten the ship for the downwind run to the finish. The event, a tradition since 1954, comes at the end of the crawfish season.

WHERE TO STAY

VERY EXPENSIVE

Four Seasons Resort Great Exuma at Emerald Bay ★★★ (Kids)   The quiet Exumas emerged from a sleep of centuries with the official opening of this resort in the winter of 2004. Its sweeping ocean vistas and tropical beauty frame an experience unique in this part of the world; the Out Islands have seen nothing like this in their history, and the resort is expected to change the entire character of the archipelago.

(**Finds**   **Life on a Houseboat**

The most offbeat way to live in the Exumas is on a brightly decorated floating houseboat. Each boat is like a hotel suite that can be used to explore Elizabeth Harbour and the coast of the Exumas. In between moving your
houseboat from anchorage to anchorage, you can go fishing, snorkeling,
scuba diving, or beachcombing. Each houseboat is fully equipped, sleeping six
to eight, with air-conditioning, hot and cold running water, a marine radio,
an inflatable dinghy, a fully equipped galley, all linens, purified water, and a
propane barbecue grill. Boats range from a one-bedroom 11m (36-ft.) to a
two-bedroom 13m (43-ft.). It doesn't take a special license or even much experience to operate one of these boats. For reservations, contact **Bahamas
Houseboats** (P.O. Box EX29031, George Town, Exuma, The Bahamas; ⓒ **242/
336-BOAT;** fax 242/336-2629; www.bahamahouseboats.com). Weekly rentals
range from $1,895 to $2,600, with a security deposit of $500 required. Amer-
ican Express, MasterCard, and Visa are accepted.

All accommodations here open onto private terraces and balconies with scenic views
of the bay. You're given a choice of rooms, from generously proportioned gardenview
units to oceanview rooms opening directly onto the bay. For the big spender, the resort
also offers a series of executive suites and beachfront properties of one and two bedrooms.

So much goes on at this resort that you may never get around to exploring the surrounding islands. The most spectacular feature is a championship 18-hole golf course
designed by Greg Norman. The full-service spa and health club is the finest in The
Bahamas, and you can swim at either the hotel's crescent-shaped white-sand beach or
in one of two pools. Currently, the best marina in the Southern Bahamas is being
reconstructed here. And the cuisine is among the best in the Out Islands, with both
indoor and outdoor dining options and a selection of Italian, Caribbean, Bahamian,
and international dishes.

Emerald Bay, Great Exuma, The Bahamas. ⓒ **800/819-5053** in the U.S. or Canada or 242/366-6800. Fax 242/336-6801.
www.fourseasons.com. 183 units. Winter $495–$775 double, $800–$1,100 suite; off season $250–$450 double, from
$550 suite. AE, DC, DISC, MC, V. **Amenities:** Restaurant; bar; 2 pools; golf course; 6 tennis courts; gym; spa; sauna; water-
sports equipment/rental; children's programs; business center; salon; 24-hr. room service; babysitting; laundry service;
dry cleaning; nonsmoking rooms; rooms for those w/limited mobility. *In room:* A/C, TV, dataport, minibar, coffeemaker,
hair dryer, iron, safe.

Hotel Higgins Landing ⓖ★   The beach at this resort is a major attraction. One of the
first eco-resorts in The Bahamas and still the only hotel on undeveloped Stocking Island,
Higgins Landing takes great care to preserve the natural beauty of its surroundings on
this gorgeous island. It's bordered by Elizabeth Harbour and the Atlantic on one side,
the crystal blue waters of Turtle Lagoon filled with colorful reefs on the other. This solar-
powered hideaway is one of the self-billed great escapes of The Bahamas.

Cottages are exquisitely decorated with antiques, mirrors, and Higgins family heir-
looms. Accommodations are furnished with queen-size beds, and each unit is given an
island accent with cool tile floors and ceiling fans, plus a well-maintained private bathroom with shower stalls. The landscaped grounds are as colorful as your imagination,

attracting many types of wildlife, ranging from herons and hummingbirds to green sea turtles. The island is reached by hotel ferry service from George Town.

Rates include a full breakfast and a candlelit first-rate dinner (nonguests are welcome, too, with advance reservations). The open-air bar overlooks the water.

Stocking Island (P.O. Box EX29146), George Town, Great Exuma, The Bahamas. ⓒ 242/357-0008. Fax 866/289-0919. www.higginslanding.com. 5 units. Year-round $360–$495 double; $540 triple; $630 quad. MAP (breakfast and dinner) included. AP (also w/lunch) $15 extra. Minimum stay of 4 nights required; 50% deposit required to secure reservation. MC, V. No children under 6. Closed Aug 1–Nov 25. **Amenities:** Restaurant; bar; watersports equipment/rentals; laundry service; nonsmoking rooms. *In room:* Kitchenettes (in some), coffeemaker, hair dryer, no phone.

EXPENSIVE

Peace & Plenty Bonefish Lodge ★   South of George Town, this is one of three Peace & Plenty properties in the Exumas—and the poshest of them all. It caters almost exclusively to fishermen and their companions. In a setting of young palms, the two-story inn is built of concrete and stone and lies on a peninsula enveloped by crystal-clear waters and sandy flats. This is the most elegant bonefishing inn in The Bahamas; you can fish all day and come back to be pampered in luxury.

The lobby is inviting, with tile floors and rattan pieces. From many of the midsize rooms opening onto the wraparound balcony, you'll have a great view of the turquoise waters, or perhaps you'd rather doze in a hammock. Accommodations are furnished in bright floral spreads and prints, with air-conditioning and ceiling fans, along with spacious, immaculate bathrooms and shower/tub combinations. You don't have to be an angler to stay here—but it helps. If you don't fish, you may be left out of the conversation at night.

The food served in the clubby dining room is excellent, with a well-trained chef who not only knows how to grill your steak to perfection, but can whip up a vegetarian platter, too. Of course, the finest way to dine here is on fish caught that day by the chef or one of the guests. After cleaning the fish, he tosses scraps to the resident sharks in the adjoining waters. This is the chief evening entertainment, although there are an honor bar and a lobby lounge upstairs with TV and VCR.

Queen's Hwy. (P.O. Box EX29173), George Town, Great Exuma, The Bahamas. ⓒ 242/345-5555. Fax 242/345-5556. www.ppbonefishlodge.net. 8 units. Year-round $777 per person 3 nights, 4 days; $1,036 per person 4 nights, 5 days. Rates include all meals, drinks, tips, airport transfers, and most activities. MC, V. **Amenities:** Restaurant; 2 bars; pool; watersports equipment/rentals; laundry service; nonsmoking rooms; rooms for those w/limited mobility. *In room:* A/C, hair dryer, no phone.

MODERATE

Club Peace & Plenty   This attractive, historic waterside inn is a classic island hotel in the heart of George Town. Once a sponge warehouse and later the home of a prominent family, it was converted into a hotel in the late 1940s, making it the oldest in the Exumas. The two-story pink-and-white hotel has dormers and balconies opening onto a water view. The grounds are planted with palms, crotons, and bougainvillea. Peace & Plenty fronts Elizabeth Harbour, which makes it a favorite of the yachting set, including former visitor Prince Philip.

The midsize units are all tastefully furnished, although there is still a lingering 1950s vibe. A refurbishment has freshened things up a bit with bright print spreads and draperies, and furnishings in white wicker or rattan. All rooms have queen, double, or twin beds, and a tiled bathroom with a shower/tub combination. Many also contain balconies opening onto harbor views; oceanfront rooms are the most desirable.

You can dine either indoors or outside, with calypso music on the terrace (see "Where to Dine," below). There are also two cocktail lounges, one of which was converted from an old slave kitchen and is now filled with nautical gear, including lanterns, rudders, and anchors. The hotel faces Stocking Island and maintains a private beach club there, offering food and bar service, as well as kilometers of sandy dunes. A boat, free for hotel guests ($8 round-trip for nonguests), makes the run.

Queen's Hwy. (P.O. Box EX29055), George Town, Great Exuma, The Bahamas. ℂ 800/525-2210 in the U.S. and Canada or 242/336-2551. Fax 242/336-2093. www.peaceandplenty.com. 32 units. Winter $160–$180 double; off season $135–$150 double. MAP (breakfast and dinner) $36 per person. Ask about bonefishing packages. AE, DC, MC, V. **Amenities:** Restaurant; 2 bars; pool; laundry service; nonsmoking rooms; rooms for those w/limited mobility. *In room:* Ceiling fan, A/C, TV, fridge, hair dryer, safe, no phone.

Coconut Cove Hotel   Set about 1.8km (1 mile) west of George Town—on a seafronting plot of land that's dotted with groves of coconut palms and palmettos and host to a brackish saltwater pond favored by bird life—this is the most recent, much-renovated incarnation of a hotel that has stood here for at least 20 years. Designed with three wings that radiate out from a central core, much like the shape of an airplane propeller, it offers simple but well-cared-for rooms, a bar where the rum-based Coconut Cove Specials are appropriately pink and heady, and a restaurant (see listing below) whose cuisine is praised as among the best on the island. The staff here can arrange access to island tours and watersports options.

George Town, Great Exuma, The Bahamas. ℂ 242/336-2659. Fax 242/336-2658. www.exumabahamas.com. 11 units. Winter $146–$172 double, $262 suite; off season $126–$152 double, $232 suite. AE, DC, MC, V. **Amenities:** Restaurant; bar; pool; babysitting; laundry service; rooms for those w/limited mobility; nonsmoking rooms. *In room:* A/C, ceiling fan, TV, fridge.

The Palms at Three Sisters   In 1994, this low-key resort opened on an isolated spot 11km (7 miles) from its nearest neighbor, on a 360m (1,181-ft.) stretch of lovely white sand. The rooms, decorated with English colonial details and simple, summery furniture, lie in a two-story, motel-like building. It's a great place for privacy and seclusion. The resort, incidentally, is named after a trio of rocks (the Three Sisters) with a composition that differs radically from the coral formations throughout the rest of the Exumas. They jut about 4.5m (15 ft.) above sea level just offshore from the beach. Bedrooms are comfortable, containing small bathrooms with shower units.

Queen's Hwy. (P.O. Box EX29215), Bahama Sound Beach (15km/9½ miles northwest of George Town), George Town, Great Exuma, The Bahamas. ℂ 888/688-4752 or 242/358-4040. Fax 242/358-4043. www.thepalmsat3sisters.com. 14 units. Winter $138 double, $155 triple, $160 cottage; off season $121 double, $135 triple, $125 cottage. Extra person $20 per day. MC, V. **Amenities:** Restaurant; tennis court; laundry service; rooms for those w/limited mobility. *In room:* A/C, TV, ceiling fan, fridge, coffeemaker, no phone.

Peace & Plenty Beach Inn   This tranquil inn is a world-class bonefishing resort, opening onto 90m (295 ft.) of white-sand beach. Its sibling, the Peace & Plenty Bonefish Lodge, is more posh, but the price tag here compensates. This is also a favorite resort for snorkelers, offering a special Jean-Michel Cousteau snorkeling program. The inn contains first-class, well-furnished double rooms, plus small bathrooms with shower/tub combinations. The bedrooms have Italian tile floors, as well as balconies overlooking Bonefish Bay and Elizabeth Harbour. For some action, and additional activities and facilities, you can go over to the Club Peace & Plenty (there are shuttles between all the Peace & Plenty properties).

An adjacent structure housing the attractive bar and restaurant was designed to reflect the colonial flavor of George Town. Very good meals are served here.

Harbourfront (P.O. Box EX29055), George Town, Great Exuma, The Bahamas. ℂ 800/525-2210 in the U.S. and Canada or 242/336-2250. Fax 242/336-2253. www.peaceandplenty.com. 16 units. Winter $170–$190 double; off season $150–$155 double. Up to 2 children under 12 stay free in parent's room. AE, MC, V. **Amenities:** Restaurant; bar; pool; watersports equipment/rentals. *In room:* A/C, ceiling fan, fridge, hair dryer, no phone.

Finds **Fresh, Sexy Conch**

The best conch salad is found at **Big D's Conch Spot No. 2,** Government Dock (*©* **242/358-0059**). "Fresh, sexy conch," as it's called here, is served daily. They'll make it right in front of you, so you know what's going into your salad. They're open Tuesday to Sunday noon to 1am. Reservations are requested.

Regatta Point 🎣 *Kids* This inn lies on a small cay just across the causeway from George Town, opening onto a small sandy beach. The cay used to be known as Kidd Cay, named after the notorious pirate. Overlooking Elizabeth Harbour, the present complex consists of six apartments, each with a full kitchen, which are not air-conditioned, although the cross ventilation is good. Ceiling fans help, too. Each of the pleasantly furnished, summery units has its own kitchen and maid service, plus a small bathroom containing shower/tub combinations. The kitchens make this a good choice for families. Those who don't wish to cook can have dinner at one of the previously mentioned hotels in town, or at a local restaurant. Nearby grocery stores are fairly well stocked if you feel like cooking. Bicycles are available at no extra charge. This colony hums in April during the Family Island Regatta.

Regatta Point (P.O. Box 6), Kidd Cove, George Town, Great Exuma, The Bahamas. *©* 800/688-0309. Fax 242/336-2046. www.regattapointbahamas.com. 6 units. Winter $168–$186 double, $242 2-bedroom apt.; off season $142–$168 double, $210 2-bedroom apt. Extra person $20 per day. No credit cards. **Amenities:** Laundry service. *In room:* Kitchen, ceiling fans, games and books, no phone.

WHERE TO DINE

With a few exceptions, the best places to take meals in George Town are in the main hotels reviewed above.

There are several casual joints in George Town where you can grab a quick meal. **Towne Cafe,** in the Marshall Complex (*©* **242/336-2194**), serves one of the best breakfasts in George Town. It's really the town bakery. Drop in any day but Sunday for a lunch of local Exumian specialties such as stewed grouper or chicken souse or a sandwich.

A former school bus was recycled and turned into **Jean's Dog House** 🎣 along Queen's Highway in George Town. Here you'll find the island's best lobster burger in a cramped but spotless kitchen on wheels. Instead of eating in the hotel dining room, we like to go here for breakfast and order the "MacJean," a robust sandwich with sausage or bacon, plus cheese, on freshly baked bread. Of course, she's also noted for her "dogs," or frankfurters. The owner is a well-loved personality known only as Jean. Visit her only from 7am to 3pm, and don't bother bringing your credit card.

MODERATE

Club Peace & Plenty Restaurant CONTINENTAL/BAHAMIAN/AMERICAN Come here for the finest island dining, with plentiful, good home-cooking that leaves everyone satisfied. You might begin with conch salad or one of the salads made with hearts of palm or artichoke hearts, then follow with local lobster. Bahamian steamed grouper regularly appears on the menu (of course), simmered with onions, sweet pepper, tomatoes, and thyme. But you can also order such special dishes as an herb-flavored Cornish game hen that is juicy and perfectly roasted and flavored. Lunch options include homemade soups, conch burgers, a chef's salad, or deep-fried grouper. Breakfast offerings range from traditional French toast or scrambled eggs and sausage to the truly Bahamian boiled fish and grits.

You sit under ceiling fans, looking out over the harbor. Windows on three sides and candlelight make it particularly nice in the evening. And who knows who will be at the next table? A celeb or two might be, or a crowd of yachters providing conversation and amusement.

In the Club Peace & Plenty, Queen's Hwy. © 242/336-2551. Reservations required for dinner. Breakfast $8.50; lunch $8–$10; dinner main courses $18–$30. AE, DC, DISC, MC, V. Daily 7:30–10:30am, noon–2:30pm, and 6:30–9:30pm.

Coconut Cove ITALIAN   Set on the premises of the previously recommended hotel, this dining room sits close to the sea, within a glassed-in, blue, white, and coral-colored dining room whose mahogany-and-glass doors slide open for maximum exposure to the breeze. American-born Pamela Chimento, in cooperation with her Bahama-born assistant, Shelia, churn out well-flavored versions of Italian and Mediterranean-inspired food that's far removed from the usual Bahamian fare you might have expected. Starters include breaded calamari with oregano and parsley sauce; linguini marinara; jalapeño peppers; breaded mozzarella sticks; onion soup; and seafood salads. Main courses feature stone crabs; different preparations of shrimp; crayfish; poached salmon served with a tropical fruit salsa; and "cowboy steaks." There's also a choice of pizzas from a "pizza bar" on-site. Most dishes, except for lobster, are priced at the low end of the scale.

In the Coconut Cove Hotel, George Town. © 242/336-2659. Reservations recommended. Main courses $12–$40, pizzas $9–$18. AE, DISC, MC, V. Wed–Sun 6–9pm.

Fisherman's Inn *(Finds* BAHAMIAN   This is the most isolated restaurant in the Exumas, a ramshackle, wood-sided hideaway that's set on a low ridge above the sea on the island of Barraterre, a 40- to 60-minute drive from George Town. Connected with two separate causeways to the "mainland" of Great Exuma Island, it's literally at the end of the line for motorists looking for a lonely, sun-bleached, and windblasted excursion from George Town. Don't come here with the assurance that there will be anything in the larder at the time of your arrival. If the season is slow, or if the supplies "didn't make it in that week," you might be faced with a smile and perhaps a somewhat erratic dialogue from the owner, and 'nary a crust of bread. The best idea involves calling ahead, surveying the gastronomic lay of the land, and then discussing with the staff what may, or may not, be available that day. Expect a roster of fish, chicken, beefsteaks, soups, salads, and stews, lots of local color, and a genuine sense of the degree to which parts of The Bahamas archipelago are isolated from the rest of the world.

Barraterre. © 242/355-5016. Reservations required. Main courses lunch $9–$15, dinner $20–$25. No credit cards. Hours vary, but in theory it's daily from 7am until around midnight.

Sam's Place BAHAMIAN/INTERNATIONAL   If Bogie were alive today, he'd surely head for this laid-back second-floor restaurant and bar overlooking the harbor in George Town. Sam Gray, the owner, offers breakfasts to catch the early boating crowd. Lunches could include everything from freshly made conch chowder to curry chicken. You'll also be able to order an array of sandwiches throughout the day. The dinner menu changes daily, but you're likely to find such well-prepared main courses as Exuma lobster tail, roast lamb, and Bahamian pan-fried grouper. At dinner, the talk here is of one of everybody's dreams—owning a private utopia, one of those uninhabited cays still remaining in the Exuma chain.

Main St. © 242/336-2579. Breakfast and lunch $6–$9; dinner main courses $12–$30. MC, V. Daily 8am–9pm.

INEXPENSIVE
Kermit's Airport Lounge BAHAMIAN   Owned by one of the island's most entrepreneurial taxi drivers, Kermit Rolle, this simple but appealing place lies across the

road from the entrance to the airport. It's the semiofficial waiting room for most of the island's flights, and it might make your wait more convenient and fun. You can usually find Kermit hanging out here. The cook will fry you some fish, and there's always beans and rice around. Johnnycake and sandwiches are also available, along with burgers and an array of tropical drinks. Until an airplane flies you to a better restaurant, this place can come in handy.

Exuma International Airport. ℂ 242/345-0002. Beer $3.50; cheeseburgers $5–$7; platters from $8. No credit cards. Daily 6:30am–5pm.

BEACHES, WATERSPORTS & OTHER OUTDOOR PURSUITS
BEACHES
Stocking Island ⍟, which lies in Elizabeth Harbour, faces the town across the bay, less than 1.5km (1 mile) away. This long, thin barrier island has some of the most gorgeous white-sand beaches in The Bahamas. Snorkelers and scuba divers come here to explore the blue holes, and it is also ringed with undersea caves and coral gardens. Boat trips leave daily from Elizabeth Harbour heading for Stocking Island at 10am and 1pm. The cost is $8 per person round-trip. However, guests of Club Peace & Plenty ride free.

If you'd like to go shelling, walk the beach that runs along the Atlantic side of Stocking Island.

The island has a beach club run by **Club Peace & Plenty** (ℂ **242/336-2551**). (Stocking Island used to be a private enclave for guests at Club Peace & Plenty, but now all visitors use it.) Snorkel gear goes for $10 a day. Visibility is great in these waters, and there are many kinds of colorful fish to see.

Yachting types and others visiting the island like to drop in at Kenneth Bowe's **Chat & Chill** ⍟ (no phone), a laid-back place that somehow manages to be both upmarket and a kind of local dive. Many of the dishes such as fresh fish are grilled over an open fire, and the Sunday pig roasts are an island event. The conch burgers are the best in the Exumas. But the seasonings? They're a secret.

BOATING
Landlocked **Lake Victoria** covers about .8 hectares (2 acres) in the heart of George Town. It has a narrow exit to the harbor and functions as a diving-and-boating headquarters.

If you come to the Exumas aboard your own boat, **Exuma Docking Services,** Main Street, George Town (ℂ **242/336-2578**), has slips for 52 boats, with water and electricity hookups. You can stock up on supplies here, get fuel, and do laundry.

Through the **Starfish Activity Center** (ℂ **242/336-3033**), you can rent Hobie Waves, high-performance sailboats that are easy to use. These stable, lightweight-yet-durable, 4.5m (15-ft.) catamarans are ideal for families, as they are simple to maneuver. With a minimum of two people, you can take a 2-hour lesson for $30 per person. Renting one of these babies runs you $35 for 2 hours, $50 for a half-day, $75 for a full day, or—if it really looks good to you—$300 for a week.

If motor boats are more your speed, **Minns Water Sports** (ℂ **242/336-3483** or 242/336-2604) based out of George Town, rents these 5-, 5.4-, and 6.7m (16-, 18-, and 22-ft.) boats for $88, $120, and $170 per day, with daily rates dropping the longer you rent. **Exuma Dive Center** (ℂ **800/874-7213** or 242/336-2390), where boat rentals start at $80 per day, also offers more economical rates when you keep a boat for a week or longer. With your boat, you can set out to sail the most stunning waters in The Bahamas, rivaled only by the Abacos. The best territory for recreational boating is the government-protected **Exumas Cays Land and Sea Park,** stretching south from Wax Cay to Conch Cay, with their magnificent sea gardens and coral reefs.

FISHING

Many visitors come to the Exumas just to go bonefishing. Arrangements for outings can be made at **Club Peace & Plenty,** Queen's Highway (© **800/525-2210** or 242/336-2551) or at **Peace & Plenty Bonefish Lodge,** Queen's Highway (© **242/345-5555**). The Exumas offer miles of wadeable flats (shallow bodies of water), where trained guides will accompany you. Fly-fishing instruction and equipment are also offered.

GOLF

The **Four Seasons Resort Emerald Bay Golf Club** ★★★, Emerald Bay (© **242/366-6800** or 358-4185), is one of the great oceanfront courses in either The Bahamas or the Caribbean. The Greg Norman design features six oceanfront holes. The par-72 course stretches a challenging 6,873 yards, yet was laid out to accommodate golfers of various skill levels. The course uses environmentally friendly seashore paspalum grass and finishes on a rocky peninsula with a panoramic view of the sea. There's also a pro shop. Greens fees are a steep $135 for 18 holes ($175 for nonguests), and reservations are required.

KAYAKING

You can best appreciate some of Exuma's most dramatic scenery from the peaceful perch of a sea kayak. In fact, many areas—including mangrove lakes, rivers, manta ray gathering spots, and bonefish flats—are too shallow for other boats to enter. Don't worry if you haven't hit the gym lately. Anyone in at least average physical condition—from children to seniors—can kayak with a smile. The **Starfish Activity Center** (© **242/336-3033**) rents sit-on-top kayaks for singles and doubles. Singles are about $10 an hour, $20 per half-day, $30 a day, or $120 a week. Doubles run $15 an hour, $30 per half-day, $40 a day, or $150 a week.

For more adventure, book one of Starfish's guided kayak trips, which are offered daily. You don't have to spend the whole time paddling your kayak. During half- and full-day excursions, lunch and beverages are served, and the price covers all gear, including snorkeling equipment. You may find yourself watching a blizzard of fish swarm a shipwreck, searching for sand dollars on a deserted beach, snorkeling into a sea cave, or finding out about bush medicine while you hike along a nature trail. Guided trips begin at $35 an hour for adults and $25 for children.

Another good outfitter is **Ecosummer Expeditions** (© **800/465-8884**). Ecosummer is especially skilled in exploring **Exuma Cays National Land and Sea Park** (© **242/357-8344**), a government-protected natural preserve with excellent wildlife-viewing opportunities.

SCUBA DIVING

Surrounding the Exumas, fields of massive coral heads, eerie blue holes, and exciting walls covered with marine life turn on scuba divers. Many excellent reefs are just 20 or 25 minutes away from the George Town area, so long boat rides don't cut into your underwater time.

For scuba divers, the great attraction here is the **Exuma Cays National Land and Sea Park,** which is 35km (22 miles) long and 13km (8 miles) wide. It draws scuba divers to its 453 sq. km (177 sq. miles) of sea gardens, with their magnificent coral reefs, flora, and fauna. The park, which was inaugurated in 1958, lies some 35km (22 miles) northeast of **Staniel Cay.** Call your hotel to ask whether it offers a hotel/dive package or try **Exuma Scuba Adventures** (© 242/336-2893; www.exumascuba.com) at Peace & Plenty Beach Inn for information about scuba diving excursions. A one-tank morning boat dive goes for $55, a two-tank dive costing $75. You can also take an afternoon one-tank boat dive for $55 or a one-tank night dive for $60. A reef boat trip for snorkeling costs $25.

SNORKELING

The best bet for snorkeling is in the magnificent waters off the coast of **Stocking Island** (see above). Boat trips from George Town depart for the island twice a day. You can also rent snorkeling equipment for $8 a day at **Minns Water Sports** in George Town (© 242/336-3483).

If you want to snorkel around some of Exuma's most well-preserved reefs, call **Exuma Scuba Adventures** (© 242/336-2893; www.exumascuba.com). Its 3-hour-plus excursions cost $25 per adult, $10 for children under 12.

EXPLORING GEORGE TOWN

There isn't much to see here in the way of architecture except the confectionery pink–and-white **Government Building,** which was "inspired" by the Government House architecture in Nassau. Under an old ficus tree in the center of town, there's a **straw market** where you can talk to the friendly Exumian women and perhaps purchase some of their handcrafts.

George Town has a colorful history, despite the fact that it appears so sleepy today. (With so little traffic, it doesn't even need a traffic light.) Pirates used its deep-water harbor in the 17th century, and those called the "plantation aristocracy," mainly from Virginia and the Carolinas, settled here in the 18th century. In the next 100 years, **Elizabeth Harbour,** the focal point of the town, became a refitting base for British man-of-war vessels, and the U.S. Navy used the port again during World War II.

There's not too much shopping, but there are a few places where you can purchase souvenirs and gifts. **Exuma Liquor and Gifts,** Queen's Highway (© 242/336-2101), is the place to stock up on liquor, wine, and beer. The **Peace & Plenty Boutique,** Queen's Highway (© 242/336-2761), stands next to the Sandpiper and across the street from the previously recommended Club Peace & Plenty, which owns it. Its main draw is a selection of Androsia batiks for women, and Androsia cloth is sold by the yard. You can also find such practical items as film and suntan lotion. The boutique stocks a large selection of men and women's sportswear, as well.

The Sandpiper, Queen's Highway (© 242/336-2084), stands across from Club Peace & Plenty. Its highlights are the original serigraphs by Diane Minns, but it also offers a good selection of Bahamian arts and crafts, along with such items as Bahamian straw baskets (or other handcrafted works), sponges, ceramics, watches, baskets, jewelry, books, and postcards. Diane designs and silk-screens T-shirts here in the shop, and she welcomes anyone to watch her at work.

One of the offshore sights in Elizabeth Harbour is tiny **Crab Cay,** which can be reached by boat. This was believed to have been a rest camp for British seamen in the 18th century.

GEORGE TOWN AFTER DARK

The best place to head for some after-dark diversion is **Club Peace & Plenty** (© 800/525-2210 or 242/336-2093), located in George Town. Although summer nights are slow, something is usually happening here in winter, ranging from weekly poolside bashes to live bands that keep both locals and visitors jumping up on the dance floor. Also consider dropping by the **Palms at Three Sisters** (© **242/358-4040**), which presents live music every Saturday night on its flowering patio. The little resort draws a lively crowd of both locals and visitors.

EXPLORING FARTHER AFIELD

Queen's Highway, which is still referred to as the "slave route," runs the length of Great Exuma, and you can travel it in either a taxi or a rented car to take in the sights in and around George Town.

Forty-five kilometers (28 miles) north of George Town, **Rolleville,** named after Lord Rolle, is still inhabited by descendants of his freed slaves. It is claimed that his will left them the land. This land is not sold but is passed along from one generation to the next.

As you travel along the highway, you'll see ruins of plantations. This land is called **"generation estates,"** and the major ones are **Steventon, Mount Thompson,** and **Ramsey.** You pass such settlements as Mosstown (which has working farms), Ramsey, the Forest, Farmer's Hill, and Roker's Point. Steventon is the last settlement before you reach Rolleville, which is the largest of the plantation estates. There are several beautiful beaches along the way, especially the ones at **Tarr Bay** and **Jimmie Hill.**

Some visitors may also want to head south of George Town, passing Flamingo Bay and Pirate's Point. In the 18th century Captain Kidd is said to have anchored at **Kidd Cay.** You, however, can stay at the previously recommended Regatta Point.

Flamingo Bay, the site of a hotel and villa development, begins just 1km (⅔ mile) from George Town. It's a favorite rendezvous of the yachting set and bonefishers.

WHERE TO DINE

Iva Bowe's Central Highway Inn Restaurant & Bar BAHAMIAN   This roadside tavern, operated by Gottfried B. Bowe, specializes in very tender cracked conch. The conch is marinated in lime, pounded to make it tender, and then fried with her own special seasonings. It's the best in the Exumas. You might also try Iva's lobster linguini or shrimp scampi. This is good Bahamian cookery.

Queen's Hwy. (.5km/⅓ mile from the entrance to the International Airport and about 9.5km/6 miles northwest of George Town). © 242/345-7014. Lunch $10–$12; main courses $10–$20. No credit cards. Mon–Sat 8am–11pm.

2 Little Exuma ⭐

This is a faraway retreat, the southernmost of the Exuma Cays. It has a subtropical climate, despite that it's in the Tropics, and lovely white-sand beaches. The waters are so crystal clear in some places that you can spot the colorful tropical fish more than 18m (59 ft.) down. The island, about 31 sq. km (12 sq. miles) in area, is connected to Great Exuma by a 182m-long (597-ft.) bridge. It's about a 16km (10-mile) trip from the George Town airport.

Less than a kilometer (½ mile) offshore is **Pigeon Cay,** which is uninhabited. Visitors often come here for the day and are later picked up by a boat that takes them back to Little Exuma. You can go snorkeling and visit the remains of a 200-year-old wreck, right offshore in about 2m (6½ ft.) of water.

On one of the highest hills of Little Exuma are the remains of an old pirate fort. Several cannons are located nearby, but documentation is lacking as to when it was built or by whom. (Pirates didn't leave too much data lying around.)

Fun Fact **A Romantic Legend & a Movie Star**

On the road to Little Exuma, you come to the hamlet of **Rolle Town,** which is another of the generation estates that was once, like Rolleville in the north, owned by Lord Rolle and is populated today with the descendants of his former slaves. This sleepy town has some 100-year-old houses.

In an abandoned field, where goats frolic, you can visit the Rolle Town Tombs, burial ground of the McKay family. Capt. Alexander McKay, a Scot, came to Great Exuma in 1789 after he was granted 161 hectares (398 acres) for a plantation. His wife joined him in 1791, and soon after, they had a child. However, tragedy struck in 1792 when Anne McKay, who was only 26, died along with her child. Perhaps grief stricken, her husband died the following year. Their story is one of the romantic legends of the island.

The village also claims a more contemporary famous daughter: the actress Esther Rolle. Her parents were born here (though they came to the United States before she was born). Rolle is best remembered for her role as the strong-willed mother on the '70s sitcom *Good Times*. She won an Emmy playing a maid in *Summer of My German Soldier;* Rolle's other film credits included *Driving Miss Daisy, Rosewood,* and *How to Make an American Quilt*. She died at the age of 78 in 1998.

Coming from Great Exuma, the first community you reach on Little Exuma is called **Ferry,** so named because the two islands were linked by a ferry service before the bridge was built. Ask around about visiting the private chapel of an Irish family, the Fitzgeralds, erected generations ago.

Along the way, you can take in **Pretty Molly Bay,** site of the now-shuttered Sand Dollar Beach Club. Pretty Molly was a slave who committed suicide by walking into the water one night. The natives claim that her ghost can still be seen stalking the beach every night.

Many visitors come to Little Exuma to visit the **Hermitage,** a plantation constructed by Loyalist settlers. It is the last surviving example of the many that once stood in the Exumas. It was originally built by the Kendall family, who came to Little Exuma in 1784. The family established their plantation at **Williamstown** and, with their slaves, set about growing cotton. But they encountered so many difficulties having the cotton shipped to Nassau that in 1806 they advertised the plantation for sale. The ad promised "970 acres more or less," along with "160 hands" (referring to the slaves). Chances are you'll be approached by a local guide who, for a fee, will show you around. Also ask to be shown the several old tombs in the area.

At Williamstown (look for the seaside marker), you can visit the remains of the **Great Salt Pond.**

If you really have to see everything, maybe you can get a local to take you over to **Hog Cay,** the end of the line for the Exumas. This is really just a spit of land, and there are no glorious beaches here. It's visited mainly by those who like to add obscure islets at the very end of the road to their list of explorations. Hog Cay is privately owned, and it is farmed. The owner seems friendly to visitors. His house lies in the center of the island.

3 Staniel Cay ⊀

Staniel Cay lies 129km (80 miles) southeast of Nassau at the southern end of the little Pipe Creek archipelago, which is part of the Exuma Cays. It's a 13km (8-mile) chain of mostly uninhabited islets, sandy beaches, coral reefs, and bonefish flats. There are many places for snug anchorages, making this a favorite yachting stopover in the mid-Exumas. Staniel Cay, known for years as "Stanyard," has no golf course or tennis courts, but it's the perfect island for "the great escape." It's home to just 80 full-time residents.

An annual bonefishing festival is sponsored here on August 5, during the celebration of Bahamian Independence Day. The **Happy People Marina** (© **242/355-2008**) arranges sportfishing trips with local guides, as well as snorkeling trips.

About 100 Bahamians live here, and there's a **straw market** where you can buy crafts, hats, and handbags.

The **Staniel Cay Yacht Club** (see below) arranges charter flights from Fort Lauderdale, costing $400 per person round-trip. Flight time is only 3 hours.

WHERE TO STAY & DINE

Staniel Cay Yacht Club   Staniel Cay is a great getaway, and the Staniel Cay Yacht Club—only a 5-minute golf-cart ride from the airstrip—is the place to get away to. Although once famous in yachting circles, drawing celebrities like the late Malcolm Forbes, the property became rundown and lost its chic clientele for several years. Now it's bounced back. Fully restored and improved, it again welcomes the yachting world to its location near a white sandy beach. Guest cottages, each with a small shower unit, have been completely remodeled and refurbished and are quite charming. Each cottage is painted a different color with different decorative features. The cottages also have west-facing balconies, which make for unimpeded views of the sun setting over the water. This is one of the few guarantees each day on Staniel Cay. Since the island is only a kilometer (⅝ mile) wide, you can easily walk to the local village, which has a grocery store, straw market, church, and post office. A Boston Whaler is docked outside each accommodation, and guests are given a map of local waters and invited to sail on their own. There are many deserted islands surrounding Staniel Cay.

An on-site clubhouse offers American/Bahamian cuisine for breakfast, lunch, and dinner, with a menu featuring steaks and seafood, nothing too foreign or experimental. The club can rent you boats for activities, from a 4m (13-ft.) Boston Whaler including

---

(*Tips*   **An Insider's Guide for Sailors & Beach Buffs**

If you want a beach to yourself, one of the uninhabited islands surrounding Staniel Cay could be yours for the day. In the unlikely event that another yachting party has arrived, just sail on to another island nearby and chances are it'll be deserted. The local map given out by the hotel pinpoints the location of **Thunderball Grotto** ⊀, where part of the James Bond hit, *Thunderball*, was filmed. This is one of the best places for snorkeling in the Exumas. To the north of Thunderball Grotto lies the curiously named **"Major Spot."** Believe it or not, **swimming pigs** will surround your boat here. They are harmless but expect to be treated to food. At another point on your nautical map, about 6.4km (4 miles) beyond Major Spot, you'll come across shallow waters where tame (at least we hope so) nurse sharks like their pictures taken. Food makes them even less camera shy.

fuel for $110 and a 5.1m (17-ft.) boat for $235 per day, to something smaller, plus scuba and snorkeling gear.

Staniel Cay, the Exumas, The Bahamas. (For information, write to: 2233 S. Andrews Ave., Fort Lauderdale, FL 33316.) ℂ **954/467-8920** in the U.S., or 242/355-2024. Fax 242/355-2044. www.stanielcay.com. 9 units. Winter $148 double; off season $121 double. MAP $35 per person. Extra person $35 per day. MC, V. **Amenities:** Restaurant; bar; outdoor pool; laundry service; nonsmoking rooms; marina; airstrip. *In room:* A/C, fridge, coffeemaker, hair dryer, no phone.

4 Sampson Cay

Tiny Sampson Cay, directly northwest of Staniel Cay and just to the southeast of the Exuma Cays National Land and Sea Park, has a certain charm. It has a full-service marina, as well as a small dive operation. Other than Staniel Cay, Sampson Cay has the only marina in the Central Exumas; thus, most visitors here arrive in their own boats, and local guides taking out sportfishers for the day provide the chief entertainment. Sampson Cay is 67 nautical miles southeast of Nassau and one of the safest anchorages in the Exumas—it's a natural "hurricane hole" (in other words, a fully protected anchorage with land all around). The cay also lies near the end of Pipe Creek, which has been called a "tropical Shangri-La."

WHERE TO STAY & DINE

Sampson's Cay Club 𝒢   This is a rather remote outpost; don't expect anything fancy. Each of the 10 units here has a tiny kitchenette (with hot plate, sink, and refrigerator, but no oven). The medium-size bedrooms were completely renovated in 2001, and are of a typical motel standard, each with a private shower/tub combination.

Norman's Cay

Throughout the Exumas, you'll see islands with NO TRESPASSING signs posted. In the early 1980s, on Norman's Cay, these signs were extremely serious: You could have been killed if you had gone ashore. Fortunately, the drug smuggling that used to occur here has been cleaned up and the area is safe for travelers. However, private NO TRESPASSING signs should still be obeyed. Even without drug activity, privacy of individual property owners has to be respected, of course.

Once upon a time, you might have run into Ted Kennedy, Walter Cronkite, or William F. Buckley Jr. enjoying the island's pleasures. The remote outpost enjoyed great popularity with the Harvard/Boston clique. During the 1980s, however, all this changed when German-Colombian Carlos Lehder Rivas purchased most of the island. Experts say it soon became the major distribution point for drug export to the United States. Millions of dollars worth of cocaine was flown from Colombia to Norman's Cay before being smuggled onward to the United States.

Eventually, the U.S. applied strong pressure on the Bahamian government to clean up the island. Lehder fled for Colombia, where he was captured and extradited to the United States. He is now in prison. Norman's Cay may one day realize its tourist potential once again, but for now it remains relatively quiet, visited only by stray yachting parties and occasional cruise vessels.

Community life here revolves around the grocery store and commissary, the fuel and dockage facilities of the marina, and a bar and restaurant favored by visiting yachters. The nautically decorated clubhouse serves drinks and sandwiches any time of day to anyone who shows up, but reservations are required before 4pm for the single-seating dinner, which is served nightly at 7:30pm.

Sampson Cay, the Exumas, The Bahamas. © **877/633-0305** or 242/355-2034. Fax 242/355-2034. www.sampson cayclub.com. 10 units. Year-round $225 double. MC, V. **Amenities:** Restaurant; bar; coin-operated laundry service; non-smoking rooms; rooms for those w/limited mobility. *In room:* A/C, kitchenette, fridge, coffeemaker, no phone.

10

The Southern Bahamas

This cluster of islands on the southern fringe of The Bahamas is one of the last frontier outposts that can be reached relatively quickly from the U.S. mainland. Their remoteness is one of the most compelling reasons to visit them—that, and a chance to see life in The Bahamas the way it used to be. Some of the islands are proud to proclaim that "we are as we were when Columbus first landed here," an exaggeration, of course, but one that certainly contains a kernel of the truth.

The Southern Bahamas have a colorful history. In the 18th century, Loyalists from the Carolinas and Virginia came here with slave labor and settled many of the islands. For about 20 years they had thriving cotton plantations until blight struck, killing crops and destroying the industry. In 1834, the United Kingdom Emancipation Act freed slaves throughout the British Empire. When the Loyalists moved on to more fertile ground, they often left behind the emancipated blacks, who then had to eke out a living as best they could.

With some notable exceptions, such as Long Island, tourism developers have stayed clear of these islands, although they have enormous potential, as most of them have excellent beaches, good fishing, and fine dive sites.

If you consider visiting any of these islands, be forewarned that transportation is inconvenient, and except for two or three resorts, accommodations are limited. For these and other reasons, the boating and yachting crowd composes the majority of visitors.

Many changes are in the wind for the Southern Bahamas. Right now, however, there's almost no traffic, no banks, no lawyers. There are, however, mosquitoes. Plan to bring a good insect repellent and a long-sleeved shirt for protection.

1 Cat Island ★★

Untainted by tourism, lovely Cat Island is the sixth-largest island in The Bahamas. The fishhook-shaped island—some 77km (46 miles) long and 1 to 6.5km (⅔–4 miles) wide—lies about 209km (130 miles) southeast of Nassau and 523km (324 miles) southeast of Miami. (Don't confuse Cat Island with Cat Cay, a smallish, private island near Bimini.)

Cat Island, named after the pirate Arthur Catt (and not wild packs of marauding cats), is located near the Tropic of Cancer, between Eleuthera and Long Island. It has one of the most pleasant climates in The Bahamas, with temperatures in the high 60s (low 20s Celsius) during the short winters, rising to the mid-80s (low 30s Celsius) in summer, with trade winds making the place even more comfortable. It is also home to some 2,000 residents, some of the friendliest in all of The Bahamas.

With its pristine virgin **beaches,** the island is beautiful to see, yet little-visited enough that it remains relatively inexpensive and undiscovered.

Many local historians claim that Cat Island residents were the first to see Columbus. The great explorer himself was believed by some to have been welcomed here by the peaceful Arawaks. Regardless of whether Columbus stopped here, the island has a rich history of adventurers, slaves, buccaneers, farmers, and visionaries of many nationalities. Cat Island remains mysterious to some even now. It's known as a stronghold of such strange practices as obeah (West Indian witchcraft) and of miraculously healing bush medicines.

A straight asphalt road (in terrible shape) leads from the north to the south of the island. Along the way you can select your own beach—and chances are you'll have complete privacy. These beaches offer an array of watersports, and visitors can go swimming or snorkeling at several places. **Fernandez Bay** is a picture-postcard, white-sand beach set against a turquoise blue sea and lined with casuarina trees. The island's north side is wild, untamed shoreline. Boating and diving are among the main reasons to go to Cat Island, and diving lessons are available for novices.

Arthur's Town, in the north, is the major town and the boyhood home of actor Sidney Poitier. (He has many relatives still living on the island, including a few amazing look-alikes.) Poitier shares memories of his childhood home in his book *This Life.*

CAT ISLAND ESSENTIALS

GETTING THERE   A commercial flight on **Bahamasair** (© **800/222-4262** in the U.S.; www.bahamasair.com) leaves Nassau for Arthur's Town on Friday and Sunday at 10:30am. There is also an airport near **New Bight,** the most scenic village on the island. Flying to New Bight from Fort Lauderdale, is **Lynx Air International** (© **888/596-9247;** www.lynxair.com), which has service between Fort Lauderdale and Cat Island three times a week.

Cat Island is also serviced by **mail boat.** The MV *Lady Rosalind* (© **242/393-1064**) departs Potter's Cay Dock in Nassau weekly, heading for Bennett's Harbour and Arthur's Town. It leaves on Thursday at 6pm and returns to Nassau on Sunday. Another vessel, the **MV** *Lady Emerald* (© **242/393-1064**), departs Potter's Cay in Nassau on Tuesday at 3pm, going to Old and New Bight, and returns on Sunday.

GETTING AROUND   Limited, but quite adequate, taxi service is available on Cat Island. Hotel owners, if notified of your arrival time, will have someone drive to the airport to pick you up. You can, however, rent a car from **Russell Brothers,** Bridge Inn, New Bight (© **242/342-3014**), to go exploring on your own. Prices begin at $70 daily, with unlimited mileage. Hours are daily from 7:30am to 6pm.

FAST FACTS   There are three medical clinics, each of which is among the simplest in The Bahamas. They are found in the settlements of Arthur's Town, Old Bight, and Smiths Bay, and they're not always open. In case of an emergency, notify your hotel staff immediately. Someone will try to get in touch with a medical person. Serious cases are flown to Nassau. If you're not in good health and might require medical assistance on vacation, Cat Island is not the island to choose. There is no central number to call for help.

SPECIAL EVENTS   The island's annual **Three-Day Regatta** takes place every summer, usually at the end of July. It attracts the largest collection of visitors to Cat Island; the inns prove inadequate to receive them. Call your local Bahamas Tourist Office (see chapter 2) for more information.

WHERE TO STAY & DINE

Bridge Inn   Lying 274m (899 ft.) from a beach, the relaxed and casual Bridge Inn is owned by Cat Islander Allan Russell, who is ably assisted by a group of family members.

The Southern Bahamas

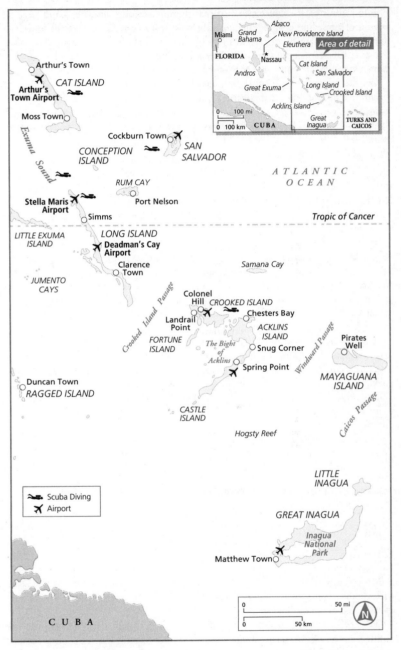

The inn offers babysitting services so that parents can play tennis or go diving, sailboarding, snorkeling, jogging, bicycling, fishing, or just sightseeing with the knowledge their youngsters are being carefully tended. Bedrooms are modest, motel-style affairs, but each unit can house three to four guests. Each of the high-ceilinged rooms does come with a private bathroom containing a shower stall.

On the premises you'll find a full bar and a restaurant that serves a rather simple Bahamian and international cuisine.

New Bight, Cat Island, The Bahamas. © 242/342-3013. Fax 242/342-3041. www.catislandbridgeinn.com. 15 units. Year-round $140 double; $190 villa. MC, V. Rates include breakfast. **Amenities:** Restaurant; bar; limited room service; laundry service. *In room:* A/C, TV, kitchenettes (in some), iron/ironing board.

Fernandez Bay Village ✦ *Finds*   Opening onto Fernandez Bay, this is the best resort on the island. Although rustic, it has a certain charm, mainly because of its position on a curvy white-sandy beach set against casuarinas blowing in the trade winds. The beach (or anywhere else for that matter) is never crowded, so come here only if you *really* want to get away from it all; this place is far too laid-back for full hotel service. Things get done, but it takes time—and no one's in a hurry.

Fernandez Bay Village has been in the Armbrister family since it was originally established on a plantation in 1870. Its rusticity and seclusion are part of its charm, and yet, if you wish, you can get acquainted with other guests with similar interests. Yachters, who moor in the water offshore—there are no marina facilities—often visit the resort to take advantage of the general store's fresh supplies. (Nearby Smith's Bay is one of the best storm shelters in the region—even the government mail boats take refuge here during hurricanes.)

The "village" consists of full housekeeping villas, each of which sleeps up to six people, as well as five double-occupancy cottages, all built of stone, driftwood, and glass. Each unit comes with a private garden bathroom with a shower stall.

Meals are served in a clubhouse decorated with antiques and Haitian art. This clubhouse, which opens onto a view of the beach and sea, also features a sitting library area, stone fireplace, and overhead fans. Dinners are served on a beach terrace adjacent to a thatched-roof Tiki bar that runs on the honor system. On many nights a blazing bonfire near the water becomes a focal point for guests who want to listen to island music.

.6km (1 mile) north of New Bight, Cat Island, The Bahamas. © 800/940-1905, 242/342-3043, or 954/474-4821. Fax 242/342-3051 or 954/474-4864. www.fernandezbayvillage.com. 15 units. Year-round $355 villa; $332–$367 houses; $220–$250 cottages. AE, MC, V. **Amenities:** Restaurant; bar; watersports equipment/rentals; bike rentals; car-rental desk; babysitting; laundry service. *In room:* Kitchen, fridge, coffeemaker, iron/ironing board, no phone.

Greenwood Beach Resort & Dive Center ✦   The location on a 13km (8-mile) stretch of the Atlantic, bordered by pink sands, is always idyllic, and there's good snorkeling right off shore. Since 1992, a German family has run this beach resort and dive center, constantly making improvements. This group of modern buildings on the most isolated section of the island has a private sandy beach and a freshwater pool. It's better run and equipped than the Bridge Inn, and it attracts mostly divers. The small oceanview double rooms are all equipped with showers and their own terraces. There is an all-purpose bar and a dining room.

The hotel's dive center is the best on the island. The inn has a 7.5m (25-ft.) and 11m (36-ft.) motorboat for diving excursions, and its Cat Island Dive Center has complete equipment for 20 divers at a time. A two-tank dive is $85, and equipment is $5 to $8 extra depending on your needs. Night dives are $55. The resort also has two fishing boats available for bonefishing ($250 for a half-day, $500 for a full day). The staff greets each arriving Bahamasair flight.

Port Howe, Cat Island, The Bahamas. Ⓒ **242/342-3053.** Fax 242/342-3053. www.greenwoodbeachresort.net. 22 units. Year-round $99–$120 double. MAP $40 per person. MC, V. **Amenities:** Restaurant; bar; pool; watersports equipment/rentals; business center; babysitting. *In room:* A/C (in some), ceiling fan (in some), no phone.

Hawk's Nest Resort & Marina   This remote getaway and marina lies on the southwestern side of Cat Island, fronting a long, sandy beach and containing its own runway for charter flights and private planes, plus an 28-slip marina attracting the yachting crowd. This intimate resort is set near the village of Devil's Point, lying some 16km (10 miles) west of Columbus Point close to the ruins of the once-flourishing but now-abandoned Richman Hill and Newfield Plantation. Bedrooms, with either two queen-size beds or a king-size bed, are well furnished and brightly decorated, each with a shower unit. Each room features a patio for those late-afternoon toddies overlooking the sunset. If you bring the family, you may want to look at the two-bedroom house on the beach, separate from the other structures. The clubhouse, the rooms, and the main house are spacious and inviting.

They serve full breakfasts (cooked to order), sandwiches for lunch, and a buffet-style dinner, with the unannounced fare changing nightly. The club can rent out snorkeling equipment for as little as $30 per 3 hours, or you can go scuba diving for $60 for a one-tank dive, $80 for a two-tank dive.

Devil's Point, Cat Island, The Bahamas. Ⓒ **800/688-4752** or 242/342-7050. Fax 242/342-7051. www.hawks-nest.com. 10 units. Year-round $345–$375 house; $135–$155 double. MAP (breakfast and dinner) $50 extra per person. MC, V. **Amenities:** Restaurant; bar; pool; tennis court; watersports equipment/rentals; bike rentals; laundry service; nonsmoking rooms. *In room:* A/C, TV, coffeemaker, hair dryer.

Pigeon Cay Beach Club   This B&B lies at the north end of the island, about a 15-minute ride from the airport and fronting a tranquil bay. The main building consists of a trio of separate but attached units, a small store, and the check-in office. Each accommodation comes with a fully equipped kitchen. In addition, there are some light and airy cottages, ranging from one bedroom to three bedrooms. Cottages are built of stucco and coral stone with beamed ceilings, along with Mexican tile floors. Each unit comes with a shower stall.

North End, Cat Island, The Bahamas. Ⓒ/fax **242/354-5084.** www.pigeoncay-bahamas.com. 11 units. Year-round $140 studio; $160 1-bedroom suite; $225–$250 2-bedroom suite; $375 3-bedroom suite. AE, MC, V. **Amenities:** Limited room service; babysitting; laundry service; nonsmoking rooms. *In room:* Kitchen, ceiling fans, coffeemaker, hair dryer, iron/ironing board, no phone.

EXPLORING THE ISLAND: PLANTATIONS, PEAKS & A HERMITAGE

There's an interesting Arawak cave at Columbus Point on the southern tip of the island. In addition, you can see the ruins of many once-flourishing plantations that saw their heyday during the island's short-lived cotton boom. Early planters, many of them Loyalists, marked their plantation boundaries with stone mounds—some of which are now nearly 200 years old. The ruined plantations include the Deveaux Mansion, built by Col. Andrew Deveaux of the fledgling U.S. Navy (who recaptured Nassau from the Spanish in 1783), and the Armbrister Plantation, which lies in ruins near Port Howe.

You can also hike along the natural paths through native villages and past exotic plants. Finally, you reach the peak of Mount Alvernia, the highest point in The Bahamas, at 62m (203 ft.) above sea level, where you will be rewarded with a spectacular view. The mount is capped by the **Hermitage,** a religious retreat built entirely by hand by the late Father Jerome, the former "father confessor" of the island, who was once a mule skinner in Canada. Curiously, the building was scaled to fit his short stature (he was a very, very short man). Formerly an Anglican, this Roman Catholic hermit priest became a legend on Cat Island. He died in 1956 at the age of 80, but his memory is kept very much alive here.

The **Cat Island Dive Center** at the Greenwood Beach Resort (② 242/342-3053) will take you out on diving or snorkeling excursions, or rent you snorkeling gear and other water toys. Our favorite spot for diving is along the west coast where **Dry Heads** is the finest reef. It gets its name because at low tide a blanket of purple sea fans stands high and dry. The drop here is 7.6m (25 ft.), and as you plunge below you'll meet butterfly fish and queen angels swimming over the coral heads.

2 San Salvador ⊕

This may be where the New World began. For some years it has been believed that Christopher Columbus made his first footprints in the Western Hemisphere here, although some scholars strongly dispute this. The easternmost island in the Bahamian archipelago, San Salvador lies 322km (200 miles) southeast of Nassau. Much of its 163 sq. km (64 sq. miles) in total area is occupied by water. There are 28 landlocked lakes on the island, the largest of which is 19km (12 miles) long and serves as the principal route of transportation for most of the island's population of 1,200. A badly maintained 64km (40-mile) road circles the perimeter of San Salvador.

The tiny island keeps a lonely vigil in the Atlantic. **The Dixon Hill Lighthouse** at South West Point, about 50m (164 ft.) tall, can be seen from 145km (90 miles) away. The light is a hand-operated beacon fueled by kerosene. Built in the 1850s, it is the last lighthouse of its type in The Bahamas. The highest point on the island is **Mount Kerr** at 41m (134 ft.).

Except for the odd historian or two, very few people ever used to visit San Salvador. Then **Club Med–Columbus Isle** opened, and the joint's been jumping ever since—at least at the Club Med property. Away from here, San Salvador is as sleepy as it ever was, although it's been known for years as one of the best dive sites in The Bahamas. The snorkeling, fishing, and lovely white-sand beaches are equally good.

SAN SALVADOR ESSENTIALS

GETTING THERE   Club Med (see listing below) solves transportation problems for its guests by flying them in on weekly charter planes from Miami. In winter there are charter flights from New York once a week. You can also rely on public transportation by land or sea, but if you do, you'll have to wait a long time before getting off the island.

Bahamasair (② 800/222-4262; www.bahamasair.com) has flights 6 days a week to the island. Departure times from Nassau are constantly changing, so check with the airline for a schedule.

From Nassau, the mail boat **MV *Lady Francis*** leaves Tuesday heading for San Salvador and Rum Cay. The trip takes 12 hours under uncomfortable conditions. For details about sailing, contact the dockmaster at **Potter's Cay Dock** in Nassau (② 242/393-1064).

GETTING AROUND

If you want to tour the island, ask your hotel staff to help you with arrangements and taxi service. If you have the staff at **Club Med** (② 242/331-2000) arrange an island tour for you, the cost is around $25 per person for a half-day ramble.

Fun Fact The Columbus Question

In 1492, a small group of peaceful Lucayan natives (Arawaks) were going about their business on a little island they called Guanahani, where they and their forebears had lived for at least 500 years. Little did they know how profoundly their lives would change when they greeted the arrival of three small strange-looking ships bearing Columbus and his crew of pale, bearded, oddly costumed men. It is said that when he came ashore, Columbus knelt and prayed—and claimed the land for Spain.

Unfortunately, the event was not so propitious for the reportedly handsome natives. Columbus later wrote to Queen Isabella that they would make ideal captives—perfect servants, in other words. It wasn't long before the Spanish conquistadors cleared the island, as well as most of The Bahamas, of Lucayans, sending them into slavery and early death in the mines of Hispaniola (Haiti) in order to feed the Spanish lust for gold from the New World.

But is the island now known as San Salvador the actual site of Columbus's landing? Columbus placed no lasting marker on the sandy, sun-drenched island of his landfall, and the result has been much study and discussion during the past century or so as to just where he actually landed.

In the 17th century, an English pirate captain, George Watling, took over the island and built a mansion to serve as his safe haven. The island was listed on maps for about 250 years as Watling's (or Watling) Island.

In 1926 the Bahamian legislature formally changed the name of the island to San Salvador, feeling that enough evidence had been brought forth to support the belief that this was the site of Columbus's landing. Then in 1983, artifacts of European origin (beads, buckles, and metal spikes) were found here together with a shard of Spanish pottery, and Arawak pottery and beads. The actual date of these artifacts most likely cannot be pinned down, although they are probably from about 1490 to 1560. However, the beads and buckles fit the description of goods recorded in Columbus's log.

National Geographic published a meticulously researched article in 1986 written by its senior associate editor, Joseph Judge, with a companion piece by the former chief of the magazine's foreign editorial staff, Luis Marden. The articles set forth the belief that Samana Cay, some 105km (65 miles) to the southeast of the present San Salvador, was actually Guanahani, the island Columbus named San Salvador when he first landed in the New World. The question may never be absolutely resolved, but there will doubtless be years and years of controversy about it. Nevertheless, history buffs still flock here every year hoping to follow in the footsteps of the explorer.

On San Salvador, you don't need to rent a car unless you want to explore far-flung places on your own. If that's the case, you can rent a car through **Riding Rock Inn Resort and Marina** (© **242/331-2631**) for about $85 a day.

Club Med guests have use of bikes for cycling around the property and for guided tours around the island. If you're not staying at Club Med, you can rent two-wheelers at Riding Rock Inn Resort and Marina for $10 a day.

FAST FACTS   The **San Salvador Medical Clinic,** a 5-minute drive north of Club Med, (℗ **242/331-2105**) serves the island's residents, but serious cases are flown to Nassau. The clinic, which also fills prescriptions, is open Monday to Friday from 8:30am to 4:30pm, and only emergencies are handled on Saturday and Sunday.

To call the police, dial ℗ **919.** (Phones are rare on the island, but the front desk at Riding Rock Inn will place calls for you.)

WHERE TO STAY

Club Med–Columbus Isle ☆☆   This is one of the most ecologically conscious, and one of the most luxurious, Club Meds in the Western Hemisphere. Set at the edge of one of the most pristine beaches in the archipelago, about 3km (2 miles) north of Cockburn Town, the resort is the splashiest pile in the Southern Bahamas. Its promoters estimate that more than 30% of the island's population works at the club.

Most of the prefabricated buildings here were barged to the site in 1991. The resort is built around a large free-form swimming pool. The public rooms are some of the most lavish and cosmopolitan in the country, with art and art objects imported from Asia, Africa, the Americas, and Europe, and assembled by a battalion of designers. Bedrooms each contain a private balcony or patio, furniture that was custom-made in Thailand or the Philippines, sliding glass doors, and feathered wall hangings crafted in the Brazilian rainforest by members of the Xingu tribe. Rooms are large (among the most spacious in the entire chain). Most have twin beds, but you might be able to snag one of the units with a double or a king-size bed if you're lucky. Each comes with a midsize bathroom with shower stall. Dozens of multilingual GOs (guest relations organizers, or *gentiles organizateurs*) are on hand to help initiate newcomers into the resort's many diversions. Unlike many other Club Meds, this one does not encourage children and deliberately offers no particular facilities for their entertainment.

The main dining room, where meals are an ongoing series of buffets, lies in the resort's center. Two specialty restaurants offer Italian and grilled food, respectively. Nonfat, low-calorie, and vegetarian dishes are also featured. Nightly entertainment is presented in a covered, open-air theater and dance floor behind one of the bars.

3km (2 miles) north of Cockburn Town, San Salvador, The Bahamas. ℗ **800/CLUB-MED** or 242/331-2000. Fax 242/331-2458. www.clubmed.com. 240 units. Winter $1,400–$1,945 weekly per person double occupancy; off season $1,277–$1,767 weekly per person double occupancy. Weekly rates include all meals, drinks during meals, and most sports activities. AE, DISC, MC, V. Children under 12 not recommended. **Amenities:** 3 restaurants; 2 bars; disco; pool; 10 tennis courts; health club; watersports equipment/rentals; laundry service or coin-operated laundry; nonsmoking rooms. *In room:* A/C, TV, fridge, beverage maker, hair dryer, iron/ironing board, safe.

Riding Rock Inn Resort & Marina   San Salvador's second resort is the motel-style Riding Rock Inn, catering largely to divers. Its simple ambience is a far cry from the extravagant Club Med. Each accommodation faces either a pool or the open sea. The most recent improvement to the inn is an 18-room oceanfront building, where the bedrooms are decorated in a tropical decor, with two double beds, satellite TV, a refrigerator, a telephone, ceiling fans, and air-conditioning. Each unit is equipped with a midsize bathroom with a tub/shower combination.

The resort specializes in weeklong packages that include three dives a day, all meals, and accommodations. Packages begin and end on Saturday and, if a client pays a $350 supplement, can include specially chartered round-trip air transportation from Fort Lauderdale. Although most of the guests are already experienced and certified divers, beginners can arrange a $120 resort course for the first day of their visit and afterward participate in most of the community's daily dives. Full PADI certification can also be arranged for another supplement of $400. There are many different dive packages—check with the hotel for specific trips.

An island tour is included in the rates, but after that, most folks rent a bike or scooter from the hotel. On the premises are a restaurant serving routine Bahamian specialties and a bar with a seating area that juts above the water on a pier. Dive packages are available.

Cockburn Town, San Salvador, The Bahamas. ℂ **800/272-1492** in the U.S.; 954/359-8353 in Florida; or 242/331-2631 in The Bahamas. Fax 242/331-2020. www.ridingrock.com. 42 units. Year-round $114–$141 double; $129–$156 triple; $161 quad. Children 11 or younger stay free in parent's room. MC, V. **Amenities:** Restaurant; bar; pool; tennis court; watersports equipment/rentals. *In room:* A/C, TV, fridge, hair dryer.

WHERE TO DINE

Rock Inn Restaurant BAHAMIAN/AMERICAN   Sit on the deck overlooking the water or eat inside; either way, you can dine on hearty portions of comfort food. Pancakes make a good choice for breakfast, and sandwiches are on the menu for lunch. The price-fixed dinners include soup, salad, main course, dessert, wine, and soft, chewy, just-baked Bahamian bread. Launch your meal with the well-seasoned conch chowder or okra soup and follow it up with steak, prime rib, veal, chicken, or fresh fish. Likewise, the Wednesday-night barbecues, featuring reggae music, are popular social events.

Cockburn Town. ℂ **242/331-2631.** Reservations recommended. Breakfast $12; lunch $15; dinner $28. MC, V. Daily 7:30–9am, 12:30–2pm, and 6:30–9pm.

Three Ships Restaurant BAHAMIAN   Since the early 1990s, Faith Jones, the owner, keeps visitors coming back for her cracked conch, steamed or fried grouper, and crab 'n' rice, served with mounds of coleslaw, potato salad, or peas 'n' rice. Spend some time here, and you're sure to strike up a conversation or two with Ms. Jones and the townspeople who stop in for food, drink, or just "to chew the fat" in more ways than one. Jones used to cater meals from her home next door before she opened this dining spot.

Cockburn Town. ℂ **242/331-2787.** Reservations not needed. Main courses $8–$15. No credit cards. Daily noon–6pm.

BEACHES, WATERSPORTS & OTHER OUTDOOR PURSUITS

If you prefer finding a stretch of sand where the only footprints on it are your own, rent a car or a bike at **Riding Rock Inn Resort & Marina** or call a taxi. Empty beaches are everywhere. Just remember to take plenty of water, and, of course, sunblock. You won't find much shade. Along the way, you can look for the island's various monuments to Christopher Columbus.

On the northeast coast, **East Beach** stretches for some 10km (6 miles). Crushed coral and shells turned the shore a rosy pink. The deep turquoise patches in the clear waters are coral heads, but the beach isn't good for snorkeling because people have spotted sharks here. Tall sea wheat or sea grass sprouts up from the sand. Off mile marker number 24 on the main road, you can pick your way to the **Chicago Herald Columbus Monument** (see below).

Scuba divers flock to this remote island—a major dive destination with some **40 dive sites** that lie no more than 45 minutes by boat from either of the two resorts. San Salvador has such stunning sea walls around it that *wall diving*—diving where the sloping shoreline suddenly drops off steeply and plummets to the ocean depths—is a major preoccupation here.

Associated with the Riding Rock Inn (see above), **Guanahani Dive Ltd.** (ℂ **242/ 331-2631**) offers dive packages, as well as snorkeling, fishing, and boating trips.

Year-round divers can book a getaway package for 5 days and 4 nights that costs from $654 to $710 per diver, including meals, transportation, diving, and rental gear. Prices are based on double occupancy.

Club Med–Columbus Isle, just north of Cockburn Town, should really be called an *almost*-all-inclusive resort, because scuba diving is not included in its rates. Resort courses run $100, and certification courses are $400. A one-tank dive costs $40 and a two-tank, $60.

With so many unpolluted and unpopulated kilometers of beaches, this area is ideal for swimming, shelling, and, of course, snorkeling. If you stay here a week, you've only begun to explore the possibilities. Places such as **Bamboo Point, Fernandez Bay,** and **Long Bay** all lie within a few miles of the main settlement of Cockburn Town on the more tranquil western side of the island. At the southern tip of San Salvador is one of our favorite places for snorkeling, **Sandy Point,** and its satellite of **Grotto Bay.** The elkhorn coral reefs off San Salvador are worth the trip to Sandy Point and Grotto Bay. A wonderful spot for snorkeling is the wreck of the SS *Frascate,* which ran aground on January 1, 1902. Filled with such marine life as moray eels and grouper, we think this is the best shallow wreck for snorkeling in the area.

Club Med–Columbus Isle offers 10 tennis courts (three lit for night play), and Riding Rock Inn Resort & Marina has one (often empty) court. Fishermen test their skill against blue marlin, yellowfin tuna, and wahoo on fishing trips, which you can arrange through Riding Rock Inn Resort & Marina (© **242/331-2631**). The trips run $400 for a half-day and $600 for a full day. Bone fishermen enjoy **Pigeon Creek,** and some record catches have been chalked up here. Rent a boat from a local or get your hotel to help set you up.

EXPLORING THE ISLAND: COMMEMORATING COLUMBUS

For such a small island, San Salvador offers a great deal of history as well as some sights that merit a look.

Rent a bike, hire a taxi, or start walking, and see how many of the **Christopher Columbus monuments** you can hit. All these monuments are supposed to mark the place where Columbus and his crew anchored the *Nina, Pinta,* and *Santa Maria* early that morning in 1492.

Just south of Cockburn Town, the **Tappan Monument,** a small, four-sided stone pillar, stands on the beach at **Fernandez Bay** (mile marker number 5 on the main road). The Tappan gas company embedded this monument here on February 25, 1951, in honor of Columbus.

The Chicago Herald Monument is located at mile marker number 24, on the east coast. To reach it, turn off the main road and drive a half-kilometer (1 mile) to **East Beach.** Unless you meet a resident who can give you a ride in a four-wheel-drive car, you have to get out and walk. Turn right and hike 3km (2 miles) parallel to the beach until the sandy road ends. You'll see a cave to the left, at the water's edge. Follow the path to the right. Cupped by vegetation, a stone structure lies on the slice of land between the ocean and the bay. Although many historians dispute the claim, the marble plaque boasts, "On this spot Christopher Columbus first set foot upon the soil of the New World, erected by the *Chicago Herald,* June 1891." The only problem with the monument's claim is that the treacherous reefs here make this a dangerous—and highly unlikely—landing spot.

At Long Bay, the **Olympic Games Memorial** to Columbus, located 5km (3 miles) south of Cockburn Town, was erected in 1968 to commemorate the games in Mexico.

Runners carrying an Olympic torch circled the island before coming to rest at the monument and lighting the torch there. The torch was then taken to Mexico on a warship for the games. Another marker is underwater, supposedly where Columbus dropped anchor on his *Santa Maria.*

Just north of the Olympic Games Memorial stands the **Columbus Monument.** On December 25, 1956, Ruth Durlacher Wolper Malvin—a leading U.S. expert on Columbus research—established a simple monument commemorating the explorer's landfall in the New World. Unlike the spot marked by the *Chicago Herald* monument, this is actually supposed to be the place where Columbus and his men landed.

Among the settlements on San Salvador are Sugar Loaf, Pigeon Creek, Old Place, Holiday Track, and Fortune Hill. United Estates, which has the largest population, is a village in the northwest corner near the Dixon Hill Lighthouse. The U.S. Coast Guard has a station at the northern tip of the island.

Except for the party people at Club Med, San Salvador is mainly visited by the boating set who live aboard their craft. If you're exploring for the day, you'll find one or two local cafes that serve seafood.

In the northeastern portion of the island, the **Dixon Hill Lighthouse,** built in 1856, sends out an intense beam two times every 25 seconds. This signal is visible for 31km (19 miles). The oil-using lighthouse rises 49m (161 ft.) into the sky, and the lighthouse keeper still operates it by hand. For permission to climb to the top, just knock on the door of the lighthouse keeper, who's almost always in the neighboring house.

After huffing and puffing your way up, you'll be surprised when you see how tiny the source of light actually is. From the top of the lighthouse, you can take in a panoramic view of San Salvador's inland lakes, a distant Crab Cay, and the surrounding islets. Ask the lighthouse keeper to show you the **inspector's log,** with signatures that date back to Queen Victoria's reign. Be sure to leave at least a $1 donation when you sign the guest book on your way out. The lighthouse lies about a 30-minute taxi ride from Riding Rock Inn Resort & Marina or Club Med.

At French Bay, **Watling's Castle,** also known as Sandy Point Estate, has substantial ruins that are about 26m (85 ft.) above sea level. The area is located some 4km (2½ miles) from the "Great Lake," on the southwestern tip of the island. Local "experts" will tell you all about the castle and its history. The only problem is that each "expert" we've listened to (three in all, at different times) has told us a different story about the place. Ask around and perhaps you'll get yet another version; they're entertaining, at least. One of the most common legends involves a famous pirate who made his living either by salvaging the wreckage from foundered ships or by attacking ships for their spoils.

Once plantations—all doomed to failure—were scattered about the island. The most impressive ruins of this former life are **Farquharson's Plantation,** west of Queen's Highway, near South Victoria Hill. In the early part of the 19th century, some Loyalist families moved from the newly established United States to this island, hoping to get rich from farmland tended by slave labor. That plan collapsed when the United Kingdom Emancipation Act freed the slaves in 1834. The plantation owners moved on, but the former slaves stayed behind.

A relic of those times, Farquharson's Plantation is the best-known ruin on the island. People locally call it "Blackbeard's Castle," but it's a remnant of slavery, not piracy. You can see the foundation of a great house, a kitchen, and what is believed to have been a jail.

COCKBURN TOWN

San Salvador's capital, Cockburn (pronounced "Coburn") Town, is a harbor village that takes its name from George Cockburn, who is said to have been the first royal governor of The Bahamas to visit this remote island. That was back in 1823.

Look for the town's landmark: a giant almond tree. Major events in San Salvador, like the Columbus Day parade held every October 12, generally take place here.

Holy Saviour Roman Catholic Church   The very first Christian worship service in the New World was Catholic. It thus seems fitting that the Roman Catholic Diocese of The Bahamas in 1992, on the eve of the 500th anniversary of the Columbus landfall, dedicated a new church on San Salvador.

Cockburn Town. Free admission. Services Sun 10am.

New World Museum   This museum, located 5.5km (3½ miles) north of Riding Rock Inn, has relics dating from Indian times, but you'll have to ask until you find someone with a key if you want to go inside. The museum lies just past Bonefish Bay in the little village of North Victoria Hill. Part of a large estate called Polaris-by-the-Sea, it's owned by Ruth Durlacher Wolper Malvin.

North Victoria Hill. No phone. Free admission. Open anytime during the day.

SAN SALVADOR AFTER DARK

Club Med (© 242/331-2000), just north of Cockburn Town, keeps its guests entertained every night, with musical revues and shows starring vacationers themselves. At **Riding Rock Inn Resort & Marina** (© 242/331-2631), also north of Cockburn Town, the Wednesday-night barbecue features reggae music, and many locals come to party. The hotel's **Driftwood Bar** is also hot on Friday nights (© 242/331-2631). If you're still game for some fun after the lodgings' festivities, head to the **Harlem Square Bar** (© 242/331-2777) across the road from Three Ships Restaurant in Cockburn Town. This friendly place is open daily from 9am to midnight.

SIDETRIPS: DISCOVERING RUM CAY & CONCEPTION ISLAND

"Where on earth is Rum Cay?" Even many Bahamians have never heard of it. Located midway between San Salvador and Long Island, this is another cay, like Fortune Island (see "The Ghost Island of Fortune," later in this chapter), that time forgot.

That wasn't always the case, though. The very name conjures up images of swashbucklers and rumrunners. Doubtless, it was at least a port of call for those dubious seafarers, as it was for ships, as well, to take on supplies of salt, fresh water, and food before crossing the Atlantic or going south to Latin America. The cay's name is supposed to have derived from a rum-laden sailing ship that wrecked upon its shores.

With the demise of the Rum Cay Club, tourist traffic to the island came to a halt except for the odd yachting party or two. But with the increased interest in tourism that followed the 1992 Columbus celebrations, the area is gaining renewed interest. At present, you can arrange for boaters on San Salvador to take you to see these islands, which remain frozen in time.

3 Long Island

The Tropic of Cancer runs through this long, thin sliver of land, located 242km (150 miles) southeast of Nassau. The island stretches north to south for some 97km (60 miles). It's 2.5km (1½ miles) wide on average, and only 5km (3 miles) wide at its broadest point.

Long Island is characterized by high cliffs in the north, wide and shallow sand beaches, historic plantation ruins, native caves, and Spanish churches. The famed **diving sites** 🏊 are offshore, including the Arawak "green" hole, a "bottomless" blue hole of stunning magnitude. The best beach bets include **Deal's Beach, Cape Santa Maria Beach, Salt Pond Beach, Turtle Cove Beach,** and the **South End beaches,** the latter offering kilometers of waterfront with powdery white or pink sands.

Most historians agree that Long Island, which has only recently emerged as a minor tourist resort, was the third island Columbus sailed to during his first voyage of discovery.

LONG ISLAND ESSENTIALS

GETTING THERE   There are two airstrips here, connected by a road. The **Stella Maris strip** is in the north, and the other, called **Deadman's Cay,** is in the south, north of Clarence Town (it's highly unlikely that you'll land here, and this one is a very expensive cab ride from most of the island's accommodations). **Bahamasair** (📞 **800/222-4262** in the U.S.; www.bahamasair.com) flies direct once a day (a 45-min. trip) from Fort Lauderdale, landing at the Stella Maris airport, which is near most of the hotels.

From Nassau, the **MV *Mia Dean*** sails weekly to Clarence Town, leaving on Tuesday. The **MV *Island Link*** departs Nassau with calls at Salt Pond, Deadman's Cay, and Seymour's also on Tuesday. Mail boat trips take a grueling 10 hours. For information contact the dockmaster at **Potter's Cay Dock,** Nassau (📞 **242/393-1064**).

GETTING AROUND   The **Stella Maris Resort Club** (📞 **242/338-2051**) can make arrangements to have you picked up at the airport upon arrival and can also arrange for a rental car.

FAST FACTS   The **police** can be reached by calling 📞 **242/337-0999** or 242/337-0444.

The **Bank of Nova Scotia** (📞 **242/338-2000**) has an **ATM** and operates a small currency-exchange facility at the Stella Maris Resort. Hours are Monday to Thursday 9am to 1pm, Friday 9:30am to 3pm.

SPECIAL EVENTS   In June, Long Island sailors participate in the big event of the year, the 4-day **Long Island Regatta.** They've been gathering since 1967 at Salt Pond for this annual event. In addition to the highly competitive sailboat races, Long Island takes on a festive air with calypso music and reggae and lots of drinking and partying. Many expatriate Long Islanders come home at this time, usually from Nassau, New York, or Miami, to enjoy not only the regatta but rake 'n' scrape music. Call your local Bahamas Tourist Office (see chapter 2) for more information.

WHERE TO STAY

Cape Santa Maria Beach Resort 🏊 *Kids*   This cozy nest has become the most luxurious resort on the island, taking over the position long held by the Stella Maris Resort Club. Cottages with two rooms are centered around a clubhouse, and the entire complex opens onto a stunning 6.5km (4-mile) strip of white sand. All units are only 18m (59 ft.) from the beach, which offers great snorkeling. Although the accommodations don't have phones or TVs, each room is air-conditioned and also has ceiling fans, plus a small bathroom with a shower/tub combination. Bedrooms have a light, tropical, and airy feeling, with marble floors and tasteful rattan furniture. There's also a screened-in porch with ceiling fans so you can enjoy the outdoors without the mosquitoes, the curse of the Southern Bahamas. The place is ideal for families, and several accommodations are configured so that children will have a separate room. The hotel's 65-seat restaurant is also good, serving a tasty Bahamian, North American, and seafood cuisine.

Cape Santa Maria, off Queen's Hwy., Long Island, The Bahamas. (℃) **800/663-7090** or 242/338-5273. Fax 242/338-6013. www.capesantamaria.com. 21 units. Winter $285 double; off season $195 double. Extra person $50 per day, $75 including all meals. AE, MC, V. **Amenities:** Restaurant; bar; health club; watersports equipment/rentals; babysitting; laundry service; nonsmoking rooms; bike rentals; car-rental desk. *In room:* A/C, ceiling fans; fridge (in some); safe (in some); coffeemaker, hair dryer, iron/ironing board, no phone. Closed Sept–Oct.

Chez Pierre (★) *Finds*   Just south of the Tropic of Cancer, Montreal expats Pierre and Anne Laurence found their little bit of heaven on 3.2 hectares (8 acres) of land opening onto a wide crescent beach of white sand. Here they built and attractively furnished a cluster of bungalows overlooking the sea, each with a screened-in porch. All the units come with private bathrooms with showers. This is the most eco-sensitive resort in the Southern Bahamas, as Chez Pierre is powered by alternative energy; the sun and the wind keep it running.

A few steps from the beach cottages is an ocean-fronting restaurant that serves the best food on the island, a blend of French, Italian, and Caribbean cuisine, using island-grown fresh produce along with fresh fish and seafood from local waters. The location is halfway between Stella Maris and Deadman's Cay.

Simms, Long Island, The Bahamas. (℃) **242/338-8809.** www.chezpierrebahamas.com. 6 units. Year-round $130–$150 double. Rates include breakfast and dinner. AE, MC, V. **Amenities:** Restaurant; bar; fishing; kayaking; reef fishing; saltwater fly fishing; snorkeling; bikes; island tours; babysitting. *In room:* Fans, no phone.

Lochabar Beach Lodge   One of the most remote retreats listed in this guide, this lodge offers escapist studios for those fleeing from the civilized world. You step from your studio to a pristine beach of white sand 23m (75 ft.) away, surrounding a "blue hole" in a natural cove. The only acceptable lodgings in the southern part of Long Island, these guest studios measure 56 or 111 sq. m (600 or 1,200 sq. ft.) each. In lieu of ceiling fans, the studios were built to take advantage of the trade winds. Guests keep their Bahama shutters and double screen doors open to capture those breezes. Each studio comes with a small bathroom containing a shower stall. Studios have kitchenettes, and a member of the staff will drive you to a nearby store to stock up on provisions.

Big Blue Hole, 1.5km (1 mile) south of Clarence Town, Long Island, The Bahamas. (℃)/fax **242/337-3123.** lochabar@hotmail.com. 3 units. Year-round $138–$180 double. Extra person $20 per day. MC, V. **Amenities:** Watersports equipment/rentals; car-rental desk; nonsmoking rooms; room for those w/limited mobility. *In room:* A/C, TV, kitchenette, fridge, coffeemaker, iron/ironing board.

Stella Maris Resort Club (★)   Situated on a ridge overlooking the Atlantic, the Stella Maris Resort Club stands in a palm grove on the grounds of the old Adderley's Plantation. Although you can swim here, the beach isn't the best, so the hotel maintains a cabana at Cape Santa Maria, a gorgeous white-sandy beach directly north, and offers shuttle service for its guests.

Accommodations vary widely—rooms, studios, apartments, and cottages with one to four bedrooms. Each accommodation has its own walk-in closet and fully equipped bathroom. Some are directly on the water. All of the buildings, including the cottages and bungalows, are set around a central clubhouse and a trio of pools. The resort makes a great honeymoon destination; everything is relaxed and informal.

The inn serves a good Bahamian cuisine, as well as continental specialties. There are rum-punch parties, cave parties, barbecue dinners, Saturday dinners, and dancing. Numerous watersports include complete diving facilities. Divers and snorkelers can choose from coral head, reef, and drop-off diving along the protected west coast of the island, at the north, and all along the east coast, around Conception Island and Rum Cay. Water-skiing and bottom- and reef fishing are also offered; there are three good bonefishing bays close by. Some 3.5m (11-ft.) Scorpion and Sunfish sailboats are free to hotel guests.

Ocean View Dr. (P.O. Box LI30105), Long Island, The Bahamas. (C) **800/426-0466** or 242/338-2051; 954/359-8238 for the Fort Lauderdale booking office. Fax 242/338-2052. www.stellamarisresort.com. 47 units. Winter $155 double, $180 1-bedroom cottage, $300–$600 bungalow or villa; off season $140 double, $165 1-bedroom cottage, $250–$515 bungalow or villa. AE, MC, V. **Amenities:** Restaurant; bar; 3 pools; watersports equipment/rentals; laundry service; nonsmoking rooms; rooms for those w/limited mobility. *In room:* A/C, fridge, hair dryer, no phone.

WHERE TO DINE

All the inns above serve food, but you should call for a reservation. In addition, you can try local joints, such as the **Forest,** Queen's Highway, Miley's ((C) **242/337-3287**), lying south of Clarence Town. Its cracked conch is the island's finest, and you can also order the standard grouper fingers or even barbecued chicken. The bar is made of seashells. On Friday nights, a live band plays for dancing, and the Forest becomes an island hot spot.

One of our favorite stopovers here is at a little roadside dive called **Max's Conch Grill,** Deadman's Cay ((C) **242/337-0056**), which serves some of the best conch on the island. Try it in a fresh salad or perhaps as conch burgers. Daily specials are also posted.

FISHING, SCUBA DIVING & SNORKELING

A lot of savvy anglers come to Long Island to **fish,** eschewing more famous places such as Andros and Bimini. The secret of the good fishing found here is the presence of a major current stream, called the North Equatorial Current, which originates in the Canary Islands. This stream washes the shores of Long Island. In its wake, the current transports huge schools of blue marlin, white marlin, sailfish, rainbow runners, yellowfin tuna, blackfin tuna, wahoo, and dolphinfish. Wahoo is best hunted from September through November. Catches weigh from 4.5 to 41kg (10–90 lb.), and some yellowfin have weighed up to 68kg (150 lb.). The small blackfin tuna (July–Dec) weigh from 4.5 to 14kg (10–30 lb.). In addition, there are kilometers and kilometers of reef fishing, with hundreds of species, including snapper or grouper that have been known to weigh 45kg (100 lb.). A jewfish caught here weighed 226kg (500 lb.). Inshore fishing for bonefish is also possible. These fish can be caught from an anchored boat, from the beach, or while wading in foot-deep water.

Although there are no watersports outfitters on Long Island, the two major resorts, the **Stella Maris Resort Club** and the **Cape Santa Maria Beach Resort** (see above) fill the void and offer more watersports than you can do in a week. Both offer bonefishing at a rate of $350 per day for up to two people; reef fishing is from $475 per day for up to six people; deep-sea fishing is $750 per day for up to six people. **Snorkeling** off the beach is complimentary at both resorts. However, boat excursions can be as little as $15 per hour at Cape Santa Maria; on Wednesday and Saturday, these excursions are complimentary at the Stella Maris. Both resorts offer scuba diving ranging from $45 to $75 per person per day, with equipment rentals ranging from $8 to $25. Both also offer kayaks, windsurfers, and bicycles. The Cape Santa Maria also offers Hobie Cats and boogie boards.

EXPLORING THE ISLAND

At **Wild Tamarind** ((C) **242/337-0262**)—1km (⅔ mile) east of Queen's Highway at the hamlet of Petty's—Denis Knight makes the best ceramics on the island. You might want to carry off one of his ceramic sculptures, or at least a bowl or vase.

Most of the islanders live at the unattractively named **Deadman's Cay.** Other settlements have equally colorful names: Roses, Newfound Harbour, Burnt Ground, Indian Head Point, and, at the northern tip of the island, Cape Santa Maria, generally believed to be the place where Columbus landed and from where he looked on the Exumas (islands that he did not visit). Our favorite name, however, is **Hard Bargain.** No one seems to know how this hamlet got its name. Hard Bargain, now a shrimp-breeding farm, is 16km (10 miles) south of Clarence Town.

Try to visit **Clarence Town** ⚶, 16km (10 miles) south of Deadman's Cay, along the eastern coastline. It was here that the stubby little priest, Father Jerome, who became known as the "father confessor" of the islands, built two churches before his death in 1956: **St. Paul's,** an Anglican house of worship, and **St. Peter's,** a Roman Catholic church. The "hermit" of Cat Island (you can visit his Hermitage there) was interested in Gothic architecture. He must also have been somewhat ecumenical, because he started his ministry as an Anglican but embraced Roman Catholicism along the way.

Many of the ruins recall the days when local plantation owners figured their wealth in slaves and cotton. The remains of **Dunmore's Plantation** at Deadman's Cay stand on a hill with the sea on three sides. There are six gateposts (four outer and two inner), as well as a house with two fireplaces and wall drawings of ships. At the base of the ruins is evidence that a mill wheel was once used. It was part of the estate of Lord Dunmore, for whom Dunmore Town on Harbour Island was named.

In the village of Grays stand the ruins of **Gray's Plantation,** where you'll see the remnants of at least three houses, one with two chimneys. One is very large, and another seems to have been a one-story structure with a cellar.

Adderley's Plantation, off Cape Santa Maria, originally occupied all the land now known as Stella Maris. The ruins of this cotton plantation's buildings consist of three structures that are partially intact but roofless.

Two underground sites that can be visited on Deadman's Cay are **Dunmore's Caves** and **Deadman's Cay Cave.** You'll need to hire a local guide to explore these. Dunmore's Caves are believed to have been inhabited by Lucayans and later to have served as a hideaway for buccaneers. The cave at Deadman's Cay, one of two that lead to the ocean, has never been fully explored. There are two native drawings on the cavern wall.

4 Acklins Island & Crooked Island

These little tropical islands, approximately 386km (239 miles) southeast of Nassau, make up an undiscovered Bahamian frontier outpost. Columbus came this way looking for gold. Much later, Acklins Island, Crooked Island, and their surrounding cays became hide-outs for pirates who attacked vessels in the Crooked Island Passage (the narrow waterway Columbus sailed), which separates the two islands. Today a well-known landmark, the **Crooked Island Passage Light,** built in 1876, guides ships to a safe voyage through the slot. Also known as the Bird Rock Lighthouse, it is a popular nesting spot for ospreys, and the light still lures pilots and sailors to the **Pittstown Point Landing Resort.** A barrier reef begins near the lighthouse, stretching down off Acklins Island for about 40km (25 miles) to the southeast.

Although Acklins Island and Crooked Island are separate, they are usually mentioned as a unit because of their proximity to one another. Together, the two islands form the shape of a boomerang. Crooked Island, the northern one, is 181 sq. km (71 sq. miles) in area, whereas Acklins Island, to the south, occupies 311 sq. km (121 sq.

miles). Both islands, which have good white-sand beaches and offer fishing and scuba diving, are inhabited mainly by fishermen and farmers.

In his controversial article in *National Geographic* in 1986, Joseph Judge identified Crooked Island as the site of Columbus's second island landing, the one he named Santa María de la Concepción.

Estimates say that by the end of the 18th century, more than three dozen working plantations were on these islands, begun by Loyalists fleeing mainland North America in the wake of the Revolutionary War. At the peak plantation period, there could have been as many as 1,200 slaves laboring in the 3,000 "doomed" acres of cotton fields (which were later wiped out by a blight). The people who remained on the island survived not only by fishing and farming, but also, beginning in the mid–18th century, by stripping the Croton cascarilla shrub of its bark to produce the flavoring for Campari liquor.

ACKLINS ISLAND & CROOKED ISLAND ESSENTIALS

GETTING THERE   There's an airport at Colonel Hill on Crooked Island and another airstrip at **Spring Point** on Acklins Island.

Bahamasair (© **800/222-4262** in the U.S.; www.bahamasair.com) has two flights a week from Nassau, on Wednesday and Saturday, to Crooked Island and Acklins Island, with returns to Nassau scheduled on the same day.

Mail-boat service, with the **MV *United Star,*** leaves Potter's Cay Dock in Nassau and heads for Acklins Island, Crooked Island, Fortune Island (Long Cay), and Mayaguana Island each week. Check the schedule and costs with the dockmaster at **Potter's Cay Dock** in Nassau (© **242/393-1064**).

A government-owned **ferry** service connects the two islands; it operates daily from 9am to 4pm. It links Lovely Bay on Acklins Island with Browns on Crooked Island. The one-way fare is $4.

Once you arrive at Crooked Island, a **taxi** service is available, but because of the lack of telephones, it's wise to advise your hotel of your arrival—they'll probably send a van to meet you.

FAST FACTS   There are several government-operated clinics. Phones are scarce on the islands, but your hotel desk can reach one of these clinics by going through the local operator. The clinic on Acklins Island is at Spring Point (© **242/344-3172**). On Crooked Island the clinic is at Landrail Point (© **242/344-2166**).

The **police** station on Crooked Island can be reached by dialing © **242/344-2599.**

WHERE TO STAY & DINE

Out Island Inn at Pittstown Point Landing ★ *(Finds)*   Located on a beach at the extreme northwestern tip of Crooked Island, this hotel is so isolated you'll forget all about the world outside. For most of the early years of its life, it was a well-guarded secret shared mostly by the owners of private planes who flew in from the mainland of Florida for off-the-record weekends. Even today, about 70% of the clients arrive by one- or two-engine aircraft that they fly themselves as part of island-hopping jaunts around The Bahamas. The island maintains its own 690m (2,263-ft.), hard-surface landing strip, which is completely independent from the one used for the flights from Nassau on Bahamasair.

Surrounded by scrub-covered landscape at the edge of a turquoise sea, it lies 4km (2½ miles) north of the hamlet of Landrail Point (pop. 50) on a sandy peninsula. Within easy access are some of the weirdest historic sites in The Bahamas, including the sun-baked ruins of a salt farm (Marine Farms Fortress) that was sacked by American-based pirates in 1812.

Spartan accommodations with shower/tub combination bathrooms lie within three low-slung, cement-sided buildings. They lie directly on the beach, usually with verandas facing the sea. Because of the constant trade winds blowing in, not all bedrooms have air-conditioning, but do contain large paddle-shaped ceiling fans. The entire resort shares only one telephone/fax, which is reserved for emergency calls.

Meals are served in a stone-sided building that was originally erected late in the 1600s as a barracks for the British West Indies Naval Squadron and later was the region's post office. The restaurant serves seafood, as well as North American and Bahamian specialties. Guests always take the meal plan here. You'll also usually find here a scattering of yacht owners or aviators who drop in spontaneously for drinks and dinner.

Landrail Point, Crooked Island, The Bahamas. (For reservations and information, contact Pittstown Point Landing, 9274 SE Hawks Nest Court, Hobe Sound, FL 33455.) ① **242/344-2507.** www.pittstownpointlandings.com. 12 units. Year-round $285–$345 double. Rates include all meals (AP). AE, MC, V. **Amenities:** Restaurant; bar; laundry service; nonsmoking rooms. *In room:* A/C (in some), no phone.

UNCOVERING A PIRATE HIDE-OUT

Crooked Island opens onto the **Windward Passage,** the dividing point between the Caribbean Sea and The Bahamas. Whatever else he may have named it, when Columbus landed at what is now Pittstown Point, he supposedly called it Fragrant Island because of the aroma of its many herbs. One scent was cascarilla bark, used to flavor Campari liquor as well as the native Cascarilla Liqueur, which is exported. For the best view of the island, climb **Colonel Hill** ☆—unless you arrived at the Crooked Island Airport (also known as the Colonel Hill Airport), which has the same vantage.

Guarding the north end of this island is the **Marine Farms Fortress,** an abandoned British fortification that saw action in the War of 1812. It looks out over Crooked Island Passage and can be visited (ask your hotel to make arrangements for you).

Hope Great House is also on the island, with orchards and gardens that date from the time of George V of England.

Other sights include **French Wells Bay,** a swampy delta leading to an extensive mangrove swamp rich in bird life, and the **Bird Rock Lighthouse,** built a century ago.

⟨Finds⟩ The Ghost Island of Fortune

Lying off the coast of Crooked Island, **Fortune Island** is truly a place that time forgot. Your hotel can put you in touch with a boater on Crooked Island who will take you here. Experts believe, based on research done for *National Geographic,* that Fortune Island (sometimes confusingly called Long Cay) is the one Columbus chose to name Isabella, in honor of the queen who funded his expedition. Its only real settlement is Albert Town, which is classified as a ghost town, but officially isn't—some hardy souls still live here. Fortune Hill, visible from 19km (12 miles) away at sea, is the local landmark. Hundreds of Bahamians came here in the 2 decades before World War I and would wait to be picked up by oceangoing freighters, which would take them to seek their fortunes as laborers in Central America—hence, the name Fortune Hill.

At the southern end of Acklins Island lies **Castle Island,** a low and sandy bit of land where an 1867 lighthouse stands. Pirates used it as a hide-out, sailing forth to attack ships in the nearby passage.

Acklins Island has many interestingly named villages—Rocky Point, Binnacle Hill, Salina Point, Delectable Bay, Golden Grove, Goodwill, Hard Hill, Snug Corner, and Lovely Bay. Some Crooked Island sites have more ominous names, such as Gun Point and Cripple Hill.

5 Mayaguana Island

The least visited of the Bahamian islands, sleepy Mayaguana seems to float adrift in the tropical sun at the remote extremities of the southeastern edge of The Bahamas, 564km (350 miles) southeast of Nassau. It occupies 285 sq. km (111 sq. miles) and has a population of about 400. It's a long, long way from the development of Nassau and Paradise Island.

Standing in the Windward Passage, Mayaguana is just northwest of the Turks and Caicos Islands. It's separated from the British Crown Colony by the Caicos Passage. Around the time of the American Civil War, inhabitants of Turks Island began to settle in Mayaguana, which before then had dozed undisturbed for centuries.

Acklins Island and Crooked Island lie across the Mayaguana Passage. Mayaguana is only 9.5km (6 miles) across at its widest point, and about 39km (24 miles) long. Its beaches are enticing, but you'll rarely see a tourist on them, other than the occasional German. A few developers have flown in to check out the island, but to date no new development has occurred.

Summer brings the rains to Mayaguana. Combined with heat and mosquitoes, it can get a little rough here. However, summer is the best time to go fishing.

GETTING THERE

Bahamasair (© 800/222-4262 in the U.S.; www.bahamasair.com) flies in here to a little airstrip. Flights depart from Nassau Wednesday and Friday at 9:15am and take approximately 2½ hours.

From Nassau, a mail boat, **MV *Trans Cargo II Inagua*** makes a stop at Mayaguana. For information, check with the dockmaster at **Potter's Cay Dock** in Nassau (© 242/393-1064).

WHERE TO STAY & DINE

Few other outposts in The Bahamas are as remote as Mayaguana, which is the main reason why many visitors come—to get away from everything. Many visitors arrive by boat and just ask around for availability at one of the ultrasimple lodgings here. Some locals are willing to house you in one of their spare bedrooms for a rate that can be negotiated up or down to almost anything.

Baycaner Beach Resort In operation since 1996, this is the only hotel on island that can even lay a claim to being that. Its owner, Ernal Brown, is called "Shorty" by all the locals, and he's the man to see if you're one of the rare visitors who ever makes it to this part of the world. You can literally jump from your simply furnished bedroom right into the water. The bedrooms contain a comfortable bed and a scattering of wicker furnishings along with a small air conditioner; each comes with a little well-maintained bathroom. The lobby adjoins the dining room and bar, the latter popular with locals. You might have the dining room to yourself, however. Dig into that Bahamian staple of brown pigeon peas 'n' rice. Most meals feature conch—perhaps in a chowder or freshly made salad—and the inevitable grouper, the most popular fish caught off island. The hotel cook makes fresh bread daily.

Pirates Well, Mayaguana, The Bahamas. ©/fax **242/339-3726.** www.baycanerbeach.com. 16 units. Year-round **$100** double. AP (breakfast, lunch, and dinner) $80 extra per person. MC, V. **Amenities:** Restaurant; bar; limited room service; laundry service. *In room:* A/C, TV.

EXPLORING THE ISLAND

Abraham's Bay is the main town on the south coast, with an excellent harbor. The other little settlement on Mayaguana is **Betsy Bay,** secluded and lost in time. Wild corn and saucy hummingbirds share this spot along with some little sun-worn cottages basking in the hot sun. At **Pirate's Well,** goats are now the chief residents, although buccaneers used to roam past here. Locals still dream of finding buried treasure. The best views of the Mayaguana Passage can be had from both Betsy Bay and Pirate's Well.

Fishing is good on the island. Locals will often take you out on one of their boats, but you've got to ask around. In summer and early autumn, temperatures can soar beyond 100°F (38°C). Winters, however, are ideal, and it never gets cold here as it can in the north Bahamas.

Mayaguana might be called The Bahamas' "great outback" or "wild west." It's a rugged and salty environment, with no organized activities of any kind. Sailing, deep-sea fishing, scuba diving, snorkeling, swimming, and walking are the main pastimes. If you need to rent any gear or want to hire a guide for an organized outing, your best bet is to inquire at your hotel; the staff can usually hook you up with the right person. The island is still too laid-back to have many organized outfitters.

6 Great Inagua ⟨★

The most southerly and the third-largest island of The Bahamas, flat Great Inagua, some 64km (40 miles) long and 32km (20 miles) wide, is home to 1,200 people. It lies 527km (327 miles) southeast of Nassau.

This is the site not only of the **Morton Salt Crystal Factory,** here since 1800, but also of one of the largest nesting grounds for **flamingos** in the Western Hemisphere. The National Trust of The Bahamas protects the area around Lake Windsor, where the birds breed and the population is said to number 80,000. Flamingos used to inhabit all of The Bahamas, but the bird is nearly extinct in many places. The reserve can be visited only with a guide. Besides the pink flamingo, you can see roseate spoonbills and other bird life.

Green turtles are also raised here, at **Union Creek Reserve,** and then released into the ocean to make their way as best they can; they, too, are an endangered species. (Tours of the reserve are not well organized, and the operation is very informal, but if you're here, inquire about getting a look.) This vast windward island, almost within sight of Cuba, is also inhabited by wild hogs, horses, and donkeys.

The settlement of **Matthew Town** is the chief hamlet of the island, but it's not of any great sightseeing interest. Other sites have interesting names, such as Doghead Point, Lantern Head, Conch Shell Point, Mutton Fish Point, and Devil's Point (which makes one wonder what happened there to give rise to the name). There's an 1870 lighthouse at Matthew Town.

Little Inagua, 8km (5 miles) to the north, has no population and is just a speck of land off the northeast coast of Great Inagua, about 78 sq. km (30 sq. miles) in area. It has much bird life, though, including West Indian tree ducks. There are also wild goats and donkeys.

GREAT INAGUA ESSENTIALS

GETTING THERE   Bahamasair (© **800/222-4262** in the U.S.; www.bahamasair. com) flies to Matthew Town Airport from Nassau on Monday, Wednesday, and Friday at 9:15am. Flight time is approximately 2 hours.

You can also go by **mail boat, MV *Trans Cargo II,*** which makes weekly trips from Nassau to Matthew Town (schedule varies). Call the **Potter's Cay Dockmaster** (© **242/393-1064**) in Nassau for details.

GETTING AROUND   Taxis meet incoming flights from Nassau. If you need a car, check with one of the guesthouses, but don't expect the vehicles to be well maintained.

FAST FACTS   The **Inagua Hospital** can be called at © **242/339-1249.** The **police** can be reached at © **242/339-1263.**

WHERE TO STAY

The choices of accommodations aren't great on this island, but most visitors are willing to forgo comfort to see the spectacular flamingos.

Morton Main House   The Main House is owned by Morton Bahamas Ltd., the salt people, whose employees often fill up all the rooms. Only five bedrooms are rented, and the furnishings are extremely modest, though everything is clean. Each unit comes with a small bathroom containing a shower/tub combination. Life here is casual and completely informal. You can order breakfast or lunch here—but no dinner. Unfortunately, it sits near a noisy power plant.

Matthew Town, Inagua, The Bahamas. © **242/339-1267.** Fax 242/339-1265. 5 units. Year-round $80–$90 double. No credit cards. **Amenities:** Nonsmoking rooms. *In room:* A/C, TV, iron/ironing board, no phone.

Walkine's Guest House   Set 1km (⅔ mile) south of Matthew Town, this simple guesthouse has a blue exterior and rosy, shell-pink bedrooms. Your hosts are Eleanor and Kirk Walkine, who built their place in 1984 across the road from the beach. Rooms are very modest but spacious, with only racks to hang your clothes in lieu of a closet. Bathrooms are large, three containing a shower/tub combination.

Gregory St., Matthew Town, Inagua, The Bahamas. © **242/339-1612.** 5 units, 3 w/private bathroom. Year-round $74 double. No credit cards. **Amenities:** Nonsmoking rooms. *In room:* A/C, TV, coffeemaker, no phone.

WHERE TO DINE

Cozy Corner BAHAMIAN/AMERICAN   The most consistently reliable restaurant outside any of the guesthouses is this lime-green, stone-built house 2 blocks from the sea. Your hosts, Rosemary Ingraham and her daughter Veronica, maintain a friendly bar where beer, rum punch, and gossip seem to be the staples of the town. Menu items include a simple roster of mostly fried foods that are almost always accompanied by french fries. Dishes include fried conch, fried chicken, burgers and "whopper burgers," plus whatever sort of fried seafood is available from local fishermen on the day of your visit.

William St., Matthew Town. © **242/339-1440.** Lunch and dinner $7–$10. No credit cards. Daily 9am (closing time varies).

> ⎛ *Fun Fact* **With Salt, Please**
>
> Salt means a great deal to Great Inagua—not only for the Morton Salt Company's extensive operations (the company produces more than 1 million tons of salt each year), but also for the unique local wildlife.
>
> First, seawater is pumped into the interior of the island and held in dikes. Great Inagua's salt ponds, about 80 of them, cover some 4,856 hectares (11,994 acres). As the water evaporates, it turns into heavy brine. The salt solidifies at night and melts during the heat of the day, and a crystallized bed forms at the bottom of the pond. In the final stage of processing, any remaining water is drained, and the salt is bulldozed into bleached-white mountains and shipped around the world for processing.
>
> As the water evaporates from these salt ponds, brine shrimp concentrate and provide great meals for the island's colorful pink flamingos.

EXPLORING THE ISLAND: PINK FLAMINGOS & MORE

The island's vast number of **pink flamingos** ★★★ outnumbers its human population of 1,200. They're so plentiful on Inagua that some of them even roost on the runway of the island's airport, as well as at thousands of other locations throughout the flat, heat-blasted landscape. When seen in a huge flock, they present a surreal vision.

Dedicated bird-watchers who are willing to forgo comforts usually trek inland to the edges of the many brackish lakes in the island's center. About half the island is devoted to a national park; the island's most viable industry involves distilling salt from the local salt flats.

To see the birds at **Inagua National Park** ★★ is reason enough to come here in the first place. Everyone entering the park must be accompanied by a warden, and reservations and a day pass costing $25 for adults and $10 for students must be obtained in advance. Get the passes either through The Bahamas National Trust in Nassau (© 242/393-1317 for information or reservations) or by contacting one of the local wardens on Inagua, Henry Nixon, at © 242/339-1616. In addition to the park fee, you're expected to offer the wardens a large tip. Figure on about $50 a day, which is the usual payment. The best time to see our feathered friends is from November until June.

One of the best panoramas on the island is **Southwest Point,** lying 2km (1¼ miles) south of the "capital." From here you can see Cuba on a clear day, because it lies just 81km (50 miles) to the west. There's a lighthouse here dating from 1870. From it, you can wave at Cuba. The reefs off this point are treacherous, as many a captain learned when his ship was wrecked here. The lighthouse is one of the last of a quartet of hand-operated kerosene lighthouses left in The Bahamas.

Index

See also Accommodations and Restaurant indexes, below.

RESTAURANTS

A Guide for Every Type of Traveler

Frommer's® Complete Guides

For independent leisure or business travelers who value complete coverage, candid advice, and lots of choices in all price ranges.

These are the most complete, up-to-date guides you can buy. Count on Frommer's for exact prices, savvy trip planning, sightseeing advice, dozens of detailed maps, and candid reviews of hotels and restaurants in every price range. All Complete Guides offer special icons to point you to great finds, excellent values, and more. Every hotel, restaurant, and attraction is rated from zero to three stars to help you make the best choices.

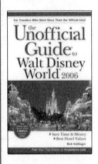

Unofficial Guides

For honeymooners, families, business travelers, and anyone else who values no-nonsense, *Consumer Reports*–style advice.

Unofficial Guides are ideal for those who want to know the pros and cons of the places they are visiting and make informed decisions. The guides rank and rate every hotel, restaurant, and attraction, with evaluations based on reader surveys and critiques compiled by a team of unbiased inspectors.

Frommer's® Irreverent Guides

For experienced, sophisticated travelers looking for a fresh, candid perspective on a destination.

This unique series is perfect for anyone who wants a cutting-edge perspective on the hottest destinations. Covering all major cities around the globe, these guides are unabashedly honest and down-right hilarious. Decked out with a retro-savvy feel, each book features new photos, maps, and neighborhood references.

Frommer's® With Kids Guides

For families traveling with children ages 2 to 14.

Here are the ultimate guides for a successful family vacation. Written by parents, they're packed with information on museums, outdoor activities, attractions, great drives and strolls, incredible parks, the liveliest places to stay and eat, and more.

Visit Frommers.com

Now you know.

A Guide for Every Type of Traveler

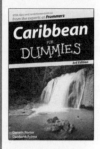

FOR DUMMIES® TRAVEL GUIDES

For curious, independent travelers.

The ultimate user-friendly trip planners, combining the broad appeal and time-tested features of the For Dummies guides with Frommer's accurate, up-to-date information and travel expertise. Written in a personal, conversational voice, For Dummies Travel Guides put the fun back into travel planning. They offer savvy, focused content on destinations and popular types of travel, with current and extensive coverage of hotels, restaurants, and attractions.

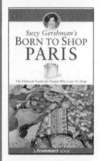

SUZY GERSHMAN'S BORN TO SHOP GUIDES

For avid shoppers seeking the best places to shop worldwide.

These savvy, opinionated guides, all personally researched and written by shopping guru Suzy Gershman, provide detailed descriptions of shopping neighborhoods, listings of conveniently located hotels and restaurants, easy-to-follow shopping tours, accurate maps, size conversion charts, and practical information about shipping, customs, VAT laws, and bargaining. The handy pocket size makes it easy to carry them in your purse while you shop 'til you drop.

FROMMER'S® $-A-DAY GUIDES

For independent travelers who want the very best for their money without sacrificing comfort or style.

The renowned series of guides that gave Frommer's its start is the only budget travel series for grown-ups—travelers with limited funds who still want to travel in comfort and style. The $-a-Day Guides are for travelers who want the very best values, but who also want to eat well and stay in comfortable hotels with modern amenities. Each guide is tailored to a specific daily budget and is filled with money-saving advice and detailed maps, plus comprehensive information on sightseeing, shopping, nightlife, and outdoor activities.

FROMMER'S® PORTABLE GUIDES

For short-term travelers who insist on value and a lightweight guide, including weekenders and convention-goers.

Frommer's inexpensive, pocket-sized Portable Guides offer travelers the very best of each destination so that they can make the best use of their limited time. The guides include all the detailed information and insider advice for which Frommer's is famous, but in a more concise, easy-to-carry format.

Visit Frommers.com

WILEY

Now you know.

Frommer's® **Portable Guides**

Destinations in a Nutshell

Frommer's®

 WILEY

Available at bookstores everywhere.

FROMMER'S® NATIONAL PARK GUIDES

Algonquin Provincial Park
Banff & Jasper
Family Vacations in the National
  Parks

Grand Canyon
National Parks of the American West
Rocky Mountain

Yellowstone & Grand Teton
Yosemite & Sequoia/Kings Canyon
Zion & Bryce Canyon

FROMMER'S® MEMORABLE WALKS

Chicago
London

New York
Paris

San Francisco

FROMMER'S® WITH KIDS GUIDES

Chicago
Hawaii
Las Vegas
New York City

Ottawa
San Francisco
Toronto

Vancouver
Walt Disney World® & Orlando
Washington, D.C.

SUZY GERSHMAN'S BORN TO SHOP GUIDES

Born to Shop: France
Born to Shop: Hong Kong, Shanghai
  & Beijing

Born to Shop: Italy
Born to Shop: London

Born to Shop: New York
Born to Shop: Paris

FROMMER'S® IRREVERENT GUIDES

Amsterdam
Boston
Chicago
Las Vegas
London

Los Angeles
Manhattan
New Orleans
Paris
Rome

San Francisco
Seattle & Portland
Vancouver
Walt Disney World®
Washington, D.C.

FROMMER'S® BEST-LOVED DRIVING TOURS

Austria
Britain
California
France

Germany
Ireland
Italy
New England

Northern Italy
Scotland
Spain
Tuscany & Umbria

THE UNOFFICIAL GUIDES®

Beyond Disney
California with Kids
Central Italy
Chicago
Cruises
Disneyland®
England
Florida
Florida with Kids
Inside Disney

Hawaii
Las Vegas
London
Maui
Mexico's Best Beach Resorts
Mini Las Vegas
Mini Mickey
New Orleans
New York City
Paris

San Francisco
Skiing & Snowboarding in the West
South Florida including Miami &
  the Keys
Walt Disney World®
Walt Disney World® for
  Grown-ups
Walt Disney World® with Kids
Washington, D.C.

SPECIAL-INTEREST TITLES

Athens Past & Present
Cities Ranked & Rated
Frommer's Best Day Trips from London
Frommer's Best RV & Tent Campgrounds
  in the U.S.A.
Frommer's Caribbean Hideaways
Frommer's China: The 50 Most Memorable Trips
Frommer's Exploring America by RV
Frommer's Gay & Lesbian Europe

Frommer's NYC Free & Dirt Cheap
Frommer's Road Atlas Europe
Frommer's Road Atlas France
Frommer's Road Atlas Ireland
Frommer's Wonderful Weekends from
  New York City
Retirement Places Rated
Rome Past & Present